Heresy and Inquisition in the Middle Ages
Volume 4

Cathars in Question

YORK MEDIEVAL PRESS

York Medieval Press is published by the University of York's Centre for Medieval Studies in association with Boydell & Brewer Limited. Our objective is the promotion of innovative scholarship and fresh criticism on medieval culture. We have a special commitment to interdisciplinary study, in line with the Centre's belief that the future of Medieval Studies lies in those areas in which its major constituent disciplines at once inform and challenge each other.

Editorial Board (2018)
Professor Peter Biller (Dept of History): General Editor
Professor T. Ayers (Dept of History of Art)
Dr Henry Bainton (Dept of English and Related Literature)
Dr J. W. Binns (Dept of English and Related Literature)
Dr K. P. Clarke (Dept of English and Related Literature)
Dr K. F. Giles (Dept of Archaeology)
Dr Holly James-Maddocks (Dept of English and Related Literature)
Professor W. M. Ormrod (Dept of History)
Professor Sarah Rees Jones (Dept of History): Director, Centre for Medieval Studies
Dr L. J. Sackville (Dept of History)
Dr Hanna Vorholt (Dept of History of Art)
Professor J. G. Wogan-Browne (English Faculty, Fordham University)

Consultant on Manuscript Publications
Professor Linne Mooney (Dept of English and Related Literature)

All enquiries of an editorial kind, including suggestions for monographs and essay collections, should be addressed to: The Academic Editor, York Medieval Press, Department of History, University of York, Heslington, York, YO10 5DD (E-mail: pete.biller@york.ac.uk).

Heresy and Inquisition in the Middle Ages
ISSN 2046–8938

Series editors
John H. Arnold, Department of History, Classics and Archaeology, Birkbeck College, London
Peter Biller, Department of History, University of York

Heresy had social, cultural and political implications in the middle ages, and countering heresy was often a central component in the development of orthodoxy. This series publishes work on heresy, and the repression of heresy, from late antiquity to the Reformation, including monographs, collections of essays, and editions of texts.

Publications of York Medieval Press in this series are listed at the back of this volume.

Cathars in Question

Edited by
Antonio Sennis

YORK MEDIEVAL PRESS

© Contributors 2016

All rights reserved. Except as permitted under current legislation
no part of this work may be photocopied, stored in a retrieval system,
published, performed in public, adapted, broadcast,
transmitted, recorded or reproduced in any form or by any means,
without the prior permission of the copyright owner

First published 2016
Paperback edition 2018

A York Medieval Press publication
in association with The Boydell Press
an imprint of Boydell & Brewer Ltd
PO Box 9, Woodbridge, Suffolk IP12 3DF, UK
and of Boydell & Brewer Inc.
668 Mt Hope Avenue, Rochester, NY 14620–2731, USA
website: www.boydellandbrewer.com
and with the
Centre for Medieval Studies, University of York
www.york.ac.uk/medieval-studies

ISBN 978-1-903153-68-0 hardback
ISBN 978-1-903153-81-9 paperback

A CIP catalogue record for this book is available
from the British Library

The publisher has no responsibility for the continued existence or accuracy of
URLs for external or third-party internet websites referred to in this book, and
does not guarantee that any content on such websites is, or will remain, accurate or
appropriate

Contents

	Acknowledgments	vii
1	Questions about the Cathars *Antonio Sennis*	1
2	The Paradigm of Catharism; or, the Historians' Illusion *Mark Gregory Pegg*	21
3	The Cathar Middle Ages as a Methodological and Historiographical Problem *John H. Arnold*	53
4	The Heretical Dissidence of the 'Good Men' in the Albigeois (1276–1329): Localism and Resistance to Roman Clericalism *Julien Théry-Astruc*	79
5	The *Heretici* of Languedoc: Local Holy Men and Women or Organized Religious Group? New Evidence from Inquisitorial, Notarial and Historiographical Sources *Jörg Feuchter*	112
6	Cathar Links with the Balkans and Byzantium *Bernard Hamilton*	131
7	Pseudepigraphic and Parabiblical Narratives in Medieval Eastern Christian Dualism, and their Implications for the Study of Catharism *Yuri Stoyanov*	151
8	The Cathars from Non-Catholic Sources *David d'Avray*	177
9	Converted-Turned-Inquisitors and the Image of the Adversary: Ranier Sacconi Explains Cathars *Caterina Bruschi*	185
10	The Textbook Heretic: Moneta of Cremona's Cathars *Lucy J. Sackville*	208
11	'Lupi rapaces in ovium vestimentis': Heretics and Heresy in Papal Correspondence *Rebecca Rist*	229
12	Looking for the 'Good Men' in the Languedoc: An Alternative to 'Cathars'? *Claire Taylor*	242

Contents

13 Principles at Stake: The Debate of April 2013 in Retrospect
    R. I. Moore   257

14 Goodbye to Catharism?
    Peter Biller   274

    Index   314

Acknowledgments

The essays collected in this volume originate in papers delivered at the conference 'Catharism: Balkan Heresy or Construct of a Persecuting Society?', which was held at University College London and at the Warburg Institute on 18–19 April 2013.

Gratitude is due to David d'Avray, for his vision and energy in co-organizing the conference; to the scholars and students who spent those two days in April discussing medieval heresies; to the UCL History Department, UCL Faculty of Social and Historical Sciences and the Warburg Institute, for their moral and financial support; to the anonymous referee, whose suggestions greatly improved the manuscript; to York Medieval Press, for accepting this volume in their 'Heresy and Inquisition in the Middle Ages' series; to Caroline Palmer at Boydell & Brewer, for her patience and kindness; to Marianne Fisher for her brilliant copyediting; to Agata Zielinska for her help with the index; and finally, to all the contributors to this volume, for being thought-provoking, curious and on time.

A. S.
London, April 2016

1

Questions about the Cathars

Antonio Sennis

At the heart of this volume is the aspiration to tackle in a comparative perspective an issue which is highly controversial and hotly debated among scholars: the existence of a medieval phenomenon which we can legitimately call 'Catharism'. Traditionally regarded as the most radical challenge to orthodox Catholicism in the medieval West, Catharism proposed that marriage is evil, just as the God of the Old Testament was evil and indeed different from the one of the New Testament, and that Christ never died in the flesh.[1]

One of the main issues at stake is the question of whether what the inquisitors called 'the heresy' was an entity with a continuous existence over the years and with international dimensions spreading from the Balkans to Italy, and to southern France. Historians are more or less in agreement that the phenomena those repressing authorities described were largely localized, both geographically and chronologically. Was heresy, therefore, just a multiplicity of local, unconnected unorthodoxies? Or, on the contrary, can we indeed find a historically grounded connection between Catharism and a Balkan heresy such as Bogomilism, so that it is actually possible to talk of dualist dissent as a distinct movement in the central Middle Ages?

Words like 'Catharism' and 'Bogomilism' have obviously to be correctly understood, and the problem of what these sects and their members were actually called in thirteenth-century sources is central to all the papers in this volume. The authors also share a specific interest in understanding the extent to which the integrated world of twelfth- and thirteenth-century Europe was reflected in the existence of a connected network of heretical groups, or if, as

---

[1] The historiography on the Cathars is comprehensively cited by all the authors in this volume. Here, for southern France, a reference to the best interpretive synthesis will suffice: M. Barber, *The Cathars: Dualist Heretics in Languedoc in the High Middle Ages*, 2nd edn (Harlow, 2013). A stimulating insight into religious deviance in medieval Italy and elsewhere is provided by the essays collected in *L'eresia medievale*, ed. O. Capitani (Bologna, 1971), especially R. Morghen, 'L'eresia nel Medioevo', pp. 61–120; R. Manselli, 'L'eresia catara come problema storiografico', pp. 121–42; C. Violante, 'Eresie urbane e eresie rurali in Italia dall'XI al XIII secolo', pp. 157–84.

recent historiographical trends have suggested, we are instead confronted with examples of local dissidence which responded to local needs and were shaped by local aspirations and cultural models.[2] Finally, the organization of the Cathars, their Churches, has been the target of a strong critique in the past decades.[3] Many of the papers here offer their view on the existence, or lack, of a structured hierarchy of religious management and control.

As is well known, R. I. Moore's book *The War on Heresy* argued that a structured 'Cathar' Church did not exist before the early thirteenth century and that, as a consequence, Catharism as a phenomenon – and, indeed, the activity, even the very identity, of its followers and the specificities of its creed – were largely the product of medieval inquisitors, on the one hand, and of modern historians, on the other.[4] According to this view, Cathars and Catharism were a construct, and the radical views attributed to them are no more than a myth. The inquisitors, who were obviously far from neutral in their observation of local realities, imposed a rigid set of preconceived labels on what in reality was a dynamic and complex amalgamation of local practices (religious and other). They did so in order to establish the conditions for, and legitimation of, repression and persecution. A corollary of this has been the calling into question of the Balkan influence of Bogomilism in western Europe, and the reconsideration of some key aspects of the political, cultural, religious and economic relationships between the Balkans and more western regions of Europe in the Middle Ages.[5]

Further to this point, alongside the works of Mary Douglas, which clearly inspire much of the discussion, readers might be reminded of the suggestions put forward by another anthropologist, Jean-Loup Amselle. He argued that nineteenth- and twentieth-century French ethnographers imposed sharp and rigid classificatory distinctions on the rather nuanced West-African social groups they were observing. In the long run what they imposed influenced, and in more than one sense determined, those groups' self-identity and customs.[6]

---

[2] See, for example, J.-L. Biget, *Hérésie et inquisition dans le midi de la France* (Paris, 2007); A. Siegel, 'Italian Society and the Origins of Heresy, in *Heresy and the Persecuting Society in the Middle Ages: Essays on the Work of R. I. Moore*, ed. M. Frassetto (Leiden, 2006), pp. 43–72.

[3] For example, C. Vilandrau, 'Inquisition et "sociabilité cathare" d'après le registre de l'inquisiteur Geoffroy d'Ablis (1308–1309)', *Heresis* 34 (2001), 35–66.

[4] R. I. Moore, *The War on Heresy: Faith and Power in Medieval Europe* (London, 2012).

[5] On the influence of Bogomilism in western Europe, see B. Hamilton, 'Wisdom from the East: The Reception by the Cathars of Eastern Dualist Texts', in *Heresy and Literacy, 1000–1530*, ed. P. Biller and A. Hudson (Cambridge, 1994), pp. 38–60.

[6] J.-L. Amselle, *Logiques métisses: anthropologie de l'identité en Afrique et ailleurs* (Paris, 1990). Translated into English by Claudia Royal as *Mestizo Logics: Anthropology of Identity in Africa and Elsewhere* (Redwood City, 1998). Among the works by Mary Douglas,

Reduced to its essentials, the argument of those who reject the early existence of a series of organized, interrelated, mutually aware groups of dualist heretics (Cathars) is that what we are actually talking about is a very dynamic, fluid and diverse cosmos of dissidence (religious, social and political), devoid of any structured and uniform system of thought, with no shared texts or recognizable doctrines. As such, these groups of dissidents were very difficult to fight. The persecutors, so the argument goes, therefore constructed and categorized those dissident beliefs in a structured and fairly rigid way, so that it would be easier to refute them.

With different perspectives and nuances, the chapters by R. I. Moore, Mark Gregory Pegg and Julien Théry-Astruc structure their argument along the lines I have just described. Moore is interested, among other things, in finding a way in which the gulf between 'traditionalists' and 'sceptics' (he qualifies his use of the two terms in his chapter and, for clarity and convenience, I adopt them here and in the following pages) can still result in a coherent, and useful, picture of religious dissent in the high and late Middle Ages. However, first of all there are issues of chronology. Moore states very clearly that the evidence for organized dualistic heresies is abundant and substantial after the mid thirteenth century. For southern France the watershed seems clearly to be the Albigensian crusade (1209–29). From the inquisitorial records it seems that, when witnesses refer to the situation before the crusade, they recall heresy as being much more spread, common, public, and that it was not so odd to see *boni homines* preaching and discussing in public. The witnesses almost give the impression that everybody was in contact with heretics, one way or the other, as part of daily life, and that this made individuals less guilty, because they simply did what everybody did. By contrast, testimonies referring to the period after the Albigensian crusade describe a much more private, secluded, secret set of behaviours, for example preaching taking place not in public, but in woods, vineyards, or isolated fields, and not during the day, but at night.[7] Moore suggests that the traditional narrative – which states that from the 1140s medieval heresy was increasingly dominated by dualism, and that this process culminated in the Albigensian crusade – makes little sense if we look at the evidence available for the twelfth century. He therefore argues that the presence of organized dualistic groups in Europe after the mid thirteenth century must be explained without presuming that they were the direct heirs of twelfth-century predecessors.

---

particularly important for this discussion are: M. Douglas, *How Institutions Think* (London, 1987); M. Douglas, 'Rightness of Categories', in *How Classification Works: Nelson Goodman among the Social Sciences*, ed. M. Douglas and D. Hull (Edinburgh, 1992), pp. 239–71; M. Douglas, *In the Wilderness: The Doctrine of Defilement in the Book of Numbers* (Sheffield, 1993).

[7] On this, see also M. G. Pegg, *The Corruption of Angels: The Great Inquisition of 1245–6* (Princeton, 2001), p. 90.

Mark Gregory Pegg begins by offering an historiographic overview, in order to frame what he sees as misapprehensions produced by a chain of academic and intellectual filiations that seek to explain the history of dissent. His views are clear: twelfth- and thirteenth-century Church intellectuals (and inquisitors) looked at some areas of southern France and applied the label of heresy *tout court* to phenomena that were mainly local – at times dissenting – social, political and religious practices; however, they never categorized those forms of dissent as Catharism in the formalized and organic way in which the term has been understood by historians since the nineteenth century. Where the traditionalists see the Cathars as structured groups of heretics who uniformly accepted theological dualism, Pegg sees local holiness, local circumstances, local customs; where the traditionalists see a long-standing Cathar hierarchical organization (in other words a Church), he sees informal networks, precepts and influence. These, he argues, began to coalesce and structure only during the Albigensian crusade, as a consequence of persecution, and even then not as formally defined Catharism.

Julien Théry-Astruc sees heresy in the Albigeois as an element of a more articulated discourse of dissent and protest against clericalism. According to him, while it was invariably labelled as heresy, this dissent did not necessarily imply the adoption of an alternative, heterodox system of religious thought. In his view, the major factor for religious dissent in the area was not so much the circulation of deviant theologies but, rather, dissatisfaction with, and hostility towards, clerical control. These are very important points. Heresy always contains instances of social discontent and protest, and the critical and alternative appropriation of the evangelical message as a strategy of resistance and opposition to the ideas of the dominating groups is a constant in popular, as well as in learned, religion.[8] In a sense, heterodoxy can be seen in fact as an act of resistance: where social protest, discontent or resistance occur, the conditions for deviating from the religious norm are created, though this does not necessarily mean that heretical thought is invariably generated. The existence of houses of heretics, and the possibility that villagers had to visit them, seems to indicate that the choice between a church and a house of heretics often depended more on local practice than on firm belief. It is also true, though, that going to visit a house of heretics was a way to make a point, locally, as opposed to going to church. During the inquisition of 1245–6 in the Lauragais, Domina Hyrlanda declared that she had stopped believing the heretics when one of them tried to convince her that she would have done

---

[8] G. G. Merlo, *Eretici e inquisitori nella società piemontese del Trecento: con l'edizione dei processi tenuti a Giaveno dall'inquisitore Alberto de Castellario (1335) e nelle valli di Lanzo dall'inquisitore Tommaso di Casasco (1373)* (Turin, 1977), p. 60.

better to burn the candle she had prepared for a vigil in the house, rather than at the local church.⁹

At the opposite end of the spectrum, readers will find the chapters by Pete Biller, Jörg Feuchter and (perhaps a little closer to the centre) John Arnold. Biller argues that heresy in southern France was indeed a reality. Far from being merely a projection on local dynamics of views elaborated centrally, in intellectual strongholds of Catholic orthodoxy such as the University of Paris and Cistercian monasteries, heresy was a genuine force that worried the papacy at least as much as any instance of political discontent. This heresy was characterized, according to Biller, by a dualism that drew clear inspiration from the East, and by a hierarchical structure, a doctrine and a complex of rituals which had been in place since at least the third quarter of the twelfth century.

Jörg Feuchter does not focus on dualism *per se*, but is more interested in the dynamics of religious dissent in medieval Languedoc – the very region which is at the heart of the sceptics' revision. According to Feuchter, the evidence at our disposal clearly points towards the existence of an organized, self-consciously dissident religious group in the region. 'Self-consciousness', 'organization' and 'religious' are key terms here, because with them Feuchter challenges some of the cornerstones of the sceptics' interpretive framework. Some of the sources on which he bases his argument have been, until now, practically unknown. This is the case of the set of charters pertaining to the Baziège family, and in particular to a woman called Ava, which Feuchter brought to the attention of scholars of heresy for the first time at the UCL conference in April 2013, and which he discusses in depth in this volume. The prospect of the impact that these discoveries will have on our understanding of medieval religious dissent is exciting to say the least.

John Arnold acknowledges that orthodox observation (and the need to control and repress deviance from the norm) does play a part in the definition of heresy, and even in how heretics ultimately perceived themselves. However, he is also clear in arguing that this does not mean that medieval Cathars were simply local dissidents to whom a religious label was applied. They were dualists, and their organization and belief were not simply the invention of their persecutors but, at least in part, the product of the circulation of texts, ideas and practices throughout Europe.

---

⁹ Toulouse, Bibliothèque municipale, MS 609 (henceforth MS 609), fol. 108r: 'audivit dici a Ramundo Gros heretico de quadam candela quam i[dem] t[estis] fecerat quam volebat portare ad vigilandum ad ecclesiam de Rocovila cuius festum fuit illa die quod melius esset ei si comburabat eam in domo, et propter hoc ulterius noluit cre[dere] h[ereticis].' On this manuscript and on the possibilites of analysis that it offers, see Y. Dossat, *Les crises de l'inquisition Toulousaine au XIIIe siècle (1233–1273)* (Bordeaux, 1959); Pegg, *The Corruption of Angels* (esp. pp. 20–7 for codicological details). A typescript of MS 609 is available online at http://jean.duvernoy.free.fr/text/listetexte.htm (this is the one I have used for this chapter). See also P. Biller, in this volume at pp. 282–3, n. 34.

As I have already mentioned, the issue of the existence and dissemination of texts and ideas is another very important point of contention. The filiation of Cathar ideas from the Balkans to southern France is strongly dismissed by the sceptics, for whom the non-existence of the connection between the two regions is a corollary of the non-existence of Catharism in southern France. The chapters by Bernard Hamilton, Yuri Stoyanov and David d'Avray aim to demonstrate the plausibility of these connections, and of the debate between different heretical groups within a largely integrated twelfth- and thirteenth-century Europe. According to Hamilton, texts and practices travelled from one region to the other, just as people did. He also shows that, with regard to the structure of the hierarchy itself, western European dualists were inspired by Balkan heretics. Adopting a purely text-oriented perspective, Yuri Stoyanov also argues for a clear connection between East and West. According to him, pseudoepigraphic, parabiblical and parascriptural narratives of western Christian dualism present clear signs of imported dualist beliefs.

Another point of discussion, which derives from the sceptics' dismissal of Cathar doctrines as a pure invention of orthodox persecutions, is whether there might have been space for doctrinal variety, even dissent, within the heretical movement itself. On the basis of non-Catholic sources, David d'Avray's chapter argues that dualist heretics were actually engaged, in the very first decades of the thirteenth century, in a heated debate among themselves about Creation. In brief, there was strong disagreement about whether the evil principle was the symmetrical counterpart of the good God, or an originally good being who had fallen. This resonates with the fact that, as Hamilton points out, since these dualists rejected the historical books of the Old Testament, they could not underpin an event so central to their belief system with any authoritative text. However, they were all in agreement that marriage and procreation were evil. According to d'Avray, this shows that western European dualism was a strong and varied reality.

Another part of the debate, and of the disagreement, centres on the existence and relevance of specific texts from which to infer the peculiarities of different heretical groups, in terms of doctrine and organization. Caterina Bruschi's chapter on Ranier Sacconi's treatise on the Cathars sheds light on the extraordinary experience of a heretic turned inquisitor. There is one aspect of Bruschi's analysis which I think deserves special mention: her firmness in arguing that heresy is, after all, a matter of individual faith which, at times, can cut against the grain of group allegiances, family ties and community bonds. The importance of individuals and of their freedom of thinking in shaping social, political, economic and religious dynamics is something that all historians should always take into account. Bruschi's interest in this issue resonates with Pegg's and Arnold's focus on the importance of agency and practice in the shaping of religious belief.

Moneta of Cremona's *Summa adversus catharos et valdenses* is another text which is central to any discussion of thirteenth-century religious dissent, as it is one of the few comprehensive discussions of heresy surviving from this period. As Lucy Sackville points out, Moneta was also one of the few to use the term 'Cathari' to describe the dualist heretics against whom he was writing. The way in which Moneta described those heretics makes it clear that, in his view, Cathars constituted a diverse group, but one which was unified by a set of common ideas and practices that set it apart from other heretical circles, such as the Waldensians. In more than one sense, Sackville argues, we can say that Moneta was describing a widespread and varied group whose doctrines and religious behaviours were, however, unified by a common intellectual and textual agenda.

The importance of texts like the treatises by Ranier Sacconi and Moneta of Cremona for grasping how churchmen understood heretical dissent appears even greater in the light of Rebecca Rist's chapter. She argues that papal letters, while expressing clear awareness of the existence in the south of France of different heretical groups, are often rather generic in labelling that local religious deviance ('heretics' is the term commonly used for southern French dissidents). This, according to Rist, constitutes evidence of the fact that, in the twelfth and thirteenth centuries, the popes were not deliberately reshuffling the cards in the attempt to control a local disobedience that was mainly political in nature. The problem of the name (Cathars? Heretics? Good Men?) remains one of the most difficult issues left to us by the surviving evidence.[10] Traditionalists and sceptics agree that 'Cathars' was used very rarely (the sceptics would say not at all) in the twelfth and early thirteenth centuries, but 'heretics' was indeed used. What did that term mean to those men and women and those churchmen who were snooping around their lives? Claire Taylor's paper investigates various possibilities and concludes that even the terms 'good men' and 'good women' were very rarely employed by these heretics to signify belonging to their group. Here traditionalists and sceptics remain distant from each other: while the former suggest that 'Cathars' is, in the end, better than nothing, just as we say 'Franciscans' or 'Dominicans', the latter reply that it is better to have no term at all.

It seems to me that there is a basic consensus among the authors of this volume in a shared emphasis on the idea that religious views and practices are part of a complex of mechanisms that regulate political and social dynamics according to relationships of force and, often, conflict. The actions of those in conflict, and the ideological tools they deploy in order to prevail over their opponents, generally provide an insight into how they view their world. Obviously, those actions are not straightforward reflections of the

---

[10] The historical validity of the term 'Cathars' is, for example, dismissed by U. Brunn, *Des contestataires aux 'cathares': discours de réforme et de propagande antihérétique dans les pays du Rhin et de la Meuse avant l'inquisition* (Paris, 2006), but see P. Biller, at pp. 275–7 in this volume.

daily lives of individuals; even the members of highly litigious social groups do many things besides arguing with each other. However, conflicts do emphasize some of the key values which operate within a community and through which, among other things, the relationships between individuals and groups are expressed and ideas about the right ordering of society are conveyed. Analysing conflicts can therefore disclose fundamental aspects of the principles that regulate power dynamics within groups, whether or not they are formalized institutions.[11] The differences start to emerge when we try to understand what this actually meant for those people who were accused of being heretics and for their accusers.

For the sceptics, where traditionally we saw men and women engaged in the formation and development of heretical religious views, we are now confronted with local dissidents, inhabitants of peripheries that the hegemonic centre endeavours to dominate through, among other things, the strategic use of local inquests and interrogations. Because the hegemonic centre was constituted by churchmen, social norms and customs were transformed by the expectations of the interrogator and turned into rigid, and deviant, religious doctrines in order for them to be refuted, and for their proponents to be crushed.

In the case of the conflict between inquisitors and local dissidents, the relationship of force was unbalanced: this was a conflict between those dominating – who could impose, create and enforce notions of what constituted good (and bad) religion – and the dominated, who, at best, could develop forms of resistance and find strategies to channel that resistance. From a formal, normative point of view ecclesiastical elites were able to exercise that control also, if not exclusively, through a carefully structured *mise par écrit* of local narratives. This is not surprising: clerics were the ones who wrote about all sorts of things, and they knew the power of writing. A complex and transnational system of values, inspired by Oriental doctrines and enriched with anachronistic elements from late antique dualistic heresies, was therefore attributed to those local communities.

It is important to stress that this view is the result of an interpretation of what constituted the hegemonic ruling culture, and of how freely this culture could be imposed, which has to be proved and tested in its regional and chronological specificities. It seems to me beyond doubt that, as Pegg argues,

---

[11] *Conflict in Medieval Europe*, ed. W. C. Brown and P. Górecki (Aldershot, 2003), esp. pp. 276–82. See also N. D'Acunto, 'Considerazioni introduttive', in *Papato e monachesimo 'esente' nei secoli centrali del Medioevo*, ed. N. D'Acunto (Florence, 2003), pp. 3–5. In using concepts such as social group – or, more broadly, society – I take into account the call for caution made, for example, by F. Barth, 'Towards Greater Naturalism in Conceptualizing Societies', in *Conceptualizing Society*, ed. A. Kuper (London, 1992), pp. 17–33 (esp. pp. 18–21).

the *inquisitio* had an impact on how the villagers reflected on themselves.¹² By equating the habits of individuals to their adherence to, or at least knowledge of, heresy, the inquisitors applied a model of consequentiality which forced lives into a rigid grid. But this model was not at all alien to the inhabitants of those villages. When deponents claimed that they did not believe the heretics even if – out of fear or convenience – they had adored them, this seems to me to indicate clearly that, among the villagers themselves, a habit, a gesture, signified adherence and complicity, to the point that one could pretend, in order to save one's face or to save even more. Social pressure could be confronted, and strategically resisted, precisely because consequentiality was part of the mental framework of the villagers.¹³

There were obviously limits to how far a deponent could go in order to save himself or herself from the accusation of complicity with the heretics. Even though they knew that certain gestures would implicate them quite heavily in dissidence, villagers could only play those gestures down to a reasonable, and credible, extent. To my knowledge there are no instances of deponents who try to minimize the significance of their gestures by saying something like, 'Yes, I did adore these good men, but this is just what we all do to everyone in the village.'

There is also a lot to agree with in the notion that communities' elaborate and structured codes of behaviour were open to the interpretation and manipulation of outsiders. Even more susceptible were the specific words that those individuals actually said to their interrogators. It is clear that the transition – not so much from vernacular to Latin, but from the mouth of a deponent to the pen of an inquisitor – affected the way in which thoughts and acts appear to us, modern readers. So, even when a deponent testified that she believed that John the Baptist was the devil, the appellation *beatus* was used.¹⁴ Similarly, in the late fourteenth century witnesses seem invariably to have called Pope Sylvester *beatus*, despite his being the great sinner in the eyes of the heterodox for having elicited Constantine's donation and ended the Church's evangelical poverty. The result is a phrase that seems paradoxical to us (though evidently not to those who wrote it): 'beatus Sylvester papa [...] unus diabolus dampnatus in inferno'.¹⁵

Can we therefore retrieve at all the voices and experiences of the local individuals? Or, on the contrary, are those voices audible only through the

---

12 See Pegg's paper in this volume and, more in detail, Pegg, *The Corruption of Angels*, pp. 114–25.
13 For example MS 609, fol. 146r: 'Poncius de Roire [...] nunquam cred[idit] nec unquam adoravisset eos nisi esset pre timore amicorum pred[ictorum] her[eticorum] [...] nec cred[idit].'
14 MS 609, fol. 142v: 'Item dixit quod cred[idit]. [...] et beatus Iohannes Babtista erat diabolus.'
15 Merlo, *Eretici e inquisitori*, p. 40, Table 8.

amplifier of the inquisitor, an amplifier that distorts them to the point of rendering their sound unrecognizable and their meaning elusive? Here we have to avoid the risk of pushing the interpretation too far. Traditionalists and sceptics are in agreement that most of the people who were interrogated faced the prospect of suffering some form of abuse if it was proved that they were dissidents. Inside their own community things might have been rather different, since some of them belonged to a dominant elite which was, almost certainly, itself prone to bullying those of lesser status.[16] But in front of the inquisitors they were all potential victims of outside persecutors. To a large extent their summoning itself was a form of coercion: they had very little choice but to go to be interrogated, and any resistance would hardly go unnoticed or be excused.[17] They also had very little choice with regard to what happened once they arrived in front of those churchmen: they had to answer (mostly hostile) questions in the formulation of which they had no negotiating power. And nothing, or so it seems, could they do about how their answers were put into writing. Thomas Bisson has suggested that, compared to the interrogations conducted at Montaillou or in Menocchio's Friuli, the Catalan memorials of complaint that he analyses present fewer distortions of evidence, because the inquirers and scribes who compiled them were not hostile to the grievances they were hearing, and were actually familiar figures in their localities.[18]

However, we must not forget that, no matter how weak they might have been when confronted with the power of hostile and unfamiliar inquisitors, those villagers tested for heresy were not passive recipients of an invented model: they were still talking about their own lives. Moreover, the self-image of the elites always contains some concessions (for example, in the case of the inquisitors, the use of a pastoral language) which, however rhetorical they might be, create an arena for the conflict. Subordinates can make political use of this small rhetorical space.[19]

That dissidents' gestures were given written form invariably and exclusively in terms of the outsiders' own categories is not necessarily true. A brief

---

[16] The bibliography concerning the relationships between lords and peasants in medieval Europe is enormous. In order to grasp the *status quaestionis* and its regional variations, two excellent points of departure are: *Señores, siervos, vasallos en la Alta Edad Media*, XXVIII Semana de Estudios Medievales (Pamplona, 2002); *Pour une anthropologie du prélèvement seigneurial dans les campagnes médiévales: réalités et représentations paysannes*, ed. M. Bourin and P. Martinez Sopena (Paris, 2004).

[17] Pegg, *The Corruption of Angels*, p. 41.

[18] T. N. Bisson, *Tormented Voices: Power, Crisis, and Humanity in Rural Catalonia, 1140–1200* (Cambridge MA, 1998), pp. 117–18.

[19] The point of reference here is J. C. Scott, *Domination and the Arts of Resistance: Hidden Transcripts* (New Haven, 1990) (p. 18 for a discussion of rhetorical concessions). On local strategies of resistance within small medieval communities, see C. Wickham, 'Gossip and Resistance among the Medieval Peasantry', *Past and Present* 160 (1998), 3–24.

analysis of the *melioramentum* (*melhoramen* in the vernacular) – the form of salutation that individuals performed when meeting a Cathar perfect – will help to clarify my point. Traditionalists and sceptics are determinedly distant from each other in their views of what this set of repeated genuflections accompanied by a structured formula actually meant. For the former, the *melioramentum* was clearly a set of codified gestures that marked acceptance of, and signified belonging (however temporary) to, a heretic sect. For the latter, it was part of a wider tradition of pious village *cortesia* shown to people who were perceived as holy. It acquired heretic connotations only when placed in the interpretive (and punitive) framework of the inquisitors, who, significantly (though not invariably – the dossier of Geoffroy d'Ablis being a case in point), called it *adoratio* rather than *melioramentum*.[20] In other words, the sceptics argue that the *adoratio*, as described by the deponents, looks more like the expression of village courtesy and esteem, which the hostile inquisitors transformed into the performance of a specific ritual and into the explicit expression of belief in a dissident creed.[21] When deponents declared that they had never adored the heretics or seen anybody do so, this might indicate an awareness that even witnessing the adoration could be construed as complicity, because that act had become so significant, secretive and private, no longer public as it had been before the Albigensian crusade.[22]

There are some specific points about the *adoratio* that make it problematic to consider it a series of widespread expressions of village courtliness. Whether they were acts of courtesy or strong statements of religious affiliation, those gestures were definitely taught by 'heretics' to some, not all, members of the community, and this complicates the argument that, whatever the villagers actually called it, what the inquisitors called *adoratio* was merely part of a shared repertoire of village gestures. When asked about this by the inquisitors at Saint-Sernin, Durand *de Bordis* testified that he and two of his friends had refused to perform the *adoratio* even though the four heretics they had just met had repeatedly showed them what to do.[23] It was also definitely understood by villagers (even those already convinced by a heterodox way of life) as a sign that an individual was, specifically, a 'heretic'. This should suggest at least a modification to the argument that *boni homines* were charismatic men widely recognized as such by the members of the community. In November 1245, Aimergarda de Mazerolles remembered how, three years before, while

---

[20] For the use of the term *melioramentum*, see *L'inquisiteur Geoffroy d'Ablis et les cathares du comté de Foix*, ed. A. Pales-Gobilliard (Paris, 1984), pp. 306, 362, 372, 388.

[21] See for example, in this volume, M. G. Pegg, at pp. 39–40 (with reference to M. G. Pegg, *A Most Holy War: The Albigensian Crusade and the Battle for Christendom* (Oxford, 2008), pp. 28–49).

[22] Pegg, *The Corruption of Angels*, p. 90.

[23] MS 609, fol. 117v: 'sed non adoravit nec vidit, licet pluries dicti heretici monstrarent eis modum adorati[o]nis.'

riding her horse near Roumengoux, she had seen Jordan of Vilar adoring two men and from this she had immediately understood that they were (fellow) heretics. Since she was pregnant at the time, she had not been allowed to get down from her horse and therefore had not adored them.[24]

That series of gestures was indeed a way to acknowledge the (religious) status of some members of the community. However, that status was not freely available and did not simply derive from the recognition of an individual's charismatic qualities, but depended on belonging to a specific (heretic) group. This makes the argument that we are, as the inquisitors were, in front of customary acts of courtesy shared by everybody in the village more problematic. Guilhelm de La Grasse confessed that he had been a heretic, because his father had long been one and he had raised him among them for some time, but stated that he had subsequently abandoned the group (*secta*) and accepted that it was bad and harmful. He also admitted that he had adored heretics so often that he could not remember how many times, and that he had been adored by many while he remained a heretic.[25]

Those gestures could also be subject to acts of negotiation and of true resistance within the community itself. People could try to get out of performing them, sometimes successfully sometimes not, and those who had done so wanted to let their interrogators know about it. A few examples will suffice. In 1245, Robert Aleman declared that, six years before, he had seen two heretics among other people in the house of Bertrand Aleman. At one point his hosts had shut the door of the room in which everyone was and had forced (*compulerunt*) him to adore them while they were doing the same.[26] Willelma Forneira said to the inquisitors that seven years before, in the house of Hysarn de Gibel, she had seen two men and had asked another woman who they were. The woman had said that they were heretics and had asked her if she wanted to adore them. When she had said she did not want to, she had been forced to do so.[27] Peter Berardi said that he had once happened to be in the presence of some heretics and that, in spite of the fact that they had

---

[24] Ibid. fols. 124r and 133r: 'invenerunt duos homines [...] quos vidit ibidem dictum Iordanum del Vilar adorantem, et tunc i[pse] t[estis] scivit eos esse hereticos, et quia i[pse] t[estis] erat tunc pregnans non descendit, nec dimiserunt eam d[icti] h[eretici] descendere de equitatura, et ideo non ad[oravit].'

[25] Ibid., fol. 133r: 'et i[pse] t[estis] fuit nutritus cum h[ereticis] bene per duos annos et dimidium, et fuit per quinquenniuum hereticus indutus, et postea recessit a dicto Bernardo Gras patre suo h[eretico] et ab aliis sociis suis h[ereticis]. Et recognovit sectam illorum esse malam et dampnosam. Et ad[oravit] tociens h[ereticos] quod non recordatur, et fuit adoratus a pluribus dum permansit hereticus.'

[26] Ibid., fol. 5r: 'Et tunc Bertrandus Aleman et dicta Austorga clauserunt hostium camere et dixerunt i[psi] testi quod adoraret h[ereticos], et compulerunt ipsum adorare predictos h[ereticos], et ipsi adoraverunt eos.'

[27] Ibid., fol. 32r: 'petiit a dicta Andreva cuiusmodi homines erant, et dicta Andreva respondit quod heretici erant et rogavit i[pse] t[estis] quod adoraret eos, et i[pse] t[estis] respondit quod non faceret, et tunc dicta Andreva compulit i[psum] t[estem] adorare.'

tried to convince them to hear their preaching, he had refused to do so, and had immediately left the house, without adoring those men, and either eating or drinking with them.[28]

In talking about their efforts and intentions, Robert, Willelma, Peter and others who, like them, claimed that they had refused to adore the heretics, were most probably influenced by the circumstances of the deposition in front of the inquisitors. Their memories were certainly framed by the questions and by how they were asked. However, their stories of resistance and disobedience to heretical influence can hardly have been invented by the interrogating churchmen, who had no reason to do so as part of their enquiry. It is indeed possible that the contrary is true, and that these men and women exaggerated, perhaps even altogether invented, their disdain for the dissidents in the attempt to find a gap in the dichotomy, Catholic–heretic, on which the inquisitorial framework relied, and to save their reputations in doing so. Their reluctance to acknowledge the charisma of these men was nevertheless perfectly credible insofar as it was manifested through those acts of petty defiance, subterfuge and animosity which constituted part of the usual repertoire of social gestures that all the villagers had at their disposal, equally, to attempt resistance against outside powers and to fight their daily battles for local positioning.[29]

It is also difficult to ignore the fact that the *melioramentum* seems to be a series of acts strongly identified with heretical behaviour throughout western Europe. In 1308, Raymund Autier of Ax told the inquisitor who was interrogating him that eight years before he was visited by two of his brothers, who were apparently returning from a period spent with heretics northern Italy. They taught him the ritual of the adoration, which was clearly distinguishable from the normal forms of affection and courtesy (a kiss on the lips and a hug) to which Raymund was accustomed when saying hello or good bye to his fellow villagers.[30] True, this source is a later one, but it seems to me difficult to explain it without accepting a connection between the adoration and heretics. The alternative is for a custom local to southern France to appear in northern Italy, where some southern Frenchmen encounter it seemingly for the first time and then present it as a novelty to a member of the very community within which it would have been widely shared some decades before.

It is beyond doubt that between the twelfth and the thirteenth centuries the discourse on heresy was ideologically framed by the papacy to embrace

---

[28] Ibid., fol. 48r: 'licet d[icti] h[eretici] incitarent ipsum et alios ad audienda verba sua, tamen ipsi noluerunt nec adoraverunt nec comederunt nec biberunt, sed statim recesserunt.'

[29] A theoretical framework is offered by J. C. Scott, *Weapons of the Weak: Everyday Forms of Peasant Resistance* (New Haven, 1985). Medieval examples in C. Wickham, *Courts and Conflict in Twelfth-Century Tuscany* (Oxford, 2003).

[30] *L'inquisiteur Geoffroy d'Ablis*, ed. Pales-Gobilliard, p. 118: 'dixit quod edoctus per dictos hereticos in dicta domo adoravit eos flexis genibus ter, dicendo: "Benedicite" et dicti heretici respondebant: "Deus vos benedicat", et hoc dicebant in qualibet adoracione.'

as broad as possible a range of dissidence, not only religious but political too. The aim was to establish the simplified equation heretic = enemy of the Church, whether on a doctrinal or a political level. Just as being a follower of a deviant creed meant being outside the Church, so did challenging the Church's *libertas*. In the heat of the struggle against the Italian cities, popes such as Honorius III explicitly framed their attempt to fight communal claims in terms of a fight against heresy. This was not a complete invention. The first half of the thirteenth century was indeed the golden age of the heretical movements in northern Italy and heretics did create problems for the Church, in the dynamic and variegated world of the Communes. But the papacy interpreted heresy in the broadest possible terms and started to impose a view of the heresy that incorporated political dissidence. This rigid model was applied almost indiscriminately to the cities of northern Italy, and this certainly caused confusion. In January 1225, confronted with a series of instances of political opposition in Brescia, Pope Honorius III ordered the bishops of Rimini and Brescia to destroy the fortified houses belonging to a number of members of important families of the city (among them the Gambara, the Ugoni and the Oriani) who had been excommunicated for having allegedly conspired with the heretics. Only after those citizens had personally gone to Rome imploring the pope's pardon was the excommunication revoked (although at least some of the fortifications had already been destroyed). In reality, however, these men were not *prima facie* heretics (though some of them might have held deviant religious views). Rather, they were political opponents engaged in struggles for supremacy within the city. And this is what they tried to explain to the pope, as a way to justify their conduct. They explained that the city had long been divided into different factions and that if they had given protection to some fellow citizens who were accused of heresy, they had done so in the name of political allegiance, not because they shared their religious convictions. Faced with a paradigm which they did not recognize as valid to explain the dynamics and politics of their lives, these men reacted. In doing so, they resisted the construction of a discourse which absorbed into heresy any instance of disobedience to the policy of the papacy.[31]

The sceptics have, in my view, somewhat complicated our understanding of religious (be it orthodox or deviant) thought. This is obviously a good thing, because it forces us to rethink our assumptions. On the one hand, they have tested our perception of how twelfth-century heresies worked. The

---

[31] *Epistolae, Epistolae saeculi XIII e regestis pontificum Romanorum selectae*, ed. C. Rodenberg, 3 vols., Monumenta Germaniae Historica (Berlin, 1883), I, no. 264, pp. 189–90; no. 275, pp. 197–8. On all this, see L. Baietto, *Il papa e le città: papato e comuni in Italia centro-settentrionale durante la prima metà del secolo XIII* (Spoleto, 2007), pp. 38–63. See also D. Webb, 'The Pope and the Cities: Anticlericalism and Heresy in Innocent III's Italy', in *The Church and Sovereignity, c. 590–1900: Essays in Honour of Michael Wilks*, ed. D. Wood (Oxford, 1991), pp. 135–52.

Waldensians are 'in'; nobody doubts their existence and the articulation of their structures and of their thought. But the Cathars are 'out': they never existed, nobody associated with heresy in the twelfth and thirteenth centuries in the region between the Garonne and the Rhône was ever called a Cathar. They were called heretics, though, and who those people called 'heretics' were is not entirely clear. On the other hand, the current discussion has greatly enriched our understanding of how orthodoxy worked. Being orthodox was not simply adhering to a system or to a set of religious teachings, it was also declaring and performing obedience to a set of political and economic allegiances. Deviance from that complex set of allegiances is what concerned the dominant ecclesiastical elites.

However, the search for a structured counter-theology as a smoking gun for heresy (and of its absence as an indicator of the non-existence of a doctrine) should not make us forget that the challenge heretics brought to orthodoxy at a local level was not particularly doctrinal. Theological reflections and proposals (which did exist, as the traditionalists have convincingly argued) were indeed marginal compared to daily practice and customs. The main point of heretical experience was, more often than not, literal adherence to the simple, original evangelical message. The sophisticated, overcomplicated, seemingly corrupted orthodox piety was therefore subject to direct daily critique through words, gestures, acts of defiance and sarcasm.[32]

I think that the authors themselves, when reading this book, will find food for their thoughts. The sceptics will have to acknowledge that we cannot expect a local dissident to express his or her animosity towards Catholic beliefs with theological sophistication as regards dualism. Their orthodox, Catholic fellow villagers would most probably not have been any more articulate on issues such as, say, transubstantiation. Sceptics will have to recognize that, if the inquisitorial investigations have to be seen only (or mostly) as acts of domination (and, conversely, of resistance), then the problem of evidence is more subtle than the narrative's simply being concocted, produced and kept by the elite for the elite. It is indeed likely that those subordinates (that is to say the heretics) in southern France played an active part in the production of a sanitized transcript, because this was a way for them to cover their tracks.[33] The sceptics will also have to appreciate that, when discussing the integrated world of twelfth-century Europe, the emergence in southern France of ideas that can be recognized as very similar to Balkan dualism does indeed point

---

[32] Merlo, *Eretici e inquisitori*, pp. 52–3. The role of irony and sarcasm in expressing religious dissent still awaits a comprehensive analysis. For an insight on how, on the other hand, heretics could be derided in the framework of inquisitorial strategies, see T. Scharff, 'Lachen über die Ketzer: Religiöse Devianz und Gelächter im Hochmittelalter', in *Lachgemeinschaften: kulturelle Inszenierungen und soziale Wirkungen im Mittelalter und in der Frühen Neuzeit*, ed. W. Röcke and H. R. Velten (Berlin, 2005), pp. 17–31.

[33] Scott, *Domination and the Arts of Resistance*, p. 87.

towards contact between those two regions. To a large extent we do not need specific, direct evidence of missionaries from Bulgaria in southern France. We have plenty of sources which indicate that people, goods and ideas had been travelling for centuries between western Europe and the Balkans. Sceptics will also have to adjust their views of a centre able to impose almost everything onto its periphery. I am convinced that it is indeed possible that some, perhaps the main part, of the local dynamics were indeed quite confusing for the distant centre, for the papacy: we have seen how Honorius III demonstrated too rigid a view of the fragmented and lively world of the Italian communes. But this does not mean that he was then able to apply his categories indiscriminately, without resistance. It is also indeed possible that when it came to describing what heretics believed in, churchmen ended up using late antique examples as artificial antecedents to those regional sets of beliefs. After all, this is exactly what Innocent III did, when writing in 1207 to the *podestà* and citizens of Treviso: he described the heretics of north-east Italy as *Manichei*, and contrasted their deviant views on marriage, creation and food with those expressed in Paul's first letter to Timothy.[34] However, it seems to me that the process has to be understood the other way round. It is the pope's need to categorize in patristic terms those dissenting beliefs that made him define the heretics *qui se appellant Catharos vel Patarenos* as Manichaeans, just as many churchmen were doing in the second half of the twelfth century. Disobeying the pope was considered as heresy already under Gregory VII, and the grounds and reasons for an individual to be considered heretic rapidly expanded after his death.[35] The tendency, on the part of churchmen, to present the political and social struggles typical of the dynamic world of the Italian communes as fights between heretics and Catholics therefore became the rule, not the exception.[36] As a result, in the course of the thirteenth century the identification of political dissidence with heterodoxy became almost a cliché in the communes of northern Italy.[37]

Meanwhile, the traditionalists will have to concede that the picture is indeed more complicated and nuanced than some have assumed, that the persecutors did often classify customs in terms that their victims found extremely difficult to negotiate explicitly, and they did so to be able to

---

[34] *Die Register Innocenz' III*, ed. O Hageneder et al., vol. 10: *Pontifikatsjahr 1207/1208: Texte und Indices* (Vienna, 2007), n. 54, pp. 85–7 (21 April 1207). See also C. Thouzellier, *Hérésie et hérétiques: vaudois, cathares, patarins, albigeois* (Rome, 1969), pp. 207–8.

[35] O. Hageneder, 'Die Häresie des Ungehorsam und das Entstehen des hierokratischen Papsttum', *Römische Historische Mitteilungen* 20 (1978), 29–47; G. G. Merlo, '"Militare per Cristo" contro gli eretici', in G. G. Merlo, *Contro gli eretici* (Bologna, 1996), pp. 11–49.

[36] C. Violante, 'Le istituzioni ecclesiastiche nell'Italia centro-settentrionale durante il Medioevo: province, diocesi, sedi vescovili', in *Forme di potere e struttura sociale in Italia durante il Medioevo*, ed. G. Rossetti (Bologna, 1977), pp. 83–111 (esp. pp. 84 and 111).

[37] N. J. Housley, 'Politics and Heresy in Italy: Anti-Heretical Crusades, Orders and Confraternities, 1200–1500', *Journal of Ecclesiastical History* 33 (1982), 193–208.

understand and dominate them better. They will have to recognize that power relations were extremely significant in shaping the way in which local people expressed their belief, and that any attempt to reconstruct that system of belief has to take this into account. By being verbalized, translated and written down, the experiences and ideas of dissidents became a constituent part of the relations among people. This does not mean, obviously, that they became objective – that is to say empirically given – facts. It does mean, though, they that ceased to be purely formal and abstract entities and became subject to relations of meaning. And we have to take into account that meaning, as is well known, is the product of constructive and interpretive intentionality.[38] To say things a little more simply, this means that we should always keep in mind that individuals have the inclination, not necessarily devious, to construct meanings that suit them.

This is true not only for medieval clerics. Putting together, one after the other, the chapters included in this volume almost made me feel as if I was in the presence of those medieval disputants (and I am not being facetious here). The way in which the chapters characterize each other's argument is, it seems to me, extremely honest and, at the same time, a powerful reminder that, now just as back then, whenever we characterize an argument which we want to refute, we select and construct a picture of it that suits our own line of thought. At times we even emphasize aspects of the past that give an episode a completely different meaning.[39]

Since it is culturally specific, though, meaning takes shape within models that dictate what is socially acceptable and politically viable. Its construction is therefore not a completely free, boundless open play. To give an example related to our volume, no traditionalist, however vehement and cunning a disputant he or she might be, would ever present a sceptic's views in such a distorted way that the sceptic would appear to be a proponent of the existence of Catharism. The same would obviously be true *vice versa*. As happens with other social practices, the construction of meaning tends to be dominated by those who are provided with the best sense of the game.[40] Moreover, social forces are in place to control the context in which meaning is constructed, accepted, contested. In this sense, the ways in which the materials (gestures, acts, rituals, beliefs etc.) that made up people's lives were organized and

---

[38] J. K. Swindler, 'Normativity: From Individual to Collective', *Journal of Social Philosophy* 39/1 (2008), 116–30 (p. 126).

[39] See, for example, p. 48 n. 114 in Mark Pegg's paper and text preceding n. 40 at p. 284 in Pete Biller's paper. They relate to the same episode, which occurred during the conference held at UCL, but, legitimately, emphasize diametrically opposite aspects of it to make their respective (and conflicting) arguments.

[40] P. Bourdieu, *In Other Words*, trans. M. Adamson (Cambridge, 1994), pp. 9–13, 63, discusses the notion of 'sense of the game', a simpler way of explaining his concept of *habitus*, the latter introduced especially in his *Outline of a Theory of Practice*, trans. R. Nice (Cambridge, 1977), p. 72, and *The Logic of Practice*, trans. R. Nice (Oxford, 1990), p. 53.

expressed can be treated as discursive practices, as a grammar for personal experiences which, once they were reformulated in that specific cultural context, played an important role in determining the rules of the social game. This means that those testimonies can actually be analysed taking into account the fact that the language used to express them dramatically contributed to and influenced the logic of political and social relations.

Disagreement among scholars ran quite deep before our conference: it would be pointless to deny this. Disagreement, it seems to me, does not run much less deep in this volume. This is, however, one of the important features of *Cathars in Question*. I decided not to edit out any sharpness in its various chapters not only because I abhor censorship, but also because the vivacity of the debate is reflected in the vivacity of the writing style of the various authors. The conference ended without consensus, and the volume reflects that. From a methodological point of view, it is interesting to see how historians of different convictions deploy a variety of tools to refute their opponents' arguments. In part, the disagreement has focused on specific empirical details which continue to be, it goes without saying, hotly disputed. For example, there has been an ongoing discussion over the credibility of a reference to a heretical book which, according to the testimony given in 1276 by Peire Perrin from Puylaurens, had been read by some heretics *in Bulgaria*. According to the traditionalists, this indicates a clear a link between Balkan heresies and dissidents in the south-west of France.[41] The connection has been dismissed by the sceptics as a fantasy, due to the fact that this mention would be a *unicum* (this is, in my view, not a very strong point) and, more significantly, because the reading *Bulgaria*, which appears in a seventeenth-century Doat manuscript, is a *lapsus calami* for *vulgaria*.[42] However, we should not forget that, even if this was true, this piece of evidence should not necessarily be dismissed at once, as *vulgaria* is a fairly common alternative spelling for Bulgaria throughout the Middle Ages.[43] Nonetheless, the sceptics' core

---

[41] See for example *Inquisitors and Heretics in Thirteenth-Century Languedoc: Edition and Translation of Toulouse Inquisition Depositions, 1273–1282*, ed. P. Biller, C. Bruschi and S. Sneddon (Leiden, 2011), p. 621 n. 3.

[42] See, for example, Pegg, p. 48 in this volume. For an overview of the mid seventeenth-century transcriptions of inquisitorial records included in the Collection Doat at the Bibliothèque nationale de France, see C. Sparks, *Heresy, Inquisition and Life Cycle in Medieval Languedoc* (York, 2001), pp. 14–15.

[43] Just a few examples among many: *Annales Cavenses*, ed. F. Delle Donne, Fonti per la storia dell'Italia medievale: Rerum Italicarum Scriptores, 3rd s. 9 (Rome, 2011), p. 11: 'et in nono huius imperii anno gens Vulgarorum cum rege suo nomine Asparuch ingressi sunt in terram Romanorum, quae nunc Vulgaria dicta est.'; F. Lošek, *Die Conversio Bagoariorum et Carantanorum und der Brief des Erzbischofs Theotmar von Salzburg*, Monumenta Germaniae Historica, Studien und Texte 15 (Hanover, 1997), p. 122: 'Interim exorta est inter illos aliqua dissensio. Quam Priwina timens fugam iniit in regionem Vulgariam cum suis'; R. Cessi, *Origo civitatum Italie seu Venetiarum (Chronicon altinate et Chronicon gradense)*, Fonti per la storia d'Italia 73 (Rome, 1933), p. 110: 'Mense Iulii 25 die interfectus est Nichoforus

demand – that we interrogate all our sources and inherited paradigms anew, keeping in mind the instability of texts as they are read, re-read, transcribed and copied – remains compelling.

Alongside these, and other, specific empirical points, most of the discussion focuses on issues of interpretation and (at times) of ideology, and this is why it is so interesting. This collection of essays is a powerful reminder to all historians of a profound problem: what constitutes, both in qualitative and quantitative terms, reliable evidence for the construction of a credible historical argument? In a sense, there is perhaps an element of one-upmanship among historians as to who has got the better evidence at their disposal (as if one could say that we will always be able to find someone who is just a little bit more 'early medievalist' than we are). More importantly, though, the issue is whether the inferences we can make are seriously undermined by the various filters that came into play when a set of depositions were elicited and then put in writing by an inquisitor. In other words, how much do our sources really tell us? The sceptics say, very little; the traditionalists say, quite a lot. This obviously does not mean that the latter should be accused of being naive, uncritical readers of their sources who accept unthinkingly any fragment of information that happens to come their way; quite the contrary, the point is to understand what we can infer from the available evidence and, in particular, how far back we can extend the information we find in a document. Here I have to abandon my editorial fence-sitting and say that, in my view, we should be realistic about how much we ask of our sources and deponents. Ideally, of course, we would all subscribe to Moore's suggestion that analyses and interpretations of, say, twelfth-century dynamics should be undertaken exclusively on the basis of evidence produced in the twelfth century. At times though, sources can be read retroactively, because it would be hard to imagine that the situation they illustrate sprang out of nowhere, all of a sudden. So, it is difficult to see why a 1232 copy of a charter issued in 1167 should not be taken as credible evidence that the Council of Saint-Félix-de-Caraman happened when, and how, it is described in the document (obviously provided that, as seems to be the case, the copy from 1232 can be considered genuine).[44]

This is an old issue, central to the work of historians and to how historians relate to their own work and to each other. This volume constitutes an attempt

imperator in Vulgaria a Crumo principe Vulgaro.' (*Vulgaria* appears in the thirteenth-century Dresden, Sächsische Landesbibliothek, Cod. F 168); *Fundatio monasterii sancti Pauli in Carinthia*, ed. O. Holder-Egger, Monumenta Germaniae Historica, Scriptores 15/2 (Hanover, 1888), pp. 1057–60 (p. 1060): 'Hunc in reditum a Ierusalem defunctum et in Vulgaria sepultum'.

[44] On this, see *L'histoire du catharisme en discussion: le 'concile' de Saint-Félix (1167)*, ed. M. Zerner (Nice, 2001), as well as, in this volume, M. G. Pegg (pp. 46–7), J. H. Arnold (pp. 71–2), B. Hamilton (pp. 140–9), C. Bruschi (p. 203), R. I. Moore (p. 258) and P. Biller (pp. 292–301).

to move the debate forward and also, hopefully, to be a source of ideas for future analysis. After all, even when disagreeing with each other, the essays here collected all contribute to make medieval religious and political deviance emerge in all its complexity, richness and specificity. The series of religious and institutional crises which occurred in Europe at the cusp between the eleventh and twelfth centuries provide the backdrop to the stories and names, big or small, evoked in the following pages. On the one hand, in the first half of the twelfth century popes such as Callixtus II, Honorius II and Innocent II reorganized the structures of the Church and, as a result, bishops were in general able to regain those privileges which, in previous centuries, had been gradually eroded by many monastic institutions.[45] On the other, the emergence, throughout Europe, of collective and individual uncertainties, of a general resentment towards centralized institutions, of the widespread quest for new forms of religious charisma which could be verified individually and locally, resulted in new ways of looking at Christianity and in original, subjective and instrumental ideas about salvation.[46]

In discussing the dynamics and the effects of this clash between the normative efforts of centralized institutions and the aspirations of individual, residual forms of religiosity, the various chapters of this volume address issues that are of key interest for historians of any period: what constitutes popular belief; how orthodoxy, in all its acceptations, is the result of a continuous process of conflict and negotiation; in what ways, and to what extent, societies are based on the suppression (whatever shape it might take) of dissidents; to what degree heresy, in its broader sense, can be seen as an invention. Ultimately, they bring back to the attention of readers the significance and meaning of the stories of people, beliefs and ambitions that, whoever, wherever and whatever they were, ended up being largely wiped out by repressing authorities.

---

[45] G. M. Cantarella, 'Un problema del XII secolo: l'ecclesiologia di Pietro il Venerabile', *Studi medievali*, 3rd s. 19 (1978), 159–209 (especially pp. 159–64), with bibliography. See also G. M. Cantarella, 'Cluny, Lione, Roma (1119–1142)', *Revue bénédictine* 90 (1980), 263–87. On the institutional effects of the Reform, see *Il monachesimo e la riforma ecclesiastica (1049–1122): atti della quarta settimana internazionale di studio, Mendola, 23–29 agosto 1968* (Milan, 1971).

[46] O. Capitani, 'Eresie nel Medioevo o Medioevo ereticale?', in *Eretici ed eresie medievali nella storiografia contemporanea: atti del XXXII convegno di studi sulla riforma e i movimenti religiosi in Italia* = *Bollettino della Società di studi valdesi / Bulletin de la Société d'histoire vaudoise* 111/174 (1994), 5–15 (p. 15).

2

The Paradigm of Catharism; or, the Historians' Illusion

Mark Gregory Pegg

Catharism was neither a Balkan heresy, a construct of the persecuting society, or, for that matter, even a medieval phenomenon, as it has never existed, except as an enduring invention of late nineteenth-century scholars of religion and history. The historical and epistemological paradigm shaping and guiding research on Catharism for more than a century is moribund. Great (if misguided) scholarship was achieved within this paradigm, including some of the methods and insights now leading to its obsolescence. What distinguishes historians who persist in accepting (and defending) the reality of Catharism is, as Thomas Kuhn argued about scientists wedded to conventional wisdom, 'how little they aim to produce major novelties, conceptual or phenomenal'.[1] This blinkered competence, where the achievements of older scholars are solemnly replicated, and all new research is wilfully ignored, consistently misunderstood, or vehemently rejected (and, every so often, a curious mix of all three), encourages either a studious treading of intellectual waters, hoping against hope that the tide is not turning, or a learned backstroke to around 1970, although, depending on the current, it is, more often than not, 1870. It is this retreat by many (really, too many) historians recently into earlier academic accomplishments and assumptions, along with a debating style closer to soapbox moralism than scholarly analysis, that, more than anything else, reveals how profound and threatening is the ongoing paradigm shift – for that is what it is – of a Middle Ages without Catharism.

The old paradigm of Catharism was, and still is, shaped by two seemingly incompatible methodological approaches to the past. The first and dominant approach views the study of religion and heresy as an exercise in intellectual history. This intellectualist bias presumes that what defines heresies are coherent theologies and doctrines compiled and disseminated in canonical

---

[1] T. Kuhn, *The Structure of Scientific Revolutions*, 4th edn (Chicago, 2012), p. 35. Now, see the collected essays edited by M. D. Gordin and E. L. Milam reflecting on Kuhn's book fifty years after its publication: *Historical Studies in the Natural Sciences* 42 (2012), 476–580.

texts by heretical leaders.² Although this bias was implicit in most scholarly research into religion before the late nineteenth century, it was only after 1870 that this idealist inclination was explicitly codified as a method, especially by German academics practising the new *Religionsgeschichte*.³ This 'religious-historical school' approached the study of religion, especially Christianity, by comparing seemingly similar philosophies, symbols, and myths among different systems of belief. Religious origins and mythical connections were made across Eurasia from ancient empires to modern in this comparative search for ideal resemblances. Crucially, before such similarities were even discerned, it was necessary for scholars to classify some belief systems as 'world religions' or 'universal religions' resembling Christianity (and, for the most part, Protestant Christianity). A world religion was characterized as possessing an elaborate clerical hierarchy, evangelical missionaries, fixed rituals, foundational sacred texts, and a clear distinction between the secular and the religious. Hinduism, Confucianism, and Buddhism, for instance, were constructed as world religions, but so too were late antique paganism, Gnosticism, and Manichaeism.⁴ When Johann Joseph Ignaz von Döllinger (who, unusually for a scholar influenced by *Religionsgeschichte*, was Catholic, albeit excommunicated in 1871 for his anti-Ultramontanism) published his influential history of Catharism and Waldensianism in 1890, the former was a world religion and a medieval continuation of Gnosticism and Manichaeism (and the accompanying volume of edited sources was, and remains, a remarkable achievement).⁵

---

2   On the intellectualist bias generally in the study of religion, see M. Douglas, 'Rightness of Categories', in *How Classification Works: Nelson Goodman among the Social Sciences*, ed. M. Douglas and D. Hull (Edinburgh, 1992), pp. 239–71, and M. Douglas, *In The Wilderness: The Doctrine of Defilement in the Book of Numbers* (Sheffield, 1993), pp. 26–9. Specifically, on medieval heresy, see M. G. Pegg, *The Corruption of Angels: The Great Inquisition of 1245–1246* (Princeton, 2001), pp. 15–19, and M. G. Pegg, 'Albigenses in the Antipodes: An Australian and the Cathars', *Journal of Religious History*, 35 (2011), 577–600.
3   On *Religionsgeschichte*, see Suzanne Marchand's superb *German Orientalism in the Age of Empire: Religion, Race, and Scholarship* (Washington DC, 2009), esp. pp. 259–67. See also, J. Turner, *Philology: The Forgotten Origins of the Modern Humanities* (Princeton, 2014), pp. 357–80.
4   Marchand, *German Orientalism in the Age of Empire*, pp. 259, 262, and, on Buddhism, pp. 270–9, 298, 319–20, on Hinduism, pp. 193, 317–18, on Confucianism, pp. 372, 476, on Gnosticism, pp. 268, 286–7; T. Masuzawa, *The Invention of World Religions; or, How European Universalism was Preserved in the Language of Pluralism* (Chicago, 2005), pp. 107–20, on inventing Buddhism as a 'world religion', pp. 121–46; C. S. Adcock, *The Limits of Tolerance: Indian Secularism and the Politics of Religious Freedom* (Oxford, 2013), esp. pp. 1–84 on the invention of Hinduism; A. Sun, *Confucianism as a World Religion: Contested Histories and Contemporary Realities* (Princeton, 2013), esp. pp. 17–44, 97–111, on Confucianism as a 'world religion' paradigm; and K. King, *What is Gnosticism?* (Cambridge MA, 2003), pp. 71–110, on *Religiongeschichte* and the making of Gnosticism.
5   J. von Döllinger, *Beitrage zur Sektengeschichte des Mittelalters: Geschichte der gnostisch-manichäischen Sekten* (vol. 1) and *Dokumente vornehmlich zur Geschichte der Valdesier und Katharer* (vol. 2) (Munich, 1890).

The Paradigm of Catharism; or, the Historians' Illusion

The most important exponent of the 'religious-historical school' for medieval heresy was Herbert Grundmann, whose *Religiöse Bewegungen im Mittelalter* (1935) represents what was once so innovative about this methodology in the nineteenth century, and what ultimately was and remains so limiting about it.[6] By comparing the beliefs of individual heretics, wandering preachers, early mendicants, and specific religious women in the twelfth and thirteenth centuries, he argued that the religious motivation underlying all of them, such as adopting an 'apostolic life', was similar. Indeed, he suggested there was one general religious movement shaping Latin Christendom before 1200, which only fractured into heterodox and orthodox movements during the papacy of Innocent III.[7] These were undeniably interesting (if not necessarily correct) insights, even if they were barely noticed until after 1960.[8] Religion possessed a naturalism for Grundmann, in that it was an innate human quality manifested in ideas, ready-made for comparative study and, most importantly, scientific generalizations. In the late nineteenth century such naturalistic presumptions, particularly in Germany, were what defined history as a science. The past challenged the historian in the same way as nature confronted the scientist. Scholars engaged in *Religionsgeschichte* approached religion as a natural process rather than a historical one.[9] They wanted to study religion 'objectively', freeing it from the confessional identities (principally Catholic, Protestant, and to a lesser extent, Jewish) defining scholars of religion before 1850. This *Objektivität* was seen as different from the pure historicism associated with Leopold von Ranke, not so much *wie es eigentlich gewesen* ('as it essentially was') – focused on nations, politics,

---

6 H. Grundmann, *Religiöse Bewegungen im Mittelalter: Untersuchungen über die geschichtlichen Zusammenhänge zwischen der Ketzerei, den Bettelorden und der religiösen Frauenbewegung im 12. und 13. Jahrhundert und über die geschichtlichen Grundlagen der deutschen Mystik*, 2nd edn (Hildesheim, 1961 [1st edn 1935]). Translated by Steven Rowan as *Religious Movements in the Middle Ages: The Historical Links between Heresy, the Mendicant Orders, and the Women's Religious Movement in the Twelfth and Thirteenth Century, with the Historical Foundations of German Mysticism* (Notre Dame, 1995), and see esp. Robert E. Lerner's insightful 'Introduction', pp. ix–xxv. For other observations on Grundmann's influence, see J. Van Engen, 'The Christian Middle Ages as an Historiographic Problem', *American Historical Review* 91 (1986), 523–4; S. Farmer and B. H. Rosenwein, 'Introduction', in *Monks and Nuns, Saints and Outcasts: Religion in Medieval Society: Essays in Honor of Lester K. Little*, ed. S. Farmer and B. H. Rosenwein (Ithaca NY, 2000), pp. 2–3; P. Biller, 'Through a Glass Darkly: Seeing Medieval Heresy', in *The Medieval World*, ed. P. Linehan and J. L. Nelson (London, 2001), p. 309; and G. Constable, 'From Church History to Religious Culture: The Study of Medieval Religious Life and Spirituality', in *European Religious Cultures: Essays Offered to Christopher Brooke on the Occasion of his Eightieth Birthday*, ed. M. Rubin (London, 2008), pp. 8–9.
7 Grundmann, *Religiöse Bewegungen im Mittelalter*, esp. pp. 5–156.
8 Lerner, 'Introduction', p. xxii.
9 R. G. Collingwood, *The Idea of History* (Oxford, 1946), esp. pp. 135–204, remains insightful on this question of 'scientific history' among European scholars in the late nineteenth and early twentieth centuries.

and institutions – as a scientific search for the beginnings of (and the connections between) world religions, a neo-Romantic quest for ineffable historical truth hidden within (and between) texts.[10] (Ranke's 'objectivity' was itself a Romantic reaction against the universal rationality of the eighteenth century, and more a statement of narrative intention than a philosophical ideal.)[11] The 'religious-historical school' collected doctrines as if they were exotic plants, regarding such compilations as empirical research. The question of origins was answered by finding the first person to think a thought or the first text to expound a belief. Grundmann's scholarship suffered from these faults, and yet, unlike many of his imitators, his acumen transcended the limitations of his method.

That is, apart from Catharism, as Grundmann followed the standard account established in the nineteenth century by scholars such as Döllinger, and which the great Ernst Troeltsch endorsed as recently as 1919.[12] Although Grundmann argued the Cathars initially shared some similarities with western apostolic groups when they entered Europe around 1140, they remained outsiders, never completely fitting into his religious movement model, even if their dualism conveniently provided the philosophical 'superstructure' (*Überbau*) supporting the ideas of various heretics in the twelfth century.[13] The 'severely eastern foreignness' of Catharism always meant it was an 'alien import', separate from, even if it was partially shaped by, medieval Latin Christianity.[14] The enthusiasm for discovering eastern influences within western religiosity was and remains a hallmark of the 'religious-historical school'.[15] This *Orientalistik* (and it was and remains a particularly German

---

[10] Marchand, *German Orientalism in the Age of Empire*, p. 260.

[11] On Leopold von Ranke and 'as it essentially was', see H. White, 'Ranke: Historical Realism as Comdey', in his *MetaHistory: The Historical Imagination in Nineteenth-Century Europe* (Baltimore, 1973), pp. 163–90; W. P. Fuchs, 'Was heisst das: 'bloss zeigen, wie es eigentlich gewesen'?', *Geschichte in Wissenshaft und Unterricht* 11 (1979), 655–77; A. Grafton, *The Footnote: A Curious History* (Cambridge MA, 1997), p. 69; J. D. Shaw, 'Vision as Revision: Ranke and the Beginning of Modern History', *History and Theory* 46 (2007), 45–60; P. Müller, 'Doing Historical Research in the Early Nineteenth Century: Leopold Ranke, the Archive Policy, and the *relazioni*', *Storia della storiografia* 56 (2009), 80–103; F. Rexroth, 'Geschichte erforschen oder Geschichte schreigen? Die deutschen Historiker und ihr Spätmittelalter 1859–2009', *Historische Zeitschrift* 289 (2009), 120–1; G. G. Iggers, 'Introduction', in L. von Ranke, *The Theory and Practice of History*, ed. G. G. Iggers, trans. K. von Moltke and W. A. Iggers (New York, 2011), pp. xi–xlv, esp. p. xiv.

[12] E. Troeltsch, *Die soziallehren der christlichen Kirchen und Gruppen* (Tübingen, 1919), p. 385: 'die gnostisch-manichäthe Sekte der Katharer, die vom Orient her auf Handelswegen und von den byzantinischen Enklaven Italiens sich ausbreitete und van da in die nordalpinen Gebiete vordrang.' Now, see Biller, 'Through a Glass Darkly', p. 322, for his discussion of Troeltsch's model of *Verkirchlichung* ('Churchification') and its application to the Waldensians.

[13] Grundmann, *Religiöse Bewegungen im Mittelalter*, p. 26.

[14] Ibid., p. 496.

[15] Marchand, *German Orientalism in the Age of Empire*, p. 266.

variety of 'Orientalism') undergirding Catharism is largely ignored by adherents of the paradigm. Even more conveniently, Grundmann asserted that Waldensianism was in part a lay Catholic reaction to Catharism.[16] All contemporary scholarship working within the old paradigm of Catharism replicates the religious naturalism of *Religionsgeschichte*, even if it is only through emulating Grundmann, and the assumption that the history of religion is more or less an exercise in the history of ideas.[17] Grundmann's notion that the Waldensians were provoked as much (if not more so in the twelfth century) by Cathar heresiarchs as the hierarchy of the Church is adopted, largely implicitly, by many scholars. Peter Biller, for example, follows Grundmann in arguing that Catharism as an established eastern philosophy and 'counter-Church' must have existed before Waldensianism, otherwise the latter could not have come into existence as a coherent western religious movement.[18] Catharism was a dynamic world religion for Grundmann, as it still is for anyone who believes in the existence of this heresy, whether they realize it or not.

The second, and less influential, methodological approach underpinning the conventional picture of Catharism is studying the social history of towns and villages where Cathars supposedly lived and compiling prosopographies of heretical individuals. Such social historians of Catharism almost defiantly turn away from studying ideas, taking for granted the traditional narrative as defined by scholars such as Grundmann, so that despite some remarkable studies on, for example, heretical families (or rather, families accused of heresy) in Toulouse by John Hine Mundy,[19] the Quercy by Claire Taylor,[20] Orvieto by Carol Lansing,[21] or Montauban by Jörg Feuchter,[22] all the evidence sorted and analysed, especially from archives, exists not so much as

---

[16] Grundmann, *Religiöse Bewegungen im Mittelalter*, p. 494.

[17] For example, M. Lambert, *Medieval Heresy: Medieval Popular Movements from the Gregorian Reform to the Reformation*, 3rd edn (Oxford, 2002), pp. 7–8, acknowledges his narrative and methodology is mostly shaped by Grundmann.

[18] P. Biller, 'Goodbye to Waldensiansm?' *Past and Present* 192 (2006), 3–33 (esp. pp. 7–8).

[19] Among his many works, see esp. J. H. Mundy, *Men and Women at Toulouse in the Age of the Cathars* (Toronto, 1990), and J. H. Mundy, *Society and Government at Toulouse in the Age of the Cathars* (Toronto, 1997).

[20] C. Taylor, *Heresy, Crusade and Inquisition in Medieval Quercy* (York, 2011). Taylor does address belief to some extent, implicitly recognizing that a history of heresy must be more than thoughts and philosophies, that the communities in which heretics lived must have some relationship to the beliefs they supposedly held, but as she never articulates any connection between ideas and society, her oscillating chapters between traditional social history and even more traditional intellectual history do not cohere. What holds the book together is the conviction that heresy in Latin Christendom was shaped by a dualism imported from the East and institutionalized in a 'Cathar Church'.

[21] C. Lansing, *Power and Purity: Cathar Heresy in Medieval Italy* (New York, 1998).

[22] J. Feuchter, *Ketzer, Konsuln, und Büßer: Die städtischen Eliten von Montauban vor dem Inquisitor Petrus Cellani (1236/1241)* (Tübingen, 2007).

a complement to the old paradigm, as detached acquiescence to it. (Feuchter, while describing his exceptional study as a *totale Mikrostudie*, demonstrates, more than anything else, the widespread confusion about what actually constitutes a 'microhistory'. There is a tendency to assume that this approach relates to questions of scale, rather than methodology. A traditional social history steadfastly within the paradigm of Catharism, no matter how sophisticated, is not a 'microhistory', total or otherwise.)[23] Much of this scholarly predisposition derives not just from the conventions of social history, but from a particular kind of religious history, once again largely systematized in the late nineteenth century and equated with Christianity, where studying parishes, bequests, tithes, property rights, clerical governance, in other words, all manner of ecclesiastical institutions, was a way of confirming the mundane aspects of a religion already defined by theology and doctrine. Obviously, if a religion is designated by such social and structural elements, then Catharism is composed of them as well.

It is only in the last twenty or so years that religion and heresy have become pivotal topics in medieval history in English-speaking countries. Since the late nineteenth century and for most of the twentieth the scholarly emphasis was on constitutional, institutional, legal, and intellectual history, with occasional forays into the history of art and economics. When David Knowles lectured on a century of trends in medieval history among British scholars in 1968, 'pride of place' belonged to English constitutional history, with no one (including himself apparently) studying religion.[24] A year later Joseph Strayer lectured on the future of medieval history in the United States, and while he warned against complacency – 'We should never forget we began as antiquarians and we could end again as antiquarians' – the destiny of American medievalists was definitely not in studying religion or heresy, it was in social-economic history (even if he had reservations about such a trajectory).[25] Ironically, two years later, in what at first seems like a brilliant

---

[23] Feuchter, *Ketzer, Konsuln, und Büßer*, p. 5. Now, see C. Ginzburg, 'Our Words, and theirs: A Reflection on the Historian's Craft, Today', in *Historical Knowledge: In Quest of Theory, Method and Evidence*, ed. S. Fellman and M. Rahikainen (Newcastle-upon-Tyne, 2012), pp. 97–120, esp. pp. 114–16, for a lucid statement on what constitutes 'microhistory' (even if, it must be admitted, he has caused some of the confusion about the model himself). For an interesting discussion of microhistory and global history, see J.-P. A. Ghobrial, 'The Secret Life of Elias of Babylon and the Uses of Global Microhistory', *Past and Present* 222 (2014), 51–93.

[24] D. Knowles, 'Some Trends in Scholarship, 1868–1968, in the Field of Medieval History', *Transactions of the Royal Historical Society* 5th s. 19 (1969), 139–57 (esp. p. 154). Also, see Constable, 'From Church History to Religious Culture', p. 6.

[25] J. R. Strayer, 'The Future of Medieval History', *Medievalia et Humanistica*, n.s. 2 (1971), 179–88 (esp. p. 181). This is a remarkably prescient analysis about the past and future of medieval history as a field, which, in some respects could have been written within the last decade. See E. A. R. Brown, 'Another Perspective on Alterity and the Grotesque (1932–)', in *Women Medievalists and the Academy*, ed. J. Chance (Madison, 2005), pp.

riposte to himself, he published *The Albigensian Crusades*; except, as far as he was concerned, there was nothing new to say about the 'Cathar Church', whereas what was important for him was how crusaders and inquisitors reshaped the political, legal, and institutional history of the French monarchy and the papacy, leading to the 'crisis of late medieval civilization'.[26] Religion and heresy were secondary (and more often than not, tertiary) concerns for Strayer, as they were for his own teacher, Charles Homer Haskins, where they were auxiliaries to writing intellectual or institutional history.[27] The trouble for Haskins, Strayer, and four generations of American historians was that religion and heresy were unable to be studied 'objectively' in the Rankean manner – or at least as American historians transformed *Objektivität* and *Wissenschaft* into an 'objective science' of history between 1880 and 1930, translating *wie es eigentlich gewesen* without Ranke's nuance into 'as it really was' – as they were topics still imbued with scholastic confessionalism.[28] The 'objectivity' of the 'religious-historical school' convinced few American historians before the 1960s. British historians (even Knowles, who was a Benedictine monk) were tacitly of the same opinion.

What this means is that religion and heresy for most of the twentieth century were divorced from mainstream historiographic trends among English-speaking historians. At best, they were taken for granted, supporting players to more important research; at worst, they were ignored, subjects only fit for philosophers, theologians, vicars, and monks. There were notable exceptions, such as R. I. Moore's seminal *The Formation of a Persecuting Society* (1987), which, while powerfully reshaping discussion about heresy in the eleventh and twelfth centuries (and Judaism, leprosy, and homosexuality), was,

919–21, 927, for her memories of Strayer and when this article was initially given as a plenary lecture at the Midwest Medieval Conference at the University of Illinois, Champagne-Urbana, on 15 November 1969.

[26] J. R. Strayer, *The Albigensian Crusades: With a New Epilogue by Carol Lansing* (Ann Arbor, 1992), p. 174.

[27] For example, see C. H. Haskins, 'Robert Le Bourge and the Beginning of the Inquisition in Northern France', *American Historical Review* 7 (1902), 437–57, which, while still a remarkably useful article, was only interested in the institutional history of the medieval inquisitions; see also his *The Renaissance of the Twelfth Century* (Cambridge MA, 1927), pp. 43, 63, 176, 346–9, 353, for heresy and intellectual history.

[28] P. Novick, *That Noble Dream: The 'Objectivity Question' and the American Historical Profession* (Cambridge, 1988), pp. 21–46, is excellent as a study of 'objectivity' among American historians and as an exemplum of the uncertainty about studying religion, as the topic barely rates a mention, except in relation to anthropologists like Mary Douglas and Clifford Geertz, pp. 546–63, and then tangentially, occuring within Part IV, 'Objectivity in Crisis'. There is no entry in the Index on 'Religion' or 'Religious History'. See also Constable, 'From Church History to Religious Culture', p. 4: 'When I first went to the University of Iowa (than called the State University of Iowa) in 1955 religion was taught by professors who were each supported by their own denominations, since the university was forbidden to teach religion; and in some universities church history is still taught in a separate department and even a separate faculty.'

nevertheless, largely uninterested in the problem of religion.[29] Interestingly, Moore at the time still took Catharism for granted, even if the implications of his argument suggested otherwise. Then again, it is a far-reaching argument, some of whose ramifications are only now coming into startling clarity. Another exception was Caroline Walker Bynum's equally influential *Holy Fast and Holy Feast* (1987), which, apart from following Grundmann's model of religion, relies to a surprising extent upon the paradigm of Catharism (especially dualism) for understanding the 'extravagant asceticism' of late medieval women.[30] (It is worth noting that Bynum's understanding of twelfth-century theologians is the opposite of Moore's, seeing evolving 'moderation' where he saw developing persecution.)[31] Surprisingly, Paul Freedman and Gabrielle Spiegel, surveying what they called 'the rediscovery of alterity' among American medievalists in 1998, said nothing about heresy (or religion for that matter), revealing not only the wearisome conventionality within so much scholarship influenced by postmodernism, but also that, however much heretics exemplified 'otherness', what was known about them was as much as we were ever going to know.[32] This grand and long-lasting isolation of religion and heresy inevitably led to theoretical and methodological stagnation, which, despite renewed interest since the 1970s, and the current prominence of these topics since 2001, remains difficult to overcome.[33] The retrograde paradigm of Catharism, and the scholarly practices underpinning it, exemplifies this enduring inertia.

It is surprising (and disappointing) just how tenacious are so many modern scholars in clinging to 'Catharism' as a descriptor, even when they know that very few heretics were called 'Cathars' in the Middle Ages, and that, like so much else about this 'heresy', the term is a learned misnomer from the nineteenth century. Crucially, no one accused of heresy or identifying as

---

[29] R. I. Moore, *The Formation of a Persecuting Society: Authority and Deviance in Western Europe, 950–1250*, 2nd eds (Oxford, 2007), esp. pp. 144–96, for his reflections on the debate around the 'persecuting society'.

[30] C. Walker Bynum, *Holy Fast and Holy Feast: The Religious Significance of Food to Medieval Women* (Berkeley, 1987), esp. pp. 16–20, 64, 238, 243, 252–3, 266.

[31] Ibid., esp. p. 238 and *passim*.

[32] P. Freedman and G. Freedman, 'Medievalisms Old and New: The Rediscovery of Alterity in North American Medieval Studies', *American Historical Review* 103 (1998), 677–704.

[33] In the essays collected by Constance Hoffman Berman in *Medieval Religion: New Approaches* (New York, 2005), heresy is barely mentioned – again revealing the tendency among many scholars to think there is nothing new to be said on the subject; each article, for the most part, envisions religion as an exercise in intellectual history, demonstrating that there is nothing very 'new' in these approaches, except perhaps some of the topics. What is topically innovative and methodologically innovative is not the same thing, though this distinction is frequently blurred. Now, see Christine Caldwell Ames's perceptive survey of some of this malaise in her, 'Medieval Religious, Religions, Religion', *History Compass* 10 (2012), 334–52.

a heretic in the twelfth and thirteenth centuries between the Garonne and Rhône rivers, the supposed heartland of Catharism, was ever called by the name, or adopted it for themselves. Then again, the stubborn white-knuckle embrace of the term by many historians goes back no further than 2001, when, largely for the first time, its Wilhelmine and Edwardian imprimatur was actually noticed.[34] What is so intriguing is that within the paradigm of Catharism there was and is an emphasis on discovering and editing texts. Philological precision is usually respected within such a tradition, and yet, when push comes to shove, it is dismissed as a trifling technicality. (The work of palaeographers and editors, for all their great skill, rarely if ever challenges historiographic conventions.) It could be argued, rather like the debate about 'feudalism', that, despite such a poor and anachronistic choice of words, the phenomenon identified as 'Catharism' was real and, until some more suitable term comes along, it is better than nothing.[35] Unfortunately, the whole edifice of Catharism collapses without the name, for when scholars use it, promiscuously stamping almost every instance of heresy in the twelfth and thirteenth centuries with the label – that is, apart from the Waldensians – they create the very reality they supposedly discover.

The epitome (and lodestar) of this self-fulfilling method is Arno Borst's *Die Katharer* (1953), which, beginning in the eleventh century with the scattered references to heretics by Latin Christian intellectuals and ending in the thirteenth with the surfeit of polemics, manuals, and inquisition records, compiles citation after citation to Cathars by deciding that any reference to 'Manicheans', 'Arians', 'Patarenes', 'the heretics', or accusation of dualism, however vague or inconsistent, was a reference to Catharism.[36] Borst, who was briefly Grundmann's assistant,[37] added very little to the established narrative of Catharism, but then that was not his concern. Rather, as a third-generation exponent of the 'religious-historical school', having studied at Göttingen with the medievalist Percy Ernst Schramm and the Orientalist Hans Heinrich Schaeder (who worked on Iranian Manichaeism),[38] he diligently confirmed convention through compilation and resolutely disavowed any relationship of religion or heresy with society, going so far as

---

[34] Pegg, *The Corruption of Angels*, pp. 15–19, and M. G. Pegg, 'On the Cathars, the Albigensians, and Good Men of Languedoc', *Journal of Medieval History* 27 (2001), 181–95.

[35] Taylor, *Heresy, Crusade, and Inquisition*, p. 6, questions the applicability of the terms 'feudal' and 'feudalism' for the Aquitaine, ultimately deciding they suggest a consistency and coherence she considers spurious, unlike the paradigm of Catharism, which she adopts without reservation.

[36] A. Borst, *Die Katharer* (Stuttgart, 1953).

[37] Borst discussed the life and work of Grundmann (it reveals much about both men) in 'Herbert Grundmann (1902–1970)', in Herbert Grundmann, *Ausgewählte Aufsätze*, 3vols., Monumenta Germaniae Historica Schriften 25 (Stuttgart, 1976), I, 1–25.

[38] I would like to thank Jörg Feuchter for reminding me of Arno Borst's Göttingen teachers, especially Hans Heinrich Schaeder.

to disparage (with deliberate Cold War overtones) the rather unexceptional social and institutional historical methodology of Austin Evans (who was Mundy's teacher) as a 'sozialistische These'.[39] A search key and a database largely eliminates the 'compilation school' of scholarship associated with historians like Borst, if not the intellectual history that rides upon such compendiums.[40] A year after Borst's monograph appeared, Arsenio Frugoni forcefully argued against the pervasive influence of the philological and idealist method in the history of heresy in his *Arnaldo da Brescia nelle fonti del secolo XII*, which, regrettably, has had little influence, especially among English-speaking scholars.[41] Every scholar trapped within the paradigm of Catharism engages in the same word-play as Borst. This palimpsestic approach to the past scrubs out more than just words, it erases the context in which they once had meaning, so that the paradigm of Catharism explains the very texts supposedly explaining it.

Around 1900, though, designating heretics attacked by crusaders and interrogated by inquisitors as 'Cathars' permitted some scholars to either abandon or absorb within Catharism the so-called 'Albigenses' or 'Albigensians'. When Pope Innocent III proclaimed a crusade against the heretics and mercenaries infesting the lands of Raimon VI, count of Toulouse, in 1208, he never mentioned 'Albigensians' or 'Cathars', only ever referring to 'the heretics' or the 'Provençal heretics'.[42] In the first two years of the crusade some northern French nobles used 'Albigenses' or 'Albigensian lands' as terms signifying

---

[39] Borst, *Die Katharer*, p. 49. Now, see A. Evans, 'Social Aspects of Medieval Heresy', in *Persecution and Liberty: Essays in Honor of George Lincoln Burr* (New York, 1931), pp. 93–116, and J. H. Mundy, *The Repression of Catharism at Toulouse* (Toronto, 1985), p. 57 n. 49.

[40] D. Armitage, 'What's the Big Idea? Intellectual History and the Longue Durée', *History of European Ideas* 38 (2012), 493–507, for the remarkably blinkered affirmation that, far from undermining this model of intellectual history, a database and search key will just make it easier to do, and on an even bigger scale.

[41] A. Frugoni, *Arnaldo da Brescia nelle fonti del secolo XII* (Rome, 1954). Now, see G. G. Merlo, *Eretici del medioevo: temi e paradossi di storia e storiografia* (Brescia, 2011), pp. 34–9 on Frugoni.

[42] M. G. Pegg, *A Most Holy War: The Albigensian Crusade and the Battle for Christendom* (Oxford, 2008), pp. 60–1. Almost all contemporary historians of the Albigensian crusade, when not reciting the old narrative of Catharism, avoid any discussion of heresy. Laurence W. Marvin's fine political and military study of the crusade, *The Occitan War: A Military and Political History of the Albigensian Crusade, 1209–1218* (Cambridge, 2008), dismisses the problem of heresy in a few sentences as a meaningless distraction for him and the crusaders: 'The Cathar heresy, the darling of those who study "the other", plays a very small role in this account', he writes (p. xiv), 'just as it did once the broadswords were withdrawn from their sheaths and the first crossbow bolt shot'. His position is more nuanced in 'The Albigensian Crusade in Anglo-American Historiography, 1888–2013', *History Compass* 11 (2013), 1126–38. Now, see M. G. Pegg, 'Innocent III, les "pestilentiels provençaux" et le paradigme épuisé du catharisme', *Innocent III et le Midi = Cahiers de Fanjeaux* 50 (2015), 225–79.

southerners or lands in the south, without any implication that this terminology involved heresy.[43] These designations derived from Albi's being the southernmost diocese within Bourges, the southernmost archdiocese of France. After 1209 'Albigensian' applied to individuals opposing or accused of opposing Simon de Montfort as lord of the Albigeois and leader of the crusade, and by 1211 it was the common name given to all southern heretics by northern crusaders, historians, preachers, biographers, and poets.[44] Admittedly, when the Cistercian historian Peter les Vaux-de-Cernay was writing around 1215, he specified that 'Albigensian' only applied to southern heretics who were not Waldensians.[45] By the eighteenth and early nineteenth centuries, the 'Albigensians' were parochial proto-Protestants from southern France, victims of the Catholic Church and the depredations of the northern French monarchy.[46]

The shift away from viewing the Albigensians within an exclusively confessional and national narrative, and so weaving them into the new story of the Eurasian universal religion of the Cathars, while in full swing by 1900, was already occurring a half century earlier, and mostly among Protestant scholars. 'The denomination of the Albigensians has been used by historians and other writers', began an eponymous entry in the London *Penny Cyclopaedia* (1833), 'often indiscriminately'. These heretics, stressed the anonymous (and very smart) author, were a 'branch of the Cathari, who were themselves the descendants of the Paulicians, a branch of the Manicheans, from the East'.[47] Charles Schmidt anticipated the methodology eventually

---

[43] D. Power, 'Who went on the Albigensian Crusade?' *English Historical Review* 128 (2013), 1047–85, is excellent on demonstrating that the term 'Albigensian' was used around 1208 by some northern French nobility before going on crusade in 1209. He claims this undermines the arguments of J.-L. Biget's *Hérésie et inquisition dans le midi de la France* (Paris, 2007), pp. 142–69, and Pegg, *A Most Holy War*, pp. 21–2, 117, that 'Albigensian' was associated with heresy a few years later, 1209 for Biget, and 1210 or 1211 for Pegg. Crucially, what he does not show is that 'Albigensian' was a synonym for heresy between the Garonne and Rhône Rivers before the beginning of the crusade – he merely assumes the name always had this meaning. Interestingly, he only mentions 'Cathars' once, arguing it is inappropriate for the crusade; nevertheless, wary of explicitly taking a side in the debate on Catharism, he studiously avoids discussing the question of heresy in any detail.

[44] Pegg, *A Most Holy War*, pp. 21–2, 117.

[45] *Petri Vallium Sarnaii monachi hystoria Albigensis*, ed. P. Guébin and E. Lyon (Paris, 1926), Preface, §4, pp. 3–4, and Part 1, §§10–19, pp. 9–20.

[46] S. Pott [Richter], 'Radical Heretics, Martyrs, or Witnesses of Truth? The Albigenses in Ecclesiastical History and Literature (1550–1850)', in *Heresy in Transition: Transforming Ideas of Heresy in Medieval and Early Modern Europe*, ed. I. Hunter, J. C. Laursen, and C. J. Nederman (Aldershot, 2005), pp. 181–94.

[47] *The Penny Cyclopaedia of the Society for the Diffusion of Useful Knowledge* (London, 1833), I, 265. The anonymous author either was, or derived most of his knowledge from, S. R. Maitland, *Facts and Documents Illustrative of the History, Doctrine, and Rites of the Ancient Albigenses & Waldenses* (London, 1832).

codified as *Religionsgeschichte* when he published his *Histoire et doctrine de la secte des cathares ou albigeois* in 1849.[48] He was professor of Theology at Strasburg, and studied at Göttingen with Johann Karl Ludwig Gieseler. He was convinced that the heretics persecuted by the Church in southern France in the twelfth and thirteenth centuries (and who were not Waldensians) were part of a Cathar dualist sect extending across the Mediterranean, whose origins could be traced back to Bogomils and Paulicians in ninth-century Byzantine Bulgaria.[49] Although he acknowledged that these heretics were known by many names, particularly 'Albigensian', he preferred the obscure 'Cathar' because it was not burdened by older confessional and national histories. Schmidt did not completely cast aside his confessional tendencies, as his Cathars typified a rudimentary form of *Kulturprotestantismus*, and so, while no longer direct evangelical ancestors like the Albigensians, they were culturally Protestant, with their modest Christian dualism part of a larger concern with scriptural purity and irenicism aimed at reconciling various doctrines within Christianity.[50] This is why he rejected Gnostic or Manichaean continuities from late antiquity for his Cathars, for that would have defined them as members of a separate, eastern world religion.[51] *Kulturprotestantismus* was also a political, social, and intellectual attitude for Protestant scholars like Schmidt, affirming that the proper venue for studying religion was the secular academy.[52] Schmidt's Cathar history expanded upon the narrative already outlined by Gieseler in the fourth edition of his *Lehrbuch der Kirchengeschicte* in 1844, including the implicit cultural Protestantism, except that whereas the former wished to escape national traits, the latter framed his history as a message to the divided Germanies.[53]

It was another four decades before Schmidt's vision of Catharism, now framed within the new scientific study of religion, reached a wider academic

---

[48] C. Schmidt, *Histoire et doctrine de la secte des cathares ou albigeois*, 2 vols. (Paris, 1849). On Schmidt, see Y. Dossat, 'Un initiateur: Charles Schmidt', *Historiographie du catharisme = Cahiers de Fanjeaux* 14 (1979), 163–84; B. Hamilton, 'The State of Research: The Legacy of Charles Schmidt to the Study of Christian Dualism', *Journal of Medieval History* 24 (1998), 191–214; and R. I. Moore, 'The Cathar Middle Ages as an Historiographical Problem', in *Christianity and Culture in the Middle Ages: Essays to Honor John Van Engen*, ed. D. C. Mengel and L. Wolverton (Notre Dame, 2014), pp. 59–60.

[49] Schmidt, *Histoire et doctrine*, I, 255–6.

[50] On *Kulturprotestantismus* before 1850, see Marchand, *German Orientalism in the Age of Empire*, pp. 76–7.

[51] Schmidt, *Histoire et doctrine*, II, 253.

[52] On *Kulturprotestantismus* after 1850, see G. Hübinger, *Kulturprotestismus und Politik: zum Verhältnis von Liberalismus und Protestismus im wilhelmischen Deutschland* (Tübingen, 1994), esp. pp. 7–17.

[53] J. K. L. Gieseler, *Lehrbuch der Kirchengeschicte*, 2 vols., 4th edn (Bonn, 1844), I, 404–6, II, 530–653, 670–8. His recent editions of Euthymius Zigabenus, *Narratio de Bogomilis* (Göttingen, 1842), and Peter of Sicily, *Historia Manichaeorum* (Göttingen, 1846), also shaped the theology of Schmidt's Cathars.

audience in Döllinger,⁵⁴ in *risorgimentale* Felice Tocco's *L'eresia nel medio evo* (1884),⁵⁵ and, most particularly, Henry Charles Lea's magisterial *A History of the Inquisition* (1887).⁵⁶ Charles Molinier, who corresponded with Lea and merged the methods of the École des chartes (where his younger brother Auguste was a professor) with the 'religious-historical school', was confidently writing about a *sociéte cathare* in the medieval Midi by 1907.⁵⁷ The Molinier brothers were prominent Dreyfusards and anti-Ultramontanes. Catharism aligned with their vision of a more tolerant and less clerical France.⁵⁸ Seven years earlier, even the bishop of Beauvais, Célestin Douais, in his edition of inquisition documents referred to the 'neo-dualist heretics' of Languedoc as 'Cathars', although in some footnotes he preferred the older name of 'Albigensian'.⁵⁹ For him, Catharism was less a world religion from the East, than a widespread Christian heresy of the West, which, possessing the structures of a 'Church', forced the Catholic Church into reacting with regrettable violence (and, even now, this premise is implicit among some Catholic scholars.)⁶⁰ The splendid eleventh edition of the *Encyclopaedia*

---

54 Döllinger, *Beitrage zur Sektengeschichte des Mittelalters*, I, 35, 75, 100, 117.
55 F. Tocco, *L'eresia nel medio evo* (Florence, 1884), esp. pp. 73–134 on Catharism.
56 H. C. Lea, *A History of the Inquisition of the Middle Ages*, 3 vols. (New York, 1887), esp. I, 88, 92, 107, 110–18, 123, 194. On Lea, see E. Peters, 'Henry Charles Lea (1825–1909)', in *Medieval Scholarship: Biographical Studies on the Formation of a Discipline*, vol. 1: *History*, ed. H. Damico and J. B. Zavadil (New York, 1995), pp. 89–100.
57 Ch. Molinier, 'L'église et la société cathares', *Revue historique* 95 (1907), 263–91. Now, see R. Fox, *The Savant and the State: Science and Cultural Politics in Nineteenth-Century France* (Baltimore, 2012), pp. 252–3, on Gabriel Monod, who (with his student Gabriel Fagniez) founded the *Revue historique* in 1876 as a 'scientific' and patriotic journal modelled on German research techniques and attitudes. Monod was a Protestant who studied medieval history with Georg Waitz at Göttingen in 1867–8.
58 Auguste Molinier even gave evidence during the 1899 retrial of Alfred Dreyfus as a handwriting expert. Now, see R. Harris, *Dreyfus: Politics, Emotion, and the Scandal of the Century* (New York, 2010), pp. 143, 145, 161, 421, on Monod as a Dreyfusard and Protestant, the *Revue historique* and German historical methods, and Auguste Molinier; and A. Roach, 'Occitania Past and Present: Southern Consciousness in Medieval and Modern French Politics', *History Workshop Journal* 43 (1997), 1–22 (p. 13), on Auguste Molinier and the *Revue historique*.
59 C. Douais, *Documents pour servir à l'histoire de l'inquisition dans le Languedoc* 2. vols. (Paris, 1900), 1, pp. xxii, xxxii, xci. In some footnotes he kept the older designation of 'Albigensian'. For example, 2, pp. 79 n. 1 for 'hérétiques albigeois', 109 n. 1, 'Les hérétiques sont les cathares, et tous ceux qui s'y rattachent directement, comme les Albigeois.' Auguste Molinier reviewed these volumes in 'Moyen âge', *Revue Historique*, 79 (1901): 347–50, where he criticized Douais' palaeographic skills (compared to his own), his knowledge of the inquisition (compared to Lea), and his understanding of Catharism (compared to his older brother Charles). Douais, 'Lettre', replied to these criticisms, while Molinier offered a curt 'Réponse', in *Revue Historique*, 80 (1902): 326–7. Now, see Roach, 'Occitania Past and Present', 13, on Molinier and Douais and his intriguing sympathy for the historical vision of the latter over the former.
60 For example, G. Wills, *Why I am a Catholic* (Boston, 2002), p. 137: 'As fatal as the tool of

Britannica (1910), while retaining a soberly outmoded entry on 'Albigenses' (no longer proto-Protestants, merely *indigènes* imbued with religious primitivism) by Paul Daniel Alphandéry, included a sparklingly up-to-date article on 'Cathars' ('the débris of early Christianity' seeking refuge in western Europe as a dualist diaspora) by Frederick Conybeare (also a passionate Dreyfusard).[61] That same year Conybeare, revealing the influence of not only *Religionsgeschichte* but also the comparative religion of William Robertson Smith, A. H. Sayce, and James Frazer, prefaced his study of Christian origins, *Myth, Magic, and Morals,* by stressing that 'those who imagine that Christianity is the one religion in the world entitled to respect' were severely shortsighted. '[T]he faith of Mahomet or the following of Buddha, the spell of the Malay or *Consolamentum* of the Cathars of Albi', were all beliefs and rituals of world religions equal (and so comparable) to Christianity.[62] After more than sixty years of construction the apotheosis of Catharism, and so medieval Christianity, was reached just before the First World War.[63] Catharism as a name (and so a paradigm) was a sign of historical modernism.

Although such bracing modernism – the romantic meshing with the scientific, cosmopolitan urbanity overcoming inward-looking provincialism – can be admired for inventing Catharism, as striking in its own way as a lithograph by Henri de Toulouse-Lautrec (with a similarly precarious grasp of the real), it was wrong then and it is wrong now. Its most serious error was, and remains, that the historical reality of the men, women, and children accused of being heretics between the Garonne and Rhône rivers in the twelfth and thirteenth centuries, and ultimately persecuted as such by crusaders and inquisitors, was, and remains, completely forfeited by the paradigm. Nothing about the lives of these supposed heretics resembles what a century of scholarship has

---

the inquisition would prove for later persecution, it should be recognized that even this was, in its origins, a populist development. Heretics are often extremely unpopular [...] The Cathars [...] denigrated marriage and the ordinary joys of life. Neighbors rarely look on such attitudes with composure.' Before this passage, Wills quotes most of p. 33 from Pegg, *The Corruption of Angels,* as a demonstration of the benign and populist nature of the early inquisitons.

[61] P. D. Alphandéry, 'Albigenses', in *Encyclopaedia Britannica,* 11th edn (Cambridge, 1910), I, pp. 505–6; F. Conybeare, 'Cathars', in *Encyclopedia Britannica* V, 515–17. The anonymous authors of 'Albigenser' and 'Katharer', in *Brockhaus' Konversations=Lexikon* (Berlin, 1901–2), I, 329–30, and X, 229–30, similarly reflected this learned shift in nomenclature and meaning. On Conybeare as an ardent Dreyfusard, see Harris, *Dreyfus,* p. 199. He even published a polemical report, *The Dreyfus Case* (London, 1898).

[62] F. Conybeare, *Myth, Magic, and Morals: A Study of Christian Origins,* 2nd edn (London, 1910), p. xxii.

[63] For example, Edmond Broeckx's Louvain dissertation, *Le catharisme: étude sur les doctrines, la vie religieuse et morale, l'activité littéraire et les vicissitudes de la secte cathare avant la croisade* (Hoogstraten, 1916), is merely a consolidation of what had been established since Schimdt.

said about them, and even when a few individuals after 1230 appear to fit the modernist (and now traditional) story, it is a false congruence, whereas what was actually happening is much more complex. The trouble is that most scholars labouring under the weight of Catharism were, and are, not only uninterested in the lives of ordinary people, but, due to the methodological strictures of the paradigm, unable to fully imagine quotidian existence in the past, even if inclined to do so. This leads to the extraordinary historiographic fact that, while almost everything we know about the men, women, and children accused of heresy comes from their testimonies to the early inquisitions into heretical depravity after 1233, it was not until the 1960s and 1970s that scholars began examining such evidence for more than just legal history, theological curios, intimations of dualism, or prosopographical appendices.

Döllinger and Douais may have skilfully edited inquisition records, but what those records contained was largely irrelevant in shaping how they understood them; for that, there was the new paradigm of Catharism. Or Yves Dossat's *Les crises de l'inquisition toulousaine au XIIIe siècle* (1959), which, for all of its beautiful palaeographic, institutional, and prosopographic precision, says next to nothing about heresy or the individuals accused of it (which, considering what he wrote later, was a deliberate choice).[64] Unfortunately, whatever inspiration about using inquisition records in new ways (and largely influenced by the methods of anthropology) was suggested forty years ago, nothing disturbed the paradigm of Catharism – or the whole question of heresy was sidestepped, as in Emmanuel Le Roy Ladurie's famous *Montaillou* (1975), where the issue is dismissed in five bland paragraphs on Cathars and Albigensian heretics (the categories were interchangeable for him) in the *Avant-propos*[65] – so that even now, when historians analyse inquisition testimonies from the Toulousain, Lauragais, Carcassès, Albigeois, Ariège, or Quercy, they still find Cathars, no matter what is written in front of them.

Why such stunningly poor vision? Most scholars only see 'jumble', as Biller calls it, in the records of the inquisitions into heretical depravity, a blurry mess only coming into focus when viewed through Cathar-coloured glasses (or, more appropriately, fin-de-siècle pince-nez). Undeniably, testimonies in these records are fragmented and patchy, alternating between confessions of various lengths (most of them short), transcribed half-thoughts, formulaic statements, boring longueurs, titbits of village gossip, repetitive repentance, and seemingly irrelevant if vivid digressions. Obviously, they lack the comforting coherence of Cistercian polemics, inquisitorial manuals, or overwritten Italian Dominican histories of heresy, and so are apparently poor fodder for conventional (intellectual) histories of heresy; but this ignores the many internal consistencies within individual and collective testimonies,

---

[64] Y. Dossat, *Les crises de l'inquisition toulousaine au XIIIe siècle (1233–1273)* (Bordeaux, 1959).
[65] E. Le Roy Ladurie, *Montaillou, village occitan de 1294 à 1324* (Paris, 1975), pp. 12–14.

which, while frequently recollections without a linear chronology, even if the inquisitors were trying to impose such a structure, powerfully demonstrate, over and over again, a sharp awareness of change over time. This is why it is so remarkable that sophisticated historians, such as John Arnold (a student of Biller's), Caterina Bruschi, or Chris Sparks (another student of Biller's), consistently report testimonies without any temporal reference, as if it makes no difference what a man remembered doing in 1245 as opposed to 1190, or what a woman recalled happening in 1273 rather 1237.[66] Such nonchalance towards the passing of time fits with Biller's presupposition that inquisition records only give 'a snapshot of a movement which has existed for some time'.[67] Catharism was always there, just out of sight, with the inquisitors 'only *sometimes*' glimpsing 'only *something*' about it, so piecing together a picture from testimonies wildly divergent in time (and often place) is perfectly acceptable for a paradigm convinced that the core beliefs of any heresy, and particularly one understood as a world religion, are unchanging over the centuries.[68]

Bernard Hamilton, taking this *sometimes, something* attitude to its logical conclusion, considers inquisition records largely irrelevant, as 'Cathar religious experience' can never be derived from them. 'An understanding of Cathar spirituality can only be gained through a study of the Cathars' own writings', he says.[69] Leaving aside that this assumption epitomizes the familiar intellectual bias in the study of religion and heresy, though Hamilton is less influenced by the 'religious-historical school' than by traditional British intellectual history along the lines of Richard Southern, who defined worthwhile academic history as 'the study of the thoughts and visions, moods and emotions and devotions of articulate people',[70] there is the inconvenient fact that no theological books written by Cathars have survived, apart from alleged extracts in the *summae* of Dominican inquisitors or a few ambiguous texts from the late thirteenth century.[71] This bothersome

---

[66] J. H. Arnold, *Inquisition and Power: Catharism and the Confessing Subject in Medieval Languedoc* (Philadelphia, 2001); C. Bruschi, *The Wandering Heretics of Languedoc* (Cambridge, 2009); C. Sparks, *Heresy, Inquisition and Life Cycle in Medieval Languedoc* (York, 2014).

[67] P. Biller, 'Christians and Heretics', in *Christianity in Western Europe, c. 1100–c. 1500*, ed. M. Rubin and W. Simons, The Cambridge History of Christianity 4 (Cambridge, 2009), pp. 170–86 (p. 177).

[68] Ibid., p. 185.

[69] B. Hamilton, 'The Cathars and Christian Perfection', in *The Medieval Church: Universities, Heresy, and the Religious Life: Essays in Honor of Gordon Leff*, ed. P. Biller and B. Dobson (Woodbridge, 1999), p. 6.

[70] R. Southern, *History and Historians: Selected Papers of R. W. Southern*, ed. R. J. Bartlett (Oxford, 2004), p. 100.

[71] These 'Cathar' writings are the Occitan New Testament and Ritual edited by Leon Clédat in *Le Nouveau Testament traduit au XIIIe siècle en langue provençale, suivi d'un Rituel cathare* (Paris, 1887), pp. 470–82; a Latin Ritual ed. C. Thouzellier in *Rituel cathare: introduction, texte critique, traduction et notes*, Sources chrétiennes 236 (Paris, 1977); 'The Book of the

technicality is brushed aside by saying the theological books of the Cathars are lost.[72] Destroyed or missing documents are common for the medievalist, and sometimes what has disappeared did once exist. This is not the case with the lost books of the Cathars, which are as much a fantasy as Catharism itself. Underlying these learned daydreams is the genuine conviction that without conventionally 'religious' texts from a religion or a 'Church', texts that can be analysed by the intellectual historian, then there is nothing meaningful to say about a heresy or a religion. It is only by studying the thoughts and visions of articulate people in coherent texts that we can 'see things their way',[73] see through the 'jumble', even if that requires misreading actual documents so as to support a library of imaginary books.

What, then, is written in front of a scholar looking at inquisition records from the thirteenth century in what is now southern France? When the Dominican inquisitors Bernard of Caux and John of Saint-Pierre interrogated almost six thousand men, women, and children in Toulouse between 1245 and 1246, every person swore he or she would 'tell the full and exact truth about oneself and about others, living and dead, in the matter of the fact or crime of heresy

---

Two Principles' edited in C. Thouzellier, *Livre des deux principes* (Paris, 1973); a 'Gloss on the Lord's Prayer' and an 'Apologia for the Church of God' found in Trinity College Dublin and edited by T. Venckeleer (the first in 'Un recueil cathare: le manuscrit A.6.10 de la "collection vaudoise" de Dublin: I – "Une apologie"', *Revue belge de philologie et d'histoire* 38 (1960), 815–34; the second in 'Une glose sur le Pater', *Revue belge de philologie et d'histoire* 39 (1961), 758–93); a 'Cathar' treatise in the polemic of Durand of Huesca, edited by Christine Thouzellier in *Un traité cathare inédit du début du XIIIe siècle, d'après le Liber contra Manicheos de Durand de Huesca* (Louvain, 1961); extracts from a lost book of the 'Cathar' Tetricus quoted by Moneta of Cremona, *Adversus Catharos et Valdenses libri quinque*, ed. T. A. Ricchini (Rome, 1743 [repr. Ridgewood NJ, 1964]), 1.3.2, 1.6.2–3, 1.8.3, 3.3.4, 4.1.9, pp. 42, 71, 94, 248, 292; and the lost 'Cathar' *Stella* referred to by Salvo Burci in his *Liber supra stella* that has been partially edited by Ilarino da Milano, 'Il *Liber supra stella* del piacentino Salvo Burci contro I catari e altre correnti ereticali', *Aevum* 19 (1945), 307–41, and now expertly edited by Caterina Bruschi as *Salvo Burci Liber suprastella: edizione critica e commento storico* (Rome, 2002).

72 P. Biller, 'Editions of Trials and Lost Texts', in *Valdesi medievali: bilanci e prospettiva di ricerca*, ed. M. Benedetti (Turin, 2009), p. 32; Biller, 'Christians and Heretics', p. 184; and Hamilton, 'The Cathars and Christian Perfection', *passim*.

73 Now, see *Seeing Things their Way: Intellectual History and the Return of Religion*, ed. A. Chapman, J. Coffey and B. Gregory (Notre Dame, 2009), where Coffey and Chapman, 'Introduction', pp. 1–3, explains that their approach to religion is adopted from Quentin Skinner's general assumption about intellectual history in his 'Introduction: Seeing Things their Way', in Q. Skinner, *Visions of Politics, Regarding Method* (Cambridge, 2002), I, 1–8, esp. p. 47. Now, see B. Gregory, 'Can we "See Things their Way"? Should we Try?', in *Seeing Things their Way*, ed. Chapman et al., pp. 24–45, and his 'The Other Confessional History: On Secular Bias in the Study of Religion', *History and Theory* 45 (2006), 132–49, where he considers all methodological models in the study of religion, apart from the most traditional (and confessional) approach of the historian of ideas, to be imposing a 'metaphysical materialism' on the sincerity of why individuals were religious in the past.

or Waldensianism'.[74] Out of all these confessions, only a handful mentioned Waldensians, whereas testimony after testimony referred to 'good men, that is, the heretics', or 'good women, that is, the heretics', and their 'believers'.[75] A century earlier similar good men and good women were not heretics (and, obviously, there were no 'believers'). This point needs stating very explicitly, as it has been widely misunderstood. Arguing that Catharism never existed is not an argument for it to be replaced with the 'heresy of the good men and good women'. Taylor (a student of Hamilton's) argues against this straw man (constructed out of her own misunderstanding of what she disagrees with) as a way of proving the utility of Catharism as name and concept.[76] Carol Lansing likewise confuses scholarly exactitude with an argument for a 'heresy of the good men and good women', though what worries her is that such names are reminiscent of sixteenth-century Protestantism, 'and of course much of the intellectual baggage we carry to this material derives from that era', and so (with no hint of irony) she recommends 'Cathar' as a 'less value-laden term'.[77] Apart from misrepresenting the historiography, this is an argument for imprecision based on misapprehension. Again, let there be no ambiguity: *between the Garonne and Rhône rivers in the twelfth century there was no Catharism and there was no 'heresy of the good men and good women'*.[78]

Of course, some good men and good women were accused of being heretics by Latin Christian intellectuals, especially Cistercians after 1170, but being accused of heresy is not the same thing as being a heretic, especially when such accusations, for the most part, were easily dismissed, as they were until around 1210. *What transformed these individuals into heretics, what turned the accusation into actuality, was the violence of the Albigensian Crusade and the persecution of the early inquisitors.* This is why the records of the inquisitions into heretical depravity from the 1230s and 1240s are so crucial, especially the great inquisition of Bernard of Caux and John of Saint-Pierre, as they reveal this social and religious metamorphosis, particularly giving insight into what the world between the Garonne and Rhône rivers was like before it changed.[79]

---

[74] Pegg, *The Corruption of Angels*, pp. 45–51.

[75] Ibid., pp. 57–62.

[76] C. Taylor, 'Evidence for Dualism in Inquisitorial Registers of the 1240s: A Contribution to a Debate', *History* 98 (2013), 319–45 (esp. pp. 325–6).

[77] C. Lansing, 'Popular Belief and Heresy', in *A Companion to the Medieval World*, ed. C. Lansing and E. D. English (Oxford, 2009), p. 287.

[78] See the thoughtful observations of J. Théry, 'L'hérésie des bons hommes: comment nommer la dissidence religieuse non vaudoise ni béguine en Languedoc (XIIe–début du XIVe siècle)?', in *Heresis: hérétiques ou dissidents? Réflexions sur l'identité de l'hérésie au Moyen Âge* 36–7 (2002), 75–117.

[79] I am frequently criticized for my emphasis on the tribunal of Bernard of Caux and John of Saint-Pierre, as if the largest inquisition in the Middle Ages were too narrow a resource, or that my whole argument against Catharism collapses if I dare (as if I never did) glance sideways at other sources.

The Paradigm of Catharism; or, the Historians' Illusion

Before 1210 the epithet 'good man' (*bon ome* in Occitan, *bonus homo* in Latin) was a courteous title for any man (high or low) between the Garonne and Rhône rivers. Sometimes, following local custom in particular situations, such a man was known as a 'prudent [proven, honourable, perfected] man' (*prodome* in Occitan, *probus homo* in Latin).[80] The prestige and pervasiveness of the good men derived from an intense localism focused upon a particular village, town, or even a city like Toulouse, where fourteen 'prudent men of Toulouse and the bourg' shared authority with the comital court as early as 1120.[81] By around 1170, however, the good men seem to be largely a phenomenon associated with rural villages. While all men could be good men, the men designated as 'good' or 'prudent' – judging boundaries, adjudicating fractional rents, deciding fights over vineyards between claimants – varied from dispute to dispute. A possessive cats-cradle knotted some men as 'good' or 'prudent' together in one place and time and released them elsewhere. Deference and loyalty were in constant flux, and no man could honourably arbitrate every dispute. Yet in each village, at least after 1140, there were one or two very special good men who, by contrast, were always 'good' and 'prudent', embodying courtliness, honour, and holiness.[82]

Every man or woman over forty questioned by Bernard of Caux and John of Saint-Pierre remembered being courteous to the holy good men, genuflecting thrice and saying: 'Bless us, good men, pray God for us.'[83] This holy *cortezia* involving the good men exemplified the daily cycles of *cortezia* shaping the lives of every man, woman, and child. This was a world where the sacred ebbed and flowed through (and around) all humans, so that questions of holiness as much as questions of honour were answered through courtliness. The courtliness given to the holy good men was known as the 'melioration' (*melhoramen* in Occitan, and transcribed by inquisitorial scribes as *melioramen* or *melioramentum* in Latin), meaning at once improvement, betterment, perfection, moderation, accumulation of honour, the accretion of wisdom, and the reciprocal process of giving and receiving holiness. The inquisitions into heretical depravity collected and classified any *cortezia* involving the good men as 'adoration' – recalling the worship and rituals of

---

[80] Pegg, *The Corruption of Angels*, pp. 95–6.
[81] J. H. Mundy, *Liberty and Political Power in Toulouse, 1050–1230* (New York, 1954), p. 32, and his *Society and Government at Toulouse*, Appendix Four, p. 386, for the names of these *probihomines de Tolosa et burgo*.
[82] Now, see Monique Bourin's excellent, 'Les dissidents religieux dans la société villageoise languedocienne à la fin du XIIIe et au début du XIVe siècle', in *L'hérétique au village: les minorités religieuses dans l'Europe médievale et modern: Actes de XXXIe Journées internationales d'histoire de l'abbaye de Flaran, 9 et 10 octobre 2009*, ed. P. Chareyre (Toulouse, 2011), pp. 201–16, esp. pp. 210–13, on Pegg, *The Corruption of Angels*.
[83] Pegg, *The Corruption of Angels*, pp. 92–103.

ancient heretics – obscuring the fine-tuned meaning, careful performance, and sheer ubiquity of courtliness.[84]

The holy good men continually exchanging 'meliorations' were living embodiments of holiness being made and perfected. The more words and bows a good man received, the more holiness he possessed, so his divinity was incrementally revised everyday by *cortezia*. As a consequence, some good men were more holy than other good men. Older men, in this social and spiritual meliorism, were favoured over younger. Indeed, before 1210 almost all holy good men were widowers. Whether young or old, they lived openly as tradesmen, artisans, farmers, or nobles, supporting themselves through work, rents, and landholdings. Little boys were sometimes good men. Raimon de Eclezia, for example, became a good man when he was ten in 1205. He was dying, so his father left him in a house with two good men. He was given the 'consolation' or 'comforting' (*consolamen* in Occitan, transcribed by inquisitorial scribes as *consolamentum*) by the good men, transforming him into one of them, so that he might die a holy death. He survived, staying with the two good men for a decade. Along with everyone else in his village, he offered the melioration to these older good men, 'so many times so often, that I can't remember'. When Raimon de Eclezia stopped being a holy good man (and his holiness was certainly lesser than his more mature companions) in 1215, with his world being broken apart by the crusaders, and many older good men fleeing as fugitives, he married an adolescent girl who had recently been a child good woman herself for two years.[85]

Unlike the good men, the good women before 1215 were all noble matrons and prepubescent girls. Hundreds, if not thousands, of noble little girls were made into good women for as little as a few weeks or for as long as three or four years. All these holy children, after their months or years of being good women, married upon reaching their majorities at twelve. When Dominic of Caleruega founded a house at Prouille in 1206 for good women, especially the little girls, he was not only defining all good women as heretics, he was also trying to redirect a few of them into what he thought more Catholic practices, even if he misunderstood that all child good women eventually married.[86] No woman was a good woman during her years of fertility, the years of her youth, the years when she married, had children, and was a wife. Marriage was an episode in the lives of all women, a fecund season to be survived. The

---

[84] Pegg, *A Most Holy War*, pp. 28–49.
[85] Toulouse, Bibliothèque municipale, MS 609 (henceforth MS 609), fol. 55v.
[86] S. Tugwell, 'For whom was Prouille Founded?', *Archivum Fratrum Praedicatorum* 74 (2004), 5–125 (esp. p. 6), which, despite being textually erudite, simply cannot grasp the complexity of the lives of the good women, devoting page after page to the question of whether girls, as opposed to older women, could be 'heretics', and whether Prouille was intended for such girls, 'forced by their parents' poverty to spend their childhood in Cathar households'.

older noble matrons were women beyond the years of fertility, no longer able or willing to marry, sometimes widows, sometimes separated from elderly husbands, living together in twos or threes in village houses, nursing and teaching little-girl good women. Older holy good women rarely left their houses, never preached, and were given few if any gifts of *cortezia*, unlike the very public repetitive cycles of courtliness for good men. 'In any one week, I adored the female heretics in three or more exchanges', as Ermengart Boer recalled with precision for Bernard of Caux about two good women staying in her house in 1209.[87]

In 1189 three noble brothers from a Toulousain village (probably Bazièges, which had a *scriptor* for charters) settled substantial *honor* (fractions of mills, vineyards, gardens, ponds, fields, and *cortezia*, as courtly 'honour' was always attached to material 'honour') on their widowed mother, Ava, 'who has given herself over to the men who are called heretics'.[88] Although demonstrating that two decades of Cistercian preaching persuaded the sons that becoming a good woman (although they never used that title) was submission to men (no mention of 'good') known as heretics, their jibe (for that is what it was) revealed how annoyed they were with their mother for fracturing their familial *honor*. The sons even inserted a clause reflecting the rising intensity of heresy accusations, allowing that, if 'a scandal arises, and Ava cannot remain in this land, she may mortgage all the aforesaid *honor* for 150 shillings of Toulouse, or for 300 shillings of Mauguio, to do with as she wishes'.[89] Either way, becoming a good woman, even with the sneer of heresy, did not affect the wishes of Ava or her proprietorial rights.

The name 'good woman' was a faint echo of the social and moral complexities resounding within 'good man'. The holiness of a good woman, deprived of meliorations, remained mediocre and imperfect. Whatever sacrality the good women possessed derived from their resemblance to the good men. Indeed, it was only an older good man, suffused with meliorations, overflowing with holy *cortezia*, that was able to make a woman into a 'good woman' – by giving her a fraction of his holiness as a rare gift of melioration. This was why the sons of Ava noted that their mother was giving herself to the '[good] men who are called heretics', as it was taken for granted that, once transformed into a good woman by a good man, Ava would live a secluded life with other good women. All nuance and historical reality regarding the good women is forfeited when, ensnared within the paradigm of Catharism, scholars try to make them fit preconceived notions of a 'Church', as does

---

[87] MS 609, fol. 20v.
[88] For a discussion of Ava see F. L. Cheyette, *Ermengard of Narbonne and the World of the Troubadours* (Ithaca NY, 2001), p. 321, and J. Feuchter's chapter in this volume (pp. 123–7). On Feuchter's discovery of this material, see A. Sennis, in this volume, p. 5. On the *scriptor* at Bazièges, see Pegg, *The Corruption of Angels*, p. 59.
[89] Cheyette, *Ermengard of Narbonne*, p. 150.

Biller in regretting that 'there are no *vitae* of holy Cathar women to analyse'.⁹⁰ Again, a mischievous allusion to lost books suggests structures and attitudes that actual texts do not support.

The early Dominican inquisitors deliberately classified all occasions when good men and good women were made, like little girls or mothers becoming good women, like little boys or dying lords experiencing 'comforting', as acts of 'heretication', and so, by making contingently precise practices into a standard ritual for becoming a 'heretic', they fabricated the liturgy of a 'heresy'.⁹¹ What they did not do was refer to the good men or good women as 'perfects'. Neither did the good men or good women refer to themselves in this way, nor did anyone else between the Garonne and Rhône rivers call them such a name. Yet the *perfecti* will be found littering all modern histories of Catharism, and, once again, this erroneous habit began in the late nineteenth century as such terminology went with the 'priesthood' of a world religion (and was suggestive of Manichaeism). Apart from a handful of references by inquisitors before 1300, there was only Peter of les Vaux-de-Cernay calling the good men the 'perfected' around 1215. He devised this term to explain the making of a good man, at least as he understood it, more than likely deriving his word from 'prudent man'.⁹² In the fourteenth century, *heretici perfecti* was a little-used inquisitorial category, meaning 'fully fledged' or 'finished' heretics, with no relevance to the good men.⁹³ As Lucy Sackville (a student of Biller's) politely observes, when scholars write and talk about perfects it 'creates an impression that is at odds with the infrequency with which it was used'.⁹⁴

The good men, and to a lesser extent the good women, embodied a holy and honourable aesthetic, where the vicissitudes of being human were moderated by courtliness. They demonstrated an art to living in the world, one that was distinctly Christian, post-Gregorian Reform (or rather post-First Crusade),

---

⁹⁰ P. Biller, 'Women and Dissent', in *Medieval Holy Women in the Christian Tradition, c. 1100–c. 1500*, ed. A. Minnis and R. Voaden (Turnhout, 2010), pp. 133–62, esp. p. 140. See also, J. H. Arnold, 'Heresy and Gender in the Middle Ages', in *The Oxford Handbook of Women and Gender in Medieval Europe*, ed. J. M. Bennett and R. M. Karras (Oxford, 2013), pp. 496–510, esp. pp. 500–2, for a conventional survey in general, and not just the usual old-fashioned narrative of Catharism.

⁹¹ Pegg, *A Most Holy War*, p. 40.

⁹² *Hystoria Albigensis*, Part 1, §13, pp. 13–14.

⁹³ For example, Bernard Gui, *Practica inquisitionis heretice pravitatis*, ed. C. Douais (Paris, 1886), iv.3, p. 218. Biller, 'Christians and Heretics', p. 181 and n. 23, notes the word was rarely used.

⁹⁴ L. J. Sackville, *Heresy and Heretics in the Thirteenth Century: The Textual Representations* (York, 2011), p. 201. For a convoluted justification of *perfectus* and *perfecta*, see C. Léglu, R. Rist, and C. Taylor, 'Historical Introduction', in their *The Cathars and the Albigensian Crusade: A Sourcebook* (London, 2014), pp. 5–6. Although this is an exemplary collection of sources, Léglu, Rist, and Taylor never mention the debate on Catharism, writing as if the historiography stopped in 1970. This approach may be ameliorative to traditional scholars, but it is unclear how it helps students.

intensely local, and not at all heretical. The good men were not antithetical to the Church; rather, they assumed they could live alongside priests, monks, and bishops, complementing and even enhancing what was being preached in village churches and squares, especially the ideas and practices associated with *imitatio Christi*. The holiness of the good men was, unlike a late antique or early medieval holy man, imitable, potentially attainable by any man or boy.[95] Equally, they personified the courtly ethos celebrated by troubadours, the power and beauty of which derived likewise from its being available for men, women, and children to copy. However, unlike the linear model of existence being articulated by Latin Christian intellectuals as they promoted their version of living like Christ, existence for good men, good women, and everyone else for that matter between the Garonne and Rhône rivers, was a shifting and changing labyrinth, and not a straight path. The boy or girl at ten was not accountable to the man or woman at forty in this nonlinear universe. An individual life was made from countless transient and mutable episodes that, while meaningful and intense at specific times and places, did not necessarily proceed, sequentially, one into the other. Baptism was not, in and of itself, wrong (the good men thought it harmless), only the idea that it had any continuous redemptive worth for an individual. A resurrected body (proof of individual linear continuity from life into death) made no sense. Marriage, which happened sooner or later to everyone during adolescence, was not a threshold to salvation. As the troubadour Marcabru put it around 1140, marriage was 'the cunt game', a necessity without virtue, 'which is why the cunt becomes a thief'.[96] Many testimonies to the early inquisitors involve references to the uselessness of marriage, or that 'marriage is prostitution', or 'there is no virtue in marriage', all of them run-of-the-mill slurs known to anyone who heard a troubadour sing, and which, while paradoxically an element of *fin'amor*, were not intimations of dualism until the inquisitors reframed them as such.[97]

---

[95] See P. Brown, 'Enjoying the Saints in Late Antiquity', *Early Medieval Europe* 9/1 (2000), 1–24, esp. 16–17.

[96] 'Dirai vos e mon latin', in *Marcabru: A Critical Edition*, ed. and trans. S. Gaunt, R. Harvey and L. Paterson (Cambridge, 2000), no. XVII, pp. 230–1.

[97] Pegg, *The Corruption of Angels*, pp. 30, 77. On evidence of dualism in inquisition records, see P. Biller, 'Cathars and the Material World', in *God's Bounty? The Churches and the Natural World: Papers Read at the 2008 Summer Meeting and the 2009 Winter Meeting of the Ecclesiastical History Society*, ed. P. Clarke and T. Claydon (Woodbridge, 2010), pp. 89–110, where he strip-mines inquisition records for supposedly dualist references, taking every testimony (and every piece of evidence in a testimony) out of its original context. See also Z. Zlatar, 'What's in a Name? A Critical Examination of Published and Website Sources on the Dualism of the Cathars in Languedoc', *Journal of Religious History* 35 (2011), 546–67, who similarly engages in a preconceived philosophical framework of what constitutes dualism, and then finds it. Taylor, 'Evidence for Dualism', p. 326, even asks, 'where did the concept of "dualism" of which the good men were accused by inquisitors *originate*?' Obviously, she concludes, from surreptitious dualist missionaries from the East. On the

This is why the good men and good women cannot be dualists in any way, shape, or form that is attributed to them by the paradigm of Catharism. Dualism, at least as articulated by Latin Christian intellectuals in the twelfth century and inquisitors in the thirteenth, presupposed that an individual was consciously turning away from a linear sense of self, with body and soul united. This was simply not the case for the good men and good women, or any ordinary Christian living between the Garonne and Rhône rivers before 1240, or arguably anywhere in Latin Christendom, as no layperson thought of their identity in this way. There was dualism in the twelfth century, but only, as Hilbert Chiu has powerfully demonstrated, in the classroom among Latin Christian intellectuals.[98] There was a reformation in the twelfth century, as Giles Constable has masterfully framed it, but this *reformatio* was confined to the Church, and even then to the intellectuals, and to forget that outside the cloister or curia millions of ordinary Christians did not fit this developing *ordo*, is, once again, to only understand religion as defined by the 'religious-historical school' more than a century ago.[99] (There is still work to be done on how much the medieval Church's formulation of religion affected the formulas of nineteenth-century scholars, despite many of them being Protestant.) Accusations of heresy were an essential part of this reformation. Initially, these accusations were made by intellectuals against one another; eventually, though, they were directed at ordinary Christians – peasants and counts alike. *There were no pre-existing heresies in the twelfth and early thirteenth centuries until the thinking of Latin Christian intellectuals invented them.* The 'reality' of heresy that these intellectuals so genuinely feared was actually fabricated by them. Of course, the fact that it was an invention makes it no less real for a Cistercian preacher or Dominican inquisitor, just not for those they accused or persecuted.[100] When historians fail to comprehend that Catharism was an invention of academic modernism, they fail to comprehend the medieval invention of heresy by Latin Christian intellectuals throughout the twelfth and into the early thirteenth centuries.

Around 1190, the troubadour Giraut de Borneil bitterly reflected on how the vilification of the good men was becoming more acceptable (such as by the sons of Ava). 'And since good men have lost the supremacy, and vile wretches and cackling slanderers have stolen it with their sly, stubborn, hard

---

troubadours supposedly singing a 'counter-doctrine' to the Church, see W. M. Reddy, *The Making of Romantic Love: Longing and Sexuality in Europe, South Asia, and Japan, 900–1200 CE* (Chicago, 2012).

[98] H. Chiu, 'The Intellectual Origins of Medieval Dualism' (unpublished MPhil, dissertation, University of Sydney, 2009), and his 'Alan of Lille's Academic Concept of the Manichee', *Journal of Religious History* 35 (2011), 492–506.

[99] G. Constable, *The Reformation of the Twelfth Century* (Cambridge, 1996).

[100] R. I. Moore's superb *The War on Heresy: Faith and Power in Medieval Europe* (London, 2012), pp. 87–240, supersedes all other scholarship on heresy in the twelfth century (including his own *The Formation of a Persecuting Society*).

hearts, what will those good men do if God takes no revenge? Will they cease to show forth His will [in the world]?' Nevertheless, 'I advise them against this', sang a suddenly optimistic Giraut de Borneil, 'so God grant me a good year!'[101] Three decades later all the holy good men and good women were fugitives, struggling to show forth His will in a world destroyed by crusade.

By 1220 the holy good men and good women were clandestine figures, wandering throughout the countryside, mostly at night, from one hiding place to another.[102] There were no longer any little-girl good women. The communal structures of honour and courtesy that once needed (and made) the good men and good women were wrecked by war. But the name 'good man', or new variations like 'just man', never completely disappeared, though, beginning in the middle of the thirteenth century, the designation 'good Christian' became more common. After 1220 the surviving 'good women' usually preferred 'good ladies', stressing their nobility more than their holiness. Courtliness, once so carefully watched and performed, declined into either indifference, profligacy, or rigidly one-sided performances, such as a good man at Puylaurens greeting noble believers around 1243, 'like a monster sitting there in his seat, as immovable as a tree trunk'.[103] As courteous village rhythms dissolved into decorous clichés, some good men instituted a 'coming together' (*aparelhamen* in Occitan, and transcribed as *apparellamentum* by inquisitorial scribes) once a month, so that they and their believers could act out wistful (and often overwrought) versions of courtliness and meliorations. In this violent and clandestine world, offering the consolation became the most important act of the good men for their believers. The good men and good women now exemplified sacred and social nostalgia for a world that was no more. It was this hearth and holy sentimentality motivating the men and women who consciously were 'believers of heretics'. A few holy good men were called 'deacons' around 1210 (though this title was possibly used a year or two earlier). More remarkably, some good men were named 'bishops' by 1220. In 1225 'up to a hundred' fugitive good men and their male believers from the Toulousain and Carcassès gathered in a house at Pieusse for a *concilium generale* (as Raimon Joan termed this gathering for the Dominican inquisitor Ferrer thirteen years later) where some male believers from Razès

---

[101] Giraut de Borneil, 'No s pot sufrir ma lenga q'ill non da', in *The Cansos and Sirventes of the Troubadour Giraut de Borneil: A Critical Edition*, ed. and trans. R. V. Sharman (Cambridge, 1989), pp. 440–1.

[102] Bruschi, *The Wandering Heretics of Languedoc*, pp. 142–89, is very good on the fugitive existence of the good men. See also, M. Cassidy-Welch, 'Memories of Space in Thirteenth-Century France: Displaced People after the Albigensian Crusade', *Parergon* 27 (2010), 111–31.

[103] Paris, Bibliothèque nationale de France (henceforth BnF), Collection Doat, MS 24, fol. 137v. Bruschi, *The Wandering Heretics of Languedoc*, p. 135, mentions this 'monster', but gives no date.

'petitioned and requested for a bishop to be given to them'.[104] The use of such titles by some good men were attempts at remaking their identities amid the communal and holy chaos around them.

This is the only way to understand the famous 'Charter of Niquinta'. This document exists as a three-page appendix in Guillaume Besse's *Histoire des ducs, marquis et comtes de Narbonne* (1660).[105] The original parchment (if it ever existed) is lost. The 'Charter of Niquinta' is a mishmash of excerpts from three supposed twelfth-century Latin documents copied for the good man and 'bishop' Peire Izarn in August 1223. It begins with a description of an assembly of good men in the village of Saint-Félix-de-Caraman (just outside Toulouse) in 1167; then comes an extract from a sermon given at this assembly by a *papa* Niquinta (or Nicetas) from Constantinople; and finally a demarcation of new heretical dioceses in the Toulousain, Carcassès, and Agenais (and the 'consoling' of the new bishops by the Byzantine heresiarch). For many scholars a lost document, once again, is proof of a 'Cathar Church' already existing in the twelfth century.[106] The 'Charter of Niquinta' was (if it was anything) a forgery by Peire Izarn undertaken sometime after 1230.[107] He

---

[104] Paris, BnF, Collection Doat, MS 23, fols. 269v–270r.

[105] G. Besse, *Histoire des ducs, marquis et comtes de Narbonne, autrement appellez princes des Goths, ducs de Septimanie, et marquis de Gothie: dedié à Monseigneur l'Archevesque Duc de Narbonne* (Paris, 1660), pp. 483–6. Besse obtained the parchment from 'M. Caseneuue, Prebendier au Chapitre de l'Eglisle de Sainct Estienne de Tolose, en l'an 1652'.

[106] B. Hamilton, 'The Cathar Council of S. Félix Reconsidered', *Archivum Fratrum Praedicatorum* 48 (1978), 23–53, and his 'Introduction' in Hugh Eteriano, *Contra Patarenos*, ed. and trans. J. Hamilton, with a description of the manuscripts by S. Hamilton and an historical introduction by B. Hamilton (Leiden, 2004), pp. 79–98. P. Biller, 'Popular Religion in the Central and Middle Ages', in *Companion to Historiography*, ed. M. Bentley (London, 1997), pp. 239–40, adopts Hamilton's view on the 'Charter of Niquinta'. C. Taylor, *Heresy in Medieval France: Dualism in Aquitaine and the Agenais, 1000–1249* (Woodbridge, 2005), pp. 172–7, and P. Jiménez-Sanchez, *Les catharismes: modèles dissidents du christianisme médiéval (XIIe–XIIIe siècles)* (Rennes, 2008), pp. 53–75, both defend the 'Charter' as revealing a 'Cathar' hierarchy in the twelfth century. D. J. Smith, *Crusade, Heresy, and Inquisition in the Lands of the Crown of Aragon (c. 1167–1276)* (Leiden, 2010), pp. 77–85, supports conventional opinion on the 'Charter', though it is unclear why he supports its veracity, or how this aids his overall argument about heresy in Aragon. Now, see the exemplary essay collection *L'histoire du catharisme en discussion: le 'concile' de Saint-Félix (1167)*, ed. M. Zerner (Nice, 2001).

[107] Y. Dossat, 'Remarques sur un prétendu évêque cathare du Val d'Aran en 1167', *Bulletin philologique et historique (jusqu'à 1715), années 1955 et 1956* (1957), 339–47, and his, 'À propos du concile cathare de Saint-Félix: les Milingues', *Cathares en Languedoc = Cahiers de Fanjeaux* 3 (1968), 201–14, in which he argued the 'Charter of Niquinta' was a seventeenth-century forgery (probably) by Besse. Monique Zerner cautiously agrees with Dossat in her 'La charte de Niquinta, l'hérésie et l'erudition des années 1650–1660', in *L'histoire du catharisme en discussion*, ed. Zerner, pp. 203–48. Michel Roquebert responded to Zerner's doubts about the 'Charter of Niquinta' with savage hostility in his 'Le "déconstructionnisme" et les études cathares', in *Les cathares devant l'histoire: mélanges offerts à Jean Duvernoy*, ed. M. Aurell (Quercy, 2005), pp. 105–33. Zerner responded to

invented a history justifying 'bishops' like himself and why the fugitive good men still deserved to be honoured. The good men were now priests in all but name of a 'Church' with a long institutional memory. A bureaucratic fiction replaced anarchic reality. The grandly named *concilium generale* at Pieusse functioned in a similar way. Bruno de Renneville even told Bernard of Caux that he gave a gift to some heretics from the 'church [*ecclesia*] of Avignonet' during the summer of 1245, suggesting that, while the localism of the good men survived, these particular holy men now saw themselves as members of their own distinct Christian community separate from the Catholic Church.[108] Peire Izarn, like the good men at Pieusse or the good men from Avignonet, adopted (and adapted) what Catholic intellectuals said about men such as themselves after 1220.[109]

What gives validation to the fallacious notion that the missing 'Charter of Niquinta' was stitched together from three missing twelfth-century documents is the equally fictitious assumption of a correspondence between Byzantine Bogomils and heretics in Latin Christian Christendom, either beginning in the eleventh century, or by 1140 at the latest.[110] This has consistently been the weakest part of the contemporary affirmation of Catharism, and yet, almost in acknowledgement that the paradigm is shifting, claims for such Orientalist connections are making a comeback, as last-ditch efforts at buttressing what

---

Roquebert (and others) in her, 'Mise au point sur *Les cathares devant l'historie* et retour sur *L'histoire du catharisme en discussion*: le débat sur le charte de Niquinta n'est pas clos', *Journal des savants* 2 (2006), 253–73. See D. Zbíral, 'La charte de Niquinta et le rassemblement de Saint-Félix: état de la question', in *1209–2009: cathares: une histoire a pacifier?*, ed. A. Brenon (Portet-sur-Garonne, 2010), pp. 31–44.

[108] MS 609, fol. 51r–v. Sparks, *Heresy, Inquisition and Life Cycle*, p. 137 and n. 82, mentions Bruno de Renneville and the 'church of Avignonet', but gives no date, even arguing this is proof of a 'Cathar Church'.

[109] Pegg, *A Most Holy War*, pp. 169–71.

[110] On Bogomil influence in Latin Christendom before the twelfth century, see, for example, S. Runciman, *The Medieval Manichee: A Study of the Christian Dualist Heresy* (Cambridge, 1947), pp. 117–18; A. Dondaine, 'L'origine de l'hérésie médiévale', *Rivista di storia della Chiesa in Italia* 6 (1952), 47–78 (p. 78: 'les Cathares occidentaux étaient fils des Bogomils, eux-mêmes héritiers du lointain Manichéisme'), and Borst, *Die Katharer*, 71–80. Bernard Hamilton, more than any other English-speaking historian, has argued for the influence of Bogomils (and other Byzantine dualists) on the 'Cathars' in Latin Christendom, and while he is sceptical of links in the eleventh century, he thinks it is possible. In particular, see his 'Wisdom from the East: The Reception by the Cathars of Eastern Dualist Texts', in *Heresy and Literacy, 1000–1530*, ed. P. Biller and A. Hudson (Cambridge, 1994), pp. 38–60; 'Bogomil Influences on Western Heresy', in *Heresy and the Persecuting Society in the Middle Ages: Essays on the Work of R. I. Moore*, ed. M. Frassetto (Leiden, 2006), pp. 93–114; and 'Introduction', in Eteriano, *Contra Patarenos*, pp. 56–72. Taylor, *Heresy in Medieval France*, although ardently supporting a connection between dualist heretics across the Mediterranean, even before 1100 (pp. 55–140, esp. p 123), acknowledges that 'it is none the less the case that not one single incident in the west corresponds in more than a handful of ways' to any Byzantine account of eastern Bogomils (p. 66).

was always insupportable. Every claim for a relationship between heretics in the Byzantine Empire and Latin Christendom rests upon the flimsy methodological and philosophical assumption that if two ideas look alike to a historian, then there must be a link between them.[111] The scientific foundation of *Religionsgeschichte* rested upon this notion that similarity was not what the scholar contrived, rather it was something discovered between religions, as natural as detecting similarities between bird beaks or pollen grains from one end of the Mediterranean to another.[112] Similarity is not an inherent quality of anything, and so a likeness between two ideas means nothing in and of itself.[113] Once again, the fact that there is no evidence for Bosnian or Bulgarian missionaries is deemed irrelevant, because, just like the lost books of the Cathars, the paradigm of Catharism assumes they must have been there, so there they must have been. This leads to all sorts of contortions. For example, in 1276, when Peire Perrin from Puylaurens told the Dominican inquisitor Pons de Parnac he heard that the heretics had a book they looked at during stormy weather, *et hoc in vulgaria*, Biller, Bruschi, and Shelagh Sneddon see *et hoc in Bulgaria*, despite the fact that it makes no sense in the context of the confession, and would be the only such testimonial reference to Bulgaria in the thirteenth century.[114] After 1220 some Latin Christian intellectuals did claim heretical links between the western and eastern Mediterranean, and

---

[111] Smith, *Crusade, Heresy, and Inquisition*, p. 72: 'Given the similarities in terms of belief and practice between the Bogomils and some of the diverse range of heretical groups which were developing in the west in the first half of the twelfth century, it is not implausible to suggest some link between them.'

[112] M. Lorenz, 'Bogomilen, Katharer und bosniche "Christen": der Transfer dualistischer Häresien zwischen Orient und Okzident (11.–13. Jh)', in *Vermitten–Übersetzen–Begegnen: Transferphänomene im europäischen Mittelalter und in der Frühen Neuzeit: interdisziplinäre Annäherungen*, ed. B. J. Nemes and A. Rabus (Göttingen, 2011), pp. 87–123, is a recent exercise modelled on the 'religious-historical school'.

[113] N. Goodman, 'Seven Strictures against Similarity', in his *Problems and Projects* (Indianapolis, 1972), p. 446. Now, see N. Goodman, 'The New Riddle of Induction', in N. Goodman, *Fact, Fiction, and Forecast*, 4th edn (Cambridge MA, 1983), pp. 59–83; N. Goodman, *Of Mind and Other Matters* (Cambridge MA, 1984); and N. Goodman and Catherine Elgin, *Reconceptions in Philosophy & Other Arts & Sciences* (Indianapolis, 1988), p. 446. On the problem of 'grue' put forward in Goodman's 'The New Riddle of Induction', see also the collected (philosophical) essays in *Grue! The New Riddle of Induction*, ed. D. Stalker (Chicago 1994), esp. Ian Hacking, 'Entrenchment', ibid., pp. 193–224, and the collected (historical, philosophical, anthropological) essays in *How Classification Works*, ed. Douglas and Hull.

[114] *Inquisitors and Heretics in Thirteenth-Cenury Languedoc: Edition and Translation of Toulouse Inquisition Depositions, 1273–1282*, ed. P. Biller, C. Bruschi and S. Sneddon (Leiden, 2011), pp. 620–1, where Paris, BnF, Collection Doat, MS 25, fol. 217r, is transcribed as *et hoc in Bulgaria* and translated as 'and this in Bulgaria'. Hamilton, 'Wisdom from the East', p. 57 and n. 93, supports this misreading. Biller in a personal communication, while disagreeing with my reading of *vulgaria*, nevertheless acknowledges *Bulgaria* could be a scribal error from the seventeenth century.

some good men, like Peire Izarn, fabricated such associations as well. Not one of them is proof of earlier heterodox connections, or even proof of connections in the thirteenth century.[115]

All the good men, good women, and their believers functioned after 1220 within a sacred and social illusion that, while partially of their own making, was mostly shaped by their persecutors. In other words, they were now heretics not only to their accusers but to themselves. It is a harsh irony that the heresy investigated by inquisitors in the middle of the thirteenth century was only atrophied nostalgia for the complex and distinctive world of the good men and good women before 1208, that is, before the Albigensian crusade. This does not make it any less profound, but scholars should not read backwards from this point, assuming this was the way it always was. By 1250 men and women choosing to be 'good Christians' were self-consciously heretics, actually needing the violence of the inquisitors to make them the glorious martyrs of the early Church they now imagined themselves to be. It went both ways, as Christine Caldwell Ames has impressively argued, with the early Dominican inquisitors equally needing the threat of violence by heretics to be martyrs.[116] Violence as a redemptive act in the world defined both heterodoxy and orthodoxy in the thirteenth century. In 1273 the inquisitor Ranuf de Plassac was told about a heretic (who was not identified as a good man, although, intriguingly, he was a friar of the Holy Cross) saying that 'the Church of the heretics was the true Church' and that this heretic wished to suffer martyrdom, as 'there was no death so beautiful as that by fire.'[117] This was a radical change within three decades, and an understanding of the good men that bears no relationship to the twelfth century. Or rather, the only meaningful connection between heretics over this period, the only element giving any sense of continuity, was the series of inquisitions into heretical depravity. By transforming the good men into a 'heresy' the inquisitors transformed them into a 'religion', or more correctly, transfigured them into a 'Church', one in which holiness was achieved by the persecuted through their persecution.

'I suspect some historians will question', David Nirenberg commented at the end of his review of Moore's *The War on Heresy* (2012), in the all-too-common brew of misunderstanding and sanctimony facing anyone doubting Catharism, 'the argument that so many men and women were willing to die for beliefs that were only someone else's construction'.[118] When a scholar this

---

[115] Pegg, *A Most Holy War*, pp. 167–71.
[116] C. Caldwell Ames, *Righteous Persecution: Inquisition, Dominicans, and Christianity in the Middle Ages* (Philadelphia, 2008).
[117] *Inquisitors and Heretics in Thirteenth-Cenury Languedoc*, pp. 178–9; Paris, BnF, Collection Doat, MS 25, fol. 3v.
[118] D. Nirenberg, review of Moore, *The War on Heresy* in *Speculum* 88 (2013), 1133.

brilliant gets so much wrong in one sentence, it reveals just how enduring is the paradigm of Catharism, and just how difficult it will be for many to accept its demise. Interestingly, Nirenberg in his sweeping history of anti-Judaism in western thought, a contemporary exercise in *Religionsgeschichte* if ever there was one, 'speaks scarcely at all about the thoughts and actions of people who would have identified themselves as Jews', as he assumes no matter how intellectuals used 'anti-Judaism as a mask, that is, as a pedagogical fear' for three millennia, 'living Jews' existed.[119] Leaving aside for the moment whether a methodology that ignores living Jews is justified, the assumption that, no matter what Latin Christian intellectuals said about heresy (especially as a pedagogic fear) in the twelfth or thirteenth centuries, 'living Cathars' existed, still forms the core of contemporary scholarly faith in Catharism. Like those great Dreyfusard historians who helped invent the paradigm of Catharism, Nirenberg implicitly regards Cathars (or Albigensians, as he also calls them) as analogous to Jews; and, like those fin-de-siècle scholars, he explicitly promotes the intellectual bias in the history of religion and heresy, even saying, as way of justifying conventional outcomes from conventional models, '[d]ifferent methodologies are appropriate to different goals'.[120] No they are not, and never have been, particularly when they lead you down the garden path of Catharism.

Biller initially singled me out as the foremost 'deconstructionist' and 'sceptic' of Catharism.[121] Lately, there is Moore,[122] and together we lead the 'demolition corps' in an 'onslaught on the conventional picture of Catharism'.[123] Biller cleverly gives the impression that we are wilfully tilting at windmills, contrarians for the sake of being contrary. By calling us 'sceptics', he implies we only disagree with what has always been said about Catharism on a personal, even emotional, level. By labelling us 'deconstructionists', he suggests we knowingly 'demolish' cogent evidence, only keeping what supports our views. There is even the sly intimation of postmodernism and all its relativist evils lurking beneath the surface.[124] He concocts a genealogy for

---

[119] D. Nirenberg, *Anti-Judaism: The Western Tradition* (New York, 2013), pp. 7, 10.
[120] Nirenberg, review of *The War on Heresy*, p. 1133.
[121] Biller, 'Goodbye to Waldensiansm?', p. 9.
[122] See esp. P. Biller, review of Moore, *The War on Heresy* in *Reviews in History* 1546 (13 February 2014), http://www.history.ac.uk/reviews/review/1546.
[123] Biller, 'Cathars and the Material World, pp. 91–2. Now, see A. Roach and J. Simpson, 'Introduction', in *Heresy and the Making of European Culture: Medieval and Modern Perspectives*, ed. A. Roach and J. Simpson (Farnham, 2013), pp. 1–27, esp. p. 6, providing an important statement of current historiographic trends, in which the positions of Moore ('forensic scalpel') and Pegg ('meat cleaver') are seriously addressed, if largely misunderstood and slightly caricatured, which is not surprising, as the paradigm of Catharism remains unquestioned.
[124] Taylor, *Heresy, Crusade and Inquisition*, pp. 4–5, goes along with this suggestion of postmodernism.

our scepticism and deconstruction, beginning with Robert Lerner (who, while a student of Strayer, studied with and remains influenced by Grundmann) and his dismantling of the so-called heresy of the Free Spirit in 1972, which was itself inspired by an article of Grundmann's from 1965.[125] Nothing could be further from the truth. Nevertheless, it is a cunning way of domesticating dissent, so to speak, by implying Moore and myself are ultimately the heirs of Grundmann, and though him, *Religionsgeschichte*. (By the way, the arguments of Moore and myself, while very close, and obviously compatible, are not always the same.) I am neither sceptic nor deconstructionist, never having been the latter, and moving well beyond the former more than a decade ago. I am leading no onslaught on the 'conventional picture of Catharism', largely because, apart from its modernist drafting a century ago, *any* contemporary picture of Catharism, conventional or otherwise, is fraudulent.

Arnaldo Momigliano insisted the history of historiography must judge between 'truth and falsehood' among paradigms, methods, and narratives, building upon the factual, dismissing the fictitious; otherwise, we are left with the platitude 'that every historian and every historical problem is historically conditioned'.[126] That the paradigm of Catharism has escaped serious historiographic judgement for so long is testament not so much to its late Victorian and Edwardian craftsmanship, though that is part of it, as to the fact that for much of the last century heresy and religion were not topics addressed by mainstream historians, especially in Great Britain and the United States. This is the paradox about the making of Catharism. It was created by historians and historically inclined theologians formulating methods for examining religion scientifically at the same time as, and in response to, general agreement in the historical profession that religion could never be analysed scientifically or objectively. The paradigm survived largely through indifference, relegated to the sidelines, as was religion for the most part, even by historians who never thought that what they did was a science. It was only in the 1970s that heresy and religion became mainstream topics for historians. Unfortunately, what also came along were the methodological conventions of the late nineteenth century, and rather than being replaced over the last five decades, these practices and assumptions have only intensified. Understanding religion has never been more critical, and yet most of the tools being used for its comprehension, including the very subject to be comprehended, were

---

[125] Biller, 'Goodbye to Waldensianism?', pp. 7–8; R. E. Lerner, *The Heresy of the Free Spirit in the Later Middle Ages* (Berkeley, 1972), influenced by H. Grundmann, 'Ketzerverhöre des Spätmittelalters als quellenkritisches Problem', *Deutsches Archiv für Erforschung des Mittelalters* 21 (1965), 519–75. Taylor, *Heresy, Crusade and Inquisition*, pp. 4–5, and Taylor, 'Evidence for Dualism, p. 320, repeat Biller's genealogy of scepticism deriving from Lerner.

[126] A. Momigliano, 'Historicism Revisited', in A. Momigliano, *Essays in Ancient and Modern Historiography* (Chicago, 2012), pp. 372–3.

manufactured more than a century ago. Indeed, I would argue that apart from the resurrection of the *Religionsgeschichte* model almost unchanged, a new naturalism (epitomized by evolutionary psychology, so-called 'deep history', and the history of emotions) and even a new confessionalism (where only the religious can truly understand religion) is ascendant.

A new history of heresy needs to be written, without Catharism.[127] It must be one that captures the complicated relationship between the invention of heresy by medieval intellectuals and the invention of Catharism by modern scholars; one that is more historically precise and methodologically sophisticated, more focused on the men, women, and children accused of heresy, and upon those individuals who consciously chose to be heretics, leaving behind the traditional assumptions of the nineteenth century. The study of heresy and religion must break away from the intellectualist bias, and while not giving up research on Latin Christian intellectuals, scholars need to be more aware that these individuals and their texts (real and imaginary) are not the only guides into the past. The old nineteenth-century notion that if we can only find that one text, that one smoking gun, then everything we 'just know' to be true will be proven, needs replacing by a broader understanding that if a past world is evoked as fully as possible, with historical and anthropological depth, where ideas and society entrench each other, then this evocation itself functions as the smoking gun, proving many things at once, giving sense to fragmentary texts, giving meaning to evidence never noticed before, revealing consequential relationships between beliefs and habits. This is why I stress evoking the world of the good men and good women, always trying, as Milan Kundera poignantly writes about such intellectual and aesthetic intentions, 'to enclose an action, a gesture, a response within a larger whole; to dissolve them into the running water of the everyday'.[128] It is the running water of the everyday that erodes Catharism, revealing it as a modernist invention, with no relationship to medieval reality. It is rare in scholarship to witness, let alone participate in, a paradigm shift in knowledge. Most scholarship is not about overturning a field, but merely adds to what is known and accepted. As much as Catharism was a revolution in the history of heresy a century ago, it seems fitting that a new revolution in the history of heresy – it was the best of times, it was the worst of times – is now overthrowing it.

---

[127] An outstanding start on this new history is C. Caldwell Ames, *Medieval Heresies: Christianity, Judaism, and Islam* (Cambridge, 2015).

[128] M. Kundera, *The Curtain: An Essay in Seven Parts*, trans. Linda Asher (New York, 2006), p. 19.

3

The Cathar Middle Ages as a Methodological and Historiographical Problem

John H. Arnold

Introduction: making and unmaking heresies

We have been here before. Ideas and arguments transmigrate between locales, reappearing reworked in different contexts, undoubtedly changed somewhat but hopefully subtly improved with each cycle of rebirth and revision. The sense of 'heresy' as a construct of orthodoxy – accompanied in its strongest ('absolute') version by the implication that the reality of heresy is 'made up' by orthodoxy – is not by any means limited to current debate around Catharism. Other 'heresies' in other times and places have similarly been taken apart, demonstrated to be wholly or (in the 'mitigated' version of the idea) partly phantasmic, and then, after a pause, often put back together again, albeit differently and more subtly, in a rush of post-revisionist enthusiasm.[1]

One of the earliest and most influential incarnations of the debate was Robert Lerner's demonstration, in 1972, that the 'Heresy of the Free Spirit' was an inquisitorial fantasy, woven together from disparate threads of lay reformist enthusiasm, torture, and the willingness of a few idiosyncratic witnesses to flesh out the picture in accord with the inquisitor's script.[2] Ten years later there followed, of course, R. I. Moore's hugely inspiring analysis of how medieval Europe became a 'persecuting society', and how, in so doing, it amplified and fantasized elements and connections (rhetorical or real) between disparate marginal groups. Discussion of late antique heresiography – 'handbooks of

---

[1] 'Taken apart' and 'put back together': I am deliberately avoiding using the word 'deconstruction', as it seems unnecessarily misleading in this context: I can see nothing in this debate related to Derrida's notion of deconstruction (notwithstanding Michel Roquebert's belief that such postmodernist practices must lie behind it all; see M. Roquebert, 'Le déconstructionisme et les études cathares', in *Les cathares devant l'histoire: mélanges offerts à Jean Duvernoy*, ed. A. Brenon and C. Dieulafait (Cahors, 2005), pp. 105–33).

[2] R. E. Lerner, *The Heresy of the Free Spirit in the Later Middle Ages* (Berkeley, 1972) – in this case, a taking-apart that has thus far *almost* withstood any revisionist attempt at reconstruction; though see R. Vaneigem, *The Movement of the Free Spirit* (New York, 1984).

heresy' and the like – has long recognized that, in a period when orthodoxy was notably fluid, a main purpose of such texts was to provide rhetorical tools for the denunciation of one's opponents, and in that sense to 'make up' at least the more *outré* and scurrilous elements of the heresies they condemned. More recently Karen King has given us a very interesting sense of what this means for the reality or otherwise of one particular heresy itself.[3] To zoom to the other chronological pole of these debates, for some long while early modernists have been arguing over the reality or otherwise of 'Puritanism' and of particular Puritan sects. Discussion here has ranged from Colin Davis's attempt to bludgeon the radical 'Ranters' out of existence (and to argue that the texts can only tell us about the issues which current orthodoxy wished to debate); to Patrick Collinson's elegant framing of 'Puritanism' as a fluctuating identity; and most recently (the swing of the pendulum heading back here toward reconstruction) to Peter Lake's extremely acute sense of particular 'Puritans' in specific locales, and the complicated interplay between their own sense of identity and that imputed to them by hostile others.[4] Regarding the English heresy of Wycliffism or Lollardy (or the Wycliffites, or Lollards, or Lollaerts, or lollards – here, also, there are ongoing debates on what names are appropriate), interpretation has partly swung away from Anne Hudson's earlier magisterial picture of heretical connection and coherence, and scholars now focus more on the local meanings of dissent, and the picture of 'heresy' imputed by orthodox power, with a particular emphasis on the political utility of heresy accusations in a time of regnal instability.[5] Most recently, however, work both by literary and historical scholars has found different ways of positively addressing Lollardy, no longer taking as given the idea that it inherited wholesale a Wycliffite theological programme, but allowing nonetheless that ideas, texts and practices could build a 'Lollard' identity independent of orthodox projections.[6]

So, as I say, we have been here before. If we were Cathars (or those whom many of us are still wont to call 'Cathars', meaning by this at the very least

---

[3] K. L. King, *What is Gnosticism?* (Cambridge MA, 2003)

[4] J. C. D. Davis, *Fear, Myth and History: The Ranters and the Historians* (Cambridge, 1986); P. Collinson, *Godly People: Essays on English Protestantism and Puritanism* (London, 1983), esp. chs. 1 and 20; P. Collinson, 'Antipuritanism', in *The Cambridge Companion to Puritanism*, ed. J. Coffey and P. C. H. Lim (Cambridge, 2008), pp. 19–33; P. Lake, *The Boxmaker's Revenge: 'Orthodoxy', 'Heterodoxy' and the Politics of the Parish in early Stuart London* (Manchester, 2001), esp. pp. 389–415. For similar issues, see also C. W. Marsh, *The Family of Love in English Society, 1550–1630* (Cambridge, 1993).

[5] A. Hudson, *The Premature Reformation: Wycliffite Texts and Lollard History* (Oxford, 1988); P. Strohm, *England's Empty Throne: Usurpation and the Language of Legitimation, 1399–1422* (New Haven, 1998); A. Cole, *Literature and Heresy in the Age of Chaucer* (Cambridge, 2008); *Wycliffite Controversies*, ed. M. Bose and K. Ghosh (Turnhout, 2013).

[6] F. Somerset, *Feeling Like Saints: Lollard Writings after Wyclif* (Ithaca NY, 2014); see also J. P. Hornbeck III, *What is a Lollard? Dissent and Belief in Late Medieval England* (Oxford, 2010).

A Methodological and Historiographical Problem

that they held dualist beliefs about material creation) we would hope that the process of transmigration would lead eventually to transcendence. Historians should surely not set their sights so high or on such an ultimately disengaged goal. But we could be alert to traces from these past 'lives'. There is a Cathar tale – it appears a couple of times as something told or preached to the laity in the early fourteenth century – which aimed to persuade believers of the fact of metempsychosis. A Cathar good man is out walking with a friend, and remembers that when, in a previous life, he was a horse traveling this same path, he had thrown a shoe close by; looking through the immediate landscape, they find the horseshoe – a material proof of that previous worldly existence.[7] I will present nothing so bluntly literal in this chapter. But I think we should nonetheless be on the look-out for metaphorical horseshoes: for the echo of other, earlier ideas and intellectual practices still reverberating in our current debate; and awake also to the possibilities engendered by the slightly *different* shapes of argument, and wider contexts for those arguments, taken when different kinds of 'heresy' are taken apart – and sometimes put back together.

There is a still longer background to these debates, pre-dating Lerner's high-point of revisionism. A couple of years after Lerner published his study, Norman Cohn produced *Europe's Inner Demons*, a book building upon his earlier *The Pursuit of the Millennium*.[8] Whereas in *Pursuit* Cohn had tended to see reports of the more *outré* elements of heresy as substantive evidence for the psychopathology of medieval society, in *Europe's Inner Demons* he turned his lens in the direction of the persecutors, unearthing the repeated calumnies visited upon religious radicals, and emphasizing the elements of projected fantasy generated by those in power. (Behind this lay a profound interest in the history of the 'blood libel' against the Jews, and the roots of the irrational persecution that culminated in the Holocaust.) In a more limited and technical fashion, elements of how orthodoxy stereotyped 'heresy' – and thus manipulated what was at heart a 'reformist' movement of popular enthusiasm into something more organized, co-ordinated and threatening – can be found in earlier works, pre-eminently Herbert Grundmann's *Religiöse Bewegungen im Mittelalter* (and in various other articles by Grundmann).[9] If one goes back to

---

7 *Le registre d'inquisition de Jacques Fournier, évêque de Pamiers (1318–1325)*, ed. J. Duvernoy, 3 vols. (Toulouse, 1965), II, 36, 408.
8 N. Cohn, *Europe's Inner Demons: An Enquiry Inspired by the Great Witch Hunt* (London, 1975). Note also T. Szasz, *The Manufacture of Madness: A Comparative Study of the Inquisition and the Mental Health Movement* (New York, 1970).
9 H. Grundmann, *Religiöse Bewegungen im Mittelater: Untersuchungen über die geschichtlichen Zusammenhänge zwischen der Ketzerei, den Bettelorden und der religiösen Frauenbewegung im 12. und 13. Jahrhundert und über die geschichtlichen Grundlagen der deutschen Mystik* (Berlin, 1935), trans. S. Rowan as *Religious Movements in the Middle Ages* (Notre Dame, 1995); H. Grundmann, 'Der Typus des Ketzers in mittelalticher Anschauung', in *Kultur- und Universalgeschichte: Festschrift für W. Goetz* (Leipzig, 1927); H. Grundmann, 'Ketzerverhöre

the great historian of inquisition Henry Charles Lea one finds, among many other things, a strong emphasis on the popular appetite for 'heresy' as an outcome of the desperate need for reform, and that therefore the orthodox representation of 'heresy' inevitably distorted the real phenomena. The very strong Protestant bias of this final witness reminds us that one very old root for the taking-apart-of-heresy is the re-presentation, by early Protestant writers, of medieval heretics as 'forebears' of their own Church (leading not infrequently to some quite large distortions of their own in the process). 'Heresy is not heresy but reform' – this view, most recently and eloquently restated by Moore, has a very long pedigree, and in one sense is ineluctably correct: unorthodox religious radicals, whether they wish to improve the existing Church or absolutely 're-form' it in their own more narrow (and frequently apostolic) image, can only be 'heretics' precisely because they are 'Christians', and hence always potentially part of a reformist move.

But within this historiographical tradition, it should be admitted that 'Cathars' have often occupied a different position from other putative sects. Waldensians, Spiritual Franciscans, Wycliffites, Hussites: elements in their radicalism have found at least partial echo in later forms of Protestantism. As a consequence, if one wishes to emphasize how much they are 'made up' as a heresy, some reformist identity can still remain, and can form the basis for some perduring claim to an independent existence. ('Heresy is not heresy but reform; and these reformers, who really existed, were called heretics.') But Cathars, if understood as full-blown dualists, do not sit so comfortably. If one decides that all the dualist elements, along with the other accoutrements of what might be posited as a 'counter-Church', were made up and thrust upon them by orthodoxy, the process of stripping away these impositions leaves one with very little that looks actively reformist. An apostolic model, yes; but not one that seems to encourage others to 'leave their families and follow' in their footsteps. Preaching, yes; but not preaching that seems to speak much, if at all, to moral reform by the laity.[10]

There are, one should then note, several different lines of interconnected argument in the modern taking-apart of Catharism. One aspect has related to connections, or the lack thereof: do French Cathars connect to Italian Cathars? Do both connect to Bogomils? Do any connect back in time to earlier dualist groups and traditions (Paulicians, Manichaeans)? Another aspect relates to the nature of the Cathar Church: an organized and hierarchical entity with a full-blown diocesan structure and administration? The 'gathered faithful',

---

des Spätmittelalters als quellenkritisches Problem', *Deutsches Archiv für Erforschung des Mittelalters* 21 (1965), 519–75. Although clearly holding the view that Catharism was a dualist religion with its roots in the Balkans, Arno Borst also paid close attention to orthodox stereotyping and modes of representation in his *Die Katherer* (Stuttgart, 1953).

[10] See J. H. Arnold, 'The Preaching of the Cathars', in *Medieval Monastic Preaching*, ed. C. Muessig (Leiden, 1998), pp. 183–205.

in the more loose and general sense of *ecclesia*, often localized to a particular area or diocese (as would also be the case in some orthodox locutions)? Or nothing that should be called a 'Church' at all? A third line relates to names, in relation to geography: is there any reason to call southern French heretics 'Cathars'? or 'Perfects'? or 'Albigensians'? And what aspects of these 'taking-aparts' matter most, and for what reasons? It is particularly interesting to note here the œuvre of Jean-Louis Biget, whose study from the 1980s onwards has simultaneously worked hard to reconstruct the 'reality' of heretical groups, particularly in southern French civic contexts (pointing out, *en passant*, that the name 'Cathar' never appears in southern French sources),[11] while also emphasizing the important political elements governing the prosecution of this heresy, and arguing that though the heresy is undoubtedly dualist, it should not be seen as dependent on any external proselytizing factor, but as arising 'autocthonically', out of local needs and spiritual reflections, and indeed out of the experience of persecution.

What interests me in the current return of the debate are the methodological and historiographical issues embedded therein. While historians' confessional commitments were an important element informing past interpretations (and perhaps still inflecting current ones), these have now more clearly been joined by other aspects that connect to wider questions of methodology and historiographical practice. For example: how one should use hostile and partial evidence to 'reconstruct' or otherwise; how to untangle the complex interplay of voices in legal court records; how much agency we should seek to impute to past historical subjects; and how much power – and 'power' of what nature – we should impute to the medieval Church.

Most of these are issues which apply to the discussions that surround every kind of 'heresy', from ancient Gnosticism to Puritanism. But the debates in each particular area are marked also by certain, more particular, aspects, arising from the specific nature of the source-base and the legacies of particular Grand Narrative frames. Thus discussion around 'heresy' in late antiquity has issues of 'rhetoric' (understood in a particularly technical sense, derived from classical traditions of learning and politics) thrust very much to the fore, because of the predominantly rhetorical nature of the source material and its cultural context; and the question of orthodox authority is framed within wider debates regarding what the establishment of the Church under Constantine actually achieved, over what time-scale, and how settled or otherwise key theological issues were at different moments.[12] With Lollardy,

---

[11] J.-L. Biget, 'Les albigeois: remarques sur une dénomination', in *Inventer l'hérésie? Discours polémique et pouvoirs avant l'inquisition*, ed. M. Zerner (Nice, 1998), pp. 219–56 n. 2: 'Les hérétiques méridionaux n'ont jamais pris, ni reçu, au cours du Moyen Âge, le nom de cathares.' For Biget's perspective more broadly, see the articles collated in J.-L. Biget, *Hérésie et inquisition dans le midi de la France* (Paris, 2007).

[12] V. Burrus, *The Making of a Heretic: Gender, Authority and the Priscillianist Controversy*

the source-base includes much textual material that is customarily treated in a literary fashion (sermons, spiritual treatises, poetry), and discussion has consequently been informed by a more literary-critical approach, embracing issues of political and religious discourse, spiritual affect, and a certain fluidity of identity. At the same time, 'the Reformation' continues to loom large in the wider interpretive landscape surrounding Lollardy, and, perhaps as a consequence, even recent scholars of the subject have sometimes found it difficult not to frame things in terms of 'good' or 'bad' religious ideas and practices.

With regard to our current debate – the new Cathar wars – the wider questions sketched above very definitely pertain, but I think one can also identify certain issues that are more particular to this specific un-making or re-making of heresy. Among other things, I would like to suggest that a key aspect is a difference in methodological praxis – or even, one might say, methodological *habitus*, the 'taken-for-granted' bit of our professional and intellectual practices – between 'earlier' and 'later' medievalists (the watershed between the two falling sometime in the late twelfth century). In the remainder of this chapter, I want to explore, first, how these differences play out in contrasting modes of source criticism; second, different practices by which historians tend to set about building larger pictures from the evidential pieces; and finally, different inherited ideas on how one should interpret the medieval ideological context.

Sources and source criticism

My division between 'early' and 'late' is of course primarily about the nature and extent of surviving textual sources. The divide pertains to a degree to medieval history in general (though one recognizes of course that there are some areas where we have early medieval sources – and non-textual sources – in abundance), but is particularly evident in the case of sources relating to heresy and its repression. For 'heresy' before the late twelfth century, all sources are the product of hostile report. Most are either chronicle reports or letters, plus a few highly polemical sermons. The three genres intertwine on several occasions, as when a chronicle reports the letter Bishop Wazo of Liège had been sent by another bishop, asking for advice on how to deal with heretics, or in the chronicle report on Bishop Gerard of Arras-Cambrai's encounter with heretics, which includes the lengthy 'sermon' that he delivered to convert them.[13] Bishop Gerard's full 'sermon' is in fact more of a theological treatise, setting out a large number of aspects of Christian faith in a way not

---

(Berkeley, 1995); C. Humfress, *Orthodoxy and the Courts in Late Antiquity* (Oxford, 2007).
[13] Translated in *Heresies of the High Middle Ages: Selected Sources*, ed. and trans. W. L. Wakefield and A. P. Evans (New York, 1969), pp. 89–93 (pp. 82–5).

dissimilar to works by earlier Carolingian writers such as Amalarius of Metz or Walahfrid Strabo; but as we move through the twelfth century we see treatises specifically written *against heresy* start to figure also in the 'early' camp, thinking here particularly of Peter the Venerable's *Contra Petrobrusianos* and, later, Alan of Lille's *De fide Catholica*. By the Third Lateran Council of 1179 we also have, of course, papal proclamations and conciliar decisions, which are interesting in terms of orthodox 'policy' but often frustratingly (or tellingly) terse regarding the heretical 'threat'.

This is not at all an insubstantial corpus, but it does not vary hugely in generic form. What, then, of the 'late' corpus on heresy? This continues to provide examples of similar texts: chronicle reports, letters sent by bishops to each other and to the papacy, sermons against heretics in the south of France in particular. But some genres grow larger: there is a huge explosion of anti-heresy treatises in the thirteenth century, in terms of both number and length;[14] and, in contrast to the earlier bits of legislation, conciliar and synodal statutes on 'what to do with heretics' get ever more detailed and nuanced.[15] Some genres grow into new ones: preaching *exempla* appear in vast numbers in the thirteenth century, and as a large subset within this, stories either specifically about heresy, or else – often more interestingly – framed by heresy as a contextual fact, get recorded, shared, and one presumes preached ever more frequently. Other genres of evidence start to mention 'heresy' as a circumstantial detail for the first time: in southern France, we have a number of charters and other forms of legal document from the mid thirteenth century dealing with property transactions, where the key or contextual fact of earlier confiscation from a landholder 'because of heresy' is mentioned.[16] Occasionally we have documents of this kind that attest to some particularly noted figure, not in connection with their involvement in heresy but because of other issues: thus the will of Stephen of Anse, including within it mention of the 'oven which belonged to Valdes', makes somewhat more 'solid' both the heresiarch and the man who translated the New Testament for him.[17] Similarly, a letter setting out record of the gift of lands to the abbey of Villelongue, lands that had formerly belonged to Guillaume

---

14 See L. Sackville, *Heresy and Heretics in the Thirteenth Century: The Textual Representations* (York, 2011).
15 Discussed in detail in H. Maisonneuve, *Études sur les origines de l'inquisition* (Paris, 1960); see also analysis in J. H. Arnold, *Inquisition and Power: Catharism and the Confessing Subject in Medieval Languedoc* (Philadelphia, 2001), pp. 33–47.
16 For example, in 1259 the seneschal of Carcassonne sold property confiscated from various named people accused of heresy from Villeneuve-Minervois: Paris, Bibliothèque nationale de France (henceforth BnF), Collection Doat, MS 65, fol. 143; extracted in *Cartulaire et archives des communes de l'ancien diocèse et de l'arrondissement administratif de Carcassonne*, ed. M. Mahul, 6 vols. (Paris, 1857–71), IV, 385–6. There are various other examples from this same collection of materials.
17 A. Patschovsky, 'The Literacy of Waldensianism from Valdes to *c.* 1400', in *Heresy and*

Bernard d'Airoux, and other lands held by 'the heretic' Raymond de Saint-Martin, allows us a tiny sideways glimpse of two 'Cathars' clearly visible in inquisition records.[18] We have, for the first time, a few sources created by 'the heretics' themselves: theological treatises in Italian manuscripts, a lengthy liturgical text explaining how and when to perform the ritual of the *consolamentum* surviving in both an Italian and a southern French manuscript, dualist treatises written in southern France, including one in the vernacular.[19] And we have the inquisition records, in their vast and varying abundance: varying both because different documents from different stages of the process survive in different places – detailed depositions, brief sentences of guilt and punishment, some subsequent appeals and negotiations of sentence – and because the kinds of questions asked and the depth of detail recorded changed over time (the evidence from the late thirteenth and early fourteenth century is on the whole much richer than that of the mid thirteenth century) and in different contexts (for example the evidence given in 1247 by witnesses against Pierre Garcias of Toulouse: perhaps because they were themselves friars, these witnesses related much more theological detail than is found in other depositions of the period – theological detail that includes explicit discussion of dualist belief).[20]

This list of material is not meant to impute greater authority to those working on the 'later' period. It is, rather, an attempt to set out the different possibilities and problems presented by a (relative) dearth of sources on the one, earlier, hand, and a (relative) wealth on the other, later, one. Let us take narrative sources – chronicles for the most part – which necessarily form a large part of the focus of R. I. Moore's most recent taking-apart of heresy. As narrative sources produced by individual authors, they are particularly amenable to certain kinds of source-critical question. One can focus on each author, viewing him as the creative nexus of the text, ask questions about his position geographically, politically and spiritually, and thus reconstruct

---

Literacy, 1000–1500, ed. P. Biller and A. Hudson (Cambridge, 1994), pp. 112–36; the will is reproduced as plate 6, p. 115.

[18] Paris, BnF, Collection Doat, MS 70, fol. 137, letter of Mathieu de Marly, knight, 1229 (see *Cartulaire*, ed. Mahul, I, 231); Guillaume Bernard d'Airoux (not named explicitly in that document as a heretic) was highly active as a medic as well as, or as part of his role as, a Cathar good man; see P. Biller, 'Cathars and Material Women', in *Medieval Theology and the Natural Body*, ed. P. Biller and A. J. Minnis (York, 1997), pp. 61–108 (pp. 104–5). Raymond de Saint-Martin was an active Cathar good man for many years, and is noted by several deponents; among other things, he brought money out of Montségur just before it fell in 1244: see Paris, BnF, Collection Doat, MS 23, fol. 168r; MS Doat 24, fols. 81r, 171v.

[19] *Heresies*, ed. Wakefield and Evans, pp. 447–630.

[20] On Pierre Garcias, see depositions from Paris, BnF, Collection Doat, MS 22, edited in C. Douais, *Documents pour servir à l'histoire de l'inquisition dans le Languedoc*, 2 vols. (Paris, 1900), II, 90–114; partial translation in W. L. Wakefield, *Heresy, Crusade and Inquisition in Southern France, 1100–1250* (London, 1974), pp. 242–9.

a possible context and 'agenda' behind his presentation of 'heresy'. That 'agenda' can be linked to a wider, political context, because with a single author (and perhaps particularly with a chronicler) there is a reasonable expectation that the work has been written as a commission or in the hope of gaining patronage from some powerful figure. So on the one hand, there is a source-critical tendency to pull apart and atomize, treating each source as most obviously and securely evidence only for its own moment of production; a source that tells us most of all about its author. On the other hand, the focus on the context of production also allows an opposite 'push' toward conformity: one can link specific narrative productions to a wider set of cultural expectations, and can point to a shared educational and ideological background for the relevant authors. Again, this is a source-critical approach inviting reflection most of all on the 'author'.[21] Much the same is true with the earlier examples of treatises against heresy: produced by specific, named authors writing in very particular contexts, where elements shared with other texts are most immediately indicative of how indebted and influenced they are by a shared, inherited discourse (going back particularly to Augustine of Hippo and Isidore of Seville). Once again, the approach invites us to reflect more on the authorial mindset rather than any external phenomena.

However, a question can then be asked about any specific text's relationship to earlier discussions, and how those discourses should be viewed in general – as available rhetorical resources, as indications of an imprisoning *mentalité*, as optional or essential 'authorities', as a unified and monovocal discourse or as different shifting strands of orthodox reaction to heterodoxy? The answer may of course differ for particular authors. One might suspect that Guibert de Nogent's evocation of 'Manichaean' orgiastic practices by the heretics he denounces at Laon in the early twelfth century is a fully witting (and consciously distorting) use of the Augustinian anti-heresy legacy. In contrast, in Eberwin of Steinfeld's letter to Bernard of Clairvaux, one may note reference to that same legacy, but deployed as part of genuine confusion and uncertainty over both what he has encountered and what to do.[22] There is a lack of clarity, to my mind, in the most recent historiographical discussions over whether those medieval authors depicted as inventing 'Cathars' are self-consciously and wittingly taking up a particular rhetorical tool to achieve

---

[21] See, thus, R. I. Moore, *The War on Heresy: Faith and Power in Medieval Europe* (London, 2012); D. Iogna-Prat, *Order and Exclusion: Cluny and Christendom face Heresy, Judaism and Islam, 1000–1150* (Ithaca NY, 2002); U. Brunn, *Des contestataires aux 'cathares': discours de réforme et propagande antihérétique dans les pays du Rhin et de la Meuse avant l'inquisition* (Paris, 2006); T. Head, 'Naming Names: The Nomenclature of Heresy in the Early Eleventh Century', in *History in the Comic Mode: Medieval Communities and the Matter of Person*, ed. R. Fulton and B. W. Holsinger (New York, 2007), pp. 91–100.

[22] *Heresies*, ed. Wakefield and Evans, pp. 101–4, 127–32. For Guibert, see the most recent translation of this passage in Guibert de Nogent, *'Monodies' and 'On the Relics of the Saints'*, trans. J. McAlhany and J. Rubinstein (London, 2011), pp. 168–71.

other, less visible, purposes (as justification for political action, or as a means of beating down other lines of religious 'reform'); or whether they are honest believers in their own discourse, trapped into viewing the world around them through a particular kind of 'anti-heresy' frame.

How one decides this does matter quite considerably. All authors of all kinds inherit discourses and templates and rhetorics and topoi. But it makes a difference if one thinks that they are deploying these almost willy-nilly, or as part of a concerted and conscious propagandistic plan, or whether certain ideas have gained *de facto* hegemony because of other factors: for example, as twelfth-century orthodox theology begins to focus on Christ's incarnated humanity, this might tend to make the spectre of 'dualism' loom large as a particularly apposite theological 'Other'. Or, perhaps we should consider whether external phenomena have prompted the choice of *particular* tools at certain apposite moments. To consider the latter case does not at all collapse 'representation' simply into 'reality' – indeed, it can still incorporate a degree of all the preceding possibilities. But it does suggest that the historian might be able to make some analytical headway by examining the particular rhetorical choices made by medieval authors, even if they are writing propagandistically, engaged in current orthodox theological reflection, or so forth. For most of those historians currently engaged in taking 'heresy' apart, the second option (*de facto* cultural hegemony) is perhaps that most favoured, implicitly or explicitly: that certain images of heresy, drawn from late antiquity and fuelled by influential texts in the twelfth century, came to dominate in the larger discussion around 'reform'. But other questions again arise: 'dualist heresy' was only one possible inheritance from Augustine and others, and if it forms a hegemonic viewpoint, why is it not imputed to *all* unorthodox movements as-and-when they arise? Why not allege it against any enemy of the Church – the Waldensians, for example? In the latter case, the answer must in part surely be to allow some sense of the 'real' heresy exercising influence: even when denouncing Waldensian heretics, orthodox authorities did not try to make them into dualists, because the charge simply wouldn't 'fit'. If some elements of the reality of the Waldensian heresy affect how it is represented in hostile sources, is that not something one might have to consider for other heresies also?

Let me turn now to methodological and interpretive issues raised by the greater volume of 'later' sources. While we continue to have a number of important texts written by specific people, for the overall corpus of material the questions and approaches invited by a focus on individual 'authorship' diminish as the documentary record thickens. I don't mean by this that individual authors and their perspectives cease to matter: clearly we want to reflect on how inquisitorial practices and texts inform, for example, Bernard Gui's *Practica inquisitionis*, and we would surely note the fact that Rainier Sacconi was a Cathar who converted to the Dominicans, as context both for what he will present as 'insider' knowledge, and also perhaps for the vehemence of his denunciation of his former faith (though in both cases we might also reflect on how the prompts to authorship have moved away from 'patronage' to something more like 'professional duty'). However, the overall volume of material does start to raise different issues. Just focusing on authored (albeit sometimes anonymous) texts such as the various treatises and inquisition manuals produced in the thirteenth century, one notes the huge increase in overall volume – both in the number of treatises produced, and their length – and the degree to which, on the one hand, the treatises purport to be informed by sustained engagement with contemporary heresy (either debating with or prosecuting it), and, on the other hand, that texts start to borrow from other contemporary works, rather than relying quite so heavily on Isidore and Augustine.

One also has to note the variation in style and purpose of different treatises: whether they figure themselves as 'debates', or denunciations, or lofty overviews, or technical manuals. Even where shared elements of discourse appear, their meaning can be different. A key element here is the emphasis on 'Manichaeans' and what we take different authors to mean by it. I have already noted a potential difference, for the earlier period, in how one thinks about Guibert de Nogent or Eberwin of Steinfeld's uses of the term. One can add to this the tendency of thirteenth-century authors to talk about *new* Manichaeans – quite consciously drawing upon a patristic category, but also explicitly reworking it to establish that the heretics viewed 'now' are different from 'then'. This we find, for example, in book five of Bernard Gui's *Practica*, and in the much earlier treatise against heresy written by the ex-Waldensian Durand of Huesca, who at one point talks of 'the Manichees, that is to say the modern Cathars who live in the dioceses of Albi and Toulouse and Carcassonne, and their accomplices'.[23] In other words, the ancient Manichaean sect, while important to thirteenth-century discussion of dualism, is more of a backdrop and patristic reference point than an ideological straight-jacket.

The *Tractatus fidei contra diversos errores* by Benedict d'Alignan, bishop of Marseille, written across the period 1240–60, is rather interesting in this regard. Benedict's treatise seeks to refute (through 'authorities, reasons and examples') *all* error against the Christian faith, whether heretical, philosophical, or from other traditions – Judaism, Islam, Greek Orthodoxy and so forth.[24] 'Manichaeans', named as such, appear only a couple of times in the *Tractatus*, and most prominently when the topic of believing in two gods is

---

[23] *Une somme anti-cathare: Le* Liber contra Manicheos *de Durand de Huesca*, ed. C. Thouzellier (Louvain, 1964), ch. 13, p. 217.

[24] See P.-A. Amargier, 'Benoît d'Alignan, évêque de Marseille (1229–1268): le contexte et l'esprit d'une théologie', *Moyen Âge* 72 (1966), 443–62; J. H. Arnold, 'Benedict of Alignan and *Tractatus fidei contra errores*', in *Christian-Muslim Relations: A Bibliographical History*, ed. D. Thomas *et al.*, 5 vols. (Leiden, 2009), IV, 422–4. I hope to publish further on this treatise in the near future.

first mentioned, at which point Benedict, in one of the very few moments of the treatise to mention violence, emphasizes that dualism is so 'pestilential' that they must be 'persecuted by fire and sword'.[25] A folio later he references Augustine to explain that dualism is the root of their other beliefs, namely that:

> They say that neither meat nor cheese nor eggs should be eaten. Another [belief] is that the Old Law [= Testament] was given by the Prince of Darkness and was evil. The third [belief] is that the Fathers of the Old Testament were evil and damned. The fourth: that souls are not newly created to enter bodies. Fifth: that Christ did not truly take on human nature. Six: that John the Baptist was evil.[26]

These and other errors strongly associated with dualism are denounced at various points throughout the *Tractatus fidei*: 'Against those who say that the God of the Old Testament is not the God of the New Testament', 'Against Paterniani and Patriciani who say that the substance of human flesh was made by the devil', 'Against those who say that the angels who fell [from Heaven] were created to be bad, and did not through free will decide to do this maliciously', 'Against those who say that one soul can enter many bodies successively, and make many bodies come to life', 'Against those who say that the soul travels from body to body or can even transmute itself into certain animals'.[27] In each case, biblical passages are then provided to 'refute' these mistaken beliefs, and on various occasions (such as an extended discussion on those who did not believe in the necessity of marriage) a sequence of heretics' further 'objections' to these refutations are noted, with responses to those objections then also provided.[28] Perhaps because Benedict's treatise is so focused on this process of rebuttal – aiming to be a handbook that can tackle

---

[25] Paris, BnF, MS Lat. 4224, fol. 114r–v. One should note that Benedict had been in the midst of the Albigensian crusade, as abbot of the monastery of Lagrasse, and had also later gone on crusade to the Middle East; see M. Segonne, *Moine, prélat, croisé: Benoît d'Alignan, abbé de La Grasse, seigneur-evêque de Marseille, 1190–1268* (Marseille, 1960).

[26] MS Lat. 4224, fol. 116r. It is worth noting that while this list of errors clearly overlaps with Augustine's description of Manichaeans in *De haeresibus*, it also diverges from it, as Augustine does not here assign Manichaean beliefs regarding Christ's nature or John the Baptist. The former topic is discussed at length in Augustine's *Contra Faustus*, but again belief regarding John the Baptist is absent. In short, Augustine provides Benedict with an authoritative framing device, but not a straightforward template.

[27] MS Lat. 4224, fols. 77r–v, 155r, 171v, 275r, 284r. Paterniani and Patriciani are both notional 'sects' listed in Augustine's *De heresibus*, the former holding the belief that human flesh was created by the devil, the latter that the lower parts of the human body were likewise satanic.

[28] MS Lat. 4224, fols. 422v–423v; this section briefly draws upon Alan of Lille to make the *Tractatus*'s only reference to 'Cathars', but seems to do so primarily because of their presence in a key passage in canon law, itself drawing on Isidore of Seville: Gratian, *Corpus iuris canonici*, Q24, q3, c. 39 'Quidam', *Corpus iuris canonici*, ed. E. Friedberg, 2 vols. (Leipzig, 1879–81 [repr. Graz, 1959]), I, cols. 1001–1006.

all deviation from western orthodoxy by providing the right tools to refute any error whenever it pops up – the 'Manichaean' ascription is not repeated. Moreover, in contrast to certain other thirteenth-century treatises, Benedict includes almost no invective or polemical denunciation, and 'dualism' is not so much built up into an edifice as treated in a largely *ad hoc* fashion, taken apart specific belief by specific belief.

My argument is not that Benedict gives a 'better' or more accurate view of real thirteenth-century heretics; on the contrary, it is in fact quite hard to get any very clear picture of heretics as such from his treatise, as it arranges everything by individual 'error' rather than by 'sect'. The point rather is that with the thirteenth-century evidence, one cannot help but be struck by the fact that while Benedict borrows profusely from various other sources – both ancient and recent – his *Tractatus* is by no means identical in tone, purpose, viewpoint or discursive effect to other treatises of the same period. Though the historian working on these 'later' sources finds it hard to ignore the contemporaneous cross-referencing between these authors, who at various points are demonstrably borrowing intertextually (Benedict, for example, makes use of Moneta of Cremona's *Summa adversos Catharos et Valdenses*, a work completed *c*. 1241; this is evidence in itself of how swiftly anti-heresy treatises could circulate in the mid thirteenth century), the historian also notes the considerable *differences* between those texts and their apparent purposes and perspectives. That they share in wider discourses 'against heresy' is indisputable; but the texts look much more like specific instantiations and adaptations of those discourses than simple iterations of some hegemonic *ur*-text.[29] That something 'beyond' each text may be influencing their composition, something more than a shared cultural milieu, once again tends to suggest itself as an interpretive possibility.

That is perhaps even more the case with the new genre of source that dominates the interpretations of those working on the 'later' period: inquisition registers. We should of course note that inquisition trials come with their own tradition of source-critical suspicion. Those working on similar records for witchcraft in a later period would emphasize how distorting the inquisitorial process can be, as of course did Lerner in his discussion of the Free Spirit. There are very good reasons for being suspicious of certain records produced in the late thirteenth century, bound up with civic politics in Carcassonne and Albi, where various contemporaries (including at some points Philip IV of France, and several different popes) suspected that inquisitors had been either coercing false confessions, or doctoring records to frame important townspeople.[30] But those were alleged misrepresentations regarding *who* rather than *what*. Nobody in the current debate wants, I think,

---

[29] On this point, see further Sackville, *Heresy and Heretics*, esp. pp. 198–200.
[30] See A. Friedlander, *The Hammer of the Inquisitors: Brother Bernard Délicieux and the Struggle against the Inquisition in Fourteenth-Century France* (Leiden, 2000).

to jettison all inquisitorial sources, and it should be noted that a key element compromising the reliability of later trials – namely torture – is almost entirely absent from the thirteenth-century records.

The sheer volume of inquisition sources raises other methodological questions. These are not 'authored' records in the same fashion as chronicles or treatises, and it is hard to read them as 'inventing' in the same mode as we might impute to other narrative sources. Mark Pegg, in particular, has argued that certain key elements to the picture of 'Catharism' are inquisitorial distortions; and the sense of heterodox reality being falsified or re-interpreted by the inquisitorial eye is certainly an important methodological issue.[31] However, if various of those key elements – the presence of a Cathar hierarchy, Cathar connections between and travel to different areas of Europe, a sense of internal 'ecclesial' organization, and above all the theological tenets associated with dualism – are the product of inquisitors rather than witnesses, why are they only *intermittently* present in the records? We have depositions in which witnesses name certain people as Cathar 'bishops', sometimes even bishops of particular 'dioceses'; but equally there are depositions where those same heretics, at an earlier point in time, are not thus designated.[32] There are depositions where no heretic is claimed to be part of a hierarchy. There are others where a much more detailed 'knowledge' of Cathar ecclesial organization is attested. If this is all inquisitorial invention, why the variation? Why not label every prominent heretic as a 'bishop', and why not question witnesses much more rigorously about such issues? Similarly, we have evidence in several depositions of large-scale meetings – 'councils' as they are reported in the sources – where heretics debate and sort out matters of hierarchy and organization. This is a key element in the picture of Catharism as a 'counter-Church'; again, if it is wholly the product of a hostile 'making-up-of-heretics' by inquisitors, why does it appear in only a *few* depositions?

---

[31] M. G. Pegg, *The Corruption of Angels: The Great Inquisition of 1245–1246* (Princeton, 2001), ch. 7; revisited and expanded in Pegg, 'Questions about Questions: Toulouse 609 and the Great Inquisition of 1245–6', in *Texts and the Repression of Medieval Heresy*, ed. C. Bruschi and P. Biller (York, 2003), pp. 111–26.

[32] For example, Raymond John of Albi, giving evidence in 1238, mentions the heretic Bernard of Lamothe's activities *c.* 1221, without according them any formal status (though elsewhere in his deposition he ascribes the title of 'deacon' and 'bishop', to other heretics, and relates how the Cathar good men held a 'General Council' at Pieusse, at which heretics from Razes petitioned to have their own bishop, rather than relying on the Cathar bishops of Toulouse or Carcassonne); whereas other evidence names Bernard of Lamothe as 'Elder Son' of the Cathar 'diocese' of Toulouse, and then 'Bishop'. Compare Paris, BnF, Collection Doat, MS 23, fols. 260v–273v (Raymond John's deposition) with Toulouse, Bibliothèque municipale, MS 609 (henceforth MS 609), fol. 62r ('She also said that she once went to a sermon of heretics at Montesquieu. And then Bernard of Lamothe was confirmed as bishop of the heretics. And there many Ladies adored Bernard de Lamothe, bishop of the heretics, and other heretics on bended knees, saying, "Bless".')

Blunt statements of dualism are admittedly rare until the early fourteenth century, when the much more detailed sources produced by the inquiries of Geoffroy d'Ablis, and subsequently by Jacques Fournier, reveal absolutely explicit – and theologically detailed – discussion of such ideas, and how Cathar good men might preach those beliefs. But there are a few moments in earlier sources in which dualism is made plain: the mid thirteenth century evidence relating to Pierre Garcias, mentioned above; various witnesses who recalled heretics saying 'that God had not made visible things';[33] and frequent mention of various beliefs and practices that 'fit' with dualism, such as the vehement rejection of marriage, and even an occasional mention of the transmigration of souls.[34] It is certainly not methodologically wise to see inquisition registers as open windows into the past; but nor should we dismiss them as mere articulations of an unvarying orthodox script, as immersion in these records inevitably makes one aware of how much small elements vary between otherwise repetitious depositions.

In an earlier book, I argued that we should see the encounter between inquisitor and deponent as certainly distorting the 'reality' of prior Cathar experience, in a way that chimes in large part with the work that Mark Pegg was simultaneously undertaking.[35] For example, inquisitorial questions tended to emphasize familial links, and tended to assume that family connections indicated adherence to the faith (an assumption that has subsequently influenced various historians); in fact, one can identify various families divided rather than united by heresy, and if reading carefully one can also note that various events, coded by inquisitors as evidence of heretical adherence, might alternatively be seen as rooted in familial connection. Thus, for example, if someone visits an aunt who is a Cathar good woman, or attends the death-bed heretication of a father, these may clearly indicate 'heretical support' to an inquisitor, but might have meant rather different things to the witness. Similarly, the rituals involved in Catharism – blessing bread, ritual greetings, the *melioramentum* and so forth – may gain different or additional meanings when viewed through an inquisitorial eye.[36] Where

---

[33] For example MS 609, fol. 5r; the same witness denied having heard errors on other topics, so cannot be read as simply repeating what the inquisitor wanted to hear.

[34] For example MS 609, deposition of Pierre de Mazerolles, Lord of Gaja-la-Selve, fol. 124r: 'He believed that the aforesaid heretics were good men, and had a good faith, and that one could be saved through them, although he knew that the Church persecuted them. And he heard the heretics saying that God had not made visible things, and that the consecrated host was not the body of Christ, and that there was no salvation in baptism or marriage, and that the bodies of the dead do not rise up again. And he heard them saying that each soul of a man went around so many bodies until it could be saved.'

[35] Our monographs were the outcome of doctoral study, Pegg's doctorate submitted in November 1997, mine a year earlier, but neither of us aware of the other at that stage.

[36] Arnold, *Inquisition and Power*, particularly ch. 4. See also Arnold, 'Inquisition, Texts and Discourse', in *Texts*, ed. Bruschi and Biller, pp. 63–80.

Pegg and I part company is, again, on a methodological question. For Pegg, at least in his 2001 monograph, large parts of the 'Cathar' edifice are invented wholesale by inquisitors; and wholly quotidian (rather than in any way ritualized) practices are manipulated by inquisitors into formalized heretical rites. For me, it seems very unlikely that inquisitorial discourse and practice 'makes things up' *ex nihilo*. I would argue, rather, that inquisitorial discourse structures and consequently determines how the world is viewed at a profound level, but that it does this by 're-coding', and forcing into a framework of categories, what are nonetheless real human experiences. Where the distortion seems most profound – and also effective – is, for me, in relation to the question of 'belief'. Deponents were confronted by a stark binary choice, in the very process of inquisition, to give definitive meaning to their actions and adherences – to admit to having 'believed' or to claim to have ceased to 'believe' in the heresy of the good men. In this sense, we should see inquisition as actively 'reshaping' reality, in an unequal dialogue with the witness: they are required to come to an agreed version of that reality through the very process of being questioned. But this again is a process of inquisition taking existing memories and words and experiences and giving them potentially new (or at least more formalized) meanings; not inventing that reality from scratch. Moreover, as I have argued in that earlier book, even as it seeks to categorize and control, the process of inquisition inadvertently tends to demand and produce an 'excess' of speech and meaning, which in turn provides variation and complexity – and provides the historian with an analytical opportunity.

To recap: because of the relative sparsity of sources relating to heresy in the 'earlier' period – roughly speaking, before 1200 – historians are encouraged toward a forensic analysis of individual sources, and a strong focus on the strength or weakness of the specific claims made in each text for each specific moment in time, which can be largely detached from other moments (or, equally, subsumed within some very powerful common discourse that is understood to be largely dictating how and what is depicted). When we move from the twelfth to the thirteenth century, the vast increase in the volume of sources is also an increase in the number of voices, cross-references, interconnections and confusions; and the possibility of treating these as 'authorial' (and hence amenable to the kind of source-criticism one can use for chronicles and so forth) recedes rapidly. Other methodological issues arise, pushing harder at how we understand the relationship between dominant discourses, specific texts, and external 'reality'. What any individual text from the later period can actually 'prove', particularly when it may be largely tangential to the main issue of heresy (as with various charters, property records, letters of agreements and so forth), may be quite limited. And yet these texts, and the many voices they contain, all *nag* at the historian, in a way that the early sources do not. That 'nagging' affects how one tries to build larger pictures from the surviving records.

A Methodological and Historiographical Problem

Building pictures

Pre-modern people, looking up at the sky on a clear night, could see quite a lot of stars; on many other nights, they could see only some; from those that shone forth brightly, they could make clear and bold patterns – the plough, Taurus the bull, the Pleiades. Modern astronomers looking up with radio telescopes see vast numbers of stars, and although the old patterns can still be discerned, they would find it difficult to invent any new ones in quite the same way. Those stars are still surrounded by blackness, but the vast deluge of bright spots tends to militate against drawing such bold images.

Something of the same situation applies between early and late medieval history (though without any imputation of zodiacal superstition on part of early medievalists, or better instruments on the part of late medievalists). With early medieval history, the number of stars in the sky is smaller, the surrounding darkness more obvious; the necessity of supposing the connections across the blackness is consequently that much more pressing. The result is often to produce much bolder and more exciting hypotheses. I think here of work on the early medieval economy, where relatively small numbers of objects and texts can nonetheless be used to suggest complex and widespread trade connections, and to argue eloquently and broadly about economic and political power. I think, for a later period, of arguments around the eleventh-century Peace of God movement, based on a few church councils and narrative sources, where a case can be made for the Peace being a key prompt to fundamental changes in European society and economy.[37] I even think, dare I say it, of the Carolingian 'empire' itself, where much of the nature of that 'empire' and the kind of power it wielded depends in large part on the interpretation of a relatively small corpus (in comparison to the chancery productions of late medieval government) of proscriptive or aspirational texts. That there are inescapable gaps in our knowledge – the blackness between the stars – demands that historians reach out imaginatively to fashion useable interpretations. This methodological *habitus* is also then liable to sudden reversals and challenges, as each specific element has that much more resting upon it: move or block out a couple of 'stars' and the image drawn on the blackness can be radically altered, or even made to fall apart.

Once we move into the thirteenth century, this kind of picture building becomes that bit harder. The volume of data overwhelms, while yet leaving much blackness in between. Late medievalists of course realize that what they can see remains a small proportion of the unknowable whole. In this sense, their *habitus* is quite unlike that of the modernists, who confront an

---

[37] M. McCormick, *Origins of the European Economy: Communications and Commerce, AD 300–900* (Cambridge MA, 2002); R. Landes, 'Economic Development and Demotic Religiosity', in *History in the Comic Mode*, ed. Fulton and Holsinger (New York, 2007), pp. 101–16.

exponentially greater wave of data by making consciously selective choices before they begin (and who are aided – whisper it – by the relative ease with which they can work on their data, and a more robust and generally accepted narrative framework within which they can fit their interpretation).[38] But nonetheless, for those working after *c.* 1200, the sheer volume of surviving records, and the amount one might yet discover from them given time, makes it that bit harder to draw confident lines across the blackness. It is notable that later medievalists tend not to produce books with theses as striking and exciting as those of the early medievalists, and that later medievalists – particularly the 'later' they get – are reluctant to write as readily across European borders, in part because the political entities they are dealing with did not presume to sprawl so widely as in the earlier period, and in part because it becomes steadily harder to deal with materials and archives beyond one area. Looking back across the historiography produced in the second half of the twentieth century, later medievalists have also been more prone to finding an initial framework in narrative sources – so helpfully edited and canonized by nineteenth-century scholarship – and then filling in the blackness with a lot more documentary detail (whereas early medievalists have more often begun by treating their scantier narrative sources with considerable suspicion). However, that later medieval 'detail' has sometimes allowed a considerable remoulding of the texture of history, the working of processes in lived reality rather than aspirational theory: one thinks, for example, of the turn from ecclesiastical history to 'lived religion', of the vast explosion of work in social history, and, in a different sense, the recent focus on 'bottom-up' processes of state formation in the later Middle Ages, where the quotidian experience in particular localities is now seen as a fundamental element in the creation of centralized power.[39]

To emphasize, if such is needed: I am not arguing that late medievalists' practices are better than those of early medievalists. They are just necessarily different – different forms of *habitus* as much as conscious methodologies, arising from intellectual inheritances but also from the inescapable demands

---

[38] Lest this be read as seeming to suggest that modern history is a calm and peaceful field marked by little disagreement, I am aware of how fraught the arguments are here also, and how radically divergent opinions may be on, for example, the causes and consequences of the First World War, the changing nature and role of the working class in the West, the short- and long-term effects of international empires. And yet it is still the case that the basic fact and brute extent of the First World War, the existence of a working-class, the reach and governmental processes of empire, and so forth, are all well established and not liable to revision; unlike, say, the nature and extent of violence in the eleventh and twelfth centuries, the nature of 'feudalism' and lordship, and what calling something an 'empire' means in the medieval period.

[39] For example, J. Sabapathy, *Officers and Accountability in Medieval England, 1170–1300* (Oxford, 2014); I. Forrest, *The Detection of Heresy in Late Medieval England* (Oxford, 2005); W. M. Ormrod and A. Musson, *The Evolution of English Justice* (Basingstoke, 1999).

of the surviving sources. The 'later' *habitus* has two concomitant aspects. One is that we expect to be able to move between the 'bright stars' of particular narrative or epistolary sources by means of at least some documentary records (reaching for roughly parallel records to at least suggest what might have been there, if the archives no longer exist); and, when we look back, we tend to think about what might once have existed between those gaps in this documentary fashion. Thus, when I (counting myself clearly as a 'late' person) in another article looked back to popular uprising in the twelfth century, for which we only have fragmentary chronicle materials, part of what helped me to think my way through those sources was to consider how different our interpretation might be if we possessed the kinds of documentary materials produced around late medieval revolts.[40] One can contrast this with R. I. Moore's approach in *The War on Heresy*: look only at the individual source itself in its present moment, he counsels us, do not project 'back' at all from later materials. In doing this, Moore fundamentally recasts the picture. Looking at each source only in its own moment in time, and being extremely wary of any back-projections from later sources, is a powerful methodology: by a similar process, Constance Berman has prompted a radical reappraisal of the early history of the Cistercians.[41] But it is hard for those working on later periods to see it as a sufficient methodology post-1200, when there are so many other voices nagging at one's elbow. Moreover, for the topic of heresy, some of those other voices speak 'backwards' in time themselves: deponents recount memories of events long before the moment of the document's creation. Thus a number of people questioned by inquisitors in the mid thirteenth century describe events that occurred before 1209 and the beginning of the Albigensian crusade, and in some cases stretching back to the 1170s.

Second concomitant aspect: for those working post-1200 the effects of destabilizing one particular source, while potentially important, are unlikely to immediately topple the larger picture. Take one star out of the constellation of Taurus, and it will cease to look like a bull's horns. Take one star out of the Milky Way, and it still looks like a galaxy. I overstate the scale, but the point remains. The pictures made from larger volumes of material are less amenable to swift and radical alteration by the removal of one or two pieces, even when those pieces are of considerable importance. Take the disputed Council of Saint-Félix text. The French project convened between 1999 and 2001 on the status of the document concluded that, despite some questions still remaining over certain details, it could not have been forged by Guillaume Besse (the

---

[40] J. H. Arnold, 'Religion and Popular Rebellion: From the Capuciati to Niklashausen', *Cultural and Social History* 6/2 (2009), 149–69.
[41] C. Berman, *The Cistercian Evolution: The Invention of a Religious Order in Twelfth-Century Europe* (Philadelphia, 2000).

seventeenth-century antiquary who provides the only extant exemplar).⁴² Nonetheless, as a thought experiment, what happens if we extinguish this particular star? Do we lose a key part of the picture? Yes, of course – we lose details regarding different 'Churches' or dioceses of those Cathars, and the date of particular contacts between French and Bulgarian dualists. If our evidence for Catharism ran out at the turn of the thirteenth century, the loss of the Saint-Félix document might suggest that the whole edifice was nothing but an orthodox mirage. But given that the evidence does not in fact thus cease, do we lose everything as a result? Not if we are at all willing to look elsewhere. We have plenty of other evidence of bishops, dioceses and organization in depositional evidence; other evidence of 'councils' deciding things within the Cathar faith; very considerable evidence of contacts between Cathars in southern France and northern Italy, in terms of witness's statements and even the transmission of texts; and one slender moment of contact with Bulgaria, and other evidence of strong similarities between liturgy and ritual in Bogomil and Cathar faith (and particularly of manuscript transmission from Bulgaria to northern Italy).⁴³ One can continue kicking away at these blocks, particularly by refusing them any 'backwards reach' in time – but if so, one ends up with a Catharism that leaps up, like a spring-form easy-erect tent, apparently only after the Albigensian crusade against it had ended.⁴⁴

One could see Mark Pegg's use of Toulouse, Bibliothèque municipale, MS 609 as a very interesting attempt to treat a mid thirteenth century source as if one were working pre-1200: to look at it, and only it, to think radically and imaginatively about what it really does and does not show. It is a highly effective process (although as various reviewers have noted, it depends also

---

⁴² *L'histoire du catharisme en discussion: le 'concile' de Saint-Félix (1167)*, ed. M. Zerner (Nice, 2001). Note the conclusion of the editor: 'it is not possible to hold that Besse invented all the contents of the charter of Niquinta' (p. 250).

⁴³ See B. Hamilton, 'Wisdom from the East: The Reception by the Cathars of Eastern Dualist Texts', in *Heresy and Literacy*, ed. Biller and Hudson, pp. 38–60; the slender bit of depositional evidence is cited at p. 57 n. 93: a witness remembering a particular book, 'et hoc in Bulgaria' (Paris, BnF, Collection Doat, MS 25, fol. 216v). Pegg has dismissed this as a misreading of the manuscript (stating that it reads 'et hoc in vulgaria'). The Doat scribe could have made a mistake when copying, but as others who have examined the Doat manuscript attest, and as Peter Biller clearly demonstrated at the conference, where he produced a photostat for inspection, it indisputably reads 'Bulgaria'. For further discussion of the wider issue, see B. Hamilton, 'Introduction', in Hugh Eteriano, *Contra Patarenos*, ed. and trans. J. Hamilton, with a description of the manuscripts by S. Hamilton and an historical introduction by B. Hamilton (Leiden, 2004).

⁴⁴ One notes that R. I. Moore does seem to admit to the existence of dualist Catharism in northern Italy by the mid thirteenth century – see *War on Heresy*, ch. 18 – but the question then arises of whence it came, and why one would see it as hermetically sealed from southern France. His discussion on pp. 323–4 in particular seeks simultaneously to admit to close contacts between Italian and French heretics, while emphasizing their differences and suggesting that they had no originary, intellectual or ecclesial connection; how and why they ever made contact is therefore left rather mysterious.

on ignoring certain elements within the source that do not fit with the main thesis). Treating MS 609 in this way allows Pegg to conjure up a lot of 'black space' around the bright star, into which a very powerful anthropological imagination can make people and stories come alive. But in doing so, it shuns other methodological choices, isolating that one inquisition register from other similar archives, and eschewing, for example, the kind of detailed prosopographical work that Jörg Feuchter has performed in order to situate a different set of deponents into their wider social and political landscape.[45] Both approaches are 'productive', in the sense of allowing us to see 'heresy' differently in the mid thirteenth century; but the approach taken by Pegg is inevitably the more precarious, as, for the rest of us, the whole of the night sky continues to twinkle around the one star he has fixed his sights upon.

Culture and ideology

None of the anglophone scholars currently fighting the new Cathar wars are, I think, either small-c or big-C conservative; on the contrary, one suspects that they would all see themselves as left-leaning to at least some degree. What, then, is at issue ideologically in our methodological choices and interpretive positions? I would suggest that a fundamental question is how one conceives of 'power', particularly the political power of the medieval 'state' and the cultural power of the medieval Church; and again I would suggest that one element in play is a difference between early medievalist and late medievalist viewpoints. For the early medievalists, the Carolingian empire looms large as a model of real power, and one where ecclesiastical authority is tightly bound to secular governance (arguably more tightly bound than in any other period until the Reformation). What comes immediately after the Carolingians is another hotly debated topic. But as more centralized authority appears to coalesce once again in the twelfth century (the period that Moore depicts very powerfully as the 'first European revolution'), there is a tendency, I think, to see 'power' as once again strongly top-down, with no real resistance or sustainable response to its incursions. And this holds true whether this centralized power is seen as a desirable attribute (as would be the case, for example, in Thomas Bisson's *Crisis of the Twelfth Century*)[46] or as something largely to bewail (as is Moore's position). That power is seen as powerful, as it were, is again in part connected

---

[45] J. Feuchter, *Ketzer, Konsuln und Büsser: die städtischen Eliten von Montauban vor dem Inquisitor Petrus Cellani (1236/1241)* (Tübingen, 2007). For similar methodological developments, see M. Jurkowski, 'Lollardy and Social Status in East Anglia', *Speculum* 82 (2007), 120–52; and L. A. Burnham, *So Great a Light, So Great a Smoke: The Beguin Heretics of Languedoc* (Ithaca NY, 2008).

[46] T. N. Bisson, *The Crisis of the Twelfth Century: Power, Lordship and the Origins of European Government* (Princeton, 2009).

to the nature of the sources: documents which record aspirations, orders, which seek to dispose and mandate, and which are archived by the surviving victors; very few of them sources which allow one meaningfully to talk about resistances at a 'popular' level. In contrast, for the later period, one could note how the greater variety of records – various in both nature and locale – have led to revisionist treatment of entities previously assumed to be powerful. Thus, for example, later medievalists have reflected on the gap between the ambitions of the French regnal state and its ability in reality to extract taxation; on the very considerable chasm between the papal notion of *plenitudo potestatis* and the claims of *Unam sanctam*, and the reality of Boniface VIII's political position. Similarly, and – again – prompted by the nature of the surviving sources, early modern historians of the Inquisition have recently tended to emphasize the gap between its aspirations and how partial, precarious and relatively limited the actual power it possessed was in certain areas.[47]

Thus those working on texts from the pre-1200 period tend to see them as potentially extremely powerful (and hence as distorting or inventing 'reality') because they are so often connected to political entities which are themselves understood to wield very considerable power. In contrast, while those working on later texts continue to see those texts as powerful, they also tend to look for ways in which that power was challenged or limited or offset by other factors. Where this then leads is to a curious paradox with regard to those subjected to crusade and inquisition. All parties feel considerable sympathy for them; but the kind of agency they see those past subjects possessing – the degree to which medieval people had any chance of challenging that to which they were subjected – is dependent on how that 'power' is viewed. For Moore, I would suggest, they are often unwitting victims, caught up in wider power-plays around 'reform' and international politics. For Pegg, in contrast, they are southern French natives, hopelessly misunderstood and brutally oppressed by the invading foreign colonists who wreck their culture. For Moore they never 'answer back', because any text which looks like it might constitute an independent 'Cathar' reality must be seen as the product of an overwhelming top-down power. For Pegg they do speak, but only in the tones of their native culture – informed in part (as he suggested at the conference at University College London) by the idea of *cortesia*, the particularly southern French notion of 'courtliness' associated with troubadour culture.[48] Pegg's deponents have a voice, but very little, if

---

[47] See for example N. Davidson, 'The Inquisition', in *The Ashgate Research Companion to the Counter-Reformation*, ed. A. Bamji, G. H. Janssen and M. Laven (Farnham, 2013), pp. 91–108.

[48] An interesting idea, though also one which depends (a) on a concept that is nowhere named in the surviving inquisition records, and (b) in large part on reading texts from northern Italy as helpfully illuminating southern France – both methodological moves that Pegg would rule out of court when it comes to Cathar dualism. For an earlier,

any, 'dialogue' with inquisition, other than (it would appear) to be brainwashed by inquisitors into eventually adopting the inquisitorial voice as their own. For Moore, and for Pegg in particular, they are *local* above all else; from which follows the sense that these local natives are very unlikely to have the kind of connections, or the possibility of travel and communication beyond their locality, upon which the wider 'Cathar Church' analysis depends.[49]

One can be sympathetic to these perspectives, but there are problems also. Some years ago, the French historian and theorist Jacques Rancière commented on Emmanuel Le Roy Ladurie's *Montaillou* that, while seeking to give a voice to heresy, it in fact dissolved any sense of challenge or agency into a static, structuralist, anthropological landscape:

> The inquisitor suppresses heresy by eradicating it: he marks it, he locks it up, he kills it. The historian, on the contrary, suppresses it by giving it roots. He removes it, as it were retrospectively, from the inquisitorial condemnation by giving it the colour of the earth and the stones, by rendering it indiscernible from its place.[50]

The poetic vibrancy of Pegg's evocation of the 'good men' and their followers follows very clearly in this line; and Pegg's propensity for having the inquisition witnesses speak in the first person (and with somewhat florid elaborations on the actual Latin in the record) imputes a kind of limited, immediate agency while evacuating any larger, structural agency. These are people who live local lives, rooted in local embodied practices and local storytelling; they are not, as Pegg sees it, people who might share theological texts, discuss spiritual ideas, travel to other countries, act to create or sustain any formalized 'counter-Church' structure. The men and women questioned in Toulouse MS 609 are undoubtedly 'given life' in *The Corruption of Angels*, but it is a life which allows only the performance of a sense of localism and indigenous culture: they must remain 'the natives' because otherwise they might become 'the heretics'. And this is also the flip-side of Pegg's 'intellectualist bias' argument: that to save them from the tyranny of ideas they must not themselves have ideas, but only a local *habitus*.[51]

---

quixotic but quite inspiring attempt to link Catharism and Troubadour culture, see Denis de Rougemont, *Passion and Society*, trans. M. Belgion (London, 1940).

[49] There is a degree of overlap here with Jean-Louis Biget's insistence that Catharism is local and not imported; though his case is that Catharism is still clearly *dualist*, and his argument is more that local conditions create and sustain the dualist response to orthodox Catholicism.

[50] J. Rancière, *The Names of History* (Berkeley, 1993), p. 73.

[51] It is worth noting that Pegg's perspective here starts to slide toward a tradition of Occitaniste nationalism, some of which is staunchly socialist, but other strands of which have roots in the Vichy regime. See A. Roach, 'Occitania Past and Present', *History Workshop Journal* 43 (1997), 1–22; R. Soula, *Cathares, entre légende et histoire: la mémoire de l'albigéisme du XIXe siècle a nos jours* (Puylaurens, 2005).

However, imputing the ability to travel and to make connections and to share texts and ideas is not a denial of agency – it is, rather obviously, the opposite.[52] And in any case, we know that people did travel, and more than that, we know that they carried with them their texts and thoughts and reflections, as various examples from across all the inquisition registers would attest. Part of the earlier medieval case against organized heresy rests, implicitly, on the basic unlikelihood of texts and radical ideas moving across large areas of Europe. But this is a weak *a priori* assumption: we absolutely know that texts and ideas could travel in medieval culture generally, or else there would have been no processes of Christianization. Even Moore's counter-construction – that everything represented as 'heresy' is in fact reform – depends itself on the transmission across Europe of radical ideas and practices, because that was what 'reform' itself also was. There is a sense, also, that that which is being demolished in the recent taking-apart of heresy – the notion of the Cathar 'Church' as a transnational superstructure – is itself formed in the image of the traditional Church, as seen by Moore and others: that is, as something powerful, capable of extensive strategy and concerted action. But there can be other ways in which one might imagine a Cathar 'Church': I do not think that anybody believes the dualists had the same kind of apparatus available – in terms of regularized finance, legal systems, archiving systems, and legacies of political power – as did orthodoxy by this period. A different model would be the 'Church' of late antiquity – very much resting upon the charismatic power of particular bishops, 'organized' in aspiration, but without any central systems of bureaucracy and audit.

Conclusion

To make 'heresy' only a product of itself – to blame the victim – is undoubtedly wrong, as Moore powerfully argued in the introduction to *Formation of a Persecuting Society*. But to make 'heresy' only the product of orthodox power is to impute to that power an overwhelming hegemony that is in danger of making the people subjected to it disappear. In the discussion around 'making up heresy' in late antiquity, one of the most interesting aspects has been re-envisioning the power of orthodoxy – recognizing that orthodox condemnation of heresy does not emanate from a pre-given and unassailable position of authority, but is precisely a part of staking a claim for, and attempting to maintain, that authority (while in fact sometimes adapting in practice to

---

[52] There are parallels here with the debates around postcolonial studies, which also saw a move from a focus on passive victimhood to a more complex sense of agency and negotiation. For the wider issues in that setting, the classic problematic is given in G. C. Spivak, 'Can the Subaltern Speak?', in *Marxism and the Interpretation of Culture*, ed. C. Nelson and L. Grossberg (Chicago, 1988), pp. 271–313.

some of the 'heretical' challenge). The context is undoubtedly different 800 years after Augustine; but the questions raised are still valid. What does the encounter with heresy *change* in orthodoxy? If we allow that 'heresy' has some real, independent existence, how securely and easily does orthodoxy denounce (and then yes, in part, 'make up') heresy? My sense is that this is a more complex and not straightforwardly linear process.[53]

In the classic article to which my title alludes, John van Engen warned of the danger of positing a blunt 'two-cultures' model of lay/clerical relations in the Middle Ages, and emphasized the importance of taking seriously the agency and engagement of the orthodox laity. We should, he argued, take 'homo religiosus' seriously, just as economists treat 'homo economicus' and political scientists 'homo politicus'.[54] The task it seems to me is to take 'homo hereticalis' seriously (recognizing also that s/he is a subset of 'homo religiosus'). My own interest has always been fundamentally in the agency – and conditions of, and limits to, the agency – of the ordinary laity; and my sense of heresy, Catharism included, is informed by that perspective. Thus, on the question of what we should call 'the heretics', it seems to me perfectly reasonable to talk of 'the good men and women' in regard to their southern French locale, but also to talk of 'Cathars' when discussing the links and activities that extended beyond that locale – much as one might talk of 'friars' acting pastorally in a specific moment, but discuss 'the Franciscan or Dominican orders' when talking about wider strategic issues. It seems quite clear to me that the Cathars were dualists, and that this dualism was informed, in part, by the transmission of texts, ideas and practices between southern France, northern Italy, and eastern Europe. But it is also quite clear to me that that does not by any means explain all that might be said about particular people – whether good men or believers or lay bystanders – in particular times and places. Medieval Christianity is a monotheistic religion informed, in part, by the spread of texts, ideas and rituals between the Middle East, north Africa, and Europe. But that by no means tells us everything – or even the most important things – about medieval Christianity.

In this discussion, I have sought to suggest that some of the reasons that we find ourselves in disagreement rests upon different methodological inheritances; and have argued that some of the taking-heresy-apart interpretations may have interpretive implications not fully intended by the authors (and with which I fundamentally disagree). But part of the irony of the debate is just how much shared ground there actually is. Reflecting on the argument of the preceding paragraph, and its invocation of the task of analysing 'lived

---

[53] Elements of this are sketched in J. H. Arnold, 'Repression and Power', in *Christianity in Western Europe, c. 1100–c. 1500*, ed. M. Rubin and W. Simons, The Cambridge History of Christianity 4 (Cambridge, 2009), pp. 355–71.

[54] J. van Engen, 'The Christian Middle Ages as an Historiographical Problem', *American Historical Review* 91 (1986), 519–52.

religion', I find a route back towards the perspectives of Moore, Pegg and Biget. With Moore, I would concur that issues arising around 'reform' are part of the context within which unorthodox religious notions and behaviours summon up support. With Biget, while demurring from the position that Catharism is totally *autocthonique*, I very much see its development as addressing, and embedded within, local needs and issues. And with Mark Pegg, I share the paramount sense of importance in looking at *how* ordinary people believed, how their spiritual and social lives entwined, and how much their 'belief' was to do with practices and culture as much as with intellectual discussion. I would argue that that project and perspective still *works* even if one gives up on the attempt to demolish the edifice of a 'Cathar Church'.

4

The Heretical Dissidence of the 'Good Men' in the Albigeois (1276–1329): Localism and Resistance to Roman Clericalism*

Julien Théry-Astruc

On 25 January 1286, before an inquisitorial court presided over by Bernard of Castanet, the bishop of Albi, a citizen from Castres known as Raimon de Baffignac, who had been arrested for the crime of heresy, mentioned in his confession a conversation that he claimed to have had about seven years beforehand with a knight named Guilhabert Lantar, who came from the area of Guitalens. They were lunching together in Albi where they had just met. Both had come to the episcopal city to appear before the ecclesiastical court. As related by Raimon de Baffignac, their observations were so compromising that the judges, or their notary, made sure that they were recorded in direct style, as reported speech, within the interrogation minutes. The two diners were rather unhappy with their affairs at the ecclesiastical court and began by deploring the *potentia cleri*, the power of the clergy, who had now set science above nobility, depriving the latter of the honours formerly bestowed upon it, which were now cornered by the clerics.[1] According to the document lodged by the Inquisition and that has survived in the form of a single copy made in the sixteenth century, the discussion proceeded as follows:

> He also said that he, Raimon, said to the aforementioned Guilhabert Lantar: 'Sire, in the olden days, we took delight in many things, I mean in courting the ladies,[2] in singing, in making love,[3] but nowadays we spend

---

* My thanks to Anita Saxena Dumond for translating this paper into English, to the Centre d'Étude Médiévales (EA 4583) of the Université Paul-Valéry de Montpellier for funding the translation, and to the anonymous reviewer for his/her observations.

[1] Paris, Bibliothèque nationale de France (henceforth, BnF), MS lat. 12856, fol. 8v. This first passage in direct style was translated with commentary by J.-L. Biget, 'Les cathares devant les inquisiteurs en Languedoc', *Revue du Tarn* 146 (1992), 227–42.

[2] *Domiciare*, a verb deriving from Occitan, is very rare. See C. Dufresne du Cange, *Glossarium mediae et infimae latinitatis*, ed. G. A. L. Henschel and L. Favre, 10 vols. (Paris 1883–7), *ad voces domneiare* and *domuciare*.

[3] It seems that here the Latin verb *psallere* is a distortion, by the archpriest of Lauzerte who

too much time thinking about the payments and pilgrimages imposed upon us by the clerics, from which we have no means to escape; our predecessors were not made to pay such a high price for these things, or so I have often heard.' He also said that to what he, Raimon, said to the aforementioned Guilhabert Lantar, the same Guilhabert Lantar replied to the same Raimon as follows: 'Raimon, Raimon, have no doubt, as we still have a few people who can and do have us pay a fair price for these things; and we will introduce you to them, if you come to visit us on our shore.'[4]

The following year, as we learn from reading the rest of the confession – now recorded in indirect style – Raimon de Baffignac travelled to Guitalens to levy a tithe from a lease. He once again met Guilhabert Lantar, who, 'remembering the friendship that they had forged in Albi', invited him first to go fishing with him on the Agout river. Then, after taking him home to cook the fish they had caught, the knight led him to a hideout set up in a 'very remote and secret' place on the river banks, to eat their catch in the company of 'the two persons that he had mentioned to him' and who were hiding there.[5]

In one of their customary interpolations, the minutes state that when speaking of these 'persons', whom he had greeted with a triple genuflection, Raimon de Baffignac 'meant heretics' ('due de personnis de quibus fecerat mentionem – intelligens de hereticis – debebant prandere cum ipso'). But in truth, the citizen from Castres had fallen into the hands of the Inquisition not because he had believed these individuals to be 'heretics', but because he thought them *boni homines*, 'good men', despite ecclesiastical teachings and repression against them. The discussion recounted to the Inquisitors, regardless of the reasons why the accused reported it and regardless of the deformations it may have suffered from the time it was written down, in Latin, by the court scribe, to the translation proposed here, affords an illustration of the prime motivation for religious dissent: dissatisfaction and the hostility aroused by clerical control.

---

copied the document in the sixteenth century, of the Occitan verb *salhir*. A rather modest translation of the verb is given here.

4 'Dixit etiam quod ipse Ramundus qui loquitur tunc dixit dicto Guillaberto *Lantar*: "Domine, tempore antiquo solebat esse quod multimode letabantur, scilicet domiciando, cantando, psallendo, modo vero satis habemus facere cogitando de premiis et peregrinationibus quas nobis clerici sciunt injungere, quibus non possumus evadere quoquomodo; solebat enim nostris predecessoribus, ut sepe refferri audivi, melius forum fieri de predictis"; dixit etiam quod hiis a se Ramundo dictis dicto Guillaberto *Lantar* idem Guillabertus *Lantar* ipsi Ramundo respondit: "Ramunde, Ramunde, non dubitetis, quoniam adhuc sunt nobis alique persone que sciunt et possunt de predictis facere bonum forum, quas vobis ostenderemus si in nostra riperia veniretis"' (Paris, BnF, MS lat. 12856, fol. 8v).

5 Ibid., fol. 9r.

'Heresies' were born, in the twelfth century, out of the protest raised by the Gregorian reform and of the criminalization of opposition movements by the new Church.[6] The construction of an autonomous ecclesiastical institution was based on a far stricter separation between the laity and the clergy than before,[7] the latter being bound by new rules and invested with new powers. Radical evangelism and traditional evangelical forms of religious life in southern France were proclaimed to be heresy because those involved refused this redefinition of the clergy. As suggested by the recent analyses undertaken by Jean-Louis Biget and Mark G. Pegg,[8] it was only in a late stage – that is, in Languedoc, from the end of the first quarter of the thirteenth century onward – that the Church's intransigence and persecution made certain dissidents sway towards a dualistic Christianity that portrayed the entire material world as the work of the cunning Devil. The 'labelling theories' of deviance developed by sociologists such as Howard Becker and Erwin Goffman, as well as Michel Foucault's pattern of 'perverse implantation', certainly provide useful suggestions to understand how some dissenters finally came to embrace, to a certain extent, some of the features and ideas that ecclesiastical categorization had rather improperly and arbitrarily ascribed to so-called 'heretics' for more than two centuries.[9] The fact remains, however, that the commitment to and support for dissidence, in the thirteenth century and even into the beginning of the fourteenth century, corresponded to a protest against pastoral discipline, ecclesiastical levies and clerical domination as a whole, which were stronger than ever before. Clericalization was a part of the Gregorian project and was compounded in the thirteenth century with the

---

[6] See *Inventer l'hérésie? Discours polémiques et pouvoirs avant l'inquisition*, ed. M. Zerner (Nice, 1998); U. Brunn, *Des contestataires aux 'cathares': discours de réforme et propagande antihérétique dans les pays du Rhin et de la Meuse avant l'inquisition* (Paris, 2006); R. I. Moore, *The War on Heresy: Faith and Power in Medieval Europe* (London, 2012). For recent synthetical accounts, see, for instance, J. Théry, 'Les hérésies, du XIIe au début du XIVe siècle', in *Structures et dynamiques de la vie religieuse en Occident, 1179–1449*, ed. M.-M. de Cevins and J.-M. Matz (Rennes, 2010), pp. 373–86; I. Bueno, *Le eresie medievali* (Rome, 2013).

[7] See J.-C. Schmitt, 'Clercs et laïcs', in *Dictionnaire raisonné du Moyen Âge*, ed. J. Le Goff and J.-C. Schmitt (Paris, 1999), pp. 214–29.

[8] J.-L. Biget, 'Réflexions sur l'hérésie dans le midi de la France', *Heresis* 36–7 (2002), 29–74 (pp. 43–8), repr. in J.-L. Biget, *Hérésie et inquisition dans le midi de la France au Moyen Âge* (Paris, 2007), pp. 106–41; J.-L. Biget, 'Réflexions sur l'hérésie au Moyen Âge: l'exemple des "cathares"', in *Religion et politique: dissidences, résistances et engagements*, ed. L. Albaret, H. Latger and J.-F. Wagniart (Paris, 2006), pp. 22–35; M. G. Pegg, *The Corruption of Angels: The Great Inquisition of 1245–1246* (Princeton, 2001), pp. 80–1; M. G. Pegg, *A Most Holy War: The Albigensian Crusade and the Battle for Christendom* (New York, 2008), pp. 25–7, 46; M. G. Pegg, 'The Paradigm of Catharism; or, the Historians' Illusion', in the present volume.

[9] J. Théry, 'L'hérésie des bons hommes: comment nommer la dissidence religieuse non vaudoise ni béguine en Languedoc? (XIIe–début du XIVe siècle)', *Heresis* 36–7 (2002), 75–117 (pp. 97–107).

implementation of the triumphant papal monarchy's theocratic ambitions. Clericalism was particularly oppressive in Languedoc, where the clergy's temporal powers were widely developed. The negative concept of anticlericalism is thus relevant to the study of 'heresy' in Languedoc, especially after the Albigensian crusade, so long as the content of this inherently flexible term is precisely defined to suit this particular case.[10]

The denigration of the clergy and the denunciation of their excessive hold over government or social life did not necessarily mean that their role as mediators between men and God, the very essence of their condition, was questioned. The hostility towards the clerical culture or power did not, moreover, involve only heretics. For example, it also permeated knightly culture. This hostility was, in fact, proportional to the influence of those that it targeted – Boniface VIII thus bitterly lamented it, at the very time when the Church's power was at its zenith, in his famous bull *Clericis laicos* (which, in 1296, imposed the pope's prior authorization for the temporal princes to levy taxes from the clergy).

It is rather difficult to distinguish clearly between two forms of anticlericalism, one superficial in that it directed hostilities solely at certain of the clerics' behaviours or values, the other radical and heretical as it rejected the holy authority of the clergy. Hostile attitudes towards the clerics no doubt veered between these two positions. Each might have been separated from the other by mere degrees of intensity. Their distinction is made all the more difficult due to the Church's endeavour to amalgamate them. Indeed, the Church justified its institutional forms by making an inseparable link between its spiritual mission and its necessary temporal powers. Hence the pope's *plenitudo potestatis* and the claimed superiority of clerical authority over secular power; hence, also, the resort to canonical sanctions against those who, by causing prejudice to the ecclesiastical institution's economic or political interests, were also considered to jeopardize its work of salvation. At the beginning of the fourteenth century, any form of persistent disobedience

---

[10] About medieval anticlericalism in general, see in particular *Anticlericalism in Late Medieval and Early Modern Europe*, ed. P. A. Dykema and H. A. Oberman (Leiden, 1994); *Pfaffen und Laien: eine mittelalterlicher Antagonismus? Freiburger Colloquium, 1996*, ed. E. C. Lutz and E. Tremp (Fribourg, 1999); *L'anticléricalisme en France méridionale (milieu XIIe–début du XIVe siècle)* = *Cahiers de Fanjeaux* 38 (2003). About heretical anticlericalism in the Middle Ages, see in particular W. L. Wakefield, 'Some Unorthodox Popular Ideas of the Thirteenth Century', *Mediævalia et humanistica* 4 (1973), 25–35; R. I. Moore, *The Birth of Popular Heresy* (Toronto, 1995 [1st edn 1975]), pp. 27–71; J. Chiffoleau, 'Vie et mort de l'hérésie en Provence et dans la vallée du Rhône du début du XIIIe siècle au début du XIVe siècle', *Effacement du catharisme (XIIIe–XIVe s.)* = *Cahiers de Fanjeaux* 20 (1985), 73–99; G. Despy, 'Hérétiques ou anticléricaux? Les "cathares" dans nos régions avant 1300', in *Aspects de l'anticléricalisme du Moyen Âge à nos jours: hommage à Robert Joly*, ed. J. Marx (Brussels, 1988), pp. 23–34; D. M. Webb, 'The Pope and the Cities: Anticlericalism and Heresy in Innocent III's Italy', in *The Church and Sovereignty, c. 590–1918: Essays in Honour of Michael Wilks*, ed. D. Wood (Oxford, 1991), pp. 135–52.

to the Church, regardless of its anticlerical nature, could be qualified as heresy.

Lastly, so as better to evoke the complex nature of the protests against clericalism during the first post-Gregorian centuries, we should note that the acknowledgment of alternative religious mediations, although considered a crime of heresy, did not necessarily go hand-in-hand with the rejection either of orthodox sacraments or of clerical authority as a whole.

Albi and its region in the last quarter of the thirteenth century and the first quarter of the fourteenth century is fertile ground for the study of the relationships between the 'heresy' of the good men of Languedoc and the clericalism of the theocratic Church stemming from the Gregorian reform. The energetic action of the character who heard Raimon de Baffignac's confession, the bishop Bernard of Castanet, establishes a unit of time – from the appointment of this papal chaplain to the see of Albi, in 1276, until 1329, date of the final conviction for heresy based on the denunciations recorded during the Inquisition trials that he held. This militant episcopate, devoted to subduing the circles that resisted ecclesiastical order, gave rise to violent conflicts which only came to an end many years after Bernard of Castanet had been transferred to the see of Le Puy, in 1308. This half-century of Albi's history is well documented. The numerous studies dedicated to this field by Jean-Louis Biget, from a fundamental article published in the *Cahiers de Fanjeaux* in 1971 to more recent publications, have provided great insight into Languedoc heresy.[11]

For the perspective adopted here, the analysis will successively focus on two aspects. We shall first briefly examine the elements that can be pieced together, with more or less ease, of the religious life of Albi heretics, while questioning the relationships between dissident practices and ecclesiastical order. This examination will be mainly based on a critical reading of the textual material produced by the inquisitorial activities in the Albigeois, in which Bishop Bernard of Castanet played a crucial part. Then, moving on to the second aspect, we shall present the place of 'heresy' – and, more broadly, the discord between ecclesiastical government and secular society – within

---

[11] J.-L. Biget, 'Un procès d'inquisition à Albi en 1300', *Le credo, la morale et l'inquisition* = *Cahiers de Fanjeaux* 6 (1971), 273–341; J.-L. Biget, 'Aspects du crédit dans l'Albigeois à la fin du XIIIe siècle', in *Castres et Pays Tarnais: XXVIe congrès de la Fédération des sociétés savantes, Languedoc-Pyrénées-Gascogne* (Albi, 1972), pp. 1–50; J.-L. Biget, 'La restitution des dîmes par les laïcs dans le diocèse d'Albi à la fin du XIIIe siècle', *Les évêques, les clercs et le roi (1250–1300)* = *Cahiers de Fanjeaux* 7 (1972), 211–83; J.-L. Biget, 'Extinction du catharisme urbain: les points chauds de la répression', *Effacement du catharisme (XIIIe–XIVe s.)* = *Cahiers de Fanjeaux* 20 (1985), 305–40, also in Biget, *Hérésie et inquisition*, pp. 206–28; J.-L. Biget, 'Sainte-Cécile et Saint-Salvi: chapitre de cathédrale et chapitre de collégiale à Albi', *Le monde des chanoines* = *Cahiers de Fanjeaux* 24 (1989), 65–104; J.-L. Biget, 'La législation synodale: le cas d'Albi aux XIIIe–XIVe siècles', *L'Église et le droit dans le Midi (XIIIe–XIVe s.)* = *Cahiers de Fanjeaux* 29 (1994), 181–213.

the political history of Albi, in the twilight of the good men's resistance. Inquisition, as we shall see, was but one of the weapons – though it was the supreme one – used by Bernard of Castanet in his long struggle to impose his ultra-clericalist rule on the local oligarchy.

The para-ecclesial religion of the good men and their friends: insight gained from the Inquisition archives

Inquisitorial sources: shortcomings, deformations and difficulties of interpretation

To attempt to describe the religious lives of heretical good men and their 'friends' or 'followers' is a perilous undertaking with certain prerequisites and a number of necessary methodological precautions. The notion of 'religion' is understood here in a sense close to that held by the word in the Middle Ages, when it referred to a religious lifestyle, the way in which people lived their faith. The term did, however, frequently refer to a specific rule, which will not be the case here. In what follows 'religion' simply refers to a set of ideas, feelings and singular practices; these are not external to Christianity and are far from being sufficiently formalized to define any unit of a denominational nature.[12]

If twelfth- to fourteenth-century 'heresy' in Languedoc was centred on forms of religious life, it is because there were people in the region who actually practised that lifestyle, and were venerated by others for doing so. This was in contrast to the erudite heresies of former centuries, which mainly consisted in dogmatic positions upheld by extremely small circles of scholars. However, the resistance nourished by the good men of Languedoc in the last decades of the thirteenth century and the first decades of the fourteenth century was not really a 'popular' heresy according to the two usual meanings of the adjective, as has been shown – and contrary to common assumptions – by J.-L. Biget.[13] It was, for one thing, rather restricted: the quantitative analyses undertaken to date, though approximate given the condition and nature of the documents, establish that the good men's friends

---

[12] See P. Biller, 'Words and the Medieval Notion of "Religion"', *Journal of Ecclesiastical History* 36 (1985), 351–69.

[13] Biget, 'Extinction du catharisme', pp. 317–19. Biget, 'Réflexions sur l'hérésie', pp. 60–1. See also, for another area in Languedoc, J.-L. Abbé, 'La société urbaine languedocienne et le catharisme au XIIIe siècle: le cas de Limoux (Aude)', in *Religion et société urbaine au Moyen Âge: études offertes à Jean-Louis Biget*, ed. P. Boucheron and J. Chiffoleau (Paris, 2000), pp. 119–39. J. H. Mundy's findings for Toulouse are in line with this view. See J. H. Mundy, *The Repression of Catharism at Toulouse: The Royal Diploma of 1279* (Toronto, 1985), and the review of this book by J.-L. Biget in *Annales: économies, sociétés, civilisations* 1 (1987), 137–40.

rarely represented more than ten to fifteen percent of the population in the areas studied and, more often than not, represented five to ten percent at the most. In Bernard of Castanet's time (1276–1308), the dissidents probably amounted to barely ten percent of the 8,000 to 10,000 inhabitants of the city of Albi, one of the greatest strongholds of heretical resistance to the clerical order. When the entire diocese is taken into account, the proportion was even smaller, and the group had practically disappeared by the final years of the episcopate. For another thing, and countering the second sense of the term 'popular', dissidence gained only very few followers from humble backgrounds; the sociology of accused individuals reported to the Inquisition confirms that the good men's friends came from the rural minor aristocracy and, above all, urban social classes born of the economic growth since the eleventh century, the well-off or rich middle classes formed of craftsmen and merchants.[14]

The inquisitorial records are practically the only source from which a glimpse of heretical religious life can be gained. Prescriptive, narrative or polemical sources hardly mention this topic, and only for the purpose of providing a distorted and very negative picture; they above all provide information on their authors and their attitudes, rather than on the heretics themselves. The surviving texts related to dissident liturgy or theology are few and far between; we know nothing of their diffusion; they do not teach us much about the life of the followers, and they reveal, at the very most, only ritual rules. Only the confessions recorded by the Inquisition offer matters of any substance. We are thus reduced to studying 'heresy' through the sources produced from its persecution. This perverse situation obviously greatly limits access to the reality of dissidence.

The inquisitorial records are the written recomposition, after their translation into Latin, of oral discussions. As such, they barely allow the voices of the accused to be heard, though they often create the illusion of doing so upon reading. Even if we acknowledge that snippets of the dissidents' real discourse can be gathered from the texts stemming from their statements, the fact remains that these addresses were severely restrained by the conditions in which they were uttered. Besides the impediments caused by the recording procedures, the content of the confessions was first and foremost determined by the inquisitors' questions.[15] Historical research is thus fully dependent on

---

[14] Biget, 'Un procès d'inquisition', pp. 298–304; Biget, 'Extinction du catharisme', pp. 319–24; J.-L. Biget, 'Cathares des pays de l'Agout', in *Europe et Occitanie: les pays cathares, actes de la 5e session d'histoire médiévale organisée par le Centre d'études cathares* (Carcassonne, 1995), pp. 259–310 (pp. 270–2, 283, 306–7).

[15] See in particular J. H. Arnold, *Inquisition and Power: Catharism and the Confessing Subject in Medieval Languedoc* (Philadelphia, 2001); Pegg, *The Corruption of Angels*; *Texts and the Repression of Medieval Heresy*, ed. C. Bruschi and P. Biller (York, 2002); L. J. Sackville, *Heresy and Heretics: The Textual Representations* (York, 2011); *Inquisitors and Heretics in Thirteenth-Century Languedoc: Edition and Translation of Toulouse Inquisition Depositions,*

their interests. These vary greatly according to the context of the case.[16] This is easy to note when comparing the two main inquisitorial sources related to Albi and its region during the period under review.[17] In 1299–1300, Bernard of Castanet and the inquisitor of Carcassonne, Nicolas d'Abbeville, held extremely swift trials, judging up to thirty-five defendants in barely four months of hearings, whereas in 1286–7, the same bishop and the inquisitor Jean Galand had conducted trials against eleven individuals that lasted more than twenty months. Tellingly, the two sets of trials produced roughly equal volumes of data, despite the disparity in the number of defendants. In the earlier series, Bernard of Castanet took all the time he needed to gather as much information as possible on those of his diocesans who mixed with the good men. From the file thus compiled he was able effectively to organize control of dissident groups and targeted repression, within a long-term strategy. In the later series, by contrast, the bishop was acting urgently. His objective this time was rapidly to condemn the arrested guilty parties, in order to bring a severe blow to the circle that was on the verge of neutralizing his temporal power. In the first series, the confessions therefore provide far greater details on the dissidence. Yet it remains true that the inquisitorial interrogations mostly sought to prove heresy in legal terms. Thus, the records are more often than not reduced to the repetitive recording of stereotyped facts which, according to the law, were sufficient to establish the crime – in this case, the ritual greeting of the good men, the receiving of their blessing and of their 'sacrament', administered *in articulo mortis* and named *consolament*. As for the rest, Bernard of Castanet was quite obviously not seeking to learn about the specific nature of heresy (the great attention paid by Jacques Fournier to the detail of the deviances, in the Inquisition trial that he conducted in Pamiers in 1318–25, is a unique case).[18] To this we may add another major difficulty (to which we shall return): the inquisitorial discourse that shaped the source material describing dissident practices was systematically inflected with the very hostile prejudices and distorting vocabulary of the Church.

    1273–1282, ed. P. Biller, C. Bruschi and S. Sneddon (Leiden, 2011), especially ch. 3 of the introduction.

[16] Good examples of the crucial importance of context for the understanding of a particular series of inquisitorial trials are Biget, 'Un procès d'inquisition', and C. Vilandrau, 'Inquisition et "sociabilité cathare" d'après le registre de l'inquisiteur Geoffroy d'Ablis (1308–1309)', *Heresis*, 34 (2001), 35–66.

[17] For what follows, see also Biget, 'Un procès d'inquisition', and Biget, 'Cathares des pays de l'Agout'.

[18] *Le registre d'inquisition de Jacques Fournier (1318–1325)*, ed. J. Duvernoy, 3 vols. (Toulouse, 1965). See in particular E. Le Roy Ladurie, *Montaillou, village occitan* (Paris, 1975); and M. Benad, 'Par quelles méthodes de critique des sources l'histoire des religions peut-elle utiliser le registre de Jacques Fournier?', in *Autour de Montaillou, un village occitan: histoire et religiosité d'une communauté villageoise au Moyen Âge*, ed. E. Le Roy-Ladurie (Castelnaud-la-Chapelle, 2001), pp. 147–55.

Yet, despite the extent of these shortcomings and distortions, the archives of persecution do allow us to retrieve certain significant elements related to dissident religious life.

'Good men', 'good life', 'good words', 'good faith'

About one year ago, or thereabouts, *Magister* Raimon Calvière, notary at the Lord King's court in Albi, *compater* of the said witness, asked him to walk with him to his dovecot. [...] Upon entering the said dovecot, they found two men; the aforementioned witness asked *Magister* Raimon to tell him who the men were and enquired as to their condition. And the said *Magister* Raimon replied to the said witness that they were some of those good men who were called heretics, that they lived well and in a holy manner and that they fasted three days a week and did not eat meat. Then the said witness, who was astounded (as he said), told the said *Magister* Raimon that they would be dead if ever word got around. Then the said *Magister* Raimon added that he should not say such things and that several other good people of Albi were to come and visit the heretics and that the said witness should do as the others, because there would arise many good things from friendship and familiarity with the said heretics.

(Confession of Guiraud Delort, 16 December 1299)[19]

One day, [...] late at night, Ermengaud Vena, from Réalmont, came to see the said witness and told him that two of those good men who were called heretics [...] were in Guilhem de Maurian's home and were preaching there, and that he should come to hear and see them, because they were good men and that they taught many good things. So the said witness and the said Ermengaud Vena went together to the said Guilhem de Maurian's home and found the said Raimon del Boc, heretic, who had almost finished his sermon and was saying that God had not made these temporal and transitory things, but celestial and eternal things; and the said heretic said many other things that the said witness did not remember (he said). [...] When required to say why the said witness and the other aforementioned persons had worshipped the said heretics in the manner described, he said

---

[19] G. W. Davis, *The Inquisition at Albi, 1299–1300: Text of Register and Analysis* (New York, 1948), pp. 156–7: 'Annus est vel circa, magister Raymundus Calverie, notarius curie Albie domini regis, compater ipsius testis, rogavit eum quod iret spatiatum cum eo ad columbarium suum. [...] Et intrantes domos dicti columbarii, invenerunt ibi duos homines, de quibus quesivit ipse testis a dicto magistro Raymundo cujusmodi homines erant illi seu cujus conditionis erant; et ipse magister Raymundus respondit ipsi testi quod erant de illis bonis hominibus qui dicebantur heretici et vivebant bene et sancte et jejunabant tribus diebus in septimana et non comedebant carnes. Tunc ipse testis atonitus (ut dicit) dixit dicto magistro Raymundo quod mortui essent si sciretur. Tunc dictus magister Raymundus subjunxit quod non diceret talia, quia et aliqui alii boni de Albia debebant convenire ibidem et dictos hereticos visitare et quod ipse testis faceret sicut alii, quia de amicicia et familiaritate dictorum hereticorum provenirent ei multa bona.'

that it was because they believed the latter to be good men, and to have a good faith.

(Confession of Garnier de Talapie, 1 March 1300)[20]

Maybe twenty-eight or thirty years ago [...], two men from Albi [...] came to his shop and said: '*Signeur Peyre*, two prudent men have come to this town, they are good, holy men, they are well advised and they know many good words; this is why it would be good for us to go and visit them.'

(Confession of Peire Astruc, February 1325)[21]

We could multiply the examples of this type of passage in which are described, within the defendants' confessions, the circumstances of their first direct contact with the good men. Compiling these short accounts would form a good starting point from which to study the reasons why people chose to join the dissidence, as they appear through the reading of the inquisitorial records. Of course, the concern of the defendants to minimize their errors, possibly to protect one person or to incriminate another, is the most obvious of the factors which oblige us to grant very little factual truth to these narrative sequences. But the present texts, like many others of the same kind, taken from the confessions of two citizens (*cives*) of Albi and a notary from Réalmont, recurrently show the authority of the heretical good men and the spiritual concern of those who acknowledged it.

What is hidden behind the evasive monotony of the words 'good' and 'well'? Their repetitive use to describe the virtues ascribed to the good men is certainly not due solely to the inquisitorial format. Why are the leaders of dissidence of 'good faith'? The only explicit justification that regularly appears in the confessions is the one mentioned by Guiraud Delort in the

[20] 'Quadam die de qua non recolit, de sero tarde, Ermengaudus Vena de Regali Monte venit ad ipsum testem, dicens sibi quod duo de illis bonis hominibus qui dicuntur heretici, quorum unus vocabatur Raymundus *del Boc*, maritus olim de *na* Cabriaga de Albia, et socius ejus, cujus nomen ignorat ipse testis, ut dicit, erant in domo Guillermi de Mauriano et predicabant ibi et quod ipse testis veniret ad audiendum et videndum eos, quia erant boni homines et docebant multa bona. Tunc ipse testis et dictus Ermengaudus Vena simul venerunt ad domum dicti Guillermi de Mauriano et invenerunt dictum Raymundum *del Boc*, hereticum, dicentem quasi in fine sermonis sui quod ista temporalia et transitoria non fecerat Deus set celestia et eterna, et multa alia dixit tunc dictus hereticus, de quibus non recolit ipse testis, ut dicit. [...] Requisitus quare ipse testis et alii predicti adoraverunt predictos hereticos modo predicto, dixit quod propter hoc quia tunc credebant ipsos esse bonos homines et habere bonam fidem' (ibid., p. 216).

[21] 'Viginti octo anni vel triginta potuerunt esse vel circa, [...] duo homines de Albia [...] venerunt ad operatorium suum et dixerunt sibi sic: "*Signeur Peyre*, in villa ista venerunt duo probi homines qui sunt sancti homines et boni et bene consulti et sciunt multa bona verba, quare bonum est quod vadamus ad eos visitandum"' (Paris, BnF, Collection Doat, MS 27, fol. 34r).

quoted extract: the good men fasted very frequently and banned meat from their diet. Those who helped them in their clandestine life had to find them fish, as did Guilhabert Lantar and Raimon de Baffignac, according to the latter's tale. More generally, the good men 'led a good and holy life', say the accounts registered in the Inquisition records. A good share of their authority obviously stemmed from their personal asceticism. Their deeds and their pure and modest lifestyles seemed to be in agreement with their evangelical message, establishing it as genuine – as opposed, of course, to the less rigorous life of the secular clergy and, more broadly, to the power of the Church (which was easily perceived, by the populations who disliked its political and economic influence, as contradictory to its mediatory ambitions). Here we find the echo of eminently anticlerical themes, the leitmotif of the protest movements since the Gregorian reform: a pure and humble existence as the primary requirement of the apostolic life.[22]

In the case of the heretical dissidence in Languedoc in the last quarter of the thirteenth century and the first quarter of the fourteenth century, it should be noted that the good men, although they lived modestly, did not profess a general contempt of wealth, unlike the Waldensians. Contrary to the 'Poor Men of Lyon' (or the 'Poor Men of Christ'), who travelled around Languedoc during the same period, they obviously did not believe money to be impure in itself, as they handled it frequently. Money-lending (*commenda*, in the texts) was, indeed, part of their everyday business. The sections of the minutes that broach this subject are far too numerous and circumstantial to correspond to forced confessions intended to corroborate the inquisitors' scurrilous views. One defendant at the trials of 1299–1300, for example, described how the good men Raimon del Boc and Raimon Didier obtained a refund of fifteen pounds which the mother and aunt of *Magister* Garnier de Talapie 'had borrowed from them [...], as they could see in their entries' ('scriptis seu memorialibus'); this tells us that the good men kept accounts. As the two debtors were either dead or had gone missing, they obtained payment from their son and grandson.[23] There is a lack of information as to the details of this practice. It is not known if the loans granted by the good men gave rise to the payment of interest. The money may have come from deposits, and certainly from donations made by followers (many of whom, we may here recall, were affluent). The good men in particular received payment for the administration of the 'sacrament' *in articulo mortis* (during the trials of 1286–7, the judges systematically enquired about the sum of money given; the deed was obviously sinful from their point of view, as it had been a capital crime for clerics to practise simony since the Gregorian reform). Moreover, defendants sometimes mentioned that the

---

[22] For a recent and suggestive account, see Moore, *The War on Heresy*, pp. 45–161.
[23] Davis, *The Inquisition at Albi*, pp. 131–3. See the examples cited and discussed by Biget, 'Les cathares devant les inquisiteurs', p. 239, and Biget, 'Cathares des pays de l'Agout', pp. 302–3.

good men or their friends had made promises of wealth to encourage them to join the dissidence.[24] This did not necessarily mean in the form of loans but maybe, more broadly, the possibility of benefiting from specific economic solidarity thanks to the dissident network. We might also wonder whether the defendants were not seeking, in this case, to be somewhat excused for their crime by claiming non-spiritual motivations for their socializing with the heretics. Whatever the case, the good men's particular affinity with money deserves to be underlined. It is no doubt related to a major driving force of the dissidence. Indeed, its members overwhelmingly belonged to social groups that were doomed to spiritual indignity and deprived of all chance of salvation because of the opprobrium the Church cast on of the very practices that made them affluent: interest-bearing loans, trade and all business based on monetary speculation.

The dissident ministers, who were persons who led a 'good life' and were of 'good faith', brought 'much good' to their followers, as Guiraud Delort stated in his confession. Of course, possible loans from the good men or mutual assistance from their followers were not among the main motivations for dissident support, which remained a principally religious engagement. What, therefore, was the substance of the *multa bona* granted to the good men's friends? Mostly, it consisted in 'good words', as declared in Peire Astruc's confession. These *bona verba* corresponded to two kinds of practices: rituals and preaching.

Only two types of ritual appear in the confessions: the blessings and the *in articulo mortis* 'sacrament'. The first was mainly administered upon addressing a ritual reverence to the good men *in adventu et recessu*, upon greeting or parting. This was a series of three genuflections (certain confessions specified that the followers, who had previously removed their hats, placed their hands on the ground) accompanied thrice by a request to be blessed, such as: 'Bless us, good Christians, keep us from harm', to which the good men replied each time 'God will save you' or an equivalent phrase ('Pray to God', for example).[25] Moreover, the good men blessed the bread before eating in the company of their friends (this fact, however, is rarely mentioned).[26] The only

---

[24] See Biget, 'Cathares des pays de l'Agout', p. 303. See also, for instance, Davis, *The Inquisition at Albi*, p. 190 (first encounter of Bertran de Montagut with the *boni homines*).

[25] See for instance, in Raimon de Baffignac's confession: 'Dixit etiam quod cum fuerunt ad dictam boariam et viderunt dictos hereticos, ipsos reverenter, flexis genibus, adoraverunt, ter flectendo genua et manus ponentes singulis vicibus super terram et singulis etiam vicibus dicendo: "Benedicite, *bon chrestia*, parcite nobis"; et singulis etiam vicibus respondentibus ipsis hereticis: "*Dious en sia pregats*"' (Paris, BnF, MS lat. 12856, fol. 6v). About this ritual as documented in the records of the first inquisitions in Languedoc, see Pegg, *The Corruption of Angels*, pp. 92–103.

[26] See for instance Guilhem de Maurian's confession: 'Dixit etiam dictus testis quod illo sero quo venerunt ad domum predicti Raymundi, adhuc dicti heretici erant jejuni et tunc, parata mensa, Raymundus *del Boc*, hereticus predictus, qui erat antiquior alio,

'sacrament', the *consolament*, was exclusively referred to in the confessions using the inquisitorial term *hereticatio*, that equated it with a ritual for joining a sect. For the persecutors, it was the stamp of full adhesion to 'heresy'. The records often associate it with the vocabulary of *receptio* (though it remains unclear how far this agrees with the dissidents' concepts, if at all): 'ipse hereticus recepit eum et hereticavit'. The descriptions of the *hereticatio* were generally reduced to the form imposed by the judges: they thus provide very little detail. The dying persons first expressed their desire to place their souls in the hands of the good man by placing their hands within his while calling upon him to help them, in terms that were not specified. The good man then placed 'a book' (no doubt containing part of the Gospel), or his hands, above the believer's head while speaking the ritual words and genuflecting.[27]

The dissidence was thus distinguished by sacred practices that were reduced to the bare minimum. Significantly, the lack of any other heretical liturgy encouraged the inquisitors, who sought to portray dissidence as a fully fledged sect, to interpret the ritual greeting of followers as a ceremony of *adoratio* (the only word used to describe it in the confessional texts). In orthodoxy, by contrast, the status of the clerics, which formed the basis for a clerical society that stood separate from lay persons, was upheld through the intensive practice of numerous and elaborate mediations.[28] By rejecting the sacraments and with the absence of any real worship, the religious life of the good men and their friends was in contrast with the evolution of the orthodox religious practice since the eleventh century, which had been even further accentuated since the beginning of the thirteenth century.

The good men's 'good words' also included their sermons (which the Inquisition minutes normally referred to as *monitiones*). Between the *in adventu* and *in recessu* blessings, the heretical ministers' religious activity, apart from any possible *hereticatio*, consisted in speaking to followers. Information as to the content of their preaching is scarce within the Albi trials. The brief indications provided by the confession of *Magister* Garnier de Talapie, mentioned above, represent the dualism that characterized the good men's teachings, according to inquisitorial sources from the end of the thirteenth century and the beginning of the fourteenth.[29]

---

accepta mapa super humerum suum, tenens una manu panem et alia cultellum, dictis quibusdam verbis de quibus ipse testis non recordatur, distribuit panem ipsi testi et dicto Raymundo hospiti eorum et dicto consocio suo heretico' (Davis, *The Inquisition at Albi*, p. 124).

[27] See for instance ibid., pp. 147, 173–4.
[28] On the connection between the denial of the sacraments (especially of the Eucharist) and the rejection of clerical power, see in particular Biget, 'Réflexions sur l'hérésie', pp. 34–5.
[29] See in particular some texts (dated 1301–5) edited from volume 34 of the Collection Doat at the BnF by R. Manselli, 'Per la storia della fede albigese nel secolo XIV: quattro documenti dell'inquisizione di Carcassona', in *Studi sul Medioevo cristiano offerti a Raffaello Morghen per il 90o anniversario dell'Istituto storico italiano (1883–1973)*, 2 vols. (Rome, 1974),

The lack of details found in the confessions regarding the doctrinal content of the *monitiones* is probably not solely due to a lack of attention on behalf of the inquisitors. Frequently, as in the case of Garnier de Talapie, the defendants did not remember what the good men had said (*non recolit*, say the texts). Also, the minutes systematically report that the defendant had 'not understood' (*non intellexit*) the words spoken by the dissident ministers during the *hereticationes* (though the insertion *ut dixit* often casts doubt on this lack of understanding). The possibility that defendants claimed not to have understood so as to minimize their transgressions certainly cannot be entirely disregarded. But this no doubt also provides insight into the limited internalization that seems to have characterized dissident religious life. More generally, dissidence seems to have been marked by the highly passive role played by followers. It would seem that the good men 'friends of God' at the end of the thirteenth century and beginning of the fourteenth, a little like the monks of the high Middle Ages, took sole responsibility for the celestial relationship on behalf of the believers – thus relieving those believers of the need to attain purity, or to understand the precise meaning of their holy words and gestures. The 'magical' (in the broad sense as defined by Durkheim and Bourdieu) efficiency of the rituals took precedence, excluding any mysticism; the spiritual commitment and the personal piety of the believer did not, or so it would seem, hold much importance.[30] This is very different from all heretical movements in the twelfth century, which were notable for their trend towards a universal calling and evangelical proselytism:[31] the good men of the late thirteenth century, by contrast, did not at all require their followers to live according to any particular demands.

The dualist theology of the dissident ministers, regardless of the mythological subtleties, did not provide the followers with much substance to guide their conduct.[32] What was important for the latter was no doubt to be reassured by 'holy, good and wise' men, whose pure life ensured their authority, that any form of materiality was evil and that salvation was ensured not (only or necessarily) by obedience to the Church, but simply by the administration of a sacrament *in extremis*. The behaviours for which the Church condemned to damnation the lower nobility or merchant middle-class (usury, trade, birth control and other breaches of pastoral discipline, or denial of the clergy's authority) were hence no longer to be seen as particularly sinful actions – no more than any other aspect of life. Finally, to use the venal words attributed to

---

I, 499–518. For a recent account of references to dualism in inquisition depositions, see P. Biller, 'Cathars and the Material World', in *God's Bounty: The Churches and the Natural World*, ed. P. Clarke and T. Claydon (Woodbridge, 2010), pp. 89–110.

[30] For the broad use of the term 'magical', see É. Durkheim, *Les formes élémentaires de la vie religieuse* (Paris, 1912); P. Bourdieu, *Langage et pouvoir symbolique* (Paris, 2001).

[31] Moore, *The War on Heresy*, pp. 45–161.

[32] See, for instance, J. H. Arnold, 'The Preaching of the Cathars', in *Medieval Monastic Preaching*, ed. C. Muessig (Leiden, 1998), pp. 183–205; Biller, 'Cathars and the Material World'.

Raimon de Baffignac in the extract referred to at the beginning of this article, the good men had the power to 'make a fair price' ('bonum forum facere possunt'), a far better price than the clerics, for the peace of the followers' souls. Their mediation was far less cumbersome, while what we might call their soteriological offer was infinitely more advantageous.

The triviality of these comparative short cuts must not eclipse the reason why people adhered to the good men's religion: spiritual anxiety and the followers' absolute need to ensure their salvation. The fact that the resistance continued for almost a century after the beginning of the inquisitorial campaign in Languedoc might in itself suggest the extent of the existential unease that compelled people, despite the ensuing dangers, to socialize with the good men. There are a number of clues in the confessions as to the deep desire that stirred the good men's friends. A royal official named Peire de Mézens, for example, travelling with Guilhem de Maurian, seized the opportunity, when they passed two men bearing crosses (as a sign of penitence for the crime of heresy), to talk to him (Guilhem) about the good men, telling him that he would sorely like ('multum vellet') to meet them – obviously already aware that Guilhem knew them well enough to occasionally act as their guide and messenger. Subsequently, as Guilhem told the inquisitors, Peire had repeated this wish to him 'on many occasions, possibly as many as ten or more times, upon different occasions'. When, eventually, Guilhem finally told Peire that he was to meet the heretics, it was 'with great joy', *cum magno gaudio*, that the latter asked him where they were to be found.[33] There is no reason to believe that these details were pure invention on behalf of Guilhem before the judges. (Guilhem might have been seeking to minimize his wrongs by exaggerating the personal resolve of those he had presented to the heretics, but it should be noted that the inquisitors had already promised him a pardon; his interest, therefore, was mostly to inform on a sufficient number of the good men's friends to satisfy the court.) The insistence and enthusiasm of Peire de Mézens were corroborated by the declarations of another defendant at the 1299–1300 trials, Raimon Augier, concerning the *hereticatio* of the very same Peire, who was said to have issued an ardent request on his death bed: 'the said sick man [...] told the said witness that he absolutely wanted

---

[33] 'Dixit quod XII anni possunt esse et ultra, ut sibi videtur de tempore, quod ipse testis ivit in Franciam cum magistro Petro de Medenco seu de Medano, tunc procuratore domini regis in senescallia Carcassonensi et Bitterrensi; et intrantes per civitatem de Turonis, in ingressu civitatis, obviaverunt duobus hominibus pro heresi crucesignatis et ex hoc sumpta occasione, idem magister P. dixit ipsi testi quod multum vellet videre hereticos et scire sectam eorum. Et extunc multociens, forte X vicibus et amplius, diversis temporibus, repeciit eadem verba idem magister P. eidem testi, videlicet quod libenter videret hereticos et sciret sectam eorum. [...] Tandem anno immediate preterito [...] dixit idem testis dicto magistro Petro quod modo posset videre illos bonos homines, videlicet hereticos, de quibus multociens rogaverat eum. Et tunc dictus magister cum magno gaudio quesivit ubi erant' (Davis, *The Inquisition at Albi*, pp. 128–9).

to be welcomed into the heretics' sect and that he shouldn't reject his wish, as this was, in any case, what he wanted.'[34] (This account was not, at least not solely, a ploy of Raimon's to exonerate himself from having encouraged Peire to commit *hereticatio*, as it coincides with a detail found in Guilhem de Maurian's statement, according to which Peire became impatient because Raimon was taking a long time to bring the good men to his bedside.)[35] The numerous known cases of people returning to heresy after disavowal, in particular to receive the *consolament* at their time of death,[36] also bear witness to the strength of the religious feeling that led them to overlook the Church's outright condemnation of dissidence.

The religious life of the good men and their friends: three general characteristics

The summary analysis of the good men's religion and that of their friends, as seen through the Inquisition archives, highlights three general characteristics which all question, to different degrees, the relationships between dissidence and orthodox clericalism. These characteristics are non-exclusivity, informality and localism.

It is important first to underline the actual compatibility, within dissident practice, of favouring both the good men and the orthodox religion. There are abundant examples. Thus, Peire Aymeric, a merchant from the Albi region who became a 'heretic' in 1287, first received the last rites from the Church before asking the good men for the *consolament*, according to his nephew's confession.[37] Moreover, the cases of churchmen who were friends of the good men are not rare – such as the six canons of the church of Saint-Salvi d'Albi,[38] or the priest from Guitalens[39] denounced during the 1286–7 trials. Although

---

[34] 'Ipse testis venit ad dictum infirmum, qui dixit eidem testi quod omnino volebat recipi in sectam hereticorum et quod nullo modo contradiceret ei, quia modis omnibus sic volebat' (ibid., p. 147).

[35] Ibid., p. 130.

[36] See, for instance, Biget, 'Cathares des pays de l'Agout', p. 290 and n. 106.

[37] 'Item dixit quod mensis est vel circa, cum predictus Petrus Aymerici, avunculus ipsius testis qui loquitur, infirmaretur infirmitate de qua obiit, postquam jam communicasset, una nocte, […] pulsatum fuit satis suaviter ad ostium et cum ipse testis vellet ire ad fenestram ad videndum quis pulsaret, dixit sibi dictus infirmus: "Vade, et aperi ostium"; et iens inferius, aperuit ostium et invenit ibi Poncium Nycolay predictum et duos hereticos […], qui omnes ascenderunt superius et intraverunt cameram ubi dictus infirmus infirmabatur; et accedentes ad dictum infirmum, unus illorum hereticorum, receptis manibus dicti infirmi inter manus suas, recepit eum secundum ritum et modum hereticorum in sectam suam, ipso infirmo hoc volente et petente' (Paris, BnF, MS lat. 12856, fol. 23r).

[38] Confession of Vital Vignal. See J.-L. Biget, 'Sainte-Cécile et Saint-Salvi', pp. 88–9 and n. 126.

[39] Paris, BnF, MS lat. 12856, fol. 9r. See Biget, 'Cathares des pays de l'Agout', p. 297 and n. 130.

it seems obvious that the dissident followers could not avoid the religious obligations imposed by the Church, as to do so would risk them being accused of heresy, nothing proves that they actually had any desire to avoid them.

Some examples demonstrate that the good men's friends maintained a clear interest in orthodox ecclesiastical mediation concurrently, or simultaneously, with their resort to dissident mediation. Thus, a certain knight of Montdragon, named Matfred Baudrac, whom the Inquisition obliged to do penance at a non-determined date, had nevertheless made a donation to the nuns of La Salvetat in 1266.[40] The same was true for Bérenguier Azémar and Peire Baudier, citizens of Albi who, according to the above-mentioned confession (in 1299) of their fellow citizen Guiraud Delort, went to hear mass after having 'worshipped' the good men in Raimon Calvière's dovecot.[41] The phenomenon has been noticed by historians[42] (not just for Languedoc 'heresy', moreover),[43] and is sometimes referred to as Nicodemism or irenicism – labels taken from notions in the Reformation period. The first of these two terms presupposes a certain duplicity, to which it would no doubt be simplistic (and anachronistic) to reduce the dissidents' attitudes. The good men's friends, contrary to the nicodemites vilified by Calvin, did not necessarily feel that they had to choose between two clearly defined options.[44] They faced, in all likelihood, not an intimate choice between two entirely separate pathways, between two possible and exclusive Churches, but rather a doubt as to the best way to ensure their salvation, and a lack of confidence in ecclesiastical mediation. Their desire was to find the best solutions to their religious concerns. This was more of an indecisive quest, a wandering, than devotion to a new Church. The Languedoc dissidence, furthermore, had no institutional dimension. In the late period contemplated here, religious life with the good men was so scantly organized that the term 'church', even in its loosest sense of a simple community of followers, is hardly appropriate when referring to the 'heretics'.

This leads us to the second characteristic emerging from the Inquisition archives: the informal nature, in all ways, of heterodoxy. In the last quarter of

---

[40] Davis, *The Inquisition at Albi*, p. 126 and n. 11.
[41] See Biget, 'Extinction du catharisme', p. 334 and n. 116.
[42] See, for instance, Y. Dossat, 'Les cathares dans les documents de l'Inquisition', *Cathares en Languedoc = Cahiers de Fanjeaux* 3 (1968), 71–104 (esp. pp. 97–100: 'Irénisme à Sorèze'); Arnold, *Inquisition and Power*, pp. 20–1; Biget, 'Réflexions sur l'hérésie', p. 66.
[43] See, in particular, G. G. Merlo, *Eretici e inquisitori nella società piemontese del Trecento, con l'edizione dei processi tenuti a Giaveno dall'inquisitore Alberto De Castellario (1335) e nelle Valli di Lanzo dall'inquisitore Tommaso di Casasco (1373)* (Turin, 1977), p. 102.
[44] See C. Ginzburg, *Il nicodemismo: simulazione e dissimulazione religiosa nell'Europa del '500* (Turin, 1970). É. Labrousse, 'Perspectives plurielles sur les frontières religieuses', in *Les frontières religieuses en Europe du XVe au XVIIe siècle*, ed. R. Sauzet (Paris, 1992), pp. 205–13. T. Wanegffelen, *Ni Rome ni Genève: des fidèles entre deux chaires en France au XVIe siècle* (Paris, 1997), about 'l'entre-deux confessionnel' in the early modern period.

the thirteenth century, a heretical hierarchy existed no more in the region of Albi than in the rest of Languedoc; there were merely good men who travelled around, attempting with diminishing success to perpetuate their tradition, communicating among themselves with difficulty, possibly attempting to maintain tenuous ties with their dissident friends in Lombardy.[45] A more or less general tendency to dualism was not sufficient to bestow upon their theology the precision and stability of a dogma, as views no doubt differed between ministers, whose varying level of education did not guarantee a uniform or very sophisticated magisterium.[46] The followers' convictions were obviously even more varied and were no doubt mostly lacking in doctrinal consistency. Lastly, dissident religious practice had all the appearances not of a structured church life, but of simple sociability, and was not very specific despite its clandestinity.[47] The words used in the confessions to talk of the relationships with heretic 'ministers' were those of friendship and familiarity. People went to 'visit' the good men; eating, drinking and talking in their company was evidently very important. The substance of dissidence mostly consisted in this everyday, though transgressive, exchange with the *boni homines*, as well as in actions to support their secret rituals and their illegal, rootless existence.

The informal condition of 'heresy' was not unknown to the Church, even though the latter took care, in the legal, theological or narrative texts, to present it as a subversive counter-Church. The inquisitorial documents relevant to the Albi region at the end of the thirteenth century and the beginning of the fourteenth century do not report any institutional heretic structures; they confirm that, in practice, the inquisition did not consider the dissidence to be very well organized. The minutes speak only of 'heretics' – as they named the good men – and of 'believers'. The latter term, unlike the former, was not used systematically and did not refer to a particular status that might have been conferred upon the relevant individuals. In most cases, 'believer' was obviously used as a synonym for 'friend' of the heretics.

Furthermore, the vocabulary associated with belief appears in two types of context. In one, it presupposes an affiliation with a well-structured organization; in the other, to the contrary, it proves the informal nature of dissidence. The records do indeed speak of the 'heretics' believers', as if the fact of mixing with the good men went hand-in-hand with joining a sect under their authority and with devotion to a specific religion.[48] And yet, according to the

---

[45] See Théry, 'L'hérésie des bons hommes'. Biget, 'Réflexions sur l'hérésie', pp. 42–3.

[46] For instance, we learn from a confession recorded by the inquisitors that two *boni homines* who lived in the Agout region between 1270 and 1285 could not read. See Biget, 'Cathares des pays de l'Agout', p. 283 and n. 73.

[47] See Vilandrau, 'Inquisition et "sociabilité cathare"'.

[48] See, for instance, Paris, BnF, MS lat. 12856, fol. 6v: 'Dictus Augerius et ipse recognoverunt se credentes eorum, scilicet hereticorum'. Ibid., fol. 7r: 'Bernardus Arnaldi de

minutes of the confessions and sentences, the defendants' guilt resided only in the fact that they 'had believed that the heretics were good men', which tended to clear the notion of 'believer' of any imputation of conversion to a faith or engagement in a sect-type group.

As already mentioned, only the *consolament* ritual, from the inquisitorial point of view, marked the admission of the 'believer' into the 'heretics' sect' (hence the notion of *hereticatio* used in the documents to refer to that which the inquisitors considered to be an induction ceremony, during which the 'believers', according to them, formally expressed their desire to be *recepti*, that is, 'admitted'). Thus, the 'heretical sect' as defined by the Inquisition only included those who had received the *consolament*, that is to say, almost exclusively the good men. Except for this very limited group, the large majority of individuals liable to inquisitorial sanction were only judged according to their degree of socialization with the 'heretics'.

To legally qualify the misconduct that could be attributed to the good men's friends (and more generally to the supporters of all other types of 'heretics' around whom dissident movements developed), canonical legislation had first only defined two categories of offenders: the 'defenders of heretics' (*defensores*) on one hand and, on the other hand, their 'hosts' (*receptatores*), meaning all those who 'welcomed them or helped them in their homes or on their lands', according to the terms of the canon *Sicut ait beatus Leo* promulgated by Alexander III at the third Lateran council of 1179.[49] The simple fact of giving credit to the good men's words and of believing in the effectiveness of their rituals was therefore not clearly, at that time, considered to be a crime against the orthodox faith. The same canon of Lateran III merely regretted the fact that the 'heretics' of Gascony and Toulouse 'convinced the weak and simple to embrace their views' ('ad consensum suum simplices attrahant et infirmos').[50] In the text, these credulous persons were plainly

---

Dosans significavit dictis hereticis quod de credentibus et amicis eorum de Carcassona intellexerat sinistra'.

[49] X 5.7.8; *Corpus iuris canonici*, ed. E. Friedberg, 2 vols. (Leipzig, 1879–81 [repr. Graz, 1959]), II, 780: 'Eos et defensores et receptatores eorum anathemati decernimus subiacere et sub anathemate prohibemus ne quis eos in domo vel in terra sua tenere vel fovere aut negociationem cum eis exercere presumat'. The third canon of the council of Toulouse (1119) and the twenty-third canon of the second Lateran council (1139) only spoke of *defensores*: *Sacrorum conciliorum nova et amplissima collectio*, ed. J.-D. Mansi, 31 vols. (Venice, 1759–98), XXI, 226–7, 532. The fourth canon of the council of Tours (1163) prohibited 'ne receptaculum quisquam eis in terra sua prebere aut presidium impertire presumat' and excommunicated 'tanquam particeps inquitatis eorum' anyone who didn't conform to the prohibition of all contact with the heretics, but it did not mention *credentes*, although it referred to the possible existence of *conventicula*, that is of small heretical houses or communities (ibid., 1177–8).

[50] Ibid.: 'Quia in Vasconia, Albigesio et partibus Tolosanis et aliis locis ita hereticorum, quos alii Catharos, alii Publicanos, alii Patarenos, et alii aliis nominibus vocant, invaluit damnanda perversitas, ut jam non in occulto, sicut alibi, nequitiam suam exerceant,

different from the *defensores* and the *receptatores*, mentioned afterwards, who were the only ones to be formally condemned. Under Innocent III, when the repressive process was stepped up (concomitant, we should note, with the beginning of a crucial phase in the construction of pontifical theocracy and with the development of the ensuing ecclesiological contestation), the legal texts – for example the decretal *Vergentis in senium* (1199) or the *Excommunicamus* canon of the fourth Lateran council (1215) – added two ancillary categories: the 'partisans' (*fautores*) and the 'believers' (*credentes*).[51] And in another *Excommunicamus* canon dated 1229, and included in the *Liber Extra* five years later, Gregory IX assimilated the fact of being a heretic with that of 'believing in the errors of heretics', with the formulation 'we similarly consider to be heretics all those who believe in their errors' ('credentes autem eorum erroribus similiter hereticos judicamus').[52] In an article of the bull *Ad Extirpanda* (1252, dealing with heretics in the Italian cities), Innocent IV added to a passage taken from *Vergentis in senium* a sentence that summarized this legal evolution: 'Those who believe in their errors should be punished as heretics too' ('Credentes quoque erroribus hereticorum tanquam heretici puniantur').[53]

The loose, vague, poorly outlined forms of adhesion – or, to use a more appropriate term, of participation – in dissident religious life had therefore made it necessary, in order to render persecution technically possible, to legislate on the crime of simply 'believing' and on its equivalence to the crime of heresy itself. It remains the case that the distinction between *heretici* and *credentes*, between 'good men' and the 'good men's friends', was perfectly clear in the reports drawn up under the inquisitors' authority. The imprecision and the variability of the actual content of the *credentes*' guilty 'belief' were clearly present in the minds of the jurists – who were the only ecclesiastics in any way concerned (due to professional reflexes) with the nuances of this particular classification. The Languedocian jurist Bernard de Montmirat (the renowned *abbas antiquus*), for example, made a careful distinction in his comments on the *Decretals* (drawn up between 1259 and 1266) between those who 'believed in the errors of the heretics' and those who 'believed that

---

sed errorem suum publice manifestent et ad consensum suum simplices attrahant et infirmos, eos et defensores et receptatores eorum'.

[51] *Vergentis in senium* (X. 5.7.10; *Corpus iuris canonici*, ed. Friedberg, II, 782): 'Contra defensores, receptatores, fautores et credentes hereticorum aliquid severius duximus statuendum'; *Excommunicamus* (X. 5.7.13; *Corpus iuris canonici*, ed. Friedberg, II, 788): 'Credentes preterea, receptatores, defensores et fautores hereticorum excommunicationi decernimus subiacere'.

[52] X. 5.7.15; *Corpus iuris canonici*, ed. Friedberg, II, 789.

[53] *Ad extirpanda*, §27, Latin text and French translation in P. Gilli and J. Théry, *Le gouvernement pontifical et l'Italie des villes au temps de la théocratie (fin XIIe–mi-XIVe s.)* (Montpellier, 2010), pp. 569–88 (pp. 580–1).

certain heretics were good men'[54] – though this did not prevent him from recommending the same sentence for all. In practice, in dealing with the accused, it would indeed have been tricky for the Inquisition to distinguish between these two types of belief. And the formulation 'having believed that the heretics were good men' used in the sentences as we saw, reveals the truth: the dissidence did not consist in an alternative faith. It was first and foremost the recognition of a religious Christian authority outside the Roman Catholic Church.

This brings us to the final topic of reflection inspired by the inquisitorial archives, concerning the notion of 'good man'. *Bos homs* was the name most commonly used for the dissident ministers by their friends (the records also show, though less frequently, the expressions 'prudent men' (*probi homines*), 'good Christians' and 'friends of God'). The expression became common as early as the twelfth century: the first occurrence appears to be found in a famous letter, dated 1165, that relates a confrontation between Languedoc prelates and good men.[55] It was still part of the 'heretics' everyday language' ('comunis loquela hereticorum') at the end of the thirteenth century, as we see in the terms of a form from the apostolic penitentiary written by Cardinal Bentevenga in 1289 regarding a case concerning some inhabitants of Carcassonne: 'Fuissetque eis indicatum quod essent de illis hereticis qui juxta communem loquelam hereticorum boni homines nuncupantur.'[56] Yet this name was not specific to dissidence, or even to religion. This is a fact that deserves very careful consideration if we are to grasp the nature of Languedoc 'heresy'.[57] Since the early Middle Ages, the term *boni homines* or *probi homines* had been used to refer to the most affluent people in local society, those who

---

[54] Cited by H. A. Kelly, 'Inquisitorial Due Process and the Status of Secret Crimes', in *Proceedings of the Eighth International Congress of Medieval Canon Law (1988)*, ed. S. Chodorow (Vatican City, 1992), pp. 407–27, repr. in H. A. Kelly, *Inquisitions and Other Trial Procedures in the Medieval West* (Aldershot, Burlington, 2001), no. II (p. 414). See also H. Maisonneuve, *Études sur les origines de l'inquisition*, 2nd edn (Paris, 1960). A. Boureau, *Satan hérétique: histoire de la démonologie (1280–1330)* (Paris, 2004), pp. 46–8.

[55] *Sacrorum conciliorum nova et amplissima collectio*, ed. Mansi, XXII, 157–68. Roger of Howden, *Gesta Regis Henrici Secundi*, ed. W. Stubbs, 3 vols. (London, 1868–70), II, 105–17.

[56] *Der Registerband des Cardinalgrosspönitentiars Bentevenga*, ed. C. Eubel, Archiv für katholisches Kirchenrecht 64 (Mainz, 1890), pp. 3–69 (pp. 39–40), cited by A. Fossier, 'La pénitencerie pontificale en Avignon (XIVe s.), ou la justice des âmes comme style de gouvernement', *Les justices d'église dans le Midi, XIe–XVe s. = Cahiers de Fanjeaux* 42 (2007), 199–239 (p. 232).

[57] See in particular M. G. Pegg, 'On the Cathars, the Albigensians, and Good Men of Languedoc', *Journal of Medieval History* 27 (2001), 181–95; Théry, 'L'hérésie des bons hommes', esp. pp. 107–16; R. I. Moore, 'When did the Good Men of the Languedoc Become Heretics?' (unpublished lecture in Berkeley, 2006, online: http://rimoore.net/GoodMen.html); M. Bourin, 'Les dissidents religieux dans la société villageoise languedocienne à la fin du XIIIe et au début du XIVe siècle', in *L'hérétique au village: les minorités religieuses dans l'Europe médiévale et moderne*, ed. P. Chareyre (Toulouse, 2011), pp. 201–16; Moore, *The War on Heresy*, pp. 201–2.

played a key role in the socio-political life of communities (members of the juries that dispensed justice, representatives of the authorities in dealings with the lords, etc.).[58] The name 'good man' referred to an authority whose main characteristic was *that of being native to a place*. This was indeed the case with the authority of the dissident good men in Languedoc, whose 'heresy' was due to their rejection of an ecclesiastical institution that had been profoundly clericalized and centralized. Regarding this matter, we may note that the monks belonging to the Grandmont order, founded at a time when the boundaries between reform movements and heresy remained unclear, were called 'good men'.[59] Now, the rule established by the founder Étienne de Muret (deceased in 1124), which obliged the good men of Grandmont to lead an evangelical life, specifically forbade any difference in status between the clerics and the laymen within the order.[60]

Moreover, the heretics referred to here were not the only dissidents in Languedoc to be called good men by their followers. The inquisitorial documents provide proof that the name was also used by the Waldensians.[61] Ultimately, the specificity of the dissidence of the good men who were not

---

[58] See, in particular, G. Musca, 'Una famiglia di *boni homines* nella Terlizzi normanna e sveva', *Archivio storico pugliese* 21 (1968), 34–62; K. Nehlsen-von Stryk, *Die* boni homines *des frühen Mittelalters: unter besonderer Berücksichtigung der fränkischen Quellen* (Berlin, 1981); M. Bourin-Derruau, *Villages médiévaux en Bas-Languedoc: genèse d'une sociabilité*, 2 vols. (Paris, 1987), I, 315–24, and II, 177–9; P. Ourliac, 'Juges et justiciables au XIe siècle: les *boni homines*', in *Justice et justiciables: mélanges Henri Vidal*, Recueil de mémoires et travaux publié par la Société d'histoire du droit et des institutions des anciens pays de droit écrit 16 (Montpellier, 1994), pp. 17–33; A. Guillou, 'Gérontes et bons hommes d'Orient et d'Occident', *Jahrbuch der österreichischen Byzantinistik* 44 (1994), 125–34; H. Gilles, '*Probi homines*', in *Lexikon das Mittelalters* (Munich, 1995), VII, 234; M. Bourin, 'Les *boni homines* de l'an mil', in *La justice en l'an mil* (Paris, 2003), pp. 53–65. And see for instance a letter from Pope Alexander III (1159–81) to the people of Città di Castello, in *Papsturkunden in Italien: Reiseberichte zur Italia pontificia*, ed. P. F. Kehr, 6 vols. (Vatican City, 1977), V, 177: 'Dilectis filiis bonis hominibus majoribus et minoribus de civitate que dicitur Castelli tam presentibus quam futuris in perpetuum'.

[59] My thanks to Didier Méhu, who long ago drew my attention to this use of *boni homines* to name the members of the order of Grandmont. See Giles Constable, *The Reformation in the Twelfth Century* (Cambridge, 1996), pp. 58–9, 74. See also the striking fact observed by R. I. Moore, 'When did the Good Men of the Languedoc Become Heretics?', that according to Roger of Howden (*Gesta Regis Henrici Secundi*, I, 7, 194), King Henry II of England, when he fell ill in 1170, insisted that he did not want to be buried at the abbey of Fontevraud, and demanded instead that his body be given to the holy *boni homines* of Grandmont.

[60] About the order of Grandmont, see A. Leclerc, *Histoire de l'abbaye de Grandmont, paroisse de Saint-Sylvestre (Haute-Vienne)* (Saint-Prouant, 1999 [1st edn 1909]); C. A. Hutchinson, *The Hermit Monks of Grandmont* (Kalamazoo, 1989); J. Becquet, *Études grandmontaines* (Ussel, 1998).

[61] See, for instance, *L'inquisition en Quercy: le registre des pénitences de Pierre Cellan (1241–1242)*, ed. J. Duvernoy (Castelnaud-la-Chapelle, 2001), pp. 74, 76, 84, 112, etc. Also G. Audisio, *Les vaudois: histoire d'une dissidence (XIIe–XVIe siècle)* (Paris, 1998 [1st edn Turin, 1989]), pp. 53–4 (an occurence from the diocese of Castres, 1327).

Waldensians, and that of their friends, was rather a lack of one: *they did not have their own name*.[62] This is a very important piece of historical information in itself; one that has been hidden beneath the names arbitrarily attributed to the dissidents in the anti-heretic treaties and repeated, since that time, throughout historiography. The notions of 'Cathars' and 'Catharism' in particular, which have been commonly used since the nineteenth century, hide the informal reality of the dissidence of these nameless good men by giving it an identity that it never had.[63] These terms are absent from the archives of the Languedoc inquisition (which never refer to the non-Waldensian good men other than by the generic name 'heretics').[64] In his highly important doctoral thesis, Uwe Brunn determined that Eckbert von Schönau, the Benedictine monk who introduced the use of the word 'Cathar' to refer to the heretics of Cologne in 1163, took it directly, along with its definition ('catharos, id est mundos' – 'cathars, meaning pure'), from the writings of Innocent I, a fifth-century pope, on the subject of heresy in late antiquity.[65] This clearly demonstrates the importance of abandoning this terminology.

To a large extent, a study of the religious practices and beliefs of the heretical good men and of their followers, based on a critical reading of the sources related to inquisitorial practices, remains to be done. These documents have rarely been taken into consideration for themselves, and even less frequently in relation to the precise socio-political environment in which they were produced; the historiography of 'Catharism' has often been restricted to searching them for elements to confirm the data systematically put forward by doctrinal or narrative sources.[66] Thus, the ecclesiastical construction of

---

[62] See Théry, 'L'hérésie des bons hommes', 108–17, for further reflections on this fact.

[63] See Pegg, *The Corruption of Angels*, pp. 15–19; Pegg, 'On the Cathars, the Albigensians, and Good Men of Languedoc'; Théry, 'L'hérésie des bons hommes'; Pegg, 'The Paradigm of Catharism'.

[64] In his *Practica inquisitionis* (a treatise, not a source immediately produced by inquisitorial activity, although it uses inquisitorial material), Bernard Gui speaks of 'Manichees', as opposed to Waldensians. *Practica inquisitionis heretice pravitatis auctore Bernardo Guidonis*, ed. C. Douais (Paris, 1886), pp. 129, 223, 239, etc.

[65] U. Brunn, '*Cathari, catharistae et cataphrigii, ancêtres des cathares du XIIe siècle?*', Heresis 36–7 (2002), 183–200 (pp. 190–1 and nn. 23, 25); Brunn, *Des contestataires aux 'cathares'*.

[66] But see the new approaches, for instance, of Biget, 'Les cathares devant les inquisiteurs'; Biget, 'Cathares des pays de l'Agout'; P. Biller, 'The Cathars of Languedoc and Written Material', in *Heresy and Literacy, 1000–1530*, ed. P. Biller and A. Hudson (Cambridge, 1994), pp. 61–82; Arnold, 'The Preaching of the Cathars'; P. Biller, 'Cathar Peacemaking', in *Christianity and Community in the West: Essays for John Bossy*, ed. S. Ditchfield (Aldershot, 2001), pp. 1–24; Arnold, *Inquisition and Power*; Pegg, *The Corruption of Angels*; Vilandrau, 'Inquisition et "sociabilité cathare"'; *Texts and the Repression of Medieval Heresy*, ed. Biller and Bruschi; I. Bueno, 'A Comparison of Interrogation in Two Inquisitorial Courts of the Fourteenth Century', *Annual of Medieval Studies at CEU* 12 (2006), 49–68; *Inquisitors and Heretics in Thirteenth-Century Languedoc*, ed. P. Biller, C. Bruschi and S. Sneddon; Sackville, *Heresy and Heretics*, pp. 114–52.

heresy and of the myths that it produced ultimately led historians to view the dissidence of the nameless good men as an alternative Church.

As can be gleaned from the Inquisition archives of the Albi region from the last quarter of the thirteenth century, the real situation was quite different. That which the Church persecuted as heresy was the practice of Christian religion with two main characteristics: it was para- or extra-ecclesial, and those who held a mediation function (the *boni homines*) did not impose any constraint on the believers' lifestyle. The power derived from the holy authority of the good men was reduced to a bare minimum: they may have given advice on evangelical life, but made no demands that carried the threat of not attaining salvation, as that was ensured by their *in extremis* sacrament, regardless of the kind of life lived by the believer. The dissidence arose from a 'malaise', as formerly described by Gabriele Zanella in a series of pioneering articles on heresy in northern Italy.[67] It emerged from the feelings of dissatisfaction and anxiety aroused by the new ecclesiastical mediation, and was felt particularly within certain circles that formed a minority and were socially rather privileged: prosperous citizens, and members of the nobility who had remained marginal to the changing economic and socio-political landscape, and thus found their traditional status under threat. More specifically, the malaise which led such people to socialize with the good men was induced by the demands of the Church – demands clearly related to its new institutional form, that is, to clericalism. By transposing, *mutatis mutandis*, a notion recently proposed for the modern and contemporary periods, we might say that the good men's dissidence, doubtless as for most 'heresies' in the medieval West, fell within 'religious anticlericalism'.[68]

Heretical dissidence and episcopal theocracy in Albi: the ultra-clericalism of Bernard of Castanet

A belligerent bishop appointed by the pope to regain control

Due to a lack of sources – meaning due to the lack of intense repression – we know practically nothing of 'heresy' in Albi between the middle of the 1240s and the end of the 1270s, which marked the beginning of a period covered with some precision by the confessions recorded during the inquisition trials held by Bernard of Castanet from 1285. The bishop Durand de Beaucaire (1228–54), during the last decade of his rule, followed by his successor, Bernard de Combret (1254–71), did not put much zeal into

---

[67] G. Zanella, *Hereticalia: temi e discussioni* (Spoleto, 1995).
[68] See *L'humaniste, le protestant et le clerc: de l'anticléricalisme croyant au XVIe siècle*, ed. T. Wanegffelen (Clermont-Ferrand, 2004); *L'anticléricalisme croyant: jalons pour une histoire, 1890–1914*, ed. C. Sorrel (Chambéry, 2004).

combatting the good men's dissidence. J.-L. Biget has shown that their lack of eagerness stemmed from the need to maintain good relations with the consular bourgeoisie in order to secure their support in resisting the French king's claims to the feudal lordship in Albi.[69] The city, held by the bishop since the elimination of Viscount Trencavel as a result of the Albigensian crusade, was the object of increasingly hardy undertakings by the royal officials, following the surrender, to King Louis IX, of the count of Toulouse Raimon VII (1243), the last opponent to Capetian power in Languedoc. Outside Albi, however, for the entire diocese, the documents left by the more ardent inquisitorial affairs give proof that 'heresy' was prosperous during this period.[70] This was no doubt also the case in the episcopal city.

It is likely that the dissidence was further stimulated by Bernard of Castanet's government. The new bishop's relentless combat against 'heresy' was but one of the elements (although a key one) of a general policy that aimed to bring to heel a local society which had forever been recalcitrant with regard to the Roman Church's central authority. The ruthless wielding of a true episcopal monarchy, fashioned according to the *plenitudo potestatis* model claimed by the thirteenth-century popes for all Christianity, exacerbated all of the reasons for the para-ecclesial religious practices around the good men.

In 1276, Innocent V appointed Bernard of Castanet to the Albi episcopate under his own authority, after a five-year vacancy of the see brought about by the canons' inability to agree upon Bernard de Combret's successor. To rule a diocese that had been renowned as a land of heresy since the twelfth century,[71] the first Dominican pope thus chose a zealous servant of pontifical sovereignty, a tough man who had found employment, during the previous decade, in situations of strife between the Roman Church and secular societies. A jurist from the region of Montpellier, Bernard of Castanet had entered the Curia in 1265 and had soon reached the positions of Papal Chaplain and auditor of causes of the Sacred Palace. He had in particular carried out two difficult missions: in 1266 against the Ghibellines of Piacenza and Cremona,[72] and from 1268 to 1270 against the Rhineland rebels who were holding the archbishop of Cologne prisoner. Upon this occasion, he had resorted to particularly harsh canonical sanctions, in particular promulgating

---

[69] Biget, 'Un procès d'inquisition', pp. 312–13.
[70] *Inquisitors and Heretics*, ed. Biller, Bruschi and Sneddon. See also Biget, 'Un procès d'inquisition', pp. 277–8.
[71] See J.-L. Biget, 'Les "Albigeois": remarques sur une dénomination', in *Inventer l'hérésie?*, ed. Zerner, pp. 219–56, repr. in Biget, *Hérésie et inquisition*, pp. 142–69; Moore, *The War on Heresy*, pp. 118–22.
[72] Gilli and Théry, *Le gouvernement pontifical*, pp. 113–99; J. Théry, '"Cum verbis blandis et sepe nefandis": une mission pontificale en Lombardie après la bataille de Bénévent (1266–1267)', in *Legati e delegati papali: profili, ambiti d'azione e tipologie di intervento nei secoli XII–XIII*, ed. M. P. Alberzoni and C. Zey (Milan, 2012), pp. 195–218.

major excommunication against all citizens of Cologne, obliging all of the clergy to desert and forbidding all supplies for its inhabitants.[73] The same dogged fighting spirit, directed at gaining the submission of the local clergy and laity to the Church's power, presided over his actions as the bishop of Albi.

On the day following his arrival in the city, in January 1277, Bernard of Castanet announced that a new cathedral was to be built. The tremendous financial needs generated by the Sainte-Cécile building site, further increased by extensive construction work on the episcopal palace, went side-by-side with a forceful policy to retrieve any of the Church's property that lay within the hands of the non-clergy, in particular through the compulsory so-called 'recovery' of tithes (those who failed and refused to pay were excommunicated),[74] and with the systematic enforcement of episcopal pre-eminence within a rigorous and rationalized administration of the diocese's temporal goods, often taken badly by the lower clergy. At the beginning of the fourteenth century, the bishopric of Albi had become one of the richest in France. The fruits of this success, the massive fortifications of the episcopal palace of La Berbie and the first formidable walls of the new church, heralded the new power of the ecclesiastical magisterium.

Exceptionally intransigent Christian discipline

In the field of Christian discipline, the policy implemented by Bernard of Castanet was particularly authoritarian – one could call it a policy of terror.[75] In order to drive straying groups back to the Church, the very notion of pastoralism, which involved efforts to persuade the soul and thus required a certain amount of comprehension, seems to have been largely discarded by the new bishop in favour of systematic repression.

Castanet waged an outright war against moneylending. The first canon to be added to the diocese's synodal statutes shortly after his advent proclaimed the excommunication of moneylenders and obliged priests to publicly denounce them every Sunday and on holidays.[76] Campaigns were soon organized to flush out the guilty parties and to oblige them to hand over their profits. The ecclesiastical court was particularly hard on the accused, who on occasion seem to have suffered mistreatment and, it seems, were denied

---

[73] See J. Théry, 'Les Albigeois et la procédure inquisitoire: le procès pontifical contre Bernard de Castanet, évêque d'Albi et inquisiteur (1307–1308)', *Heresis* 33 (2000), 7–48 (pp. 13–16).

[74] Biget, 'Aspects du crédit'; Biget, 'La restitution des dîmes'.

[75] See J. Théry, 'Une politique de la terreur: L'évêque d'Albi Bernard de Castanet et l'inquisition', in *Les inquisiteurs: portraits de défenseurs de la foi en Languedoc (XIIIe–XIVe siècle)*, ed. L. Albaret (Toulouse, 2001), pp. 71–87.

[76] See Biget, 'La législation synodale'.

all right to appeal. The bishop thus chose to attack, head on, the ordinary practices of merchants, who were not only condemned to eternal damnation, but were also harassed in their earthly life by the episcopal system of justice. In 1302 the inhabitants of Cordes presented the royal reformers with a list of grievances against Bernard of Castanet; this contained five articles dedicated to the abuse used in the repression of moneylending.[77]

Measures taken to control the sexual practices of the faithful were also exceptionally stringent.[78] Bernard of Castanet particularly endeavoured to be personally made aware of and to condemn forms of behaviour in this area that were forbidden (there is evidence, in particular, of a Sainte-Cécile canon who was sentenced to prison for life when found guilty of sodomy). The additions made to the diocese synodal statutes, in 1280, have no known equivalent in the Capetian kingdom of that period. They explicitly mention sodomites, proclaiming the excommunication of all those who sinned against nature, and they compelled those among the clerics who had cure of souls, if they had committed a sin of the flesh, to *repeat* their confession; if they failed to do this they would be suspended. This measure even seems to have been extended to laymen who infringed the new and very precise synodal regulation of sexual practices. In synod, Bernard of Castanet did indeed impose upon the confessors a particularly extensive conception of *contra naturam* sin that included any carnal intercourse that was beyond a very narrowly defined 'natural mode'. As specified by the members of the clergy who were questioned during a papal enquiry in 1307–8,[79] any coupling that was not performed 'as is commonly done, meaning embracing each other [that is, from the front] or from the side' or during which the man 'shed his seed in whatsoever manner outside the due repository' (*nisi in instrumento debito*), was assimilated to an act contrary to nature, for which the authors were *ipso facto* excommunicated and could only be absolved after having confessed to the bishop in person.[80] The inhabitants of Albi who failed to

---

[77] Archives du Tarn, AC Cordes, FF 49. See C. Portal, *Histoire de la ville de Cordes, Tarn (1222–1799)* (Albi, 1902), pp. 30–1.
[78] See Biget, 'Législation', and Théry, 'Les Albigeois', pp. 28–30.
[79] The records of this enquiry, kept at the Vatican Archives (Archivio Segreto Vaticano, henceforth ASV, *Collectoriae* 404), are edited in my doctoral thesis (2003): J. Théry, 'Avec le vrai et le faux: l'enquête sur les crimes de l'évêque d'Albi Bernard de Castanet (1307–1308)', forthcoming. See Théry, 'Les Albigeois', and the abstracts of the doctoral thesis in *Revue Mabillon* 15 (2004), 277–9, and in *Heresis* 40 (2004), 192–7.
[80] ASV, *Collectoriae* 404, fol. 67v (deposition of Raimon Delort, a priest from Albi): 'Ipse episcopus mandavit eis quod quicumque, esset masculus vel femina, qui venirent ad eorum confessionem et confiterentur eis quod inter se commixti fuissent carnaliter aliter quam comuniter fiat, videlicet se amplexando vel utroque a latere jacendo per modum naturalem, tamen quod ipsi curati non absolverent eos, sed quod eos remitterent ad ipsum episcopum absolvendos ab illis peccatis; et hoc eis imposuit quod nisi facerent quod ipse eos faceret poni in carcere. Item dixit ipse qui loquitur quod aliqui, tam masculi quam femine, fuerunt sibi qui loquitur confessi predictum modum commixtionis carnalis; et cum eis diceret quod

report their transgressions to their confessors, or who subsequently refused to seek pardon from the bishop, had to live with the notion of their excommunication and knew that they might die in a state of mortal sin. This situation necessarily led to a certain alienation from the Church. The legal framework established by Bernard of Castanet for the sexuality of his subjects was, moreover, in all likelihood designed to prevent people from practising birth control – a practice which, like the loan of money with interest, was particularly prevalent among the new merchant middle-classes, who wished to limit the division of assets to protect their wealth.

The immoderate use of spiritual sanction completes this portrait of Bernard of Castanet's excessively repressive spiritual government. Excommunication, traditionally used flexibly, for persuasive purposes, was applied with the obvious aim of permanently excluding any black sheep. Similarly, the sentences of interdict, which were applied in particular to lands belonging to those who refused to hand back Church goods as demanded by the bishop, were applied to the bitter end, seemingly with no mercy at all. There are traces of *funera per arbores*, meaning that the bodies of believers living on lands that were under interdict were left to hang from trees, as they had died while being refused the last rites and a Christian burial.[81]

The battle against the consular oligarchy to preserve the episcopal temporal lordship

This stringent Christian discipline represented only one facet of the clerical power exerted over the citizens of Albi. Political life too was marked by a highly authoritarian clericalism. As lord of the city, Bernard of Castanet practised a temporal government that was no less intransigent that his spiritual administration.

Insofar as the documents show, the bishop seems to have dispensed secular justice with extreme severity. The testimonies of the inhabitants of Albi recorded by the papal inquisitors in 1307–8 (which obviously stem from sources that did not shed good light on the bishop but are partly corroborated by the rare archives that were kept) mention the merciless repression of crimes through spectacular and bloody punishments. Apparently, Bernard of

---

irent ad episcopum predictum ad obtinendum absolutionem super predictis, quia ipse testis qui loquitur non audebat eos absolvere, illi confitentes dicebant quod ipse eos absolveret si vellet, quia ipsi nunquam irent ad episcopum propter hoc'. Ibid., fol. 131v (deposition of Peire Enjalran, a priest of the cathedral of Albi): 'Dixit quod ipse audivit recitare in sinodo sentenciam excommunicationis lata per dictum episcopum in illos qui comiterent peccatum contra naturam, et audivit dici quod episcopus interpretabatur illam sentenciam qualitercumque vir effunderet semen, nisi in instrumento mulieris debito'.

[81] Ibid., fol. 163r (deposition of Peire Ferreol, a Franciscan friar from the house of Albi): 'Item non vidit eum reconciliantem ecclesias vel cimiteria; et tamen vidit terram domini Bertrandi vicecomitis et totam terram Lautraguesii interdictam et funera per arbores.'

Castanet often stepped in to increase the sentences. Even for children or for a young pregnant woman guilty of theft, the bishop seems to have refused all mercy, imposing death sentences despite the families' pleas.[82]

This harshness cannot be explained solely by the will to inculcate subjection, but should be considered with a more specific stake in mind: that of municipal autonomy in Albi. The bishop was in this case seeking to establish his pre-eminence despite the charter obtained by the bourgeois in 1269, which entrusted the judgement of criminals to a jury of *probi homines* (reputable men) gathered together with the episcopal bayle. The subordination of the municipal institutions required a relentless fight against the ambitions of the city's elite, who were eager to extend their meagre powers. Bernard of Castanet blocked the establishment of autonomous municipal notaries, banned the regulation of professions or the free distribution of taxes by the consuls, contested the *universitas*'s right to a common house and probably attempted to restrict the freedom acquired under the episcopate of his predecessor. However, by encouraging the infringements of a triumphant royal jurisdiction, with systematic appeals lodged against the judgements of the *Temporalité* (the secular court of the lord bishop), the oligarchy did succeed in implementing a strategy particularly dangerous to the episcopal power. As from 1278, Bernard of Castanet was obliged to defend his rights before the seneschal of Carcassonne. The history of the episcopacy was also that of the continuous advancement of the king's justice in a city that was beyond his reach until the see became vacant in 1271. Leaving no hope for communal emancipation, the bishop's intransigence

---

[82] See for instance the deposition of the merchant of Albi Raimon Baudier (ASV, *Collectoriae* 404, fol. 58r): 'Item dixit se vidisse et audivisse quod cum quidam nomine Fabianus, comorans Albie, esset condempnatus per consules et alios proceres de Albia usque ad XX, ut est moris, ad bulliendum in oleo, episcopus, ipso teste presente et vidente, dixit quod volebat quod dictus Fabianus primo traheretur seu rossegaretur per totam Albiam usque ad furcas de *Sang Amaran* et quod bulliretur ibi in oleo et truncaretur capite et suspenderetur ibidem. [...] Item dixit quod vidit quod cum tres pueri de Albia acusarentur quod furati fuissent carnes et cutellos et marsupia et dicti consules et proceres usque ad XX non possent bene concordare in sentencia, magister G[uillelmus] de Tribus Virginibus venit coram dicto episcopo et episcopus tunc dixit: "Quid est hoc?"; et dictus magister G[uillelmus] dixit: "Domine, tres pueri qui furati fuerunt carnes et cutellos et marsupia; et consules et proceres non concordant in sentenciando eos"; et episcopus dixit: "Suspendatis eos apud Vallem Cabreriam". [...] Interrogatus si scit quod ita fuerint suspensi sicut episcopus dixit, dixit quod sic, quia ipse qui loquitur sequtus fuit eos usque ad pontem et in crastinum vidit eos suspensos in Valle Cabreria. [...] Item dixit quod vidit quod cum quedam mulier pregnans filia Jacobi *Regambal* et uxor d'*en Rizols*, galopodiarii de Albia, esset condempnata per consules et proceres de Albia usque ad XX ad submergendum pro furto lini et dragmarum et quarundam aliarum rerum de quibus ipse testis non recordatur, venit dictus Jacobus *Regambal* cum quibusdam amicis suis, ipso teste presente et vidente, coram episcopo et supplicabat quod, cum dicta mulier esset pregnans, quod vellet dictam sentenciam mitigare vel saltim differre quousque peperisset; et dictus episcopus dixit quod si portaret duos vel plures quod volebat quod sentencia mandaretur exsequtioni.'

brought about a shift in alliances; the elite of the city consequently joined ranks with the royal officials against the episcopal lordship.[83]

The progressive escalation, over more than twenty years or so (1277–99), of the conflict between the oligarchy and the bishop, and its final explosion in the first years of the fourteenth century (1300–8) into an open combat, give a clear idea as to the interconnection of religious dissidence and political contestation, as well as to the social establishment of the 'heresy' of the good men.

The Inquisition as the supreme weapon against the two facets of dissidence

The Inquisition was used by Bernard of Castanet as the centrepiece of a policy aimed at monitoring and intimidating the small circle of good men's friends. As seen previously, the very long trial of 1286–7 was used to methodically collect denunciations – more than four hundred in all, half of which concerned the inhabitants of Albi. Practically all of the latter belonged to the city's elite. For the twelve following years, Bernard of Castanet used this file to strike, at the time of his choosing, certain individuals who had been reported, freely singling out for arrest, according to the context and the status of his relationship with the Albi citizens, those who were the most severely compromised and contributed significantly to the existence of 'heresy', or those who were the most active participants in the opposition formed by the municipal oligarchy. Whoever had reason to believe that they were among those denounced lived in fear of being arrested at any time and must have hesitated before engaging in battles for the autonomy of the consular institutions.

As from 1297, and for a period of more than two years, Bernard of Castanet was faced with a trial that he was powerless to put a stop to; it was led by the bourgeois before the royal courts to neutralize his secular justice to the benefit of the king.[84] The bishop's temporal jurisdiction was at risk of being paralysed. It was at this crucial point that the second series of Inquisition trials was launched, between December 1299 and March 1300. The twenty-five inhabitants of Albi who were among the accused were all from the most influential families and were also among the most active opponents to episcopal power. Bernard of Castanet thus found confirmation of his theocratic convictions, according to which those who opposed the temporal interests of the Church were also those who opposed the true faith that it defended. His own intransigence in the exercising of episcopal power had, of course, largely contributed to this state of affairs. He was rightly able to identify municipal opposition and 'heresy' as being two facets of the same enemy.

The ensuing events even further corroborated this point of view. Struck hard by the trials of 1299–1300, the city elite were more than ever exposed to

---

[83] See Biget, 'Un procès d'inquisition', pp. 316–22.
[84] Ibid., pp. 322–5.

new arrests that could at any time, at the bishop's whim, deliver anyone who had been denounced to the Inquisition, with no hope of return. Bernard of Castanet seems to have chosen a strategy of terror to overcome the resistance of his defiant diocesans. In 1300–1, the situation had become unbearable, inciting most of the oligarchy to engage in an anti-inquisitorial movement which had a truly political dimension. Indeed, the Albi bourgeois forged an alliance with those of Carcassonne and of several other Languedoc cities, naming a Friar Minor, Bernard Délicieux, as leader, and they strove under his command, by all possible means, to discredit the inquisitors before the pope and the king of France.[85] Bernard of Castanet was one of the main targets. At the beginning of the year 1302 a riot, orchestrated by the bourgeois, forced him to flee from the city, which remained in a state of semi-insurrection for a number of years.

After the failure of the anti-inquisitorial movement between 1303 and 1306, the oligarchy did not cease trying to get rid of the bishop. They finally succeeded in a roundabout manner. In the spring of 1307 two canons from Sainte-Cécile cathedral, both members of eminent local families, presented a series of terrible accusations against Bernard of Castanet to the Papal Curia. Unlike the complaints elaborated by the citizens of Albi in previous years, these did not allege the arbitrary arrests justified by heresy. They did not even mention the Inquisition. However, the canons reported the numerous crimes, negligences and pastoral abuse of a tyrannical episcopal government, as well as denouncing Bernard of Castanet for his depraved morals. Pope Clement V, whose accession had marked within the Curia the defeat of those who took a hard line against the secular resistance generated by the ecclesiastical government, grasped the opportunity to launch an enquiry that in itself looked like a repudiation of the bishop and weakened his position, thus justifying his transfer to the episcopal see of Le Puy (July 1308). The prosopographical study of the 114 prosecution witnesses auditioned in Albi provides a clear confirmation of the identity of those who opposed the episcopal temporal lordship and of the good men's friends, revealing that the groups were one and the same.[86]

The repression of 'heresy' clearly played a major role in the turbulent political life of Albi during the time of Bernard of Castanet. In terms of the sequence of events and from the structural point of view, it would be difficult to separate it from the other aspects of the theocratic government enforced by the bishop. Faced with religious dissidence born out of the local discontent aroused by Roman clericalism, Bernard of Castanet opted for outright war, for a full-on attack that left no room for compromise, through the immoderate pursuit of an ultra-clerical policy.

---

[85] A. Friedlander, *The Hammer of the Inquisitors: Brother Bernard Délicieux and the Struggle against the Inquisition in Fourteenth-Century France* (Leiden, 2000).
[86] Théry, 'Les Albigeois'. Théry, 'Avec le vrai et le faux'.

Julien Théry-Astruc

Conclusion

The heretical dissidence of the good men swiftly disappeared, both in the region of Albi and elsewhere in Languedoc, in the twenty years that followed Bernard of Castanet's transfer to Le Puy (1308).[87] The accession of John XXII, in 1316, sparked off an inquisitorial reaction following the appeasement brought by Clement V (1305–14) – and the new pope hastened to offer a resounding promotion to the old theocrat bishop by appointing him cardinal of Porto at the end of the year 1316. The city of Albi, in 1319, just as that of Cordes in 1321, was subject to solemn penance for its past opposition to Bernard of Castanet and to the Inquisition.[88] The former bishop of Albi may have been the author of an initial list of articles of accusation drawn up for the trial of the leader of the anti-inquisitorial movement Bernard Délicieux, arrested by order of John XXII in 1317.[89] Sentenced to life in prison, the Franciscan Brother died in the dungeon. Ultimately, his wrongdoing was to have led protest actions (in favour of different groups of outcasts: the good men's friends, the beguines and spiritual Franciscans) in which the common principle was to reject the very category of heresy[90] a 'self-terminating' and criminalizing category that historiography can now be freed from, by ceasing to consider heresy as a fact in itself, and by approaching dissidence in terms of resistance to Roman clericalism. Until 1329, the inquisitors of Carcassonne continued to condemn a few Albi citizens denounced almost thirty years beforehand, during the Albi trials of 1299–1300.[91]

Persecution, however, even if it played a major role in the extinction of dissidence, is unlikely to have been the only reason.[92] The Franciscans' accommodating pastoral approach was far more decisive, together with a marked relaxation of the ban that the Church had established on mercantile business,

---

[87] See Biget, 'L'extinction du catharisme'.

[88] The records of the collective penitence of Cordes are edited in *Le livre des sentences de l'inquisiteur Bernard Gui, 1308–1323*, ed. A. Palès-Gobilliard, 2 vols. (Paris, 2002), II, 1218–39. Those of the collective penitence of Albi are edited in Théry, 'Avec le vrai et le faux'.

[89] A. R. Friedlander, *Processus Bernardi Delitiosi: The Trial of Fr. Bernard Délicieux, 3 September–8 December 1319* (Philadelphia, 1996). See M. de Dmitrewski, 'Fr. Bernard Délicieux, OFM: sa lutte contre l'inquisition de Carcassonne et d'Albi, son procès, 1297–1319', *Archivum Franciscanum historicum* 17 (1924), 455–88 (pp. 474, 486).

[90] Théry, 'L'hérésie des bons hommes', pp. 103–5. See for instance Délicieux's claim that even St Paul and St Peter would have been declared heretics by the inquisitors: 'Item dixit ibidem quod si sanctus Petrus et sanctus Paulus essent coram inquisitoribus, quantumcumque fuerint et sint boni christiani, inquisitores eos ita male tractarent quod facerent eos heresim confiteri' (Friedlander, *Processus Bernardi Delitiosi*, p. 72).

[91] See Biget, 'L'extinction du catharisme'.

[92] See Biget, 'L'extinction du catharisme', and Biget, 'Autour de Bernard Délicieux: franciscanisme et société en Languedoc entre 1295 et 1330', *Revue d'histoire de l'Église de France* 70 (1984), 75–93.

and also the stronger royal power of the Capetians in Languedoc, in a region where the secular authorities had always been quite slack, giving free rein to para-ecclesial religious life just as they did to excessive ecclesiastical power. These three factors had reduced the need for dissidence by slightly restricting and by adapting the clericalism that had been part and parcel of ecclesiastical mediation since the Gregorian reform. And, probably much more important: by 1320–30, the localist (and thus anti-Gregorian and anticlerical) tradition represented by the good men had completely disappeared. It had taken a century and much violence for it to die.

5

The *heretici* of Languedoc: Local Holy Men and Women or Organized Religious Group? New Evidence from Inquisitorial, Notarial and Historiographical Sources

Jörg Feuchter

In what follows I shall present three examples of new evidence for the existence of an organized religious group among the people persecuted for heresy in medieval Languedoc. I shall thus try to make a case against the radical scepticism or 'deconstructivism' brought forward – in various degrees of intensity and on diverse points – by Mark G. Pegg, Robert I. Moore, Julien Théry, Monique Zerner, Uwe Brunn and other scholars.[1] I shall not, however, argue for or against a 'Balkans' connection, that is to say, a link between the Languedocian group and the Bogomils or other forms of eastern dualism. In fact, I shall not deal with the question of dualism at all. This is simply not within the scope of my text. Rather, I take up a simpler but essential question raised by R. I. Moore: 'whether there was in fact any division in the society of the lands between the Rhône and the Garonne that corresponded in the eyes

---

[1] M. G. Pegg, *The Corruption of Angels: The Great Inquisition of 1245–1246* (Princeton, 2001) (see review by J. Feuchter, in *H-Soz-u-Kult* (2002), online at http://hsozkult.geschichte.hu-berlin.de/rezensionen/id=880); M. G. Pegg, 'On Cathars, Albigenses, and Good Men of Languedoc', *Journal of Medieval History* 27 (2001), 181–95; M. G. Pegg, 'Albigenses in the Antipodes: An Australian and the Cathars', *Journal of Religious History* 35 (2011) 577–600; R. I. Moore, *The War on Heresy: Faith and Power in Medieval Europe* (Cambridge MA, 2012); J. Théry, 'L'hérésie des bons hommes: comment nommer la dissidence religieuse non vaudoise ni béguine en Languedoc (XIIe – début du XIVe siècle)?', *Heresis* 36–7 (2002), 75–117; U. Brunn, *Des contestataires aux 'cathares': discours de réforme et propagande antihérétique dans les pays du Rhin et de la Meuse avant l'inquisition* (Paris, 2006); *Inventer l'hérésie? Discours polémiques et pouvoirs avant l'inquisition*, ed. M. Zerner (Nice, 1998); *L'histoire du catharisme en discussion: le 'concile' de Saint-Félix (1167)*, ed. M. Zerner (Nice, 2001). For more bibliographical references and an overview of the 'deconstructivist' approach see Moore's afterword in *The War on Heresy* ('Afterword: The War among the Scholars', pp. 332–6), and R. I. Moore, 'The Cathar Middle Ages as an Historiographical Problem', in *Christianity and Culture in the Middle Ages: Essays to Honor John van Engen*, ed. D. C. Mengel and L. Wolverton (Notre Dame, 2014), pp. 58–86.

The Heretici of Languedoc

of its inhabitants to the distinction between catholics and heretics.'[2] Moore has answered this question in the negative, mostly by discarding all sorts of evidence. I shall try to present new evidence supporting an affirmative answer.

Before I start, I want to make it clear that I think that the 'deconstructivist' case has at least some merit in that it leads every scholar in the field to question both his own presuppositions and those of the sources. However, it is my firm opinion that the critics are overstepping any sensible boundary in their rejection of the ample textual evidence – for example, in inquisitorial records – for the existence of an organized, self-consciously dissident religious group. They also ignore or underplay the critical approaches to the concepts of heresy present in the work of earlier scholars who wrote long before the deconstructionists, such as Herbert Grundmann or Arno Borst.[3] To accuse Grundmann of naivety or lack of awareness, as some among the deconstructivists do, does him wrong and it is itself based on a misunderstanding of his work, as can easily be demonstrated. Thus, when Mark G. Pegg charges him with having introduced an 'intellectualist bias' into heresy studies, he defines that bias as follows:

> What supposedly makes a heresy or religion, and so what makes someone heretical or religious, is solely defined by doctrines, philosophies, and ideals. Scriptural consistency and theological cogency are what make heresies or religions, not poorly articulated thoughts or anomalous habits, which either get tossed aside as notional and habitual irrelevancies or (like square pegs in round holes) made to fit conventional narratives like 'Catharism'. [...] Unfortunately, too many scholars assume that ideally gathering ideas, or thoughtfully paraphrasing thoughts, or notionally laying out notions, says everything that needs saying about heresy or religion.[4]

---

[2] '[...] a question that has not been confronted, or perhaps even formulated – whether there was in fact any division in the society of the lands between the Rhône and the Garonne that corresponded in the eyes of its inhabitants to the distinction between Catholics and heretics. To Innocent III it was so fundamental that he could not conceive of a world without it. Yet to ask how many of these heretics, however designated, there were before the Albigensian crusade is rather like asking how many witches there were in Europe on the eve of the great witch craze of the sixteenth and seventeenth centuries. It assumes the objective, measurable existence of a category that was actually in the process of being constructed by the interrogators themselves, and which in that process was described in language that meant different things to different people.' (Moore, *The War on Heresy*, pp. 261–2).

[3] H. Grundmann, 'Ketzerverhöre des Spätmittelalters als quellenkritisches Problem', *Deutsches Archiv für Erforschung des Mittelalters* 21(1965), 519–75; H. Grundmann, 'Der Typus des Ketzers in mittelalterlicher Anschauung', in *Kultur- und Universalgeschichte: W. Goetz zu seinem 60. Geburtstag* (Leipzig, 1927), pp. 91–107; A. Borst, *Die Katharer*, Monumenta Germaniae Historica Schriften 12 (Stuttgart, 1953).

[4] Pegg, 'Albigensians', pp. 585–6, with n. 36 (in almost identical phrasing and with

In a footnote to the last sentence quoted here Pegg traces back the alleged bias in heresy studies explicitly and firstly to Grundmann:

> For example, an intellectualist bias defines Grundmann's influential *Religiöse Bewegungen im Mittelalter. Untersuchungen über die geschichtlichen Zusammenhänge zwischen der Ketzerei, den Bettelorden und der religiösen Frauenbewegung im 12. und 13. Jahrhundert, und über die geschichtlichen Grundlagen der deutschen Mystik*, 2nd ed. (Hildesheim, 1961, orig. 1935), esp. 396ff., 503.

Yet the reader who looks up these pages in Grundmann is left puzzled. First he finds that the indication '396ff' leads to pages in *Religiöse Bewegungen* with no relevance at all to the subject of heresy (they are about the dry history facts of a Dominican nunnery). Obviously a typo has occurred and the references should read '496ff., 503'.[5] For page 496ff indeed deals with heresy, and the Cathars in particular. There Grundmann supports the theory of an eastern origin of their dualism. But he also expresses just the opposite of the bias of which Pegg accuses him. For he states that the foreign doctrine of the Cathars was not important:

> Their dualistic dogma only gradually distinguished itself from Catholic doctrine. For the mass of the believers, the *credentes*, the religious attitude and moral rigorism of their preachers, the *perfecti*, was always more impressive than their dualistic speculation. In the religious movement of the West, the question of a truly evangelical way of life as the path to salvation was always more important, more vital, than all doctrinal matters of theology or cosmology'.[6]

---

identical references to Grundmann already in Pegg, *The Corruption of Angels*, p. 142, and Pegg, 'On Cathars', p. 183).

[5] Note that these pages are from a text by Grundmann that was not even part of the original *Religiöse Bewegungen*. It is a follow-up essay written twenty years later and titled 'Neue Beiträge zur Geschichte der religiösen Bewegungen im Mittelalter'. First published in 1955 it was reprinted as an addition ('Anhang') on pp. 485–538 in the second edition: H. Grundmann, *Religiöse Bewegungen im Mittelalter: Untersuchungen über die geschichtlichen Zusammenhänge zwischen der Ketzerei, den Bettelorden und der religiösen Frauenbewegung im 12. und 13. Jahrhundert, und über die geschichtlichen Grundlagen der deutschen Mystik*, Anhang: neue Beiträge zur Geschichte der religiösen Bewegungen im Mittelalter (Hildesheim, 1961).

[6] H. Grundmann, *Religious Movements in the Middle Ages*, trans. S. Rowan (Notre Dame, 1995), p. 215. The original text: 'Erst allmählich tritt ihr dualistisches Dogma in schroffem Gegensatz zur katholischen Lehre deutlicher hervor; aber für die Masse ihrer Gläubigen, die *credentes*, ist wohl immer das religiöse Verfahren und der moralische Rigorismus ihrer Prediger, der *perfecti*, eindrucksvoller gewesen als deren dualistische Spekulation. Überhaupt erscheint in der religiösen Bewegung des Abendlandes die Frage des wahrhaft christlichen, evangelienmäßigen Lebens als Weg zum Seelenheil wichtiger, vitaler als alle theologisch-kosmologischen Lehrfragen' (Grundmann, *Religiöse Bewegungen im Mittelalter*, p. 496).

It is more than clear that Grundmann is emphasizing here (as well as on p. 503, the other page cited by Pegg) the priority of actual religious practice over doctrine. For Grundmann, mendicants, beguines and religious dissidents all started from the same non-doctrinal motivation, the urge to imitate the apostolic life (*vita apostolica*). For him heresy was all about religious forms of life ('religiöse Lebensformen') and hardly at all about doctrine – even in the case of the Cathars. Pegg simply misses Grundmann's most basic legacy to heresy studies and instead imputes to him the contrary.

But this is also not the point of my text. Rather, I shall accept for the sake of the argument the deconstructivists' discarding of everything in inquisition documents that can be subjected to scepticism about falsification or even invention by inquisitors or their scribes, such as narratives about religious tenets, dualist myths, clerical hierarchy, and so on. In the same way, and again for the sake of argument, I shall accept their criticism of thirteenth-century historiographical accounts of what went on in Languedoc. Instead I shall try to ask what we might know about the *heretici* of Languedoc if we leave aside the contested narratives and look for (i) other ways of interpreting inquisition records, (ii) other kinds of documents not susceptible to clerical distortion, and (iii) earlier historiographical evidence.

I shall begin with the presentation of clues drawn from a thirteenth-century inquisition document that are not dependent on the narrative structure of the text, yet point towards the existence of clearly demarcated dissident religious groups. Second, I shall present a document written by a notary from the Toulouse region dating from the twelfth century. It explicitly mentions a group of 'heretical' people but was not produced in a context of hostility towards that group. The third source analysed is a twelfth-century chronicle from outside the region, even outside Roman Christianity, which makes explicit mention of an episcopal structure among the dissidents in Languedoc.

Two groups of religious dissidents in the 'Paenitenciae' of Peter Sellan (Petrus Cellani), 1241

In the middle of the 1230s the Dominican inquisitor Peter Sellan[7] carried out a series of inquisitions in several localities of the Quercy region, the bishopric and county to the north of the Toulousain.[8] The deposition records are not

---

[7] For a biography of Peter Sellan see J. Feuchter, *Ketzer, Konsuln und Büßer: die städtischen Eliten von Montauban vor dem Inquisitor Petrus Cellani (1236/1241)* (Tübingen, 2007) (henceforward *Ketzer*), pp. 257–8, superseding J. Feuchter, 'Pierre Sellan, un viellard expérimenté', in *Les inquisiteurs: portraits de défenseurs de la foi en Languedoc (XIIIe–IVe siècles)*, ed. L. Albaret (Toulouse, 2001), pp. 41–55.

[8] On Sellan's campaign in Quercy in the context of the early inquisition in Languedoc, see *Ketzer*, pp. 278–306.

extant, yet a document by the inquisitor from 1241 – giving a reduced version of the depositions together with the corresponding levels of penance – is. It is known by the heading 'Paenitenciae fratris Petri Sillani' given to it in the only version of the text, the transcription in the seventeenth-century Collection Doat in the Bibliothèque nationale de France.[9] This document was composed as the basis for a tour of public announcements of the penances in the region in the years 1241 and 1242.[10] This sort of text was made in order to facilitate the attribution of sanctions, as Bernard Gui in his manual *Practica inquisitionis* (beginning of the fourteenth century) describes. Bernard labels it as an 'extractio summaria et compendiosa' or 'brevis extractio'.[11] There is a full, yet rather flawed, edition by Jean Duvernoy[12] and a newer edition of the parts concerning the city of Montauban, which I prepared myself.[13]

The document consists of 653 individual names with short texts (between five and 200 words). In each text, the first part sums up the deposition, the second gives the penitential sanction. It is obvious that the first part is still very close to the original deposition records. Thus it frequently starts with the words 'dixit quod'. After that follows an enumeration of the contacts of the individual with *heretici* and *Valdenses*, with standardized categories and the frequencies of each contact. A comparison with the deposition records of the great 1245/6 inquisition of Bernardus de Cautio (Bernard of Caux) in the Lauragais[14] shows a great likeness in syntax and lexis. Both texts are structured by terminologically exactly classified contacts, given in chronological order from the first to most recent, each phrase subsuming one chronological period, the next phrase beginning with 'Item'. The biggest difference between the 'Paenitenciae' and the deposition records is that 'Paenitenciae' lacks indications of time at the end of each phrase and of the names of other persons involved. These indications were not necessary for establishing the penances. In fact their omission was the point of the 'brevis extractio' as described by Bernard Gui; only the 'substantia confessionis [...] sine expressione nominis alicujus persone' should be given in this sort of text.[15] The second part with the penances consisted in a single sentence starting with 'Ibit' ('He/She will

---

[9] For an extensive description and analysis of the document see *Ketzer*, pp. 54–75.
[10] See *Ketzer*, pp. 63–6.
[11] *Practica inquisitionis heretice pravitatis, auctore Bernardo Guidonis*, ed. C. Douais (Paris, 1886), p. 83; see *Ketzer*, pp. 65–6.
[12] *L'inquisition en Quercy: le registre des pénitences de Pierre Cellan, 1241–1242*, ed. J. Duvernoy (Castelnaud-la-Chapelle, 2001).
[13] *Ketzer*, Appendix I (pp. 453–89) (henceforward *Ketzer* App. I). In this edition, each of the Montauban individuals receiving a penance is referenced by a number (1–253). I will use this reference system in the present text too.
[14] Toulouse, Bibliothèque municipale, MS 609 (henceforth MS 609); see extensive analysis by Y. Dossat, *Les crises de l'inquisition toulousaine au XIIIe siècle (1233–1273)* (Bordeaux, 1959). MS 609 is the subject of Pegg, *The Corruption of Angels*.
[15] *Practica*, ed. Douais, p. 83; see *Ketzer*, pp. 65–6.

go') and then naming the directions of the penitential pilgrimages (from one to seven) imposed on the individual, e.g. to Le Puy, Santiago de Compostela, Canterbury or Rome, and – in some cases – additional sanctions such as the obligation to take part in the defence of the Latin Empire in Constantinople.[16] The 'Penitenciae' are singular in that they name both the 'offences' and the sanctions. No other document of this kind has survived from the inquisition of medieval Languedoc.[17]

The depositions which form the basis of the 'Paenitenciae' were given under special circumstances. After initial failure, the inquisitors in the Toulousain and the Quercy had introduced in 1235 the 'tempus gratiae', a 'grace period' of a few days in which depositions went without heavy sanctions, provided they were made fully and truthfully.[18] The inhabitants of Quercy made extensive use of this provision, with only very few exceptions (mentioned specifically in the 'Paenitenciae').[19] In Montauban, the town which will be our focus, a political decision to comply fully with the inquisitor was made in 1236, as can be inferred from a reconstruction of the chronology and circumstances of Sellan's entry into the town.[20] Each deponent was thus aware that everybody else in the city in contact with religious dissent would also give a full deposition. Concealment was not a sensible strategy under these circumstances. For some of the depositions in Montauban we even have proof for their completeness and truthfulness, as they correspond exactly to the depositions of a native of that town given in another inquisition. This woman, Arnalda de la Mota, lived elsewhere yet received visits from her kin from Montauban. What she said about the contacts fits exactly what was recorded for her relatives in the 'Paenitenciae', who at this moment, in 1236, could not know that Arnalda would be caught years later, in 1243.[21]

In the 'Paenitenciae', 256 individuals from Montauban are given a penance, by far the greatest number for a single location and indeed the highest proportion of people implicated in 'heresy' in any single Languedoc location.[22] In a general population of a few thousand[23] the individuals contained in the

---

[16] For the historical context and an explanation for this rather unique penance see *Ketzer*, pp. 325–30.
[17] For an overview on documents of inquisitorial sanctions in medieval Languedoc, see *Ketzer*, pp. 315–20.
[18] On the introduction of the measure see *Ketzer*, p. 287.
[19] Paris, Bibliothèque nationale de France, Collection Doat MS 21, fol. 186v: 'et fuit captus pro haeresi et non fuit in tempore gratiae'; and fol. 220r: 'Item non venit in tempore gratiae.'
[20] See *Ketzer*, pp. 297–305.
[21] *Ketzer*, pp. 77–8.
[22] Compare with the overview by J.-L. Biget, 'L'extinction du catharisme urbain: les points chauds de la répression', *Effacement du catharisme (XIIIe–XIVe s.)* = *Cahiers de Fanjeaux* 20 (1985) 305–40 (esp. pp. 317–19), and *Ketzer*, p. 68.
[23] *Ketzer*, pp. 163–4.

'Paenitenciae' make up about five to ten percent. Another exceptional fact was that reference is made to two religious groups, *heretici* and *Valdenses*. The Waldensians, the followers of an apostolic religious movement originating in Lyons in the 1170s,[24] do not appear frequently in the rest of Languedoc inquisition records, but in Montauban and two other Quercy locations[25] references to them are almost on a par with those to *heretici*. The latter is clearly not a catch-all name for religious dissidents of all sorts, but the designation for a certain group distinct from the *Valdenses* and which non-deconstructivists would identify, with due awareness of the conceptual problems, as 'Cathars' or 'Albigenses'. A third important fact to mention is that Montauban has rich documentation in the town's cartulary, the 'Livre Rouge', containing transcriptions of texts mostly from the thirteenth century.[26] This enables the individuals in the 'Paenitenciae' to be 'placed' in the political and social structures of the town.

If we compare the references to the two religious groups, some differences are obvious. There are the frequent mentions that the *heretici* were 'adored' by the (later) penitents,[27] that is, that a genuflection and a demand for an intercessory prayer was made towards the 'heretic'. This was never the case with the *Valdenses*. They, on the other hand, are often described as having 'cured' people[28] (in a medical, not in a spiritual sense, as there is mention of practical action),[29] something which is never said of the *heretici*.

Apart from this, the references to both groups in the 'Paenitenciae' seem hardly to differ, at least at a first glance. They are about hearing sermons, eating together with the 'heretics' and 'Valdenses', and supporting them with material gifts, shelter or company. A somewhat puzzling phenomenon is that many people from Montauban had contact with members of both groups. It is only when we take a closer look that significant differences emerge. For instance, the circumstances of the sermons (sixty-five mentions for the

---

[24] On the Waldensians see C. Papini, *Valdo di Lione e i 'poveri nello spirito': il primo secolo del movimento valdese (1170–1270)* (Turin 2001); G. Audisio, *Les vaudois* (Turin, 1989); P. Biller, *The Waldenses, 1170–1530: Between a Religious Order and a Church*, Variorum Collected Studies Series 676 (Aldershot, 2000).

[25] Gourdon and Montcuq. On these places see C. Taylor, *Heresy, Crusade and Inquisition in Medieval Quercy* (York, 2011).

[26] Archives municipales de Montauban, AA 1. A calendar of all texts is given in *Ketzer*, Appendix V (pp. 537–63). My edition is in preparation.

[27] *Ketzer* App. I, nos. 1, 8, 13, 16, 17, 20, 45, 54, 56, 57, 61, 109, 111, 132, 138, 139, 145, 148, 150, 151, 159, 160, 161, 164, 175, 182, 185, 197, 201, 203, 223, 224, 226, 227, 229, 231, 234.

[28] *Ketzer* App. I, nos. 4, 5, 16, 20, 21, 25, 29, 30, 31, 35, 36, 38, 43, 58, 59, 62, 69, 74, 76, 76, 77, 78, 80, 82, 85, 86, 88, 90, 92, 95, 97, 104, 107, 113, 117, 120, 121, 122, 123, 124, 136, 140, 153, 159, 163, 166, 169, 171, 172, 174, 176, 177, 178, 180, 181, 185, 186, 187, 189, 191, 194, 195, 199, 200, 208, 213, 219, 221, 230, 231, 236, 238, 243, 244, 246, 248, 251.

[29] On Waldensian healing see P. Biller, '*Curate infirmos*: The Medieval Waldensian Practice of Medicine', *Studies in Church History* 11 (1982), 55–77.

heretici,³⁰ 100 for the *Valdenses*)³¹ are not the same. The Waldensians' sermon is often described as having taken place either 'in public'³² or in their proper building, and only very rarely in the houses of the inhabitants. By contrast, the sermon of the *heretici* only takes place in the private 'domus', with just one exception mentioned.³³ There is also a major difference when it comes to eating. The *heretici* accompanied each meal and each drinking with a blessing, but the meal itself was not a special religious occasion, just ordinary consumption of food.³⁴ The *Valdenses*, however, had a specific religious ritual called the 'caena' (holy supper), taking place in their own building, where bread, fish and wine were consumed. Sometimes it is mentioned specifically that it took place on Maundy Thursday. This 'caena' is mentioned for no fewer than forty-six individuals in Montauban,³⁵ and it is clearly differentiated from other, non-ritualistic eating where a *Valdensis* was present.³⁶

The two religious groups held public disputations about their faith. Eight individuals from Montauban are described as having admitted to the attendance of such occasions.³⁷ Such 'disputationes haereticorum et Valdensium' fall into a larger picture of public religious arguing in the region.³⁸

It thus seems improbable that people in Montauban were unaware of the differences between the two groups. That is why it seems so confusing

---

30 *Ketzer* App. *I*, nos. 1, 3, 8, 10, 13, 16, 17, 18, 34, 48, 48, 56, 57, 60, 61, 62, 75, 76, 76, 78, 80, 98, 103, 104, 109, 110, 111, 117, 126, 130, 132, 135, 138, 139, 145, 148, 149, 150, 151, 157, 159, 160, 161, 165, 173, 175, 181, 183, 184, 185, 195, 196, 200, 201, 202, 203, 223, 226, 227, 231, 232, 234, 235, 242.

31 *Ketzer* App. *I*, nos. 11, 12, 21, 23, 26, 27, 28, 29, 33, 35, 36, 37, 39, 46, 49, 53, 58, 59, 61, 63, 65, 66, 68, 69, 78, 80, 81, 82, 83, 84, 85, 86, 87, 88, 89, 91, 92, 94, 96, 97, 111, 121, 122, 123, 124, 125, 129, 131, 132, 136, 137, 141, 142, 143, 146, 147, 152, 153, 154, 155, 158, 159, 162, 165, 166, 167, 168, 169, 172, 173, 174, 178, 179, 180, 181, 186, 189, 192, 193, 194, 198, 200, 204, 205, 208, 209, 210, 213, 214, 215, 216, 219, 220, 221, 225, 228, 240, 241, 243, 244, 245, 247, 250, 253.

32 For instance 'in plateis Montisalbani', 'in platea', or 'in plateis' (*Ketzer* App. *I*, nos. 136, 141, 153, 169, 178–80, 189, 192–4, 215, 220, 225, 250), 'publice in viis' (no. 39), 'publice' (nos. 58, 111).

33 *Ketzer* App. *I*, no. 104: 'publice praedicantes'.

34 There are twenty-eight penitents described as having eaten with *heretici*: *Ketzer* App. *I*, nos. 2, 42, 45, 57, 61, 77, 103, 109, 112, 118, 123, 126, 148, 150, 151, 155, 156, 160, 164, 175, 223, 224, 226, 227, 229, 233, 234, 242.

35 *Ketzer* App. *I*, nos. 11, 12, 21, 23, 25, 26, 27, 28, 29, 31, 35, 37, 46, 49, 53, 65, 70, 83, 91, 94, 96, 123, 125, 129, 131, 136, 141, 143, 146, 153, 154, 158, 159, 162, 166, 169, 173, 179, 180, 198, 213, 216, 218, 225, 250, 253.

36 *Ketzer* App. *I*, no. 27: 'Item interfuit caenae valdensium et comedit de pane et pisce benedictis ab eis et audivit praedicationem eorum. Item iacuit et comedit cum valdensibus cerasas'; see also no. 129.

37 *Ketzer* App. *I*, no. 11: 'interfuit disputationi haereticorum et valdensium', and very similar words in nos. 17, 23, 24, 104, 127, 143. Different, because expressing partisanship, is no. 169: 'fuit cum valdensibus quando disputaverunt cum haereticis'.

38 See *Ketzer*, pp. 234–8.

to read that many individuals entertained contacts with both. For instance, Geralda de Biele gave of her own (from her belongings) to her sister, who was a 'heretic', and also went to a house where female heretics lived, and ate with them. Yet she also gave alms to the *Valdenses* and thought that they were 'boni homines'.[39] And Caturcinus de la Vernha had *Valdenses* help him during his illness, listened to their sermon, gave them alms and held them to be 'good people'. But he also went to the house of a female 'heretic'.[40] Or take Ioannes Toset, who had been frequently and in diverse places in contact with 'heretics', had heard their sermons and had 'adored' them, whose uncle was a 'heretic' and who had attended the 'making' of a 'heretic': nonetheless he consulted the *Valdenses* because of some ailment.[41] Petrus Carbonelz senior, who supposedly gave bread and wine fifty times over and meat ten times over to the Waldensians, listened to their preaching frequently and participated in their supper, ate as well with 'heretics' and slept together with them.[42] Arnaldus de Castillo celebrated the 'caena' with the Waldensians but ate also with the 'heretics'.[43] Ioannes Austorcs attended the sermons of both groups 'frequently' ('multotiens'), but gave goods to the Waldensians and thought of them as good people.[44] Bernardus Tessender also had no problem with listening frequently to Waldensian sermons and going three times to the *heretici* to hear what they preached.[45] There are many others who had a habit of listening to both sermons.[46]

In total, fifty-five individuals from Montauban had such 'double' contacts. Was this a kind of syncretism, of 'double religiosity', where lay people did not care about differences between the groups – or were the differences less than inquisitors, polemical sources and scholarship want to make us believe?

Further examination shows us that that was not the case. Rather, with the individuals who had 'double' contacts, a case can be made for a clear distinction between the adherents of both groups. For double contacts only obtained before and until a specific 'liminal rite'. The individual who had passed through this gateway into one of the two groups, never did so with the other. But this is not easy to spot, as the two 'liminal rites' of the *heretici* and the *Valdenses* in Montauban are different. With the latter, it was the participation in the holy supper, with the *heretici* it was the attendance at the sermon. Once this is established, a very clear picture emerges. Although both rites are very frequent in the Montauban 'Paenitenciae' – forty-six participations in

---

[39] *Ketzer* App. I, no. 103.
[40] *Ketzer* App. I, no. 122.
[41] *Ketzer* App. I, no. 16.
[42] *Ketzer* App. I, no. 131.
[43] *Ketzer* App. I, no. 123.
[44] *Ketzer* App. I, no. 132.
[45] *Ketzer* App. I, no. 200.
[46] *Ketzer* App. I, nos. 61, 78, 80, 111, 159, 173, 181.

the Waldensian holy supper, sixty-five in the preaching of the *heretici* – there is virtually no overlap. Only two individuals did both, Raimundus Gastaudz and Naufressa Hospitalaria.[47] Every other combination of contacts with both Waldensians and 'heretics' is much more frequent.

Yet we have to ask ourselves why attending the sermon of the *heretici* was a liminal rite, but not that of the Waldensians? The reason is to be found in the different character of their preaching. The public talk of the Waldensians was directed towards what we might call 'walk-in customers'; the sermon of the *heretici* was a 'private function', taking place in private homes and not attended casually or by chance. This was not the result of greater pressure exerted on the *heretici* by the Catholic Church. Rather, 'heretical' preaching was the preserve of a certain social stratum. Take, for instance, Beneit Ioculator, a man whose second name, meaning 'joker', betrays his humble origin. He often served as a paid messenger and guide to the 'heretics', and also 'adored' them; he certainly had their full confidence that he would not betray them. Still, no attendance at the sermon of the 'heretics' is reported for him.[48] Nor is it for the day labourers P. de Pomareda, Arnaldus Sarralhier and P. Magistris, though they ate together with some female 'heretics'.[49] Not even Guillelma Maurina – the personal maid of a female 'heretic', who had very close contacts with the 'heretics' – reported attending a sermon.[50] The Waldensian supper on the other hand seems to have been less socially exclusive. For example, one of the above-mentioned day labourers, Arnaldus Sarralhier, attended it.[51]

The sermon of the 'heretics' took thus place before a socially selected, invited audience, in a 'closed shop', and attending it was a mark of adherence to the group. The public Waldensian preaching, however, seems to have been pretty well unavoidable, taking place as it did, for example, in the market place at Montauban. Listening to it is, therefore, hardly evidence of close affiliation with the Poor of Lyons. Only participation in the holy supper provides such a marker. Notable here is Peter Sellan's quick appreciation of this: he gave very light penances for listening to Waldensian preaching but very heavy ones for attendance at 'heretical' sermons and Waldensian suppers.[52]

People in Montauban thus chose deep commitment to one or other group through taking the step of one of these two liminal rites. If we look at the two exceptions to this rule, we see that they do not really contradict it. The first is Naufressa Hospitalaria. She had only attended a 'heretical' sermon as a

---

[47] *Ketzer* App. *I*, nos. 159, 173.
[48] *Ketzer* App. *I*, no. 182. See also G. Aymerici (no. 133).
[49] *Ketzer* App. *I*, nos. 155, 179, 220.
[50] *Ketzer* App. *I*, no. 197.
[51] *Ketzer* App. *I*, no. 179. This day labourer, however, became a consul in 1254; see *Ketzer*, p. 535.
[52] *Ketzer* App. *I*, no. 332.

girl. After that, she participated only in the 'caena' of the Waldensians.[53] Her affinity to each group thus seems to have been exclusive to a particular period of her life. The second case is similar but just the other way around: A man called Raimundus Gastaudz had first only contacts with the Waldensians, including attending the holy supper. Afterwards, however, he became an assiduous participant in the predication of the 'heretici', with no further mention of Waldensian rites.[54]

Moving beyond inquisition records, and into the Montauban cartulary, we can inquire into the position of the adherents of both groups in the town's society. The results are very interesting. Among the thirty names of members of the executive council, the 'consuls', recorded between 1221 and 1241, we see that seventeen of them appeared before the inquisitor in 1236 and received a penance in 1241.[55] Ten of the thirty consuls attended the 'heretical' sermon, none the supper of the Waldensians. Thus the political elite of the town contained only adherents of the 'heretics', not of the 'Waldensians', as far as we can tell from our document. Similarly, from the list of 134 citizens of Montauban who took an oath to keep the peace of Lorris (between Raymond VII, count of Toulouse, and Louis IX of France) in 1243, fifty-eight were among the penitents. Here we find twenty-one participants in 'heretic' preaching, and only five in the Waldensian holy supper.[56] Here too, the adherents of the Cathars are significantly bunched among the important men of the town.

Turning to the kinship structure of the adherents of the two religious groups, the evidence is also very clear: there are no divergences in adherence (defined by participating in the liminal rites described above) between parents and children, between siblings, or even between husband and wife.[57] Differentiation may even be found in the field of anthroponomy:[58] only among the adherents of the Waldensians do we find the new apostolic first names so popular in Latin Europe since the end of the twelfth century. This wave reached southern France and the town of Montauban rather late. Names like Bartholomew, Jacolb, Philip, Simon or Thomas are only found once each in the 'Paenitenciae', but always among the Waldensians. T[homas] Caudier, Bartholomaeus de Posaca, Simeon Agulher and Philippus Donadeu were all participants in the 'caena'.[59] For a fifth bearer of an apostolic name, Iacobus Carbonel, the supper is not mentioned. Yet according to our source he often went to the Waldensian 'school' (their building) when he was a youngster, in

---

[53] *Ketzer* App. I, no. 173.
[54] *Ketzer* App. I, no. 159.
[55] In chronological order of their consulates: *Ketzer* App. I, nos. 64, 3, 17, 177, 18, 2, 24, 76a, 223, 16, 161, 170, 175, 248, 50, 34, 104 (see also *Ketzer*, pp. 501–2).
[56] *Ketzer*, pp. 501–2.
[57] See *Ketzer*, pp. 246–8.
[58] On anthroponomy in Montauban see *Ketzer*, pp. 164–71.
[59] *Ketzer* App. I, nos. 27, 29, 35, 198.

order to 'read there with the Waldensians'.[60] The first names of the Montauban adherents of the *heretici*, on the other hand, are quite unremarkable: they are simply old-fashioned.

The result of the analysis of our first source could not be clearer: there were two very clear-cut religious dissident groups in the urban society of Montauban, the *Valdenses* and the *heretici*. There was little fluidity in adherence to these groups, and they were mutually exclusive. The *heretici* group was also closed off from the lower levels of society. This evaluation of the 'Paenitenciae' of Peter Sellan has not relied on interpretation of the narrative parts of the depositions preserved in our document, but on a structural approach which is independent of the existence of clerical stereotyping or even the invention of religious dissidents.

'Heretici' in a notarial document from Baziège (near Toulouse), 1189

The Italian notariate was introduced to Languedoc in the late twelfth century. Toulouse has its first mention of a 'publicus scriptor' in 1186.[61] Only three years later, in February 1189, a public scribe in the 'castrum' (fortified settlement) of Baziège, twenty kilometres to the south-east, wrote a unique document. Religious dissidence is usually absent from the charters of Languedoc, but in this particular piece the scribe explicitly mentioned it. The charter is about an annuity a woman, Ava, is to get from her three sons. They are one nucleus of the extended family that holds lordship over the *castrum* of Baziège. Arnaldus, Guillelmus and Ugo of Baziège guarantee their mother, Ava, certain possessions and revenues in and around Baziège for lifetime use. The charter is part of a remarkable ensemble of twenty-five charters preserved in the Archives nationales de France, Paris, all relating to the Baziège family and their possessions at Baziège, dating between 1175 and 1232. This family archive has not been recognized up to now, as the charters were dispersed over different historical 'layettes' (i.e. shelves in the old archives), which, however, all held documents pertaining to the archives of the counts of Toulouse which were integrated into the royal 'Trésor des chartes' after 1271. Except for the first charter and the last three, all (i.e. twenty-one, dating from 1181 to 1208) are written by one scribe, Andreas. All show his characteristic handwriting, scribe's formula, notary's sign and trademark flawed Latin, the 1189 document included, which makes a strong case for its authenticity.

---

[60] *Ketzer* App. I, no. 24.
[61] See Y. Dossat, 'Unité ou diversité de la pratique notariale dans les pays du droit écrit', *Annales du Midi* 68 (1956), 175–83 (p. 182); more generally on the introduction of the notariate in southern France, see A. Gouron, 'Diffusion des consulats méridionaux et expansion du droit romain aux XIIe et XIIIe siècles', *Bibliothèque de l'École des Chartes* 121 (1963), 26–76.

The last two charters of the family archive, both from 1232, document a convention between Raymond VII, count of Toulouse, and Arnaldus, Ava's last living son. Arnaldus surrenders his dominion over Bazièege and all his allod there to the count. In exchange he receives the *castellum* of Gardouch and other possessions. In Languedoc it was not unusual in land deals to hand over all charters pertaining to the land in question. This is how the charters of the family of the lords of Bazièege entered the count's archives, which would later themselves be integrated into the royal French archive. This might explain why the highly compromising 1189 document is still extant. It was no longer in the hands of those for whom it was potentially very dangerous, the Bazièege family.

Most of the Bazièege charters figure Ava's sons as one of the contracting parties, some (all before 1189), Ava herself. Apart from their very early date, twenty-four of the charters are not very remarkable. What makes the 1189 convention so special is the mention, right in its first sentence, of its occasion: it was made 'when she gave herself to the men whom they call "heretics"':

Sciendum est et manifestum omnibus hominibus presentibus atque futuris sit quod Arnaldus Vadeie et fratres eius Guillelmus et Ugo bonis eorum voluntatibus et absque ulla vi donaverunt et fecerunt donum talem ex quibus honoribus habebant Ave matri eorum tunc quando se tradidit illis hominibus quibus [*recte*: qui] vocantur *heretici*.

[It shall be known and evident to all men present and future that Arnaldus of Bazièege and his brother Guillelmus and Ugo voluntarily and without any coercion made the following gift from the possessions they had to their mother Ava when she gave herself to the men whom they call heretics'][62]

The convention was thus made on the occasion of Ava becoming a heretic! Indeed we find a woman called Ava living as a 'heretic' in Bazièege or nearby places in many inquisition depositions of the thirteenth century from parishioners of Bazièege or of Montgaillard and Renneville. All in all, fourteen witnesses mention her,[63] one of them explicitly as 'Ava of Bazièege, heretic,

---

[62] Paris, Archives nationales de France, J 320, 11. The text of the charter is fully edited in the calendar of *Layettes du Trésor des chartes*, ed. A. Teulet *et al.*, 5 vols. (Paris, 1863), I, 149–50 (charter no. 353), but with some errors (in the sentence quoted above: 'eius fratres' instead of 'fratres eius'; 'tunc' omitted). Until recently, the only scholar to have noticed the document was, at least to my knowledge, F. L. Cheyette, *Ermengard of Narbonne and the World of the Troubadours* (Ithaca NY, 2001), pp. 320–1, with some brief comments. See now M. G. Pegg's chapter in this volume (p. 4).

[63] In chronological order (according to the dates attributed in the depositions to the events reported): MS 609, fols. 43r, 44v, 46v, 53v, 59r, 60r–61r, 60v, and also in a fragment of a manuscript with depositions collected by the inquisitors Jean de Saint-Pierre and Reginald de Chartres in 1256, a.k.a. fragment Bonnet: *Les sources de l'histoire de l'inquisition dans le midi de la France aux XIIIe et XIVe siècles, mémoire suivie du texte authentique et complet*

lady of the castrum of Baziège' ('Avam de Vazega hereticam dominam castri de Vazega').[64] According to these references, dated in the record between c. 1215 and c. 1227, Ava lived in her own house at Baziège, but was also seen in other *castra* of the region. We even have a report of her interment in a wood nearby, around 1226 or 1227.[65] I intend, in a future publication, to provide a full analysis of Ava's life, the full document of the convention between her sons and her, its context within the other Baziège charters, and its general value for the history of female heretics. For the present purpose, we will concentrate on the reference to the *heretici*. It stands in clear contradiction to the deconstructivist claim that 'heretic' was a category of thought imposed upon Languedoc society by extraneous churchmen. Thus Mark G. Pegg writes:

> The *heretici* whom the inquisitors did ask about, and whom they heard about in thousands of testimonies, were the 'good men', the 'good women', and their believers.[66]

And:

> A 'good man' (*bon ome* in Occitan, *bonus homo* in Latin) was a 'heretic' for the inquisition by the middle of the thirteenth century. A good man knew and accepted this about himself by 1250, as did any person who welcomed and sheltered him. This was not the case a century earlier. Apart from 'good man' being a courteous epithet for any man (high or low) between the Garonne and Rhône Rivers, in every village there were one or two very special good men who were the embodiments of courtliness, honour, and holiness. [...] These holy good men did not think they were heretics, and even after 1170 when travelling Cistercian preachers accused them of heresy, they and most villagers dismissed the accusation.[67]

In the case of the 1189 document's use of *heretici*, although the circumscription 'qui vocantur' ('who are called') is added, it would be absurd to speak of an extraneous category forced upon the Languedoc population by churchmen, as the charter was commissioned by and served the purposes of a member of the very group in question, Ava. The scribe of the text was, as we have seen, a public notary who had written many charters for the same family before and would do so after. It also antedates the beginning of the Albigensian crusade (1209) by two decades and that of the Dominican inquisition in the region (1233/34) by about forty-five years. The only palpable

---

de la Chronique de Guillem Pelhisso et d'un fragment d'un régistre de l'inquisition, publié pour la première fois, ed. C. Douais (Paris, 1881), pp. 119–32 (p. 128).

[64] MS 609, fol. 59a.
[65] *Les sources*, ed. Douais, p. 128.
[66] Pegg, 'Albigenses', p. 584.
[67] Pegg, 'Albigenses', p. 590.

action of the Church in Languedoc between 1150 and 1200 had been the very ineffective council of Lombers in the mid-1160s, and the Cistercian mission under Henry of Marcy in 1178/79 to Toulouse and his armed incursion in 1181 to Lavaur.[68] In the 1178/79 mission, a few men were accused of and sanctioned for 'heresy'. It is possible that the terminology was already widespread then. Still it is quite unlikely that its negative meaning was preponderant if the term could be accepted in a document commissioned by a member of the group itself. It would have made no sense at all to use such a term inside a charter whose purpose was just to keep a record of a convention made on the occasion of the entry of one of the contractors into the group in question. It is obvious that there is no other accepted, specific 'indigenous' name for the group (obviously, 'good men/women', a widespread honorific designation, was not such a name). This, however, does not imply that there was no such group. First, a certain reticence in applying names to groups which were self-evident social realities is a distinct feature of Languedoc/Toulouse society, as has been demonstrated.[69] Second, it is important to note that the formula used by the notary to describe Ava's act of self-donation to this group is in close parallel to similar terminology for self-donations to Catholic religious houses in the area. In the region of Toulouse, the new institution of the 'donatus', which emerged in Roman Christianity around 1180 – an adult lay person giving his/her possessions in turn for a life-long annuity taken from these possessions and the warranty to be taken in as a brother/sister at the end of this life – was flourishing.[70] The usual words in this context were 'se et sua reddere' and 'se et sua donare'.[71] Yet in our charter Ava gave herself neither to the Templars (closely associated to this new institution), nor to some other Catholic convent like the nearby abbey of Lézat, but to 'the people who are called *heretici*'. This demonstrates social acceptance of, and trust in, the group's stability. It was not merely a few local holy men and women characterized by exemplary behaviour; it was an institution in society which could

---

[68] See Cheyette, *Ermengarde*, pp. 314–20, and B. M. Kienzle, *Cistercians, Heresy and Crusade in Occitania, 1145–1229: Preaching in the Lord's Vineyard* (York, 2001).

[69] Not using a designation for themselves was a central part of the self-conceptualization of the urban elites of the city of Toulouse, according to J. Rüdiger, *Aristokraten und Poeten: die Grammatik einer Mentalität im tolosanischen Hochmittelalter*, Europa im Mittelalter: Abhandlungen und Beiträge zur historischen Komparatistik 4 (Berlin, 2001), pp. 64–5. Rüdiger writes: 'Das "Patriziat", die "Aristokratie" hatte nicht nur kein Wort für sich, sondern kein Wort zu haben, war ein zentrales Element ihres Vokabulars' (p. 64). See similarly, for Montauban, *Ketzer*, pp. 143–5.

[70] See C. de Miramon, *Les 'donnés' au Moyen Âge* (Paris, 1999), pp. 105–11. On *donates* in the region, see also J. Oberste, 'Donaten zwischen Kloster und Welt: das Donatenwesen der religiösen Ritterorden in Südfrankreich und die Entwicklung der städtischen Frömmigkeitspraxis im 13. Jahrhundert', *Zeitschrift für Historische Forschung* 29 (2002), 1–37 (pp. 3–4).

[71] de Miramon, *Les données*, pp. 106–9, with examples from the abbey of Lézat to the west of Toulouse.

take the place of a Catholic convent, and could be referred to openly at this time in a document which had juridical force.

'Bishops' among the heretics in France according to the Syrian Patriarch Michael the Great, before 1179

Michael the Great (1126–99) was, from 1166 until his death, the patriarch of the Syrian Orthodox (Jacobites), that is to say, of a church of Eastern Christians independent from Roman Catholicism. His official see was in Antioch. He composed a universal chronicle, a 'description of the times' from the Creation up to 1195, written in the Syriac language, focusing on the fate of the Eastern Christians.[72] In the twentieth book, when he is dealing in his narrative with the end of the 1170s, Michael reports that the pope of Rome invited the Latin patriarchs of Antioch and Jerusalem to join him in a council on account of a heresy that had arisen 'there' (that is, in the religious realm of the pope). The Latin patriarch of Antioch sent the bishop of Tarsus, together with two priests, to ask Michael to join him in the journey on this business (evidently the council in question was the third Lateran council).[73] Michael rejected this proposal, but he wrote a long treatise on similar heresies and how they had been refuted by several Church fathers. Unfortunately, this treatise is lost. But in his chronicle Michael gives an account of the information he could glean about the new heresy (I quote from the French translation and add an English one):

> Nous nous informâmes et nous apprîmes que Satan avait fait tomber dans l'hérésie quelques hommes de la race des Francs, qui étaient dans ce pays, et qui brillaient par leur amour des pauvres. Ils disaient qu'il n'est pas possible que le pain et le vin deviennent la chair et le sang de Dieu; qu'il n'y a d'autre vertu que les aumônes et la miséricorde envers les pauvres, la charité et l'union des hommes entre eux. Or, ils s'associèrent nombreux, au point d'être des milliers et des myriades; ils avaient des évèques, et les comtes, seigneurs des pays, s'étaient unis à eux. Ils firent en outre dans

---

[72] *Chronique de Michel le Syrien, patriarche jacobite d'Antioche (1166–1199)*, ed. and trans. J.-D. Chabot (Paris, 1905), 3 vols. The best introduction to and analysis of the work is D. Weltecke, *Die 'Beschreibung der Zeiten' von Mor Michael dem Großen (1126–1199): eine Studie zu ihrem historischen und historiographischen Kontext* (Leuven, 2003). I am indebted to Dorothea Weltecke (University of Constance) for pointing out to me the references to the French heretics in Michael's work, and for discussing their context and the specific meaning of Syriac terms.

[73] 'La même année, pendant que nous étions à Antioche, le pape de Rome envoya des messagers aux patriarches des Francs d'Antioche et de Jérusalem, et les invita à se rendre près de lui, à cause d'une hérésie qui avait surgi là. Le patriarche d'Antioche nous adressa de sa part l'évêque de Tarse et deux prêtres, et nous demanda d'aller avec lui pour cette affaire' (*Chronique*, ed. Chabot, III, 377).

leur association quelque chose de très honteux, car ils mirent leurs femmes en commun. Quand cette impiété fut dévoilée, en vue de la faire cesser, le patriarche de Rome, qu'ils appellent Apostolos, résolut de tenir un synode œcuménique.

[We informed ourselves and we learned that Satan had made fall into heresy some men from the race of the French, who were from that country, and who shone for their love of the poor. They said that it was not possible that the bread and the wine became the flesh and the blood of God; that there was no other virtue than alms and being compassionate towards the poor, love and the union of men among them. And they gathered in high numbers, until they were in their thousands and ten thousands; they had bishops, and the counts, the lords of the lands, had joined them. Also, they did something very shameful in their group, because they shared their women. When this abomination was discovered, in order to stop it the patriarch of Rome, whom they call 'Apostolos', decided to hold an ecumenical synod.][74]

The report by Michael raises many questions, which will be discussed at length elsewhere.[75] For the present purpose we will concentrate on Michael's knowledge about bishops among the heretics worrying the pope in Rome. But first we have to establish that he is really talking about the heretics in Languedoc usually referred to as 'Cathars'. In this context, it is important to note that the words corresponding to 'la race des Francs' in the original Syriac text point specifically to France, not to all the Frankish people (that is to say, all Latin Europeans, from the Oriental point of view).[76] Michael provides us with the additional information that the lords of the land in question were 'counts', which fits the region of Languedoc, where the counts of Toulouse and the viscounts from the Trencavel family were the main rulers. It is also important to note that the word used for 'counts' in the original ('qumisi') is not a Syriac word, but that Michael here is transcribing a Latin word, 'comes', and pluralizing it (Michael did not have Latin).[77] Because it is an original term unknown to him and his readers, he then adds 'the lords of the lands' to explain it. This adds even more strength to this particular information and makes it clear that it is really about a region of France where counts ruled (not

---

[74] Ibid., pp. 377–8.
[75] In a future joint article by Dorothea Weltecke and myself. One of the most important questions is whether Michael was invited to join the Latin patriarch because of his competence in the Bogomils, which seems most likely – he describes them elsewhere in his work (ibid., p. 277, see Weltecke, *Die 'Beschreibung der Zeiten' von Mor Michael*, p. 235).
[76] I thank Dorothea Weltecke for this information.
[77] Information provided by courtesy of Dorothea Weltecke. On Michael's politics of using foreign-language expressions to add credibility to his reports, see a forthcoming contribution by D. Weltecke, in *Locating Religions: Contact, Diversity and Translocality*, ed. R. F. Glei and N. Jaspert (forthcoming).

dukes, and not the king). These counts were said to make common cause with heretics – a description which only fits the County of Toulouse.[78]

The fact that Michael reports rejection of transubstantiation excludes heresies like Waldensians and many others from the list of candidates. If we accept, then, that Michael is really writing about the 'Cathars' of Languedoc, he is providing us with one of the earliest pieces of evidence that they had an episcopal structure. Of course we do not know whether the information is true – for it is clear that Michael did not get it first hand from the 'heretics' themselves, but from their enemies – but still it shows that the heretics in the Languedoc were strongly associated with having bishops even shortly before 1179,[79] when this was first reported much more incidentally by Henry de Marci (to the same third Lateran council).[80] Having bishops was a narrative element about the heretics of the Languedoc that made its way from France to the Levant; this is evidence that an episcopal structure was one of a few traits considered fundamental to the group very early on by its enemies, not some idea that evolved only with and after the Albigensian crusade.[81]

Conclusion

All the evidence analysed in this contribution points towards the existence of structured and self-conscious religious group dissenting from Roman Catholicism in the Languedoc. The charter from Baziège and the Syriac chronicle do this even for very early points in time, 1189 and 1179 (or shortly before). These dates are long before the onset of the Albigensian crusade (1209) or the Dominican inquisition (1233/34), that is to say, long before the events credited by the deconstructivists with the framing of 'heresy' in medieval Languedocian minds as a concept for the (mis-)understanding of an

---

[78] See the 1177 letter of Count Raymond V of Toulouse in which he lamented that the nobles of his land were implicated in heresy, probably implying the Trencavel viscounts (Gervase of Canterbury, *Opera historica*, ed. W. Stubbs (London, 1879), pp. 270–1).

[79] There is very little likelihood of Michael making up this information after Lateran IIII, for he most probably had finished book XX of his chronicle before 1180; see Weltecke, *Die 'Beschreibung der Zeiten' von Mor Michael*, p. 133.

[80] *Patrologia Latina*, ed. J.-P. Migne, 217 vols. (Paris, 1844–64), CCIV, 235–40 (p. 236): 'Interim praevaluerat pestis in terra, quod ibi sibi non solum sacerdotes et pontifices fecerant, sed etiam evangelistas habebant' ('the plague was so strong in the land that the heretics had not only their own priests and bishops, but their own evangelists as well'; translation taken from Moore, *The War on Heresy*, p. 192).

[81] Compare the statement in Moore, *The War on Heresy*, p. 302, relating to memories of witnesses as given in inquisition records: 'There is no mention of "bishops" among them before the crusade and very few after it'; on bishops as an (allegedly) imposed and then self-accepted concept see also Pegg, 'Albigenses', pp. 592–3. Reports on the Cathars from the Rhineland also mentioned 'bishops', but for our present purpose we do not take this into consideration, for the sake of the deconstructivist argument.

indigenous local style of life not connected to any religious dissent. This leads us to suggest an affirmative answer to that sceptical question formulated by R. I. Moore, of whether there was indeed a 'division in the society of the lands between the Rhône and the Garonne that corresponded in the eyes of its inhabitants to the distinction between Catholics and heretics.'[82]

---

[82] Moore, *The War on Heresy*, p. 261.

6

Cathar Links with the Balkans and Byzantium

Bernard Hamilton

'In the days of the good Christian Tsar Peter [927–69], there was a priest [*pop*] called Bogomil [...] who started for the first time to preach heresy in the country of Bulgaria.'[1] So wrote Cosmas the Priest in his *Discourse against the Bogomils*. Pop Bogomil was a moderate dualist, who taught that there was only one creator God, who had two sons, Christ and Lucifer.[2] Lucifer had fashioned the phenomenal world from the elements created by the good God, and had imprisoned angelic souls in material bodies. Christ, God's other son, had come to this earth in the appearance of a man in order to teach the angelic souls how to be reunited with the good God their creator. The early Bogomils described by Cosmas the Priest were unsophisticated: they rejected the Orthodox Church and its material sacraments together with the Old Testament, but they accepted the New Testament as authoritative, claiming that it had been given to them by Christ. The Bogomils called themselves Christians (by implication denying this title to the Orthodox) and adopted an ascetic lifestyle, rejecting sexual intercourse completely, and abstaining from meat and wine. They met frequently and prayed together, continually repeating the Lord's Prayer, and confessed their sins to each other.[3]

The Byzantine authorities labelled the Bogomils Manichaeans, but though they shared a dualist view of Creation with the ancient Manichaeans, there was no direct historical link between the two movements. Obolensky defined them as Neo-Manichaeans, but I prefer the term Christian Dualists because they accepted no authority apart from the New Testament, which they read in the canonical text, but interpreted in a dualist sense.

---

[1] *The Discourse of the Priest Cosmas against the Bogomils*, trans. Y. Stoyanov, in *Christian Dualist Heresies in the Byzantine World, c. 650–c. 1450*, ed. J. Hamilton and B. Hamilton (Manchester, 1998), p. 116.

[2] *Pop* is the Old Slavonic word for priest. It was open to misunderstanding in the West and gave rise in some cases to belief in a 'pope of the heretics' living in the Balkans.

[3] For a full account of Bogomil history and faith see D. Obolensky, *The Bogomils: A Study in Balkan Neo-manichaeism*, 2nd edn (Twickenham, 1972); for a masterly survey of the place of this movement in the history of dualist belief see Y. Stoyanov, *The Other God: Dualist Religions from Antiquity to the Cathar Heresy* (London, 2000).

During the eleventh century Bogomilism spread into the Greek provinces of the Byzantine Empire, a process facilitated by the annexation of the Bulgarian Empire by Basil II (d. 1025). No action was taken against the Bogomils by the imperial authorities until Alexius I arrested Basil the leader of the sect in Constantinople in c. 1100. Basil was examined by the emperor's personal theologian, Euthymius Zigabenus, who wrote the fullest account of Byzantine Bogomilism, which forms Book XXVII of his *Dogmatic Panoply*. All the Byzantine sources affirm that the Bogomils made a distinction between hearers, who listened to Bogomil teachers, and the initiated members of the sect.[4]

Zigabenus describes the initiation rite, which consisted of two parts. Each was preceded by a long period of instruction in the Bogomil faith and in the practice of the ascetic life of the initiates. In the first ceremony, the successful candidates were brought before the assembly of the initiated and were given the right to say the Lord's Prayer. After an interval of further training a second ceremony was held at which the candidate received what the Bogomils described as the true baptism, not, like Orthodox baptism, performed with water, but the baptism with fire and the Holy Spirit of which Christ had spoken.[5] The ritual culminated with the officiating minister holding a copy of the Gospel of St John over the candidate's head, while the initiates of both sexes who were present placed their hands on his shoulders. The Bogomils taught that the souls of initiates would, if they persevered in the faith, return when they died to the realm of the good God.[6] All Byzantine sources agree that initiated Bogomils dressed like Orthodox monks and that when they spoke in public their discourses were entirely Orthodox. The true doctrines of the sect were only revealed to committed adherents who sought initiation.

Although it is not correct to speak of a schism between the papacy and the Orthodox Church of Byzantium in the twelfth century, official relations were very largely restricted to the exchange of embassies charged with the discussion of specific issues. One consequence of this is that the Roman curia showed no awareness of the existence of Bogomilism, but this did not mean that the entire Latin Church was ignorant of the heresy. There was a large Latin community in twelfth-century Constantinople. The great maritime cities of Italy – Venice, Pisa, and Amalfi – all had colonies there, as after 1155 did Genoa. But there were also other western groups living in the

---

[4] Zigabenus, together with the other important Byzantine sources on Bogomilism, is translated in *Christian Dualist Heresies*, ed. Hamilton and Hamilton.

[5] Matthew 3. 11; Acts 1. 5.

[6] Euthymius Zigabenus, *Panoplia dogmatica*, in *Patrologia Graeca*, ed. J.-P. Migne, 162 vols. (Paris, 1857–86), CXXX, 19–1362. The description of the initiation ceremony is in bk XXVII, ch. xvi, 1312; G. Ficker published a variant text of Zigabenus, *Euthymii Zigabeni de haeresi Bogomilorum narratio*, in his *Die Phundagiagiten: ein Beitrag zur Ketzergeschichte des Byzantinischen Mittelalters* (Leipzig, 1908), pp. 89–111.

city, the French, Germans, Scandinavians and English, who had their own churches. Eustathius of Thessalonica estimated the western population of Constantinople on the eve of the Latin massacre of 1182 at 60,000.[7] The context certainly existed in which western people might form links with Bogomils, and there is evidence to suggest that that happened.

An earlier generation of scholars, of whom Sir Steven Runciman was an influential example, argued that the outbreak of heresy in various parts of western Europe in the years c. 980–1056 was explicable largely in terms of Bogomil influence.[8] R. I. Moore has rightly challenged the view that all the incidents reported were cases of dualism. But some of these incidents are specifically described in western sources, particularly by Adhemar of Chabannes, as occasioned by Manichaeans. Those who wish to discount his evidence point out that Adhemar did not attribute dualist belief to those heretics, and argue that he was labelling them Manichaeans because their behaviour corresponded to that described by St Augustine in his *Liber de haeresibus*. In this short work, which is an annotated list of eighty-eight heresies, Augustine gives detailed information about the theology and cosmogony of the Manichaeans, and explains how their asceticism is a corollary of their dualist beliefs.[9] Educated medieval churchmen believed that they were answerable to God for the transmission of the apostolic faith to their flocks, and, indeed, Moore has drawn attention to the way in which they equated heresy with disease.[10] The corollary of this was that such clergy were trained to identify heresy correctly: if they diagnosed a heresy as Manichaean it was because they considered that the characteristics of the dissent which they had described were an index of a belief in a dualist cosmology.

The objection that there is no evidence of Bogomils being present in western Europe in the eleventh century is not a significant one. Even in the Byzantine Empire at that time Bogomils were difficult to detect because they were indistinguishable in appearance from Orthodox monks, and the same would have been true had they travelled to the West. A substantial number of Orthodox monks was present in western Europe in the first half of the eleventh century.[11] Yet if there were contacts between Bogomils and western Europe in the first half of the eleventh century they had no discernible

---

[7] Eustathius of Thessalonika, *The Capture of Thessalonika*, ch. 28, trans. J. R. Melville Jones (Canberra, 1988), p. 35; P. Magdalino, 'The Maritime Neighbourhoods of Constantinople: Commercial and Residential Functions, Sixth to Twelfth Centuries', *Dumbarton Oaks Papers* 54 (2000), 209–26.

[8] S. Runciman, *The Medieval Manichee: A Study of the Christian Dualist Heresy* (Cambridge, 1947); R. I. Moore, *The Origins of European Dissent* (London, 1977), pp. 23–45.

[9] Augustine, *De haeresibus*, xlvi, ed. R. Vander Plaetse and C. Beukers, Corpus Christianorum Series Latina 46, Aurelii Augustini Opera XIII.2 (Turnhout, 1969), pp. 312–20.

[10] R. I. Moore, 'Heresy as a Disease', in *The Concept of Heresy in the Middle Ages (11th to 13th C.)*, ed. W. Lourdeaux and D. Verhelst (Louvain, 1976), pp. 1–11.

[11] B. Hamilton and P. A. McNulty, '*Orientale lumen et magistra latinitas*: Greek Influences

long-term effect.¹² New links with Byzantine Bogomilism were formed in the West during the twelfth century.

In 1143 Eberwin, abbot of the Praemonstratensian house of Steinfeld in the Rhineland, reported the presence in the neighbourhood of Cologne of a group of heretics, led by a bishop and his companion, who claimed when interrogated that 'This heresy has remained hidden from the time of the martyrs until the present day, and it has survived in Greece and in certain other lands' ('hanc haeresim usque ad haec tempora occultatam fuisse, a temporibus martyrum, et permansisse in Grecia et quibusdam aliis terris'). They claimed to be members of the True Church, and were divided into hearers (*auditores*) and the elect, who had received baptism in the Holy Spirit by the laying-on of hands. The elect emphasized that, unlike Catholic clergy, they owned no property, and that they spent their days and nights in fasting and prayer. They did not celebrate the Eucharist, but consecrated their daily food by reciting the Lord's Prayer over it. They condemned marriage, although they would not tell Eberwin their reasons for this. Finally, they abstained from what Eberwin describes as 'the food of coition', by which he means all animal products, including milk. There is no doubt that these dissenters were Bogomils, since not only did they claim links with the Byzantine world, but also their teachings and way of life were identical with those ascribed to the Bogomils in Byzantine sources. It is therefore worthy of note that there is no suggestion in Eberwin's narrative that the leaders of this group were not from the West.

Eberwin's account of this group, and of another group of dissidents in the Cologne area he had examined, is contained in a letter of appeal which he sent to St Bernard of Clairvaux.¹³ R. I. Moore has explained the reason for this appeal very convincingly in terms of ecclesiastical politics, and he considers that this invalidates all of Eberwin's evidence. That part of his argument is not convincing. Although it is clear that Eberwin was magnifying his role and that of his order in the defence of the Catholic faith, there is no reason to suppose that he ingeniously invented the heresies with which he claimed to have wrestled. This would be like saying that because we now have a clear understanding of the political dynamics of the Profumo affair, none of the men involved slept with Christine Keeler and Mandy Rice Davies.

For the same reasons, I disagree with Moore's interpretation of the evidence relating to the Albigensians. His *War on Heresy* is a lucid and

---

on Western Monasticism (900–1100)', in *Le millénaire du Mont Athos, 963–1963: études et mélanges*, 2 vols. (Chevetogne, 1963), I, 181–216.

¹² For a defence of the presence of Bogomils in eleventh-century Aquitaine see D. F. Callahan, 'Adhemar of Chabannes and the Bogomils', in *Heresy and the Persecuting Society in the Middle Ages: Essays on the Work of R. I. Moore*, ed. M. Frassetto (Leiden, 2006), pp. 31–41.

¹³ Eberwin of Steinfeld, *Epistola ad S. Bernardum*, in *Patrologia Latina*, ed. J.-P. Migne, 217 vols. (Paris, 1844–64) (henceforth *PL*), CLXXXII, ep. 472, cols. 676–80.

convincing exposition of the secular and ecclesiastical politics which led to action against groups of heretics in southern France and culminated in the Albigensian crusades. This does not prove that there was no organized heretical movement in twelfth- and early thirteenth century Languedoc, although it might indicate that the movement had far fewer adherents and far less influence than its Catholic opponents claimed, and perhaps believed.[14]

Eberwin's intervention at Cologne did not halt the spread of the western Bogomil sect in the Rhine valley and Flanders. Eckbert of Schönau, while a canon at Bonn, had met and talked with members of this group, and at some time before 1167 he wrote a series of thirteen sermons against the 'Cathars'.[15] He was the first writer to use this name, and says that these dissenters were called 'Cathars' in Germany, 'Piphles' in Flanders and 'Texerant' [weavers] in France. Cathars is a Greek word, κάθαροι, meaning 'the pure', and if the heretics of the Rhineland used it to describe themselves it would be further evidence of their Byzantine origins. Some scholars, such as Patschovsky, have argued that the Germans gave the sectarians this name because they believed that they were Satanists, who worshipped the Devil in the form of a cat, but there is no evidence to support that opinion.[16] Eckbert was convinced by what he learned of this sect that they were some form of Manichaeans. They believed that Satan had made the bodies of human beings and animals and that they were therefore evil, and for that reason they abstained from eating meat. They held a docetic Christology, and rejected the Catholic Church and its material sacraments, and they had their own initiation rite, baptism in the Holy Spirit by the laying-on of hands. Eckbert consulted St Augustine's *De haeresibus*, but did not suppose that the heretics could be Cathars, who were defined in this way by the saint in Heresy 38: 'Cathars, who proudly and repulsively call themselves by that name on account of their purity, do not admit second marriages and deny [the need for] penitence. They are followers of the heretic Novatus and so are called Novatians.'[17] Eckbert thought that their name must indicate that they belonged to a branch of the Manichaeans called Catharistae by Augustine. This was an obscure sect: Augustine is the only source to mention them, and he does so only in the *De haeresibus*. As he describes them, they appear to have been avatars of Aleister Crowley and to have mixed semen with the grain from which their bread was prepared.[18] R. I. Moore has argued that Eckbert called the heretics of the Rhineland Cathars

---

[14] R. I. Moore, *The War on Heresy: Faith and Power in Medieval Europe* (Cambridge MA, 2012).
[15] This text can be dated to before 1167 because it was dedicated to Archbishop Rainald of Dassel, who died in that year: Eckbert of Schönau, *Sermones tredecim contra Catharos*, in PL 195, 11–102.
[16] A. Patschovsky, 'Der Ketzer als Teufelsdiener', in, *Papsttum, Kirche und Recht im Mittelalter*, ed. H. Mordek (Tübingen, 1991), pp. 117–34.
[17] Augustine, *De haeresibus*, xxxviii, pp. 306–7.
[18] Ibid., p. 208.

because he identified them with the Catharistae, and that the name Cathar originates with him. But if that is so, it is difficult to see why: why would Eckbert call his sermons *Contra Catharos* and not *Contra Catharistas*? The actual title implies that he was using the name already given to the sect in Germany, one which he considered misleading for theological reasons. It is also difficult to see how German public opinion could have fixed on this name unless the sectaries had first used it of themselves, in which case it would be further evidence of their Byzantine origins.

In the long term the name Cathar has won out over all others to describe these dissidents. In that regard it is like the name Protestant: some of the leading reformers of the sixteenth century were indignant at being called Protestants, but that name has subsequently come to be accepted by all the Churches which became independent of Rome at that time. In this article I have used the word Cathar to designate all those dissenters who used a common form of public worship and of Christian initiation, shared a common form of organization and, with some variation, held dualist Christian beliefs.

In twelfth-century Italy these dissidents were known as Patarenes. This term had first been used in eleventh-century Milan to describe a group of militant supporters of the reforms advocated by Pope Alexander II (1061–73), notably the suppression of simony and the enforcement of clerical celibacy. The name, according to Arnulf, the historian of the church of Milan, was given them by their opponents, the supporters of the imperialist Archbishop Guido, and meant 'ragpicker', or, in English idiom, 'ragamuffin'. This was polemic, since the Patarenes included clergy and noblemen. The movement spread to other Lombard cities and had full papal support, and in 1095 Urban II licensed the cult of two of its first leaders, Arialdus and Erlembald, who had been killed in fighting with their opponents.[19] The name Patarene was not used at all in the first seventy years of the twelfth century, but from *c.* 1170 it began to be applied to the Italian Cathars.

An early, perhaps the first, instance of the use of this word to mean a heretic is that of the Pisan theologian, Hugh Eteriano, in his tract *Contra Patarenos*.[20] Hugh had been trained in the schools of Paris and during most of his life remained a layman. In the early 1160s he went to Constantinople in search of Greek patristic texts and became an adviser to the Emperor Manuel I (1143–80) on western Church affairs. He made a decisive contribution at the synod convoked by Manuel in 1166 to consider the teaching of Demetrius of Lampe about the relation between the humanity of Christ and God the Father. His intervention undoubtedly established his reputation as a theologian among the Byzantine ruling class, and it was almost certainly after

---

[19] H. E. J. Cowdrey, 'The Papacy, the Patarenes and the Church of Milan', *Transactions of the Royal Historical Society* 5th s. 18 (1968), 23–48.

[20] Hugh Eteriano, *Contra Patarenos*, ed. and trans. J. Hamilton, with a description of the manuscripts by S. Hamilton and an historical introduction by B. Hamilton (Leiden, 2004).

1166 that he was approached by 'certain men of rank and influence' to advise about whether 'the wicked sect of the Patarenes' should be rooted out.[21] The treatise which he composed in response to this request may therefore be dated between 1166 and 1180, the year of Manuel's death.

Hugh collected information about the sect and learned that they preached in secret and not publicly. They taught that sinful clergy could not perform valid sacraments; they rejected Catholic teaching on Eucharistic sacrifice and were opposed to marriage. He was led to suspect, but was not certain, that they rejected the authority of the Old Testament. They refused to swear oaths, and would not pay reverence to religious images, and they rejected the cult of the Holy Cross. While not directly attributing dualist views to them, Hugh considered that their beliefs and behaviour were reminiscent of those of the Manichaeans: 'And perhaps a Patarene would say, as a Manichaean would, that reverence is not shown to an ass because Christ rode on an ass, so therefore honour should not be paid to the cross because the same Christ was nailed to the cross' ('Ac forsitan Patherenus dicit ut Manicheus si asine non exhibetur reverentia, eo quod Christus super asinam sederit, neque dandus cruci honor ex eo quod idem Christus in ea confixus fuerit').[22] He recommended that his patrons should 'try to persuade the most intelligent Emperor Manuel [...] to order a black *theta* to be placed on the foreheads of the men of this most damnable sect'.[23] *Theta* is the first letter of the Greek word *thanatos*, meaning death, and would be a public sign that their teaching was not from God, but would lead to damnation.

The Patarenes about whom Hugh was writing must have been members of the western community in Constantinople. Had they been Byzantine Greeks or Slavs, the Byzantine noblemen who commissioned Hugh's work would not have approached a western theologian, but would have referred the matter to the Orthodox Patriarch. But the Latins of Constantinople had no bishop and were subject to the ecclesiastical authorities of their communities of origin. Such an environment was friendly to the growth of dissenting movements. The Patarenes described by Eteriano shared many of the characteristics of Byzantine Bogomils, except in their refusal to take oaths, which was not a tenet of any of the Byzantine dualist groups. Oath-taking, apparently prohibited by Christ,[24] was a problem particularly for western dissidents, because in medieval western European society the oath occupied a central place in the social and legal systems. Hugh evidently considered that the Patarenes were dualists, but he could only obtain limited information about their teachings. The Byzantine nobles who had identified them as dissidents did not identify them as Bogomils, perhaps because they did not look

---

[21] Ibid., p. 155.
[22] Ibid., p. 173.
[23] Ibid., p. 192.
[24] Matthew 5. 33–7.

like Bogomils, who normally dressed like Orthodox monks. Hugh makes no comment about the use of distinctive dress by the Patarenes, who presumably looked like western laymen.

He does not explain whether he had labelled these dissidents Patarenes himself, or whether it was a name which the Byzantines had given them. Dujčev suggested that the name was given by the Byzantines to Bogomils because they kept repeating the Lord's Prayer in Greek, the opening words of which are *Pater emon*.[25] No Byzantine source uses this name for Bogomils, but it may have been used by the Byzantines to describe Latins in Constantinople who were Bogomil converts. If so, this would explain why members of this group who proselytized in Italy were known as Patarenes. This was the name they had been given in Constantinople, but it sounded exactly like the eleventh-century term *Patarini*, so that no distinction was made in Italy between the two names, although they represented two completely different movements.

Hugh's tract is evidence that some members of the western community in Constantinople had been converted to Bogomilism by the 1160s. They formed a crucial link in the transmission of Byzantine dualism to Italy, and, of course, were not distinguished by speech or dress from other Italians who had spent time in Constantinople.[26]

The first recorded instance of the presence of Patarenes in Italy dates from Low Sunday 1173, when Florence was placed under an interdict because of Patarene activity.[27] Then towards the end of the reign of Archbishop Galdinus of Milan (1166–76): 'The heresy of the Cathars began to break out in the city. It had grown to such a point that many people publicly preached that heresy.'[28] The names Cathar and Patarene had become interchangeable in north and central Italy, and Canon 27 of the third Lateran council (1179) legislates about the heretics 'whom some call Cathars, others Patrines, others Publicani, and others call them by other names' ('quos alii Catharos, alii Patrinos, alii Publicanos, alii aliis nominibus vocant').[29]

The evidence about the spread of Catharism and its links with the Byzantine world in the twelfth century is fragmentary. The early Cathars do not seem to have been very interested in their own history, while the Catholic authorities were primarily concerned to identify the doctrinal errors of the dissidents rather than their historical origins. The attitude of the Cathars to their past changed when a schism occurred in the movement, which is best

---

[25] I. Dujčev, 'Compte-rendu', *Byzantino-Slavica* 19 (1958), 318–19.
[26] Just as the Cathar bishop and his companion at Cologne in 1143 had not been described as alien in speech or dress.
[27] *Annales Florentini*, ed. G. H. Pertz, Monumenta Germaniae Historica, Scriptores 19 (Hanover, 1860), p. 224.
[28] *Vita S. Galdini*, ed. G. Henschenius, in *Acta sanctorum quotquot toto orbe coluntur vel a Catholicis scriptoribus celebrantur* […], vol. 11: *Aprilis, pt. II* (Paris, 1865), ch. 9, col. 592.
[29] *Decrees of the Ecumenical Councils*, ed. N. Tanner, 2 vols. (London, 1990), I, 224.

recorded in the Italian sources. Three of these are of particular importance: the anonymous *De heresi Catharorum in Lombardia*, written in the early thirteenth century and before 1215; the *Tractatus de hereticis* written by the Dominican Anselm of Alessandria between 1260 and 1270, to which he later added a few notes; and the *Summa de Catharis et Pauperibus de Lugduno* by Rainier Sacconi, written c. 1250.[30]

Rainier Sacconi had been a member of the Cathar hierarchy, possibly a deacon, for seventeen years when, in 1235, he was converted to Catholicism and joined the Dominican order. He gives a clear exposition of the way in which the Cathar hierarchy was organized. A Cathar bishop was appointed in each region where the movement attracted sufficient followers, and he was assisted by two coadjutors known as his Elder and Younger sons. When he died, his Elder Son succeeded him, his Younger Son became his Elder Son, and a new Younger Son was chosen by the fully initiated members of that Church (the term which Cathars used to describe a diocese). The bishop was assisted by Cathar deacons, who, in his absence and that of his Sons, could perform most of his functions. The initiated members of the Cathar Church who held no office were called simply Christian men and women.[31] All those who wrote about the Italian Cathars used the word *Ordo* (a technical term, analogous to the Catholic concept of Apostolic succession), to describe the succession and tradition of the Cathar sacrament of initiation. The Cathars believed that their rite of spiritual baptism could be traced to Christ and his apostles.

The Cathar rite of initiation was baptism in the Holy Spirit by the laying-on of hands and was known as the *consolamentum*. This act freed the souls of the recipients from the power of evil and guaranteed that, if they persevered in the faith, they would return to the realm of the good God when they died. The normal minister of the sacrament was the bishop or one of his Sons, or a deacon deputizing for him, but in cases of emergency the *consolamentum* might be administered by any initiated Cathar of either sex, and in this it resembled the Catholic sacrament of baptism. Yet, as Sacconi explained, the validity of the Cathar sacrament depended on the worthiness of the minister. If a Cathar minister committed a mortal sin, and the most readily identifiable of these was fornication, then all the sacraments which he had conferred were by that act invalidated. The consequences of this were serious for the whole community, particularly if a bishop were found guilty of such a sin. This belief made the Cathar Churches specially vulnerable to schisms.[32]

---

[30] A. Dondaine, 'La hiérarchie cathare en Italie: I – Le *De heresi Catharorum in Lombardia*', *Archivum Fratrum Praedicatorum* 19 (1949), 280–312; A. Dondaine, 'La hiérarchie cathare en Italie: II – Le *Tractatus de hereticis* d'Anselme d'Alessandrie, OP', *Archivum Fratrum Praedicatorum* 20 (1950), 234–324; Rainier Sacconi, *Summa de Catharis et Pauperibus de Lugduno*, ed. F. Šanjek, *Archivum Fratrum Praedicatorum* 44 (1974), 31–60.

[31] Sacconi, *Summa*, pp. 47–9.

[32] Sacconi, *Summa*, p. 49.

Both the *De heresi* and Anselm of Alessandria's *Tractatus* are in broad agreement that the first Cathar bishop, with charge of Lombardy, Tuscany and the Marches, was named Mark and that he had been initiated in the *Ordo* of Bulgaria. The *De heresi* relates that subsequently 'a certain man called papa Nicheta from the region of Constantinople' ('quidam, papas nicheta nomine, de Constantinopolitanis partibus') came to Lombardy and criticized the *Ordo* of Bulgaria, and that consequently Mark and all his followers were reconsoled in the *ordinem drugonthie*.[33] As his name shows, Nicetas was a Byzantine Greek. He used the title *papa/pop* as all leaders of the movement had done since the time of Pop Bogomil. Pop Bogomil was the founder of the Bulgarian *Ordo*, but Nicetas represented a new *Ordo*, that of Drugunthia.[34] Dujčev has argued convincingly that this is an attempt to Latinize the name Dragvista, a region to the south of Philippopolis, a city which was a centre of Paulicianism in the twelfth century.[35] The Paulicians were absolute dualists who believed in the existence of two co-equal gods, one good and the other evil, and unlike the Bogomils they did not have an ascetic lifestyle.[36] It would appear that a group of Bogomils in twelfth-century Dragvista had come under Paulician influence and adopted an absolute dualist theology while preserving an ascetic lifestyle in the Bogomil tradition.[37] The Bogomil Church of Drugunthia was in schism with the older Bogomil Church of Bulgaria. It not only held a different theology, it also claimed to be the source of a different *Ordo*, and condemned the Bulgarian *Ordo* as invalid.

The *De heresi* does not date Nicetas's mission, and nor does Anselm of Alessandria. But Anselm later added a note to his text reporting that Bishop Mark first brought heresy to Lombardy in about 1174.[38] He does not cite any authority for this precise date, but if it is approximately accurate, then Nicetas's visit must have taken place later.

Moore has pointed out that the sources do not say that Nicetas visited Languedoc, but this is asserted in the Saint-Félix document.[39] This document is known only in the printed text published in 1660 by Guillaume Besse in his History of Narbonne. Besse claimed that this was a copy of a document

---

[33] Dondaine, 'La hiérarchie cathare en Italie: I', p. 306; Dondaine, 'La hiérarchie cathare en Italie: II', pp. 307–8.

[34] D. Obolensky, 'Papa Nicetas: A Byzantine Dualist in the Land of the Cathars', *Harvard Ukrainian Studies* 7 (1983), 489–500.

[35] I. Dujčev, 'Dragvista-Dragovitia', *Revue des études byzantines* 22 (1964), 215–21.

[36] Peter of Sicily, *Historia Manichaeorum qui et Pauliciani dicuntur*, ed. C. Astruc et al., *Travaux et mémoires* 4 (1970), 3–67; Anna Comnena, *Alexiad*, ed. B. Lieb (Paris, 1945), bk XIV, viii, pp. 177–82.

[37] B. Hamilton, 'The Origins of the Dualist Church of Drugunthia', *Eastern Churches Review* 6 (1974), 115–24.

[38] Dondaine, 'La hiérarchie cathare en Italie: II', p. 319.

[39] R. I. Moore, 'Nicétas émissaire de Dragovitch, a-t-il traversé les Alpes?', *Annales du Midi* 85 (1973), 85–90.

lent to him by M. Caseneuve, a canon of St Étienne, Toulouse, but the original has never been seen since and some writers have cast doubt on the authenticity of the text, claiming that it was forged by Besse. I have stated elsewhere my reasons for considering the text authentic.[40] In 1999 Monique Zerner convened a conference to consider this text. Among the participants were Jacques Dalarun and four colleagues from the Institut de recherches et d'histoire des textes, none of whom are specialists in the history of heresy and whose judgment is therefore impartial. They concluded their report on the examination of the text printed by Besse: 'The final impression which this record presents [...] is that it is a homogenous document, written at the same time as the events which it describes and that it is the work of a single scribe' ('L'impression finale que l'on retire [...] est celle d'un document homogène, contemporain des évènements relatés et dû à un même redacteur'). I think that this report has vindicated the authenticity of this document, even though some points of detail in the transcription remain controversial. I do not consider it possible that Besse could have forged this source, since he was writing before the study of palaeography had been inaugurated by Dom Jean Mabillon.[41] Monique Zerner remains sceptical, because she has discovered among the Baluze manuscripts in the Bibliothèque nationale two other copies of the Saint-Félix document made by Besse, which she considers are earlier attempts to forge this charter; they appear to me, however, to be different attempts by Besse to transcribe the unfamiliar script and abbreviations of the original.[42]

The document is a vidimation of a charter made by Peter Pollan for the Lord Peter Isarn on Monday 14 August 1232. Peter Isarn was Cathar bishop of Carcassonne, first mentioned in inquisition records in 1223, and according to Dom Vaissète, citing a record from Montpellier which has not survived, was burned for heresy in 1226.[43] Peter Pollan was his Younger Son. Clearly the date of the transcription has been miscopied, since Peter Isarn was dead by

---

[40] G. Besse, *Histoire des ducs, marquis et comtes de Narbonne* (Paris, 1660), pp. 483–6. One of the most rigorous critics was Y. Dossat, 'À propos du concile cathare de Saint-Félix: Les *Milingues*', *Cathares en Languedoc = Cahiers de Fanjeaux* 3 (1968), 201–24; Dossat, 'Remarques sur un prétendu évêque cathare du Val d'Aran en 1167', *Bulletin philologique et historique du Comité des travaux historiques et scientifiques, années 1955–6* (1957), 339–47; I have made a detailed defence of the authenticity of this source: B. Hamilton, 'The Cathar Council of Saint-Félix Reconsidered', *Archivum Fratrum Praedicatorum* 48 (1978), 23–53.

[41] J. Dalarun et al., 'La charte de Niquinta: analyse formelle', in *L'histoire du catharisme en discussion: le 'concile' de Saint-Félix (1167)*, ed. M. Zerner (Nice, 2001), pp. 135–201.

[42] M. Zerner, 'La charte de Niquinta, l'hérésie et l'érudition des années 1650–1660', and 'Copies de la charte de Niquinta de la main de Guillaume Besse', both in *L'histoire du catharisme*, ed. Zerner, pp. 203–48, and pp. 274–8, repectively. There are photographs of the Besse copies between pp. 248–9.

[43] C. Devic and J. Vaissète, *Histoire générale de Languedoc*, ed. A. Molinier, 16 vols. (Toulouse, 1872–1915), VI, 619; E. Griffe, *Le Languedoc cathare au temps de la croisade (1209–1229)* (Paris, 1973), pp. 209–10.

1232, and I have argued that the text was originally dated 1223, an hypothesis supported by the fact that 14 August fell on a Monday in 1223, but not in 1232.[44]

The document which was copied is dated May 1167 and relates to an assembly hosted by the Cathar Church of Toulouse in the castle of Saint-Félix at which Papa Niquinta presided. There are various places in Languedoc called Saint-Félix, but Besse identified it with Saint-Félix-de-Caraman, near Lavaur. This identification is possible, since that was certainly a centre of Catharism in the early thirteenth century.[45] It would strain coincidence to suppose that Niquinta was a different Bogomil leader from Nicetas, who happened to be in western Europe at about the same time.[46] The source records that the assembly was attended by three Cathar bishops: Mark of Lombardy, Robert de Spernone, who was bishop of the Church of France [that is northern France], and Sicard Cellarier, the bishop of Albi. Also present were delegations from the Cathar communities of Toulouse, Carcassonne and the *Ecclesia Aranensis*. It has been suggested that the latter was a wrong transcription of *Ecclesia Agenensis,* for there was certainly a Cathar bishopric at Agen in the early thirteenth century, but this is speculative and it is possible that there once was a bishopric in the Val d'Aran which proved to be ephemeral.[47] Niquinta/Nicetas reconsoled all the Cathars present, reconsecrated the three existing bishops, and consecrated three new bishops: Bernard Raymond for Toulouse, Gerald Mercier for Carcassonne and Raymond de Casalis for the *Ecclesia Aranensis*. Nicetas then spoke of the Bogomil Churches of the East: the *Ecclesia Romana* (that is, the Church of Constantinople, the New Rome, his own see), the Church of Dragometia (another variant of Dragvista/Dragovitsa/Drugunthia, whose *Ordo* he represented), the Church

---

[44] It would appear that Besse had difficulty in reading this date. As Monique Zerner has pointed out, one of the two copies written in his hand, now in the Baluze manuscripts in the Bibliothèque nationale de France, is dated 1223: *L'histoire du catharisme*, ed. Zerner, p. 212; the manuscript (Paris, Bibliothèque nationale de France, Collection Baluze, vol. 275, fols. 38, 39r.) is photographed following p. 248. If the document was worn, the date MCCXXIII might have been misread as MCCXXXII. Hamilton, 'The Cathar Council', pp. 26–8.

[45] During the Albigensian crusade it was said: 'Few men die at Lanta, at Caraman or at Verfeil without being hereticated', cited by E. Griffe, *Le Languedoc cathare de 1190 à 1210* (Paris, 1971), p. 91.

[46] Jacques Dalarun has pointed out that the form Niquinta, written by a not-very-well-educated notary, 's'est fait l'écho phonétique de la forme courante [de Nicétas]' 'reproduces the sound of the word Nicetas as it was pronounced at the time': *L'histoire du catharisme*, ed. Zerner, p. 154.

[47] The Agen hypothesis was accepted, for example, by F. Šanjek, 'Le rassemblement hérétique de Saint-Félix-de-Caraman (1167) et les églises cathares au XIIIe siècle', *Revue d'histoire ecclésiastique* 67 (1972), 786–7; but Denis Muzerelle and his colleagues do not consider this emendation palaeographically plausible: *L'histoire du catharisme*, ed. Zerner, pp. 194–5.

of Melenguia (that is, the Peloponnese), and the Churches of Bulgaria and Dalmatia. All of them had territorial boundaries and he advised the western Cathars to adopt this practice. The rest of the document is concerned with the definition of the boundaries between the Cathar Churches of Toulouse and Carcassonne.

There is no inherent conflict between the Italian sources for Nicetas's mission and the Saint-Félix document. I have discussed elsewhere the possibility that the date of 1167 at the head of that document may have been wrongly transcribed, since the Italian sources suggest a date in the 1170s for Nicetas's visit.[48] What is certain is that it occurred before 1177, since in that year Raymond V of Toulouse complained to the Chapter-General of Cîteaux that the doctrine of two principles, that is absolute dualism, was being preached in his lands, and that, as is known from the Italian sources, was the new doctrine introduced by Nicetas as the teaching of the *Ordo* of Drugunthia.[49]

No southern French source contradicts the account of Cathar organization contained in the Saint-Félix document, and some of them corroborate it. When a legatine commission came to Toulouse in 1178 to investigate heresy, Bernard Raymond, whom Nicetas had consecrated bishop of Toulouse, and his companion Raymond of Barmiac, named as a member of the Church of Toulouse in the Saint-Félix charter, were summoned to appear before it as leaders of the Cathar community. They claimed to be orthodox in faith and no action was taken against them because they had come to the tribunal under safe conduct.[50] In 1181 Henry de Marcy, the new papal legate to Languedoc, organized a successful siege of the castle of Lavaur, where the two men were living. They both recanted and were reconciled to the Catholic Church. Bernard Raymond was appointed canon of Toulouse cathedral and Bernard of Barmiac canon of St Sernin, Toulouse. The chronicler William of Puylaurens, born *c.* 1200, related that Bernard Raymond had still been alive in his very early childhood and was nicknamed 'Bernard the Arian', a popular name for a heretic.[51]

There is also independent evidence about Sicard Cellarier, named in the Saint-Félix document as the first Cathar bishop in Languedoc. William of Puylaurens reports that he lived at Lombers in the reign of the long-lived Catholic bishop William of Albi (1185–1227), while Durand of Huesca, in his *Liber contra Manicheos*, written in 1222–3 while he was still a Waldensian,

---

[48] Hamilton, 'Cathar Council', pp. 28–30.
[49] Gervase of Canterbury, *Chronica*, ed. W. Stubbs, 2 vols., Rolls Series 73 (London, 1879–80), I, 270.
[50] Roger of Howden, *Chronica*, ed. W. Stubbs, 4 vols., Rolls Series 51 (London, 1868–71), II, 150–5.
[51] William of Puylaurens, *Chronica*, ch. 2, ed. with French trans. J. Duvernoy (Paris, 1976), pp. 28–30.

named Sicard Cellarier as the heresiarch of Catharism in Languedoc, that is as the founder of the Cathar Church there.[52] This probably explains why in Languedoc the Cathars were known as Albigensians, since their first bishop had been called bishop of Albi. Durand also named the three important Cathar leaders in his own day as Gaucelm, Bernard de Simorra and Vigouroux de [la] Bacona, who, as is known from inquisition records, held the Cathar sees of Toulouse, Carcassonne and Agen respectively.[53] Peter Isarn had succeeded Bernard de Simorra as bishop of Carcassonne by August 1223, which is probably why he had a copy made of the Saint-Félix document, which set out the boundaries of his diocese. He is mentioned by Raymond Affre in his deposition to the inquisition in November 1243 as 'bishop of the heretics, living at Cabaret in the diocese of Carcassonne some twenty years ago'.[54]

As the copying of the Saint-Félix document shows, the Cathars of Languedoc remained aware of their links with Byzantine dualism fifty years after the visit of Papa Nicetas. The popular conception of Cathar origins in Languedoc at the time of the Albigensian crusade also linked them with the Balkans. William of Tudela, the Catholic author of the first part of *La chanson de la croisade albigeoise*, describes the participants at the colloquy of Carcassonne in 1204 in this way:

> Si que l'avesques d'Osma ne tenc cort aramia
> Et li autre legat, ab cels de Bolgaria,
> Lai dins e Carcassona, on mota gent avia,
> Que'l reis d'Arago y era ab sa gran baronia.
>
> Then the bishop of Osma and the other legates held a colloquy with those of Bulgaria/the Bulgarian group. It was held at Carcassonne and a large number of people were present, including the king of Aragon with his chief barons.[55]

'Cels de Bolgaria', 'those of Bulgaria/the Bulgarian group', reflects the *Ordo* in which Sicard Cellarier had originally been ordained, and which appears to have stayed fixed in the popular memory.

The Cathar Churches of Languedoc remained in the *Ordo* of Drugunthia to which Nicetas had introduced them, and no challenge was made to

---

[52] William, *Chronica*, ch. 4, p. 34; C. Thouzellier, *Une somme anti-cathare: Le Liber contra Manicheos de Durand de Huesca*, Spicilegium Sacrum Lovaniense: études et documents 32 (Louvain, 1964), p. 78.
[53] Thouzellier, *Une somme anti-cathare*, pp. 77–8; E. Griffe, *Le Languedoc cathare au temps de la croisade, 1209–1229* (Paris, 1973), pp. 167–71, 176, 207–9.
[54] Cited by A. Dondaine, 'Les actes du concile albigeois de Saint-Félix-de-Caraman', in *Miscellanea Giovanni Mercati* 5 (Studi e Testi 125) (Vatican City, 1946), p. 347 n. 46.
[55] William of Tudela, *La chanson de la croisade albigeoise*, ed. with modern French trans. E. Martin-Chabot, 3 vols., 2nd edn (Paris, 1960), I, 8, 10.

this settlement until the 1220s, when the Cathar bishop of Sclavonia (i.e. Bosnia and Dalmatia) appointed Bartholomew of Carcassonne as his vicar in Languedoc. He represented the moderate dualist Bulgarian *Ordo* and converted Vigouroux de la Bacona, the Cathar bishop of Agen, to his cause. News of this reached Conrad of Porto, papal legate in Languedoc, who supposed that the bishop of Sclavonia was 'the pope of the heretics', a mirror image of the Catholic pope of Rome, with authority over all the Cathar Churches.[56] There is some evidence that this led to a division among the Cathars of Languedoc during the next few years, but it would seem to have had no long-term consequences.[57] The inquisition records suggest that Guilhabert of Castres, Cathar bishop of Toulouse, restored Vigouroux de la Bacona and his followers to the unity of the Drugunthian *Ordo*.[58]

The Italian Cathars had fresh contacts with the Bogomil Churches soon after Papa Nicetas had left. This is recorded in the *De heresi* and independently in the *Tractatus* of Anselm of Alessandria, which, while differing in detail from the earlier account, broadly substantiates it.[59] After Bishop Mark's death a delegation led by Petracius, whom the *De heresi* describes as 'certain men from overseas' ('quidam de ultramarinis partibus'), came to Lombardy and reported that Bishop Simon of Drugunthia, from whom Papa Nicetas's consecration derived, had been found guilty of fornication. If the report was true, it would have meant that no valid *consolamentum* had been conferred by those in his succession, including Nicetas. The source does not give any further details about Petracius: his name is Italian, but he came from the Byzantine Empire and he may have been a member of the Latin Cathar community in Constantinople. This news proved divisive to the fledgling Cathar community of Lombardy. It led to a disputed election of Mark's successor, and ultimately to multiple schisms in the Lombard Church. One group sent their candidate, Garattus, to Bulgaria to be consecrated in the moderate dualist *Ordo*, while another group chose John the Fair and sent him to 'Dragovitsa' to be consecrated in the *Ordo* of Drugunthia; the Cathars of Mantua and Vicenza, meanwhile, sent candidates to be consecrated by the bishop of Sclavonia. Those who remained true to the tradition of Nicetas and the *Ordo* of Drugunthia were known as the Church of Desenzano, or, more commonly, as the Albanenses – after one of their early bishops. They were

---

[56] *Sacrorum Conciliorum nova et amplissima collectio*, ed. J.-D. Mansi, 31 vols. (Venice, 1759–98), XXII, col. 1204.

[57] See the case of the Cathar believer imprisoned at Narbonne who refused to be consoled by two perfects because 'they were not of the faith of the heretics of Toulouse', cited by R. W. Emery, *Heresy and Inquisition in Narbonne* (New York, 1941), p. 93.

[58] Y. Dossat, 'Un évêque originaire de l'Agenais, Vigouroux de la Bacone', *Bulletin philologique et historique (jusqu' à 1610)*, année 1965 (1968), 623–39; Hamilton, 'Cathar Council', pp. 44–8.

[59] Dondaine, 'La hiérarchie cathare en Italie: I', pp. 306–8; Dondaine, 'La hiérarchie cathare en Italie: II', pp. 309–10.

absolute dualists, and according to Rainier Sacconi the Cathar Churches of Languedoc shared their beliefs. The other Cathar Churches of Lombardy and Tuscany, of which that of Concorrezzo was largest, were moderate dualists, some adhering to the Bulgarian *Ordo,* and others receiving their consecrations from the moderate dualist Church of Sclavonia. Sacconi reports that whereas the Albanenses and the Cathar Churches of Languedoc regarded themselves as the only true representatives of Catharism in the West, the moderate dualist Churches all recognized each other as part of the same Church despite some differences in doctrine.[60]

The *De Heresi,* dating from the early thirteenth century, concludes with a list of Cathar bishops currently holding office in Italy. This begins: 'Bishop Garattus, ordained in Bulgaria, still holds office at Concorezzo, and his Elder Son is Nazarius.'[61] Nazarius maintained contact with the Bulgarian Church. Rainier Sacconi had met him while he was a Cathar minister. Nazarius was then a very old man and had succeeded Garattus as bishop of Concorrezzo, and he asserted that Christ's mother had been an angel, not a woman, a doctrine which he had been taught by the bishop of Bulgaria and his Elder Son 'almost sixty years ago' ('iam fere elapsis annis LX'). As Rainier was writing *c.* 1250, that visit would have taken place *c.* 1190.[62] Anselm of Alessandria reported that Nazarius had brought back a secret book from Bulgaria which he treated as authoritative. This caused division among his followers: his Elder Son, Desiderius, rejected this book, which he considered evil. Anselm later obtained a copy of it and made an additional note to his treatise: 'This is the Secret Book of the Heretics of Concorrezzo, brought from Bulgaria. It is full of errors and written in bad Latin.'[63]

The work survives in two Latin versions: an incomplete manuscript now in Vienna, and a complete text, formerly in the archive of the inquisition at Carcassonne. The colophon to the Carcassonne manuscript reads: 'This is the *Secret* of the heretics of Concorrezzo, brought from Bulgaria by Nazarius their bishop. It is full of errors.' One of the chief weaknesses of the papal inquisition in the Middle Ages was that it had no central organization. Each local inquisitor was personally responsible to the pope, and there was no regular method of exchanging information between the inquisitors in different areas. Thus the presence of this text in the inquisition archive at Carcassonne implies that this work was read by the Cathars of Languedoc as well as by those of Lombardy. The 'Secret Book' claims to be an account of the revelation made by Christ to the apostle St John at the Last Supper about the mysteries of the universe. There is general consensus that this book was written, either in Greek or in Old Slavonic, by the Bogomils, and was not an adaptation by

---

[60] Sacconi, *Summa,* p. 59.
[61] Dondaine, 'La hiérarchie cathare en Italie: I', p. 312.
[62] Sacconi, *Summa,* p. 58.
[63] Dondaine, 'La hiérarchie cathare en Italie: II', pp. 310–12, 319.

them of some older apocryphal work. The text is known only in the Latin translation made from it, and this must have been produced by the western Cathars, almost certainly those of Concorezzo, near Milan.[64]

The Cathars also received from the Bogomils an adaptation of the apocryphal early Christian Greek Gnostic work *The Ascension of Isaiah*. This gives an account of how the prophet Isaiah was taken up to Paradise in the spirit and granted a vision of the cosmology of the universe and its spiritual significance. In the eleventh century a section of this work, chapters 6–11, was adapted to Bogomil beliefs and translated into Old Slavonic.[65] Durand of Huesca, writing *c*. 1222–3, Moneta of Cremona, writing in *c*. 1241, and the author of the late thirteenth-century Cathar work the Occitan Gloss on the Lord's Prayer, all provide evidence that the Cathars read this text in its Bogomil adaptation.[66] It was available to them in a Latin translation, which has only survived in a printed text.[67]

The work which is fundamental to an understanding of the Cathar faith is the Ritual. The same liturgical forms were used by all Cathars irrespective of the *Ordines* to which they belonged, which is evidence that their use pre-dated the divisions in the Cathar and Bogomil Churches resulting from the foundation of the Church of Drugunthia and the mission of Papa Nicetas to the West. The Ritual is first mentioned by Eckbert of Schönau *c*. 1163, describing the rite of initiation used by the Cathars in the Rhine valley: 'The wretched man who is to be baptized, or rather catharized, stands in the middle, and the Archcathar ministers to him, holding in his hand the book appointed for this rite' ('Statuitur in medio infelix ille qui baptizandus sive catharizandus est. Et assistit ei archicatharus, tenens in manu libellum deputatum ad officium hoc').[68] The Cathar Ritual survives in two copies: an incomplete Latin text, written in Italy *c*. 1235–50, and a complete Provençal text written in the end-leaves of a manuscript now at Lyons, containing a copy of the New Testament in Occitan and dating from the second half of

---

[64] *Le livre secret des cathares: Interrogatio Iohannis, apocryphe d'origine bogomile*, ed. with French trans. E. Bozóky (Paris, 1980).

[65] R. H. Charles, *The Ascension of Isaiah, translated from the Ethiopic version, which together with the new Greek fragment, the Latin versions and the Latin translation of the Slavonic, is here published in full* (London, 1900), pp. 93–139; J. Knight, *Disciples of the Beloved One: The Christology, Social Setting and Theological Context of the Ascension of Isaiah* (Sheffield, 1996), pp. 21–8.

[66] Thouzellier, *Une somme anti-cathare*, pp. 256–7, 287–8; Moneta of Cremona, *Adversus Catharos et Valdenses libri quinque*, ed. T. A. Ricchini (Rome, 1743 [repr. Ridgewood NJ, 1964]), bk. II, ix, 4, p. 218; 'Un recueil cathare: le manuscrit A. 6. 10 de la "Collection vaudoise" de Dublin: II – Une glose sur le Pater', ed. T. Venckeleer, *Revue belge de philologie et de l'histoire* 39 (1961), 764.

[67] This text was printed at Venice in 1522 and edited by Antonio de Fantis. I have never seen a copy and know it only in the reproduction of A. Dillmann, *Ascensio Isaiae Aethiopice et Latine cum [...] additis versionum Latinarum reliquiis* (Leipzig, 1877), pp. 70–83.

[68] Eckbert, *Sermones* VIII, ii, in *PL* 195, 51.

the thirteenth century.[69] The differences between the texts are in matters of detail: the overall construction of the liturgies is the same. Although Borst argued that the Latin text had been translated from Provençal, M. Roy Harris has shown that there is no evidence to support this view. Indeed, the use of common forms of worship – the Lord's Prayer and the prologue of St John's Gospel – in Latin in the Provençal text implies that they were already familiar in the Latin form when the vernacular translation was made. It therefore seems likely that the Ritual was originally written in Latin, and that the Provençal translation was made later.[70] The full text of the Ritual consists of four parts: first, a section on common forms of prayer used in communal worship; second, the administration of the *consolamentum*, which is in two parts (part I, in which the candidate is granted the right to say the Lord's Prayer, and part II, in which the candidate is baptized with the Holy Spirit by the laying-on of hands); third, a set of rules of conduct for the initiated; and fourth, a shortened form for administering the *consolamentum* to the dying. The Latin Ritual only contains the two-part office for administering the *consolamentum*, and begins in the middle of the first part, the granting of the right to say the Lord's Prayer.

The shape of the liturgy of the *consolamentum* contained in these Rituals corresponds exactly to the initiation rites of the Bogomils of Constantinople in the early twelfth century described by Euthymius Zigabenus.[71] It is tempting to argue that the Cathar Ritual is a translation of a Bogomil Ritual, which must have existed even though no Greek or Old Slavonic text has survived. A Bosnian manuscript from the mid fifteenth century made for Radoslav the Christian contains an Old Slavonic version of the first section of the Provençal Ritual, and it is possible that this might be a late copy of part of a Bogomil Ritual, but that is speculative.[72] In her edition of the Latin Ritual, Christine Thouzellier sought to prove that the text was derived entirely from western sources, but as Duvernoy has pointed out, she only succeeded in doing so in regard to the Gloss on the Lord's Prayer (the explanation given by the officiating minister to the candidate in the first part of the *consolamentum*). Yet, Duvernoy points out, that was the one part of the rite which could be extemporized by the presiding minister.[73] It seems probable that the first

---

[69] *Le Nouveau Testament traduit au XIIIe siècle en langue provençale, suivi d'un Rituel cathare*, ed. and trans. L. Clédat (Paris, 1887); the Latin text is edited by C. Thouzellier, *Rituel cathare: introduction, texte critique, traduction et notes*, Sources chrétiennes 236 (Paris, 1977).

[70] A. Borst, *Die Katharer* (Stuttgart, 1953), p. 280; M. R. Harris, 'Prologomènes à l'histoire textuelle du Rituel cathare occitan', *Heresis* 6 (1986), 7.

[71] See above p. 32.

[72] Christine Thouzellier has printed the Slav text of the Radoslav manuscript, together with a French translation, in the end-papers of her edition of the Latin Ritual, and discusses the date of that manuscript with full bibliographical references on pp. 63–70.

[73] J. Duvernoy, *Le catharisme*, vol. 1: *La religion des cathares* (Toulouse, 1976), unnumbered pages at the end of the book headed 'Addition au chapître: le baptême'.

Bogomil missions to the West used a Latin translation of their traditional rite of initiation and their other liturgical ceremonies.

Papa Nicetas, in his address to the assembly at Saint-Félix, numbered the *Ecclesia Dalmatiae* among the Bogomil Churches of the East. This is a Byzantine usage: Dalmatia was the name given by them to the theme, or province, on the east coast of the Adriatic, which western writers at that time referred to as Sclavonia. Anselm of Alessandria was told that that Church had been founded by the Bogomil Church of Constantinople.[74] Unlike the other Bogomil Churches named by Nicetas, that of Dalmatia was not situated in an area subject to the ecclesiastical authority of the Orthodox Patriarchate of Constantinople, for the coastal cities of Dalmatia and the inland province of Bosnia formed part of the western Church and were under papal jurisdiction.

Exaggerated reports of the spread of Bogomilism in Bosnia reached Innocent III at the beginning of his reign, and he persuaded King Andrew II of Hungary as overlord to bring pressure to bear on Ban Kulin to conform to Catholicism. Kulin endorsed the Agreement of Belino Polje in 1203, negotiated by a papal legate, by the terms of which the seven priors 'of those who until now have been uniquely privileged to be called Christians in the land of Bosnia' undertook to adopt Catholic practices. They were not directly charged with heresy, but it is clear from the conditions that were imposed on them that the priors were the heads of Bogomil communities.[75] In practice the Agreement was never strictly enforced and the Bogomil Church of Sclavonia continued to exist in the thirteenth and fourteenth centuries, though the number of initiated members may well have been quite small.[76]

Because some of the Cathars rejected the Old Testament, and all of them, apart from the followers of John of Lugio in mid thirteenth century Italy, rejected the historical books of the Old Testament,[77] they lacked an authoritative account of the Creation, even though what had happened then was central to their belief system. In practice this led them to adopt a mythology which underpinned their belief.[78] This was a problem which they had

---

[74] Dondaine, 'La hiérarchie cathare en Italie: II', p. 308.
[75] *Acta Innocentii III*, ed. T. Haluščynskyj, Pontificia Commissio ad redigendum codicem iuris canonici Orientalis, Fontes, 3rd series 2 (Vatican City, 1944), pp. 235–7; English trans. in *Christian Dualist Heresies*, ed. Hamilton and Hamilton, pp. 254–9.
[76] The later history of Bosnian Bogomilism is complex. A minimalist view of the role of Bogomilism is taken by J. V. Fine, *The Bosnian Church: A New Interpretation* (Boulder, 1975). This receives some support from Rainier Sacconi's estimate in *c*. 1250 that the number of initiated members in the Churches of Sclavonia, Philadelphia in Romania, Bulgaria, Drugunthia and the Church of the Greeks of Constantinople was only 500 in total (Sacconi, *Summa*, p. 50).
[77] Sacconi, *Summa*, pp. 51–2, 58.
[78] A. Greco, *Mitologia catara: il favoloso mondo delle origini* (Spoleto, 2000).

inherited from the Bogomils, and they derived much of their mythology from them.[79]

Rainier Sacconi, a former Cathar minister, clearly thought that the Cathar Churches of the West and the Bogomil Churches of the East formed a single communion. He named them as the Churches of the Albanenses, the Concorezzenses, the Bagnolenses, and those of Vicenza, Florence and the valley of Spoleto in Lombardy and Tuscany; the Church of (northern) France, which, when he was writing, had its headquarters in exile in Lombardy; and the southern French Churches of Toulouse, Carcassonne and Albi. To the east of the Adriatic were the Churches of Sclavonia, the Church of the Latins in Constantinople and the Church of the Greeks in Constantinople, the Church of Philadelphia in Romania (that is, in the Byzantine Empire of Nicaea), the Church of Bulgaria and the Church of Drugunthia. Any pope who read that list would have seen it as evidence of a counter-Church, but Sacconi was anxious not to create a false impression. He is the only writer to give any indication of the numbers of Cathar perfects, and he concludes his statistical survey: 'in the whole world there are not as many as four thousand Cathars of both sexes, and the computation given has been made many times among them'.[80]

In 1325, when the last traces of Cathar perfects had virtually disappeared from western Europe, Pope John XXII wrote to Stephen Katromanić of Bosnia that 'a great crowd of heretics from many different regions have gathered together and migrated to Bosnia'.[81] If Pope John was accurately informed, the links between Cathars and Bogomils persisted to the end.

---

[79] Stoyanov, *The Other God*, pp. 260–86.
[80] Sacconi, *Summa*, pp. 49–50.
[81] *Acta Johannis XXII*, ed. A. L. Tautu, Pontificia Commissio ad redigendum codicem iuris canonici Orientalis, Fontes, 3rd series 7.2 (Vatican City, 1952), p. 160, no. 78.

7

Pseudepigraphic and Parabiblical Narratives in Medieval Eastern Christian Dualism, and their Implications for the Study of Catharism

Yuri Stoyanov

Naturally enough, the interrelations between medieval Christian dualist doctrinal traditions, on the one hand, and medieval redactions of early Jewish and Christian pseudepigraphic literature on the other, were not among the main subjects of early scholarly study of medieval European dissent and heresy. But in the nineteenth and twentieth centuries that study was revolutionized by the publication of major primary sources for the history and doctrines of medieval Eastern and Western Christian dualism, which triggered substantial revisions of the assumptions and theses of early modern Protestant and Catholic polemical heresiology. However, the early scholarly exploration and, to some extent, even the modern study of medieval dualist heresy remain affected by the legacy of Catholic–Protestant polemical controversies that began as early as the sixteenth century, concerning the nature and teachings of medieval heretical, dissenting and reformist groups.

In these disputes Protestant scholars frequently understood the Cathars as dissenters reviving the spirit of early Christian communities in the face of the corruption and oppressions of the medieval Church; such scholars saw the Cathars as antecedents of the Waldensians (and hence forerunners of the Reformation), and routinely treated the accounts of their dualist and docetic doctrines as deliberate polemical misrepresentations by their Catholic adversaries.[1] Medieval Catholic polemics and heresiology had habitually located the origins of the Cathars among medieval eastern dualist sectarians: these

---

[1] For early Protestant views on the connections between eastern and western dualist sects and the reformist movement, see, for example, J. Chassanion, *Histoire des albigeois: touchant leur doctrine & religion & de la [...] guerre qui leur a este faite* (Geneva, 1595), pp. 29ff.; J. Perrin, *Histoire des vaudois et des albigeois* (Geneva, 1618), *passim*; J. Léger, *Histoire générale des églises evangeliques des vallées du Piemont ou vaudoises*, 2 vols. (Leiden, 1669), I, 18, 126–31; II, 328; E. Gibbon, *Decline and Fall of the Roman Empire*, ed. J. B. Bury, 7 vols. (London, 1903–13 [1st edn 1778–88]), VI, 111–15, 124–5; J. L. Oeder, *Dissertatio inauguralis prodromum historiae Bogomilorum criticae exhibens* (Göttingen, 1743).

were considered the offspring of the ancient Manichaean heresy, and held to be the vehicle by which that heresy was transmitted to the western heretical communities identified as 'Cathar'.[2] Accordingly, early Protestant scholarship was liable to minimize and de-emphasize the existence, nature or provenance of dualist (routinely defined as 'Manichaean') teachings among the eastern dualist groups, due to their assumed and posited genealogical link (via the Cathars and Waldensians) to the later reformed Churches. Post-Reformation Catholic heresiological authorities like Benoist or Bossuet could reconstruct similar genealogies linking the eastern dualist communities to the Cathars and then to the Huguenots,[3] but in their case with the goal of the exploiting these postulated heretical dualist connections to dent the theological and political credibility of their Protestant opponents.

The progress of the historical-critical and source-based study of medieval western dualist heresy from the mid nineteenth century onwards started to demonstrate that these polemical reconstructions of doctrinal and sectarian genealogies linking medieval dualist communities (eastern or western) and the reformed Churches were untenable. In addition, in the course of the nineteenth century the study of Eastern Christian dualist movements was enhanced by the identification of new relevant primary sources that shed fresh light both on the rise of Paulicianism in early medieval Armenia (with its distinctive religious complexity and tensions) and Byzantium, and the emergence of Bogomilism in the tenth-century newly Christianized Bulgarian realm. The nineteenth-century study of Bogomilism also began to assimilate newly formulated and influential Slavophile or Slavophile-inspired approaches, which eventually influenced Russian and Balkan scholarly and public discourses on the role of heretical currents in the religious history of the Orthodox Slavonic world.[4] Some of these discourses later absorbed

---

[2] For the development of post-Reformation Catholic approaches to eastern–western dualist connections with the reformist movements, see, for example, C. du Cange, *Glossarium ad scriptores mediae et infimae latinitatis*, 10 vols. (Niort, 1893–7 [1st edn 1678; repr. Graz, 1954]), I, 688, 722; VI, 211, 412; C. Baronio, *Annales ecclesiastici*, 12 vols. (Antwerp, 1597–1612), IX, 28–30, 235, 502, 577; X, 24, 740; XI, 57, 59, 195, 215; XII, 659–60, 663, 714–15, 716–18; J. B. Bossuet, *Histoire des variations des églises protestantes*, 2 vols. (Paris, 1688), II, 146–7, 154–5, 201; C. Fleury, *Histoire ecclésiastique*, (Paris, 1858 [1st edn 1722]), III, 223, 225–7, 229, 243–4, 259, 319, 487–8, 645; L. A. Muratori, 'Dissertatio LX, Quaenam haereses saeculis rudibus Italiam divexarint', *Antiquitates Italicae Medii Aevi*, 6 vols. (Milan, 1738–42), V, 79–153.

[3] J. Benoist, *Histoire des albigeois et des vaudois ou barbets*, 2 vols. (Paris, 1691); Bossuet, *Histoire des variations*, II, 121, 144, 155, 162, 200, 244.

[4] Some Slavophile tendencies can be discerned in the pioneering and source-based study of F. Rački, 'Bogomili i Patareni', in F. Rački, *Borba Južnih Slovena za državnu neodvisnost u XI vieku* (Belgrade, 1931), pp. 337–599 (1st edn in *Rad Jugoslavenske Akademije Znanosti i Umjetnosti* 7, 8, 10 (1869–70), respectively pp. 84–179, 121–87. For further elaborations of the Slavophile approach to Bogomilism, see, for example, M. Drinov, 'Iuzhnye slaviane

additionally (sometimes in varied combinations) socio-economic,[5] Marxist and ethnocentric approaches (with the Marxist interpretation becoming dogmatically largely institutionalized in the Eastern Bloc countries and their historiographies in the Cold War era).

A derivative and intermittently influential approach to Bogomilism reconstructs it as a popular Slavonic reaction against the religious and political expansionism of the Byzantine Empire, rendering Bogomil theological dualism as a religious manifestation of alleged Slavonic–Byzantine collisions in the political and ecclesiastical spheres, whether persistent or periodic. Another version of this socio-political interpretation of Bogomilism assumes a more precisely defined ethnocentric character by linking Bogomilism exclusively with one or another Balkan Slavonic group, though retaining the tendency to interpret its dualist theology within the framework of some kind of conflictual dual socio-political model.[6] Similar Armeno-Byzantine models also continue to be employed in the study of medieval Paulicianism and its theology, despite the fact that critical investigation of the sources for Eastern Christian dualist heresies has shown that none of them can be approached and explained on a social, regional or national basis, and that they completely elude simplistic methodologies along these lines.

As a rule none of these Slavophile, socio-economic, socio-political and ethnocentric approaches has been particularly concerned with the traces of earlier pseudepigraphical and parabiblical literature in the doctrinal and narrative traditions of medieval Eastern Christian dualism. Within the fields of religious and Church history the contact–diffusion model has long been the preferred method of reconstructing sectarian historical continuities and genealogies. In the case of the fortunes, migrations and resettlements of the historic Paulician communities in Armenia, Anatolia and the Balkans – and of the Paulician groups that were Catholicized in the early modern period in Bulgaria, the Banat and Transylvania (and the historiographic and theological disputes regarding the roots and evolution of Paulician dualism) – the historical records present some considerable gaps and obscurities, but still

---

i Vizantiia v X veke', in M. Drinov, *Sŭchineniia*, 3 vols. (Sofia, 1911 [1st edn 1875]), I, 371–520; N. P. Blagoev, *Pravni i sotsialni vŭzgledi na bogomilite* (Sofia, 1912).

[5] For early expositions of the socio-economic approach, see, for example, D. Ilijć, 'Srpska demokratija u srednjem veku', *Letopis 'matice' srpske* 163–4 (1890), 17–42; D. Blagoev, *Prinos za istoriiata na sotsializma v Bŭlgariia* (Sofia, 1956 [1st edn 1906]), pp. 38–40; M. Popović, 'Bogomilen und Paterener: ein Beitrag zur Geschichte des Sozialismus', *Die neue Zeit* 24/1 (1905), 348–60; I. Klincharov, *Pop Bogomil i negovoto vreme* (Sofia, 1927).

[6] For some early studies of Bogomilism, displaying various degrees of ethno-centric and ethno-confessional bias, see, for example, B. Petranović, *Bogumili, Crkva bosanska i krstjani* (Zadar, 1867); F. Milobar, 'Ban Kulin i njegovo doba', *Glasnik Zemaljskog Muzeja* 15 (1903), 351–72, 483–525; V. Glušac, 'Srednjevekovna crkva bosanska bila je pravoslavna', *Prilozi za knjizevnosti, jezik, istoriju i folklor* 4 (1924), 1–55; L. Petrović, *Kršćani bosanske crkve* (Sarajevo, 1953; published *post mortem*).

provide important indications of the dynamics of the rise, expansion and suppression of dualist heterodoxy and heresy in the Caucasus, Anatolian and Balkan regions. The study of Bogomil, Bogomil-related and Bogomil-labelled communities, groups and individuals in the medieval Byzantine and Balkan world is equally affected by major historical uncertainties and gaps in the record, but has been lately enriched by the advance of source-oriented research that has transcended and superseded the earlier scholarly predilection for elaborating on medieval heresiological definitions of Bogomilism as a 'Manichaean heresy' or a combination of earlier heresies, whether Manichaeism and Paulicianism, Paulicianism and Messalianism or Manichaeism and Messalianism.[7]

Thus, along with the study of antecedent dualist, heretical and heterodox traditions as possible sources for Paulician and Bogomil dualism, the possibility that both movements could have developed largely independently of such external influence has been also considered and explored.[8] New vistas have opened in the study of Bogomil theological dualism, with arguments that in medieval Balkan and Byzantine heterodox and learned milieux new dualist theologies could have evolved from versions of Byzantine Neo-Platonism[9] or extreme forms of monastic mysticism. Such arguments draw on telling analogies between the terminology and practices in the Byzantine mystical tradition, dualist Paulicianism and Bogomilism. In the case of Bogomilism and the practices and teachings described by medieval polemicists as 'Bogomil-Messalian',[10] these analogies concern asceticism,

---

[7] See, for example, Theophylact Lecapenus, *Epistula*, ed. I. Duichev in 'L'epistola sui Bogomili del patriarca constantinopolitano Teofilatto', in *Mélanges Eugène Tisserant*, 7 vols. (Vatican City, 1964), II, 89–91; Anna Comnena, *Alexiad*, XV.10.3–4, in vol. 3 of Bernard Leib's edition (Paris, 1945), pp. 227ff. For a lucid discussion of the use of heresy designations in Byzantine heresiology, its main patterns and tendencies as well as the still unresolved research questions it poses, see A. Cameron, 'How to Read Heresiology', *Journal of Medieval and Early Modern Studies* 33/3 (2003), 471–92. It has been argued that heresiological labelling in the Comenian era was part of a greater imperial project to categorize the 'other'/'outsider' in the Byzantine *oikoumene* in response to the changing religio-political circumstances of the time: see H. Kusabu, 'Comnenian Orthodoxy and Byzantine Heresiology in the Twelfth Century: A Study of the *Panoplia dogmatica* of Euthymios Zigabenos' (unpublished PhD dissertation, University of Chicago, 2013).

[8] Cf. J. Hamilton and B. Hamilton, 'Historical Introduction', in *Christian Dualist Heresies in the Byzantine World, c. 650–c. 1450*, ed. J. Hamilton and B. Hamilton, assist. ed. Y. Stoyanov (Manchester, 1998), pp. 7–8; Y. Stoyanov, *The Other God: Dualist Religions from Antiquity to the Cathar Heresy* (London, 2000), pp. 125–9.

[9] See, for example, N. Garsoïan, 'Byzantine Heresy: A Reinterpretation', *Dumbarton Oak Papers* 25 (1971), 87–114.

[10] On the development of the equation between Bogomilism and Messalianism, see A. Rigo, 'Messalianismo = Bogomilismo: un equazione dell'eresiologia medievale bizantina', *Orientalia christiana periodica* 56 (1990), 53–82; for a discussion of the 'cases' and accusations of 'Messalianism' in the framework of developments in the Byzantine mystical tradition and its equation with Bogomilism, see J. Gouillard, 'L'hérésie dans l'empire

contemplation and divine vision, and ideas such as man's ability to ascend directly to God. The parallels and the substantial contrasts illustrate the points of convergence and divergence between Byzantine mysticism and Eastern Christian dualist heresies (or between Christian mysticism and dualism in general), yielding some important clues about how the considerable differences and doctrinal borders between the two currents of religiosity could on occasion be obscured or traversed in the quest for 'pneumatic' Christianity.[11]

Likewise, Byzantine alternative demonology, especially in its popular forms in Anatolia and the Balkans (with all their pre-Christian residues), sometimes approximated modes of diabology in Christian dualism. Both its elite and popular variations often attributed to demons powers greater than mainstream Christianity could tolerate, and recent research has highlighted the areas in which Bogomilism evolved and exercised an appeal as a 'particularly well structured and clearly thought out version' of this alternative demonological tradition.[12]

It is thus becoming increasingly evident that the anti-somatic and anti-cosmic aspects of Paulician and Bogomil dualism (and analogous dualist-leaning developments in lay and monastic mysticism) need to be investigated in the wider context of the undercurrents of heresy, heterodoxy and alternative demonology in the Byzantine and Eastern Christian world in general (given the Paulician and Messalian earlier axes of diffusion from north-east Mesopotamia to Syria, Armenia and Asia Minor). At the same time, the growing amount and availability of diverse source material has led

---

byzantin jusqu'au XIIe siècle', *Travaux et mémoires* 1 (1965), 299–324 (pp. 319–23). On the reuse of the old heresy title of the "autoproscoptae" as equivalent to Messalians in fourteenth-century Bulgaria to denote contemporary monastic heterodoxy, see J. Wolsky, 'Autoproscoptae, Bogomils and Messalians in the Fourteenth-Century Bulgaria', *Studia Ceranea* 4 (2014), 233–41.

[11] On the 'narrowing' or 'thinning' of the borders between Christian asceticism/mysticism and dualist heresy, see, for example, D. Obolensky, *The Bogomils: A Study in Balkan Neo-Manichaeism* (Cambridge, 1948), p. 21; Garsoïan, 'Byzantine Heresy', pp. 109–13; M. Angold, *Church and Society in Byzantium under the Comneni, 1081–1261* (Cambridge, 1995), pp. 472–3, 478. For the parallels and differences between the teachings of Symeon the New Theologian and Bogomilism, see H. J. M. Turner, 'St Symeon the New Theologian and Dualist Heresies – Comparisons and Contrasts', *St Vladimir's Theological Quarterly* 32 (1988), 359–66; H. J. M. Turner, *St Symeon the New Theologian and Spiritual Fatherhood* (Leiden, 1990), pp. 66–8. For arguments that trends in Byzantine heresiology could use designations of dualist heresy to categorize monastic groups or vagrant holy men practising deviant forms of mysticism and asceticism as part of their religious non-conformism or popular syncretism, see Kusabu, 'Comnenian Orthodoxy and Byzantine Heresiology', pp. 221–35; H. Kusabu, 'The Byzantine View of the Bogomils: A Heresiological Approach', paper delivered at the 21st International Congress of Byzantine Studies, London, 2006.

[12] R. P. H. Greenfield, *Traditions of Belief in Late Byzantine Demonology* (Amsterdam, 1988), p. 175, with a general discussion of Bogomil demonology on pp. 166–76; see Angold, *Church and Society*, p. 470; Hamilton and Hamilton, 'Historical Introduction', pp. 42–3.

to a greater understanding of the importance of various earlier pseudepigraphic and parabiblical traditions in the formation and elaboration of some of medieval Eastern Christian dualism's principal cosmological, diabological, Christological and eschatological narratives and ideas. Some of the pseudepigraphic affinities of these dualist elements are especially evident in a crucial internal source for Eastern Christian dualism: the Bogomil apocryphon *Interrogatio Iohannis*.[13] This is certainly significant, and, indeed, these affinities received scholarly attention in the early phases of the text's study.

The current state of evidence and research regarding Paulician dualist teachings does not allow as yet an assessment of the role pseudepigraphical literature in Armenia and Byzantium may have played in the formative or later stages of Paulician doctrinal traditions. In the evidence of Bogomil dualism, however, one may detect ideas and narratives variously related, for instance, to parabiblical embellishments of the Genesis Creation and Flood stories, apocryphal and heretical Satanologies and Christologies, and so forth, that cannot be discerned in the teachings of anticlerical, heterodox and heretical groups and movements preceding the emergence of Bogomilism. These ideas and narratives find immediate and close parallels in the pseudepigraphic works that came to be translated and circulated in diverse Slavo-Byzantine contexts and milieux before and during the formation and elaboration of Bogomil dualist theology and its accompanying parabiblical amplifications.

These parallels are clearly a symptom and outcome of the accelerated institutionalization of Slavo-Byzantine Orthodox theology, culture and learning in the newly Christianized Bulgarian kingdom in the late ninth and early tenth centuries, and its subsequent spread in what was to become the

---

[13] The apocryphon is extant only in Latin and divides into two main versions; the first version derives from a manuscript once in the archives of the Inquisition at Carcassonne but subsequently destroyed: it survives in two late manuscripts and one printed text, published for the first time by J. Benoist (*Histoire des albigeois et des vaudois*, I, 283–96). Benoist's text was reprinted in *Fortgesetzte Sammlung von alten und neuen theologischen Sachen* (Leipzig, 1734), pp. 703–13; J. C. Thilo, *Codex apocryphus Novi Testamenti* (Leipzig, 1832), I, 884–96; C. U. Hahn, *Geschichte der Ketzer im Mittelalter*, 3 vols. (Stuttgart, 1845–50), II, 815–20. The second version is represented solely by a manuscript preserved in the National Library of Vienna, dating from the late twelfth/early thirteenth century. The Carcassonne version was published alongside the Vienna version by M. Sokolov, *Slavianskaia kniga Enokha pravednago* (Moscow, 1910), pp. 165–75; also by I. Ivanov, *Bogomilski knigi i legend* (Sofia, 1925), pp. 73–87; R. Reitzenstein, *Die Vorgeschichte der christlichen Taufe* (Leipzig, 1929), pp. 297–311; and in the most recent critical edition of text, *Le livre secret des cathares*, ed. E. Bozóky (Paris, 1980), pp. 41–94. For the other two manuscripts of the Carcassonne version see their description in Bozóky, *Le livre secret*, pp. 19–21; one of these manuscripts, that from the Dôle library, is used as a representative of the Carcassonne version in Bozóky's critical edition. On *Interrogatio Iohannis* as a source for Catharism, see G. Rottenwöhrer, *Der Katharismus: Quellen zum Katharismus, Anmerkungen*, 4 vols. (Bad Honnef, 1982), I.ii, 49–56; G. Rottenwöhrer, *Der Katharismus: Glaube und Theologie der Katharer*, Bd 4 (Bad Honnef, 1993), I, 313–28; III, 239–77.

medieval *Slavia Orthodoxa*.[14] Significantly, during this period the translation of the Scriptures into a language not far remote from the vernacular inevitably aroused tensions characteristic of the multifaceted interrelationships and interdependencies between orthodoxy, literacy and heresy in medieval Christian culture and religiosity.

It is also symptomatic that in the Slavonic indexes of forbidden apocryphal books[15] local priests were sometimes denounced for possessing and disseminating banned texts. This situation almost certainly applies also to the initial phases of the reception of Byzantine canonical and non-canonical literature in Slavonic Orthodox literary circles and schools, and accounts for the wide-ranging translation and diffusion of apocryphal texts in these early stages. The influx of parascriptural narratives, themes and ideas in the newly translated apocryphal works from late antiquity obviously carried the potential for the formulation of new heterodoxies, especially since some of these texts comprised proto-Gnostic, Gnostic-like and dualist-leaning elements (which, in the first place, were among the reasons these texts were censored by the Church in late antiquity and the early Middle Ages). Their early availability in the clerical, monastic and lay learned circles that were forming Slavo-Byzantine literary culture made it possible for heterodoxies to emerge or be embellished by direct borrowings of apocrypha-derived narratives, themes and ideas, combined with idiosyncratic and creative exegesis of the Scriptures, especially the New Testament, which could be preached and spread in the vernacular.

There is growing evidence that this creative appropriation of pseudepigraphical material combined with an allegorical exegesis of the New Testament was, at the very least, a significant element in the formation and

---

[14] There is voluminous literature on this process in Bulgaria following the end of the mission of St Cyril and St Methodius in Moravia: see, for example, F. Dvornik, *Les slaves, Byzance et Rome au IXe siècle* (Paris, 1926), pp. 312–13; D. Obolensky, 'Sts. Cyril and Methodius, Apostles of the Slavs', *St Vladimir's Seminary Quarterly* 7 (1963), 3–13 (pp. 6–7).

[15] For the texts and the history of the Slavonic indexes of forbidden books, see, for example, A. Pypin, 'Dlia obiasneniia stat'i o lozhnykh knigakh', *Letopis' zaniatii Arkheograficheskoi kommisii* 1 (St Petersburg, 1862 for 1861), 1–55; A. Pypin, 'Lozhnye i otrechennye knigi russkoi stariny', *Russkoe slovo* 1.2 (1862), 48–130; A. Gorskii and K. Nevostruev, *Opisanie slavianskikh rukopisei Moskovskoi sinodal'noi biblioteke*, 3 vols. in 6 parts (Moscow, 1867), II.3, pp. 641ff; I. I. Porfir'ev, *Apokrificheskie skazaniia o vetkhozavetnykh litsakh i sobytiiakh* (Kazan, 1872), pp. 142–68; O. Reusch, *Der Index der verbotenen Bücher*, 2 vols. (Bonn, 1883–5); N. S. Tikhonravov, *Pamiatniki otrechennoi russkoi literatury*, 2 vols. (Moscow, 1863), I, 1–11; I. I. Iatsimirskii, *Bibliograficheskii obzor apokrifov v iuzhnoslavianskoi i russkoi pis'mennosti*, vol. 1: *Apokrify vetkhozavetnye* (Petrograd, 1921), pp. 1–75; B. S. Angelov, 'Spisŭkŭt na zabranenite knigi v starobŭlgarskata knizhnina', *Izvestiia na instituta za bŭlgarska literatura* 1 (1952), 107–59; N. A. Kobiak, 'Indeksy "lozhnykh" i "zapreshchennykh" knig i slavianskie apokrificheskie evangeliia', in *Iz istorii kul'tury i obshtestvennoi mysli narodov SSSR* (Moscow, 1984), pp. 19–30.

amplification of Bogomil theological dualism and its parabiblical narrative conflations and embellishments. The interrelations between Slavo-Byzantine pseudepigraphical literature and Bogomilism became the subject of scholarly scrutiny with the study and publication of the so-called Old Church Slavonic pseudepigrapha. Some of these, like *The Book of the Secrets of Enoch* (2 Enoch)[16] and *The Apocalypse of Abraham*,[17] are extant only in Slavonic, whereas others, such as the Slavonic versions of *The Vision of Isaiah*[18] and *The Greek Apocalypse*

---

[16] The first edition of 2 Enoch as a whole was prepared by A. I. Popov (based on a late seventeenth century Russian manuscript of the long recension): A. I. Popov, 'Bibliograficheskie materialy sobrannye A. N. Popovym', *Chteniia v imperatorskom obshchestve istorii i drevnostei Rossiiskikh* 3 (1880), 66–139. Soon afterwards was published for the first time a manuscript of the short recension: S. Novaković, 'Apokrif o Enohu', *Starine* 16 (1884), 67–81. The subsequent discoveries of more manuscripts belonging to both recensions led to a continuous textual debate focused on the problem of which one of the two is closest to the original Slavonic translatio and, occasionally, whether there exists a third, intermediate, version. For a bibliography of the editions, translations and studies of 2 Enoch, see A. Orlov, 'Selected Bibliography on the Transmission of the Jewish Pseudepigrapha in the Slavic Milieux', in A. Orlov, *Selected Studies in the Slavonic Pseudepigrapha* (Leiden, 2009), pp. 203–435 (pp. 222–43). On 2 Enoch and Bogomil doctrinal and narrative traditions, see Y. Stoyanov, 'Apocryphal Themes and Apocalyptic Traditions in Bogomil Dualist Theology and their Implications for the Study of Catharism' (unpublished PhD dissertation, University of London, 2000), pp. 73–90.

[17] Like 2 Enoch and *The Ladder of Jacob*, *The Apocalypse of Abraham* is extant only in Slavonic manuscripts. The Slavonic version of *The Apocalypse of Abraham* has been preserved in a more or less full form in nine Russian manuscripts, the earliest of which dates from the fourteenth century and was published separately by Tikhonravov, *Pamiatniki*, I, 32–53, and by I. Sreznevskii, 'Kniga Otkorivenie Avraama', *Izvestiia imperatorskoi akademii nauk po otdeleniiu russkogo iazyka i slovesnosti* 10 (1861–3), 648–65. Recent critical editions of the apocalypse were published separately by B. Philonenko-Sayar and M. Philonenko, *L'apocalypse d'Abraham: introduction, texte slave, traduction et notes* (Paris, 1981), and by R. Rubinkiewicz, *L'apocalypse d'Abraham en vieux slave: introduction, texte critique, traduction et commentaire* (Lublin, 1987). The recent important textual critical study of the apocalypse includes an English translation of the text: A. Kulik, *Retroverting Slavonic Pseudepigrapha: Toward the Original of the Apocalypse of Abraham* (Atlanta, 2004), pp. 9–37. For a bibliography of the editions, translations and studies of *The Apocalypse of Abraham*, see Orlov, 'Selected Bibliography', pp. 246–56. On *The Apocalypse of Abraham* and Bogomil doctrinal and narrative traditions, see Stoyanov, 'Apocryphal Themes', pp. 99–104.

[18] *The Vision of Isaiah* forms the second section (chs. 6–11) of the *Martyrdom and Ascension of Isaiah*, a pseudepigraphon which weaves together important Jewish and early Christian traditions about Isaiah. The latest critical edition of the text is prepared by L. Perrone and E. Norelli, 'Ascensione di Isaia profeta: versione etiopica', in *Ascensio Isaiae: textus*, ed. P. Bettiolo et al. (Turnhout, 1995), pp. 3–129. The complete text of the pseudepigraphon is extant only in several Ethiopic manuscripts, the earliest of which dates from the fourteenth–fifteenth centuries. Only a fragment of the Greek and Coptic texts has been found as yet, while the extant Latin translations divide into two different textual families. The first Latin translation (Lat1) is preserved in two Latin fragments from the pseudepigraphon, dating from the fifth or sixth centuries, which belong to the textual tradition of the Ethiopic and Greek texts and were first published by A. Mai, *Scriptorum veterum nova collectio e Vaticanis codicibus edita*, vol. 3 (Rome, 1828), pp. 208–39. The second Latin

of Baruch (3 Baruch),[19] preserve early and valuable textual traditions which often are earlier than those represented in the other redactions. The identification and exploration of the various redactional layers and earliest strata of these pseudepigrapha have assumed wider significance and implications in several areas of Jewish and Christian religious history after recent research has indicated their importance for the investigation of early Jewish and Christian apocalypticism, Gnosticism and the development of the Jewish Merkabah ('Divine Chariot') tradition. Since their texts have been edited at various stages of their transmission, and in various cultural and religious milieux, the separation and dating of the original material and the various secondary interpolations has become the most imperative task for research.

translation (Lat2), the so-called *Visio Isaiae*, covering chapters 6–11, was first published by A. de Fantis, *Opera nuper in lucem prodeuntia* (Venice, 1522). Like the Latin *Visio Isaiae*, the Slavonic version of the pseudepigraphon contains only chapters 6–11 of the *Martyrdom and Ascension of Isaiah* and largely belongs to the same textual tradition, which clearly represents a separate recension of the pseudepigraphon. The original Slavonic version of the *Vision of Isaiah* is preserved in six Slavonic manuscripts, the earliest of which is included in the twelfth-century Russian manuscript, the so-called 'Uspenskii sbornik', first published by A. Popov, 'Bibliograficheskie materialy sobrannye A. N. Popovym', *Chteniia v imperatorskom obshchestve istorii i drevnostei Rossiiskikh* 1 (1879), 3–20. For up-to-date commentary and discussion of the family stemma of the manuscripts, along with a new edition of Slavonic text, see A. Giambelluca Kossova, '*Visio Isaiae*: versione paleobulgara', in *Ascensio Isaiae: textus*, ed. Bettiolo *et al.*, pp. 235–319. For a bibliography of the editions, translations and studies of the Slavonic version of the the *Vision of Isaiah*, see Orlov, 'Selected Bibliography', pp. 276–8. The beginner in this field will find an accessible introduction and translation in *The Apocryphal Old Testament*, ed. H. F. D. Sparks (Oxford, 1984), pp. 775–812. On the *Vision of Isaiah* and Bogomil doctrinal and narrative traditions, see Stoyanov, 'Apocryphal Themes', pp. 104–14. On the *Vision of Isaiah* and Catharism in Italy and France, see Rottenwöhrer, *Der Katharismus: Quellen zum Katharismus*, pp. 56–66.

[19] *The Greek Apocalypse of Baruch* (3 Baruch) has been a subject of academic study for more than a century. The text of a Slavonic version of the apocalypse was published (from a fifteenth-century Serbian manuscript) for the first time by S. Novaković, 'Otkrivenjie Varuhovo', *Starine* 18 (1886), 203–9, and an edition of the Greek text by M. R. James, 'The Apocalypse of Baruch', in *Apocrypha Anecdota II* (TS 5/1), ed. J. A. Robinson (Cambridge, 1897), pp. li–lxxi; 83–94. The subsequent discoveries and publications of more manuscripts of 3 Baruch led to a continuous textual debate focused on the problem of the relationship between the Greek and Slavonic versions and the Slavonic textual tradition. The study of 3 Baruch was greatly enhanced by the critical editions of the Greek version of the apocalypse by J.-C. Picard, *Apocalypsis Baruchi Graece* (Leiden, 1967), and its Slavonic version by H. Gaylord, 'The Slavonic Version of 3 Baruch' (unpublished PhD dissertation, Hebrew University of Jerusalem, 1983). These were followed by the major studies of the apocalypse by D. C. Harlow, *The Greek Apocalypse of Baruch (3 Baruch) in Hellenistic Judaism and Early Christianity* (Leiden, 1996), and most recently, A. Kulik, *3 Baruch: Greek-Slavonic Apocalypse of Baruch* (Berlin, 2010), which includes a very valuable new English translation of, and commentary on, the apocalypse, at pp. 89–386. For a bibliography of the editions, translations and studies of 3 Baruch, see Orlov, 'Selected Bibliography', pp. 278–84. On 3 Baruch and Bogomil doctrinal and narrative traditions, see Stoyanov, 'Apocryphal Themes', pp. 90–9.

The principal controversies surrounding the relationship between Bogomilism and the development of pseudepigraphical literature and its principal genres in the Orthodox Slavonic world concern possible Bogomil editorial interventions in the extant versions of the texts. Furthermore, the analogies between Bogomil teachings and apocryphal and popular cosmogonic traditions which circulated in the medieval Orthodox Slavo-Byzantine world has attracted the attention of investigators of both Bogomilism and the pseudepigraphical genre, as well as folklorists, anthropologists and medievalists in general.

Some early, and more recent, studies have assigned the Bogomil movement an important role in the adaptation and transmission of pseudepigraphical literature in the Slavonic Orthodox world, and considered it responsible for various interpolations and changes in the texts.[20] However, these views, especially their more sweeping variants, have been also subjected to criticism in the early phases of research on this problematic;[21] indeed, the major

---

[20] For early views on the links between the spread of Bogomilism and the dissemination of apocryphal literature and Bogomil theology see, for example, F. Rački, *Bogomili i patareni*, pp. 575–89; A. N. Pypin and V. D. Spasovich, *Obzor istorii slavianskikh literature* (St Petersburg, 1865), pp. 64ff.; V. Jagić, *Istoriia serbsko-khorvatskoi literatury*, trans. M. Petrovskii (Kazan, 1871), pp. 95ff., 100–9; A. N. Veselovskii, *Slavianskie skazaniia o Solomone i Kitovrase i zapadnye legendy o Morol'fe i Merline* (St Petersburg, 1872); E. Golubinskii, *Kratkii ocherk pravoslavnykh tserkvei* (Moscow, 1871), p. 165; M. Gaster, *Ilchester Lectures on Greco-Slavonic Literature* (London, 1887), pp. 16–45, 64–74 *passim*, 146–205; M. Popruzhenko, *Sinodik tsaria Borila* (Odessa, 1899), pp. 139 ff; A. Pypin, *Istoriia russkoi literatury*, 4 vols. (St Petersburg, 1907), I, 410ff.; M. Murko, *Geschichte der älteren südslavischen Litteraturen* (Leipzig, 1908), pp. 82ff.; D. Tsukhlev, *Istoriia na bŭlgarskata tsŭrkva* (Sofia, 1910), I, 708–50. For the classical treatment of the theory that the Bogomil scribes edited a number of Old Church Slavonic apocryphal texts see I. Ivanov, *Bogomilski knigi i legendi* (Sofia, 1925); cf. the approach to the problem in Obolensky, *The Bogomils*, pp. 154–5, 226, 228, 272, 281, 282ff.; H.-C. Puech and A. Vaillant, *Le traité contre les bogomiles de Cosmas le prêtre* (Paris, 1945), pp. 130ff.; S. Runciman, *The Medieval Manichee: A Study of the Christian Dualist Heresy* (Cambridge, 1947), pp. 77–8, 84; for more recent statements on the relationship btween Bogomilism and apocryphal literature, generally reinstating Ivanov's position see, for example, D. Angelov, *Bogomilstvoto v Bŭlgaria*, 3rd edn (Sofia, 1980), pp. 63, 66, 208, 212–14, 351–2; I. Begunov, *Kozma prezviter v slavianskikh literaturakh* (Sofia, 1973), pp. 245–8; and the recent revival of Ivanov's thesis by P. Dimitrov, 'Bogomil' and 'Bogomilski skazaniia i legendi', in *Petŭr Chernorizets* (Shumen, 1995), pp. 116–67 and 140–67; D. Dimitrova, 'Tainata kniga na bogomilite v sistemata na starobŭlgarskata literatura', *Preslavska knizhovna shkola* 1 (1995), 59–69.

[21] See, for example, F. I. Buslaev, *Slavianskie skazaniia o Solomone i Kitovrase i zapadnye legendy o Morol'fe i Merline, Sochinenie A. V. Veselovskogo* (St Petersburg, 1873), pp. 12–13; M. Sokolov, *Materialy i zametki po starinnoi slavianskoi literature*, 1. Kompiliatsiia apokrifov bolgarskogo popa Ieremi (Moscow, 1888), pp. 142ff.; K. F. Radchenko, 'Etiudy po bogomilstvo. K voprosu ob otnoshenii apokrifov k bogomil'stvu', in *Izbornik Kievskii* (Kiev, 1904), pp. 29–38; E. Anichkov, 'Manihei i Bogumili. Povodom knige I. Ivanova 'Bogomiliski knigi i legendi', Sofia, 1925', *Glasnik srpskog nauchnog drushtva* (Skopje, 1929), pp. 151–2.

advance of the study of Old and New Testament pseudepigrapha in the wider context of early Jewish and Christian studies since World War II has demonstrated that a number of the posited Bogomil-edited passages in the Slavonic pseudepigrapha actually belong to the earlier strata of the texts, or at least to a stage preceding the Slavonic redaction.[22]

Another set of controversies focuses on the problem whether the term 'Bogomil apocrypha' should be understood in a wide context as including all apocryphal texts, even earlier ones, that were used or adopted by the Bogomil scribes,[23] or in a narrower context including only texts that were actually composed and compiled in Bogomil circles.[24] Further debate surrounds the posited analogies or similarities between Bogomil teachings and certain elements in Slavonic and Greek folklore and Slavonic popular cosmogonies.[25]

Significantly enough, direct or indirect references to Bogomil use of apocryphal works can be discovered in the early sources for the heresy such as Presbyter Cosmas's *Sermon against the Heretics*, where there are references to the 'fables' ('блѫди ихъ плетеныѧ') of the heretics, in general, or a specific heretical 'fable': 'Хощє [...] повѣсть еретическоую повѣдати';[26] another example

---

[22] See É. Turdeanu, 'Apocryphes bogomiles et apocryphes pseudo-bogomiles', *Revue d'histoire des religions* 138 (1950), 22–52, 176–218; M. Loos, *Dualist Heresy in the Middle Ages* (Prague, 1974), pp. 84, 85, 88, 134, 143–4, 340; Dragojlović, *Bogomilstvo na Balkanu i u Maloj Aziji*, pp. 186–95. See also D. Dragojlović and V. Antić, *Bogomilstvoto vo srednovekovnata izvorna graga* (Skopje, 1978), pp. 31–45 (cf., however, V. Antić's different approach in her 'Dualistichkoto knizhevno nasledstvo', in V. Antić, *Niz stranitsite od juzhnoslovenskite knizhevnosti* (Skopje, 1977), pp. 188–253).

[23] Ivanov, *Bogomilski knigi i legendi*, pp. 49–327; cf. Dimitrov, 'Bogomil', pp. 116–40; 'Bogomilski skazaniia i legendi', pp. 140–67; Dimitrova, 'Tainata kniga na bogomilite v sistemata na starobŭlgarskata literatura', pp. 59–69; A. Miltenova, 'Bogomilska knizhnina' and 'Tiveriadskoto more', in *Starobŭlgarska literatura, Entsiklopedichen rechnik*, ed. D. Petkanova et al. (Sofia, 1992), pp. 60–2, 464–5.

[24] Turdeanu, 'Apocryphes bogomiles'; Dragojlović and Antić, *Bogomilstvoto vo srednovekovnata izvorna graga*; cf. N. Minissi, 'La tradizione apocrifa e la origini del bogomilismo', *Ricerche slavistiche* 3 (1954), 97–113.

[25] I. Polakova, 'Materialy o razvitii dualisticheskikh narodnykh skazok u slavian', *Slavia* 3 (1965), 456–68; V. Antić, 'Bogomilskiot dualizm i folklorot', *Sovremennost* 26 (1976), 7–8, 58–84; V. Antić, 'Dualisticheski elementi vo makedonskiot folklor', in *Bogomilstvoto na Balkanot vo svetlinata na najnovite istrazhuvania* (Skopje, 1982), pp. 113–26; V. Antić, 'Narodni umotvoreniia so dualistichka orientatsiia zabelezhani od Marko K. Tsepenkov' and 'Dualisticheski elementi vo folklorot', both in V. Antić, *Niz stranitsite od juzhnoslovenskite knizhevnosti*, pp. 191–200 and 272–306; G. Wild, 'Die Bogomilische häresie in einigen südslavischen Volksliedern', *Die Welt der Slaven* 9.3 (1964), 258–76; D. Petkanova, 'Bogomilstvoto i apokrifnata literatura', *Starobŭlgaristika* 6 (1982), 143–63; D. Petkanova, *Apokrifna literatura i folklore* (Sofia, 1978), pp. 150–210 *passim*; T. Koleva, 'Auffasungen der Bogomilen im Spiegel der bulgarischen Volkskultur', *Jahrbuch für Volkskunde und Kulturgeschichte* 21, n.s. 6 (1978), 70–6.

[26] New edition of the text in I. Begunov, *Kozma prezviter* (for the quotes of Cosmas's references to the heretical 'fables', see pp. 340, 347) Translation into French and comments in Puech and Vaillant, *Le traité contre les bogomiles*; partial translation of the anti-Bogomil

is Euthymius of Peribleptos's *Epistola*, which refers to the Bogomil use of an apocryphal *Revelation of Peter*.[27] References to heretical 'fables' can also be found in Ioan Ekzarkh's *Shestodnev*, in a passage providing evidence of the spread of heretical dualist teachings in tenth-century Bulgaria before the rise of Bogomilism.[28] In some Orthodox polemical traditions, reflected in the Slavonic indexes of forbidden books, the founder of the Bogomil heresy, the priest Bogomil, could be credited with writing apocryphal works and identified with another priest renowned for his heterodox exploits and authorship of apocryphal texts, Jeremiah.[29] The extant evidence suggests that the apocryphal works of Jeremiah, though heterodox and drawing on diverse sources, largely lack dualist tendencies; nonetheless, it is significant that the association between him and the priest Bogomil is maintained in other Orthodox polemical traditions, in which he could appear as a son and disciple of the heresiarch of Bogomilism.[30]

The principal line of divergence in the debate on the exact nature of the interrelations between medieval dualist heresy and pseudepigraphical

---

section of the tract into English in *Heresy and Authory in Medieval Europe*, ed. E. Peters (London, 1980), pp. 108–17; new translation of the anti-Bogomil section in *Christian Dualist Heresies*, ed. Hamilton and Hamilton, pp. 114–34. For Cosmas's references to the heretical 'fables', see the text in Begunov, *Kozma prezviter*, pp. 341–2. On Cosmas's tract as a source for the Bogomil reliance and use of apocryphal traditions, cf. M. Weingart, 'Pocatky bogomilstvi prvniho opravneho i hnuti u Slovanu', *Slovansky prehled* 16.1 (1913), 17; Begunov, *Kozma prezviter*, pp. 245–9; Antić, 'Dualistichkoto knizhevno nasledstvo', pp. 189–90; Dimitrov, 'Bogomilski skazaniia i legendi', pp. 142–3, 145–56.

[27] The *Epistola* is contained in *Patrologia Graeca*, ed. J.-P. Migne, 162 vols. (Paris, 1857–86) (henceforth *PG*), CXXXI, 47–58, but is erroneously attributed to a later theologian, Euthymius Zigabenus. Another edition is to be found in G. Ficker, *Die Phundagiagiten: ein Beitrag zur Ketzergeschichte des byzantinischen Mittelalters* (Leipzig, 1908), pp. 3–86; English translation in *Christian Dualist Heresies*, ed. Hamilton and Hamilton, pp. 142–64.

[28] New edition of the text in R. Aitzetmüller, *Das Hexameron des Exarchen Johannes*, 7 vols. (Graz, 1958–75). On the pasage on the 'Manichaeans' and their 'fables', see Ivanov, *Bogomilski knigi i legendi*, p. 22; M. G. Popruzhenko, *Kozma prezviter bolgarskii pisatel'* X *veka* (Sofia, 1936), p. ccxix; Antić, 'Dualistichkoto knizhevno nasledstvo', p. 188.

[29] See texts in Gorskii and Nevostruev, *Opisanie slavianskikh rukopisei*, p. 641; Pypin, *Istoriia russkoi literatury*, I, 451 n. 2; on the evidence concerning the figure of the priest Jeremiah and his apocryphal works, see A. N. Pypin and V. D. Spasovich, *Obzor istorii slavian-skikh literarur* (St Petersburg, 1865), pp. 72–8; V. Jagić, 'Prilozi k historiji knjzevnosti naroda hravatskoga i srbskoga', *Arkhiv za povjestnicu jugoslovensku* 9 (1869), 92–104; A. Popov, *Pervoe pribavlenie k opisaniiu rukopisei i katalogu knig tserkovnoi pechati biblioteki A. I. Khludova* (Moscow, 1875), pp. 31ff.; Sokolov, *Materialy i zametki*, I, 108–42; Tsukhlev, *Istoriia na bŭlgarskata tsŭrkva*, p. 718ff.; Ivanov, *Bogomilski knigi i legendi*, pp. 50–1; E. Georgiev, 'Prokulnatiiat starobŭlgarski pisatel pop Ieremiia', *Ezik i literatura* 1 (1964), 1–30; B. Angelov, 'Knizhovnoto delo na starobŭlgarskiia pisatel Ieremiia', *Ezik i literatura* 3 (1976), 26–30; Petkanova, *Apokrifna literatura i folklor*, pp. 126–37; P. Dimitrov, 'Prezviter Ieremiia', in Dimitrov, *Petŭr Chernorizets*, pp. 167–90.

[30] See, for example, Iatsimirskii, *Bibliograficheskii obzor*, p. 51; on the sources for and the nature of Jeremiah's apocryphal works, see the references in n. 26 above.

Pseudepigraphic and Parabiblical Narratives in Medieval Eastern Christian Dualism

and parabiblical literature translated, edited or compiled in the medieval Eastern Orthodox world still concerns conflicting approaches to the 'wider' or 'narrower' definition of the term 'Bogomil apocryphon'.[31] Recent revised and updated reformulations of Ivanov's classical thesis of the wider meaning of the term have sought to fortify it with new observations and material, and to reconstruct the complex interrelations between the Bogomil heresy and pseudepigraphical and parabiblical literature in a chronological framework conditioned both by changes in the development of medieval Orthodox Slavonic literature and by hypothesized modifications within Bogomilism itself.[32] According to one of these lines of interpretation, the interrelationship between Bogomilism and pseudepigraphical and parabiblical literature passed through three main stages. First, the appearance of the initial cycle of 'Bogomil apocrypha' (understood in the wider sense), in which texts were adopted (*The Vision of Isaiah*) or composed (*Interrogatio Iohannis*) in Bogomil circles; this stage was facilitated by the wide-ranging translation of canonical and non-canonical works in the formative phases of Slavo-Byzantine culture and occurred between the mid tenth and early eleventh centuries. In the second stage a second cycle of Bogomil apocrypha appeared, including such texts as *The Battle between Archangel Michael and Satanael* and *The Sea of Tiberias*; this occurred during the eleventh–thirteenth centuries. In the new religio-cultural context of this period, the narratives acquired and integrated more popular features, while their theological and cosmological dualism was further mitigated. Finally, the creation of this cycle of Bogomil apocrypha eventually led to the third theorized stage: the emergence of long-lasting popular folk legends and traditions exhibiting variously pronounced dualist features in the sphere of cosmogony, diabology, Christology or biblical history. Approaches which adhere to more minimalist views on the relationship between the development of pseudepigraphical literature and Bogomil or Bogomil-influenced heresy and heterodoxy still could accept that on certain occasions passages in the Slavonic versions of pseudepigraphical works which reflect heterodox or dualist ideas were introduced by medieval Bogomil editors of the texts.[33]

One of the problems still affecting the study of interrelations between Bogomil/Christian dualist traditions and pseudepigraphical and parabiblical literature in the Byzantine Commonwealth is the insufficient focus (usually in

---

[31] See nn. 20 and 21 above.
[32] Dimitrov, 'Bogomil', pp. 116–40; 'Bogomilski skazaniia i legendi', pp. 140–67; Dimitrova, 'Tainata kniga na bogomilite', pp. 59–69; A. Miltenova, 'Bogomilska knizhnina', pp. 60–2; Miltenova, 'Tiveriadskoto more' pp. 464–5.
[33] Turdeanu, 'Apocryphes bogomiles', pp. 213–18; É. Turdeanu, 'La *Vision d'Isaie*: tradition orthodoxe et tradition hérétique', repr. in É. Turdeanu, *Apocryphes slaves et roumains de l'Ancien Testament* (Leiden, 1981), pp. 145–72; R. Rubinkiewicz, *L'apocalypse d'Abraham* (Lublin, 1987), pp. 66–9.

medieval studies) on the historical and theological provenance of the cosmological and apocalyptic material they share. Ongoing research on the earliest versions of these pseudepigrapha, which date from the early Christian era, and the efforts to identify the oldest authentic strata of those preserved only in their medieval versions, have demonstrated that during the initial phases these texts exercised an influence and gained reception in Jewish and/or Christian sectarian or heretical circles. Some of the relevant pseudepigrapha have thus been the subject of continued heretical interest, and certain of their dualist-leaning and proto-Gnostic tendencies were already subject to heterodox interpretations and modifications during their early transmission in sectarian and heretical milieux. Some of these tendencies allowed a more radical dualist interpretation, which was eventually provided by Bogomil scribes in the medieval stage of the texts' circulation, and via these channels such tendencies found their way (modified and adapted or not) into medieval dualist teachings.

The analysis of these different stages, earlier and medieval, of the heretical appropriation of pseudepigraphical material will naturally have significant implications for understanding the character of Christian dualist exegetical approaches to canonical and non-canonical narratives and themes: it will allow scholars to distinguish between those cases in which medieval Christian dualist exegesis offered continuations of classical Gnostic lines of interpretation of biblical accounts and protagonists, and those in which medieval commentary introduced innovative developments and elaborations.

The existence of, and future research on, pseudepigraphical and parabiblical material in medieval Eastern Christian dualist doctrinal and narrative traditions is also of direct significance to another area: the recent and ongoing scholarly efforts to refine and redefine the methodology and terminology used in studying intertextuality and metatextuality in ancient, late antique and medieval pseudepigraphy and apocryphal and parascriptural literature. Starting with reformulations and reassessments of the heuristic usability of the terms 'apocryphon' and 'pseudepigraphon',[34] 'rewritten Bible/Scriptures'[35]

---

[34] See, for example, C. Torrey, *The Apocryphal Literature: A Brief Introduction* (New Haven, 1975).

[35] G. Vermes, *Scripture and Tradition in Judaism: Haggadic Studies* (Leiden, 1961 [2nd edn 1973]); G. W. E. Nickelsburg, 'The Bible Rewritten and Expanded', in *Jewish Writings of the Second Temple Period: Apocrypha, Pseudepigrapha, Qumran Sectarian Writings, Philo, Josephus*, ed. M. E. Stone (Assen, 1984), pp. 89–156; P. S. Alexander 'Retelling the Old Testament', in *It is Written: Scripture Citing Scripture: Essays in Honor of Barnabas Lindars*, ed. D. A. Carson and H. G. M. Williamson (Cambridge, 1988), pp. 99–121; G. Brooke, 'The Rewritten Law, Prophets and Psalms: Issues for Understanding the Text of the Bible', in *The Bible as Book: The Hebrew Bible and the Judaean Desert Discoveries*, ed. E. D. Herbert and E. Tov (London, 2002), pp. 31–40; the contributions in *Reworking the Bible: Apocryphal and Related Texts at Qumran: Proceedings of a Joint Symposium by the Orion Center for the Study of the Dead Sea Scrolls and Associated Literature and the Hebrew University Institute*

and 'parabiblical literature',[36] these efforts have recently culminated in two major interdisciplinary projects that have transformed the study of parascriptural and paratextual ancient and medieval literature (and its modern *nachleben*): *In the Second Degree: Paratextual Literature in Ancient Near Eastern and Ancient Mediterranean Culture and its Reflections in Medieval Literature*, and *Between Text and Text: The Hermeneutics of Intertextuality in Ancient Cultures and their Afterlife in Medieval and Modern Times*.[37] Some of the theoretical and methodological advances arising from these publications and projects have been successfully and usefully applied in the field of Old Slavonic apocryphal literature,[38] where they are of central importance both in classification and in refining the existing models and differentiations between quasi-canonical, non-canonical and anti-canonical apocryphal texts.[39]

In view of these advances in the study of late antique and medieval pseudepigraphical and parascriptural literature and the provenance of the theological and apocalyptic material in the earliest strata of the relevant Old Slavonic pseudepigrapha, the use of the term 'Bogomil apocrypha' in reference to these works, whether in its wider or narrower meaning, seems unjustified, and even potentially misleading, despite the fact that some of

---

for Advanced Studies Research Group on Qumran, ed. E. G. Chazon, D. Dimant and R. A. Clements (Leiden, 2008); the relevant contributions in E. Tov, *Hebrew Bible, Greek Bible, and Qumran: Collected Essays* (Tübingen, 2008). Cf. M. J. Bernstein, '"Rewritten Bible": A Generic Category which has Outlived its Usefulness?', *Textus* 22 (2005), 169–96.

[36] See, for example, H. W. Attridge *et al.*, in consultation with J. C. VanderKam, *Qumran Cave 4.8. Parabiblical Texts, Part 1* (Oxford, 1994); M. Broshi *et al.*, in consultation with J. C. VanderKam, *Qumran Cave 4.14: Parabiblical Texts, Part 2* (Oxford, 1995); D. K. Falk, *The Parabiblical Texts: Strategies for Extending the Scriptures among the Dead Sea Scrolls* (London, 2007); A. Lange, 'The Parabiblical Literature of the Qumran Library and the Canonical History of the Hebrew Bible', in *Emanuel: Studies in Hebrew Bible, Septuagint, and Dead Sea Scrolls in Honour of Emanuel Tov*, ed. S. M. Paul *et al.* (Leiden, 2003), pp. 305–21; on the use of 'paratextual', see, for example, A. Lange, 'Pre-Maccabean Literature from the Qumran Library and the Hebrew Bible', *Dead Sea Discoveries* 13/3 (2006), 277–305.

[37] The former ed. P. Alexander, A. Lange and R. Pillinger (Leiden, 2010); the latter ed. M. Bauks, W. Horowitz and A. Lange (Göttingen, 2013).

[38] A. Miltenova, 'Paratextual Literature in Action: Historical Apocalypses with the Names of Daniel and Isaiah in Byzantine and Old Bulgarian Tradition (11th–13th Centuries)', in *In the Second Degree*, ed. Alexander, Lange and Pillinger, pp. 267–84; A. Miltenova, 'Intertextuality in the Orthodox Slavic Tradition: The Case of Mixed-Content Miscellanies', in *Between Text and Text*, ed. Bauks, Horowitz and Lange, pp. 314–28; see also the relevant contributions on the typology, terminology and genre specifications employed in the field of the study of Old Slavonic apocryphal literature in *Biblia Slavorum Apocryphorum: I – Vetus Testamentum = Fundamenta Europaea* 6–7 (2007); *Biblia Slavorum Apocryphorum: II – Novum Testamentum*, ed. G. Minczew, M. Skowronek, and I. Petrov (Łódź, 2009).

[39] See A. Naumow, *Apokryfy w systemie literatury cerkiewnosłowiańskiej* (Wrocław, 1976), and the more recent treatment of the problematic in A. Miltenova, 'Marginality, Intertextuality, Paratextuality in Medieval Bulgarian Literature', in *Marginality in/of Literature*, ed. R. Kuncheva (Sofia, 2011), pp. 108–33.

their Slavonic textual traditions do betray some traces of Bogomil dualist editing.[40] The application of the term 'Bogomil apocrypha' to apocryphal texts preserved only in their medieval versions (such as *The Dispute of Christ with the Devil* and *The Battle between Archangel Michael and Satanael*), and conjectured to have been compiled in Bogomil circles to render Christian dualist teachings more popular and widely accessible, could be similarly misleading and does not rest on conclusive evidence.[41] Similar caution needs to be exercised in arguments for analogies or interdependencies between Bogomil and apocryphal cosmogonic concepts and scenarios (as well as cosmogonic ideas in Greek and Slavonic folklore).[42] Such arguments have often been advanced without making the necessary distinction between the theological dualism underlying Bogomil cosmogony, and the variants of cosmophysical dualism and binary cosmogonies found in apocryphal and popular traditions (or, for that matter, between dualist Bogomil Satanology and a mere preoccupation with the history and the power of the Devil which is evident in a number of Greek and Slavonic apocryphal and folklore traditions, but without approaching or evolving into a religious dualism proper).[43]

These considerations and methodological caution should also be applied in studying the relationship between medieval Eastern Christian cosmogonic traditions and archaic and Christianized popular earth-diver cosmogonies, particularly in view of the arguments that the latter's medieval Slavonic apocryphal version, *The Sea of Tiberias*, was composed as a Bogomil apocryphon. The early and later forms of these popular earth-diver cosmogonies present a suggestive variety of dualist tendencies, including approximations of dualist diabology, which require careful interdisciplinary and cross-cultural examination. At the same time, as with some of the apocryphal works already mentioned, while the textual traditions of *The Sea of Tiberias* do display traces of Bogomil editorial intervention, it would be misleading to treat or label it as a 'Bogomil apocryphon' on a par with *Interrogatio Iohannis*. This again highlights the distinction to be made between works actually composed in Bogomil circles and those which, along with textually or orally transmitted popular (archaic and Christianized) cosmogonies in the south and east Slavonic worlds, served as a source for Bogomil cosmogonic and diabological traditions.[44]

I have already, in my existing work, provided a detailed investigation of the important ideas in Bogomil diabology, cosmogony, expansions on

---

[40] Stoyanov, 'Apocryphal Themes', pp. 89–91, 99–101, 104–5, 114–16, 231–6.
[41] Ibid., pp. 116–25.
[42] See n. 26 above.
[43] For the distinction between religious/theological dualism and archaic systems of dual symbolic classifications, see U. Bianchi and Y. Stoyanov, in *Encyclopedia of Religion*, ed. L. Jones *et al.*, 15 vols., 2nd edn (Detroit, 2004), IV, 506–14.
[44] Stoyanov, 'Apocryphal Themes', pp. 158–90.

biblical history, Christology and apocalypticism which were adopted from earlier pseudepigraphical and parabiblical works and often subjected to dualist reinterpretation.[45] A few suggestive examples will be put forward here to highlight and illustrate the parameters and extent of this Bogomil dependence on earlier parascriptural literature. It should be noted first that, being at the core of Bogomil theological dualism, Bogomil diabology preserved its main tenets throughout the history of the heresy, whereas other Bogomil doctrinal traditions (such as cosmogonic ideas and narratives) were not a stable fixed system that was developed in the early stages of the heresy and remained unaltered afterwards. Indeed the extant evidence suggests that Bogomil cosmogonic systems were always fluid and heterogeneous, initially formulated to reinforce and supply appropriate cosmological background to the heresy's original moderate dualism, and subsequently subjected to expansions and modifications that drew upon new dualist reinterpretations and appropriations of canonical and extra-canonical traditions.

In the case of early Bogomil diabology, the extant sources indicate that in its dualist elaboration of the tradition of Satan's revolt (developed from the traditional diabological exegesis of Isaiah 14. 12–15, and the recognition of the 'evil one' as the 'Prince of this World' in 1 John 5. 19 and John 12. 13), Bogomil moderate dualism drew on both newly translated apocryphal literature and normative Christian diabology. In the formative stages of Slavo-Byzantine religious culture normative Christian diabology was available both in works translated from Greek, such as the diabological section in John of Damascus's *Ekthesis akribēs tēs orthodoxou pisteōs* (in the translation of Ioan Ekzarkh),[46] and in the works of new Slavonic Orthodox authors, for example Kliment of Okhrid's *Eulogy of Archangels Michael and Gabriel*.[47] In these texts Satan was depicted as one of the highest angels, who was entrusted with an important role in the order of Creation but who rebelled against his Creator and was hurled from heaven. Both the *Palaea historica* and *Palaea interpretata*, which incorporate heterodox and apocryphal elements and narratives in their compilatory texts, develop the tradition of Satanael's revolt in heaven, which was deemed to have taken place on the fourth day (when the sun, moon and stars were created), interpreting the motifs of the revolt through the medium of Isaiah 14. 12–15. According to *Palaea historica*, after his fall Satan was deprived of his divine light and angelic garments;[48] significantly, the theme

---

[45] Ibid., pp. 191–230.
[46] New edition by L. Sadnik, *Des Hl. Johannes von Damaskos 'Ekthesis akribēs tēs orthodoxou pisteōs' in der Übersetzung des Exarchen Johannes*, 4 vols. (Freiburg, 1967–83), II, 16–19.
[47] New edition in *Kliment Okhridski: Sŭbrani sŭchineniia*, ed. B. St Angelov et al., 3 vols. (Sofia, 1971), I, 281–2.
[48] See the Greek text of *Palaea historica*, ed. A. Vassiliev, in *Anecdota-Graeco-Byzantina* (Moscow, 1839), p. 189, and the Slavonic text, edited by A. N. Popov, 'Kniga bytiia nebesi i zemli', *Chteniia v Imperatorskom Obshchestve istorii i drevnostei rossiskikh* 1 (1881), 2; for the

of Satan's deprivation of his divine garments is shared in the diabological sections of Zigabenus's account of Bogomil dualist theology, and in *The Battle between Archangel Michael and Satanael*.

At the same time, a condemnation of a heretical diabology, preceding the appearance of Bogomilism and described as 'Manichaean', occurs in Ioan Ekzarkh's *Shestodnev*. In this reported diabology the Devil figures as the eldest son of God,[49] a belief later attributed to Bogomil monarchian dualism. In his *Sermon against the Heretics* Cosmas reproduces a Bogomil reading of the parable of the Prodigal Son (Luke 15. 11–32) according to which Christ was taken to represent the elder and the Devil the younger brother: 'They make Christ the elder son and the younger son, who has deceived his father, the Devil' ('Х(ри)с(т)а ѹбо творѧть старѣишаго с(ы)на, меньшааго же, еже есть заблѫдилъ ѡ(т)ца, дїавола мѣнѧть').[50] In Euthymius Zigabenus's account of Bogomil monarchian dualism Satanael (Samael, Σαμαὴλ) was the Father's first-born (πρωτότοκον); thus, 'Satan is the steward, second to the Father, having the same form and dress as He does, and he sits at His right hand on a throne, and deserves honour next after His' ('Εἶναι τὸν Σαταναὴλ οἰκονόμον, καὶ δευτερεύοντα τόῦ Πατρὸς τὴν αὐτήν αὐτῷ περικείμενον καὶ μορφήν, καὶ στολὴν, καὶ ἐν δεξιᾷ αὐτοῦ καθήμενον ἐπὶ θρόνον').[51] This version of Bogomil monarchian dualism also develops the tradition of Satanael's loss of the syllable '-el' in the wake of his rebellion, attested in earlier pseudepigraphical and parabiblical texts such as 2 Enoch 31. 5, the Slavonic version of 3 Baruch 4. 7, *The Questions of Bartholomew* 4. 25 and *The Martyrdom of St Paul and St Juliana*.[52]

Slavonic text of *Paleiia Tolkovaiia po spisku, sdelannomu v Kolomne v 1406 g. Trud uchenikov N. S. Tikhonravova*, 2 vols. (Moscow, 1892–1896), I, 37.

[49] Text reproduced in Ivanov, *Bogomilski knigi i legendi*, p. 20; on the reference cf. the different approaches of Obolensky, *The Bogomils*, p. 95, and M. Loos, 'Le prétendu témoignage d'un traité de Jean Exarque intitulé 'Šestodnev' et relatif aux Bogomiles', *Byzantinoslavica* 13 (1952–3), 59–67; for arguments that the allusion to the 'Manichaeans' in Ioan Ekzarkh's tract refers to Paulicians or Paulician missionaries in Bulgaria, see Angelov, *Bogomilstvoto*, pp. 88–9; Hamilton and Hamilton, 'Historical Introduction', p. 26 (with a clarification that this specific view of the Devil as the eldest son of God did not derive from Paulicianism).

[50] Tranlsation in *Christian Dualist Heresies*, ed. Hamilton and Hamilton, p. 128; original from Begunov, *Kozma prezviter*.

[51] Euthymius Zigabenus, *Panoplia dogmatica*, in PG 130, 1293; the Bogomil section comprises cols. 1289–1331; another version of the Bogomil section is also edited by Ficker in *Die Phundagiagiten*, pp. 89–111. English translation of the relevant section in *Christian Dualist Heresies*, ed. Hamiton and Hamilton, pp. 180–207 (quotation from p. 183). See also the detailed recent study of the transmission history of *Panoplia dogmatica* (especially focused on its Greek *editio princeps*, published in Tîrgovişte, Walachia, in 1710 and the single Athonite manuscript of the treatise– Iviron 281): N. Miladinova, *The* Panoplia dogmatike *by Euthymios Zygadenos: A Study on the First Edition Published in Greek in 1710* (Leiden, 2014).

[52] See the edition of the Greek text of the *Questions of Bartholomew* in A. V. Vassiliev, *Anecdota graeco-byzantina* (Moscow, 1893), pp. 17–21: *Quaestiones S. Bartholomaei apostoli;*

Pseudepigraphic and Parabiblical Narratives in Medieval Eastern Christian Dualism

Cosmas's statement that in Bogomil diabology it was Christ who was the elder, and the Devil the younger, son of God the Father can be perhaps best explained as referring to that stage in the cosmic drama when Christ defeats Satanael, takes the divine syllable '-el' from his name, acquires the rights of a first-born son and sits on his brother's throne at the right hand of the Father, as detailed in Zigabenus's account.[53] Satanael's original status as God's first-born son in Bogomil monarchian dualism also represents an idea that can be traced to *The Questions of Bartholomew* 4. 25–9, where Satanael is depicted as the first angel created by God, from a handful of fire, though he is not named explicitly the 'first-born' or the 'eldest son' of God. The identification of Satanael as a son of God could have been reinforced by the Bogomil dualist interpretation of the parable of the Prodigal Son in Luke 15. 11–32, and of the parable concerning the unrighteous steward in Luke 16. 1–9, as attested in Cosmas's text discussed above, and by the Bogomil predilection for the use of parables and allegories, as expounded in Zigabenus's account.[54]

Moving on to Bogomil cosmogony and cosmology, Euthymius of Peribleptos's account of Bogomil cosmogony is the earliest source which attributes to the Bogomils a cosmology with multiple heavens (seven, to be precise).[55] This is also attested in some later sources for the heresy, including the *Sermon against the Bogomils for the Sunday of All Saints* attributed to Patriarch John Xiphilinus (1064–75)[56] and an anti-Bogomil anathema added to the *Synodicon of Orthodoxy*.[57] The anathema explicitly links the Bogomil doctrine of a superior Trinity residing in the uppermost of the seven heavens to their use of the apocryphon *The Vision of Isaiah*,[58] and this is one of the rare cases when the Orthodox anti-Bogomil sources explicitly link Bogomil teachings

---

for the Slavonic manuscripts of the work, see A. de Santos Otero, *Die handschriftliche Überlieferung der altslavischen Apocryphen*, 2 vols. (Berlin, 1978–81), II, 58–9. On the use of the name 'Satanael' instead of 'Satan', 'Samael', 'Lucifer' or the 'Devil' and the theme of Satanael losing his theophoric suffix '-el' following his fall in pre-Bogomil doctrinal and apocryphal traditions, cf. M. Dando, 'Satanael', *Cahiers d'études cathares*, 2nd s. 85 (1979), 3–21; Turdeanu, 'Apocryphes bogomiles', pp. 177–81; H. E. Gaylord, 'The Slavonic Version of 3 Baruch', p. xxxii; H. E. Gaylord, 'How Satanael lost his "-el"', *Journal of Jewish Studies* 33 (1982), 303–9; R. Stichel, 'Der Verführung der Stammeltern durch Satanael nach der Kurzfassung der Slavischen Baruch-Apocalypse', in *Kulturelle Traditionen in Bulgarien*, ed. R. Lauer and P. Schreiner (Göttingen, 1989), pp. 116–28.

53 Euthymius Zigabenus, *Panoplia dogmatica*, col. 1305; see H.-C. Puech and A. Vaillant, *Le traité contre les Bogomiles de Cosmas le prêtre* (Paris, 1945), pp. 190–2.
54 Euthymius Zigabenus, *Panoplia dogmatica*, cols. 1321–2; see M. Loos, 'Satan als erstgeborene Gottes: ein Beitrag zur Analyse des bogomilischen Mythus', *Byzantinobulgarica* 3 (1970), 23–36 (esp. pp. 30–1).
55 Euthymius, *Epistola*, p. 34.
56 Published in *PG* 120, 1289–92; for the reference to a Bogomil seven-heaven cosmology, see col. 1292.
57 Edited in J. Gouillard, 'Le Synodicon de l'orthodoxie', *Travaux et mémoires* 2 (1967), 1–316 (p. 65).
58 Ibid.

to pseudepigraphical works. Apart from *The Vision of Isaiah* the conceptualization of Bogomil seven-heaven cosmology was undoubtedly influenced by the other apocalypses offering seven- or plural-heaven cosmologies, such as 2 Enoch, *The Apocalypse of Abraham* and 3 Baruch (a five-heaven cosmology, with the existence of more heavens above implied in the apocalypse).

In *Interrogatio Iohannis*, after his fall Satan takes his seat in the firmament ('in firmamentum'; Carcasonne version 64) or above the firmament ('super firmamentum'; Vienna version 70), and initiates the cosmogonic process. The association between Satan and the firmament is also present in Zigabenus's account, in which it is Satanael who creates and adorns the firmament as his second heaven.[59] The association between the realm of the firmament and Satan and his ministering powers finds a parallel in, and may have been borrowed from, the *Vision of the Isaiah* 7. 9–11, where it is also depicted as a place of constant strife among the fallen angelic orders. The link between Satanael and the firmament is also evident in *The Battle between Archangel Michael and Satanael*, where, after his escape from the God-created seven heavens, Satanael creates his own heavens and erects his throne on the heavenly clouds/firmament, an act which marks the beginning of the creation of his parallel, satanic universe.[60] The theme of the firmament as a sphere ruled by Satan is further enhanced in the section of Bogomil exegesis of Matthew in *Panoplia dogmatica*, where the high mountain in the episode of Jesus's temptation by the Devil is interpreted as being the second heaven or firmament created by Satan.[61] On the other hand, the strong association between the water element and Satanael and his rebellious angels in *Interrogatio Iohannis* finds an analogy in *The Sea of Tiberias*, where Satanael participates in the demiurgic process of creation through his implied mastery of the waters of the primordial sea.

The indebtedness of certain cosmogonic ideas in *Interrogatio Iohannis* to traditions peculiar to 2 Enoch is discernible in several passages. In its account of Enoch's 'throne vision' one of the manuscripts of the long version of 2 Enoch (22. 1) employs somewhat unorthodox imagery: 'іакѡ желѣзо ражеженѡ ѿ огнѣ изнесено и искры испоущает и жежё'[62] ('like iron made burning hot in a fire and brought out, and it emits sparks and is incandescent').[63] *Interrogatio Iohannis* adopts this imagery to depict the transformation of Satan's face after his fall: 'et facies eius sicut ferrum fuit fervens ab igne' (Vienna version 61); 'et facta est facies [eius] sicut ferrum calefactum' (Carcassonne version 55).

---

[59] Euthymius Zigabenus, *Panoplia dogmatica*, cols. 1295–7.
[60] *The Battle between Archangel Michael and Satanael*, Ma. Sofia, Church Historico-Archeological Museum No. 1161, fol. 41r.
[61] Zigabenus, *Panoplia dogmatica*, cols. 1324–5.
[62] The quote is from the Khludov manuscript of 2 Enoch: Sokolov, *Slavianskaiia kniga Enokha pravednago*, p. 21.
[63] F. Andersen, '2 (Slavonic Apocalypse of) Enoch', in *The Old Testament Pseudepigrapha*, 2 vols. (New York, 1983–5), I, 91–223 (p. 136).

Likewise, the theme of the primeval 'restlessness' of the Creator, motivating the beginning of his demiurgic exploits (which finds interesting parallels in some Gnostic texts),[64] is articulated in both the long and short versions of 2 Enoch 24. 4–5 as: 'азъ єдй прохождхъ въ невйдймы́. аз же не шбрѣтѹ́ покоа, зане всѧ бествора'[65] ('I, the One, moved around in the invisible things [...] yet I did not find rest because everything was not created').[66] Similar ideas appear in *Interrogatio Iohannis* to describe the state of Satan after his fall from heaven to the firmament, and again precede his demiurgic activity: 'Et descendens de celo Sathanas in firmamentum hic nullam requiem poterat facere neque hii qui cum eo erant' (Vienna version 65); 'Et descendens Sathanas in firmamentum hic nullam requiem potuit facere sibi nec qui cum eo erant' (Carcassone version 59).

Furthermore, according to 2 Enoch 7. 18 the fallen angels dwell in the second and the fifth heavens, whereas in the Carcassonne version of *Interrogatio Iohannis* (39) Satan seduces the angels from the first five heavens (according to the Vienna version, the first three heavens). The angelic hierarchies set to minister over thunder, rain and hail in 2 Enoch 5. 2, 40. 8–11 (a theme which is also found in *The Questions of Bartholomew* 4. 45)[67] are mirrored in the Satan-created orders presiding over thunder, rain and hail in *Interrogatio Iohannis* (Vienna version 84; Carcassonne version 75). Another motif which is peculiar to 2 Enoch (both versions 29.3) – the derivation of fire from rock and the creation of the angelic orders from this fire – becomes in the Vienna version of *Interrogatio Iohannis* another demiurgic exploit of Satan's: 'Et de lapidibus fecit ignem et de igne fecit omnem militiam et stellas' (80); the Carcassonne version states only that Satan created his hosts from stone: 'et de lapidibus fecit omnes militias stellarum' (71). The motif is also shared in *The Sea of Tiberias*, where God and Satan create separate angelic hierarchies respectively from the right and left part of a stone or flint brought from the bottom of the sea.

Apart from 2 Enoch the multi-heaven cosmology and the angelic hierarchies dwelling in the different heavens in *Interrogatio Iohannis* are paralleled in apocalypses like *The Vision of Isaiah*, *The Apocalypse of Abraham* and *3 Baruch*, traces of whose influence can be seen in other sections of the Bogomil apocryphon. As already noted, *Interrogatio Iohannis* shares with *The Vision of Isaiah* 7. 9–11 the idea of Satan residing on the firmament; given the currency of apocalyptic traditions developed in *The Vision of Isaiah* among Bogomil and Cathar

---

[64] Cf. the 'restlessness' of the pre-existent redeemer in the Gnostic *Kerygmata Petrou* (according to the Pseudo-Clementine *Homilies* 3:20.2), and the primal 'restlessness' of Sophia in the Gnostic *Apocryphon of John*.

[65] The quote is from MS Belgrade, National Library, No. 321, ed. in Sokolov, *Slavianskaiia kniga Enokha pravednago*, pp. 24–5.

[66] Andersen, '2 (Slavonic Apocalypse of) Enoch', p. 142.

[67] *Quaestiones S. Bartholomaei apostoli*, in Vassiliev, *Anedocta graeco-byzantina*, pp. 17–18.

groups, it is very probable that this idea was adopted in Bogomil Satanology and cosmology through a dualist reading of that apocalypse text. Another theme where one can discern the influence of *The Vision of Isaiah* on *Interrogatio Iohannis* is the latter's portals of the air and water in heaven and their angelic guardians, which are paralleled by the gates of the heavens and their angel guards in the former – a theme which is also developed in Jewish Merkabah and Gnostic traditions.[68] Otherwise, the two angels respectively presiding over the air and water find parallels both in canonical and apocryphal traditions, such as the reference to the demonic 'commander of the spiritual powers of the air' in Ephesians 2. 2; the angels of the four winds in Revelation 7. 1–3 and the angel of the waters in Revelation 16. 5; the angels of the air in *The Vision of Isaiah* 10. 30; the account of the contents of the first heaven in 2 Enoch 4–6, with the angels governing the stars and the angels flying over the waters (only in the short version); the angels ruling over the winds of the air and the waters of the sea in *The Questions of Bartholomew* 4. 31–6.[69]

Considering now the sphere of Bogomil sacred history and cosmography narratives, it is worth highlighting the indebtedness of crucial elements of the dualist renditions of the Genesis Paradise story and the fall of Adam and Eve in *Interrogatio Iohannis* and Zigabenus's account to themes variously developed in 2 Enoch, 3 Baruch and *The Apocalypse of Abraham* (such as Satan's planting of Paradise, Eve's seduction by Satan/Samael, the association between Paradise's primal tree (or trees) and human carnality, etc. – some of which also find parallels in other medieval parabiblical works and compilations).[70] Generally, textual evidence indicates that in its dualist expansions on biblical history and anthropogony Bogomil teachings and their attending narratives have borrowed and developed themes and imagery from 2 Enoch, 3 Baruch, *The Apocalypse of Abraham*, the Slavonic versions of *The Life of Adam and Eve* and *The Legend of the Cross* and *The Sea of Tiberias*.[71] Although less well recorded and discussed in the sources, there are clear textual indications that Bogomil Christology adopted some elements from the Christology of *The Vision of Isaiah* and also drew on apocryphal and popular traditions concerning the struggle between the archangel Michael and Satanael, as developed in *The Sea of Tiberias* and *The Battle between Archangel Michael and Satanael*.[72] Finally, in the sphere of eschatology, while most of the themes and imagery in the eschatological section of *Interrogatio Iohannis* are traceable to canonical New Testament sources, some of its ideas find parallels in earlier

---

[68] Cf. the Gnostic Ophite teachings in Origen, *Contra Celsum* 6:24–38; for parallels in Merkabah literature, see *Hekhalot Rabbati*, 17:1–20:3; 3 Enoch 18. 3, 48D:5.
[69] *Quaestiones S. Bartholomaei apostoli*, in Vassiliev, *Anedocta graeco-byzantina*, pp. 17–18.
[70] Y. Stoyanov, 'Medieval Christian Dualist Perceptions and Conceptions of Biblical Paradise', *Studia Ceranea* 3 (2013), 149–66.
[71] Stoyanov, 'Apocryphal Themes', pp. 208–16.
[72] Ibid., pp. 216–18.

apocryphal works such as 4 Ezdras 4. 35–7 and the Slavonic version of the *Apocryphal Apocalypse of John*.[73]

This wide-ranging dependence on, and use of, earlier pseudepigraphic and parabiblical material (including its possible oral renditions) in Bogomil dualist teachings and narratives certainly indicates that the formulation and elaboration of the Bogomil new version of Eastern Christian dualism was stimulated to a great extent by the influx of teachings, themes and ideas into a nascent Slavo-Byzantine religious and literary culture, which were absorbed along with the newly translated non-canonical works from late antiquity.

The above summary of the evidence of the main trajectories of the relationship between parascriptural literature and Bogomilism has significant implications for the study of medieval Western Christian dualism in several important areas, including, for example, the perceived and actual links between heresy and literacy in medieval Christendom in general, and medieval western heresy, in particular.[74] It is also of direct significance to the ongoing scholarly debate regarding the nature and chronology of the interrelations between medieval Eastern and Western Christian dualism. This debate has become increasingly vigorous and intense since the 1990s after the reassertion of the minimalist, or hyper-critical, approach to the spread, existence and nature of Christian dualist heresy in medieval western Europe, which questions or rejects the reality of a coherent dualist doctrinal system or organizational structures and hierarchy among groups labelled as 'Cathar' in medieval Catholic polemical and historical sources.[75]

Among the positive outcomes of this 'inventionist' or deconstructivist approach to medieval dualist heresy in western Europe has been the renewed critical attention paid to some of the relevant primary sources, their sociopolitical provenance and agendas. Revisiting these sources with some novel empirical and theoretical insights has reignited a number of far-reaching interdisciplinary debates which have undoubtedly greatly benefited scholarship and our understanding of a number of areas in the study of religious dissent in medieval Europe, such as the strategies and socio-political goals informing the construction of heresy and deviance in elite ecclesiastical and secular discourses, the dynamics of heresy and authority, the continuation of late

---

[73] Ibid., pp. 218–19.
[74] See the contributions in *Heresy and Literacy, 1000–1530*, ed. P. Biller and A. Hudson (Cambridge, 1994).
[75] See the most recent summaries of the debate in A. P. Roach and J. R. Simpson, 'Introduction', in *Heresy and the Making of European Culture: Medieval and Modern Perspectives*, ed. A. P. Roach and J. R. Simpson (London, 2013), pp. 1–31; C. Taylor, 'Evidence for Dualism in Inquisitorial Registers of the 1240s: A Contribution to a Debate', *History* 98 (2013), 319–45 (pp. 319–29); cf. P. Jiménez-Sanchez, *Les catharismes: modèles dissidents du christianisme médiéval (XIIe–XIIIe siècles)* (Rennes, 2008), pp. 21–53; D. Zbíral, 'Définir les "cathares": le dualisme dans les registres d'inquisition', *Revue de l'histoire des religions* 227.2 (2010), 195–210.

antique heresiological models and rhetoric in medieval anti-Cathar polemics, the phenomenon of 'lived religion' and the formation of non-conformist and local group identities, socio-economy, and the sociology of religious behaviour and practice – to name but a few.

At the same time, the source-criticism and theorizing underlying the arguments that medieval western dualist heresy was largely a medieval clerical construct imposed on the variety of sources about the groups defined as Cathar in western Christendom has so far not included historical-critical analysis of the diverse parabiblical material and (discernible or potential) echoes of earlier pseudepigraphic texts in these sources. This certainly seems a glaring omission of, and disregard for, a highly significant primary source-base which customarily is included, at least partially, in discussions and analyses of what is often styled the 'mythology' or 'mythic' narratives of medieval western dualist heresy.[76] What makes this omission even more surprising is that far-reaching assertions that Western Christian dualism was fabricated in polemical and inquisitorial contexts have been made without a proper preliminary consideration of the textual reality and provenance of this doctrinal and narrative material, whether in polemical or internal sources. Methodologically, it is especially problematic in cases where this material is ignored or downplayed, while the generalized conclusions of a local study or documentation are being projected on the diverse and complex evidence of medieval dualist heresy as a whole.

One of the reasons for this lack of attention to or analysis of the parascriptural material in the evidence for western dualist heresy in these minimalist and deconstructivist models of interpretation probably lies in the nature of the sources themselves, and their difference from those relating to Eastern Christian dualism. Eastern Christian dualism had intertextual relationships with diverse and relatively widely disseminated pseudepigraphic literature, but that was not the case in medieval western Christendom. This is admittedly a very different type of material from that which is found in the western historical chronicles, trial registers and inquisitorial interrogatories which have been lately the predominant focus of western heresy research, with its various insights informed and enriched by methodologies drawn from the

---

[76] See, for, example, Loos, *Dualist Heresy*, chs. 7 and 11; Bozóky, *Le livre secret des cathares*, pp. 186–217; Bozóky, 'La part du mythe dans la diffusion du catharisme', *Heresis* 35 (2001), 45–58; Y. Stoyanov, *The Hidden Tradition in Europe* (London, 1994), ch. 6, pp. 211–26; Stoyanov, *The Other God*, pp. 262–87 *passim*; B. Hamilton, 'Wisdom from the East: the Reception by the Cathars of Eastern Dualist Texts', in *Heresy and Literacy*, ed. Biller and Hudson, pp. 38–61; B. Hamilton, 'Old Testament History: A Cathar Dilemma', *Scripta & e-Scripta* 12 (2013), 211–26; L. Paolini, 'Italian Catharism and Written Culture', in *Heresy and Literacy*, ed. Biller and Hudson, pp. 87–103; H. Fichtenau, *Heretics and Scholars in the High Middle Ages, 1000–1200*, trans. D. A. Kaiser (University Park, 1998), pp. 155–72; M. Lambert, *The Cathars* (Oxford, 1998), pp. 163ff., 197ff.; A. Greco, *Mitologia catara: il favoloso mondo delle origini* (Spoleto, 2000); Jiménez-Sanchez, *Les catharismes*, pp. 215–54 *passim*.

fields of sociology and social and cultural anthropology. Due to an increasing compartmentalization of scholarship, historians of western heresy tend not to follow closely developments and newly published material in the study of heresy in eastern Christendom, even when it is of comparable nature – such as historical accounts or records of heresy trials.

As in the case of the western evidence, external sources for medieval dualism in eastern Christendom pose a series of hermeneutic challenges and problems arising from the use and recontextualization of inherited or revived heresiological constructs and rhetorical techniques to approach, describe and denounce outbreaks of what was considered doctrinal non-conformity and deviance. At the same time, heresy-related documentary records in the Latin West and the Byzantine/Orthodox Slavonic East show some important differences in scope, focus and underlying agendas, and exemplify differing types of evolving intertextualities in medieval Catholic and Eastern Orthodox religio-historical and theological discourses on heresy. While betraying its dependence on late antique models (by drawing on and reusing classical labels), Byzantine heresiology also showed flexibility in its efforts to describe and diagnose actual medieval heretical beliefs.[77] For example, the chapter against the Paulicians in Euthymius Zigabenus's twelfth-century *Panoplia dogmatica* was not an anachronistic reproduction of the earlier tract, *Contra Manichaeos*, of Patriarch Photius (856–67; 877–86), but rather a 'meticulously composed re-working' of the original sections of this treatise, accomplished, moreover, on the basis of actual and contemporary information concerning twelfth-century Paulician groups.[78]

A balanced and objective research methodology will need to approach the various parabiblical narratives and literary models in the evidence for medieval Christian dualist heresy, East and West (and hence one of its most important textual strands), on their own parascriptural, theological and literary terms. Moreover, the evidence of clearly discernible, unmistakable intertextual layers of late antique pseudepigraphic literature in medieval Eastern Christian dualism illustrates compilatory and exegetical techniques which certainly need to be taken into account when considering (on its own terms) the analogous parabiblical material in the sources for Catharism.

Reinstating critical analysis of primary sources in the case of the parascriptural narratives and elements in the evidence of Western Christian dualism (with a due grasp and knowledge of the latest advances in the corresponding textual studies in this area of research on Eastern Christian dualism) will facilitate reassessment of the arguments that this parascriptural material

---

[77] Cameron, 'How to Read Heresiology', *passim*.
[78] See the innovative analysis in H. Kusabu, 'Panoplia Syndrome and Comnenian Orthodoxy: Photios in the Dogmatike Panoplia', paper presented at the Workshop on Late Antiquity and Byzantium, University of Chicago, 2008; Kusabu, 'Comnenian Orthodoxy and Byzantine Heresiology', pp. 119–31.

presents secure markers of imported dualist beliefs. Such source-oriented critical analysis would help towards integrating further these western sources' parascriptural material into the expanding study of the evolution of pseudepigraphical and parabiblical literature and oral thought-patterns in medieval European Christendom.[79] Undoubtedly, there will be a number of empirical, theoretical and methodological insights to be gained if this western source material is treated within this wider framework and with a renewed focus on intertextuality. It would also reinstate some major religio-historical research questions in the study of the evidence of Eastern and Western Christian dualism, posed in recent scholarship, but never properly followed up. These questions concern a range of issues which have been left under-explored: the direct textual and indirect doctrinal echoes and developments of material from *Interrogatio Iohannis* and *The Vision of Isaiah* in the records of Italian, Languedocian and Catalonian Catharism,[80] the patterns of oral and written transmission of pseudepigraphic and parabiblical material in western dualist milieux (including the role of 'learned culture' and written materials),[81] the dynamics of what has been labelled 'Cathar scholasticism' and pursuit of high learning[82] vis-à-vis parascriptural mythic creativity and innovations (especially in Italian Catharism), and, last but not least, the associations between pseudepigraphy, visionary mysticism and religious secrecy in eastern and western dualist and non-dualist medieval sectarian settings.

---

[79] On the significance of the 'surplus', non-formulaic material in sources for western dualism such as the inquisition depositions (including parascriptural material), cf. C. Bruschi, *The Wandering Heretics of Languedoc* (Cambridge, 2009), *passim*; P. Biller's 'Cathars and the Material World', in *God's Bounty? The Churches and the Natural World: Papers Read at the 2008 Summer Meeting and the 2009 Winter Meeting of the Ecclesiastical History Society*, ed. P. Clarke and T. Claydon (Woodbridge, 2010), pp. 89–110; Taylor, 'Evidence for Dualism', *passim*; Taylor, 'Heresy in Quercy in the 1240s: Authorities and Audiences', in *Heresy and the Making of European Culture*, ed. Roach and Simpson, pp. 239–57 *passim*.

[80] A. Colin, 'L'*Ascension d'Isaïe* à travers la prédication d'un évêque cathare en Catalogne au quatorzième siècle', *Revue de l'histoire des religions* 185/2 (1974), 157–78; J. Duvernoy, *Le catharisme*, vol. 1: *La religion des cathares* (Toulouse, 1976), pp. 33–4; Bozóky, *Le livre secret des cathares*, pp. 196–202; A. Acerbi, 'La *Visione di Isaia* nelle vicende dottrinali del catarismo lombardo e provenzale', *Cristianesimo nella storia* 1 (1980), 77–122; Hamilton, 'Wisdom from the East', pp. 52–9; Stoyanov, *The Other God*, pp. 264–74; Jiménez-Sanchez, *Les catharismes*, pp. 218–23. On the use of the *Vision of Isaiah* in late Catharism (by the 'last missionaries', Pierre Autier and Guillaume Bélibaste), see Rottenwöhrer, *Der Katharismus: Quellen zum Katharismus*, pp. 66–9; M. Frassetto, *Heretic Lives: Medieval Heresy from Bogomil and the Cathars to Wyclif and Hus* (London, 2007), pp. 112ff.

[81] Paolini, 'Italian Catharism and Written Culture'; P. Biller, 'Northern Cathars and Higher Learning', in *The Medieval Church: Universities, Heresy, and the Religious Life: Essays in Honour of Gordon Leff*, ed. P. Biller and B. Dobson (Woodbridge, 1999), pp. 25–52.

[82] Paolini, 'Italian Catharism and Written Culture'; P. Biller, 'The Cathars of Languedoc and Written Materials', in *Heresy and Literacy*, ed. Biller and Hudson, pp. 61–81.

8

The Cathars from Non-Catholic Sources

David d'Avray

A convenient starting point for the history of dualist heresy in medieval Europe is R. I. Moore's *The War on Heresy: Faith and Power in Medieval Europe* (London, 2012). Moore leaves the attentive reader in no doubt that dualist heresy flourished in the thirteenth century. It is worth collecting some of the data he provides together, since one or two reviewers appear to have missed it.[1] (How did they do so? The key passages occur near the end of the book, by which time it would be easy for a reader to have decided what its central argument was and to miss Moore's conscientious record of evidence that complicates the overall picture, especially since the central thrust of the argument is foregrounded and the complexities are fitted in smoothly and quite unobtrusively, as in an *Economist* article.) Writing about an inquisition in 1245–6, Moore comments that:

> Dualism is certainly suggested by occasional comments incidental to the inquisitors' immediate concerns – that God did not make the world, that the devil did, that a man who slept with his wife could not be saved (and so might just as well sleep with somebody else.)
>
> (p. 304)

Or again:

> Testimony presented [...] by a group of Franciscan friars [in 1247] [...] was more revealing. [...] The unique value of the friars' stories [...] is that they record a spontaneous account of Pier's beliefs, given of his own volition. The God who had given the law to Moses, he said, was a malevolent scoundrel [...] Marriage was prostitution, and nobody who slept with a woman, even his own wife, could be saved.
>
> (pp. 304–5)

Turning from southern France to Italy, Moore gives a good deal of space to the inquisitorial treatise written *c.* 1250 by Rainier Sacconi, 'who had been

---

[1] Page references in brackets in the text are to R. I. Moore, *The War on Heresy: Faith and Power in Medieval Europe* (London, 2012).

a Cathar for seventeen years and occupied a leading position among them [...] before joining the Dominicans' (p. 315) – and so presumably knew what he was talking about. He quotes Sacconi's words: 'All Cathars believe that the devil made the world and everything in it [...] they regard as mortal sins reproductive sex, the consumption of its fruits, meat, eggs and cheese' (pp. 315–16). Rejection of all forms of sex, especially reproductive, is a theme emerging clearly from Moore's treatment of Catharism. That he and most other scholars are right to emphasize the rejection of marital sex is conclusively confirmed by a key Cathar source, the 'Book of Two Principles', in which it emerges as common ground between warring sects.

The 'Book of Two Principles' was one of Antoine Dondaine's remarkable discoveries. His provisional edition of it was replaced by that of Christine Thouzellier, *Livre des deux principes* (Paris, 1973). She dated it to *c.* 1250, with 1254 as a *terminus ante quem*.[2] This paper is concerned with the section entitled *Contra Garatenses*. This takes us into the middle of a debate between moderate and hard-line dualists, one in which positions have already become entrenched. The 'Garatenses' believe in a creation that was good in its origins but was corrupted at an early stage by an evil principle – so in this respect their position is not so far from that of their Catholic opponents. The author of the *Liber*, however, is further removed: he presents the view that the visible world was evil right from the beginning. Here our concern is with the presuppositions about marriage taken for granted by both sides of the debate. The Latin is rather clumsy but the level of debate is fairly sophisticated, enough to make a paraphrase of the argumentation a useful preliminary to any inferences we may go on to draw.

The *Liber*'s author first addresses himself to the theory that a good God created the four elements but that the evil 'prince of this world' shaped the visible world as we know it. This evil lord was himself created by the good God, but clearly went bad and corrupted the rest of creation[3] – a Lucifer figure in effect. It was he who formed the two sexes.[4] Some skilful logical fencing follows. The *Liber* asks where the proponents of this view find scriptural proof for their version, and an imaginary *Garatensis* respondent quotes passages from Genesis including Genesis 2. 24, 'Because of this man will leave father and mother and cleave to his wife' – all this representing the work of the evil lord.[5] Then the *Liber*'s author drives his opponents onto the horns of a dilemma. Either they believe the words of Genesis or they do not (because it derives from the evil principle so cannot be trusted).[6] If they do not, they have no evidence for their story at all. But if they do, Genesis proves more

---

[2] C. Thouzellier, *Livre des deux principes* (Paris, 1973), p. 31.
[3] Ibid., pp. 364–5.
[4] '[...] ipse malus dominus masculum et feminam *formavit*' (ibid.).
[5] Ibid., pp. 366–8.
[6] Ibid., pp. 368–9.

than they want: for similar texts from Genesis, the author argues, show that the visible world was created by this evil principle from the beginning.[7] They want to have the good God creating the visible world and the bad principle corrupting it (and introducing sex), but they cannot have it both ways.

The *Liber*'s author now turns to a variant on the theory he has just demolished. Some 'indiscreet' *Garatensis* might try to escape the net by arguing (with the help of New Testament texts) that the state of affairs described in the Genesis creation narrative was indeed all good. That is, not just the four elements, but the distinction of the sexes, birds and beasts, and all visible bodies were initially good (more or less the orthodox position, incidentally).[8] This would get the *Garatenses* out of the trap into which the author forced them in the first part of the polemic. But only to walk into the punch: if they do indeed think that the Genesis creation story is about the work of the good God, on what grounds does their condemnation of marriage rest?[9]

We need to stop to reflect on this argument. When a writer argues for this or that view, it might be just his personal opinion. When a writer treats a view as an assumption shared with an opponent, and uses it as the premise of an argument, that implies a much more widespread and unquestioning acceptance, in this case the assumption that marriage is evil. This much is clear: so far from defending marriage, the author of the *Liber* is refuting the *Garatenses* by saying that their creation beliefs would lead to the absurd position that marriage is defensible. The goodness of marriage is an '*absurdum*' to which his remorseless logic drives anyone who opposes his own version of a creation which is in its entirety the work of an evil principle.

The author returns to this *reductio ad absurdum* more than once in the course of his polemic against the *Garatenses*. With crushing irony, he writes:

> For you condemn of a daily basis something created (*creaturam*) by the true lord God, by condemning his matrimony – if it is true that a most kindly and *merciful lord* created and made the male and woman and the visible bodies of this world.[10]

He makes quite clear his own credo, that it was an evil God who created man and woman.[11] The point is that his account of creation by an evil God is compatible with his condemnation of marriage, whereas the condemnation of

---

[7] Ibid., pp. 370–1.
[8] Ibid., pp. 372–5.
[9] 'Contra hoc obicio in hunc modum: Si autem dominus verus fecit in principio masculum et feminam, volucres et iumenta et alia visibilia corpora universa, quare carnale opus coniunctionis maris et femine cotidie condempnatis, illud esse opus diabolicum affirmantes? Cur non facitis filios et filias domino deo vestro?' (ibid., p. 374). He develops a similar line of argument with respect to eating meat.
[10] Ibid., p. 376, passage beginning 'Vos enim' and ending 'huius mundi.'
[11] '[…] volo sustinere et defendere fidem meam, quam habeo et coram Christi fidelibus

marriage by the *Garatenses* is undermined by their account of creation.¹² Both the author of the *Liber* and the *Garatenses* he attacks can be called dualists without hesitation. Common ground is the absolute rejection of marriage as intrinsically evil.¹³

The *Garatenses* do seem to have been in touch with the Bogomil world. The evidence of an anonymous tract from the 1220s or 1230s has been summarized by R. I. Moore:

> Mark, their bishop over 'the whole of Lombardy, Tuscany and the Marches', accepted a fresh *consolamentum* from a visitor from Constantinople, named Nicetas, who told him that his original *consolamentum*, which he had received from Bulgarian heretics, was invalid. After Mark's death, however, his followers heard from another visitor from 'across the sea' that Nicetas's own *consolamentum* had not been valid because the man from whom he received it had been found with a woman. This caused some of them to withdraw their allegiance from Mark's successor and choose a new leader. The two parties agreed to draw lots between their respective bishops. After much wrangling, including the deposition of one bishop who said he would not accept the result and the resignation of another because he thought that if chosen he would not be accepted, candidates were selected from each side and the lot fell upon Garatus [*sic*] – who was promptly reported by two witnesses to have slept with a woman. 'Because of this there were many who maintained that he was unworthy of his rank, and therefore they no longer considered themselves bound by their promise of obedience to him.'¹⁴

Nonetheless it would seem that Garattus retained a body of supporters, and these can presumably be identified with the *Garatenses*. The account given by Moore shows a movement sufficiently well developed *c.* 1230 (on his dating) to be both institutionalized and riven by factions. (That date might be pushed back even earlier: Dondaine dated the text to around 1200,¹⁵ and each of their datings is heavily affected by their respective ideas of antecedent probability. But for the sake of argument, let us stay with Moore's dating.)¹⁶ It is also impossible to airbrush out the link asserted between them and a Bulgarian sect.

---

predico evidenter, per testimonia legis et prophetarum et novi testamenti, […] quod unus malus deus est, qui "creavit […] masculum et feminam"' (ibid., p. 378).

[12] Similar reasoning again (ibid., p. 382).

[13] Also, though it is not the subject of this paper, the eating of meat, eggs and cheese.

[14] Moore, *The War on Heresy*, p. 320.

[15] A. Dondaine, 'La hiérarchie cathare en Italie: I – Le *De heresi catharorum*', *Archivum Fratrum Praedicatorum* 19 (1949), 280–312 (pp. 290, 312). Dondaine's argument is powerful. We have evidence of a Peter Gallo who was a Cathar bishop in 1214–15, but in the treatise he does not yet appear to have reached that eminence.

[16] 'Of course, an element of circularity in all these datings is pretty hard to avoid: you could say something similar about mine. The real difference is that Dondaine saw it all coming together in the 1170s and 80s, I in the 1220s' (R. I. Moore, personal communication).

The Cathars from Non-Catholic Sources

In view of connection between the *Garatenses* and Bulgaria, their ideas about the origins of sex as described and attacked in the *Liber* can usefully be compared with the account of sex in the 'Secret Book of the Bogomils', from the tenth century, which was 'originally written in Old Bulgarian and translated into Latin as Bulgarian Bogomils who fanned out West after the conquest of the country by Byzantium found a fertile soil for spreading their unorthodox beliefs in Northern Italy and Southern France':[17]

> Then he [Satan] thought and made man in the likeness of himself and ordered the angel of the Third Heaven to enter a clay body. And he took from him and made another body in the shape of a woman and ordered the angel of the Second Heaven to enter the body of the woman. The angels, seeing themselves in mortal shapes, and different ones at that, began to weep. He ordered them to copulate in their clay bodies and [they] did not understand this was sin.[18]

The ideas of the Bulgarian sect and those of the *Garatenses* as reported in the *Liber* are not very different. The *Liber* simply goes further, utterly refuting the view held by the Catholic Church, which was overwhelmingly positive about marriage as an institution and promulgated its view through preaching[19] – more on this below. While it is possible that the Balkan connections of Italian dualists had no influence on their attitudes to marriage, the hypothesis seems extreme.

To summarize the foregoing: dualist communities disagreed on the question of whether the evil principle was the symmetrical counterpart of the good God, or an originally good being who had fallen, but on marriage they were in complete agreement. For both, marriage and procreation were evil. This common assumption was so strong that the author of the *Liber* could use it as a lever to prise apart the rest of the system of the *Garatenses*. The community of the *Garatenses* goes back at the very least to the second or third decade of the thirteenth century, and seems to be one of the sects resulting from irreconcilable divisions within the larger Italian dualist community, probably one with strong Balkan connections. If the tract is 'from the 1220s or '30s' (Moore, p. 320), we may infer an Italian dualist movement that must have been around for decades before the crisis described.

Was such dualism a purely Italian phenomenon? It seems unlikely. Moore says 'it is easy to forget how much movement there actually was' in the early medieval world, while:

---

[17] K. Petkov, *The Voices of Medieval Bulgaria, Seventh–Fifteenth Century: The Records of a Bygone Culture* (Leiden, 2008), p. 83.

[18] Petkov, *The Voices of Medieval Bulgaria*, p. 85.

[19] D. L. d'Avray, *Medieval Marriage: Symbolism and Society* (Oxford, 2005), ch. 1(d). This positive message went with the view, expressed in Handbooks of Confessors, that pleasure should not be the motive for sex (though it could be a side effect).

From around the millennium such contacts grew exponentially in number, variety and regularity. [...] It is hardly possible to exaggerate the importance of evangelism in the dissemination of ideas, and of the itinerant preacher, the archetypal outsider, in prompting the questioning of habits of life and deference long accepted as simply how things are.[20]

A chance documentary survival reveals great numbers of Waldensians in fourteenth-century Bohemia.[21] They had come a long way from their origins. It would be strange if dualist heresies did not spread far and fast, as we know the Waldensian movement did. In short, and whatever the direction of influence, the default position should be to expect the presence of dualism in southern France c. 1200, rather than to seek to deny it. The argument from silence is a particularly risky basis for denial, since a scorched earth policy against heresy, and the absence of anything remotely like a dissident 'library' to preserve dualist texts, raised the odds against survival to almost insuperable heights. It is in fact astounding that we have as many dualist texts as we do from the period. This we owe presumably to the 'know your enemy' philosophy of inquisitors.

One of the most interesting heretical texts that we still have is an attack on the dualists from a Waldensian point of view: the *Liber antiheresis* of Durand of Huesca, composed before his conversion to Catholicism in 1207[22] or 1208.[23] This has a long section defending marriage against the dualists, prefaced by the following sentence:

> And since some assert that marriage is a dreadful sin and criminal, we will attack their audacity showing that it is licit for those who are not able to be continent, and permitted by God: and [we will show] this by means of authorities of the New Testament only, since they do not respect or care at all about the authorities of the Old Testament and of the doctors [of the Church].[24]

This Waldensian view of the dualists should be taken seriously. Durand was himself a member of a persecuted movement. His defence of marriage against, let me say it, the Cathars takes up more than six pages in Selge's edition. One has the impression he is dealing with argumentative opponents:

> But perhaps someone will say: Is it not one and the same act that is carried

---

[20] Moore, *The War on Heresy*, p. 322.
[21] Alexander Patschovsky, *Quellen zur Böhmischen Inquisition im 14. Jahrhundert* (Weimar, 1985).
[22] M. Lambert, *Medieval Heresy: Popular Reform Movements from the Gregorian Reform to the Reformation* (Oxford, 1992), p. 92
[23] *Die ersten Waldenser, mit Edition des* Liber antiheresis *des Durandus von Osca*, vol. 2: *Der Liber antiheresis des Durandus von Osca*, ed. Kurt-Victor Selge (Berlin, 1967), p. x.
[24] Ibid., p. 63.

out with your own wife, as with other women? To whom the following reply will be given: No, because your own wife is not forbidden to him[25] by the Lord, but other women are.[26]

This Waldensian source, written before its author's conversion to the established Church in 1207/8, attempts to rebut the same condemnation of marriage as was current among Italian dualists. This combined testimony from non-Catholic sources makes it impossible to deny that dualist heresy was firmly established in the Europe of the central Middle ages.

Cathar attitudes to marriage have been the focus of this paper because they cannot be explained as 'obvious answers to frequently recurring questions', or picked up from 'the opening chapters of the Acts of the Apostles', or ultimately derived from the programme of the eleventh-century papal reformers.[27] The last generation of research has corrected misapprehensions of the latter. Christopher Brooke wrote of one of the most influential reform leaders, Peter Damian, that he 'hated all sexuality and barely allowed marriage to be a legal cover to sin'.[28] Homer nodded here, for this is a mistake, *tout court*. Peter Damian had quite an exalted view of marriage, including sex: he could write of 'the marriage bed of mutual charity';[29] he saw marriage as a symbol of Christ's union with the Church.[30] Starting with Hincmar of Reims in the ninth century, the idea developed among orthodox intellectuals that only a sexually consummated marriage adequately symbolized that union.[31] In a different context Moore has written well about the promotion of marriage in the age of the papal reform. He links it with a change in inheritance rules: 'When the transmission of an undivided inheritance became the overriding consideration [...] the heir must be designated as clearly as possible, and the number and standing of his potential rivals minimised' (by the stigmatization of bastardy); consequently, 'Insistence on legitimacy inevitably elevated the importance of the marriage from which the heir would spring.'[32]

Rejection of marital sex is not on a continuum with the agenda of the orthodox reform movements of the eleventh to the thirteenth centuries. They were against a married priesthood, but that went with a promotion of

---

[25] The word is 'ei', to which MS P adds 'qui continere non potest', according to Selge's *apparatus criticus*.
[26] Ibid., p. 68.
[27] Moore, *The War on Heresy*, p. 319: a weak page.
[28] In his generally excellent book on *The Medieval Idea of Marriage* (Oxford, 1989), p. 61.
[29] D. L. d'Avray, 'Peter Damian, Consanguinity and Church Property', in *Intellectual Life in the Middle Ages*, ed. L. Smith and B. Ward (London, 1992), pp. 71–80 (pp. 73–4). The too-learned copy editor or typesetter of that paper tried to change the phrase to 'the marriage bed of mutual chastity'!
[30] d'Avray, *Medieval Marriage*, pp. 134–5.
[31] Ibid., ch. 4 *passim*.
[32] R. I. Moore, *The First European Revolution, c. 970–1215* (Oxford, 2000), p. 91.

marriage for the laity. It is one of the services of Professor Moore to scholarship that he has brought this out with great clarity. As he sums it up, in his synthesis on the 'first European Revolution':

> At the heart of our revolution was the unspoken agreement between the eldest son and his tonsured brother to confirm the lands and privileges of the monastery in return for recognition of the eldest as sole legitimate heir to the patrimony, and on condition that the monks would remain celibate.[33]

Celibacy and marriage with children were complementary.

The idea that sex is bad, marriage worse, and reproductive sex the worst of all makes no sense within any of the rationalities of reform, but it is entirely logical within a dualist view of the material world as created by the devil. This paper uses ideas about marriage as a symptom of the appeal of dualism the Middle Ages. No Catholic sources were used to do this: the key witnesses were a Cathar text, the 'Book of Two Principles', and a Waldensian attack on Catharism from the early thirteenth century. As for secondary sources, the key witnesses were the works of Professor Moore. There is still an argument going on about chronology, but the question is not whether dualist Catharism existed, but rather by when, how early. Contributions to this volume, notably Jörg Feuchter's, move that debate significantly forward. In the meantime, no careful reader of Moore's work (or of key non-Catholic thirteenth-century sources) can doubt the existence of Cathar dualism as a force in the medieval world. His writings should be read with greater attention.

---

[33] Ibid., p. 97.

9

Converted-Turned-Inquisitors and the Image of the Adversary: Ranier Sacconi Explains Cathars*

Caterina Bruschi

Ego autem frater Rainerius, olim heresiarcha, nunc gratia Dei sacerdos in ordine Predicatorum licet indignus, dico indubitater et testificor coram Deo, *qui scit quod non mentior*, quod aliquod illorum trium non est inter Catharos sive in penitentia eorum.[1]

It is 1250, and Brother Ranier, a middle-aged Preacher and former dualist heretic from Piacenza (Lombardy), writes a treatise about his former fellow believers, the Cathars. Following Ranier himself, who shaped his identity as an ex-heresiarch and later Brother Preacher, my approach to this subject takes into account Ranier and his work *together*, and considers that in anybody's life experience both past and present contribute to building up a whole

---

* My thanks for help and guidance in preparing this paper go to Maurizio Ulturale, Riccardo Parmeggiani, br. Marco Rainini OP, Erika Cancellu and br. Angelo Piagno, Head Librarian of Saint Dominic's convent in Bologna. Many thanks also to Beth Spacey and to the editor of this book for polishing my English prose with great care.

[1] 'I brother Ranier, once heresiarch, now for the grace of God minister, albeit unworthy, in the order of the brothers Preacher, state unquestionably and testify in God's presence, *who knows that I am not lying*, that none of those three [items: contrition of heart, confession of words, and satisfaction through works] features among the Cathars or in their way of penance'; *Summa fratris Raynerii de ordine fratrum predicatorum de Catharis et Leonistis seu Pauperibus de Lugduno*, ed. in F. Šanjek, 'Raynerius Sacconi OP *Summa de Catharis*', *Archivum Fratrum Praedicatorum* 44 (1974), 31–60 (pp. 42–60, at p. 44) (italics are mine). On Ranier, the reference work is still Šanjek's 'Introduction' to the edition; more recently this has been complemented by Marina Benedetti's analysis of Ranier's inquisitorial work and documentation, in M. Benedetti, *Inquisitori lombardi del Duecento* (Rome, 2008), pp. 39–73, and by M. Ulturale, '*Inventer l'hérésie? La controversistica antiereticale: il mito della reificazione*' (unpublished BA thesis, University of Bologna, 2011), pp. 101–8. Given the scarcity of information on Ranier's life, little has been written on him, although his name is often brought into the wider picture of Peter of Verona's life and death: see for example D. Prudlo, *The Martyred Inquisitor: the Life and Cult of Peter of Verona (†1252)* (Aldershot, 2008), pp. 75–6, 225. He is mostly focused upon through the analysis of his work, as in L. J. Sackville, *Heresy and Heretics in the Thirteenth Century: The Textual Representations* (York, 2011), pp. 136–8, 140–53, 183–7.

individual, and that this individual's writings are necessarily – at least to some extent – the expression of this entirety.[2] In other words, this ex-heretic turned-inquisitor wrote about his former companions not only as a convert who hid the acrimony and resentment typical of an apostate, but also as an inquisitor, bringing his own life, experience and problematic past into his textual construction of the heretical 'adversary'.

Ranier's work, of little literary but enormous historical value, enjoyed great success – nineteen manuscripts containing all, or excerpts of, the *Summa* have been counted in the most recent survey by Käppeli,[3] scattered throughout Europe.[4] This is a telling figure, especially if compared to the two works most closely related to the *Summa*: the treatise attributed to Peter of Verona (1230–8) – known through two manuscripts[5] – and Anselm of Alessandria's *Tractatus* (1267–70), of which only one version is extant.[6] (The nature of the connection between these works will be discussed below.) Ranier's popularity is confirmed also by his frequent contacts with the papacy after his conversion: three different pontiffs (Innocent IV, Urban IV and Alexander IV) wrote to him frequently in the decade 1252–62, addressing their letters to him *personally* ('to my beloved son in God Ranier, inquisitor in Lombardy').[7]

What surprised me most, however, is that Ranier does not feature equally prominently in his order's records and celebratory works. There are no references in the surviving provincial councils, only feeble traces in the order's chronicles and, most striking of all, no mention in Stephen

---

[2] As acknowledged by Benedetti, *Inquisitori*, p. 64.

[3] *Scriptores Ordinis Praedicatorum Medii Aevi*, 4 vols., ed. T. Käppeli and E. Panella (Rome, 1970–93), III, 293–4, and IV, 249–50 n. 3430, where they update the old survey by Šanjek, who mentioned only seventeen manuscripts (*Summa*, ed. Šanjek, p. 31), and add two manuscripts. The estimate of fifty exemplars in *Summa*, ed. Šanjek, pp. 39–41 (thus in Sackville, *Heresy and Heretics*, pp. 136–7), rests on nineteen manuscripts of Sacconi, the single manuscript of his follower Anselm of Alessandria's *De hereticis*, and the copies of Sacconi inside the compilation on heresy by the Anonymous of Passau (*c.* 1260–6) and its later recension, the 'Pseudo-Reinerius' treatise. Accessible in English on this last text is M. A. E. Nickson, 'The "Pseudo-Reinerius" Treatise: The Final Stage of a Thirteenth-Century Work on Heresy from the Diocese of Passau', *Archives d'histoire littéraire et doctrinale du Moyen Âge* 62 (1967), 255–314 (pp. 257, 261, 283).

[4] A copy was kept in the Carcassonne inquisitorial depots, and possibly in the Toulouse offices as well, as highlighted in P. Biller, 'Introduction', in *Inquisitors and Heretics in Thirteenth-Century Languedoc: Edition and Translation of Toulouse Inquisition Depositions (1273–1282)*, ed. P. Biller, C. Bruschi and S. Sneddon (Leiden, 2011), p. 8.

[5] Peter Martyr(?), *Summa*, edited in T. Käppeli OP, 'Une somme contre les hérétiques de S. Pierre Martyr(?)', *Archivum Fratrum Praedicatorum* 17 (1947), 295–335 (pp. 320–35).

[6] Anselm of Alessandria, *Tractatus de hereticis*, in A. Dondaine, 'La hierarchie cathare en Italie: II – Le *Tractatus de hereticis* d'Anselme d'Alexandrie, OP', in A. Dondaine, *Les hérésies et l'inquisition, XIIe–XIIIe siècles: documents et études*, ed. Y. Dossat (Aldershot, 1990), IV, pp. 234–324.

[7] See Benedetti, *Inquisitori*, pp. 40–5, 66–73, and p. 68 n. 106, for a full record.

of Salagnac and Bernard Gui's work on illustrious Dominican writers and thinkers (written at the end of the thirteenth / beginning of the fourteenth century)[8] or in Gerard of Frachet's (d. 1267) *Vitae fratrum ordinis praedicatorum* and Chronicle.[9] Could this paradox be a reflection of the special status of the converted-turned-inquisitor? It looks as though his renowned zeal in pursuing heretics did not secure him enduring status, and was not sufficient, even in the eyes of inquisitor Bernard Gui, to grant him the passport to a long-lasting memory. Sacconi could have 'paid' for having been a heretic through his exclusion from the celebratory works of the order, whereas Peter of Verona purified his dubious past through martyrdom. If this is the case, inquisitorial status is not the way to fame, unless it is associated with martyrdom: being an inquisitor is only one of the many duties of a Brother Preacher.[10] Thus it does not come as a surprise that the *Instructiones de officiis ordinis* by the contemporary Master General, Humbert of Romans, do not even contemplate the 'office' of inquisitor, although they very carefully list forty-seven others, including not only the prior and the preachers, but also the tailor, the gardener and the librarian.[11] Ranier Sacconi from Piacenza exists to this day as inquisitor only.

A brief sketch of his timeline should help us to place Ranier in a clearer context. We have records of him spanning from 1250 to 21 July 1262, when he disappears from our sight following an urgent and worried summons from Pope Urban IV to his court in Urbino:

> Since I wish to have a discussion with you about some present things that need doing in regard to the business of Catholic faith, and since – for this reason, your presence is to me very much appropriate [to discuss] about this matter, [...] I command that you [...] come quickly to me, and, in order for you to be quicker, [...] I grant you the permission to avoid your order's prohibitions and ride freely.[12]

---

[8] Stephen of Salagnac and Bernard Gui, *De quatuor in quibus Deus Praedicatorum Ordinem insignivit*, ed. T. Käppeli, Monumenta Ordinis Praedicatorum Historica 22 (Rome, 1949), for instance, where talking about the killing of Peter of Verona (p. 20).

[9] Gerard of Frachet, *Vitae fratrum ordinis praedicatorum necnon Cronica ordinis ab anno MCCIII usque ad annum MCCIV*, ed. B. Reichert, Monumenta Ordinis Praedicatorum Historica 1 (Louvain, 1896).

[10] C. Caldwell, 'Peter Martyr: The Inquisitor as Saint', *Comitatus* 31 (2000), 137–74 (p. 139).

[11] Humbert of Romans, *Epistolae ex capitulis generalibus ad ordinem scriptae*, in *Beati Humberti de Romanis Opera de vita regulari*, ed. J. J. Berthier, 2 vols. (Turin, 1956), II, 187–8.

[12] 'Cum super quibusdam agendis ecclesie negotium catholice fidei contingentibus, tecum velimus habere tractatum, tuaque sit nobis propter hoc presentia plurimum opportuna, [...] mandamus [...] ad nos sublata difficultate qualibet, festinanter accedas. Nos enim ad hoc ut celerius ad nos accedere valeas [...] equitandi libere, contrario tui ordinis non obstante statuto, liberam concedimus auctoritate presentium facultatem': 'Cum super quibusdam' (21 July 1262), in *Bullarium Ordinis Praedicatorum*, ed. A. Brémond and T. Ripoll, 8 vols. (Rome, 1729–40), I, 427 n. 23.

In roughly twelve years as an inquisitor Ranier had developed a privileged relationship with the popes, despite the seventeen years he spent among the Cathars as 'heresiarch', that is – he tells us – as bishop or member of the high clergy.[13] If Šanjek is correct, Ranier was now an old man in his sixties, having been born around the beginning of the century in Piacenza within a Cathar milieu. In his early forties, presumably around the mid 1240s, he meets, listens to and is converted by his contemporary Brother Peter of Verona, inquisitor in various capacities in Lombardy possibly since 1240[14] and prior in Piacenza's convent of San Giovanni in Canale since 1241.[15] Whenever Sacconi's conversion and Peter's nomination at the convent of Piacenza took place – sometime during the 1240s – it seems clear to me that in 1250 (before Peter's murder) Ranier was already an inquisitor.[16] He himself tells us so at the end of his treatise, when talking about Waldensian customs: 'and I also think that they say the same of women [that they can consecrate the Host] *because they* [the Waldensians] *did not deny it to me'*.[17] This typical passing comment has been overlooked by historians so far, but seems very revealing. Peter in fact was yet to become St Peter Martyr by being murdered in April 1252. On Peter's death, the order replaced Peter with Ranier and entrusted him five months later with the long inquest over the murder, during which Ranier eventually came to know that he too was a target, as inquisitor in Pavia. A sum had been sent there to pay for his murder.[18]

When James of the Chiusa paid to have him murdered, the inquisitor Ranier thus had already written his work. Therefore, unless he lies to us

---

[13] Ranier uses the word 'heresiarch' to indicate himself ('olim heresiarcha'; *Summa*, ed. Šanjek, p. 44) and John of Lugio ('Iohannes de Lugio heresiarcha'; ibid., p. 57); then he defines further the internal role held by John of Lugio, by glossing John's *own* self-definition, made *in writing* in official letters: 'Unde Iohannes of Lugio, qui est unus ex illis taliter ordinatis, semper describit se in epistolis suis sic: "Iohannes, Dei gratia filius maior et ordinatus episcopus"' ('Thus John of Lugio, who is one of those ordered in this manner [to the role of "episcopus"], always described himself in his letters in the following way: "John, for the grace of God elder son and ordered bishop"') (ibid., p. 49). See also Sackville, *Heresy and Heretics*, p. 136.

[14] This date, debated by some (see Prudlo, *Martyred Inquisitor*, pp. 30, 36–7, 57), derives from the words of Galvano Fiamma's *Chronica Maior*. While reporting it, Benedetti rightly allows for some leeway in that, although we might doubt Fiamma's accuracy as a chronicler, tools for a counter-argument are not available.

[15] Benedetti, *Inquisitori*, p. 55; differently Prudlo, *Martyred Inquisitor*, p. 55, who dates this (not without ambiguity) at 1249.

[16] This is compatible with Prudlo's theory that Peter of Verona's very first occurrence as an inquisitor dates back to 13 June 1251 (*Martyred Inquisitor*, p. 57): even if this was correct, it would not exclude the possibility that Ranier also could act as inquisitor, perhaps on Peter's behalf, or at his orders. Sackville dates the conversion to 1245 (*Heresy and Heretics*, p. 136).

[17] 'Credo etiam quod idem dicant de mulieribus, *quia hoc non negaverunt michi*'; *Summa*, ed. Šanjek, p. 60 (italics are mine).

[18] Benedetti, *Inquisitori*, p. 24–5.

regarding the date of composition[19] – the *Summa* should be seen as unconnected to the plotting, murders and violent events of the second half of the thirteenth century, and – most importantly – the posthumous operation of the construction of Peter of Verona's life and death into that of Saint Peter Martyr. In 1250 Ranier was only a relatively new inquisitor, with some – possibly little – experience of leading inquiries, but a massive knowledge of his former fellow believers, among whom he was as a full member of the Church, he says, for seventeen years.[20]

As a replacement for Peter of Verona, Ranier's career peaked. He led the inquest on the murder, which lasted fifteen years (well beyond Ranier's mandate) and concluded in 1267, when Stephen Confalonieri, previously convicted by Ranier but saved by the intervention of some 'friends' (probably supporters of the Ghibelline leader Oberto Pallavicino), confessed his guilt to Anselm of Alessandria.[21] Perhaps the various letters sent by Innocent IV in 1255, granting Ranier the help of eight(!) new inquisitors for the province of Lombardy, and other missives – at least five more – sent between 1256 and 1257 to the authorities of Lombardy urging them to support Ranier, bear witness to the region's *overwhelming* 'reluctance to prosecute heresy', to echo Peter Diehl.[22] On 1 August 1255 Ranier, from the church of St Tecla in Milan, pronounced an excommunication against those who *knowingly* (*scienter*) weave plots to undermine the inquisitors, obstruct their business and contravene their words.[23] Ranier carried out the order to destroy the castle of Gattedo (near Milan), a sort of Italian Montségur, where the Cathar bishops Nazarius and Desiderius were buried (the destruction was ordered in 1253).[24] This was a particularly emotional event for him, as – he tells us – he

---

[19] The *explicit* of the *Summa*, closed in a dry notarial style, runs thus: 'Anno Domini MCCL compilatum est fideliter per dictum fratrem Raynerium opus superius annotatum. (Deo Gratias)' ('In the year of the Lord 1250 the work above listed[?] has been compiled faithfully by the said brother Ranier. (Thanks be to God)'); *Summa*, ed. Šanjek, p. 60.

[20] 'Praeterea dico indubitanter quod annis XVII quibus *conversatus* sum cum eis non vidi aliquem ex eis orare secreto seorsum ab aliis' ('Moreover I say without doubt that in the seventeen years during which I was a full member of their church, I have not seen any of them praying secretly, differently from the others'); ibid., p. 45. The verb *conversare* seems not to have been chosen casually, as it identifies a full monastic profession: 'To profess a religious or monastic life', as in C. Du Cange *et al.*, *Glossarium mediae et infimae latinitatis*, ed. L. Favbre, 10 vols. (Niort, 1883–7), II, 546, online at http://ducange.enc.sorbonne.fr/CONVERSARE.

[21] Benedetti, *Inquisitori*, pp. 41–2; 65–8.

[22] Discussed and listed in Šanjek's 'Introduction' to the *Summa*, p. 33 n. 14; P. D. Diehl, 'Overcoming Reluctance to Prosecute Heresy in Thirteenth-Century Italy', in *Christendom and its Discontents: Exclusion, Persecution, and Rebellion, 1000–1500*, ed. S. L. Waugh and P. D. Diehl (Cambridge, 1996), pp. 47–66.

[23] The document, transcribed in full, is reported in P. M. Campi, *Dell'historia ecclesiastica di Piacenza*, 3 vols. (Piacenza, 1651–62), II, 402 n. 99 (1 August 1255).

[24] As per three papal letters of July 1253, see Benedetti, *Inquisitori*, p. 69 n. 108; on its

had heard Nazarius preach about various theological tenets Nazarius himself had learnt sixty years before, in Bulgaria.[25]

Perhaps as a consequence of such a significant event, Ranier was expelled in 1258 from Milan, where he was carrying out his inquisitorial duties, by order of Oberto Pallavicino, *podestà* of the city and arch-enemy of the inquisitors,[26] having already opposed and ostracized them in Piacenza a few years earlier.[27]

Aside from the clear 'success' of Ranier as inquisitor, acknowledged by the papacy, denied and jeopardized by the Ghibelline leaders and their supporters, one other element seems important to the purpose of this research, and this is the relationship linking three people: Ranier Sacconi, Peter of Verona, and Anselm of Alessandria.[28] The three share very many similarities. All are northern Italian, born in cities which – according to both Ranier and the late thirteenth century depositions of French suspects – hosted Cathar communities.[29] Peter and Ranier grew up for some time in Cathar communities, but

---

relevance, Prudlo, *Martyred Inquisitor*, pp. 59–60, 76 (dating the military operation to 1254); while Campi gives the date of 1258 (Campi, *Dell'historia*, II, p. 215).

[25] 'Nazarius vero quondam eorum episcopus et antiquissimus *coram me* et aliis multis dixit [...] et dixit quod habuit hunc errorem ab episcopo et filio maiore ecclesie Bulgarie iam fere elapsis annis LX' ('Nazarius, in truth once their bishop and very old, in front of me and many others said [...] and said that he got this error from a bishop and elder son of the church of Bulgaria nearly sixty years ago already'); *Summa*, ed. Šanjek, p. 58.

[26] 'Nam frater Raynerius placentinus inquisitor hereticorum fuit de conventu Mediolanensi per turrianos expulsus' ('In fact brother Ranier from Piacenza, inquisitor of heretics, was expelled from the Milan convent by the supporters of the de la Torre'), Galvano Fiamma, *Chronica Ordinis Praedicatorum ab anno 1170 usque ad annum 1333*, ed. B. M. Reichert, Monumenta Ordinis Praedicatorum Historica 2.1 (Rome, 1897), p. 98. Papal documents of 1260 report the event *post quem*; see Benedetti, *Inquisitori*, pp. 71–2.

[27] See C. Bruschi, 'Dissenso e presenza ereticale in Piacenza e nelle città padane tra gli anni Cinquanta e Settanta del Duecento', in *Studi sul Medioevo emiliano: Parma e Piacenza in età comunale*, ed. R. Greci (Bologna, 2009), pp. 233–60 (pp. 241–2).

[28] This study will not go into the alleged 'functionality' of Sacconi and Peter of Verona within the papacy's schemes. I consider this interpretation methodologically weak. First, because it privileges wider schemes (also seen with the benefit of hindsight, from our modern historical perspective) over the personal and inner motivations of each actor, excluding *a priori* the spiritual drive which might have led them to decision-making; secondly, becauses it ignores the energy and determination that arise from the personal situation of a convert, which was of course Sacconi's status.

[29] Ranier refers to Verona three times ('Albanenses morantur Verone et in pluribus civitatibus Lombardie', 'Ecclesia de Marchia nihil habent Verone', 'Ecclesia Francie morantur Verone et in Lombardia') ('the Albanenses live in Verona and in many cities of Lombardy', 'The church of the Marches have no supporters in Verona', 'The church of France live in Verona and Lombardy'); *Summa*, ed. Šanjek, p. 50 – where, interestingly, 'church' is taken as a collective name and carries a verb in the plural; for other references to exiled French Cathars in northern Italian cities, including Verona, Piacenza and Alessandria, see the lists in Bruschi, 'Dissenso', pp. 255–60, and C. Bruschi, *The Wandering Heretics of Languedoc* (Cambridge, 2009), pp. 76–8.

nothing is known about Anselm's origin before he made his religious profession.[30] All became Brothers Preacher, and all became inquisitors. All wrote anti-heresy treatises. In fact, they were not the only examples of inquisitors/writers, as the seventeenth-century Dominican erudite Rovetta interestingly tells us that Sacconi's partner in inquisitorial activities, a jurist named Guido da Sesto, also wrote a (lost) treatise against heresy.[31] Both Peter of Verona and Anselm of Alessandria, as we shall see, are likely to have known Sacconi personally.

Peter of Verona, already a Dominican, was named as prior in Piacenza, Sacconi's birthplace, in 1241. He was briefly in Florence during 1244–5, assisting Roger Calcagni, the Preachers' local inquisitor, in leading a major inquiry into the Florentine Cathars, which led to the arrest of – among others – the siblings Pace and Barone of Pesamigola, the former a *podestà* of Florence.[32] Peter appears in the records of the inquisition of those years simply as 'witness', at least three times.[33] There is a suggestion – not demonstrated – that it is in Florence that Ranier Sacconi was converted. I have found no trace of this in the records.[34]

How old was Ranier then? He already was inquisitor in 1250, and presumably had been so for at least a couple of years before being able to write his *summa* telling us that he had heard the declarations of Waldensians – scarcely, if at all, present in Tuscany – about the consecration of the Host. This takes us back at least to 1248. He also was a Cathar for seventeen years – how old must one be to be able to 'conversari' with Cathars? Although the canons of various councils of the 1240s state that, when it came to heretical liability, the 'age of consent' was agreed to be fourteen for boys and twelve for girls,[35] we can infer that children as young as eight could be employed in various roles in networking activities.[36] If Sacconi was really young when he started

---

[30] On Peter's background, see Käppeli, 'Une somme', pp. 313–15; Prudlo, *Martyred Inquisitor*, pp. 17–22. See also *Scriptores ordinis*, ed. Käppeli, I, 79 [on Anselm], and III, 293–4 [on Ranier].

[31] According to the seventeenth-century Dominican bibliographer Rovetta, as in Käppeli, 'Une somme', p. 314. The coincidence makes for an interesting reflection on the overlap between inquisitorial practice and anti-heretical writing, as does the fact that three out of seven of the polemicists quoted by Käppeli are preachers from Piacenza (Albert of Piacenza, Bonvisus of Piacenza and Radulph of Piacenza). On Guido as Sacconi's co-inquisitor, see BOP, I, 224–5.

[32] Käppeli, 'Une somme', p. 313; Caldwell, 'Peter Martyr', p. 140.

[33] See documents in F. Tocco, *Quel che non c'è nella* Divina Commedia; *o, Dante e l'eresia* (Bologna, 1899), no. 16, p. 54 (12 August 1245); no. 17, p. 55 (12 August 1245); no. 18, pp. 56–7 (24 August 1245).

[34] The suggestion appears, for example, in Šanjek's 'Introduction' to the *Summa*, p. 33.

[35] For example the Council of Toulouse (1246), in *Sacrorum conciliorum nova et amplissima collectio*, ed. J.-D. Mansi, 31 vols., 2nd edn (Graz, 1960–1), XXIII, cols. 722–3, chs. 31–3.

[36] As twice recorded in depositions from Toulouse, *Inquisitors and Heretics*, ed. Biller, Bruschi and Sneddon, pp. 526, 722.

to become familiar with the community, then he would have been about twenty-three when he converted to Catholicism; thus he was born sometime before 1225. If, instead, he was in his early teens – fourteen, for example – then he would have been born sometime before 1217. We can thus infer that, in either case, he must have been slightly younger than Peter of Verona (born likely at the beginning of the century, and Brother Preacher from 1220–1 onwards).[37] According to Käppeli the two acted together, as main inquisitor and non-specified assistant, after Peter's time in Florence in 1244–5.[38]

By 1252 Peter and the now-converted Ranier are both on the radar of the conspirators who plot Peter's murder. Ranier Sacconi replaced Peter as inquisitor at his death, and carried out the inquest on the killing, which he pursued with an obstinacy that is not difficult to understand. In 1262, as we have seen, Ranier Sacconi was still inquisitor. On 26 January 1267, five years later, Brother Anselm of Alessandria, who was office-holder in Genoa at least in 1256, was promoted inquisitor in Lombardy and the Genoese March (the post held by Sacconi) by the provincial John of Turin. In 1269 Anselm recorded the confession of guilt by Stephen Confalonieri, the main character behind Peter of Verona's killing. Anselm's promotion probably coincided with his becoming the holder of this tricky and delicate inquest.[39]

How can this intricate chronological sequence help our understanding? Father Dondaine once suggested personal acquaintance between Ranier and Anselm, given the chronological overlap of their inquisitorial duties.[40] In the light of modern knowledge of inquisitorial procedure, we can assume that Ranier was the main coordinator in Lombardy and the Genoese March since 1252, with Anselm based in Genoa certainly in 1256 as a 'secondary' contact, perhaps an inquisitor vicar. Even at this level there must have been some sort of contact between them, at least in writing, or even in person. Seven years later, in 1262, the pope summoned Sacconi to Viterbo to discuss matters of heresy, which suggests that Sacconi was still acting as the main figure in the Lombardy area. At this point Sacconi disappears. We could therefore suggest Sacconi left his duties at some point between 1262 and 1267, due to either old age or death.

Dondaine, again, saw a clear link between Sacconi's and Anselm's works, which look complementary. He even advanced the hypothesis that Anselm might have possessed the original *Summa* by Ranier, and aimed at its

---

[37] Käppeli, 'Une somme', p. 315; Prudlo, *Martyred Inquisitor*, p. 18.
[38] Käppeli, 'Une somme', p. 315.
[39] A. Dondaine, 'La hiérarchie cathare en Italie', *Archivum Fratrum Praedicatorum* 20 (1950), 261 and n. 57, where he refers to a document kept in the Milanese archives. The fact that John of Turin also hands over to him 'many pontifical documents concerning the activities of this tribunal' looks like the handing over of the full archive, which was normally transmitted by the main inquisitor to his successor.
[40] Ibid., p. 262.

completion when writing his *Tractatus*. It is not unlikely that, if Anselm took over from Sacconi in leading and coordinating the Lombard inquisitors, he might also have inherited his library. Anselm tells us in fact that he too possessed the Cathar text known as the *Secretum*[41] – it could be another exemplar or Sacconi's very own copy of John of Lugio's work.[42] We have other examples of how the office's library possessions are stored and catalogued into a neat archive, to be used by the next office-holder.[43] It is the same with finance books, as I myself have studied.[44] Nothing should therefore prevent us from thinking that the similarities between the two works are deliberate. The only weakness in this idea lies in the fact that – unlike Sacconi's work – Anselm's did not circulate as widely. In fact, it did not circulate at all. Something here must have gone wrong.

At the time of Sacconi's writing, other works on heresy were available, and some works had been written by dualists themselves. He certainly knew the masterpieces of Catholic controversy, among them Alan of Lille's *De fide Catholica* (pre-1202),[45] from which he takes the section on penance; and presumably he knew the texts circulating within a northern-Italian milieu: the *Manifestatio heresis Catharorum* (c. 1190),[46] and the *De heresi Catharorum in Lombardia* (1190–1214), possibly by an ex-Cathar.[47] He may also have been familiar with the *Liber suprastella* (1235) by a fellow Piacenzan notary,[48] and the *Summa* by Pseudo-James Capelli (post-1234);[49] the one attributed to Peter of Verona (1230–8), which we have incomplete, was perhaps known to him, if not in detail.[50] Being northern Italian, and Dominican, he cannot have missed the seminal *Summa* by Brother Preacher Moneta of Cremona (1240–1) – incidentally, the only one Stephen of Salagnac and Bernard Gui

---

[41] Ibid., p. 249, referring to the Budapest manuscript.

[42] '[Iohannes de Lugio] compilavit quoddam volumen magnum decem quaternorum cuius exemplarium habeo et perlegi et ex illo errores supredictos extraxi', ('[John of Lugio] compiled a large volume of ten quires, a copy of which I have, and I have read through, and from which I have extracted the above-mentioned errors'); *Summa*, ed. Šanjek, p. 57.

[43] *Inquisitors and Heretics*, ed. Biller, Bruschi and Sneddon, pp. 11–14.

[44] C. Bruschi, '*Familia inquisitionis*: A Study on the Inquisitors' Entourage (XIII–XIV Centuries)', *Mélanges de l'École Française de Rome – Moyen Âge*, 125-2 (2013), online at http://mefrm.revues.org/1519.

[45] Alan of Lille, *De fide Catholica contra hereticos sui temporis, praesertim Albigenses*, in *Patrologia Latina*, ed. J.-P. Migne, 217 vols. (Paris, 1844–64) (henceforth *PL*), CCX, 305–430.

[46] *Manifestatio heresis Catharorum quam fecit Bonacursus (Vita haereticorum)*, in *PL* 204, 775–7.

[47] For the text, see A. Dondaine, 'La hiérarchie cathare en Italie: I – Le *De heresi Catharorum in Lombardia*', *Archivum Fratrum Praedicatorum* 19 (1949), 280–312 (pp. 306–12), repr. in A. Dondaine, *Les hérésies et l'inquisition, XII–XIII siècles*, ed. Y. Dossat (London, 1990), IV.

[48] Salvus Burcius (Salvo Burci), *Liber suprastella*, ed. C. Bruschi (Rome, 2002).

[49] Pseudo-James Capelli, *Summa contra hereticos: edizione critica con saggio introduttivo e commento storico*, ed. P. Romagnoli (unpublished PhD dissertation, University of Bologna, 1991–2). Dr Romagnoli and M. Ulturale are currently preparing this work for publication.

[50] *Summa*, ed. Käppeli.

described as 'maxima et validissima'.[51] He also knew and possessed a copy of the work by the Cathar theologian and leader John of Lugio, possibly the *Liber de duobus principiis* written between 1230–5, which he quotes extensively, and had 'read over and over again'. Comparisons between Ranier's text and the text of the Cathar rituals – the Occitan and Latin manuscripts – reveal that he knew their content too, either because he had seen and read them, or because he had performed the rituals himself, had witnessed others doing so, or both. He also knows of letters written by John of Lugio, who – he says – 'always described himself in his letters as elder son and ordained bishop' ('filius maior et ordinatus episcopus').[52] This brief repertoire is meant to show what Ranier was *likely* to have seen and read before writing his own *Summa*, without stating with absolute certainty that such reading did actually occur.[53]

We should not assume that an intellectual operation of literary planning or research – as we understand research – lies beyond Sacconi's work: the idea that, because we now know those works and their rough chronology and location, our medieval predecessors did also, is historically and contextually incorrect. In particular, in Sacconi's case, one should discard the suggestion of an intellectual process going beyond the simple supply of information to inquisitors. There are no consistent how-to manuals known to us before 1248, and the ins and outs of dualist communities were not much known to churchmen at that time. Ranier's work seems as though it was meant to compensate for this lack of information by providing invaluable insider knowledge, and to provide inquisitors with a concise guide to names, places, beliefs and rituals. Lucy Sackville has recently highlighted a 'reticent tone' in Ranier's work, which is extremely similar to that detected in his continuation, Anselm of Alessandria's compendium.[54] Sackville puts forward the idea that this similarity could be due to the fact that both works were born into a specific 'Italian' current of anti-heretical writing which bore witness to a higher degree of literacy among the laity and the Cathar communities. This is certainly true if one reads Ranier and Anselm alongside certain other works (e.g. the *De heresi*, and some parts of the *Liber suprastella*, the former by an ex-heretic, perhaps a notary, and the latter also possibly by a notary, maybe working for the inquisitors). However, when comparing them to the work by Ranier's closest predecessor, Peter of Verona, and with Moneta of

---

[51] Moneta of Cremona, *Adversus Catharos et Valdenses libri quinque*, ed. T. A. Ricchini (Rome, 1743 [repr. Ridgewood NJ, 1964]); 'Moneta de Cremona, qui contra machinationes hereticorum maximam et validissimam summam scripsit' ('Moneta of Cremona, who wrote a great and very reliable *summa* against the machinations of the heretics'), Stephen of Salagnac and Bernard Gui, *De quatuor in quibus Deus Praedicatorum Ordinem insignivit*, p. 33.

[52] See above, n. 10.

[53] A close textual comparison of these works has been partly done in the dissertation by Ulturale, *'Inventer l'hérésie?'*, cited in n. 1 above.

[54] Sackville, *Heresy and Heretics*, p. 152.

Cremona, this interpretation loses strength, as both Moneta's and Peter of Verona's writings are far more theoretically refined and stylistically polished. It is true that Ranier might have not been aware of Peter's written work, but he certainly had the chance to read Moneta. And yet there is little similarity in tone between Moneta's treatise on the one hand, and Ranier's and Anselm's on the other.

Sacconi's work is – as we have said – of little literary value. Despite being called a 'compendium [*summa*] about Cathars and Leoniste, or the Poor of Lyon', most of it talks about the former. There seems to be little structural planning, as the work is complete, but heavily imbalanced. There is no recourse to *auctoritates* or biblical references, and the only references Ranier quotes come from the Cathar John of Lugio's work on the two principles (1230–5). In fact, a noticeable rise in the style, terminological choices and prose occurs when Ranier is talking about John of Lugio and his 'great work' (*magnum opus*), which suggests that Ranier is then working with John's ten quires next to him, possibly taking excerpts or inspiration from them.[55]

There is an overall 'notarial' tone – dry, far from the use of hyperbole which is typical of the preachers. There seems to be no intention to convert his readers, but only to inform them. The only incipit is a brief 'In the name of our Lord Jesus Christ', and the explicit merely 'In the year of the Lord 1250 the above annotated work has been compiled by the said brother Ranier.'[56] The length itself is telling – in the longest manuscript around twenty-three folios – an element placing Ranier in the middle ground between Anselm of Alessandria's thirteen folios and the lengthy 123 of Peter of Verona's *Summa*.[57]

There are several instances where Ranier tells us about, or hints at, the first-hand basis of his knowledge, indicating to readers that it rests upon his own experience. These disclose his desire to expose the errors of his former friends, as well as adding to the trustworthiness of his account. It is worth looking at them in greater detail.

Ranier carefully provides the Catholic and non-Catholic names for groups and their rituals (for instance, 'the imposition of hands is called by them *consolamentum* and spiritual baptism, or also baptism of the Holy Spirit'),[58]

---

[55] *Summa*, ed. Šanjek, pp. 52–7.
[56] Ibid., pp. 42, 60.
[57] The manuscripts are: Lyon, Bibliothèque publique, MS Coste 424, fols. 1r–24v; Paris, Bibliothèque nationale de France (henceforth BnF), MS Doat 36, fols. 67r–90v; and Paris, BnF, MS lat. 14983, fols. 1–46 (*recto* only).
[58] 'Manus impositio vocatur ab eis consolamentum, et spirituale baptismum, sive baptismum Spiriti Sancti'; *Summa*, ed. Šanjek, p. 43; also 'Et appellatur istud officium, ut ita loquar, "caregare servicium"' ('And this task [of the deacons] is called "caregare servicium"'), ibid., p. 48; 'Et primo de ecclesia Albanensium, qui alio nomine dicuntur de Donzenacho' ('And first about the church of the Albanenses, who are called with another name of *Donzenacho*'), ibid., p. 50; 'Vocantur autem iste Dei creature secundum eos "populus Dei" et "anime" atque "oves Israel", et etiam aliis nominibus' ('Instead

thus accounting for a multi-layered terminology.[59] His intention here is, presumably, that of providing the most accurate information. It might sound surprising, therefore, that he calls dualist non-conformists nothing but 'Cathari et Cathare', with only one exception at the very beginning of the treatise, where they are named 'Cathari vel Paterini',[60] as was the custom after 1179, when canon twenty-seven (*Sicut ait beatus Leo*) of the third Lateran council codified the naming of Italian dualists.[61] Is it surprising to find that there is no mention of *boni homines/femine* ('good men/women') in a treatise where the author wants to uncover and clarify what is secret, concealed or ambiguous, and where the intent is to do so by providing the means to recognize, below its surface, the real nature of Catharism? Why use 'Catharus/Cathara' (adjusted according to gender) if they did *not* call themselves such?[62] This omission does not seem a casual one, since Sacconi is well aware of the risk of being accused of attributing precise names and labels to a reality which is more difficult to grasp. This is evident when – interestingly – he talks about the 'churches' present in Italy, France, and eastern Europe. In this crucial demonstration, he removes any room for misunderstanding by starkly addressing his readers: 'do not blame me for calling them "churches", O reader, rather blame them [the Cathars], as they call them thus.'[63]

Through the warp and weft of doctrines, accurate refutation of Cathar texts, historical data and personal recollection of events, Ranier weaves a piece of work where effectiveness and usefulness are the paramount objective. This texture owes much to Ranier's personal contribution: what he has seen and heard. He tells us that 'without a shadow of doubt […] *I have never seen, in seventeen years of familiarity with them*, any Cathar praying individually, removed from others, or showing contrition about their sins, or crying and

---

these creatures of God are called, according to them, "people of God", and "souls", and "sheep of Israel", and also with other names'), ibid., p. 51.

[59] For Paolini, Sacconi's precision in accounting for names, events, and places is the proof of his reliability; L. Paolini, 'La chiesa di Desenzano: un secolo di storia nel panorama del Catarismo padano', in *Eretici del Garda: la chiesa catara di Desenzano del Garda*, ed. L. Flöss (Desenzano del Garda, 2005), pp. 17–39 (p. 33); Sackville, *Heresy and Heretics*, pp. 137, 152.

[60] 'Cathari sive Paterini'; *Summa*, ed. Šanjek, p. 42.

[61] *Decrees of the Ecumenical Councils*, ed. N. Tanner, 2 vols. (London, 1990), I, 224.

[62] Interestingly, the *summa* attributed to Peter Martyr nearly always talks about 'Patareni' and rarely about 'Cathari' (Käppeli, 'Une somme', p. 303). Anselm of Alessandria instead, like Sacconi, talks about Cathari, and in one case he too gives the word in the feminine gender: 'De imposicione manuum omnium catharorum, quam vocant baptismum vel consolamentum, notandum quod semper fit a pluribus, sed in necessitate magna bene fit ab uno solo, et etiam ab una sola cathara' (Anselm of Alessandria, *Tractatus*, p. 313).

[63] 'Nec imputes michi, o lector, quod eas nominavi ecclesias, sed potius eis, quia se ita vocant'; *Summa*, ed. Šanjek, p. 49. This would match what Bernard Gui tells in his *Practica*, where the counter position between churches (as in 'organizations', not as in 'assembly of believers') is highlighted: Bernard Gui, *Practica inquisitionis heretice pravitatis*, ed. C. Douais (Paris, 1886), part I, 10. See Paolini, 'La chiesa di Desenzano', p. 26.

beating their chests saying "O Lord, be propitious to me, for I am a sinner."'[64] Earlier on, he glosses a standard explanation of the way in which Cathars do penance by adding *'In addition to this, I shall also say* that many among them [...] often suffer while remembering that they did not fulfil their own sexual desire more often, when they were not yet adepts of the heresy of Cathars.'[65]

Sacconi's short phrases tell us that he was there. For instance, he recounts how confessions are public, made as an act of public penance in front of all those who attended. Then he adds: 'and many times there are 100 or more, between men and women, Cathars and their believers'.[66] One might suspect a degree of exaggeration in this number, which seems to have been added as a further factual proof within a very didactic narration. This, to a sceptical reader, could look like willingness to inflate numbers in order to make for a stronger Cathar threat; whereas – for a less suspicious one – it could appear as the more understandable falsification of reality by a rather resentful ex-Cathar. It is my opinion, however, that we should give Ranier the benefit of doubt: he is addressing his inquisitor-readers, but calls in God as a witness of his trustworthiness. Would a Brother Preacher, especially a newly converted one, lie under the eyes of God on this very hot matter? And why?

As this following example shows very well, even sections which might sound as though they were made up in an anxious attempt to discredit the adversary are actually not empty accusations. This paragraph matches realistically what we know about requisitions of heretics' possessions, and does so from the point of view of the Cathars:

> Almost everyone is very miserly and strong-minded, and this is why the poor among them – who, in times of persecution do not have what is necessary to live on, or anything with which to repay those of their hosts ['receivers', *receptatores*] whose goods or houses have been destroyed on their account – can scarcely find people willing to shelter them; but the rich Cathars can find many. And this is why, if they can manage, some among them amass and save wealth for themselves.[67]

---

[64] '[...] dico indubitanter [...] in annis XVII, quibus conversatus sum cum eis, *non vidi* aliquem ex eis orare secreto seorsum ab aliis, aut ostendere se tristem de peccatis suis, sive lacrimari vel percutere pectus et dicere: "Propitius esto, o Domine, (michi) peccatori'; *Summa*, ed. Šanjek, p. 45 (italics mine).

[65] 'Ad hec etiam dico amplius quod multi ex eis [...] sepe dolent dum recolunt quod non adimpleverunt sepius libidinem suam tempore quo nondum fuerant professi heresim Catharorum'; ibid., p. 45.

[66] 'Fit etiam ista confessio coram omnibus et publice qui sunt ibi congregati, ubi multotiens sunt centum vel plures viri et mulieres Cathari et credentes eorum'; ibid., p. 46.

[67] '[...] fere omnes sunt avarissimi et tenaces, et est causa quia pauperes eorum, qui tempore persecutionis non habent victui necessaria vel ea quibus possint restaurare suis receptatoribus res et domos, quae pro eis destruuntur, vix possunt invenire aliquem qui velit eos tunc recipere, sed divites Cathari multos inveniunt. Quare quilibet eorum, si potest, divitias sibi congregat et conservat' (ibid., p. 47).

The culpability of the 'receivers', established in the earlier great councils of Toulouse (1229), Béziers (1232) and Tarragona (1242),[68] made them liable to requisitions: goods, including houses, were to be seized and/or destroyed in the attempt to wipe out the memory, financial and social strength of sinners.[69] Sacconi gives us an account of how this practice affected non-conformist networks and communities, and does so speaking from their viewpoint.

Finally, the following example shows us Ranier's awareness of the evolution of practices over time and space. When discussing the way in which 'clergy' are ordained, he makes distinctions between an 'old' and a 'new way'. He achieves this mainly by utilizing a different tense: past 'used to happen' ('consueverat fieri'), as opposed to present 'seems that [...] he institutes' ('videtur quod [...] instituat'):

> The ordination of a bishop used to happen in this way. [...] And this ordination of the younger son has not been changed among them. In truth, what was said above about the bishop has been changed by all Cathars living on this side of the sea, saying that through such an ordination the 'son' would seem to be instituting the 'father', which looks rather incongruous.[70]

Where second-hand information would have simply reported a variation in ritual procedures, Sacconi gives an explanation for (a) the variation itself; (b) those responsible for it; and (c) the underlying theoretical motivation for such changes. This is a valuable insight which adds to the completeness of information.

That Sacconi wishes to provide insider knowledge and not a confutation is also evident by the emphasis he puts upon the idea of secrecy: this should be considered afresh, aside from preoccupations of textual construction, and instead through understanding Sacconi as an ex-Cathar. There is a difference, in fact, between the formulaic nature of a phrase like 'they [the sacraments] are not true sacraments of Christ and of his Church, but deceitful, and diabolical, and [typical of] the malignant Church',[71] and the following descriptions of

---

[68] See discussion on these categories and their shifts in meaning in J. H. Arnold, *Inquisition and Power* (Philadelphia, 2001), pp. 34–40.

[69] L. Paolini, 'Le finanze dell'inquisizione in Italia', in *Gli spazi economici della Chiesa nell'occidente mediterraneo (secc. XII–metà XIV): Atti del XVI Convegno internazionale di studi (Pistoia, 16–19 May 1997)* (Pistoia, 1998), p. 441–81; and, on a specific fourteenth-century case, M. Benedetti, 'Le finanze dell'*officium fidei*', in Benedetti, *Inquisitori*, pp. 153–78; Bruschi, '*Familia*'.

[70] 'Ordinatio autem episcopi consueverat fieri in hunc modum. [...] Et hec ordinatio filii minoris non est mutata inter eos. Illa vero que supradicitur de episcopo mutata est ab omnibus Catharis morantibus citra mare, dicentibus quia per talem ordinationem videtur quod filius instituat patrem, quod satis apparet incongruum'; *Summa*, ed. Šanjek, p. 48.

[71] '[...] quod non sunt vera sacramenta Christi et eius Ecclesie, sed deceptoria et diabolica et

how the most radical tenets of Cathar dualism and mythology are concealed from believers by the hierarchy and the clergy:

> Surely all Albanenses among themselves held the above mentioned opinions in that time, with the exception of the most simple ones, to whom some were not revealed.[72]

> And one must note that the said John [of Lugio] and his accomplices do not dare to reveal the said errors to their own believers, in order to prevent these believers from tearing themselves away from them because of these unheard-of errors.[73]

And, about mutual confession in use among the *Albanenses*, a practice followed by all, men and women: 'unless by chance one is a simple man or a novice among them, in fact they do not reveal at all their secrets [*secreta*] to many of them'.[74]

So, we have a middle-aged inquisitor, ex-heresiarch, convert and now Dominican, who was zealous, probably charismatic, certainly competent, well-read, and trained during the years of Peter of Verona's mandate, before replacing Peter after his death. He – in turn – oversees the career of another inquisitor, Anselm of Alessandria, whom the order designates, with all probability, to replace him. By inserting deliberate textual markers in his work which should prove the reliability of his information beyond any shadow of doubt – 'God knows that I don't lie' – Ranier aims at preventing criticism, the foreseeable counter-argument that would accuse him of attributing a 'Church-moulded' lexicon to the heretics' words.

Aside from his experience, clever rhetorical tricks and knowledge, the one feature which has been too often overlooked is that Ranier Sacconi is, above everything else, a convert. We know that, during Peter of Verona's mandate, there were many conversions from among dualist communities. Dominican sources attribute this wave to the extraordinary effectiveness of Peter's charismatic preaching.[75] This may or may not have been the case.

---

ecclesie malignantium'; ibid., pp. 42–3; but also 'falsa, inania, illicita et sacrilega' ('false, empty, illicit and sacrilegious'); ibid., p. 43.

[72] 'Siquidem predictas opiniones tenebant omnes Albanenses in predicto tempore generaliter, exceptis simplicioribus quibus singula non revelabantur'; ibid., p. 52.

[73] 'Et etiam valde notandum, quod dictus Iohannes et eius complices non audent revelare dictos errores credentibus suis, ne ipsi credentes discedant ab eis propter hos novos errores'; ibid., p. 57.

[74] '[…] nisi forte fuerit homo simplex vel novicius inter eos, talibus enim multis illorum secreta minime revelantur'; ibid., p. 59.

[75] For instance Humbert of Romans, *Epistolae*, ed. Berthier, p. 493; Prudlo, *Martyred Inquisitor*, p. 58 (quoting Galvano Fiamma and a letter of Romeo de Attencia to Raymond of Peñafort); Benedetti, *Inquisitori*, p. 61. Others see this phenomenon as highly

What we know for sure is that Pope Innocent IV on 17 June 1244 issued a peremptory letter to all orders following the Benedictine rule, instructing them to oblige all their novices to not less than a year of novitiate.[76] What Pope Innocent calls 'zeal of the souls', that is the 'urge to earn for God' the souls of sinners, can also be applied to the conversion of ex-Cathars. It is not by chance that, following a petition, possibly by the Dominican community of Sant'Eustorgio in Milan,[77] the same pope on 13 September 1246 released an amendment addressed to Dominican houses, 'persuaded by their supplications', whereby this one-year period could be shortened. The reason being:

> In order for those once oppressed by the obscure chain of heretical depravity [...], to be able to enter a path of salvation; we, persuaded by your supplications, allow you the licence to accept converted heretics or those who are to be converted, who have worn the gown of your community, or who aim at wearing it in the future, to the religious profession within your order after less than one year.[78]

Evidently, conversions to the Order of Preachers were many, in the Milanese territory. The order and indeed the Church were in a rush to save the souls of those who voluntarily returned to orthodoxy – Dominican orthodoxy – and were therefore 'solicitous to gain them to the Lord', to avoid losing them to the forces of evil once more.[79]

---

dependent on the waning of previous favourable conditions: Merlo, for example, talks about 'desertions' (*defezioni*) and not 'conversions'; see G. G. Merlo, *Eretici del Medioevo: temi e paradossi di storia e storiografia* (Brescia, 2011), p. 148.

[76] 'Non solum in favorem conversi' (17 June 1244), in *Bullarium Ordinis Praedicatorum*, ed. Brémond and Ripoll, I, 144.

[77] This is suggested by the clause 'vestris precibus inclinati' ('persuaded by your supplications'). In the footnote to the *Bullarium Ordinis Praedicatorum*, moreover, the editor mentions a now-lost pontifical autograph once kept in the convent of Sant'Eustorgio in Milan.

[78] 'Ut pressi quondam tenebrosa catena heretice pravitatis [...] pedem iniciant in compedes salutares, nos, vestris precibus inclinati, quod hereticos conversos et etiam convertendos, qui vestre religionis habitum assumpserunt, vel quos in posterum continget assumere ad professionem vestri ordinis possitis recipere infra annum [...] vobis concedimus facultatem' ('Ut pressi quondam', in *Bullarium Ordinis Praedicatorum*, ed. Brémond and Ripoll, I, 168, no. 162).

[79] Interestingly, however, the 1250 Chapter General of the Dominicans reintroduced the preparation period of one year, pointing out that, although the probationary period was at the time six months ('probationis vero tempus [...] VI mensium'), it should be brought back to one year ('probacionis vero tempus unius anni statuimus'), so that all applicants could experience the order's required austerity, and the friars could test the applicants' intellectual and moral qualities (*Monumenta Ordinis Praedicatorum Historica* III, p. 52). It seems that fast-tracking was found to detract from the quality of applications and religious conversions.

Why now? During the late 1240s and entire 1250s the Ghibelline front in northern Italian cities had strengthened. Ezzelino of Romano, Oberto Pallavicino and Ubertino Landi, among others, appeared frequently in sources as the 'antichrists', as they opposed with strength, stubbornness and tenacity the papacy's interference in local policies.[80] Whatever their *inner* motivations, these leaders' reluctance to subscribe to the anti-heretical legislation went hand in hand with open challenge to inquisitorial officers and the sheltering of non-conformist communities. In all northern Italian communes where this pattern emerges – Piacenza, Milan, Bologna and Rimini, for instance[81] – one can note a specific reaction from the Church, that is, a new revival of inquisitorial practices, and renewed dogmatism in prosecuting heresy when the Ghibelline front breaks down, at the death of its leaders, from the beginning of 1260s. It is not a coincidence that Peter of Verona's killing, the plot to assassinate Ranier Sacconi, and the various occurrences of inquisitors being ostracized – Ranier too is expelled from Milan by the *podestà* Pallavicino – all happen within this climate. Alexander IV's letter of December 1260 requesting the exceptional number of eight further inquisitors to be at Ranier's side attests to the stark need for a greater number of personnel in the field.[82]

Such anxious haste is very evidently echoed in Ranier's *Summa*: although formally completed – it has an incipit and an explicit – it is not structurally so, and the imbalance of sections suggests inconsistent (or insufficient) planning; it does not show a particular background of research on the anti-heretical tradition, and does not cross-refer to the Scriptures. On two occasions Ranier himself tells us that he wants to cut things short: first, within the lengthy description of John of Lugio's errors, he states 'What more? Writing the many fables written by John about the above vices and idols in order to try and state his errors is repulsive to me.'[83] Here Sacconi uses the word *tedium*. The same word recurs a few folios later, in a similar phrase about the same subject. In this second case we are at the highest point in his description of doctrinal

---

[80] See Bruschi, 'Dissenso', pp. 240–5; Diehl, 'Overcoming Reluctance', p. 61 (Diehl saw a connection between the reiteration of papal prescriptions in the 1250s and a 'continuing resistance to a forcible repression of heresy', but overlooked the link between this and the political scenario of the 1240s and 1250s); L. Paolini, 'L'eresia catara a Rimini (secoli XII–XIII)', in *Storia della Chiesa riminese*, ed. R. Savigni and A. Vasina, 2 vols. (Rimini, 2010–11), II, 293–315 (p. 311).

[81] Paolini 'L'eresia catara a Rimini', p. 312; J. Dalarun, 'Hérésie, commune et inquisition à Rimini (fin XII – début XIV siècle', *Studi Medievali* 3rd s. 29 (1988), 641–83 (pp. 647, 652–5); L. Paolini, 'L'eresia catara alla fine del Duecento', in L. Paolini and R. Orioli, *L'eresia a Bologna fra XIII e XIV secolo*, 2 vols. (Rome, 1975), I, 15–18.

[82] 'Cum super negotio', in *Bullarium Ordinis Praedicatorum*, ed. Brémond and Ripoll, I, 399.

[83] 'Quid plura? Tedium est michi scribere multa fabulosa que dictus Iohannes scripsit de superascriptis viciis et ydolis ut suos asserere conaretur errores.' *Summa*, ed. Šanjek, p. 53.

errors. Again, Sacconi says: 'Indeed the oft-quoted John of Lugio, heresiarch, made up the above-mentioned blasphemies, which would be long and even repulsive for me to list.'[84] Ranier has provided a very effective and accurate depiction of John of Lugio's exegesis and teachings, which represent the acme of Cathar radical dualistic thought. In stating the reliability of his recollection (that he even possesses the text written by John of Lugio), he wants to break off from the erroneous beliefs these teachings refer to. Could this be a mere rhetorical tool, a sort of *recusatio* from speaking about sinful beliefs? Yes, if this writer were not Sacconi. For instance, the very last recorded phrase of the *Summa* attributed to Peter Martyr is a very learned equivalent, where the author says he wishes to avoid pointless and obsolete discussion: 'There were many other heresies [...] about which, because in our days they have been completely wiped out, I did not care to write, wasting a page.'[85] When written by a newly converted Preacher phrases such as these suggest a sort of nauseous recalling of something he knows very well, and despises from the bottom of his heart, especially because Ranier knows that he himself, long ago, had believed these *fabulosa*: 'what a foolish, unsubstantiated thing to believe' – he seems to add – 'and in any case, what I have said about them is sufficient for the purpose of this work'.[86] Far from a doctrinal demonstration, Sacconi creates a repository of information on the foolishness, audacity and doctrinal weakness of those beliefs.

On taking over Sacconi's job, his inquests, and probably the contents of his library, Anselm of Alessandria also took over his task: he completed the information on Catharism by adding some discussion of the Concorezzan Church, included more on Waldensians, inserted the section on Cathar origins and migration to Europe and – most importantly to us – he set up a very effective template for mapping hierarchies within Cathar geography. All of this, again, appears to have started in a tidy – albeit rushed – way, before he loses control of his plan just after the insertion of Ranier's *summa*. Here he adds various material: more on the Poor of Lyon, some information 'heard by another' ('audita ab alio') on the Lombards, tiny glossed snippets on the *Secretum* of the Concorezzans, a formulary on the examination of heretics, more on common points on the Waldensians, *formulae* and a list of ministers of Albanenses and Concorezzans. Such a conglomeration of data strikes the reader as having been put together in a random order, or – and this is my view – as he went along.

Anselm's treatise, like Ranier's, is addressed to practitioners. The author himself informs us when talking about the imposition of hands: 'and we need

---

[84] 'Siquidem blasphemias et errores predictos et multos alios quos longum esset et etiam michi tedium ennarrare, finxit sepedictus Iohannes de Lugio heresiarcha'; ibid., p. 57.

[85] 'Fuerunt autem quam plures alie hereses [...] de quibus, quia iam temporibus nostris sunt penitus delete, non curavi cartam inutiliter occupare'; *Summa*, ed. Käppeli, p. 335.

[86] Käppeli sums up this attitude as 'sentiments un peu excessifs d'un converti'; ibid., p. 35.

to be very careful, when *we have* some suspects, that Cathars do not go near the ones who are ill, or even to the houses where these are detained'.[87] A very detailed section on rituals follows, which comes no doubt from knowledge gathered while carrying out inquisitorial duties. Such a degree of detail is most probably meant to help officials who are being trained, or who want to know more about this subject.

Both Sacconi's and Anselm's work, though, are famous for the information they provide on Cathar hierarchy, geography, history and inner fragmentation. The Churches – Ranier says – are the way in which *Cathars themselves* structure *and name* their communities. Whatever the earlier text of the Council of Saint-Félix-de-Caraman[88] wanted to achieve, it originated in the will *of non-conformists* to mould communities into a territorial, manageable and organized shape. We can trace the Cathars' desire to number themselves, as reported by Sacconi, to the same attitude. The witness detailing the decisions of the council of Pieusse in the Doat inquisitorial depositions shows the same desire.[89] And that this rooting actually occurred we know from a series of scattered – but nevertheless very effective – pieces of topographical evidence found in northern Italian cities such as Rimini, Bologna, and Verona. As we all know, topography bears witness to the already acknowledged geographical appropriation of a place, a building, an area.[90]

---

[87] '[…] et ideo diligenter cavendum est quando habemus aliquos suspectos ne cathari infirmantibus appropinquent, vel etiam domibus in quibus detinentur'; Anselm of Alessandria, *Tractatus*, p. 314.

[88] On this very controversial theme, see the latest contributions: *L'histoire du catharisme en discussion: le 'concile' de Saint-Félix (1167)*, ed. M. Zerner (Nice, 2001); F. Zambon, 'Où en est le problème des actes du concile de Saint-Félix? À propos de *L'histoire du catharisme en discussion*', in *Les cathares devant l'histoire: mélanges offerts à Jean Duvernoy*, ed. M. Aurell (Cahors, 2005), pp. 135–44; M. Zerner, 'Mise au point sur *Les cathares devant l'histoire* et retour sur *L'histoire du catharisme en discussion*: le débat sur la charte de Niquinta n'est pas clos', *Journal des savants* 2 (2006), 253–73; D. Zbìral, 'La charte de Niquinta et les récits sur les commencements des églises cathares en Italie et dans le Midi', *Heresis* 44–5 (2006), 135–62; D. Zbìral, 'La charte de Niquinta et le rassemblement de Saint-Félix: état de la question', in *1209–2009: cathares: une histoire à pacifier? Actes du colloque international tenu à Mazamet les 15, 16 et 17 mai 2009*, ed. A. Brenon (Portet-sur-Garonne, 2010), pp. 31–44; J. Dalarun, 'La charte de Niquinta: débats heuristiques, enjeux herméneutiques', *Aevum* 88 (2012), 535–48, esp. pp. 542–8.

[89] For which see Bruschi, *The Wandering Heretics*, pp. 136–7, 141, 195; A. Roach, *The Devil's World: Heresy and Society, 1100–1300* (Harlow, 2005), pp. 124–5; M. Barber, *The Cathars: Dualist Heretics in Languedoc in the High Middle Ages* (London, 2000), p. 142.

[90] Paolini, 'L'eresia catara a Rimini', p. 298, who accounts for toponyms such as *domus patarorum, vicus pataranie, fossa patara, molendinum patarenorum, via patara, locus dictum* 'la Patarina', etc; L. Paolini, '*Domus* e zona degli eretici: l'esempio di Bologna nel XIII secolo', *Rivista di storia della Chiesa in Italia* 35 (1981), 371–87; Paolini, 'L'eresia catara alla fine del Duecento', pp. 167–9; G. M. Varanini, '*Minima hereticalia*: schede d'archivio veronesi (sec. XII–XIII)', in *Chiesa, vita religiosa, società nel Medioevo italiano: studi offerti a Giuseppina De Sandre Gasparini*, ed. M. Rossi and G. M. Varanini (Rome, 2005), pp. 677–93.

Lorenzo Paolini has highlighted the fact that, beyond a supposed stereotypical organization of random communities into Churches, in both Sacconi and Anselm there is the spelling out of names and hierarchy lists, and a detailed mapping of inner groups. There is a palpable drive to make order and to tidy up what was previously scattered information, hearsay and snippets of depositions.[91] Sacconi *assumes* his readers know that – at some point – there had been a division (I avoid the word 'schism' on purpose), on account of which there are now three groups, with common points and some different ones. He tells us about them, then about the way they order their leaders and how ministers are promoted up (or down) the hierarchical scale; then he tells us where one can find them, their Churches, and the way in which these Churches reflect such doctrinal division. It makes sense.

In his mapping, Sacconi is accurate, and in all his information thorough, quoting places, multiple ways to name the internal groups, and their affiliation to each other on the basis of doctrine. Then, he ends with a discussion of the *opiniones* (that is, doctrinal tenets) of their leaders: Belesinanza, John of Lugio and Nazarius. Finally, squeezed into eight lines of the concluding section on Cathars, more is added on opinions held in Bagnolo and in the Churches in France. This approximation and succinctness shows that this last topic was not his priority. Instead, the very final paragraph is particularly telling. Sacconi says:

> Moreover, all the Cathar Churches accept each other, despite having different, or even opposite views, *except the Albanensians and the Concorezzans*, who condemn each other reciprocally.[92]

The same is stated by a notary from Piacenza, the author of the *Liber suprastella*, fifteen years before Sacconi wrote his work, in a famous passage at the very beginning:

> Against the Cathars who are called Albanenses and Concorezzans, who differ very much among themselves, that is, condemn one another to death: the Albanenses saying against the Concorezzans that they are the Church of God, and saying that the others come from them 'and have seceded from us'; and, conversely, the Concorezzans say the same. *It is well known that Albanenses and Concorezzans at various times gathered together, and held many councils, discussing the way in which they could come together to one faith:* both Albanenses and Concorezzans wanting to omit [something] from what they preached, on account of the believers of both of the Albanenses and of the Concorezzans, who were scandalized among

---

[91] Paolini, 'La chiesa di Desenzano', p. 33.
[92] 'Item omnes ecclesie Catharorum recipiunt se ad invicem licet habeant diversa set contrarias opiniones, preter Albanenses et Concorezzenses, qui se dampnant ad invicem sicut supradictum est'; *Summa*, ed. Šanjek, p. 59.

themselves by their preaching. And to this end, in order to be brought back to one ⟨shared⟩ faith, they spent much of their temporal goods going on many and various journeys, wandering hither and thither throughout the world. And some say – that is the Cathars who are called 'Caloiani' and also 'Francigene' [French-born] – that they are entirely not of the faith of the Albanenses, nor of the faith of the Concorezzans. But as they could not agree with each other, and ⟨although⟩ they devoted effort and strove with all their strength to make both sects come together in one faith, saying that *because of this division their Church suffers scandal*, and many of their believers, for this reason, have returned to the Catholic Church,[93] and although, as we have said, they often gathered together, they could not find peace among themselves. For each of these sects wanted to obtain the leadership. But fierce feuds kept going on both sides, and there are great divisions even within each person.[94]

The feud detailed in the *Liber suprastella*, Sacconi, and Anselm, is an all-Italian one, tearing apart communities, families, even individuals, split (morally and physically) between loyalty to their own people and doctrinal disagreements. The *Liber suprastella* tells us that, to some, this is the reason for the wave of conversions back to the Roman Church. If one reads in parallel Sacconi and this earlier work, it seems that the scandal of internal divisions is the disaggregating factor among Cathar communities.[95] The debated issue of a

---

[93] It seems thus that the phenomenon is not a new one during Peter of Verona's times.
[94] 'Contra Catharos qui appellantur Albanenses et Concorricii, qui inter se valde discrepant, videlicet quod unus alterum ad mortem condempnat, dicentes Albanenses adversus Concoricios se esse ecclesiam Dei et dicentes illos fuisse ex ipsis, et a nobis secessi sunt, et e converso Concorritii vero dicunt illud idem. *Manifestum est* quod Albanenses et Concorricii pluries convenerunt in unum et conscilia plurima fecerunt tractando quomodo possent in unam fidem convenire, volentes tam Albanenses quam Concorricii obmittere de eo quod predicabant propter credentes eorum tam Albanensium quam Concorrentium, qui inter se scandaliçabantur ex eorum predicatione. Et propter hoc, ut reducerentur ad unam fidem, multum de temporalibus rebus consumpserunt in diversis et multis itineribus euntes, huc atque illuc vagantes per orbem terrarum, et quidem dicunt, id est Catheri qui Caloiani vel eciam Francigene nuncupantur, qui ex toto non sunt ex fide Albanensium nec ex fide Concorritiorum. Sed con non possent ad invicem concordari et operam dedissent et pro viribus niterentur ut ambe secte simul in una fide convenirent, dicendo quod eorum ecclesia patitur scandalum pro divisione eorum, et multi de eorum credentibus propter hoc ad Romanam Ecclesiam sunt remeati, et licet multociens sicut diximus, sint congregati ad invicem pacem reperire non potuerunt, volentes enim unaqueque illarum sectarum dominium optinere. Set lites vehementer in ambabus partibus remanserunt et in una quaque persona sunt divisiones magne.' Burci, *Liber suprastella*, pp. 5–6 (italics are mine). See also ibid., p. 284 (on Poor Lombards – 'maior non potest esse divisio' – and on Concorezzans, Albanenses, the Poor of Lyon and Poor Lombards – 'hec quatuor secte sunt contrarie una alteri quasi ut ignis aque, et una ad mortem aliam condempnat'), and p. 290 ('Concorricii et Albanenses sunt due secte, deum quod unus credit bonum alter credit falsum, nulla potest esse maior divisio').
[95] This Lombard tendency to division is witnessed by earlier sources too – Stephen of

Cathar 'census', accounted for by Sacconi, also points in this direction: that of a broken community which tries to make sense of itself, both doctrinally and numerically, and to re-establish its own identity.[96] There is certainly no need to refer to the learned quotation of Isidore of Seville, to a symbolization of the hydra[97] with several heads, in these Italian writers. Reality, as it happens, exceeded stereotype. Here, in Sacconi, in the *Liber suprastella*, in Anselm, the hydra is alive. Each head has a name, many names – in fact, a sequence of names. It has followers, young and new, and leaders. Heresy is a true wedge separating communities who were once closely knitted. One can even map the hydra on a piece of parchment. Sacconi does so: here the Albanenses, in Verona, and in some other Lombard cities; here the Concorezzans, 'the Bagnolenses are in Mantua, Brescia, Bergamo, in the countryside of Milan, but few here', he adds colloquially.[98] To Sacconi and to Anselm, knowledge of this map is paramount because of the mutual excommunication of the two groups, which stems from a radically different mythological interpretation of the Scriptures. Crucially, this is not in the information the Cathars tell their sympathizers, 'credentes', simpler people, or 'novices' (say all three sources), but is reserved to those among them who are confirmed in their beliefs. Sacconi, who once was one of them, knows the 'secrets' (*secreta*) well.

The ruptures within the Cathar groups have split not only consciences but also families. We know of members of the same parental group dividing their allegiance between the Roman Church and the non-conformist ones: the Sacconi presumably did so, as did the family of Peter of Verona, the da Giussano (one Brother Minor, one Cathar, converted by the death of Peter of Verona, and then becoming inquisitor), and the da Sesto.[99] The de Cario themselves, commissioning the composition of *Liber suprastella*, are caught in

---

Bourbon (*c.* 1220) and the *De heresi Catharorum in Lombardia* (1190–1214) – and it seems to stop around the time of Sacconi's work; see Paolini, 'La chiesa di Desenzano', pp. 35–7.

[96] Sacconi tells us that there are sixteen churches of the Cathars (*Summa*, ed. Šanjek, p. 49), and refers to precise numbers of heretics in each of them (specifying that they are 'of both sexes') (p. 50), and that 'in the whole world there are 4,000 heretics of both sexes, *and this computation has been made among them many a time in the past*' ('in toto mundo non sunt Cathari utriusque sexus numero MMMM, et dicta computatio pluries olim facta est inter eos') (ibid.); see also Paolini, 'La chiesa di Desenzano', p. 36.

[97] *Isidori Hispalensis Episcopi Etymologiarum sive Originum libri XX*, ed. W. M. Lindsay, 2 vols. (Oxford, 1911) XI.3.34–5, quoting Ambrose, *De fide Catholica*, 1, 46. This symbolism is thus derived from the fathers, see for instance Iohannes Cassianus, *De incarnatione Christi*, in *PL* 50, cols. 9–272 (cols. 11–12) on Nestorius (*c.* 430); Later, and somewhat closer to our times (1199–1202), Alan of Lille, *De fide Catholica contra hereticos*, in *PL* 210, cols. 305–428, (col. 307). On the relevance of such symbolism to the historical perspective in Sacconi, see Sackville, *Heresy and Heretics*, p. 145.

[98] *Summa*, ed. Šanjek, pp. 49–50; for example: 'Etiam Baiolenses Mantue, Brixie, Bergami, et in comitatu Mediolani, sed pauci, et in Romaniola, et sunt CC' (p. 50).

[99] Well studied by Benedetti, *Inquisitori*, pp. 34–5, 61, 75–95, esp. 78–9, 88.

this mechanism.¹⁰⁰ There is, it seems, a network of very mercurial adherence to faith and nuanced allegiance to belief and communal/familial dynamics, which would confirm the idea that, in the eyes of the authorities 'heresy threatens co-existence, social peace and the quiet and orderly institutional layout of Christian societies. Heresy is disaggregating to the social order, breaks down and damages the common patrimony of the only, legitimate faith.'¹⁰¹ This aspect is still untapped ground for study. It is, to me, the fundamental proof that, well beyond political loyalties and familial ties, and beyond wider feudal dynamics of support for the papacy or its adversaries, that which we call heresy is, after all, and more than anything else, a matter of individual faith. And that, as this discussion has shown, and perhaps contrary to what we often think, was a matter of individual freedom of thought. Just as it is now.

---

[100] Burci, *Liber suprastella*, pp. xii–xiv.
[101] Paolini, 'L'eresia catara a Rimini', p. 307 (translation mine).

10

The Textbook Heretic: Moneta of Cremona's Cathars

Lucy J. Sackville

Moneta of Cremona's *Summa adversus Catharos et Valdenses* has been at the centre of the conception of Catharism for a long time. Widely used by contemporaries, both the text and its author retained a consistent place in the Dominican (and later also Jesuit) memory of anti-heretical writing from the time of its composition until it was edited by Thomas Ricchini at the Dominican convent in Rome in 1743.[1] Ricchini's edition was used in early nineteenth-century histories of the Catholic Church and of Catholic writers, but it was placed back at the centre of the history of heterodoxy with the advent of modern scholarship on heresy that began, in earnest, with Charles Schmidt in the middle of the nineteenth century.

Schmidt, really the first modern commentator to look at the Cathars as a subject in their own right, was a leading figure in a revival of interest in medieval heresy, and his *Histoire et doctrine de la secte des cathares ou albigeois* set the standard for much of the work that followed.[2] Another work on Catharism was being written at the same time, by Hahn, and Schmidt acknowledged this work, but he did not perceive it as being exactly parallel to his own project.[3] He saw himself as addressing a topic that had been

---

[1] Moneta of Cremona, *Adversus Catharos et Valdenses libri quinque*, ed. T. A. Ricchini (Rome, 1743 [repr. Ridgewood NJ, 1964]). Ricchini collects historical references to Moneta's work from Stephen of Salagnac to Franciscus Arisius in his introduction, pp. ix–xii. I expand here my earlier discussion, L. J. Sackville, *Heresy and Heretics in the Thirteenth Century: The Textual Representations* (York, 2011), pp. 13–40.

[2] C. Schmidt, *Histoire et doctrine de la secte des cathares ou albigeois*, 2 vols. (Paris, 1848–9). See P. Biller, 'Cathars and Material Women', in *Medieval Theology and the Natural Body*, ed. P. Biller and A. J. Minnis, York Studies in Medieval Theology 1 (York, 1997), pp. 61–81 (pp. 72–3); Y. Dossat, 'Un initiateur: Charles Schmidt', *Historiographie du catharisme = Cahiers de Fanjeaux* 14 (1979), 163–84; U. Brunn, *Des contestataires aux 'cathares': discours de réforme et propagande antihérétique dans les pays du Rhin et de la Meuse avant l'inquisition* (Paris, 2006), pp. 13–14.

[3] C. U. Hahn, *Geschichte der Ketzer im Mittelalter, besonders im 11., 12. und 13. Jahrhundert: nach den Quellen bearbeitet*, 3 vols. (Stuttgart, 1845–50); Schmidt, *Histoire et doctrine*, p. iii n. 1.

little covered, looking at heresy not as part of the history of the Church so much as part of the wider western intellectual tradition. That meant that his interest in reading the anti-heretical texts of the high medieval period was primarily in excavating what visible remains of heterodox thought could be discerned, rather than in the commentators and authors who wrote about it. His approach to his topic was therefore one of self-conscious and deliberate reconstruction of a sect, a process that he described as rebuilding an edifice from scattered debris.[4] These materials, his debris, were collected largely from French archives, and to a lesser extent from German and Swiss archives, but Schmidt was frank about his inability or disinclination to use Italian material: at the time he was writing, the material was too scattered, and access to it too problematic. Tellingly, he described the task of reconstruction as an exercise in reconnecting events and information which would otherwise look unrelated, in order to present a coherent whole.[5]

The two volumes of the work treat the two parts of Schmidt's subject, history and doctrine. The second volume lays out the reconstructed belief system of the Cathars and deals, in turn, with theology, morality, cult, hierarchy and character. Within those categories, the various data gleaned from his different sources are fitted into a framework that is largely drawn from anti-heretical treatises. Schmidt used some earlier texts to provide this framework, for instance Eckbert of Schönau's *Sermones contra Catharos* and Bonacursus's *Manifestatio*, but he relies most heavily on thirteenth-century texts – Ranier Sacconi's *Summa de Catharis et Pauperibus de Lugduno*, and, especially, Moneta's *Summa*. This is interesting, given that a large proportion of Schmidt's other material is French, and drawn from a much longer chronological range than that described by these treatises. In fact, an overwhelming proportion of the framework that Schmidt builds rests upon Moneta's text; indeed, even the structure of the second volume echoes that of Moneta's *Summa*. All the partial elements that Schmidt unearths in earlier material, stretching back to the tenth century, are thus given a place within the framework visible in later works, and the structure and arrangement of the discussion presents Cathar belief and doctrine as a coherent system.

Schmidt was writing a history that aimed to rebalance the view of the western tradition, and to move away from a focus on authoritarian repression of thought and liberty, towards one in which different strands or positions

---

[4] 'Nous avons tâché de reconstruire un édifice avec des débris épars et des matériaux rassemblés de différents côtés'; Schmidt, *Histoire et doctrine*, p. v.

[5] 'On nous reprochera peut-être d'être entré dans trop de détails. Mais [...] il nous a semblé que les détails étaient le meilleur moyen de faire connaître le véritable caractère de la secte [...] Un fait en apparence minutieux répand souvent un jour inattendu sur toute une période obscure; il sert d'intermédiaire pour rétablir la liaison entre des événements, qui sans cela ne paraîtraient être que des accidents sans suite et sans importance'; Schmidt, *Histoire et doctrine*, p. vi.

of thought were possible. In that context, he is reluctant to ascribe dualist thought to the groups he describes, because he clearly admires them not for their religious ideas, but for what he sees as a rational and free-thinking reaction to authority and institutional thought. He seems to regard dualism as an undesirable position, but he attributes it to his subjects because the frame that he gives them is built from texts that read them in this way. He is much more scathing of the institutions that would condemn free thought, and react with coercion rather than persuasion and reason (perhaps one of the reasons that he favours Moneta's long, argumentative and academic approach to the topic, and is dismissive of his contemporary Hahn because he does not pay adequate attention to the rational and philosophical elements of the history of the sect.) He does not, however, seek to present a monolithic sect, *per se*, but rather a counter-tradition in western thought.

Strands of this history of Catharism were picked up and taken in several directions by commentators over the next century, and Moneta's text remained at the heart of that history.[6] In 1890, Ignaz von Döllinger took up the idea of a coherent structured belief system and extended it, through a reinsertion of the Cathars into a history of alternative heterodox movements that set the development of the sect within a longer history of Gnostic-Manichaean belief in Europe.[7] Thus, beginning with the Paulicians, and encompassing the Bogomils and the reform preachers of western Europe, he devoted half of his first volume to a history of 'the Cathars', looking at origins, then teachings (dividing these latter into two main groups), and then shared beliefs. This again has much in common with the layout of the Italian thirteenth-century texts: a straightforward exposition of doctrine, it is so heavily underpinned by biblical citations as to resemble a high medieval description. All the beliefs are carefully distinguished by geography and group following Ranier Sacconi's scheme, and drawing heavily once again on Moneta and on late thirteenth and fourteenth-century inquisition records, many of which he included in the extraordinarily wide range of documents edited in the second volume. Von Döllinger's interpretation preserves the idea of a hierarchical and organized structure existing in a relatively stable state from an early stage.

Douais, writing soon afterwards, presented a two-part work that was concerned to bring original texts into the discussion.[8] In that much, Douais's

[6] For detailed discussion of the historiographical development since Schmidt see A. Borst, *Die Katharer* (Stuttgart, 1953), pp. 42–58; Biller, 'Cathars and Material Women', pp. 72–81; Brunn, *Des contestataires*, pp. 14–22.
[7] I. von Döllinger, *Beiträge zur Sektengeschichte des Mittelalters*, 2 vols. (Munich 1890).
[8] C. Douais, *Les albigeois, leurs origines, action de l'Église au XIIe siècle* (Paris, 1879). Douais was also the first scholar to produce an account of heretics in Languedoc based entirely on Toulouse, Bibliothèque municipale, MS 609: *Les hérétiques du comté de Toulouse dans la première moitié du XIIIe siècle, d'après l'enquête de 1245: compte rendu du congrès scientifique international des catholiques* (Paris, 1891), pp. 148–62.

work was moving away from what Schmidt was trying to do, and bringing this history back into that of repression and authority. The first part of his commentary is an overview of the origins of the 'Albigeois', which essentially traces the different stages of Manichaeism, from the seventh century onwards, via the Paulicians and Bogomils, the fifth and final stage being the Albigensians, established in northern France by the eleventh century. The second part examines the relationship between the Albigensians and the Church. Douais looks first at Albigensian doctrine, in metaphysical and then moral terms. Alongside this, he examines the state of the contemporary Church, with particular attention to reformers like Peter of Bruys and Valdes, but also to Jewish schools on the Mediterranean coast. The spread of Albigensians in the twelfth century is then placed in this context: the early wandering preachers, Robert of Arbrissel, Raoul Ardent, and the early legation and missions of Alberic and St Bernard. And so it goes, interweaving the history of the Cathars with that of the Church's anti-heretical mission and conciliar activity in the south of France.

The work of Arno Borst in the middle of the twentieth century was in many ways the closest to Schmidt's in outlook.[9] He too was concerned to look at 'Catharism' as part of a wider western tradition, and as part of a broader tension inherent in western religion between Christianity and dualism. (Although he did see connections to the East, it was in terms of the importation and adaptation of ideas, rather than the transplantation of a sect.) His view of the sect itself was that any homogeneity it may have exhibited was brought about as a result of external pressures from the Church, and in deliberate opposition to it. So he described a change over time in the structure of the groups holding these beliefs, which only became coherent, condensed into dogma and morality, in the face of opposition, rather than as the result of any natural evolution. He did not regard the belief system that he looked at to be homogenous, therefore, but rather a 'zusammengewürfelt' group of different beliefs and sects, brought together by the accidents of history.[10] Here he deliberately aligned his work with that of Schmidt, and set it apart from that of Döllinger and Molinier who saw this as a closed system of belief. He regarded his work as part of a reaction to this closed view, along with Grundmann, Dondaine, and Morghen in particular, who emphasized the plurality of divisions within the heretical groups described by the Church.[11] Nonetheless, Borst still relied heavily on Moneta and the thirteenth-century commentators.

Schmidt's work therefore provided a foundation for a picture of a stable, long-term system of belief, a picture that was structured largely

---

[9] Borst, *Die Katharer*, p. 6.
[10] Ibid., p. 143.
[11] Ibid., pp. v, 143. Borst did see a hierarchy visible in the later period: as a result of oppression, the Cathars founded a church, he says (p. 213).

via thirteenth-century texts, though it is worth noting that, while he saw continuities and relationships of thought as part of a counter-tradition, he did not necessarily see those as corresponding to a fixed framework of a counter-Church. Schmidt did not make the same claims for uniformity or for coherence as were made later by commentators who took that overarching structure of thought and laid it over organization and relationships as well. Duvernoy, for example, made a very neat and schematic picture out of the complex set of ideas that Schmidt was trying to present, a picture that took the principle of basing the thought system on the thirteenth-century material, and extended and simplified it to project the state of thirteenth-century heretical groups backwards as well.[12]

The edifice of 'Catharism', as a coherent and organized alternative religious institution, against which historians of heresy have argued for some time, is therefore in large part the legacy of those scholars who were first interested in medieval heresy in its own right in the second half of the nineteenth century, Schmidt in particular, but also his continuators. The picture they drew was one of an established and institutional counter-Church, with a firm and international doctrine, spanning the eleventh to fourteenth centuries. Much, if not most, of what was and is used to construct that edifice is taken from, or framed by, Moneta's work, filtered through Sacconi and Anselm of Alessandria. Isolated pieces are given longer-term significance by being slotted into that scheme. The idea of 'Catharism' as a system has been significantly complicated since then, and few would now subscribe to the old view of Catharism as a counter-Church, but the basic idea is tenacious (particularly in the popular imagination) and continues to provide a target for scholarly argument. The problems of applying an historiographical framework built from thirteenth-century material to the evidence surviving for twelfth-century heresy have been well demonstrated, most effectively through close examination of that evidence in its own immediate context. But the problem of applying that framework to the broader situation of the thirteenth century itself has been less examined, and, furthermore, there is some danger that the revisionist view of the twelfth century is now influencing interpretation of the thirteenth. Detaching thirteenth-century Italian material from an overall picture, where it has been used to talk about earlier times and other places, is as necessary for the thirteenth century as it is for the twelfth. The obvious problems with applying the later material to the earlier period also refracts a certain unreliability back to Moneta, but that obscures what he is doing and where he finding his material. To that end, I want to look in more detail at Moneta's text, so central to the received idea of 'medieval Catharism', and to understand what he is actually doing, what were his sources, his motives and models, how those shaped his text, and therefore the image of 'Catharism' that he presents.

---

[12] J. Duvernoy, *Le catharisme*, 2 vols. (Paris, 1976–9).

Moneta was a scholar at the university of Bologna, a teaching master in the Arts who, like several of his colleagues, was moved to join the new Dominican order upon hearing the preaching of Reginald of Orléans in the city in 1218 or 1219. His recruitment, part of the order's early drive to attract scholars to its ranks, must have been something of a coup since Moneta is given a prominent place in the biographical histories written by the Dominicans later in the century. The *Vitae fratrum*, compiled in the years after 1256 to preserve stories of the early brethren, begins its account of those brothers brought to the order by the Word of God with Moneta, 'tunc in artibis legens in tota Lombardia famosus'.[13] The later collection *De quatuor in quibus*, begun by Stephen of Salagnac in the 1270s and revised and completed by Bernard Gui between 1307 and 1314, which sought to show the ways in which the order had been singled out by God, includes Moneta among its illustrious academic members.[14] Moneta's fame in the memory of his order was partly based on his already established academic career, but it rested mainly on the long anti-heretical text, usually called the *Summa adversus Catharos et Valdenses*, that he wrote twenty years after joining the order, in 1241 or thereabouts.[15] It has a reasonably good manuscript survival rate, and seems to have been relatively widely read and used.[16] In the *De quatuor in quibus* it is described as a great and most effective *summa*.[17]

Moneta drily refers to his *Summa* as an 'opusculum', and everybody since has referred to it in terms that emphasize its enormous size: Biller puts it at

---

[13] Gerard of Frachet, *Vitae fratrum ordinis praedicatorum necnon Cronica ordinis ab anno MCCII usque ad MCCLIV*, ed. B. M. Reichert, Monumenta Ordinis Fratrum Praedicatorum Historica 1 (1896), p. 169.

[14] Stephen of Salagnac and Bernard Gui, *De quatuor in quibus deus praedicatorum ordinem insignivit*, ed. T. Käppeli, Monumenta Ordinis Fratrum Praedicatorum Historica 22 (1949), p. 33.

[15] For MSS, see T. Käppeli and E. Panella, *Scriptores Ordinis Praedicatorum Medii Aevi*, 4 vols. (Rome, 1970–93), III, 138–9, and IV, 201. Käppeli lists twenty-one complete copies from the thirteenth to fifteenth centuries, and six now lost. Of the twenty-seven known copies, thirteen are/were in Italian libraries. On the date of the text see Borst, *Die Katharer*, p. 17; G. Schmitz-Valckenberg, *Grundlehren katharischer Sekten des 13. Jahrhunderts: eine theologische Untersuchung mit besonderer Berücksichtigung von Adversus Catharos et Valdenses des Moneta von Cremona* (Munich, 1971), p. 4; *Heresies of the High Middle Ages: Selected Sources*, ed. and trans. W. L. Wakefield and A. P. Evans (New York, 1969), p. 744 n. 1.

[16] Both at the time and in the centuries following. The Linz Studienbibliothek copy was used by Peter Zwicker in the compilation of his *Cum dormirent homines*; see P. Biller, 'The Anti-Waldensian Treatise *Cum dormirent homines* of 1395 and its Author', in *The Waldenses, 1170–1530: Between a Religious Order and a Church*, Variorum Collected Studies Series 676 (Aldershot, 2000), pp. 237–69 (pp. 254–61). Six of the extant copies are fifteenth-century.

[17] 'Fr. Moneta, natione Lombardus, qui contra machinationes hereticorum maximam et validissimam summam scripsit'; Stephen of Salagnac and Bernard Gui, *De quatuor in quibus deus praedicatorum ordinem insignivit*, p. 33.

nearly half a million words.[18] It is in five parts, which deal with: arguments against those who assert two principles; arguments against those who assert one; matters Christological; matters sacramental; the nature of the Catholic Church. Within each part, Moneta arranges his material in chapters, each of which presents an argument or belief that conflicts with Catholic doctrine and the authorities and reasons used to support that argument, and then sets about responding to each in turn. In fact, in some ways it resembles a *disputatio*, in which a 'Catholic' and a 'heretic' speak to each other in turn.

Moneta's is one of the few full-scale, academic treatments of heresy in this period.[19] Academic theologians of his time were certainly interested in contemporary heresy, but the main focus of this interest was the impact heterodox thought might have on academic authority and practice, and academic concern with heresy is more to do with potential problems raised by the mode of discussion and the appropriate boundaries of the increasingly independent Arts. Moneta is really the only one exhaustively presenting and responding to error; this, coupled with the richness of detail presented by Moneta, and his systematic treatment of his subject, is partly why the *Summa* has proved so popular with historians. Moneta is not uninterested in contemporary debates over the use of new natural philosophical works – he spends some time engaging with ideas on the eternity of the world in his fifth book, for example – but aside from this and a relatively brief discussion of Waldensians, for the most part he is concerned with what he calls 'Cathars'.

Moneta is one of a few contemporary authors to use the term 'Cathari' to describe the heretics against whom he is writing. It is used rarely in this period, though when it is used, it is mostly by Italian and German authors.[20] Moneta never explains why he has chosen this name, or what he thinks it means; he makes no attempt at an etymology. He does give a brief account of the group's origins, as he sees them, but it is late in his text, included in book five as part of a discussion of the origins of the Catholic Church, and in order to cast into relief the superior and more ancient origins of the latter.[21] For Moneta, the crucial point is to demonstrate that the Cathars have their origins not in the Church of God but rather from pagans, Jews, and Christian apostates. He presents a picture in which teachings are selected from a variety of pagan authors, including Pythagoras, Mani, Tatianus, and Valentinus: essentially pagan authors who have expounded views that Moneta ascribes

---

[18] Moneta, *Adversus Catharos*, p. 2; P. Biller, 'Cathars and the Material World', in *God's Bounty? The Churches and the Natural World: Papers Read at the 2008 Summer Meeting and the 2009 Winter Meeting of the Ecclesiastical History Society*, ed. P. Clarke and T. Claydon (Woodbridge, 2010), pp. 89–110 (p. 93).

[19] On contemporary treatments of heresy see Sackville, *Heresy and Heretics*, ch. 1 and pp. 177–90.

[20] See Borst, *Die Katharer*, Appendix II, pp. 240–53.

[21] Moneta, *Adversus Catharos*, p. 411.

to the Cathars, such as the transmigration of souls or dualism. From some of these sources he sees all Cathars drawing shared errors, from others, only certain groups. Moneta therefore makes no direct line to any one origin, and in fact the origins he does describe are multiple, intellectual, textual, and deliberately so. He presents the Cathars as fabricators of a pastiche of beliefs and errors, a view that he has in common with the Waldensian writer Durand of Huesca.[22]

'Cathari' is a name used throughout the *Summa*, then, though not with any great frequency. Moneta employs it where he needs to distinguish one group from another, or is discussing divisions within a group – so, the *Cathari* not the *Leonistae* think this; one group of *Cathari* think this, but the rest do not. The structure of Moneta's text is usually described as dealing first with absolute dualists or Cathars, and then with mitigated dualists or Cathars, but these are terms never used by Moneta himself.[23] He does not even divide them into two groups, rather he says that the groups fall into two main types: those who believe there to be two principles, and those who assert that there is one, but that Lucifer is responsible for all that is material. He ordinarily refers to the first of these as 'primi'. He does carefully note where different groups overlap and diverge, and he also says they coincide in their lifestyle and their organization. But his primary interest is in belief, and the differentiation that he notes is mostly on those lines. He discusses practical matters – hierarchies, or ritual behaviours – only as a matter of course, in order to explain the background to a point of contention. Some sort of overall group structure is implied by the divisions he notes, and by the differentiation from other types of error, but it is 'multiplex', as he calls it. It has many parts, some of which are connected, some of which are not. This is usually only apparent where he talks about how to apply the given refutation – coincidence of ideas is usually noted so that the reader can use an argument in more than one instance – or where he wants to differentiate between different errors. He draws it as variform, heterogeneous, though also connected, overlapping.

Multiplicity is in fact part of Moneta's wider criticism of the 'Cathari' as a group when he engages in explicit criticism, which is not often.[24] He makes little comment as he writes, but on one point he is emphatic: the Catholic faith has many ways to follow one path, whereas its opponents argue about what the path is. We can perhaps understand his overall scheme in this way, that is, to show the coherence of Catholic faith and the poverty of heterodox ideas. But in that case, why present any coherence at all? To understand more

---

[22] W. L. Wakefield, 'Notes on Some Anti-Heretical Writings of the Thirteenth Century', *Franciscan Studies* 27 (1967), 285–321 (pp. 308–9).

[23] Not least by me, Sackville, *Heresy and Heretics*, p. 15.

[24] C. Caldwell Ames, *Righteous Persecution: Inquisition, Dominicans, and Christianity in the Middle Ages* (Philadelphia, 2009), p. 34; P. Biller, 'Words and the Medieval Notion of "Religion"', *Journal of Ecclesiastical History* 36 (1985), 351–69.

clearly why Moneta gives his material the shape that he does, it is necessary to look to his sources. The *Summa*'s relationships with other texts have been explored in several places, but they are worth revisiting and bringing together here in order to understand where Moneta was finding his information.[25] This means looking at the sources that Moneta was reading and using, so far as we can establish what those were, and also the texts with which the *Summa* has formal similarities.

Like a good academic, Moneta is explicit about where he finds his heretical material, namely: the texts of, and encounters with, the opponents he describes. He foregrounds this borrowing in his preface: the heretical arguments and responses that appear in his text have been drawn 'vel ex ore eorum, vel ex scripturis suis'.[26] Direct engagement with opponents was a long-standing trope of anti-heretical writing, and Moneta's formula echoes similar statements in late antique texts, though this is more than a nod to tradition, since the principle is borne out throughout the *Summa*: Moneta can be seen to use heretical texts in several places.[27] In at least one instance, he uses a heretical text still surviving today: the *Visio Isaiae*, known to be used by Cathar groups, appears in the *Summa* as an authority used by heretics to support the idea that all prophets are damned, save Isaiah, 'cuius dicunt esse quemdam libellum, in quo habetur'.[28] Moneta also cites now no-longer extant texts of two specific authors, Desiderius and Tetricus. Moneta makes three references to Tetricus, two of them mentioning a book written by the latter,

---

[25] Wakefield, 'Notes', pp. 305–15; P. Biller, 'Northern Cathars and Higher Learning', in *The Medieval Church: Universities, Heresy, and the Religious Life: Essays in Honour of Gordon Leff*, ed. P. Biller and R. B. Dobson (Woodbridge, 1999), pp. 25–53; L. Paolini, 'Italian Catharism and Written Culture', in *Heresy and Literacy, 1000–1530*, ed. P. Biller and A. Hudson (Cambridge, 1994), pp. 83–103; G. Rottenwöhrer, *Der Katharismus*, 4 vols. (Bad Honnef, 1982), I.ii, 134–89.

[26] Moneta, *Adversus Catharos*, p. 2.

[27] Late-antique texts, for example, such as Irenaeus and Epiphanius. Irenaeus: 'necessarium duxi, cum legerim Commentarios ipsorum, quemadmodum ipso dicunt, Valentini discipulorum, quibusdam autem ipsorum et congressus, et apprehendens sententiam ipsorum' (*Libri quinque adversus haereses*, ed. W. Wigan Harvey, 2 vols. (Cambridge, 1857), bk I, preface, p. 4). Epiphanius: 'Some of the things ⟨about⟩ sects and schisms which I shall be telling the reader, I owe to my fondness for study. Certain things I learned from hearsay, though I happened on some with my own ears and eyes' (*The Panarion of Epiphanius of Salamis*, trans. F. Williams, 2 vols., Nag Hammadi Studies 63, 79, 2nd edn, (Leiden, 2009–13), Proem 2.2.4, p. 14).

[28] And in the same paragraph: 'absit autem, quod ille liber unquam fuerit Isaiae, sed eorum peccatis exigentibus, sicut in aliis spiritibus errori intendunt, ita et in illo libello'; Moneta, *Adversus Catharos*, p. 218. See T. Venckeleer, 'Un recueil cathare: le manuscrit A.6.10 de la collection vaudoise de Dublin', *Revue belge de philologie et d'histoire* 38 (1960), 815–34, and 30 (1961), 759–92 (p. 764 for the *Visio*'s use by heretical groups). Some correspondence between the *Summa* and the *Liber de duobus principiis* has also been suggested, though the nature of the relationship is unclear, Wakefield, 'Notes', p. 305; Borst, *Die Katharer*, p. 272 n. 11; Rottenwöhrer, *Der Katharismus*, I.ii, 140.

and the third a particular chapter within the book.[29] The section in which Moneta responds to claims for the antiquity of souls in book one seems to be directed primarily at this book.[30]

Desiderius is more widely attested in other sources.[31] The *Vitae fratrum* reports that Peter of Verona passed by Gattedo (Giussano, not far from Milan) with his companion in the year before his death and predicted that the castle would be destroyed, and that 'the two bishops of the heretics, Nazarius and Desiderius, who are buried there, will be burned and consumed by fire in the tower of that castle.'[32] Desiderius was probably dead by the time that Moneta was writing, though not by many years: Dondaine puts his death in or around 1235.[33] Possibly Moneta heard him preaching, or heard reports, since he cites both preaching and writing as a source for Desiderius's ideas, but he seems mostly to have relied on a written source. Moneta describes a disagreement between Desiderius and others 'who assert one creator' over the humanity of Christ, a disagreement that is also reported by both Ranier Sacconi and

---

[29] 'Ex qua auctoritate voluit esse miser Haereticus Tetricus nomine, quod populus Dei antiquus sit, non novus, id est de novo creatus'; Moneta, *Adversus Catharos*, p. 61. 'Volunt autem hoc habere pluribus testimoniis, quae in scriptis cuiusdam Haeretici Tetrici nomine reperi'; p. 71. 'Sicut Thetricus Haereticus in quadam parte cuiusdam Libri sui cap. ii illius partis'; p. 79. Rottenwöhrer, *Der Katharismus*, I.ii, 138.

[30] Bk I.vi.iii, Moneta, *Adversus Catharos*, pp. 71–4.

[31] 'Quibus etiam modo consentiunt quidam ex his, qui unum asserunt Creatorem, docti a quodam Haeresiarcha, qui Desiderius vocatur, qui tamen, ut diximus, aliquando contrarium praedicavit, et scripsit'; Moneta, *Adversus Catharos*, p. 248. 'Dixit etiam Desiderius haereticus [...] Ad hoc autem induxit'; p. 347. 'Ad hoc dixit Desiderius haereticus'; p. 357. 'Dixit quidam haeresiarcha Desiderius nomine, credens per hoc fugere obiectionem [...] quod illa voluit proabare ex eo quod dicitur Apocal. I. v.3'; p. 473. 'Quod autem lex mentis sit ratio, Desiderius haeresiarcha notavit in cap. suo de resurrectione'; p. 540. A. Dondaine, 'La hiérarchie cathare en Italie: II and III', *Archivum Fratrum Praedicatorum* 20 (1950), 234–324, repr. in A. Dondaine, *Les hérésies et l'inquisition, XIIe–XIIIe siècles: documents et études*, ed. Y. Dossat (Aldershot, 1990), p. 292; Rottenwöhrer, *Der Katharismus*, I.ii, 138.

[32] 'Transiens semel beatus Petrus cum fratre Gerardo Tridentino juxta quoddam castrum hereticorum, nomine Gathe, per annum ante passionem suam dixit fratri: "Istud castrum destruetur pro fide et Nosarius et Desiderius, duo episcopi hereticorum, qui ibi sepulti sunt, comburentur et cremabuntur". Quod ita plene et per ordinem post modum factum est per ministerium fratrum inquisitorum contra hereticos, ut manifeste ostenderetur, quod per ipsum spiritus sanctus predixit'; Gerard of Frachet, *Vitae fratrum*, p. 239. The action was ordered by Innocent IV in a letter to Ranier Sacconi in 1254: see A. Potthast, *Regesta Pontificum Romanorum*, 2 vols. (Berlin, 1874–5), II, 1274, no. 15492 (19 August, 1254); 'Ad audientam', in *Bullarium Ordinis Praedicatorum*, ed. A. Brémond and T. Ripoll, 8 vols. (Rome, 1729–40), I, 254. Giussano was a town deeply implicated in heresy at that time, with an established heretical school. It was the place from which the plot against Peter Martyr was launched, and also the hometown of another heretic-turned-inquisitor, Daniele of Giussano; see D. Prudlo, *The Martyred Inquisitor: The Life and Cult of Peter of Verona (†1252)* (Aldershot, 2008), pp. 59, 74.

[33] Dondaine, 'La hiérarchie cathare en Italie: II and III', p. 292.

Anselm of Alexandria. Ranier describes a distinction between Nazarius's denial of the humanity of Christ, and the belief of others in his group that Christ did have a human form, but did not ascend with it.[34] Anselm also describes at much greater length a division between Nazarius and others of his group led by Desiderius, the humanity (or otherwise) of Christ again being one of the central points of difference between them.[35] All three authors report the same ideas, though with a difference of detail and language that makes direct borrowing from each other unlikely, and familiarity with a text such as Moneta describes more probable. Aquinas also independently ascribes a text to Desiderius, in his defence of mendicant poverty.[36]

Throughout the *Summa*, in fact, Moneta refers to texts that he has used, either in passing ('sicut quidam Catharus scripsit'; 'ut haereticus dixit in quodam suo tractatu'), or in response to an opponent ('sicut tu dixisti in scriptis tuis'; 'ego possum ostendere tibi per scripta tua').[37] Drawing on opponents' writings was standard practice not only in the long tradition of anti-heretical writing, but also in anti-heretical treatises of Moneta's own time, and, indeed, in the academic writing of his contemporaries more generally. Moneta seems to excerpt heretical statements from other Catholic texts where they are included, since several of the heretical arguments that he presents correspond to the arguments recorded elsewhere.[38] A university trained

---

[34] *Summa fratris Raynerii de ordine fratrum predicatorum de Catharis et Leonistis seu Pauperibus de Lugduno*, ed. F. Šanjek, in 'Raynerius Sacconi O.P. *Summa de Catharis*', *Archivum Fratrum Praedicatorum* 44 (1974), 31–60 (pp. 42–60, at p. 58).

[35] Anselm of Alessandria, *Tractatus de hereticis*, in Dondaine, 'La hiérarchie cathare en Italie II and III', pp. 308–24 (pp. 310–12). Anselm includes a lot of detail, and does give one supporting authority for one of Desiderius's positions, 'hoc affirmat per illud'. He may also be working from a text written by Desiderius. The *Summa contra hereticos* of Peter Martyr also seems to present a similar disagreement over the humanity of Christ and the nature of angels, Biblioteca nazionale centrale di Firenze, *Conventi soppressi*, MS 1738, fols. 45ff.

[36] 'In haereticis quibusdam qui Cathari nominantur, permansit, et adhuc permanet, sicut patet in quodam tractatu cuiusdam Desiderii haeresiarchae Lombardi nostri temporis, quem edidit contra Catholicam veritatem'; Thomas Aquinas, *Contra impugnantes Dei cultum*, cap. 6, cited by Dondaine, 'La hiérarchie cathare en Italie: II and III', p. 292 n. 36; *Sancti Thomae de Aquino opera omnia*, vol. 41A (Rome, 1882–).

[37] References to anonymous texts: 'dices etiam, sicut quidam eis adhaerens mihi respondit, et sicut quidam Catharus scripsit'; Moneta, *Adversus Catharos*, p. 42. 'non dico, quod hoc velimus ostendere per paucitatem, quae videtur notari in hac dictione Quidam, ut haereticus dixit in quodam suo tractatu'; p. 94. '[...] haereticus quasdam frivolas persuasiones, [...] et ad hoc scripsit eas'; p. 133. Rottenwöhrer suggests that all the testimony pp. 128–34 might be understood as derived from the same source. '[...] ad hoc respondit haereticus quidam, et scriptum reliquit'; p. 209. '[...] item nota haereticum docuisse, et scripsisse'; p. 292. Again, Rottenwöhrer suggests all the material on pp. 279–92 may be drawn from the same source. '[...] tu ipse posuisti, et scriptum reliquisti, [...] sicut tu dixisti in scriptis tuis'; p. 367. '[...] dixit haereticus et scripsit'; p. 398. '[...] ego possum ostendere tibi per scripta tua'; p. 472. Rottenwöhrer, *Der Katharismus*, I.ii, 138.

[38] On the *Summa*'s relationship with the *Summa contra haereticos* of the Pseudo-James

scholar like Moneta would have been inclined to approach the refutation of an opponent's position from the original source where possible. Certainly in his (admittedly much briefer) treatment of Waldensianism, Moneta can be seen to be careful about, and interested in, obtaining as accurate a picture as possible. Moneta, who manages, unlike nearly all his contemporaries, to give the correct form of Valdes's name, includes details that can only come from a knowledge of original material.[39] One detail of a division that he describes between Waldensian groups – a controversy over a brother called Thomas – is only otherwise known from a 1218 letter written by Lombard Waldensians to their brothers and sisters across the Alps.[40] He also gives an account of the

Cappelli, see Wakefield, 'Notes', pp. 309–15; the corresponding passages occur in the heretical statements rather than in the refutations. On the possible use by Moneta of the Cathar treatise discussed by Durand of Huesca, see Wakefield, 'Notes', pp. 305, 308–9, and Rottenwöhrer, *Der Katharismus*, I.ii, 139. On the relationship between the *Summa* and the *Disputatio inter Catholicum et paterinum hereticum*, see *'Disputatio inter Catholicum et paterinum hereticum': die Auseinandersetzung der katholischen Kirche mit den italienischen Katharern im Spiegel einer kontroverstheologischen Streitschrift des 13. Jahrhunderts*, ed. C. Hoécker, Edizione nazionale dei testi mediolatini 4, series I, 3 (Florence, 2001), pp. lx–lxx. Wakefield ('Notes', pp. 306–8) points to similarities between Moneta's *Summa* and the *Brevis summula*, in the discussion of ideas attributed to John of Pergamo (possibly John of Lugio) and John of Cucullio; see also *Summula contra hereticos: un traité contre les cathares du XIIIème siècle*, ed. J. Duvernoy (1987), at http://jean.duvernoy.free.fr/text/pdf/summula.pdf. Wakefield also suggests a relationship between the *Summa* and the *Quaedam obiectiones*, again in the heretical ideas presented; 'Notes', p. 308. See also Sackville, *Heresy and Heretics*, pp. 24, 27–9, 42–53.

[39] Erroneous versions of Valdes's name given by: Geoffrey of Auxerre, 'Wandesius'; Bernard of Fontcaude, making a joke, 'Valdenses, nimirum a Valle Densa'; Alan of Lille, 'Waldus'; Walter Map, 'Valde'; Richard of Poitiers, 'Valdensis'; Peter of les Vaux-de-Cernay, 'Valdio', in *Enchiridion Fontium Valdensium*, ed. G. Gonnet (Rome, 1958), pp. 46, 65, 103, 122, 165, 168. Also by Stephen of Bourbon, 'Valdensis'; *Quellen zur Geschichte der Waldenser*, ed. A. Patschovsky and K.-V. Selge (Gütersloh, 1973), p. 15. By Peter of Verona, 'Gualdese'; T. Käppeli, 'Une somme contre les hérétiques de S. Pierre Martyr(?)', *Archivum Fratrum Praedicatorum* 17 (1947), 295–335 (p. 333). And in two different formats by Salvo Burci, 'Valdexius', 'Gualdensi[s]'; Salvo Burci, *Liber suprastella*, ed. C. Bruschi (Rome, 2002), pp. 72, 74, 287. Accounts of Waldensian origins in the *Anonymous of Passau* and the Pseudo-David of Augsburg's *De inquisitione hereticorum* give no indication that the authors knew the name of the founder; *Quellen zur Geschichte der Waldenser*, ed. Patschovsky and Selge, p. 19; *De inquisitione hereticorum*, ed. W. Preger, 'Der Tractat des David von Augsburg über die Waldesier', *Abhandlungen der bayerischen Akademie der Wissenschaften* 14.2 (1879), 204–35 (pp. 205–6). The correct form of 'Valdesius' is found in the will of Stephen of Anse, plate 6 in *Heresy and Literacy*, ed. Biller and Hudson; in Valdes's profession of faith, A. Dondaine, 'Aux origines du valdéisme: une profession de foi de Valdès', *Archivum Fratrum Praedicatorum* 16 (1946), 191–235, repr. in Dondaine, *Les hérésies et l'inquisition*, p. 231, 'ego Valdesius'; in a Waldensian letter of 1218, in *Quellen zur Geschichte der Waldenser*, ed. Patschovsky and Selge, p. 24; in Durand of Huesca's *Liber antiheresis*, ed. K.-V. Selge, *Die ersten Waldenser*, 2 vols. (Berlin, 1968), II, 8, 95. Moneta gives the correct form, *Adversus Catharos*, pp. 402, 408.

[40] Moneta, *Adversus Catharos*, p. 403; *Quellen zur Geschichte der Waldenser*, ed. Patschovsky and Selge, pp. 20–43; Wakefield, 'Notes', p. 305.

Waldensians at the third Lateran council in 1179 that is more detailed than the more nearly contemporary accounts, and devoid of the hostility that can be found in them and that is especially marked in Walter Map's.

Although the accounts of Valdes and the office of preaching provided by the Anonymous of Laon and Moneta are both compatible with canon law on preaching by laymen (that it is not to be done unless requested by the clergy, 'clericis [...] nisi ipsis rogantibus'), there is a striking contrast between them. The slant in the Anonymous is negative: he describes the pope forbidding Valdes and his companions from preaching unless the condition of canon law was fulfilled, here echoing the words of the *Decretum*, 'nisi rogantibus sacerdotibus'. Moneta's slant is positive: the directness and clarity of his words – that Valdes 'accepit a papa praedicationis officium' – again suggest that Moneta has independent sources, 'cujus rei testimonium facile potest inveniri'.[41] A similar level of first-hand knowledge and clean transmission can be inferred for his use of 'Cathar' material in the rest of the treatise. Acting against heresy in the decades before writing the *Summa*, Moneta would have had access to writings deemed heretical by the Church, and there is no reason to doubt the assertion that he makes in his preface: that he is drawing at least some of the positions against which he argues from copies of heterodox texts that were circulating at the time.

The sources for Moneta's refutations of the propositions that he sets out are less direct. He is indeed largely independent in his own arguments, but the anti-heretical texts of this period and region are all bound to each other to some degree, as Hoécker has pointed out, and the practical and textual contexts of Moneta's work, the Dominican *studium* and his anti-heretical activity in Lombardy in particular, shape and inform his *Summa*.[42] If we begin with those places in which he is more dependent, then we begin to see the ways in which those contexts provide Moneta with his source material.

In book five of his *Summa*, Moneta spends some time examining contemporary philosophical arguments, primarily on the eternity of the world and the immortality of the soul. In the course of that discussion, he shows himself to be familiar with then current trends in philosophical discussion, citing a number of texts that had only relatively recently entered the discourse of the schools, including Arabic authors and Aristotelian works, and he also uses

---

[41] Moneta, *Adversus Catharos*, p. 402. D XXIII, c. 29, *Corpus iuris canonici*, ed. E. Friedberg, 2 vols. (Leipzig 1879–81 [repr. Graz, 1959]), I, col. 86. Walter Map, *De nugis curialium*, ed. M. R. James, C. N. L. Brooke and R. A. B. Mynors, Oxford Medieval Texts (Oxford, 1983), pp. 124ff. Anonymous of Laon, *Chronicon universale anonymi Laudunensis*, ed. G. Waitz, Monumenta Germaniae Historica, Scriptores 26 (Hanover, 1882), pp. 442–57 (p. 449), cited in Selge, *Die ersten Waldenser*, I, 253. K.-V. Selge, 'Caractéristiques du premier mouvement vaudois et crises au cours de son expansion', *Vaudois languedociens et Pauvres catholiques = Cahiers de Fanjeaux* 2 (1967), 110–42 (pp. 110–11). I am grateful to Pete Biller for pointing me in the direction of the Waldensian material.

[42] *Disputatio*, ed. Hoécker, p. lxix; see also Biller, 'Northern Cathars'.

contemporary theological works to support his arguments.[43] We know that he used William of Auvergne's *De immortalitate animae* to argue for the immortality of the soul, because he says so directly: 'his modis, atque rationibus usus est, in tractatu suo de animae immortalitate Magister Guillelmus de Arverni Parisiensis Episcopus'.[44] We also know that he was familiar with William of Auxerre's *Summa aurea*.[45] Given Moneta's Arts background this is not surprising, though the fact that William of Auvergne's text was written at least ten years after Moneta had left the university to join the order suggests that the intellectual environment of the Dominican order, and the *studium* at Bologna, might be an equally valid context for his knowledge of this material.[46] The Bologna *studium* in the 1240s had not quite achieved its later pre-eminence as a theological centre, though Moneta is named as a master of Theology there in 1243, but it had from the 1220s maintained a consistent practice of bringing in Paris-trained theologians and had established a significant body of expertise. It was one of the four main *studia generalia* of the order by 1248.[47] Alongside this, the *studium* had emerged over the course of the 1230s as one of the main centres of inquisitorial activity in the north of Italy, and the development of inquisitorial practice and the interaction of personnel was an integral part of its intellectual activity.[48] For Moneta, it was one of the settings for his interaction with fellow Cremonese, Roland of Cremona.

Roland appears to have been influential on Moneta's thought. Roland too wrote a *Summa*, a long commentary on the *Sentences*, and it has been

---

[43] M. Grabmann, *Forschungen über die lateinischen Aristotelesübersetzungen des XIII Jahrhunderts*, Beiträge zur Geschichte der Philosophie des Mittelalters XVII (Münster, 1916), pp. 48–9. Grabmann shows Moneta citing John of Damascus, Avicenna, Algazel, Albumazar, Maimonides and William of Auvergne, as well as Aristotle's *Metaphysics, Physics, De generatione et corruptione, De caelo et mundo*, and the pseudo-Aristotelian *De plantis*. See also *Alfred of Sareshel's Commentary on the Metheora of Aristotle*, ed. J. K. Otte (Leiden, 1988), p. 6; B. Lawn, *The Rise and Decline of the Scholastic 'Quaestio Disputata': With Special Emphasis on its Use in the Teaching of Medicine and Science* (Leiden, 1993), p. 29.

[44] Moneta, *Adversus Catharos*, p. 422.

[45] Biller, 'Northern Cathars', pp. 27–40.

[46] For the *De immortalitate animae* (dating 1228 and 1235, if we ascribe both versions to William) see *William of Auvergne, The Immortality of the Soul [De Immortalitate animae]*, trans. R. Teske, Medieval Philosophical Texts in Translation 30 (Milwaukee, 1991), p. 4. For the *Summa aurea* (1215 × 1229) see S. E. Young, *Scholarly Community at the Early University of Paris: Theologians, Education and Society, 1215–1248* (Cambridge, 2014), ch. 3 and pp. 222–3.

[47] A 'master Moneta' is named as a 'doctor of theology' in the dedication (to the mendicants of the University of Bologna) of Jean de Dieu's *De dispensationibus* in 1243; see *Dictionnaire de théologie catholique*, 15 vols. in 30 (Paris, 1923–50), X, col. 2211.

[48] M. M. Mulchahey, 'The Dominicans' *Studium* at Bologna and its Relationship with the University in the Thirteenth Century', in *Praedicatores/Doctores: Lo Studium generale dei frati predicatori nella cultura bolognese tra il '200 e il '300*, ed. R. Lambertini, Memorie Domenicane n.s. 39 (Florence, 2008), pp. 117–41; R. Parmeggiani, '*Studium* Domenicano e inquisizione', in Lambertini, *Praedicatores/Doctores*, pp. 17–30.

suggested that Moneta knew and used Roland's text.[49] It is very plausible to think of Roland as a conduit between Parisian theology and scholarship and Moneta's work.[50] The first Dominican theologian at the university of Paris, Roland was intimately familiar with the work of contemporary theologians and the debates surrounding the use of philosophical works, and his text is saturated with references to both. It may be that it was through Roland's work that Moneta knew, or was introduced to, the work of William of Auvergne and William of Auxerre, both used extensively by Roland in his *Summa*. The fact that Moneta refers to the Pseudo-Aristotelian *Liber de causis* using that title, which Borst suggests was first applied to the text by Roland, would reinforce that suggestion.[51]

Roland probably composed his work either during his time at the university of Toulouse, between 1229 and 1232, or very soon thereafter once he had returned to Italy, certainly by 1234.[52] During his time in Languedoc, Roland was deeply involved not only in university life but also in action against heresy in Toulouse, leading a preaching campaign against heresy in the city, despite objections and threats from the civic government.[53] His text was therefore clearly informed by his experience of southern French anti-heretical activity, but this does not seem to be Moneta's motivation for using it. (It is interesting to note that Roland does not use the term 'Cathar', only 'heretic' or 'Manichaean', so whatever Moneta's dependence on Roland's text, it is not from here that he has taken the name.) Moneta's principal interest in Roland's work seems to have been as a source of argument, particularly of argument from reason or philosophy. Where a relationship between Moneta's *Summa*

---

[49] A. Brungs, 'Roland von Cremona O.P., die Geschichte des geistigen Lebens im frühen 13. Jahrhundert und die definition der Tugend', in *Roma, Magistri Mundi: Itineraria Culturae Medievalis*, ed. J. Hamesse, 3 vols., Textes et études du Moyen Âge 10 (Louvain-la-Neuve, 1998), III, 27–51 (pp. 32–3); Borst, *Die Katherer*, p. 18 n. 20, p. 272 n. 11, p. 275, nn. 21, 22; G. Cremascoli, 'La "Summa" di Rolando da Cremona: il testo del prologo', *Studi Medievali* 16 (1975), 825–76 (p. 848); Wakefield, 'Notes', p. 305; R. G. Witt, *The Two Latin Cultures and the Foundation of Renaissance Humanism in Medieval Italy* (Cambridge, 2012), pp. 402–10.

[50] See also Biller, 'Northern Cathars', pp. 31–2; F. Ehrle, 'San Domenico, le origini del primo studio generale del suo ordine a Parigi e la somma teologica del primo maestro, Rolando da Cremona', *Miscellanea Dominicana* (1923), 85–134.

[51] Moneta, *Adversus Catharos*, p. 428; Borst, *Die Katharer*, p. 18 n. 20. See also Ehrle 'San Domenico', pp. 120–2; R.-A. Gauthier, 'Notes sur les débuts (1225–1240) du premier 'Averroïsme', *Revue des sciences philosophiques et théologiques* 66 (1982), 327–74 (pp. 330–1); P. Porro, 'The University of Paris in the Thirteenth Century', in *Interpreting Proclus*, ed. S. Gersh (Cambridge, 2014), pp. 264–98 (pp. 276–8).

[52] E. Filthaut, *Roland von Cremona O.P. und die Anfänge der Scholastik im Predigerorden* (1936), pp. 48–50; Cremascoli, 'La "Summa" di Rolando da Cremona', pp. 829–30.

[53] William Pelhisson, *Chronicle*, in W. L. Wakefield, *Heresy, Crusade and Inquisition in Southern France, 1100–1250* (London, 1974), pp. 207–36 (pp. 209–10). See also on Roland and heresy: R. Parmeggiani, 'Rolando da Cremona (†1259) e gli eretici: il ruolo dei Frati Predicatori tra escatologismo e profezia', *Archivum Fratrum Praedicatorum* 79 (2009), 23–84.

and Roland's can be identified, it appears to be in the reasoned arguments, rather than in the heretical arguments or scriptural responses.[54] This is not to say that Roland is not a conduit for information on heretical ideas for Moneta. He was active in northern Italy against heresy as well as in Languedoc, and Moneta worked with him in this context on several occasions.[55] But it is that context, in which Moneta interacted with and read Roland, that is more immediately influential on Moneta's text than the debt he owes him for reasoned arguments.

Moneta's own anti-heretical activity provides probably the largest source-base for his text, not only of refutations, but also of heterodox ideas. Moneta's career outside his study is not very easy to trace, but it is possible to pin him down in several places, more or less securely. After joining the order he seems to have remained in Bologna for a time (St Dominic died in Moneta's cell, and in his tunic).[56] In the late 1220s he was apparently in Cremona, founding the Dominican convent there. He was apparently involved in the foundation of another convent at Mantua in the early 1230s. We know he was back in Bologna in the early 1240s, and that he probably stayed there until his death.[57] Essentially, Moneta seems to have stayed in northern Italy, to have moved around the Milan/Lombardy region, and to have been at the forefront of much of the Dominican activity there, in particular its anti-heretical mission and the early years of inquisition. He certainly seems to consider himself as experienced in combating heretics.[58]

The inquisition of heresy in northern Italy at this stage was still in its infancy.[59] The early work of developing mendicant anti-heretical inquisition procedure was done in southern France, where it met with some

---

54 Cremascoli 'La "Summa" di Rolando da Cremona', p. 848.
55 Filthaut gives a clear chronological account of the career of the 'kampfesfrohe' Roland, including his preaching in Piacenza and Milan, his inquisitorial work, and the injuries he sustained in the process; *Roland von Cremona*, pp. 21–8.
56 Stephen of Salagnac says that he heard this from Moneta himself, and the story also appears in the documents of the canonization process; Stephen of Salagnac and Bernard Gui, *De quatuor in quibus deus praedicatorum ordinem insignivit*, p. 33 and n. line 11.
57 On Moneta's life see Käppeli, *Scriptores Ordinis Praedicatorum Medii Aevi*, IV, 137–8. His date of death is hard to establish: Käppeli puts it at 1250, though it was perhaps as late as 1260. (A more recent tradition has it that Moneta was blind by the time that he died, though the source of this is unclear; perhaps an assumption arising from commentators' experience of reading the *Summa* ...) There is also a recent doctoral study of Moneta's work by Francesca Merlo, 'Lotta all'eresia e anti-necessitarianismo nel pensiero di Moneta da Cremona' (Tesi di Dottorato, Università degli Studi di Salerno, 2013/14).
58 Moneta, *Adversus Catharos*, pp. 2, 314; Rottenwöhrer, *Der Katharismus*, I.ii, 138.
59 Parmeggiani, '*Studium* Domenicano e inquisizione', p. 123; A. Del Col, 'I rapporti tra i giudici di fede in Italia dal Medioevo all'età contemporanea', in *Tribunali della fede: continuità e discontinuità dal Medioevo all'età moderna*, ed. S. P. Rambaldi, Bollettino della Società di studi valdesi 200 (2007), 83–110 (pp. 85–6); L. Paolini, 'Il modello italiano nella manualistica inquisitoriale', in *L'inquisizione: atti del Simposio internazionale, Città del Vaticano, 29–31 ottobre 1998*, ed. A. Borromeo (Rome, 2003), pp. 95–118.

initial success. In Italy, progress was rather slower, not least because of the continuing influence of the episcopate and the resistance of the civic governments of the communes. Even relatively 'effective' inquisitors like John of Vicenza met with mixed success, and operated largely through preaching.[60] Roland of Cremona was deployed as a preacher against heresy in Lombardy in the early 1230s, in Piacenza and in Milan in particular, and was met with fierce opposition much of the time.[61] There was little momentum, in fact, until the situation was galvanized by the murder of Peter Martyr in 1252 and Innocent IV took the situation in hand. Before that, anti-heretical activity was characterized more by preaching and debate than by authority and institution, and dispute was the more normal mode of interaction in a context where few other, more powerful, weapons were available to the Church until the middle of the century.[62]

This is the mode in which Moneta most frequently casts his refutations. The *Summa* is set out as a *disputatio*, certainly, but it is littered with allusions to active debate, not just the formal structure of an academic exchange. Moneta frequently attributes material to 'a certain heretic' or 'another heretic'.[63] He presents his opponents' views and his own responses in terms that likewise reflect an immediate experience of debate. Some statements give a sense of direct report, such as: 'in dispute, when they are asked why it is evil to swear an oath, the cathari say that is it evil because it is forbidden' ('Cathari dicunt in disputatione, quando ab eis quaeritur, quare juramentum malum sit, quod ideo malum est, quia prohibitum est'). This is in evidence throughout: 'a certain adherent replied to me' ('quidam eis adhaerens mihi respondit'); 'as he once said to me' ('ut aliquando mihi dixit'); 'I can show you this from your own mouth' ('ex ore tuo [...] possum ostendere').[64] The testimony to which Moneta refers (and the form of address throughout suggests debate rather than tribunal) points again to his own experience as being one of his main sources, which would bear out the other part of his opening statement, that he has this 'ex ore eorum'.

Moneta's *Summa* is usually grouped by historians with a set of roughly contemporary anti-heretical texts, all products of Lombardy in the 1230s and early 1240s, and it is indeed related to these. He occasionally borrows from them, and also occasionally shares with them material from texts that are now lost. These works, usually called polemics, are dialectic texts which, like

---

[60] Caldwell Ames, *Righteous Persecution*, pp. 97–9, 102.
[61] Filthaut, *Roland von Cremona*, pp. 21–8.
[62] L. Paolini, 'Italian Catharism and Written Culture', pp. 83–103.
[63] Rottenwöhrer, *Der Katharismus*, I.ii, 139.4, lists material attributed to 'a certain heretic' or 'another heretic': Moneta, *Adversus Catharos*, pp. 126–9, 129–37, 174–5, 193, 195, 213, 220, 249–50, 251–4, 279, 296, 300–2, 316–30, 330–6, 332, 333, 363, 386, 387, 389–97, 471, 472–3, 529.
[64] Moneta, *Adversus Catharos*, pp. 470, 42, 174, 97, also: 'Quod quidam eorum respondit', p. 28; 'dixit haereticus aliquando', p. 296. See also Rottenwöhrer *Der Katharismus*, I.ii, 138.

Moneta's, present arguments about points of faith, and engage in debate with them, often in the form of a dialogue; in fact, this is the mode of polemic in this period, rather than the rhetorical attacks that characterize Cistercian-led polemic of southern France in the twelfth century.[65] The shape of these texts likely reflects of a common mode of encounter: the debate between orthodox and heterodox (and between heterodox) groups that Paolini has shown to be commonplace in northern Italy in the early decades of the thirteenth century. One of the polemical authors refers to dispute in this mode as typically heretical.[66] Moneta is therefore working within a relatively new but also quite widespread tradition of anti-heretical writing, and one of his models is that contemporary generic habit. But his text is much more methodical than these others, and he is also working within another model, again produced in a context of which he himself had direct experience. This was a model drawn from the manuals for preaching and debate that were compiled (in that typical habit of handbook production) by the mendicants for reference, and in particular from the *summae auctoritatum*.

The *summae auctoritatum* are lists of authorities organized under headings that provide material from which the reader can construct a refutation of a given proposition, or, more usually, defend an orthodox position.[67] They are often very brief, copied into the leaves of portable Bibles for reference, but they also survive in longer, fuller versions in which the refutation or defence is elaborated at length. Moneta's text has complex but well-established connections with several of these (he borrows from them, they borrow from him, they share originals), and the overall structure of his *Summa* is more like the *summae auctoritatum* than anything else.[68] That Moneta also includes the opposing argument and its proofs, that his elaboration of the lists follows a dialectical mode, does not alter the fact that his work has much in common with these texts born of debate and preaching. It is not quite as portable – though some of the early manuscripts of the *Summa* are as small as pocket Bibles – but these *summae* are as much his models as the polemical texts he

---

[65] Sackville, *Heresy and Heretics*, ch. 1; see also D. Iogna-Prat, *Ordonner et exclure: Cluny et la société chrétienne face à l'hérésie, au judaïsme, et à l'islam, 1000–1150* (Paris, 1998); trans. G. R. Edwards as *Order and Exclusion: Cluny and Christendom Face Heresy, Judaism, and Islam (1000–1150)* (Ithaca NY, 2002). See also B. M. Kienzle, 'Tending the Lord's Vineyard: Cistercians, Rhetoric and Heresy, 1143–1229: Part 1 – Bernard of Clairvaux, the 1143 Sermons and the 1145 Preaching Mission', *Heresis* 25 (1995), 26–61.

[66] L. Paolini, 'Italian Catharism and Written Culture', pp. 90–1. 'More hereticorum', *Disputatio*, ed. Hoécker, p. 4 and n. 6; see also Gerard of Frachet, *Vitae fratrum*, p. 236.

[67] *La somme des autorités, à l'usage des prédicateurs méridionaux au XIIIe siècle*, ed. C. Douais (Paris, 1896); R. Manselli, 'Una "Summa auctoritatum" antiereticale (MS 47 della Bibiothèque municipale di Albi): memoria di Raoul Manselli', *Atti della Accademia nazionale dei Lincei: 1 – Classe di scienze morale storiche e filologiche* 6 (1985), 324–97; Sackville, *Heresy and Heretics*, pp. 42–53.

[68] Sackville, *Heresy and Heretics*, pp. 24, 44, 51.

is usually grouped with.[69] Indeed, Moneta's work is almost a *summa auctoritatum* written by somebody with an Arts background.

The structure of Moneta's text also reflects the *summae* clearly. Like them, the material is arranged in a framework determined by orthodox doctrine. The ordering of the articles does not follow a scheme laid down by Moneta's opponents, but is determined, like the *summae*, by the category of orthodox proof to which they are relevant (especially in the last three books). Moneta's text is organized for navigation, for the ease of finding a relevant counter-argument, and for cherry picking. Its first audience is Moneta's Dominican brothers, so the arrangement of the articles is driven by the logic of the orthodoxy they defend (theology, Christology, sacramental doctrine, ecclesial doctrine), rather than any particular concern to present a coherent counter-orthodoxy. Hoécker has pointed out that the *Summa*'s manuscript survival suggests its principal use was in the preparation of Dominican preachers, and later also inquisitors, for confrontation with heretics. This also suggests that the anti-heretical activity of the *studium* was as, if not more, influential in the formulation of the *Summa* than was its general academic milieu.[70] A relationship between the *Summa* and the *summae auctoritatum* would reinforce that suggestion. In any case, Moneta's text was clearly born out of a practical interaction and purpose, rather than an abstract or closed idea of heresy.

Moneta's declared purpose in writing his *Summa*, so far as he does declare it in his prologue, is to confute heresy with the Word of God, to strengthen faith, and to defend the Church. This is a purpose that he sees very much as a continuation of St Dominic's mission, and as defining his vocation as a member of that order.[71] Its subject matter is belief and counter-belief, and its

---

[69] BnF, MS 3656, which is late thirteenth/early fourteenth century, is 185 mm × 130 mm, though 292 fols. in length. Biblioteca Apostolica Vaticana, MS Reg Lat 428, mid thirteenth century, is 245 mm × 176 mm, 357 fols.

[70] *Disputatio*, ed. Hoécker, p. lx; M. M. Mulchahey, '*Summae inquisitorum* and the Art of Disputation: How the Early Dominican Order Trained its Inquisitors', in *Praedicatores, Inquisitores* vol. 1: *The Dominicans and the Medieval Inquisition*, ed. W. Hoyer (Rome, 2004), pp. 145–56; R. I. Moore, *The War on Heresy: Faith and Power in Medieval Europe* (London, 2012), p. 314; Caldwell Ames, *Righteous Persecution*, pp. 1–2, 199.

[71] 'Tempus ergo est ex parte Dei faciendi, idest intellectum dandi mihi, et aliis pro fide eius certare volentibus; quia dissipaverunt legem eius haeretici. Tempus etiam est propter eandem caussam faciendi huiusmodi Opusculum ex divinis testimoniis mihi sua gratia inspiratis, suffragante orationum instantia, et copia meritorum B. Dominici Patris mei, cuius totum fuit desiderium, et conatus per se suosque filios spirituales spretis saeculi nugi demoliri opere et sermone haereticorum dogma perversum, et beatam credulitatem fidelium adaugere. Ad quod felicius consumandum Sancti Spiritus consilio fretus primus primum Praedicatorum excogitavit Ordinem, et erexit. Cuius Ordinis devictus precibus, adiutus meritis, et documentis edoctus imbecillis Athleta ecce vibrare audeo gladium Verbi Dei in confutationem haeresum, ad robur Fidei, et Catholicae Ecclesiae firmamentum'; Moneta, *Adversus Catharos*, p. 2. Caldwell Ames, *Righteous Persecution*, pp. 1–3.

approach is from Scripture and the discussion of its interpretation. It is a text designed to provide tools for dispute and argument, to be of use in the context of northern Italy at this time.

When Moneta cut his teeth as a Dominican in the 1220s, inquisition was a long way from being the preferred mode for combating heresy; in the 1230s, when he was more seasoned, the new and as yet undeveloped inquisitorial culture of northern Italy was still not the principal mode for anti-heretical activity. Conflict and dispute remained the predominant forms of interaction – and the Catholic side was by no means the dominant one in the arena – and Moneta's text reflects an encounter that is argumentative and disputative, not investigative. That is, the environment and tradition that informs Moneta's work also provides him with the materials and information that he needs, the models for structuring it, and the purpose for writing it, as a way of fulfilling his vocation.

The heresy that Moneta presents in his text, then, is shaped by that immediacy, and by an interest in gathering relevant information from that context, and in being accurate. The groups that Moneta describes as 'Cathars' are diverse but connected, differentiated from each other, but with enough shared ideas and characteristics to differentiate them also from other heretical groups like the Waldensians. Moneta's use of the term 'Cathar' is not particularly emphatic, and he seems unconcerned by the lack of a definite group name, content to call them 'heretics' for the most part. He gives only a brief history of the Cathars, compared to his corresponding discussion of the Waldensians, and presents their origins as intellectual, derived and constructed from historical error. That mixture, the assembly of a doctrine from various ideas, matches the contemporary diversity he describes. He sees commonality across these groups in terms of their organization (and he does use the term 'Church'), and by implication in terms of their disagreement over common points of doctrine. Essentially he presents a set of ideas in dispute, not forming a coherent whole, but shared in some aspects and consciously differentiated in others. His point is not to describe a homogeneous movement, but rather to present single articles in an order that seems logical to the Catholic faith, to prove a Catholic position, and to disprove a heretical one; any coherence that does emerge is incidental.[72] As far as his discussion of the 'Cathars' themselves is concerned, his agenda is to show multiplicity and to present refutation and offer ammunition: again, connections are incidental. Given that multiplicity is part of his overall conception of heresy, those connections that are included appear because they are useful, and because that is what he finds in the immediate context of encounter and debate, as much as in the *studium* library.

---

[72] 'Antequam tractemus de unoquoque articulo per se, ut melius pateant sequentia, fidem erroneam utrorumque catharorum describamus, et in quibus conveniant, aut differant declaremus. Sunt enim eorum duae partes principales'; Moneta, *Adversus Catharos*, p. 2.

All of this has implications for the ways in which we use the *Summa*. This is not a text produced by an institutional understanding or the work of inquiry, even though it is aligned with inquisition texts by historians (and used by inquisitors later). Moneta is working and writing before formalized procedure and approach took hold, and his text pre-dates the schematic descriptions of the developed inquisitorial texts that appear from the middle of the century, which seek to categorize sects. It is mostly concerned with ideas and beliefs, not with activity and markers, as inquisition texts tend to be (governed as they are by a different agenda, of police work and legal prosecution). Nonetheless, Moneta has been filtered by commentators from Ricchini onwards through the frameworks provided by those inquisitors, and his careful delineation has been essentially retro-fitted to what is visible in the works of Sacconi and other Italian inquisitors of the post-1250s phase.

More important, Moneta's *Summa* is used as a reservoir, as it were, of heretical doctrine. Scholars from Schmidt onwards have been attracted by its detail and size and have used it not only as a store of information, but also as a basic textbook of Cathar heresy, and then applied that model widely, through time and space. This has made a theological discussion of heresy as Moneta found it into a universal theology of heresy that was not intended by its author. The text is more useful to us if we understand it to represent a picture of Italy in the 1220s and 1230s, rather than a compendium of Catholic knowledge for the whole thirteenth century. And also, more specifically, it is a picture drawn by a Dominican working in the context of debate: a treatment of 'Catharism' that is born not only, or even mainly, of an academic theology but a pastoral one, from preaching and encounter, and a mendicant preoccupation with the correct understanding of doctrine by the laity, and with the problem of a deceptively convincing error.

Unmaking a picture of Catharism based on Moneta's work is important: Catharism in the twelfth century almost certainly did not look like the Catharism Moneta encountered, whatever we think about its existence. But drawing that scepticism forward into the thirteenth century is no less problematic; a model that seeks to explain anti-heretical writing in this period either as a reaction to an independent entity or as a self-contained construct obscures the dialectic relationship between orthodoxy and heterodoxy that can be seen in texts like Moneta's, as well as what Moneta, a careful and accurate scholar, so far as we can tell, is telling us that he saw. He is not claiming that this is a universal Church, or a centuries-wide phenomenon, he is describing and refuting what he found on the ground: an intellectually driven, textually oriented, connected set of thinkers.

11

'Lupi rapaces in ovium vestimentis': Heretics and Heresy in Papal Correspondence

Rebecca Rist

In recent years historians have debated whether the medieval phenomenon which they have called 'the Cathar heresy' or 'Catharism' was a Balkan heresy, or the construct of a 'persecuting society', or both.[1] Some historians have denied that there was a recognizable group of heretics in the late twelfth and thirteenth centuries who were called 'Cathars', arguing that such a group never existed but was rather an invention of medieval scholars and clergymen. I would disagree with these historians and argue that that, although medieval scholars, clergymen and theologians may have over-emphasized their unity and coherence, and exaggerated the threat they posed to the Catholic Church, there is undoubted evidence for Cathars. I would also argue that there are serious flaws in the 'revisionist' or 'de-constructionist' argument. For historians to claim that an organization invented or constructed a heresy – in this instance that the Catholic Church 'invented' or 'constructed' the Cathar heresy – suggests that they have failed to take into account a procedure which medieval clergy widely used: namely to attack what the attacker (the Church) saw as the *logical conclusion* of the position attacked (a neatly packaged Cathar heresy) rather than what the attacked (the Cathars) actually said. Yet this does not mean that Cathars – those who espoused beliefs fundamentally at odds with Catholic Christianity – never existed. I also believe that the medieval Church, following St Augustine of Hippo (354–430 CE), adopted the attitude of many ancient thinkers in looking at the logical conclusions of a heretical system. So, for example, some historians have suggested that Pelagianism was invented by St Augustine, but this does not mean that there were no Pelagians, or that all Pelagians reached the logical conclusions Augustine gave them. Rather, Augustine pointed out where one must logically finish up if one starts along a certain road.

---

[1] For the use of this term to describe Medieval Society from the eleventh century onwards see R. I. Moore, *The Formation of a Persecuting Society: Authority and Deviance in Western Europe, 950–1250*, 2nd edn (Malden MA, 2006), pp. 4–5.

Hence, despite the possible exaggerations of medieval commentators, there seems no doubt that 'Cathars' existed. From a wealth of sources – chronicles, annals, inquisitorial records, theological treatises and sermons – historians are able to build up a picture of these heretics' beliefs and practices. They inform us that Cathar beliefs seem to have derived from Bogomilism, a form of dualism which originated in Bulgaria in the early medieval period and probably spread to the Byzantine Empire during the eleventh century, before making its way to the West where we find it in the Rhineland by the mid twelfth century.[2] Those who adhered to this dualism were first called 'Cathars'; though they established themselves in northern Italy by the second half of the twelfth century, they were particularly associated with the south of France or Languedoc. Their beliefs were anti-sacramental and anticlerical. They rejected infant baptism, the Mass, confession, extreme unction, and the Old Testament, believing its god to be the evil, creator God, whereas the good God of the New Testament was the loving creator of souls. Their fully initiated members were commonly referred to in Latin as *perfecti* (perfect ones) or *bos homes* (good men), a term that also often in the vernacular designated a man of good character. In inquisition sources and troubadour literature they were known as 'the heretics' but some clergy referred to them as 'Patarenes', 'publicani' or 'popelicans'. In contrast to some Catholic clergy, Cathars lived very simply, owning no property, requiring no church buildings, and working for their keep. Since everything material was evil, the *perfecti* among them lived austere lives; since they believed that when a person died the soul was trapped in human and animal bodies by the creator God, they ate nothing derived from coition (i.e. meat, eggs or dairy products, although they did eat fish) and renounced sexual intercourse, which produced more bodies in which the evil god could imprison souls. They had their own ecclesiastical hierarchy and organized themselves into dioceses with their own bishops and deacons.

Two medieval popes, namely Innocent III (1198–1216) and Honorius III (1216–27), described these heretics frequently in their correspondence when calling for the Albigensian crusade. They believed it was vital for the Church to combat these beliefs in order to safeguard correct Christian doctrine and theology. Both Innocent and Honorius were at the forefront of authorizing and encouraging important initiatives against heresy in the late twelfth and early thirteenth centuries – by preaching and teaching campaigns, by the crusade and by paving the way for the implementation of the papal inquisition by their successor Gregory IX (1227–43). In order to understand what these popes knew and believed about Cathars we need to examine what papal sources themselves say about heresy and heretics, in particular the decrees

---

[2] *The Cathars and the Albigensian Crusade: A Sourcebook*, ed. C. Léglu, R. Rist and C. Taylor (London, 2014), pp. 5–6.

of Lateran III and Lateran IV, the two great ecumenical councils of the late twelfth and early thirteenth centuries, and the correspondence of popes to the south of France. As we shall discover, such primary sources are not the best place to find information on specific beliefs and practices; the historian needs to look elsewhere, to other types of source, to gain a rounded picture of who the Cathars were and what they believed. Nevertheless, papal documents are important primary sources for the study of the Cathar heresy, because they tell us so much about the 'official' view held by the medieval Church.

The papacy's concern with what it perceived to be the growing threat of heresy in the south of France was first given official expression at the third Lateran council, the ecumenical council of 1179 which was called during the pontificate of Alexander III (1159–81). Canon 27 of that council stated:

> For this reason, since in Gascony and the regions of Albi and Toulouse and in other places the loathsome heresy of those whom some call the Cathars, others the Patarenes, others the Publicani, and others by different names, has grown so strong [...] we declare that they and their defenders and those who receive them are under anathema.[3]

We can see from this statement that Lateran III did not refer specifically to a heresy with definite beliefs and practices called 'Catharism'; indeed, it did not name any particular heresy. Rather it referred to groups or sects of people: 'Patarenes', 'Publicani' and 'Cathari' ('Cathars'). This is not in itself surprising. 'Catharism' is a term used by some modern historians to describe a particular set of beliefs and practices; there was no one Latin word used to describe the heresy, and medieval legislation referred to the people concerned, i.e. 'Cathari'.[4] As we know from papal correspondence, post-Lateran III popes continued on occasion to refer to 'Cathari' among a number of other named heretical groups which they singled out for anathematization. Thus, for example, in 1184 Lucius III issued his decretal 'Ad abolendam', which placed under perpetual anathema 'the Cathari, Patarini, and those who falsely call themselves Humiliati, the Poor Men of Lyons, Passagini, Josepini and Arnaldistae'.[5] In contrast, Constitution 3 of the fourth Lateran council (1215), which took place when the Albigensian crusade had been underway for a number of years, excommunicated and anathematized 'every heresy raising itself up against this holy, orthodox and catholic faith'; it did not mention 'Cathars' by name, or indeed any other specific groups of heretics,

---

[3] *Decrees of the Ecumenical Councils*, ed. N. Tanner, 2 vols. (London, 1990), I, 224.
[4] Medieval Latin did not tend to have -*ism*, essence or abstract words for what we call 'religions' or 'religious entities'. Rather, it usually referred to a collection of persons, or the 'faith of', 'law of', 'order of', 'sect of', etc. See P. Biller, 'Words and the Medieval Notion of "Religion"', *Journal of Ecclesiastical History* 36 (1985), 351–69.
[5] *Heresy and Authority in Medieval Europe: Documents in Translation*, ed. E. Peters (London, 1980), p. 171.

as Canon 27 of Lateran III had done.[6] Rather it contented itself with a very general condemnation of 'all heretics, whatever names they may go under'.[7]

Thus, evidence for a heresy which can be instantly recognized as 'Catharism' is not described in detail in the decrees of these ecumenical councils, and the word 'Cathars', though present, is only infrequently used. How then were these heretics and the heresy itself referred to by popes involved in authorizing and organizing the Albigensian crusade? The letters of the two popes whom one would expect to have most to say about 'Cathars' – since it was they who called for the crusade to combat heresy in the south of France – were Innocent III and Honorius III. What exactly *do* they say in their correspondence? Of course, when reading papal letters it is important to consider the circumstances of their composition. It is extremely difficult to ascertain the extent to which Innocent and Honorius contributed personally to their correspondence, and how much freedom of expression they allowed their notaries. We cannot be sure quite whose 'voice' we are hearing. Nonetheless both popes did fully endorse their letters, so one might expect them to be a useful source of information on the Cathars.

Innocent III had been trained as a young man in Rome, Bologna and Paris and had been greatly influenced by the reforming ideas of Peter the Chanter and his intellectual circle in Paris, with whom it is extremely likely he would have debated the subject of heresy. He may even have known the theologian and poet Alan of Lille (1116/1117–1202/1203), who in his *De fide Catholica*, dated sometime between 1185 and 1200, set out to refute heretical views, specifically those of Cathars and another prominent heretical group, the Waldensians. Nevertheless, in Innocent's correspondence to the south of France we do not find much factual information about the heretics against whom he authorized the crusade. Rather his letters convey to the Christian faithful a sense of what they were like indirectly – in particular by his use of similes, metaphors and biblical quotations. It is through these similes, metaphors and quotations that the reader or listener could build up an understanding of the pope's fears about Cathars. So in several of his letters Innocent likened the heretics to the 'little foxes' of the Song of Songs 2. 15 and Judges 15. 4–5.[8] He wrote that just as these foxes are described as destroying 'the vineyard of the Lord', so too were the heretics metaphorically destroying the Lord's vineyard by threatening Catholicism in the south of France.[9]

---

[6] *Decrees of the Ecumenical Councils*, ed. Tanner, I, 233.
[7] Ibid.
[8] H. Grundmann, *Ketzergeschichte des Mittelalters* (Göttingen, 1978), pp. 22–8.
[9] For biblical references, see the *Biblia sacra iuxta Vulgatam versionem*, ed. R. Weber, 2 vols., 2nd edn (Stuttgart, 1975). For example, Innocent III, 'Ne populus Israel' (7 February 1205), in *Die Register Innocenz' III*, ed. O. Hageneder *et al.*, currently 14 vols. (Rome, 1964–) (henceforward *Die Register Innocenz' III*), VII, 372–4; 'Cum jam captis' (15 January 1213), in *Patrologia Latina*, ed. J.-P. Migne, 217 vols. (Paris, 1844–64) (henceforth *PL*), CCXIV,

He also likened the heretics to sheep in wolves' clothing ('Lupi rapaces in ovium vestimentis'), to tares which polluted the corn and sullied the purity of growing faith (Matthew 7. 15, Matthew 13. 25–30),[10] and to rough places which must be smoothed so that fruit-bearing vines might be planted in the vineyard of the Lord (Isaiah 5. 7).[11]

The use of such similes and metaphors is not particularly surprising. Medieval popes, and the clergy in general, were particularly fond of employing biblical ideas and language to add colour and emphasis to their rhetoric. Yet we find Innocent III elaborating on standard metaphors which had been used by his papal predecessors, and employing such literary techniques much more widely and imaginatively than many contemporaries. So in several letters he elaborated on the idea of the heretics being like 'little foxes' by claiming that 'although they have different forms their tails are bound to one another because they combine into one by reason of their vanity'.[12] Here he was deliberately reminding the reader of the story of Samson and his purging of the land and crops of the Philistines from Judges 15. 4–5:

> So Samson went and caught three hundred foxes, and took torches; and he turned them tail to tail, and put a torch between each pair of tails. And when he had set fire to the torches, he let the foxes go into the standing grain of the Philistines, and burned up the shocks and the standing grain, as well as the olive orchards.[13]

Furthermore, he was drawing upon an image which Bernard of Clairvaux (1090–1153), whom he may have known personally when a young man, had employed about heretics in his famous sermons, and thereby deliberately fostering an idea that these heretics were animalistic, strange and 'other'. By contrast, Innocent equated faithful Catholics with the Lord's flock (Luke 12. 32) and likened the Church's struggle against heresy to a ship, the barque of St Peter, tossed on the waves by a storm (Mark 4. 37–40).[14]

744–5. See P. Biller, 'Through a Glass Darkly: Seeing Medieval Heresy', in *The Medieval World*, ed. P. Linehan and J. L. Nelson (London, 2001), p. 317.

[10] For the metaphor of wheat and tares, see M. Lambert, *Medieval Heresy: Popular Movements from the Gregorian Reform to the Reformation*, 2nd edn (Oxford, 1992), p. 92.

[11] For example, Innocent III, 'Equo rufo de' (17 January 1214), in *Recueil des historiens des Gaules et de la France*, ed. Dom Bouquet, 24 vols., 2nd edn. (Paris, 1880), XIX, 587–8; 'Cum oculos nostre' (2 April 1215), in *Layettes du Trésor des chartes*, ed. A. Teulet *et al.*, 5 vols. (Paris, 1863), I, 415–16; 'Vergentis in senium' (25 March 1199), in *Die Register Innocenz' III*, II, 3–5; 'Postquam vocante Domino' (11 July 1206), ibid., IX, 221–3.

[12] Innocent III, 'Cum unus Dominus' (21 April 1198), ibid., I, 136–7; Also, for example, Innocent III, 'Ne populus Israel', pp. 372–4; Constitution 3 of Lateran IV also used the same language about heretics.

[13] *Biblia sacra iuxta Vulgatam versionem*, ed. Weber.

[14] For example, Innocent III, 'Ne populus Israel', pp. 372–4; 'Postquam vocante Domino', cols. 940–1.

Innocent's letters employed metaphors not only for heretics but also for heresy itself. Metaphors of illness and disease are particularly prominent: heresy was a deviant virus, a sickness which spreads to the sound and healthy parts of a body, even a plague.[15] One of the letters to the south of France described it graphically as a putrid festering which infected a healthy body; others likened it to cancer, quite possibly referring not to the illness which we call by that name but to common skin complaints such as sores, ulcers, tumours and scabs.[16] This last image was particularly striking but again, not innovative. We find it frequently in earlier conciliar legislation, for example in the decrees of the Council of Tours of 1163, and we know that it was staple rhetoric for a number of twelfth- and thirteenth-century polemicists. Its derivation was St Paul's description of godless chatter as a 'discourse' which 'creeps in like a cancer' (2 Timothy 2. 16–17).[17] Other letters asserted that the Church must clear the rough ground from the vineyards of the Lord and plant useful greenery, or, using only slightly different language, must extirpate vice and plant virtues.[18] So they told the reader or listener something about the nature of heresy and, even more importantly, how Innocent wanted to tackle it. By using such biblical images of cultivation and planting, the pope emphasized that carefully organized long-term measures were needed to combat heretical beliefs, which he maintained were especially deeply rooted in southern French society.[19] It is clear therefore that his employment of such metaphors was very deliberate. His aim was to convey his belief not only in the destructive power but also in the insidious and firmly lodged nature of the heresy which the Albigensian crusade had been called to combat.

What else do we learn about this heresy and the heretics themselves from Innocent's correspondence? In particular, do we find comparisons between heretics and other minority groups who might be the target of a 'persecuting society'? In one very informative letter of 1208 Innocent drew a direct comparison between heretics and Muslims and argued that those who follow heresy, namely the followers of Count Raymond VI of Toulouse (1194–1222), were morally worse than Muslims because they were more

---

[15] For example, Innocent III, 'Hanc inter corporalia' (23 December 1198), in *Die Register Innocenz' III*, I, 722–3; 'Inter cetera que' (1 April 1198), ibid., 119–20; 'Religiosa fides et' (3 February 1209), in *PL* 215, col. 1545.

[16] Innocent III, 'Etsi resecandae sint' (18 January 1213), in *PL* 216, 739–40; 'Gloriantes hactenus in' (11 November 1209), ibid., 158–60.

[17] *Corpus documentorum inquisitionis haereticae pravitatis neerlandicae*, ed. P. Fredericq, 5 vols. (Ghent, 1889–1906), I, 39; R. I. Moore, 'Heresy as Disease', in *The Concept of Heresy in the Middle Ages (11th–13th C.)*, ed. W. Lourdeaux and D. Verhelst (Louvain, 1976), p. 3.

[18] Innocent III, 'Postquam vocante Domino', pp. 221–3; 'Vineam Domini Sabaoth' (19 April 1213), in *PL* 216, 823–7. See Lambert, *Medieval Heresy*, p. 92.

[19] W. L. Wakefield, *Heresy, Crusade and Inquisition in Southern France, 1100–1250* (London, 1974), pp. 71–7.

securely entrenched in Christian society.[20] Of course the idea that the heretic was more of a threat to the Church than even those of other religious faiths was not new to Innocent. Rather the pope was closely following the tradition of prominent Church authorities including Gratian, who in Causa 23 and Causa 24 of the *Concordia discordantium canonum* (popularly known as the *Decretum*) had emphasized that the Church's struggle against heretics was more important than wars against heathens or infidels because their position within – rather than external to – Christian society meant they posed a more serious threat.[21] Bernard of Clairvaux had also argued that the heathen whose beliefs were openly opposed to the Christian faithful were less dangerous to the Church than those of heretics, while Peter the Venerable (c. 1092–1156) claimed that heathens were not only less pernicious but also less responsible for their wickedness than 'internal' heretical enemies of the Church.[22]

It is clear from such remarks, and from his use of the metaphors and similes, that one of the things Innocent feared most about heresy in the south of France was its secretive and surreptitious nature. This fear often led him to express himself in his correspondence in very black and white language: many of his letters exhorting the crusaders to stamp out heresy in the south of France were colourful, highly emotionally charged, even violent. He frequently used emotive phrases not only to express his desire to 'to exterminate wicked heresy' ('ad extirpandam hereticam pravitatem')[23] and 'to subdue heretics' ('ad expugnanados haereticos'),[24] but also 'to exterminate the followers of wicked heresy' ('ad exterminandum pravitatis haereticae sectatores').[25] Innocent feared both the heresy itself and those who in any way fostered its growth and spread. Indeed, his greatest anger was often reserved for men such as Count Raymond VI of Toulouse, whom he believed to be supporting heretics in their domains and whom he contrasted with noble

---

[20] The Latin word is 'securius': 'Sectatores ipsius eo quam Saracenos securius quo pejores sunt illis'; Innocent III, 'Si tua regalis' (10 March 1208), in *PL* 215, 1359. See R. Foreville, 'Innocent III et la Croisade des Albigeois', *Paix de Dieu et guerre sainte en Languedoc au XIIIe siècle* = *Cahiers de Fanjeaux* 4 (1969), 184–217 (p. 191).

[21] Gratian, *Concordia discordantium canonum*, in *Corpus iuris canonici*, ed. E. Freidberg, 2 vols. (Leipzig, 1879–81), I, cols. 889–1006. See Y. Dossat, 'La croisade albigeoise vue par les chroniqueurs', *Paix de Dieu et guerre sainte en Languedoc au XIIIe siècle* = *Cahiers de Fanjeaux* 4 (1969), 221–59 (p. 221).

[22] The idea that heretics were more dangerous to the Church than 'external' enemies goes back at least as far as St Augustine. See, for example, Bernard of Clairvaux, 'De Consideratione', in *Sancti Bernardi opera*, ed. J. Leclercq, C. H. Talbot and H. M. Rochais (Rome, 1957–78), III, 393–410; Bernard of Clairvaux, 'Sermo 65', in *Sancti Bernardi opera*, II, 177; Peter the Venerable, *The Letters of Peter the Venerable*, ed. G. Constable, 2 vols., Harvard Historical Studies 78 (Cambridge MA, 1967), I, 407–11.

[23] For example, Innocent III, 'Etsi nostri navicula' (28 March 1208), in *Layettes*, ed. Teulet, I, 318.

[24] For example, Innocent III, 'Quanto Montispessulani' (1 March 1209), in *PL* 216, 187.

[25] For example, Innocent III, 'Ut contra crudelissimos' (9 October 1208), *PL* 215, 1469.

crusaders. So, for example, on hearing the news of the murder, supposedly at the count's own hands, of the papal legate Peter of Castelnau, who had been sent to preach and teach Catholic doctrine in the south of France, Innocent once again employed the metaphor of disease in striking language, describing Raymond as 'a pestilential man' ('vir pestilens').[26] In stark contrast, the crusader Simon de Montfort was described in the highest terms as a 'soldier of Christ' ('miles Christi')[27] and a 'defender of the faith' ('defensor fidei').[28]

Such harsh language was consistent with the uncompromising pronouncements of Church councils relating to heresy both earlier than and contemporary to Innocent's pontificate. Innocent was in a long tradition of medieval popes and clergy who were uncompromising in their view of heresy and heretics as inimical to the Church, to the papacy and to Christian society in general.[29] Nevertheless, what is remarkable about Innocent's correspondence is how little we actually learn about the beliefs and practices of what we call 'Catharism'. As we have seen, throughout his correspondence he refers very generally to 'heretics' ('haeretici') and the problem of 'the followers of wicked heresy' ('sectatores pravitatis haereticae'). In contrast to the legislation of Lateran III and the 'Ad abolendam' of Lucius III, we do not find specific reference to 'Cathars' ('Cathari') in his correspondence to the south of France concerned with the Albigensian crusade. Nevertheless, there are clues in this correspondence which tell us that Innocent did know something about the heretics' practices and beliefs. In particular, a letter of 1207–8, sent not to the south of France but to the northern French bishops of Auxerre and Troyes, referred to *consolatores* – those who administered the Cathar right of the *consolamentum*:[30]

---

[26] Innocent III, 'Si parietem cordis' (29 May 1207), in *Die Register Innocenz' III*, X, 119.

[27] For example, Innocent III, 'Nobilitatem tuam dignis' (2 April 1215), in *Layettes*, ed. Teulet, I, 414.

[28] For example, Innocent III, 'Gaudemus in Domino' (2 April 1215), ibid., p. 413.

[29] J. Gilchrist, 'The Papacy and War against the "Saracens"', *International History Review* 10 (1988), 194.

[30] Innocent III, 'Ex tenore litterarum' (12 January 1208), in *Die Register Innocenz' III*, X, 364–6. For the debate that there were Cathars in the north of France as well as in the south see discussion in P. Biller, 'Northern Cathars and Higher Learning', in *The Medieval Church: Universities, Heresy and the Religious Life: Essays in Honour of Gordon Leff*, ed. P. Biller and B. Dobson (Woodbridge, 1999), pp. 25–53, *passim*; É. Chénon, 'L'hérésie à La Charité-sur-Loire et les débuts de l'inquisition monastique dans la France du Nord au XIIIᵉ siècle', *Nouvelle revue historique de droit français et étranger* 41 (1917), 299–345; G. Despy, 'Les débuts de l'inquisition dans les anciens Pays-Bas au XIIIᵉ siècle', in *Problèmes d'histoire de christianisme: hommage à Jean Hadot*, ed. G. Cambier (Brussels, 1980), pp. 71–104; G. Despy, 'Hérétiques ou anticléricaux? Les "cathares" dans nos régions avants 1300', in *Aspects de l'anticléricalisme du Moyen Âge à nos jours: hommage à Robert Joly*, Problèmes d'histoire du christianisme 18 (Brussels, 1988), pp. 23–33; C. Haskins, 'Robert le Bougre and the Beginnings of Inquisition in Northern Europe', in *Studies in Medieval Culture* (Cambridge MA, 1929), pp. 193–244.

From the tenor of your letter, brother of Auxerre, we gather that, although your predecessor Hugh of good memory, acting like a far-seeing and wise shepherd keeping watch over his flock through the vigils of the night, laboured with anxious care to eliminate heretical wickedness from the town called La Charité, he was still unable fully to cure that Babylon of this kind of sickness. For many people of both sexes, [...] *returned like dogs to their vomit* [Proverbs 26. 11]. Giving themselves over to perdition was not enough for them, they also strove to drag others with them to perdition, secretly bringing into *the kine of the people* [Psalms 67. 31] certain heresiarchs whom they call 'consolers' [*consolatores*], who are to kill the sheep with the poison of their pestiferous doctrine.[31]

Although the life of the *perfectus* was much too difficult for most, what was important was not how you lived, but how you died. So as long as *credentes* received the *consolamentum* on their deathbed the Cathar faith allowed them to live as they pleased until just before the point of death. According to the contemporary cleric Peter of les Vaux-de-Cernay, as long as believers of the heresy (*credentes*) received this *consolamentum* or laying on of hands – a heretication rite performed by the *perfecti* on the point of death – and did not sin subsequently, they too would be 'perfected' and their souls would escape to heaven when they died.[32]

What, if any, new information about heretics and heresy in the south of France do we learn from Innocent III's successor, Honorius III? Again it is important to consider the composition of papal letters. Again, it is important to consider the composition of papal letters. Not only is it difficult to separate the pope's own voice from the voices of his notaries, one must also be aware that Honorius's correspondence concerned with the Albigensian crusade – both general letters to the faithful and directives to individuals to carry out specific mandates – followed a long-established style of papal letters, and strict compositional rules; this means that his letters deliberately contained many of the traditional, almost formulaic, passages about heresy and heretics used by his predecessor. Even so, the fact that he authorized the letters to the south of France again suggests their utility as a source for historians.

What is immediately apparent is the intensely pragmatic nature of Honorius's correspondence to the south of France. We rarely find those flights of rhetoric so characteristic of his predecessor, and the letters tend to be shorter and much more practical. Honorius's letters only occasionally quoted from or referred to Scripture when describing the Church's struggle against

---

[31] Innocent III, 'Ex tenore litterarum', p. 365.
[32] Peter of les Vaux-de-Cernay, *The History of the Albigensian Crusade*, ed. and trans. W. A. Sibly and M. D. Sibly (Woodbridge, 1998), pp. 12–13. For details of the *Consolamentum* see, for example, M. Barber, *The Cathars: Dualist Heretics in Languedoc in the High Middle Ages*, 2nd edn (Harlow, 2013), pp. 90–4.

heresy or exhorting the faithful to action against heretics. Furthermore, such references usually occurred in general letters which were sent out to the whole body of the Christian faithful rather than correspondence to particular individuals, possibly because the particular legal judgements and instructions on lands and rights which were contained in the latter did not seem to him to merit such references.[33]

When on occasion Honorius's correspondence to the South of France does contain metaphors and similes, they tend to be very familiar – similar to those which his predecessor had employed about heresy and heretics. So, for example, one letter used a combination of established metaphors for heresy and its cure, namely those of disease, of medicine and of planting, to outline how the situation in the south of France had only recently improved.[34] Though Honorius used such metaphors and similes only infrequently, when he did employ them they were piled one on another for maximum emphasis.[35] In particular, the biblical metaphor of planting recurs in his correspondence,[36] as does the idea of heresy as an infectious disease.[37] Indeed, just like Innocent III, he continued to describe the dangerous effect of heresy on the Church, which he too likened to the barque of St Peter, tossed on stormy waves.[38] Occasionally a few 'new' and striking metaphors and similes, albeit couched in language traditionally employed by the curia, also appear. Hence Honorius described the south of France as a piece of tarnished silver that a metal worker, for all his labour, is unable to free from rust,[39] while the support for heresy of the count of Toulouse – by now Raymond VII (1222–49) – was likened to a broken hand leaning on a reed staff.[40]

In general Honorius's letters expressed many of the same ideas as those of Innocent, and in very similar ways. This was partly because, as official pronouncements of the papacy, they contained the standard, traditional

[33] Honorius III, 'Populus Israel a' (11 August 1218), in *Honorii III romani pontificis opera omnia quae extant*, ed. C. A. Horoy, 5 vols. (Paris, 1879–82) (henceforward *Horoy*), III, cols. 10–12; 'Populus Israel a' (3 January 1218), in *Horoy* II, cols. 573–5; 'Populus Israel a' (30 December 1217), ibid., cols. 567–9; 'Cum dilectus filius' (23 October 1217), ibid., cols. 524–5; 'Gratiarum omnium largitori' (21 January 1217), ibid., cols. 203–4: in this letter Honorius III granted to Dominic and his followers the office of Preachers of the Faith; 'Mirabiles elationes maris' (15 February 1225), in *Horoy* IV, cols. 781–4.
[34] Honorius III, 'Multo sudore laboratum' (19 January 1217), in *Horoy* II, cols. 189–91.
[35] For example, Honorius III, 'Multo sudore laboratum', cols. 189–91; 'Mirabiles elationes maris', cols. 781–4.
[36] Honorius III, 'Mirabiles elationes maris', cols. 781–4.
[37] Honorius III, 'Cum dilectus filius', cols. 524–5.
[38] Honorius III, 'Mirabiles elationes maris', cols. 781–4. The image was originally biblical, for example, Jonah 1. 4; Matthew 14. 22–33.
[39] Honorius III, 'Multo sudore laboratum', cols. 189–91; 'Mirabiles elationes maris', cols. 781–4.
[40] Honorius III, 'Quod de libertatis' (23 December 1223), in *Horoy* IV, cols. 497–8.

language which the curia had used for decades to describe heretics. Yet undoubtedly it was also because Innocent's letters had such an enormous influence on those of his successors, including Honorius III, both in terms of substance and style. Honorius himself said that he consulted Innocent's letters: 'Certainly we have observed it to be contained in the Registers of our predecessor, Innocent III of happy memory'.[41] This strongly suggests that he – and therefore probably also his notaries – looked to Innocent's letters for inspiration and guidance when composing his correspondence and was unwilling to deviate much from his predecessor in expressing his ideas about heresy.

Similarity in the language used to describe heretics reflected similarity of outlook. Like Innocent III, two of Honorius's letters to the south of France made direct comparison between heretics and Muslims – the only other 'minority group' with which heretics are directly compared. As we have seen, Innocent declared in one letter that the followers of Count Raymond VI of Toulouse were worse than the Muslims because more deeply entrenched in Christian society.[42] In a letter of 1218, instructing the archbishops of Vienne and Arles that half of the tax of the twentieth deputed for crusaders to the Near East should be conferred on Simon de Montfort for his campaign against the people of the town of Toulouse, Honorius echoed similar sentiments, writing that: 'since it is manifest that heretics are worse than Muslims, they must be opposed with no less zeal than the insolence of those [Muslims].'[43] And in a letter of the following year, to his legate Pelagius and concerning the despatch of money to aid crusaders in the Holy Land, he again made the same comparison when he stated that 'since the Albigensian heretics rise up against the Church, [they are] worse than the Muslims.'[44] Again, such statements accorded with the idea, by now familiar to the Christian faithful, that heresy posed a particular problem for the Church because it was an 'internal' menace within Christian Europe, threatening the fundamental tenets of Christianity itself.

Honorius's reputed gentleness, a character trait recorded by some contemporary chroniclers, is not at all evident in his letters to the south of France. Like his predecessor, the language he used to refer to heretics and heresy was harsh and uncompromising. Nevertheless, although he used forthright and colourful words and phrases, as with Innocent they were also very general and unspecific, providing little guidance to crusaders and clergy about the beliefs of the heretics, nor much detail about how campaigns were to be waged against them. This was not surprising: popes were far away in

---

[41] Honorius III, 'Justis petentium desideriis' (3 June 1220), in *Horoy* III, col. 445.
[42] Innocent III, 'Si tua regalis', col. 1359: 'sectatores ipsius eo quam Saracenos securius quo pejores sunt illis'.
[43] Honorius III, 'Cum haereticos deteriores' (5 September 1218), in *Horoy* III, col. 30.
[44] Honorius III, 'Litteris tuis' (1 October 1219), ibid., cols. 299–301.

Rome and deliberately left their legates and the local clergy on the ground to deal with specifics. So once again heretics are described in papal correspondence in traditional language and in conventional terms: their beliefs were unorthodox; the Church regards them as rebels ('rebelles');[45] their faith was an evil dogma;[46] the arguments they employed against orthodox preachers and churchmen were untrustworthy.[47] Yet, just like Innocent's, Honorius's letters contain scant discussion of the nature of the heresy to be combated and the practices of supposed heretics. There is nothing about the dualistic nature of unmitigated Catharism, which many historians believe became the prevalent form of the heresy in the south of France following the Council of Saint-Félix-de-Caraman of 1167/72, nor any specific reference to the secret rite of initiation known as the *consolamentum*.[48] Yet again there is no clear reference to a set of beliefs which we can identify as 'Catharism', nor are 'Cathars' mentioned by name.

What then can we conclude from the letters of Innocent III and Honorius III concerned with the Albigensian crusade, and the decrees of the ecumenical councils of Lateran III and Lateran IV which refer to the problem of heresy in the south of France in the late twelfth and early thirteenth centuries? Very importantly there is a distinct lack of detail about the beliefs and practices of 'Cathars'. When the papacy did refer, infrequently, to 'Cathars' this was in the context of a number of names which it claimed people popularly gave to different groups or sects of heretics which they encountered in France and northern Italy. This lack of evidence about Cathar beliefs and practices may be one reason why some recent historians have made the much greater and more controversial claim that 'Catharism' as a heresy with a particularly distinct set of beliefs and practices did not exist, that there was no particular heresy, Balkan or otherwise, against which the Church was reacting, and no group of people whose beliefs and practices were similar enough to group them together as 'Cathars'. Rather, those historians would argue that there were men and women in the south of France whom the Church wanted to persecute for a number of different reasons: political, social and theological. For this reason they constructed an organized and highly structured heresy which allowed them to implement mechanisms of persecution such as crusade and inquisition.

This argument is not convincing. The fact that popes only infrequently referred to the heretics who espoused a form of dualism as 'Cathars', thereby deliberately differentiating them from other heretical groups, does not of course mean that such beliefs and practices did not exist, or that people did

---

[45] Honorius III, 'Multo sudore laboratum', cols. 189–91.
[46] Honorius III, 'Cum reges et' (14 December 1223), in *Horoy* IV, cols. 484–7.
[47] For example, Honorius III, 'Nosti fili carissime' (14 May 1222), ibid., cols. 144–6.
[48] *Documents de l'histoire de Languedoc* (Toulouse, 1969), pp. 99–105; Barber, *The Cathars*, 2nd edn, pp. 90–4.

not practice them in some form – whether loosely and sporadically or more consistently and 'officially'. Indeed, one could argue that the fact that Church documents only infrequently referred to 'Cathars', and that popes preferred in their correspondence to use the more general word 'haeretici', shows not that it was deliberately constructing a heresy and a heretical group with the aim of scapegoating enemies in the south of France, but rather the reverse. The decrees of Lateran III and Lateran IV suggest not that the medieval papacy constructed the idea of a group called 'Cathars', but that it was fully aware that there were different heretical groups in the south of France, whom people called by different names to acknowledge that their beliefs deviated both from mainstream Catholicism and from each other. Popes feared all heretical groups as dangerous to the proper understanding and practice of the true faith, and we should not underestimate that fear. In particular the Papacy feared one such group, popularly known as 'Cathars', because it saw its dualist theology as so radically at odds with the tenets of Christianity.

Even so, the papacy's acknowledgment of a group of people who did not espouse mainstream Catholicism and who were popularly called 'Cathars' does not itself take us as far as we might like. Nowhere in the legislation of Lateran III or Lateran IV, or in the correspondence of Innocent III and Honorius III, for example, do we find specific reference to Cathars deriving their ideas from a dualist Balkan heresy. Indeed, what is so remarkable is just how little we do learn about the Cathars from papal documents, either in terms of beliefs, practices or structures. Yet here it is important to remember that the purpose of Innocent III's and Honorius III's letters was not to give a detailed description to the Christian faithful of the particular nature of the danger posed by 'Cathars', or indeed of any other heretical grouping. Rather it was to encourage the Christian faithful by means of emotional rhetoric to defend Christianity by a simple call to take part in a crusade against heresy and thereby to prevent what was seen as the pernicious and corrupting influence of heretics in the south of France. Papal letters were issued for the specific purpose of authorizing and encouraging the Albigensian crusade; their purpose was never to inform the reader or listener about the nature of Cathar beliefs or their origins. Indeed it is very likely that neither Innocent III nor Honorius III knew very much about the dualist heresy against which they authorized their crusade. In order to find detailed information on what this prominent group of heretics, popularly called 'Cathars', did and did not believe, who they were and where their beliefs and practices originated, we must look for answers not in papal documents but in other primary sources from the period.

12

Looking for the 'Good Men' in the Languedoc: An Alternative to 'Cathars'?

Claire Taylor

This volume addresses the question of whether, in the twelfth and thirteenth centuries, there existed a distinctive dualist religious movement, ranging from Asia Minor almost to the Atlantic. It seems important in this context to consider terminology and how it affects the discussion. Specifically, I am going to consider terminology used in the Middle Ages for southern French examples of what historians have come to call 'Cathars' and 'Catharism'. There is a legitimate debate about whether we should be using the terms. This is quite distinct from the debate about whether 'Cathars' were dualists. It is also distinct from the debate about whether southern French dualists, called 'Cathars' or otherwise, were connected to other pockets of dualism. However, all three elements of the traditional approach – the name, the dualism, the international phenomenon – are coming to be dealt with separately in recent, refreshingly iconoclastic, but very scholarly, francophone works. Monique Zerner *et al.* deny the evidence of dualism in the West; Jean-Louis Biget finds an indigenous dualism which was independent of external influence, and does not call it Catharism; Pilar Jiménez-Sanchez considers the western phenomena as different 'Catharisms'.[1]

In the dominant anglophone literature,[2] as in the traditional francophone, it is as though 'western dualism' and 'Catharism' were the same thing, even

---

[1] *L'histoire du catharisme en discussion: Le 'concile' de Saint-Félix (1167)*, ed. M. Zerner (Nice, 2001); J.-L. Biget, *Hérésie et inquisition dans le midi de la France* (Paris, 2007); P. Jiménez-Sanchez, *Les catharismes: modèles dissidents du christianisme médiéval (XIIe–XIIIe siècles* (Rennes, 2008). For the more traditional approach, see, most obviously, J. Duvernoy, *Le catharisme*, vol. 1: *La religion des cathares* (Toulouse, 1976), and vol. 2: *L'histoire des cathares* (Toulouse, 1979). On the response of those following in Duvernoy's footsteps to the new historiography, see Julien Théry's review of *Les cathares devant l'histoire: mélanges offerts à Jean Duvernoy*, ed. Anne Brenon *et al.* (Cahors, 2005), in *Midi-Pyrénées patrimoine* 3 (2005), 84–5.

[2] See, most obviously, Bernard Hamilton's papers brought together in the collections *Crusaders, Cathars and the Holy Places* (Aldershot, 1999), and *Monastic Reform, Catharism and the Crusades (900–1300)* (London, 1979). Picking up where this leaves off are M. Lambert, *The Cathars* (Oxford, 1998) and M. Barber, *The Cathars: Dualist Heretics in the High Middle Ages*, 2nd edn (Harlow, 2013). These works supersede the overly positivist

though we all know that 'Catharism' is an ahistorical term for the medieval phenomenon, or phenomena, under discussion. The traditionalists know that it was hardly used in, or of, southern France,[3] and not very often elsewhere either, and do not argue otherwise. But whilst it could be argued that we need some universal label for the people whom inquisitors, unhelpfully, simply called 'heretics', so that we know that we are all talking about the same phenomenon (however we interpret it), this approach presupposes an association between western heresies called 'Cathar' by their detractors; that they were alike and connected, even though they were geographically distant, and did not always use the same terminology as each other to describe themselves. My opinion is that 'alike and connected' does indeed describe what the sources reveal, and that we may legitimately use a short-hand terminology for it, while nonetheless noting significant differences between groups on account of the ways they developed.

However, the specific term 'Cathar' goes beyond this and *presupposes* what the nature of this generalized phenomenon is. The word is neither neutral, nor simply 'as good or as bad' as any other. In fact, 'Cathar' has *a priori* dualist implications. Eckbert of Schönau first proposed it, for the manifestation in the 1160s in the Rhineland, of what seemed to him to be like the *Catharistae*, a branch of the ancient, dualist, Manichaean heresy.[4] So the modern term 'Cathar' refers to a set of a phenomena in Europe which were dualist, and even connect to Manichaeism.[5] The practice of naming the sect(s) 'Cathar' only began when Charles Schmidt, the first modern historian to use the term for a generalized western European phenomenon, introduced it into modern historiography.[6] This did not matter at the time, because the

---

conclusions about the interconnectedness of all dualist heresy in S. Runciman, *The Medieval Manichee: a Study of the Christian Dualist Heresy* (Cambridge, 1947).

[3] Alan of Lille used it somewhere between 1185 and 1200: *De Fide Catholica contra haereticos libri quatuor*, in *Patrologia Latina*, ed. J.-P. Migne, 217 vols. (Paris, 1844–64) (henceforth *PL*), CCX, bk 1, 305–430. Hilbert Chiu has argued that Alan never worked in the Languedoc and never met a Cathar: H. Chiu, 'Alan of Lille's Academic Concept of the Manichee', *Journal of Religious History* 35/4 (2011), 492–506. Peter Biller has challenged this assertion, referring to work by Marie-Thérèse d'Alverny, which Chiu was evidently unaware of: M.-T. d'Alverny, *Alain de Lille: textes inédits* (Paris, 1965). See http://www.history.ac.uk/reviews/review/1546.

[4] *PL* 195, 11–98.

[5] Cf. Uwe Brunn, who limits the influence of Eckbert's heretics, whatever their nature, to the Rhineland: U. Brunn, *Des contestaires au 'cathares': discours de réforme et propagande antihérétique dans le pays du Rhin et de la Meuse avant l'inquisition* (Paris, 2006). Brunn does not refer to Robert Harrison, who stressed that Eckbert observed that the new sect was like the Catharistae, but at the same time novel and not the same: R. Harrison, 'Eckbert of Schönau and Catharism: A Re-evaluation', *Comitatus* 22/1 (1991), 41–53.

[6] Charles Schmidt was the first historian to coin this general term for what he considered to be an interconnected western European dualist movement: C. Schmidt, *Histoire et doctrine de la secte des cathares ou albigeois* (Paris, 1848–9). See B. Hamilton, 'The State of

dominant model was of a dualist heresy. Recent revisionism which does not consider the southern French phenomenon to be dualist is indeed correct in identifying a certain circularity.[7] Again this would not matter, but for the light-touch scholarly style of subsequent influential works on the subject.[8] To non-specialists, conventional readings of the sources could soon appear entrenched and complacent. The simple use of the term 'Cathar' could appear to limit the legitimacy not only of the orthodox understanding of the subject matter, but also of any attempt to rethink some of the issues, and problematize some of the evidence. This matters at an ethical level, because by being cleverly iconoclastic and populist in suggesting that those using 'Cathar' have made 2 + 2 = 5, Pegg and now Moore have 2 + 2 = 3. The missing element is a dissident religious doctrine, for which historians using a fuller range of sources[9] believe thousands of people were prepared to suffer extreme persecution and an agonizing death. As it stands, historians are entrenched, but not about all the right things: legitimate arguments over terms all too often become entangled with arguments over the very existence of heresy. In short, will it be necessary to abandon the term 'Cathar' in order to win the case for dualism?

I am not going to address here whether these heretics were dualists or not (though I am convinced that certainly their leadership and a good proportion of their followers consciously were; there is a good deal of evidence for this). Neither am I going to make a case that we should *not* call the entirety of western dualism 'Catharism'. Rather, I am acknowledging problems with the label when applied to the Languedoc, and discussing the most obvious alternative.[10]

---

the Research: The Legacy of Charles Schmidt to the Study of Christian Dualism', *Journal of Medieval History* 24/2 (1998), 191–214.

[7] This is a cornerstone of Mark Gregory Pegg's approach to the matter since his historiographical essay M. G. Pegg, 'On Cathars, Albigenses, and Good Men of Languedoc', *Journal of Medieval History* 27 (2001), 181–95. See also M. G. Pegg, *The Corruption of Angels: The Great Inquisition of 1245–6* (Princeton, 2001).

[8] See M. G. Pegg, *A Most Holy War: The Albigensian Crusade and the Battle for Christendom* (Oxford, 2008). Significant objections on the same basis as Pegg's now come from R. I. Moore, *The War on Heresy: Faith and Power in Medieval Europe* (London, 2012). Drawing heavily on Pegg, Moore has entirely rejected his former conviction that there was dualism in southern France since the 1160s, as well as the practice of referring to it as 'Cathar'. Cf. R. I. Moore, *The Origins of European Dissent* (London, 1997). For reviews of *The War on Heresy* see P. Biller in *The Medieval Review* http://www.history.ac.uk/reviews/review/1546 (together with Moore's reply), and Claire Taylor in *Journal of World History* 24/3 (2013), 681–8.

[9] Moore is an acknowledged expert on a wide range of eleventh- to early thirteenth century sources. Pegg has done more work than many on a set of inquests in the Lauragais (1245–6, and see below). Neither has tested their theory against the full range of early inquisitorial sources (see below for examples of these).

[10] This cannot be the simple term 'heretics' (*haeretici*), which was considered a specific enough label by inquisitors in southern France. What they needed to do was to

'Good Men' in the Languedoc: An Alternative to 'Cathars'?

For an alternative which could be agreeable to all, the historian apparently need look no further than the sources themselves, in which, the secondary literature tells us, the term used for heretics, both by themselves and their followers, is 'the good men'.[11] The term is *boni homines* in Latin, and in Occitan appears in a range of variants of the term *bos omes* or *bos homes*. It has been considered an appropriate term by traditionalists, by those who consider the dualist heresy to be home-grown, and by those who find little evidence of dualism. Furthermore, the term was apparently used from the period in which the sect first became established in the Languedoc, i.e. by the 1160s, through into the inquisitorial period of the thirteenth century. The purpose of this chapter is to explore this, the most commonly proposed and readily acceptable compromise label for the heretics of Languedoc.

The first question to ask is how do we know that these 'heretics' of the Languedoc called themselves 'good men'?[12] That they did so is such a commonplace in the literature on heresy that evidence for it is rarely even addressed. The scholarly consensus originates with Herbert Grundmann. Grundmann listed five key sources for the region that were composed before inquisitors come to dominate the discourse concerning what 'heretics' should be called.[13] Grundmann's first two examples appear to describe the heresy in its first flowering in the Languedoc. The earliest is the record of the Council

---

distinguish dualists, as they certainly considered them to be, from another local sect, 'Waldensians', whose 'heresy' was of another kind entirely. The Latinists called these 'Valdenses'. For historians, there are too many other kinds of medieval heresies for the exponents of one to be usefully defined as 'heretics'.

[11] On this see Biget, above, and J. Théry. 'L'hérésie des bons homes: comment nommer la dissidence religieuse non vaudoise ni béguine en Languedoc (XIIe–début du XIVe siècle)?' *Heresis* 36/37 (2002), 75–117.

[12] I set aside, for now, two other problems with the terminology. At both ends of the historiographical spectrum, from Duvernoy to Pegg, historians consider that 'good men' did not apply only to people considered 'heretics', but was a general appellation for the righteous, the upstanding, the generous, the high-born, and so on. As well as Biget, Pegg and Théry, above, see Duvernoy, *La religion des cathares*, p. 39. In what sense, therefore, and to whom, was it a useful way of simultaneously referring to a very specific subset of those people: the ones arrested and tried for heresy? Secondly, was it so ubiquitous? In general, scholars discussing heresy do not actually give many, if any, examples of its wider usage in the specific geographical regions affected by 'heresy', for example in troubadour poetry, law codes, charters or customs, where we might expect to find it. Nor do they tend to refer to secondary literature on the socio-political life of Languedoc, where there is far less discussion of the term in a secular context than we might expect, were it indeed so specific to the region and so widely used. On the use of the terminology at Montauban, see J. Feuchter, *Ketzer, Konsuln und Büßer: die städtischen Eliten von Montauban vor dem Inquisitor Petrus Cellani (1236/1241)* (Tübingen, 2007).

[13] H. Grundmann, *Religious Movements in the Middle Ages*, trans. S. Rowan (Notre Dame, 1995 [trans. from 1961 edn; 1st German edn 1935]), p. 11 n. 17 (which is at pp. 256–7). Grundmann says confidently that this was 'the actual term the heretics used for themselves' (p. 257). He drew some of the examples from A. Borst, *Die Katharer* (Stuttgart, 1953), p. 242 n. 11.

of Lombers in 1165, at which sentence was passed against people who apparently called themselves 'good men', after a debate between themselves and clerical judges. The Latin expression used for the heretics is *boni homines*, which we could translate as, 'good people', as well as 'good men'. The source then lists the bishops and abbots who attended, and says that this council took place in the presence of more 'good men', whom it lists, but this time the phrase is *bonorum virorum*. Soon after this, we again find the heretics, and again they are called *boni homines*.[14] So we have 'good men' three times if we render it in the most obvious manner for most modern European languages. But this conceals a contrast being made in the Latin between the 'heretical' 'good men/people', and the *really* 'good men', the clerics and their lay allies. On the basis of this evidence, Grundmann's assertion for this being the first time that 'heretics' are designated 'good men' seems sound. It is reasonable to assert that these people called themselves *boni homines* (presumably *bos homes*). We also learn that more than one kind of person could be called a 'good man'. The source is making a point about this.[15]

After this, the problems begin. Grundmann's next example originates in a process in 1178 whereby the kings of England and France, Henry II and Louis VII, involved themselves in rooting out and punishing heretics at Toulouse at the request of its count. The fullest narrative account is found in the *Gesta Regis Henrici Secundi*. This refers to 'faithless men, who have themselves referred to as "good men"'.[16] The *Gesta* is an earlier version of the *Chronica* of Roger of Howden, a member of Henry II's household, though it was not attributed to him until the 1950s. The *Chronica* continues where Roger left off the *Gesta*, in 1192, and continues to 1201 when he is presumed to have died. The *Gesta* version is therefore most contemporary with the Toulouse affair, and is also more detailed.[17] Roger was not present himself in Toulouse, in

---

[14] 'Anno ab Incarnatione Domine MCLXV talis diffinitiva sententia lata est super altercatione at assertione atque impugnatione fidei catholicae, quam expugnare nitebantur quidam qui faciebant se appellari Boni homines [...] in praesentia bonorum virorum tam clericorum quam laicorum [...] Interrogavit Lodovensis episcopus eos qui faciunt se nuncupare boni homines'; *Sacrorum conciliorum nova et amplissima collectio*, ed. J.-D. Mansi, 31 vols., 2nd edn (Graz, 1960–1), XXII, cols. 157–68 (at cols. 157 and 159).

[15] It is therefore not useful to translate both terms as 'good men', as W. L. Wakefield and A. P. Evans do in *Heresies of the High Middle Ages: Selected Sources* (New York, 1969), p. 190.

[16] '[...] quaedem gens perfida, quae se bonos homines appellari fecerant, in terra Tolosana congregata erant [sic]'; *Gesta Regis Henrici Secundi, Benedicti Abbatis*, in *The Chronicle of the Reigns of Henry II and Richard I, A.D. 1169–1192, Known Commonly under the Name of Benedict of Peterbrorough*, ed. W. Stubbs, 2 vols. (London, 1867), I, 198–202 (p. 198).

[17] D. M. Stenton, 'Roger of Howden and Benedict', *English Historical Review* 68 (1953), 574–82; D. Corner, 'The *Gesta Regis Henrici Secundi* and *Chronica* of Roger, parson of Howden', *Bulletin of the Institute of Historical Research* 56 (1983), 126–44; J. Gillingham, 'Writing the Biography of Roger of Howden, King's Clerk and Chronicler', in *Writing Medieval Biography, 750–1250: Essays in Honour of Frank Barlow*, ed. D. Bates, J. Crick and S. Hamilton (Woodbridge, 2006), pp. 207–20. Roger of Howden's later version is *Chronica*

spite of having spent time in France on royal business for some of the 1170s. He based his account on letters circulated by the papal legates Peter of Pavia[18] and Henry of Marcy.[19] The latter had just been made abbot of the Cistercian monastery of Clairvaux, and it was to his order that Count Raymond had appealed.[20] However, neither of these two letters uses the term 'good men' in relation to the heretics. Furthermore, Henry of Marcy also wrote to King Louis about the heretics, and does not refer to 'good men' in that letter either.[21] In addition, when Roger of Howden edited his earlier text into the *Chronica*, he erased the reference to 'good men'.[22]

So where did the term 'good men' originate in relation to the affair of 1178? On the face of it, the best explanation appears to be that Roger was informed by sources for the Council of Lombers concerning the nature of the heresy. It is not too speculative to suggest that while in France earlier in the 1170s he met people who had heard of the Lombers affair, or indeed that he might have read the record of the council at some point. However, if he made the same connection between the two sets of heretics that other clergy did, and reflected this in his account, he appears to have then repented and dropped the term when he redrafted the *Gesta*. Perhaps his change of mind marks a later suspicion that the canons of Lombers had rather over-stressed the heretics' use of 'good men' in the first place, as a result of their choosing to construct some self-righteous word-play around *homines* and *viri*. Whatever the explanation, the account of the Council of Lombers is the only extant, locally originating and reliable twelfth-century evidence that the 'heretics' of the sources were called 'good men'.

Grundmann's next example dates from the second decade of the thirteenth century. Peter of les Vaux-de-Cernay, a northern French Cistercian and chronicler of the Albigensian crusade (1209–29), writing in 1212–18, says of the heretics that some of them were called '"perfected" or "good men"', and others their supporters. Grundmann missed a further reference here, concerning the ritual of adult baptism, through which the believer became one of these '"perfected" or "good men"'. In this ceremony, Peter states, the believer is told, 'Therefore receive the Holy Spirit from the good men'.[23] But where did Peter

---

magistri Rogeri de Houedene, ed. W. Stubbs, 4 vols., Rolls Series 51 (London, 1868–1871), II, 150–5.
[18] *PL* 199, 1120–4 (copied into *Gesta Regis Henrici Secundi* at p. 202).
[19] *PL* 204, 235–40.
[20] Gervase of Canterbury, *Opera historica*, ed. W. Stubbs, 2 vols., Rolls Series (London, 1879), I, 270–1.
[21] *PL* 204, 234–5.
[22] Instead, he calls them 'Arians'.
[23] Grundmann cites Peter from a fragment of the chronicle partially transcribed by Achille Luchaire and published posthumously as 'Premier fragment d'une édition critique', in *Cinquièmes mélanges d'histoire du Moyen Âge*, Bibliothèque de la Faculté de lettres 24 (Paris, 1908), pp. 1–75. He gives the references col. 2, p. 19 ('quidam inter hereticos

get this information from? While he is an invaluable source for the Albigensian crusade, which he witnessed at first hand, he possibly had little direct contact with the heretics themselves. He was a newcomer to the Languedoc, and does not claim to have personally encountered them. Although some of his chronicle is based on the work of the southerner Ermengaud of Béziers, Ermengaud does not use the term 'good men'. Peter's most likely sources were the abbots of abbeys such as Fontfroide, Ardorel and Candeil. Once again, the evidence for the sectarians calling themselves 'good men' by the time of the crusade possibly also originates in Cistercian stories about the 1160s.

Grundmann then tells us that the inquisitor and writer against heresy Stephen of Bourbon spoke to some women in Provence who had been converted by Dominic Guzman. They referred to heretics as 'illos homines, contra quos predicas, usque modo credidimus et vocavimus "bonos homines"'.[24] But does Stephen really mean to imply that the women used 'good men' as a title or appellation? It seems just as logical to render the text as 'those men who, until now, we believed in and we called good men', i.e. the women, convinced by Dominic's teaching, now removed the heretics from a wider set of people whom they considered to be 'good' people rather than 'bad' people. Furthermore, the story in fact originates in Constantine of Orvieto's *Vita* of St Dominic, which was not composed until *c.* 1246.[25] Dominic had died in 1221. As a story drawn from a *vita*, composed no fewer than twenty years after the events it refers to, this too is flimsy evidence that 'the good men' is how the sect had wanted to be known.

A fifth specific example appears, in Grundmann's account, to have been taken from the cartulary of Le Prouille, the abbey for women established by Dominic Guzman in 1206. It is in fact to be found in the introduction to Jean Guiraud's 1907 edition of the Le Prouille cartulary,[26] and is one of the

---

dicebantur perfecti sive boni homines'), and col. 4, p. 19 ('Heretici enim a fautoribus suis boni homines vocabantur'). The more commonly consulted Latin edition is *Petri Vallium Sarnaii monachi hystoria Albigensis*, ed. P. Guébin and E. Lyon, 3 vols. (Paris, 1926–30). This supercedes Luchaire's uncompleted work, which Guébin and Lyon had in any case been involved in publishing (Guébin and Lyon discuss the editions at pp. i–v). Grundmann, who published in 1935, presumably did not have access to this fuller edition, which utilises more manuscripts. Differences between the manuscripts used are evident. Guébin and Lyon give exactly the same as Grundmann/Luchaire for the first quotation, 'quidam inter hereticos dicebantur perfecti sive boni homines' (part 1, ch. 13, p. 13), but only Guébin and Lyon give 'Ergo accipe Spiritum a bonis hominibus' (part 1, ch. 19, p. 19).

[24] *Tractatus de diversis materiis praedicabilibus*, ed. A. Lecoy de la Marche, *Anecdotes historiques, légendes et apologues tirés du receuil inédit d'Étienne de Bourbon* (Paris, 1877), p. 35.

[25] Observed by L. J. Sackville, *Heresy and Heretics in the Thirteenth Century: The Textual Representations* (York, 2011), pp. 80–1. She offers an important new evaluation of the sources for the saint and the order: pp. 76–87.

[26] *Cartulaire de Notre-Dame de Prouille, précédé d'une étude sur l'albigéisme languedocien au XIIe et XIIIe siècles* (Paris, 1907), p. lxxii n. 3.

documents extant in the archive of the castle of Merville (Haute Garonne) in 1890, when they were edited by Célestin Douais.[27] According to Guiraud, who quotes it as part of an extensive introduction to Catharism, the document reads 'Quod erant de illis bonis hominibus, qui dicebantur "heretici" [sic] et vivebant bene et sancte et jejunebant tribus diebus in septimana, et non comedebant carnem'.[28] Jean Guiraud refers to p. 185. The modern facsimile of Douais's edition does not contain pages after p. 169, so Guiraud was probably mistaken. Nothing appears to be missing from the facsimile. Neither can I locate the statement elsewhere within the Douais facsimile. Given this, and the fact that the Merville documents date from the thirteenth to seventeenth centuries, the date, origin and nature of the source from which the quotation comes are uncertain. None of this strengthens Grundmann's case. Furthermore, taken at face value – Grundmann obviously found it significant – this passage, like the previous example, makes more sense if we translate it along the lines of: 'those good men, who were called heretics and lived well and in a holy way and fasted three days a week, and did not eat meat'. This does not mean that the people living in this way were called 'the good men'. It means that some people, considered good, were called heretics (or, in other words, 'those perfectly decent people who got accused of heresy').[29]

Grundmann then notes that the term 'good men' appears 'extraordinarily often' in inquisitorial trial records.[30] He is of course correct. However, it is easy to demonstrate that, in spite of the hundreds of occasions on which the Latin words 'boni homines' appear, we find few examples using words that can safely be logically rendered 'the good men' or 'the good women', or 'the good people' as any sort of title, or even with a definite article. Here I am using sources dating to the 1240s, in which we are most likely to find reflections of an earlier usage of 'good men'. The following are very typical of the examples to be found in the register of sentences of the inquisitor Peter Sellan, originating in his inquest in the diocese of Cahors in 1241–2.[31]

We read, in a generic example, that Na Aurimonde of Moissac had believed of heretics 'quod essent boni homines, et habebat bonam fidem in eis' ('that they were good men/people, and she had great faith in them').[32] Geralda, wife of Bernard Manhe, had likewise 'credebat quod essent boni homines'

---

[27] *Les manuscrits du château de Merville* (Paris, 1890).
[28] *Cartulaire de Notre-Dame de Prouille*, pp. xix–cccxxxvii.
[29] Douais's translation in the Prouille cartulary does not use the word 'heretic', and nor does it imply that 'good men' is any kind of title. It reads, 'Ce sont, disait-on, des bonnes homes qui vivent saintement, jeûnent trios jours par semaine et ne ne manger jamais de viande' (p. lxxii).
[30] Grundmann, *Religious Movements in the Middle Ages*, p. 257.
[31] Which we have extant as a seventeenth-century copy, Paris, Bibliothèque nationale de France (henceforth BnF), Collection Doat, MS 21 (henceforth Doat 21), fols. 185r–312r.
[32] 'Item credebat quod essent boni homines et habebat bonam fidem in eis' (Ibid., fol. 290v).

('believed that they were good men/people').³³ In fact, this construction, *quod essent boni homines*, is ubiquitous in the register and accounts for the vast majority of the references to 'good men'. But 'good' is a description of the 'men/people'. Na Aurimonde and Geralda had thought them 'good', not 'bad'. It makes no sense in context to say, 'she believed that they were *the* good men', as though she might have muddled them up with some other group. The inquisitor is merely trying to ties things up neatly in the register in order to remind himself about, or explain, particular sentences. Thus many deponents 'saw' or 'heard' heretics, or even 'gave them goods'. If at the same time they 'believed that they were good people', this was a more serious matter.

Another context in which 'good men' cannot be synonymous with the people whom inquisitors called heretics is the deposition of Bernard of Lasmartres.³⁴ This is a reflection of the near ubiquitous presence of Waldensians in manuscript Doat 21. We learn that Bernard received *Valdenses*. He had given them 'goods of his [...] heard them preach [...] and believed that they were good men/people' ('et credebat quod essent boni homines'). Two depositions further on, Na Marquesa says the same of Waldensians that she believed 'that they were good men'.³⁵ Na Aymare of Montlauzun said that she believed that *Waldensian* women she met were 'good women'.³⁶ In fact, in this register there are whole clusters of people calling Waldensians 'good' people.³⁷ 'Good people', therefore, does not refer to the same people whom the inquisitors called 'heretics'.

Moving on to a source containing evidence from Bernard of Caux's inquest in Lower Quercy and the Toulousain, in 1243–6,³⁸ in which we have full depositions as opposed to summaries of crimes, we find another generic way of referring to 'good people'. It does not refer to Waldensians (the inquisitors presumably asked about them, but either did not find evidence of them, or did not record answers concerning them). By far the most common usage of 'good men' is where the deponent did, or did not believe, 'that they were good men'. Bernard of Caux introduced *boni homines* into the record for the same reason that Peter Sellan did, but the construction around it is different. In Pons Grimoard's deposition we read 'Dixit etiam quod credidit hereticos esse bonos homines et habere bonam fidem.'³⁹ Conversely, we also find, 'Dixit etiam quod nunquam credidit hereticos esse bonos homines.'⁴⁰ The

---

33   Ibid., fol. 292.
34   '[...] recepit Valdenses in domo sua et dedit eis de bonis suis et locavit eis domum et audivit predicationem eorum, et credebat quod essent boni homines (Ibid., fol. 221v).
35   Ibid.
36   Ibid., fol. 222v.
37   See Feuchter, *Ketzer, Konsuln und Büßer*, p. 231.
38   Paris, BnF, Collection Doat, MS 22 (henceforth Doat 22), fols. 1r–106v.
39   Ibid., fol. 38r.
40   Ibid., fol. 45v.

witnesses, in other words, 'believed', or had 'never believed', 'heretics *to be* good men'. Again, it simply does not make sense conceptually to translate this as 'believed them to be *the* good men'. This would only make sense if inquisitors were asking witness after witness whether or not they believed that the people the inquisitors were calling 'heretics' were the same people that other people called 'good men'. Obviously the inquisitor is not asking that. He is asking, 'Did you think that they were good people, with a good faith?' as opposed to 'bad people' with an evil faith. Sometimes we simply get, 'crediderit hereticos esse bonos',[41] in a familiar type of construction where an adjective can be read as though it were accompanied a noun: 's/he believed the heretics to be good (people)'. This takes us another step further from understanding 'the good men' as some kind of distinctly recognizable group.

Turning now to the manuscript known as MS 609, originating in the inquest of Bernard of Caux and John of Saint-Pierre in the Lauragais in 1245/6,[42] there are indeed some references which, when taken in context, could be interpreted as using 'boni homines' as an appellation. They include a reference to two 'good men' being escorted from the town by Arnold Velh, who knew them to be heretics: 'quod exirent extra villam et q(uo)d associarent duos bonos homines scilicet h(aeretici)'.[43] This could be translated as 'good men' or 'the good men'. In two cases, witnesses appear to have used the expression 'the good men' and been induced to clarify it as 'the heretics'. Gordoz Vidal's mother apparently informed him that she was told he had given himself to what can be translated as either 'good men' or '*the* good men', adding, 'that is, to heretics': 'Fili, dictum est mihi quod tu es datus bonis hominibus, id est, hereticis.'[44] Similarly, Na Matheude saw women in the home of Hugh of Canelle, and on asking what sort of women they were, was told that 'bone mulieres erant, id est, heretice' ('they were (the) good women, that is, heretical').[45] As such, 'the good people' could indeed be a recognizable group in some depositions.

Less convincingly, 'the good men' and 'the good women' are perhaps sometimes acknowledged by a title in reported speech, as in the ritual request for blessing. In the deposition of Arnold Garner we encounter a woman who had genuflected before female heretics, saying, 'Benedicite, bone mulieres, orate Deum pro nobis' ('Bless us, good women, and pray to God for

---

[41] Ibid., fol. 41v.
[42] Bibliothèque municipale de Toulouse, MS 609 (henceforth MS 609).
[43] Ibid, fol. 38r. I have not had access to a sufficiently legible copy of MS 609 and am using Jean Duvernoy's not entirely perfect transcription: http://jean.duvernoy.free.fr/text/pdf/ms609_a.pdf.
[44] This is cited by Pegg in *Corruption of Angels* at p. 178 n. 15. He gives MS 609, fol. 45v. I cannot find it in Jean Duvernoy's transcription, but Duvernoy is not always accurate.
[45] MS 609, fol. 47v.

us').⁴⁶ Should we necessarily understand 'good women' as a title or formal appellation here? The expression works just as well as an encouraging and complimentary, but informal form of address. Furthermore, the ritual request for blessing did not have to involve 'good men/women'. We commonly find 'Domini, orate Deum pro isto peccatore quod faciat me bonum christianum et perducat ad bonum finem' ('Lord' – meaning an initiated heretic – 'pray to God for this sinner, that he makes me a good Christian, and leads me to a good end').⁴⁷

However, far from the appellation '(the) good men' being ubiquitous in MS 609, 'good men' or 'good women' are most commonly recorded just as they are in Doat 21 and 22. 'Heretics' are typically being 'believed to be good men' in a sense where 'the good men' would be an unusual translation of *boni homines*. We find this in the testimony of Arnold Garner, above: 'dixit quod credebat h(aeretici) esse bonos homines et habere bonam fidem et esse veraces et amicos Dei' ('he said that he believed the heretics to be good men and to have a good faith, and to be truthful and friends of God').⁴⁸ We find 'to be good men' also in the testimony of Peter Gardog of Montgaillard.⁴⁹ Conversely, as with Doat 22, we also find 'credidit quod heretici *nunquam* fuerunt boni homines'.⁵⁰ Again, this could be, 'he *never* believed them to be good men', or 'he believed they *never* were good men'; but it makes no sense as 'he never believed that the heretics were *the* good men', or 'he believed that the heretics were *never* the good men', as though it were incorrect to mix up the two groups, 'good men' and 'heretics'. The incorrect thing – what the inquisitor is driving at – is the belief that the heretics were 'good'.

In short, every inquisitorial register has its own style, not least in its formulaic answers to formulaic questions, and in the sort of shorthand it employs. MS 609 does indeed use 'good men' and 'good women' in ways other sets of documents do not – to refer to good men in ways which may be read as 'the good men'. But more often it resembles other registers in employing 'good' as the opposite of 'bad', in terms of what *sort* of people 'heretics' were. We certainly cannot generalize about terminology appearing in inquisition documents of the 1240s without reading all of the documents generated by that wave of inquisition.

Finally, I turn to a narrow set of sources apparently originating with southern French heretics themselves, which Grundmann neglected. Surely if the heretics called themselves 'the good men', we would find this reflected here. We do not find it in Latin sources such as the Saint-Félix charter of

---

⁴⁶ Ibid., fol. 2v.
⁴⁷ Ibid., fol. 4v, and see e.g. fol. 53r.
⁴⁸ Ibid., fol. 1r.
⁴⁹ Ibid., fol. 45v.
⁵⁰ Ibid., fol. 157v.

c. 1170,[51] or the text known as the Cathar Ritual, set down by c. 1250.[52] 'Good men' is, however, used in the extant Provençal version of the Ritual, set down in writing possibly as late as 1280.[53] It is the instructions for the performance of the *consolamentum*, the ritual through which a believer became an initiated heretic. In the Latin version the heretic leading the ritual is called an *ordinatus* and is assisted by an *ancianus* (elder). In the Provençal version, however, it is the leading heretic who is *l'ancia* ('the elder'), and he is assisted by 'one of the good men' ('la us dels bos homes'). In the Provençal are examples of 'good man' being used even more obviously as an appellation. In an account of the initiation rite as having been passed down since the apostolic era, spiritual baptism is given, 'ab l'empausament de las mas dels bos homes' ('by the imposition of hands by the good men'),[54] 'de bos homes en bos homes' ('from good men through good men').[55] So *bos ome* here is indeed a category of people with initiated characteristics.

This sense of the specialness of the good men is also echoed where we read that, once the believer wishing to enter the sect was sufficiently prepared, the selected representative of the *bos homes* placed his hands on him.[56] Further on, 'one of the good men' makes his *melioramentum*' ('la us dels bos homes fasa so miloira'),[57] and soon the other 'good men' place their right hand on the initiate: 'li autri boni homi cascu la ma destra'.[58] Later, Christ is described as having taught the 'good men' how to pray: 'Aisso es la oracio que Jesu Christ aportec en aquest mon, e la ensenc als bos homes.'[59] Ironically, for those seeing only non-dualist 'good men', the strongest case that can be made for 'heretics' calling themselves and being called the 'good men' is if the Ritual is taken

---

[51] The text of the record of this heretical council survives only partially, and the oldest extant version is in Guillaume Besse, *Histoire des ducs, marquis et comtes de Narbonne* (Paris, 1660), pp. 483–6. The source is problematic, but not to the extent that we should eliminate it as a source for the heresy: *L'histoire du catharisme en discussion*, ed. Zerner, pp. 135–201.

[52] The edition is in A. Dondaine, *Un traité néo-manichéen du XIIIe siècle: le Liber de duobus principiis, suivi d'un fragment de Rituel cathare* (Rome, 1939), pp. 151–65.

[53] Lyon, Bibliothèque municipale, PA 36, fols. 325v–241v. The edition referred to is *Le Nouveau Testament traduit au XIIIe siècle en langue provençale, suivi d'un Rituel cathare: reproduction photolithographique du manuscrit de Lyon*, ed. and trans. L. Clédat (Paris, 1887); Latin text ed. C. Thouzellier, *Rituel cathare: introduction, texte critique, traduction et notes*, Sources chrétiennes 236 (Paris, 1977), Appendix 20. Cf. Wakefield and Evans, *Heresies of the High Middle Ages*, pp. 465–6. See also B. Hamilton, 'Wisdom from the East: The Reception by the Cathars of Eastern Dualist Texts', in *Heresy and Literacy, 1000–1530*, ed. P. Biller and A. Hudson (Cambridge, 1994), pp. 38–60.

[54] *Le Nouveau Testament*, ed. Clédat, p. xvi.
[55] Ibid., p. xvii.
[56] Ibid., p. xvi.
[57] Ibid., p. xx.
[58] Ibid.
[59] Ibid., p. xxiv.

at face value, as a thirteenth-century text composed by dualists,[60] operating within a counter-Church.

Certainly, modern editors of the Ritual have understood that there was something special about the 'good men'. In Clédat's edition, though 'good men' is rendered in the vernacular simply as 'bos homes', in the translation it is picked out as a significant term thus, «bons hommes». Wakefield and Evans even render it in upper case: 'Good Men'. However, it is not just that the Ritual uses language differently from inquisitorial and other sources that makes it suggest the use of 'good men' in the sense that some historians now employ the term. In addition, the Provençal makes use of definite articles where they are not used in Latin. On the one hand, it could be argued that definite articles were present in the original vernacular testimonies on which the Latin texts of depositions are based (we cannot really call the process, 'translation'). However, it is still the case that in the vast majority of depositions, were we to infer definite objects in the vernacular versions, they would make little sense logically with the addition of 'the'. (Examples include (i) *quod essent boni homines et habebat bonam fidem in eis*, (ii) *et credebat quod essent boni homines*, (iii) *credebat quod essent boni homines et habebat bonam fidem in eis* and (iv) *et credebat quod essent boni homines*.)

Another problem with the Provençal Ritual is that 'good men' is not, in fact, the way in which initiated heretics are typically referred to in the text. The handful of examples we have just discussed should not overshadow that the word used most often for those in the sect is 'christians' (*crestia*, in various grammatical forms),[61] and 'christian' with an adjective, for example: 'good christians' ('bos crestias' and 'bo crestia');[62] the 'loyal glorious christians' ('li dreiturers gloriosses crestias');[63] 'among christians we are sinners' ('entrels crestias estam peccadres');[64] 'the custom of the good christians' ('es costuma de bos crestias').[65] We also have the singular form, 'the christian' ('li crestia')[66] and 'the true christian' ('li ver crestia').[67] In fact, it is only those of the 'christians' taking a specific, most active, role in the ritual ceremony who are the 'good men.' The sect as a whole, what inquisitors would call the 'heretics', is entirely interchangeable with 'christians', and the latter term is used far more often. This reminds us also of a Latinized construction discussed above,

---

[60] Which the heretical text is explicit about: 'No aias merce de la carna nada de corruptio, mais aias merce del espirit pausat en carcer' ('do not have pity on the flesh born of corruption, but have mercy on the imprisoned within it'); ibid., p. xi. See also numerous references to their *gleisa* (ibid., p. xii and *passim*).
[61] Ibid., pp. x, xi, xv, xx, xxii (three times), xxiii, xxv (twice).
[62] Ibid., p. xi, xx.
[63] Ibid., p. ix.
[64] Ibid., p. x.
[65] Ibid., p. x.
[66] Ibid., p. xi.
[67] Ibid., p. xii.

'Good Men' in the Languedoc: An Alternative to 'Cathars'?

'Domini, orate Deum pro isto peccatore quod faciat me bonum christianum et perducat ad bonum finem'. The expression most interesting to a historian looking for alternatives to 'Cathar' is therefore 'good christian', which is not synonymous with 'good men', and is more prevalent.

Returning to Grundmann, he does give a few extra examples of the use of 'good men', but all of them are rather late to be taken as evidence that those called 'heretics' by their enemies in the early period were called 'good men' by their friends. One example is from a formula for inquisitors, the *Summa de officio inquisitonis*, found in the Laurentian Library of Florence and described by Charles Molinier. The inquisitor should establish whether the witness had at any point seen 'either heretics or good men' ('unquam hereticos aut bonos homines').[68] This seems to be good evidence that the two terms, 'heretics' and 'good men', were interchangeable in some contexts. However, the manuscript was compiled in the early fourteenth century. The earliest documents copied into it relate to inquisition in Languedoc in 1244, but other material concerns the inquisitor Sinibald of Lacu, charged with combating heresy in Italy in 1279.[69] As such, we cannot be certain that the instructions reflect southern French practice in the period in question. Next, Grundmann quotes from Célestin Douais's edition of documents relating to preachers in the Midi in the thirteenth century, using another term occasionally also applied to Cathars: 'Patarines'. We hear that these 'call themselves good men and without sin' ('se dicunt bonos homines and sine peccato').[70] 'Good men' is simply a description here and not a title, given that *dicunt* applies also to *sine peccato*. Furthermore, it is treacherous to attempt to read 'Cathar' or 'dualist' where sources say Paterines. Finally, Grundmann then moves to sources from *c.* 1300, in particular Bernard Gui, but these are far too late to interest us here.

In summary, there is no reliable first-hand, local twelfth-century evidence that these 'heretics' called themselves 'good men' except for the possible over-stressing of the concept in the record of the Council of Lombers in 1165. In fact, far from it being the case that 'heretics' called themselves 'good men', the evidence is that 'good men' itself was most often adopted by enemies of the heretics. This was possibly partly because the easily parodied *boni homines* appealed first to Roger of Howden (though on sober reflection he excised it from his work), and then to Cistercians of Peter of les Vaux-de-Cernay's generation. Certainly the sources relating to Stephen of Bourbon and Dominic

---

[68] Firenze, Biblioteca Medicea Laurenziana, Plut. vii, sin., cod. 2, fols. 156r–159v; Charles Molinier, 'Rapport à M. le Ministre de l'instruction publique sur une mission exécuté en Italie de Février à Avril 1885: Études sur quelques manuscrits des bibliothèques d'Italie concernant l'inquisition et les croyances hérétiques du XIIe et XIIIe siècle', *Archives des missions scientifiques et littéraires*, 3rd series 14 (Paris, 1888), 133–336, in which the *Summa de officio inquisitonis* is at pp. 156–65, and the relevant passage at p. 163.

[69] Molinier, 'Rapport', pp. 161–2 n. 5.

[70] *La somme des autorités à l'usage des prédicateurs méridionaux au XIIIe siècle* (Paris, 1896), p. 107, cited in Grundman, *Religious Movements*, p. 257.

Guzman do not stand up in the sense Grundmann intended them to. While the words *boni homines* appear frequently in inquisitorial documents, few such examples can be rendered 'the good men' in the sense of a title or a specific group. Ironically, it is in an indisputably dualist text that 'the good men' is most convincingly used self-referentially, but this is a later thirteenth-century source and most often refers to the sectarians as 'christians'.

This research began in an attempt to meet the revisionist scholarship on its own terms, and consider losing 'Cathar' and adopting terminology which we could all use relatively neutrally. 'Good men' seemed the obvious choice, because we understood, since Grundmann, that the contemporary evidence showed this to be what the 'heretics' called themselves. Instead, it seems this terminology may have originated in some self-righteous word-play by the clergy at Lombers, and that we do not have reliable evidence of its usage until around the middle of the next century. The obvious next question, therefore, is what *did* the 'heretics' or 'good men' actually call *themselves*? 'Good christians' is amongst those terms recorded and seems most likely.[71] It would be worthwhile to undertake a more detailed etymology of 'Christian' in 'Cathar' self-naming than has so far been the case. Of course, 'christian' is no more useful to a historian trying to find an accurate generalized terminology than 'heretic' is, because the term is obviously used by christians of the Roman Church and many other Churches besides.

Other enemies of the southern French (branch of the) 'Cathar' sect, for example crusaders, sometimes called them 'Albigensians' (*Albigenses*). Again this is an externally imposed term, but it at least has a southern French association, even though the heretics spread far beyond the Albi region. Duvernoy noted that 'Albigensians' was used by Cistercians, was perhaps first in use in 1181, and certainly by 1197. His main objection to it was that it has been confused with *Albanenses*, a term used for some of the dualists of Lombardy.[72] I can make no recommendations about an alternative to 'Cathars', but 'the good men' would appear to be even less historically appropriate than 'christians' or 'Albigensians'.

---

[71] On this see term Duvernoy, *La religion des cathares*, pp. 298–9.
[72] Duvernoy, *La religion des cathares*, pp. 308–9.

13

Principles at Stake: The Debate of April 2013 in Retrospect

R. I. Moore

The 2013 conference at University College London aimed to undertake, in the words of the preliminary announcement, a reassessment of the phenomenon traditionally known as 'Catharism' through a debate in a non-confrontational spirit, with the aim of reconsidering without assumptions the strength of the evidence for dualist beliefs and for an organized movement of adherents to them. Eighteen months on the predominant recollection of a quite exceptionally stimulating and enjoyable occasion is that it left among its participants a surprising degree of agreement on such facts as are capable of being established – and at least as profound a disagreement as before on what they mean, for there was little, either then or since, to suggest that any mind has been much changed. It was ever thus. It is hardly news that differences in reading small pieces of evidence may lead to widely divergent conclusions. Nevertheless, that despite the best efforts of all the participants discussion focused with ever sharper intensity on ever diminishing detail reinforces the suspicion that there is more at stake in the disagreement about the nature and origins of 'Catharism' than a straightforward difference of scholarly opinion. Peter Biller's comment, in his introductory remarks, that the passions run much higher in this debate than in its counterpart over early Waldensianism, even though on the face of it the issues are very much the same, has been amply fulfilled.[1] This chapter, however, eschewing wider issues, will attempt to clarify the methodological differences which still put us at cross purposes, and in particular the implications of the difference between looking forward to the crucial period in debate from an earlier standpoint, or back from a later one.

In respect of the facts divergence on the main question was not great. It was agreed that clear evidence of the presence of organized dualism in Europe, and

---

[1] Cf. Peter Biller, review of R. I. Moore, *The War on Heresy: Faith and Power in Medieval Europe* (London, 2012), together with my response, *Reviews in History* 1546, http://www.history.ac.uk/reviews/review/1546, accessed 30 September 2014. I am grateful to Biller for compelling me by the frankness of his response to consider the historiographical implications of my premises and conclusions more carefully.

a fortiori between the Rhone and the Garonne, before the Albigensian crusade is very slight at best, and that after 1250 it is both abundant and substantial. The traditionalists[2] attached considerable weight to the following: a donation of revenues in 1189 to a woman who had joined the *heretici*; the possibility that the document which describes the *'acta'* of a meeting at Saint-Félix-de-Caraman – agreed to have been composed and written in or not very long before 1232 – contains or reflects the record of a real occasion in 1167 (or 1174–7); the memories of the time 'before the crusaders came' offered by deponents before Peter Sellan in 1235–6 and Bernard of Caux and John of Saint-Pierre in 1245–6, and the phraseology associated with them. They did not, however, maintain that fragments such as these constitute strong, still less incontrovertible, evidence in themselves, but treated them rather as being consistent with, and capable of substantiating, an account of beliefs and organization derived from later sources. Conversely, the sceptics denied not the possibility of such a reading, but its necessity, and, in the absence of clear, strictly contemporary corroboration, its probability. Nor did they contest the presence in Italy in the second half of the thirteenth century of a hierarchically organized and theologically dualist movement whose adherents were known, at least to some, as 'Cathars', with close links to the Languedoc and apparent debts to Balkan heresy and mythology. That may yet be a question for another day and other disputants, but it was not an issue here. Debate turned rather on the legitimacy of reading the evidence for that situation back to the Languedoc, first in the 1230s and 1240s, with particular reference to Toulouse MS 609 and the inquisition of 1245–6, and second in the years before and during the Albigensian crusade. As to the former I have nothing to add to the comments of Mark Pegg and Julien Théry, with whom I am fully in agreement. The argument that I have to make is that what we know happened in the twelfth century both can and should be explained by evidence from the twelfth century. Some of its methodological considerations, however, also apply to the discussion about the 1220s and 1230s and the interpretation of Toulouse MS 609.

This debate is as old as the modern study of Catharism itself. Charles Schmidt's *Histoire et doctrines de la secte des cathares ou albigeois* (1849), the first to be based on a comprehensive review of the primary sources, has shaped the study of the subject ever since.[3] Schmidt, Professor of Practical Theology at the Protestant seminary in Strasbourg, concluded that the Cathars, with

---

[2] I hope it will be accepted that I refer to the participants in this discussion as 'traditionalists' and 'sceptics' only to avoid repeated circumlocution. It does not impute credulity to the one or Pyrrhonism to the other, or impugn the scholarship or integrity of either. Nor does it imply that either is indifferent to the fate of the persecuted.

[3] C. Schmidt, *Histoire des sectes des cathares ou albigeois*, 2 vols. (Paris, 1849); see also Y. Dossat, 'Un initiateur: Charles Schmidt', *Historiographie du catharisme* = *Cahiers de Fanjeaux* 14 (1979), 163–84; B. Hamilton 'The Legacy of Charles Schmidt to the Study of Christian Dualism', *Journal of Medieval History* 24/2 (1998), 191–214, whose account is largely followed here.

whom the inquisitorial treatises and records of the thirteenth century were chiefly concerned, were part of a single movement with the Bogomils of the Byzantine world, sharing a common body of doctrine, ritual, myth, and organization. Their heresy, which he distinguished definitively from that of the Waldenses, spread through western Europe and was deeply rooted in Lombardy and the Languedoc. The view that the Cathars believed in two gods or principles had hitherto usually been dismissed by Protestants as a Catholic slander, but Schmidt decided that they did indeed do so, and that they considered the material world and its inhabitants to be the domain, and for the main branch of the movement the creation, of the evil principle. Release from it could be secured only through absolute abstention from procreation and its products.

Schmidt's account, apparently supported by many subsequent discoveries both of Byzantine and of Latin sources, reigned unchallenged until the middle of the twentieth century and is still in its essentials widely accepted. It has dominated all subsequent historiography – or rather, heresiography, for most of those who have written about it until quite recently have been mainly interested, like the Professor of Practical Theology himself, in the ideas and practices associated with the heretics, rather than in the circumstances and chronology of their appearance. Much confusion, for example, arises from the fact that theologians and historians often do not mean the same thing when they speak of 'the same heresy': it may denote simply an identity of ideas to the one, but to the other implies direct personal or institutional connection. Schmidt was fully conscious that we depend for our knowledge of heretics and their beliefs almost entirely on the testimony of their enemies, whose descriptions of them should therefore be treated with caution. He concluded, however, that the resemblances between the teachings and rituals described in heresy accusations throughout the period and across the continents must mean that they were not merely invective or fabrication.

This is the argument – and now in effect the only argument – that Schmidt's followers have used ever since. 'Some have sought to contest the veracity of these witnesses in order to spare the Cathars the reproach of dualism' he wrote, 'but comparison of authors from different lands and different periods proves that the reproach is only too deserved: their adversaries are in general worthy of confidence which cannot be withheld merely on dogmatic grounds.' He therefore regarded most of those who were accused of heresy from the trial at Orléans in 1022 onwards as Cathars, or at least as influenced by Cathar teachings. It is an argument not only from resemblance, but from retrospective resemblance, to a set of beliefs and practices adumbrated only after another hundred years at least (and even that is now vigorously contested), and fully described only after two hundred.

That resemblance is not enough was the starting point of the revision launched by Raffaello Morghen in 1944, arguing that what Schmidt and his successors had seen as manifestations of dualism in the eleventh century could as readily be explained by the influence of the movements for apostolic poverty and papal reform.[4] By the 1970s almost everyone agreed that external influence was not necessary to account for any of the accusations or assertions of heresy reported before the 1140s, and that there was no evidence either of theological dualism or of an organized movement up to that time. Equally, however, everyone also agreed that the presence of an organized dualist movement originating in the Byzantine world was unmistakeably described for the first time by Eberwin of Steinfeld in a letter to Bernard of Clairvaux usually dated to 1143,[5] and that by the end of the twelfth century this movement was widely spread and deeply rooted, especially in the Rhineland, Lombardy and the lands between the Rhone and the Garonne. It was natural, therefore, to see signs of its growth and diffusion in references to heresy and heretics from that time forward (though not necessarily in all of them), and to assume that assertions of their presence and descriptions of their beliefs and practices were based on observation and experience, even if mediated or distorted by the preconceptions of the reporters. Widespread agreement – to all intents and purposes unanimity – on that view supported a striking resurgence of interest in 'the Cathars' (including the use of the word itself, in preference to 'Albigensians', which had hitherto been preferred by French and anglophone scholars) in the 1980s and 1990s. It was led from the Languedoc, and specifically from Carcassonne and Toulouse, but there were handsome contributions from Great Britain and North America, both in primary research and popularization.[6]

Nevertheless, doubts were gathering from two directions, regrettably unknown to one another. Mark Pegg's examination of Toulouse MS 609, shaped by a background in social anthropology as well as a well-honed critical edge, argued that the inquisitors' accounts of the beliefs and behaviour of the people they called *heretici* were based on their own expectations, rather on what the deponents actually said.[7] He found no persuasive evidence either of widely accepted theological dualism or of long-standing hierarchical

---

[4] R. Morghen, "Osservazioni critiche su alcune questioni fondamentali riguardanti le origini e i caratteri delle eresie medievali", *Archivio della R. deputazione romana di storia patria* 67 (1944), 97–151, repr. in R. Morghen, *Medioevo cristiano* (Bari, 1951), and followed by a series of papers culminating in 'Problèmes sur les origines de l'hérésie médiévale', *Revue historique* 336 (1966), 1–16; cf. R. I. Moore, 'The Origins of Medieval Heresy', *History* 55 (1970), 21–36; 'Afterthoughts on *The Origins of European Dissent*', in *Heresy and Persecution in the Middle Ages: Essays on the Work of R. I. Moore*, ed. M. Frassetto (Leiden 2006), pp. 291–326.

[5] *Patrologia Latina*, ed. J.-P. Migne, 217 vols. (Paris, 1844–64), CLXXXII, 676–80.

[6] R. I. Moore, 'The Cathar Middle Ages as an Historiographical Problem', in *Christianity and Culture in the Middle Ages: Essays to Honor John Van Engen*, ed. D. C. Mengel and L. Wolverton (Notre Dame, 2014), pp. 59–86. A draft of this paper was pre-circulated to the University College London conference.

[7] M. G. Pegg, *The Corruption of Angels: The Great Inquisition of 1245–46* (Princeton, 2001).

organization. Instead he postulated, and vividly described, local holiness revolving around the 'good men' whose precepts and influence arose from and corresponded to local circumstances and conditions, which began to organize, taking on the aspect of a sect, mainly under the pressure of persecution during the Albigensian crusade, and especially after the Peace of Paris of 1229. Meanwhile, a group of scholars led by Monique Zerner had been examining afresh the sources for heresy accusations up to 1208 in a series of seminars at Nice which culminated in the publication of *Inventer l'hérésie?* in 1998.[8] They showed that since patristic times churchmen had deployed a well-established discourse of heresy, especially against those regarded as political usurpers, and in defence of ecclesiastical discipline and church property.[9] Thus, for example, a text which had usually been taken as describing a Bogomil incursion into the Périgord in the 1140s or 1160s was found to date from the 1030s, and to have been designed to lampoon the liturgical elaboration associated with the 'imperial' expansion of the Cluniac order under the abbacy of Odilo.[10] By attending closely to the provenance and dating of texts which their predecessors (including this one) had taken more or less uncritically from the printed collections of the eighteenth and nineteenth centuries they showed that many of the sources on which the old story relied were much later than the events they described, and had often been preserved and/or edited as part of the late twelfth century campaign against heresy which prepared the ground for the Albigensian crusade.

For example, the well-known account of the trial at Arras in 1024–5 survives only in a copy made at Cîteaux at the end of the twelfth century. Nevertheless, Guy Lobrichon concluded after close scrutiny that the sermon preached at Arras is indeed the work of Bishop Gerard II of Cambrai-Arras in 1020s, and the report of the trial that of his clerks, thus placing it on a more secure footing than ever before.[11] Scepticism does not always lead to negative,

---

[8] *Inventer l'hérésie? Discours polémiques et pouvoirs avant l'inquisition*, ed. M. Zerner (Nice, 1998).

[9] Ibid., chs. 1–4; see further D. Iogna-Prat, *Order and Exclusion: Cluny and Christendom Face Heresy, Judaism, and Islam (1000–1150)* (Ithaca NY, 1998), pp. 99–147.

[10] G. Lobrichon, 'The Chiaroscuro of Heresy', in *The Peace of God: Social Violence and Religious Response around the Year 1000*, ed. T. Head and R. Landes (Ithaca NY, 1992), pp. 80–103; for the earlier view, H. Fichtenau, *Heretics and Scholars in the High Middle Ages* (University Park, 1998), pp. 81–2. Claire Taylor's reply to G. Lobrichon ('The Letter of Heribert of Périgord as a Source for Dualist Heresy in the Society of Early Eleventh Century Aquitaine', *Journal of Medieval History* 26 (2000), 313–49), typifies responses of the kind described at pp. 266–7 below, insisting on the significance of 'surprising resemblances' between 'Heribert's' description of his fictitious heretics and practices (for which Lobrichon accounts differently and in full) associated with the Bulgarian Bogomils.

[11] G. Lobrichon, 'Arras, 1025; ou le vrai procès d'un faux accusation', in *Inventer l'hérésie?*, ed. Zerner, pp. 67–87; see further T. M. Riches, 'Bishop Gerard I of Cambrai-Arras, the Three Orders, and the Problem of Human Weakness', in *The Bishop Reformed: Studies of Episcopal Power and Culture in the Central Middle Ages*, ed. J. S. Ott and A. Trumbore

or merely destructive, conclusions. That provenance, however, is one of many indications of the Cistercians' formative role since the 1170s in demonizing (or raising the alarm about) heresy between the Rhone and the Loire,[12] and of how the charge of protecting heresy could be exploited politically against those with designs on the county of Tolouse.[13] In this context, and in the light of John Gillingham's wholly unconnected investigation of his career and writings, the fact that all the substantive reports of heresy in the region in the 1160s and 1170s come from Roger of Howden acquires a new significance.[14] It is now clear that those reports were part of Henry II's campaign to impugn the legitimacy of Count Raymond V of Toulouse by portraying him as a protector of heretics. The Council of Tours in 1163, which identified Toulouse as a centre of heresy for the first time, and the mission to Toulouse in 1178, which exposed heresy (though not dualist heresy) among its leading citizens, and in which Roger may have participated, also enjoyed Henry's patronage.

The *coup de grâce* was the publication in 2005 of Uwe Brunn's study of ecclesiastical reform and heresy accusations in the archdiocese of Cologne, from the denunciations of Ellenhard of Utrecht and Tanchelm at the beginning of the twelfth century to the campaigns of Conrad of Marburg in the 1220s and early 1230s.[15] This is a demanding work of great complexity, particularly in its exhaustive examination of the provenances and contexts of often very fragmentary reports and the connections between them. The implications of the unfolding dialogue of confrontation and demonization that it reveals are far from having been absorbed: nobody considering any aspect of heresy in the period, whether in the Rhineland or not, can afford to neglect it. The present discussion, however, may be confined to Brunn's examination of the context of a single document, the letter of Eberwin of Steinfeld to Bernard

---

Jones (Aldershot, 2007), pp. 122–38; S. Vanderputten and D. J. Reilly, 'Reconciliation and Record Keeping: Heresy, Secular Dissent and the Exercise of Episcopal Authority in Eleventh-Century Cambrai', *Journal of Medieval History* 37 (2011), 343–57.

[12] J.-L. Biget, '"Les albigeois": remarques sur une désignation', in *Inventer l'hérésie?*, ed. Zerner, pp. 219–55, repr. in J.-L. Biget, *Hérésie et inquisition dans le midi de la France* (Paris, 2007), pp. 142–69; see also B. M. Kienzle, *Cistercians, Heresy and Crusade in Occitania, 1145–1229: Preaching in the Lord's Vineyard* (York, 2001); A. Trivellone, *L'hérétique imaginé: hétérodoxie et iconographie dans l'occident médiéval de l'époque carolingienne à l'inquisition* (Turnholt, 2009), pp. 174–88, 349–89.

[13] Biget, 'Les albigeois'.

[14] J. Gillingham, 'The Travels of Roger of Howden and his Views of the Irish, Scots and Welsh', *Anglo-Norman Studies* 20 (1998), 152–69; J. Gillingham, 'Royal Newsletters, Forgeries and English Historians: Some Links between Court and History in the Reign of Richard I', in *La cour Plantagenêt (1154–1204)*, ed. M. Aurell (Poitiers, 2000), pp. 171–86; R. I. Moore, 'Les albigeois d'après les chroniques angevines', in *La croisade albigeoise*, Actes du Colloque du Centre d'études cathares de Carcassonne, octobre 2002 (Carcassonne, 2004), pp. 81–90.

[15] U. Brunn, *Des contestataires aux 'cathares': discours de réforme et de propagande antihérétique dans les pays du Rhin et de la Meuse avant l'inquisition* (Paris, 2006).

of Clairvaux, hitherto usually dated to 1143, but convincingly by Brunn to 1147. In it Eberwin described two groups of heretics whose public quarrels had brought them to the notice of the authorities. The first were devotees of apostolic poverty appalled by the wealth and corruption of the Catholic clergy, from which they had drawn radically anticlerical conclusions. The other group was led by one whom they called a bishop and his companion, who were burned at the stake. They claimed that theirs was the true church, which despite persecution had survived in Greece and other lands since the time of the martyrs; they eliminated the fruits of procreation from their diet, and rejected the Catholic sacraments in favour of a laying on of hands by which mere hearers (*auditores*) were received into the sect as *credentes* who might then progress to become *electi* with the right to confer the status on others. Eberwin attached no name to the sect he described, and his earnest appeals to Bernard for elucidation implied that he himself had no preconceptions about who or what these heretics were.

A question posed in the 2013 debate was what the sceptics would consider 'strong evidence for dualist beliefs and for an organized movement of adherents to them' in twelfth-century western Europe. Eberwin's letter was for long accepted on all sides not only as strong, but as decisive. It reported at first hand, quoting the accused directly, a formally conducted examination which had arisen not from anonymous denunciation or over-zealous heresy hunting, but from the public quarrels of the accused among themselves; it did not stereotype, distinguishing clearly between the teaching and practice of different groups of heretics; in doing so it showed that while one of them could be readily accounted for within the familiar parameters of the 'evangelical awakening' in the eleventh- and twelfth-century West, members of the other group not only claimed to be part of a wider movement which had 'persisted in Greece and in other lands', and even had its own pope, but also observed among themselves a formal hierarchy which, as Eberwin could hardly have anticipated, closely resembled that which would be described, much later, by Dominican inquisitors and others. Eberwin himself was a reformer, in touch with Bernard because he was enlisting the eloquence of the abbot against the worldliness and corruption of Cologne's cathedral clergy, denunciation of whom Bernard combined with preaching the second crusade in the region. Corroborative traces of other manifestations and consequences of the movement Eberwin described could be discerned in a series of heresy trials and accusations in the Rhinelands and the Low Countries in the following twenty years, and more widely thereafter.

On close reading Eberwin turns out not to have based quite as much of his account directly on the words of the accused as appears at first sight, and to have derived or at least supplemented his understanding of their practices and beliefs from Augustine on the Manichees. Nevertheless, his clear, full, and circumstantial account left few scholars in doubt that the people he described shared the beliefs and organization of those who would later be identified as

Cathars, and were the first in western Europe to be unequivocally described in that way. Once that presence had been established it was both natural and legitimate to regard later descriptions of, and assertions about, heresy and those suspected of heresy as further manifestations of the same phenomenon, even in sources which might otherwise have been considered too fragmentary, or too indirect, to bear weight. Opinion differed in particular cases – whether the extent of Eckbert of Schönau's reliance on Augustine undermined his characterization as Cathars of the people with whom he debated in Bonn in the 1140s and questioned in Cologne in the early 1160s;[16] whether the charters which purported to show Jonas of Cambrai convicted of heresy in Cologne, Trier and Liège in the 1150s and early 1160s attested widespread missionary activity in the Rhineland and the Low Countries;[17] whether (as I thought but Peter Biller and others did not) William of Newburgh's affirmation that the people tried at Oxford in 1165 'answered correctly on the nature of Christ' – that is, did not subscribe to the docetist heresy – meant that they were not Cathars,[18] and so on. But such differences related to the extent and rapidity of the movement's diffusion, not whether there was such a movement at all.

Eberwin's credibility, unquestioned in the twentieth century as a 'matter of fact, first-hand account' ('einen nüchternen Tatsachenbericht'),[19] was severely challenged on every point by Brunn's discussion.[20] In the first place, extraordinary though it may now seem, previous commentators on this letter (Moore again included) had paid no attention to Eberwin himself, beyond repeating his title, Provost (*prepositus*) of the Premonstratensian house at Steinfeld. Nor had anyone mentioned in this connection the fact (familiar enough in itself) that the Premonstratensians were at the very heart of ecclesiastical reform

[16] R. Manselli, "Eckberto di Schönau e l'eresia catara', in *Arte e Storia: studi in onore di Leonello Vincenti* (Turin, 1965), 311–38; R. I. Moore, *The Origins of European Dissent* (London, 1977), pp. 176–82; R. Harrison, 'Eckbert of Schönau: A Reevaluation', *Comitatus* 22/1 (1991), 41–54.

[17] P. Bonenfant, 'Un clerc cathare en Lotharingie au milieu de XIIe siècle', *Le Moyen Âge* 69 (1963), 271–80; M. Suttor, 'Le *Triumphus sancti Lamberti de castro Bullonio* et le catharisme à Liège au milieu du XIIe siècle', *Le Moyen Âge* 91 (1985), 227–64; cf. Brunn, *Des contestataires*, pp. 366–72.

[18] P. Biller, 'William of Newburgh and the Cathar Mission to England', in *Life and Thought in the Northern Church, c. 1100–c. 1700: Studies in Honour of Claire Cross*, ed. D. Wood (Woodbridge, 1999), pp. 11–30; M. Barber, 'Northern Catharism', in *Heresy and Persecution*, ed. M. Frassetto, pp. 125–6; Moore, *Origins of European Dissent*, p. 184.

[19] H. Fichtenau, *Heretics and Scholars*, p. 63. Even so, Eberwin did not know as much about dualism as Fichtenau thought he ought to have, since he says they claimed that initiation qualified their *electi* to consecrate the body and blood even though they could not, as dualists, have believed in it: 'On this point Eberwin must have misunderstood his sources' says Fichtenau (ibid., p. 80), thus illustrating to perfection the point repeatedly made by sceptics, that believers in the presence of dualism, from the inquisitors onwards, have habitually heard what they expected to hear, or read their conviction into what their witnesses actually said.

[20] Brunn, *Des contestataires*, pp. 80–160.

in the region. They had become so at the initiative of Frederick, archbishop of Cologne (1100–31), who fashioned the famously devout, often learned and rapidly multiplying followers of Norbert of Xanten into the weapon he needed against his diocesan clergy, which was headed by the notoriously wealthy and worldly cathedral canonry. To this end Frederick charged Premonstratensian canons with parochial services, supported by the revenues of endowed or re-endowed churches. The first such house, established in 1121 on the site of a former Benedictine house, and exempt from all authority save that of the archbishop, and from all payments and other obligations to the dean and chapter of Cologne, was Steinfeld. Eberwin was its first superior. This was a model which spread throughout the German lands, though hardly at all beyond them, and appears in retrospect as a major success of the reform movement. It was not, however, plain sailing at the time. The dean and chapter did not surrender their position lightly, and Eberwin's invocation of Bernard's eloquence against them came after two and a half decades of unremitting and many-sided conflict.

That was not the only cross Eberwin had to bear. Among the hermit preachers who thronged Europe in his generation Norbert of Xanten was not only the most spectacularly successful but also among the most uncompromising in his devotion to apostolic poverty and the absolute separation of its devotees from worldly affairs. Discreet as the sources are, it is clear that he consented even to allow them to be settled at Premontré and so many other places only under severe ecclesiastical pressure. We do not know his view of Archbishop Frederick's arrangements, which, however worthy their objective, seem flatly in contradiction to Norbert's principles, but he was removed from the scene soon afterwards by being summarily relocated to the distant archbishopric of Magdeburg.

As in other instances when eremitical communities were reorganized in the generation after their formation, some of Norbert's followers regarded the acceptance of property and revenues, including tithes, and of parochial duties, as a betrayal of his legacy, irrespective of the motives that had inspired it. Their disaffection naturally intensified as growth and, with it, institutionalization continued, and especially when the decision was taken in the 1130s to segregate the sexes in their communities, all of which had originally been mixed. The betrayal became more bitter as, in the years that followed, the newly separated female communities were increasingly and relentlessly marginalized until most of them simply withered away, and was the more cruel because so many had embraced the apostolic life as husband and wife.[21]

'This is their heresy' Eberwin's description of his major group of heretics begins:

---

[21] H. Grundmann, *Religious Movements of the High Middle Ages*, trans. S. Rowan (Notre Dame, 1995), p. 21; G. Constable, *The Reformation of the Twelfth Century* (Cambridge, 1996), pp. 72–4, 233–5.

They claim that they are the true Church, because the heritage of Christ survives in them alone. They are the true followers of the apostolic life, because they do not seek the things of this world, houses or land or any other sort of property, just as Christ did not seek them, and did not allow his disciples to possess them. They said to us, 'You join house to house and field to field and seek the things of this world. Those who are thought most perfect among you, monks and canons regular, possess things, not individually but in common: nevertheless they do possess all of these things.'

His letter concludes:

These apostles of Satan have women among them who are – so they say – chaste, widows or virgins, or their wives, alleging that they follow the apostles, who permitted them to have women among them.

It is hardly coincidental that Eberwin's account begins and ends with exact statements of the two most fundamental points of contention among Norbert's followers, and the chief grievances of those who had lost not – they would have said – the argument, but the long and bitter battle against the developments of which Eberwin himself was a leading proponent. In doing so it reveals not only the principles at stake, but the emotions familiar whenever a successful radical movement faces the inevitable necessity of reaching an accommodation with the world it set out to reform. There is no need to imagine Eberwin as a ruthless or cynical manipulator. He had worked and suffered in his cause, which many thought and still think a noble one. He had been, it is not extravagant to surmise, baffled and frustrated, undermined for more than twenty years by the denunciations of the very people who ought most keenly to have appreciated his achievements. It is not to be wondered at if he entertained the darkest suspicion of their inspiration and motives, and came to regard them as instruments of Satan.

At first sight this looks like one more episode in a pattern of discussion that has been much the same since the 1940s. Closer readings of a rather small body of texts relating to eleventh- and twelfth-century heresy accusations, and sharper scrutiny of their provenance, in combination with a fuller understanding of the changing religious climate of the period in its political and social as well as its pastoral and devotional dimensions (loosely referred to as 'reform'), have consistently concluded that accusations of heresy regularly originated in conflicts and misunderstandings that arose from a variety of causes other than its preaching or presence. Details of heretical belief and practice, it has been suggested, were often the fruit of expectation rather than observation, the constructions of the accusers rather than the convictions of the accused. Those conclusions have as regularly been countered by increasingly ingenious (and sometimes very learned) explanations of the anomalies of the documentation, together with assertions that resemblances between the reported beliefs of people accused of heresy at widely varying times and places amount to at least *prima facie* evidence of direct links between them. Some of Brunn's reviewers, noticeably in Germany, have responded in that way.[22] But even if that were an adequate response to his findings in itself, which in my view it is not, it would be vitiated in this case by the unique position in the historiography hitherto accorded to Eberwin's letter. For half a century it had been accepted by the most sceptical not only as strong evidence of an organized dualist movement in itself, but also as being so strong as to validate a similar reading of subsequent episodes much less clearly and fully recorded. That special status is gone for good. Eberwin's testimony is subject to the same doubts and difficulties as all the rest. There is now no evidence of organized dualism before the Albigensian crusade that can be said unequivocally to meet ordinary scholarly criteria of credibility. It is still possible with sufficient determination and ingenuity to construct the jigsaw, but not a single piece falls naturally or securely into place.

A remaining question, posed by Peter Biller,[23] goes to the heart of the methodological issue at stake in this debate. Could not both be right? Might it not be the case that, in all the conditions and circumstances described by Brunn, Eberwin and his colleagues had indeed come across dualist heretics who were part of a movement that originated outside the region, even possibly in Constantinople? Certainly it might, though the coincidences would be remarkable. A charge is not necessarily false because the accuser had a vested interest. However scarlet the sins of their clerical superiors, or lurid the imaginations of their chroniclers, for example, it is impossible to doubt that some of those (though it is not at all easy to be sure which ones) accused at this time of holding the sacraments administered by corrupt priests invalid were guilty as charged of having taken that short but crucial step from the instruction of Gregory VII and his successors that such sacraments were to be boycotted.[24] On the other hand, the profession of heretical doctrine was neither a necessary nor a sufficient condition of being charged with heresy. The question is why we should continue to accept not only Eberwin's description itself, but also the viewpoint from a century later that makes 'Cathars' of the organized dualist movement he seemed to describe. Eberwin's account remained compelling for so long because it seemed well founded, complete and, as these things go, tolerably detached, but also and especially because he appeared to describe beliefs and organization that could not be explained without invoking some new, external factor – until Brunn showed that they could. To superimpose the old explanation on the new would be to postulate a superfluous entity. The logical error inherent in doing

---

[22] G. Rottenwöhrer, in *Zeitschrift für Kirchengeschichte* 119 (2008), 408–10; J. Given, in *Speculum* 83/4 (2008), 961–3. James Given, not generally sympathetic to the sceptical position, acknowledges that Brunn 'has provided much ammunition' for it.
[23] In his opening remarks at the 2013 conference.
[24] Moore, *The War on Heresy*, chs. 5–7.

so can be obscured only by focusing attention exclusively on the perceived similarities to 'Catharism' and ignoring (rather than rebutting, or even denying) the explanation proposed by Brunn. To offer an analogy – it is not meant to give offence, but to clarify the point with a more clear-cut example – it is possible to sustain more or less indefinitely a circumstantial and plausible case[25] that Shakespeare's plays were written by the earl of Oxford, but only by ignoring or explaining away the considerable body of evidence that they were written by William Shakespeare, a simpler hypothesis that readily accounts for all the available facts. Many reviewers sidestepped, though with great courtesy, the subtle and nuanced account of the religion of the good men in *The Corruption of Angels*[26] to rally their defences against its critique of 'Catharism'; and sidestepped *The War on Heresy*'s account of the vicissitudes and political applications of 'reform', again with great courtesy, to spotlight its negative assessment of the evidence for the traditional story of 'the Cathars'. The authors of those works, like Brunn, offered alternative, not additional explanations. I hope they may be forgiven for regretting that their substantive conclusions have not been more seriously addressed.

It may seem churlish, even arrogant, so uncompromisingly to dismiss the possibility of compromise; certainly, to my regret, the manner in which *The War on Heresy* did so appeared to some in that way.[27] The persistent tendency of academic culture to seek a middle way, resisting intellectual absolutes in the expectation that even exploded theses may contain something of value, is rooted in wisdom as well as courtesy: certainly I have benefited greatly from having been compelled to re-examine the historiographical context of this discussion, and my own possibly simplistic positivism. But as to the main point at issue middle ground does not exist. We cannot agree to settle for half a Cathar. Either there was an organized movement of adherents to dualist beliefs in twelfth-century Europe or there was not. Nor will it serve to use 'Cathar', as textbook writers occasionally seem to, to denote a religious tendency or outlook rather than an organized movement or sect, much as scholars of Tudor and Stuart England use the word 'Puritan'. That would simply be to muddy the waters still further, and readmit by the back door the confusion that we are driving out through the front. The whole history of the word invokes and is meant to invoke the organized and widely diffused dualism described by Schmidt, as Fernand Niel explained in adopting the title

---

[25] Biller wondered in the concluding discussion whether a criterion of plausibility might help to resolve our differences. I fear not. Like resemblance, it is not enough.

[26] Pegg, *The Corruption of Angels*, chs. 13–17.

[27] As Robert Lerner pointed out in a personal communication in respect of my comments on 'The War Among the Scholars' (in Moore, *The War on Heresy*, pp. 332–6); I am glad to have been able somewhat to mitigate the brusqueness of my rejection of the traditional position in the UK paperback edition (London, 2014), pp. 332–41, and more fully, I hope, in this paper.

Albigeois et cathares for his *Que sais-je?* volume: 'the Albigensian heresy which developed in the south of France in the twelfth and thirteenth centuries was only the local manifestation of a far more important movement, Catharism.'[28] That is a proposition that admits no compromise. It is either true or untrue.

That it removes the possibility of compromise is what makes the renewed critique of the foundations of the traditional story in the 1990s and 2000s more consequential than the debate of the 1940s–1960s. The latter ended in general agreement that a period of heresy without dualism up to the 1140s was followed by one of heresy increasingly dominated by dualism, which culminated in the Albigensian crusade. I have suggested elsewhere that this was symptomatic of, and even contributed to, a wider rapprochement between secular and religious traditions of historiography in the 1960s and 1970s, following the second Vatican council.[29] Conversely, there must be at least a possibility that the collapse of the consensus has revived, or threatens to revive, some of those old tensions and anxieties. If I have unwittingly contributed to such a revival, especially by a superfluous exuberance of language, I very much regret it. On the other hand, if we are now finding that the rapprochement left fundamental questions about the limits and constraints of historical methodology unresolved, it behoves us to define them and address them afresh, however delicately.

The end of consensus also raises more straightforwardly historical issues. Shifting the appearance of an organized heretical movement from the 1020s to the 1140s involved much to excite specialists, but did not materially alter its place in the broader narrative of European history (whatever that place was thought to be) up to the Albigensian wars and their immediate aftermath. Its total collapse under the scrutiny of Monique Zerner and her colleagues, including Zerner's student Uwe Brunn, and its replacement by an alternative narrative, sweeps away a plethora of explanatory clichés and raises an entirely different set of questions. For the twelfth century this is refreshing, but not especially problematic. The manifestations of religious dissent, as far as they are discernible, and the reactions of authority to it, including both anxiety about what it might betoken and appreciation of ways in which the spectre of it might be open to exploitation, can be comfortably accommodated within, and may even enrich, the current historiography of the period: that, in effect, is what *The War on Heresy* tried to show. The relations between 'reform' and dissent, the bureaucratization of power in both Church and State, and the formation and dissemination of an ideology of religious unity under the impetus of an emergent clerical elite, were already well to the fore. Understanding of resistance to those forces, of the role of religion and of the Church in the formation and restructuring of communities in response to

---

[28] F. Niel, *Albigeois et cathares* (Paris 1955), p. 5.
[29] Moore, 'The Cathar Middle Ages'.

social change, and of the formation of a heightened sense of evil and its active presence in the world, are newer questions which both illuminate and can be illuminated by systematic reappraisal of the evidence for accusations of heresy and the circumstances in which they arose.

The questions that arise from the perspective of the mid thirteenth century seem to be more complicated, and I am not well equipped to assess them. There appears to be agreement that after c. 1250 there was in Italy, as described chiefly by Dominican inquisitors, a profusion of enthusiastic and dissenting communities of belief, known at least by some as 'Cathars'. Several of them explicitly articulated dualist theologies, and some or all of the following: hierarchical organization headed by 'bishops'; gnostic legends apparently with Balkan antecedents; apparently related rituals; and collective memories of their own history. Among them were émigré communities from the Languedoc which maintained contacts with that region, where there were similar communities with similar beliefs, and made a number of efforts to re-establish there the Church which they believed to have been destroyed and driven out by crusaders and inquisitors.

Such knowledge as I have of this is entirely second-hand. I do not assert it or endorse it on my own account. Neither do I contest it. I have no reason (without prejudice to the conclusions of future work, in which I have no present intention of engaging) to do so, and no difficulty in reconciling it with my conclusions on heresy and its repression in the twelfth century and the first third of the thirteenth. Where I differ from those who are expert in this period and material, among whom Peter Biller is pre-eminent, is that I do not accept their account of how this situation came about. It is natural that they should have started from the presumption that it was the outcome of a direct historical continuity, just as it was natural that both the inquisitors and the heretics themselves thought so, and natural that all three groups should lay particular stress on pieces of evidence (however small), memories and perceived resemblances consistent with that presumption. The difficulty is that extensive and sophisticated investigation from many directions has left this explanation without support by contemporary evidence from the period in which the members, inquisitors and modern scholars of the post-1250 sects in question located their origins and early history.

It must be emphasized that I do not propose an alternative. There is no 'Moore thesis' as to the origin and development of these sects. I do, however, point to a number of things in the early thirteenth century which seem likely to contribute to such a new explanation.[30] Most directly, more systematic and effective persecution forced dissenters to organize secretly, to identify members and supporters and insist on clear commitment from them, and hence to create and elaborate group identities, memories and history, or

---

[30] Moore, *The War on Heresy*, chs. 17, 18.

to accelerate and intensify whatever tendencies in those directions already existed among them. On the other side, a growing conviction in the schools of the comprehensive power of evil and its agents made churchmen look out for traces of dualist belief and expect to find sects motivated by it.[31] Institutional commitment to that conviction and political demand for legitimation by it, notably in papal policy and the factional communes in Italy, and in the links between the university of Paris and the French royal court around Louis VIII as dauphin and king, were intensified by the extreme social instability of the early decades of the century. I do not imagine for a moment that those observations amount to an exhaustive account of the circumstances that fostered the rising fever of heresy fears and accusations during the pontificates of Innocent III, Honorius III and Gregory IX, or claim that they describe or explain the real beliefs of real heretics. But they do help to account for how they were imagined and perceived by their persecutors, and became the objects of intense anxiety amounting to universal panic.

After the debate of 2013, but reflecting its main preoccupation, Peter Biller suggested that in *The War on Heresy* I did not give enough thought to the implications of the massively greater availability of source materials for the thirteenth than for the twelfth century.[32] It is an entirely fair comment, and an important one, but I do not find that it leads in the direction he pointed. Clearly, information from the thirteenth, and especially the later thirteenth, century, however diverse or profuse, cannot be treated as direct evidence for what was the case in the twelfth. It is, in one way or another, evidence of collective or inherited memory, fascinating and revealing but difficult to assess, shaped and reshaped by the needs and concerns of successive generations, its interpretation subject to complex and contentious methodological difficulties.[33] Its value, like that of all comparisons across time and space, is that it may suggest possibilities for filling lacunae in the direct evidence that can then be tested

---

[31] I would add that over time that conviction may also have been self-fulfilling. We need not look far to see that given enough publicity almost any set of ideas, however absurd or wicked, will find adherents. In the early twentieth century many sophisticated people, including eminent scholars, believed in the reality of the medieval witch cult, and some of them practised the Satanism on which (following the inquisitors) they held it to have been based. No serious scholar now thinks that the existence and activity of such believers constitutes evidence of continuity, or that there were 'real' Satanists at some time in the past. I have often been assured, however, by people who describe themselves as witches, that they belong to an underground tradition active since the Middle Ages, and indeed much longer; anyone who lectures publicly on these matters has probably had the same experience.

[32] In the review cited above, n. 1.

[33] For a fine overview of the problems and possibilities see J. Fentress and C. Wickham, *Social Memory* (Oxford, 1992), including a suggestive discussion of the formation of memories of the Camisard revolt (pp. 92–6). The issues include, but necessarily go beyond, some of those addressed with great subtlety by J. H. Arnold, *Inquisition and Power* (Philadelphia, 2001).

against it. But that is exactly what Schmidt and his followers did, and their conclusions have now been exhaustively tested against the direct evidence, most recently by *The War on Heresy*, and found wanting. There are still many deficiencies in our understanding of non-Catholic Christians in the twelfth century, especially between Rhone and Garonne, where narrative sources are so lacking. There is no doubt that insights derived from the far richer sources of the thirteenth century can be immensely valuable in alleviating them, and may on occasion point to continuity. For example, Pegg's reconstruction of the ways in which the values and demeanour of the good men responded to the needs and tensions of a petty nobility faced with acute resource deprivation is highly illuminating in itself.[34] It also combines with Feuchter's demonstration of the continuity of the division between *heretici* and Catholics among the noble families of Montauban, to point to the 'crisis of the villages' in the 1140s as a decisive moment in the emergence and consolidation of religious affinities in the region.[35] Though Feuchter himself does not agree, I cannot see that the social continuity he has demonstrated so brilliantly between the foundation of Montauban in 1145 and its inquisition by Peter Sellan in 1236 requires or implies continuity of religious teaching and organization, even if it were agreed that Sellan confronted organized dualism; nor can I see that Claire Taylor's fascinating account, making extensive use of the same source, of the diffusion and social value of heresy in the Agenais and Quercy either requires or is enhanced by her insistence that the heresy in question was 'Catharism'.[36]

Comparison between the poverty of the twelfth century in respect of sources and the wealth of the thirteenth therefore emboldens me to suggest that the boot is now on the other foot – that it is time for those who study heresy and its ramifications after the sack of Constantinople and after Lateran IV to explore the advantages of doing so without the assumption that it was directly transmitted or inherited from the twelfth century, or that its completest penetration, if not its *fons et origo*, was in the county of Toulouse. Late and fragmentary as they are, it would be rewarding to establish a convincing context in the West for the traces of gnostic tradition and Balkan folklore which Bernard Hamilton has contemplated for so long,[37] and which

---

[34] M. G. Pegg, *A Most Holy War: The Albigensian Crusade and the Battle for Christendom* (Oxford, 2008), pp. 28–49.

[35] J. Feuchter, *Ketzer, Konsuln und Büßer: die städtischen Eliten von Montauban vor dem Inquisitor Petrus Cellani (1236/1241)* (Tübingen, 2007), esp. pp. 243–56.

[36] C. Taylor, *Heresy in Medieval France: Dualism in Aquitaine and the Agenais, 1000–1249* (Woodbridge, 2005), esp. pp. 225–61; C. Taylor, *Heresy, Crusade and Inquisition in Medieval Quercy* (Woodbridge, 2011), esp. pp. 154–208.

[37] Notably in his influential 'Wisdom from the East', in *Heresy and Literacy, 1000–1530*, ed. P. Biller and A. Hudson (Cambridge, 1994), pp. 38–60. As far as western Europe is concerned the chronology of this learned and beguiling essay is largely, and for the period before 1230 or so entirely, conjectural. Some of the problems associated with the dating of the texts in question, going well beyond the Saint-Félix document, are pointed

Andrew Roach and Yuri Stoyanov elucidated at the 2013 conference.[38] Mark Pegg, and in France Jean-Louis Biget, Julien Théry and others, have placed what they do not call the 'Cathar phenomenon' in fuller and richer social and political contexts. But so has Peter Biller, by relating it to far wider developments in Catholic piety and scholastic thought.[39] Lucy Sackville has developed those insights and added her own to show how, irrespective of what the reality of dissent on the ground may have been, the ways in which it was perceived, imagined, recorded and classified contributed substantially to the reshaping of ideas in many areas.[40] In doing so she points, with Biller, to the prospect that 'thinking with Cathars' might be as fruitful an approach to the later medieval centuries as 'thinking with demons' to those that followed, irrespective of the realities of the witch craze.

In reviewing Sackville's book I rebuked her for sitting on the fence in respect of the present argument about organized dualism in the twelfth and early thirteenth centuries.[41] I was wrong to do so, not only because, as the 2013 debate showed so clearly, the differences between the contested views have proved not to be susceptible of resolution by the ordinary procedures of historical method alone, but also because from the perspective of the mid thirteenth century they are much less momentous than they seem in that of the twelfth. That is not to belittle the questions of why, how, when, where and to what extent the Cathar Churches and theology described by Moneta and Ranier came into being. They remain, obviously, of great interest and importance in themselves. But even on their own terms they are part of a teeming landscape of heresy, dissent, and reaction more complex and various by far than that of the earlier period. In the still wider context of the completion of the world picture of the later Middle Ages they will continue to command all the attention that Biller and his influence have accorded them. Our differences as to the mundane reality of 'the phenomenon known as "Catharism"' are unlikely to be resolved, but they may yet turn out to be smaller than our agreements.

---

out in *L'histoire du catharisme en discussion: le 'concile' de Saint-Félix (1167)*, ed. M. Zerner (Nice, 2001), e.g. at pp. 49–56, 96–102.

[38] See also M. Angelovska-Panova and A. Roach, 'The Bogomils' Folk-Heritage: False Friend or Neglected Source?', in *Heresy and the Making of European Culture*, ed. A. Roach and J. Simpson (Farnham, 2013), pp. 129–49.

[39] Notably in 'Cathars and the Material World', in *God's Bounty? The Churches and the Natural World: Papers Read at the 2008 Summer Meeting and the 2009 Winter Meeting of the Ecclesiastical History Society*, ed. P. Clarke and T. Claydon (Woodbridge, 2010), pp. 89–110. See also S. Hamilton, 'The Virgin Mary in Cathar Thought', *Journal of Ecclesiastical History* 56/1 (2005), 24–49.

[40] L. J. Sackville, *Heresy and Heretics in the Thirteenth Century: The Textual Representations* (York, 2011).

[41] *H-France Review* 12 (2012), 44, online at http://www.h-france.net/vol12reviews/vol12no44moore.pdf.

14

Goodbye to Catharism?*

Peter Biller

Should we say 'Goodbye'? For anglophone readers such a farewell was heralded by Mark Pegg's *The Corruption of Angels*, a monograph on inquisition and heresy in the Lauragais region of Languedoc, published in 2001.[1] This paved the way for, and heavily influenced, the account of heresy in Languedoc contained in the second half of a book which has been at the forefront in the dismantling of Catharism since its publication in 2012, R. I. Moore's *The War on Heresy*.[2] Since the two key terms historians use when talking about heresy in Languedoc (i.e. 'Cathars' and 'Catharism') are regarded as problematic in both books – and because we have to have a policy about words – we shall begin with words (§1 below). Discussion of *The Corruption of Angels* and *The War on Heresy* occupies the rest of the chapter. This is introduced by a lightning sketch of modern works, in order to place these books within the field (§2). The next section (§3) is devoted to *The Corruption of Angels*, while the one after (§4) discusses the general trajectory of Moore's earlier works on heresy. Then follow five sections providing closer examination of *The War on Heresy*'s major themes. These are the Bulgars (§5), heresy in the Toulousain (§6), ivory-tower dualism (that is, the idea that dualism was projected onto heretics in the south by Cistercians and Paris theology, both largely detached from the real world) (§7), the alternative to this – local knowledge of the doctrines of heretics (§8) – and heretics' bishops (§9). There are three appendixes: Appendix A is on names; Appendix B provides a brief summary of events at Montségur; Appendix C discusses the translation of two texts.

---

* I am grateful for comment to John Arnold, Malcolm Barber, John McClay, Lucy Sackville, Antonio Sennis and Shelagh Sneddon, and to Marianne Fisher for her fine copy-editing.

[1] M. G. Pegg, *The Corruption of Angels: The Great Inquisition of 1245–1246* (Princeton, 2001); henceforth cited as *Corruption*.

[2] R. I. Moore, *The War on Heresy: Faith and Power in Medieval Europe* (London, 2012), cited henceforth as *War*.

Goodbye to Catharism?

§1 Words

We begin with words. There was use of the word 'Cathar' in Languedoc in the early thirteenth century. The Waldensian Durand of Huesca wrote of 'the Cathars who live in the dioceses of Albi and Toulouse and Carcassonne'.[3] But this was rare.[4] The fact that the word used in Languedoc was not usually 'Cathar' raises questions and a practical problem. Does modern historians' use of the word 'Cathar' indicate their lack of awareness of the semantic problem? Does it lead insidiously to the attribution of unity and identity where there was none? In practice, what words should modern historians use?

There is a long history of high awareness. The medieval Church's writers were anxious to document regional variation in the names that were applied to these heretics. Stephen of Bourbon is an example, writing that 'They are called "Albigensians" for this reason, that they infected first of all that part of the province ⟨of Narbonne⟩ [...] By the Lombards, also, they are called "Cathars" or "Patarenes"; by the Germans, "Cathars" or "Catharists". They are also called "Bulgars", because their special lair is in Bulgaria.'[5] This has continued in the modern world. The fundamental modern account, Arno Borst's *Die Katharer*, devotes a massive appendix to the various names given by the heretics to themselves, and by others to them.[6]

---

[3] *Une somme anti-cathare: Le* Liber contra Manicheos *de Durand de Huesca*, ed. C. Thouzellier (Louvain, 1964), p. 217: 'Kathari qui in Albiensi et Tolosanensi et Carcassonensi diocesibus commorantur'. 'Cathars' also appear on pp. 89, 106, 135, 160, 210, 226, 254, 297, 306, 319. They are sometimes – as here – 'moderni Kathari', in a phrase where Durand airs his patristic learning.

[4] 'Cathar' is also used in a *Summa auctoritatum* from Albi around 1200; 'Edizione della Summa auctoritatum contenuta nel MA. 47 della Bibliothèque municipale d'Albi', ed. F. Šanjek, *Atti della Accademia Nazionale dei Lincei = Classe di scienze morali, storiche e filologiche* 8th s. 28 (1985), 355–95. The statement that 'Cathar' was not used of heretics in this area between 1179 and 1250 (M. G. Pegg, 'Albigenses in the Antipodes: An Australian and the Cathars', *Journal of Religious History* 35 (2011), 577–600 (pp. 581–2)) is incorrect.

[5] 'Dicti sunt Albigenses, propter hoc quia illam partem Provincie que est versus Tolosam et Agennensem urbem [circa fluvium Albam] primo in Provincia infecerunt; dicuntur a Lombardis Gazari vel Pathari, a Theotonicis Katari vel Kathaariste; dicuntur eciam Burgari, quia latibule eorum speciale est in Bulgaria'; *Anecdotes historiques, légendes et apologues tirés du recueil inédit d'Étienne de Bourbon, dominicain du XIIIe siècle*, ed. A. Lecoy de la Marche (Paris, 1877), p. 300 and n. 1, where there is comment on the section in parentheses which we have left untranslated. It is a geographical problem, which may be solved in Jacques Berlioz's future edition of this part of Stephen's treatise.

[6] A. Borst, *Die Katharer* (Stuttgart, 1953), 'Anhang II: Namen der katharischen Sekte', pp. 240–53. The use of *perfecti* for the elite among the Cathars features in the controversy. Borst devoted two pages to these names (whose heavy annotation is still the starting-point for scholars). He used a German word that translates *perfecti* as a past participle with the sense 'fully fledged' or 'finished', carefully placing it within quotation marks. His precision and scruple have been erased in French. So 'Nur die "Vollendeten" dürfen

What have been the consequences of semantic usage on thought about heretics, in particular about the unity of heretical phenomena? We do not need to apply this question to Stephen of Bourbon and his contemporaries. With them it is worth remembering that the ideal type of a sect or heresy, which they inherited from patristic writings, stressed the small size and membership, geographical confinement and internal divisiveness of sects, in contrast to the large size, universality and unity of the Catholic Church, and that this overshadowed whatever words were used. Even the names used for sects, in their large number and variety, conveyed the point. If we continue on to the modern world and, again, turn to Borst and his *Die Katharer*, we find a historian who fastidiously discriminates when tracing different strands among religious movements and among the heretics he is examining, not someone led by his work's title into the conflation of different phenomena.

There is no need therefore to jettison 'Cathars', or even the key-words ending in '-ism'. They may sound anachronistically modern but, in fact, the inquisitors of Languedoc also used '-ism' words in their registers. Alongside the words for the two main groups of people regarded as heretics – *Valdenses* (Waldensians) and *heretici* (meaning, when paired with Valdenses, dualist heretics, Cathars) – are the terms *Valdesia* and *heresis*. When paired with each other in the interrogations and depositions of Languedoc, the first meant Waldensianism and the second Catharism. Or, we could say, 'the -ism of the dualist heretics'. The awkwardness and length of the last example provide a hint. In an ideal world, when writing about the religious before 1500, we would write 'a member of the Order of Preachers' or 'a member of the Order of Minors'. But it is more practical simply to use the post-1500 names, 'Dominican' and 'Franciscan'.

Nevertheless, there are good grounds for using a wide range of words. We need to keep reminding ourselves of the variety of semantic fields in the thirteenth century. We could even occasionally take a medicinal semantic pill, by referring to Catholic priests as 'heretics' – a salutary reminder of what the Good Men called them. We have just used their own term for themselves. Here again we need to keep in mind the semantic fields beyond the heretics themselves – in plain language, other groups of people among whom 'good men' had different meanings. We need to remember ordinary variety in the use of a phrase, within a particular group of people or just in the speech and writing of one individual. 'Good men' could be used in a purely secular sense, denoting solid citizens in a community, or office-holders. The same words could be used simply to make a precise point about some people's morals – they were good men – or to make an approximate point about them, or with

das Vaterunser beten' became 'Seuls les parfaits étaient en état de dire le Pater'; *Die Katharer*, pp. 192, 295–6; *Les cathares*, trans. C. Roy (Paris, 1974), p. 164.

irony. We misunderstand if we ignore the many uses of these words, and we also misunderstand if we try to elide all of them. One very clear and distinct meaning was prominent when the heretics were talking. The Good Man was the Good Christian that someone became when receiving the *consolamentum*. They insisted on use of the phrase. They themselves *make* their followers *designate* them 'the "Good Men" or "Good Christians"', as Durand of Huesca said, when writing around 1223 about the dualist heretics of Languedoc.[7] The heretics' emphasis warrants modern orthographic underlining through the use of indefinite or definite articles and initial capital letters.

In this chapter we shall sometimes use their own terms, sometimes the Church's, and sometimes the convenient 'Cathar'.

§2 *The general place of* The Corruption of Angels *and* The War on Heresy *in the field*

In order to place *The Corruption of Angels* and *The War on Heresy*, we need a quick sketch of the field of modern writing about the Cathars.

It has an academic core and a popular periphery. Most of the core can be split into work in German, Italian, French and English. The earliest serious work was in German, beginning with Charles Schmidt's long article on 'Die Katharer in Südfrankreich' in 1847.[8] Schmidt, who was from the Alsace, also produced a general history in French in 1848–9, and fundamental research in French was especially strong in the decades around 1900. Most of the important Italian work came after the Second World War, from Raffaello Morghen and Raoul Manselli, and then after the 1970s from Lorenzo Paolini and Grado Merlo. 'Anglophone scholarship' covers two camps, on the one hand the 'Columbia school' of American historians in the second half of the twentieth century, especially Walter Wakefield, and on the other hand a group of English scholars, principally Malcolm Lambert, Bernard Hamilton, R. I. Moore, Malcolm Barber and myself, who did not constitute a school but together made England one of the most fertile fields of heresy scholarship from the 1970s onwards.[9]

---

[7] *Une somme anti-cathare*, ed. Thouzellier, p. 105: 'seipsos "bonos homines" vel "⟨bonos⟩ christianos" a suis faciunt fautoribus vocitari'. Note Durand's emphasis, when choosing *vocitari* rather than *vocari*, 'designated' rather than simply 'called'. In the first occurrence of the term – in the 'Acts of the Council of Lombers', a meeting and debate between Catholics and heretics in 1165 – the conscious deliberateness of the naming is spelled out: 'they *had* themselves named "Good Men"' ('faciebant se appellari boni homines'); Mansi, *Concilia*, XXII, 157; translated in *Heresies of the High Middle Ages: Selected Sources*, ed. and trans. W. L. Wakefield and A. P. Evans (New York, 1969), p. 190.

[8] In *Beiträge zu den theologischen Wissenschaften von den Mitgliedern der Fakultät zu Strassburg* 1 (1847), 85–157. Schmidt's later work on the heretics was in French.

[9] For a long time the confinement of my research to inquisition in later medieval

Let us look more closely at the Germans and the French. The Germans developed a critical approach to medieval Church texts on heresy very early, beginning with Herbert Grundmann's article on the 'type' of the heretic in 1927, and continuing with his later article on the influence in this area of biblical exegesis.[10] In his *Die Katharer* Borst laid the foundations for text-genre criticism, laying out in an historical line and analysing the main sequence of types of writers on heretics: the chroniclers, the letter-writers, the polemicists, the scholastics and the inquisitors.[11] Grundmann and, later, Alexander Patschovsky (on this occasion writing in Italian) turned their attention to the source-critical problems of inquisition depositions.[12] Two points stand out. First, although the German critical approach did not preclude dismantling in one area – Grundmann's article on depositions paved the way for Robert Lerner's removal of the 'heresy' of the Free Spirit[13] – its aim was not crude scepticism. Rather it was the analysis of the characteristics of genres and individual examples of texts; it led to a view of texts as positioned by genre and author, and in turn shaping the presentation or direction of material. Scepticism is part of the armoury, but not the only weapon. This approach has mainly meant that Grundmann, Borst and Patschovsky, and now, in the younger generation, Jörg Feuchter, have been and are exceptionally sophisticated readers of texts. Second, the influence of the Germans among non-German readers has been muted, because most of their writing has been not translated, or in a few cases only translated after a very long delay.[14]

Let us turn to the French. The inquisition records of Languedoc survive in larger quantities than elsewhere and are conveniently accessibly in just a few places, mainly Paris, Toulouse and the Vatican. Some are medieval, but a large proportion are seventeenth-century copies of medieval registers, and these are now held in the national library in Paris, in the 'Collection Doat'. The records from Languedoc attracted a great deal of attention in the years

---

Germanophone areas and the Waldensians, together with publication only in articles, gave me a lower profile in this English field.

[10] H. Grundmann, 'Der Typus des Ketzers in mittelalticher Anschauung', in *Kultur- und Universalgeschichte: Festschrift für W. Goetz* (Leipzig, 1927), repr. in H. Grundmann, *Ausgewählte Aufsätze*, 3 vols., Monumenta Germaniae Historica Schriften 25 (Stuttgart, 1976–8), I, 313–27. This collection also reprints '"Oportet et haereses esse": das Problem der Ketzerei im Spiegel der mittelalterlichen Bibelexegese', pp. 328–63.

[11] Borst, 'Die Katharer im Spiegel von Quellen und Forschung', in *Katharer* (ch. 1, parts 1–5).

[12] Grundmann, 'Ketzerverhöre des Spätmittelalters als quellenkritisches Problem', reprinted in his *Ausgewählte Aufsätze*, I, 364–416; A. Patschovsky, 'Gli eretici davanti al tribunale', in *La parola all'accusato*, ed. J.-C. Maire Vigueur and A. Paravicini Bagliani (Palermo, 1991), pp. 242–67.

[13] R. E. Lerner, *The Heresy of the Free Spirit in the Later Middle Ages* (Berkeley, 1972).

[14] First published in 1935, Grundmann's *Religiöse Bewegungen* was not translated into English until sixty years later; *Religious Movements in the Middle Ages*, trans. S. Rowan (Notre Dame, 1995). Borst's book was eventually translated into French, as *Les cathares*, trans. C. Roy (Paris, 1974).

around 1900.[15] Although most of the records remained unpublished for a long time – and many still are – their ransacking in these years led to a long succession of very detailed histories of Cathars in Languedoc that are essentially constructed from deposition records. These go from Célestin Douais in the late nineteenth century through Jean-Marie Vidal, Jean Guiraud in the early twentieth, later Jean Duvernoy and Elie Griffe, and most recently Michel Roquebert.[16] Their volumes are extraordinarily rich in stories and they feature thousands of named individuals. Because of the concrete nature of the data in inquisitions, these scholars have all been writing history that amounts to the 'lived religion' of the Cathars. The earlier names in this catalogue – especially Guiraud – were doing this long before Jean Delumeau and others around 1960 argued for the idea of this sort of history.

Two things stood out in this 'lived' Catharism of Languedoc. The first was its long continuity. There are many thousands of depositions. Those interrogated in the 1240s included a reasonable proportion of very old people who remembered back to the 1180s, 1190s – and especially to the 1200s, 'before the advent of the crusaders', as many said, that is, before 1209.[17] Historians went forward from these, to those interrogated in the 1270s and in the early fourteenth century. The consequent history of the sect comprised an extraordinary complex of people, a visible sequence of Good Men and their followers in a long line of great-grandparents, grandparents, parents and children, grandchildren and so on. It is a Venn diagram of overlapping circles of people. Second, for some time the Good Men had been centred at Montségur. The fortress fell in March 1244, and in many of the interrogations

---

[15] Célestin Douais can be taken as just one example from the French heresiologists of this period; we select just two items from his prodigious output to represent him. In 1891 and 1907 he published an article containing a *tour de force*, a brief, but extraordinarily rich, analysis of 1245–6 interrogations in Toulouse, Bibliothèque municipale MS 609 (henceforth MS 609) (the manuscript which is the object of Pegg's *Corruption*): the manuscript is gutted and served up on a plate for later historians. The 1907 part is cited here, 'Les hérétiques du comté de Toulouse dans la première moitié du XIIIe siècle d'après l'enquête de 1245', *Bulletin théologique, scientifique et littéraire de l'Institut catholique de Toulouse* n.s. 3 (1907), 161–73 and 206–9. In 1900 he produced the large and still fundamental *Documents pour server à l'histoire de l'inquisition dans le Languedoc* (Paris).

[16] For Douais, see previous note. Guiraud's first account was in his book-long introduction to his edition of the *Cartulaire de Notre-Dame de Prouille*, 2 vols. (Paris, 1907), his second in the French sections (which predominate) of his *Histoire de l'inquisition au Moyen Âge*, 2 vols. (Paris, 1935–8); É. Griffe, *Les débuts de l'aventure cathare en Languedoc (1140–1190)*; *Le Languedoc cathare de 1190 à 1210*; *Le Languedoc cathare au temps de la croisade (1209–1229)*; and *Le Languedoc cathare et l'inquisition (1229–1329)* (Paris, 1969–80); J. Duvernoy, *Les cathares*, vol. 1: *La religion des cathares* (Toulouse, 1976), and vol. 2: *L'histoire des cathares* (Toulouse, 1979); M. Roquebert, *L'épopée cathare*, 5 vols. (Toulouse, 1970–98). E. Le Roy Ladurie's monograph on Montaillou lies outside the picture of more conventional histories that I am sketching here.

[17] The most spectacular example is provided by the memory of one deponent from Fanjeaux, interrogated in 1245, which reached back seventy years; MS 609, fol. 159r.

over the next year the questions were about Montségur. Who had been there? What went on? The inquisitors were able to put these questions to the co-lord of Montségur, and many others of high rank – people who had had daily dealings with leaders among the heretics. An exceptionally 'churchy' picture of the heretical sect appears in the records of their replies. It is not surprising. If we had witnesses questioned about goings-on at the papal curia we would get a very churchy view of Catholic Christianity. Just so here with heresy, for Montségur had been for some years the 'headquarters of the heretics' church', the *caput* of the *ecclesia hereticorum*. A reminder is provided in Appendix B at the end of this chapter.

In the 1980s a critical school emerged among French historians of heresy and inquisition. It was particularly linked with the name of Monique Zerner, important conferences held by her, and some fine fundamental scholars, Jean-Louis Biget, Jacques Chiffoleau and (later) Julien Théry. The titles of books – *Inventer l'hérésie?*[18] and *L'hérétique imaginé*[19] – convey the interests of the school, as also the aim of one of the conferences: to delve more deeply into forgery and its ramifications in the case of 'Le supposé concile cathare de Saint-Félix'.[20] There is no apparent connection with the German critical school, and the preoccupations are epistemologically narrower: the demonstration of lack of credibility, imaginative fabrication and forgery. Finally – though it only gets one sentence here – we need to remember what lies outside the academic core: an enormous, various and highly coloured popular view of Catharism.

In broad terms, what is the location of *The Corruption of Angels* and *The War on Heresy* books in this field? Some of the older Italian scholarship appears in the earlier and more academic work of the author of *The War on Heresy*, but in general *The Corruption of Angels*[21] and *The War on Heresy* do not face in the direction of the German part of the field.[22] Neither work squares up to Borst's

---

[18] *Inventer l'hérésie? Discours polémique et pouvoirs avant l'inquisition*, ed. M. Zerner (Nice, 1998).

[19] A. Trivellone, *L'hérétique imaginé: hétérodoxie et iconographie dans l'occident médiéval, de l'époque carolingienne à l'inquisition* (Turnhout, 2009). The point here is about one of the ways this title can be read, not the precise arguments of this valuable study of iconography.

[20] The acts were published in *L'histoire du catharisme en discussion: le 'concile' de Saint-Félix (1167)*, ed. M. Zerner (Nice, 2001).

[21] Its author has just started to incorporate references to earlier German scholars, especially Ignaz von Döllinger, into the exposition of his theory that Catharism is a construction of modern scholarship; M. G. Pegg, 'Innocent III, les 'pestilentiels provençaux' et le paradigme épuisé du catharisme', *Innocent III et le Midi = Cahiers de Fanjeaux* 50 (2015), 279–310. Since German historians regarded Döllinger as one of the poorest of all scholars, such a theory needs to establish that any worthwhile historian took him seriously; Borst, *Katharer*, pp. 42–3, 46 n. 41.

[22] The appearance of 'Börst' as a short form of Borst's *Die Katharer* in the list of abbreviations in R. I. Moore, *The Origins of European Dissent* (London, 1977), p. 290, its use once

account of the Cathars. In place of this *The Corruption of Angels* holds up for display and ridicule old encyclopaedia articles and the images of Catharism peddled to tourists.[23] The German critical approach has not influenced it. *The War on Heresy* also ignores the German critical school, stating that the critical approach arose in the 1980s, among the French – whose value for *The War on Heresy* is simple: their preoccupation with the fragility of sources.[24]

Both *The Corruption of Angels* and *The War on Heresy* sidestep the deposition-based histories of Catharism written by Douais, Guiraud, Griffe, Duvernoy and Roquebert. This runs along with the broad contrast between the angles of vision of their lenses: French historiography used wide-angle lenses, taking in all the inquisition records, while *The Corruption of Angels* uses a microscope on one set of depositions contained in just one manuscript (this is described more fully below). Although *The War on Heresy* does make direct use of one tiny set of inquisition records from Languedoc (about 0.01% of the extant inquisition records of this region),[25] its reliance on *The Corruption of Angels* is so heavy, and its retailing of the latter's conclusions so pervasive, that the angle of vision of its lens, when turned towards inquisition in Languedoc, is roughly similar. The significance in both cases is exclusions. Since *The Corruption of Angels* does not spell out for the reader the extent of the exclusions and their consequences, let us supply the gap. First, an example: the manuscript considered in *The Corruption of Angels* contains the confessions of the lord of Gaja, Peter of Mazerolles, so Peter is in the book.[26] But the confession of Peter's mother, Helis of Mazerolles, is in another manuscript,[27] so she is not in his book. An extraordinary *cordon sanitaire* is thrown around the book. The consequences are the removal of the long-duration account of Catharism, and Montségur.

(ch. 8 n. 3) and reference to an article of Borst's published in French (ch. 7 n. 9) suggest that an exhaustive trawl through the large number of articles published by its author would show a steady trickle of similar references, without affecting the general point. Nor is it affected by the use in *War*, pp. 298–9, of J. Feuchter's *Ketzer, Konsuln und Büßer: die städtischen Eliten von Montauban vor dem Inquisitor Petrus Cellani (1236/1241)* (Tübingen, 2007), whose contents are detailed at great length in Anglophone reviews, e.g. the online *H-Soz-u-Kult* (21 April 2010).

[23] *Corruption*, p. 17.
[24] *War*, pp. 335–6.
[25] *War*, pp. 304–6. The inquisition records of Languedoc amount to about 1.8 million words, the largest caches being the enquiries of 1245–6 used in *Corruption* (about 425,000 words), Paris, Bibliothèque nationale de France (henceforth BnF), Collection Doat, MSS 21–6 (about 250,000 words), Bernard Gui's sentences (about 200,000 words), and the inquisition register of Jacques Fournier (about 700,000 words). Electronic registration of these records would modify these estimates, which are based on counting sample pages, taking an average, and multiplying by numbers of pages or folios.
[26] *Corruption*, pp. 66, 118.
[27] Paris, BnF, Collection Doat, MS 23, fols. 162r–180r. She may be outside Pegg's *Corruption*, but she is not an obscure figure; it would be difficult to find any deposition-based history of the last century that omitted her. For a modern example see M. Barber, *The Cathars: Dualist Heretics in Languedoc in the High Middle Ages*, 2nd edn (Harlow, 2013), pp. 43–4.

Though Montségur does have index entries, five in *The Corruption of Angels*,[28] three in *The War on Heresy* (which does briefly allude to the testimony of the co-lord of Montségur on bishops),[29] it has virtually no presence in either book. Many thousands of depositions given by people who attested their belief in the Good Men, stretching over a very long period, and the mass of evidence relating to the organized activities of the Good Men at Montségur, are removed from view. Students fresh to this area are not going to know this.

Let us now look more closely at these books.

§3 *The Corruption of Angels*

We shall look first at *The Corruption of Angels*, published in 2001. Subsequently its author has published another book and several articles on the subject.[30] Since these have gone over the same ground, recycling footnotes[31] and repeating the same claims, we shall look mainly at the first book. This was an exercise in the use of just one manuscript, which survives in Toulouse: a copy from about 1260 of records mainly from 1245–6 which contain the depositions of over 5,000 people; it is a fraction of a once larger set of records. The manuscript's serious use began with a short article that gutted it very efficiently, published in different versions in 1891 and 1907,[32] and it was the object of a *thèse d'état* by Yves Dossat, published in 1959, which contained a superlative analysis of the manuscript itself and a fundamental and unsurpassed account of inquisition in the Toulousain.[33] Two modern typescript transcriptions exist, one of them difficult to locate;[34] one can find modern

---

[28] *Corruption*, p. 232.
[29] *War*, pp. 289, 375. One of the pages in the index-entry, 310, is a mistake.
[30] M. G. Pegg, *A Most Holy War: The Albigensian Crusade and the Battle for Christendom* (Oxford, 2008); 'On Cathars, Albigenses and the Good Men of Languedoc', *Journal of Medieval History* 27 (2001), 181–95; 'Questions about Questions: Toulouse 609 and the Great Inquisition of 1245–6', in *Texts and the Repression of Medieval Heresy*, ed. C. Bruschi and P. Biller (Woodbridge, 2003), pp. 111–25; 'Heresy, Good Men and Nomenclature', in *Heresy and the Persecuting Society in the Middle Ages: Essays on the Work of R. I. Moore*, ed. M. Frassetto (Leiden, 2006), pp. 227–39; 'Albigenses in the Antipodes: An Australian and the Cathars', *Journal of Religious History* 35 (2011), 577–600.
[31] See, e.g., 'On Cathars, Albigenses and the Good Men of Languedoc', pp. 187–8, and 'Heresy, Good Men', pp. 236–8.
[32] See n. 15 above.
[33] Y. Dossat, *Les crises de l'inquisition toulousaine au XIIIe siècle (1233–1273)* (Bordeaux, 1959).
[34] One is a transcript made at Columbia University. *Corruption* comments on it extensively, but does nothing to help the reader find it, saying only that it is uncatalogued (pp. 26, 159–60). It is in fact in the catalogue of the Butler Special Collection at Columbia, which states that it is photocopy of a transcript, lacking twenty-five folios, with the title 'Interrogatoires subis par des hérétiques albigeois', and the call marks BX4890, B47 1255. The other is the typescript of the late Jean Duvernoy, scanned and made available at http://jean.duvernoy.free.fr/text/listetexte.htm.

works of scholarship on inquisition and heresy in Languedoc that do not use the text.

The depositions are grouped by parishes, beginning with a very long set of deponents from Mas-Saintes-Puelles. Many of their depositions take up only one line. Richarda appears, takes an oath, says she never saw heretics or believed in them, and abjures: that is it. But some deponents had seen heretics, and with these the two inquisitors, Bernard of Caux and John of Saint-Pierre, persisted; these depositions can be long. With the high-ranking and well-informed witness Peter of Mazerolles, the record of questions and answers occupies two folios. Four categories of people were envisaged by the inquisitors: (1) 'heretics' (fully fledged Cathars); (2) believers in the heretics; (3) Waldensians; and (4) believers in the Waldensians. The third and fourth categories only came up rarely, and the deponents were almost all in the second category. The question-list used in interrogations reflected the inquisitors' ideal type of the actions of support and belief of someone who believed in the Cathars, distilled from observation and experience in dealing with heretics and their supporters, and also legal consultations about how to define and distinguish varies sorts of support. Deponents were asked whether they had seen heretics, when, who else was there; whether they had 'adored' the heretics, when, who else was there; whether they had been present at the administration of a *consolamentum*, when, who else was there. After further questions about actions, a quintet of the heretics' doctrines was put to them, that God did not create visible things, that the Eucharist was not the body of Christ, that there was no value in baptism, or in marriage, and that there will be no resurrection of the body.[35]

As translated into Latin and recorded by the inquisitors' scribes, the deponents' answers were varied, rich and colourful. They constitute a great treasury for an historian who sees what can be done with them, comparable to the even more fertile early fourteenth century depositions whose opportunities were seized by Emmanuel Le Roy Ladurie and worked into his famous *Montaillou*. The parallel should not be pushed too far. While *The Corruption of Angels* shares the colour of *Montaillou*, in its literary form it resembles rather Carlo Ginzburg's *Cheese and the Worms*. And Mary Douglas's name (she is one of the book's dedicatees) is a banner for the anthropological colouring of *The Corruption of Angels*'s use of the inquisition records in a remarkable depiction of the land, ecology, buildings, social structures and relationships, culture and religion of the Lauragais region of Languedoc. *The Corruption of Angels*'s

---

[35] See P. Biller, 'Cathars and the Material World', in *God's Bounty? The Churches and the Natural World: Papers Read at the 2008 Summer Meeting and the 2009 Winter Meeting of the Ecclesiastical History Society*, ed. P. Clarke and T. Claydon (Woodbridge, 2010), pp. 89–110; P. Biller, 'Intellectuals and the Masses: Oxen and She-asses in the Medieval Church', *The Oxford Handbook of Medieval Christianity*, ed. J. H. Arnold (Oxford, 2014), pp. 323–39 (pp. 329–31).

interest in colour, surface, sound and texture and the wonderful capacity of its prose to evoke place and time are evident everywhere – 'it was in the dark of the night amid the tangle of woods'[36] – and they help explain the great impact the book has had.

The Corruption of Angels has been commented upon extensively in reviews,[37] and here we confine ourselves to two points about the book and its author. The first point is that some things stated in the book are not true. Let us begin with small examples and proceed to larger ones. There is an interest in undermining the validity of the seventeenth-century copies of medieval inquisition registers. The appearance of the word *perfectus* in them is used to serve this end:

> It seems that *perfectus*, if it was transcribed, has only survived in the Collection Doat (e.g. Doat 26, fol. 258r–259r). This apparent fact, in stark contrast to original manuscripts surviving from the thirteenth and fourteenth centuries, should suggest that the seventeenth-century copyists employed by Jean de Doat perhaps took more transcribing liberties than is often realised.[38]

It is not true that the word appears in Doat 26, fols. 258r–259r, as Chris Sparks has pointed out. The passage contains *boni homines* and *heretici*. There is no trace of *perfectus*.[39] (It should also be pointed out that the starting-point of the argument here – that *perfectus* was not in use in the inquisition texts, *ergo* its presence in an early modern copy of a medieval manuscript would suggest early modern tampering – is wrong: *perfectus* is found in legislation about the repression of heresy in Languedoc, in inquisitor's formulae and in Bernard Gui's sentences.)

Another example is the attempt to discredit what Bernard Hamilton has written about Bulgarian influence. Hamilton has been guilty, it is alleged, of 'misreading *et hoc in vulgaria* (about a book) in a seventeenth-century copy of an inquisition record (Doat 25, fol. 217r) as *et hoc in Bulgaria*'. This is not true. The manuscript's *et hoc in Bulgaria* is plain and unproblematic. When the evidence was presented at the University College London conference, an invitation to withdraw the statement was declined.[40]

---

[36] *Corruption*, p. 122.
[37] See J. Feuchter, http://www.hsozkult.de/publicationreview/id/rezbuecher-880; B. Hamilton, *American Historical Review* 107 (2002), 925; P. Biller, *Speculum* 78 (2003), 1366.
[38] 'On Cathars, Albigenses and the Good Men of Languedoc', pp. 192–3 n. 28.
[39] C. Sparks, *Heresy, Inquisition and Life Cycle in Medieval Languedoc* (Woodbridge, 2014), p. 15 n. 70.
[40] Pegg, 'On Cathars, Albigenses and the Good Men of Languedoc', p. 190 n. 20. The passage is edited in *Inquisitors and Heretics in Thirteenth Century Languedoc: Edition and Translation of Toulouse Inquisition Depositions, 1273–1282*, ed. P. Biller, C. Bruschi and S. Sneddon (Leiden, 2011), p. 620. Misrepresentation is found even in insignificant points.

These examples provide the leitmotiv for something of more general significance regarding *The Corruption of Angels*'s chapter 13, 'Words and Nods'.[41] This is an important chapter in the book (and also for *The War on Heresy*, which reproduces the conclusions). *The Corruption of Angels* takes a ritual which inquisitors called 'adoration' and used in their questioning: 'Did you adore a heretic?' A 'yes' was one of the clear signs of complicity. The case starts with social relations and courtesies among the inhabitants of the Lauragais. Inquisitors over-interpreted these, *The Corruption of Angels* argues, raising them into a formal ritual: 'the friar-inquisitors objectified a style of highly contingent politeness into the classifiable form, *adoratio*, so that it forced people to see their past and future nods and benedictions as much more formulaic than they ever were.'[42] At this point the prose of *The Corrupting Angels* is packed with persuaders, words and phrases such as 'respectful nod', 'being civil', 'habitual politeness', 'an etiquette', 'courteous hellos and goodbyes', 'civilities', 'honours', 'mark of respect', and 'routine *cortesia*'.

Deponents in the Toulouse manuscript did not put it like this. They described a complex ritual, involving three genuflections accompanied by a repeated formula requesting blessing. It had to be *taught*. Deponents described how heretics – going back at least as far as 1206 – 'taught' and 'instructed' (*docere, instruere*) them how (*quomodo*) to perform it, showing (*ostendere*) them its exact form (*modum*).[43] One deponent tried to fool the inquisitor, by saying he and others 'had only bowed their heads' with the bland formula 'God give you good thanks'. Later he retracted, admitting that they had, in fact, 'adored them, genuflecting three times and saying, "Bless, Good Men, pray to God on our behalf"'.[44] *The Corruption of Angels* keeps its readers in ignorance about all of this, and omission of this evidence is the only way it can maintain its thesis.

Compare, for example, the statement that an editorial comment in *Inquisitors and Heretics* is made 'anonymously' ('Albigenses in the Antipodes', p. 585), to the fact that the first footnote in every chapter in *Inquisitors and Heretics* states which editor wrote which section. See n. 31 above.

[41] Pegg, *Corruption*, ch. 13.

[42] Pegg, *Corruption*, p. 234.

[43] MS 609, fols. 5v, 117v, 124r–v, 175r, etc. Two examples, at fols. 117v, 160r. 'He did not adore nor see (them adored), though the said heretics often demonstrated to them the mode of adoration' ('non adoravit nec vidit, licet pluries dicti heretic monstrarent eis modum adoracionis'). 'She adored the heretics often, just as the same heretics taught her. And this was forty years ago or thereabouts (*c.* 1206)' ('Et adoravit hereticos pluries, sicut ipsi heretici docebant ipsam. Et sunt xl anni ve l circa'). What they were doing already around 1206 – *teaching* the performance of the ritual – they were still doing a century later; *Le livre des sentences de l'inquisiteur Bernard Gui*, ed. A. Pales-Gobilliard, 2 vols. (Paris, 2002), I, 612, 618, 624, 662, etc.

[44] MS 609, fol. 169r: 'in domo domine Cavaers [...] inclinaverunt eis tantum capita sua, dicentes, "Deus referat vobis bonas gracias." [...] Item, dixit postea quod, quando vidit supradictos hereticos in domo predicta dicte domine Caverz [...] adoraverunt eos ter flexis genibus dicendo, "Benedicite, boni homines, orate Deum pro nobis."'

The second point is a question about what is excluded from *The Corruption of Angels*. We need to ask, while the oils are being mixed on the palette and the artist is at the easel, looking at the landscape, what *proportion* of that landscape is being transferred into this highly coloured pointillist painting? Consider a Catholic example. Suppose Catholic lay men and women rather than Cathars were the heretics, and we were mining their depositions in order to produce our picture of their 'lived religion', including, for example, the myriad different responses to and understandings of rituals. The insight provided by the extraordinary contrasts between aspersion with blessed water among parishioners in the dioceses of Lincoln in England and Rieti in Italy would be fascinating. But if this is all we did, and we deliberately left out the structure of the Church, its dioceses, bishops, councils, and theological, legal and liturgical texts, ours would only be half a picture of Catholic Christianity. *The Corruption of Angels* includes in its painting the 'lived religion' of people of the Lauragais. But it excludes the heretics' church's structure, their bishops, their ordinations and regularized succession, relations with fellow heretics in Lombardy, learned theology, formal liturgy, the long continuity of the heretics, and the traces still occasionally evident of their earlier connections with Bulgaria. The result is a picture of only half the landscape.

§4 The War on Heresy: the trajectory of its author's works on heresy and persecution

The milestones of the author's monographs on heresy and its persecution are *The Origins of European Dissent* (1977, 2nd edn 1985), *The Formation of a Persecuting Society: Power and Deviance in Western Europe, 900–1250* (1987, 2nd edn 2007), and *The War on Heresy: Faith and Power in Medieval Europe* (2012). They describe several broad trajectories. The first is postponement of dualism. Dualism was swept away from the heresy accusations of the first half of the eleventh century. The scene became the mid and late twelfth century: dualism was there, but its appearance was delayed. Finally, with *The War on Heresy*, it has been swept into the thirteenth century and put as late as possible, both in the past (mainly after 1250) and in the book's exposition: most positive evidence is deposited in the book's last chapter.

The second trajectory regards subject matter. Heretics and heresy between around 1000 and the late twelfth century were surveyed in *The Origins of European Dissent*. Then *The Formation of a Persecuting Society* made those who were persecuting the object of study, and *The War on Heresy* took this further. The title's witty allusion to President Bush's 'War on Terror' deftly implanted the idea of a parallel between an American President starting at shadows and launching weapons against something as indefinable as 'terror', and the Church launching crusade and inquisition against 'heresy'.

Third, between 1977 and 2012 there was a change in the author's modes of research and exposition. *The Origins of European Dissent* had one focus. Topics and texts were paraded steadily, expounded straightforwardly, and carefully underpinned with reference to the editions of texts and specialist literature that had been read. The widening of focus in the second book and its large overarching thesis – a society that not only persecuted people upon whom the author was a specialist but also others upon whom he was not – meant that there was a wider range of topics and material. Putting them over needed broader brush strokes, and – this is not a criticism – no-one could be an original research scholar in all the areas about which Moore was writing. In some areas there had to be heavy reliance on the scholarship of others, always, it goes without saying, scrupulously acknowledged. An example from *The Formation of a Persecuting Society* is provided by the pages depicting the segregation of lepers, ranging from the 1140s to around 1200. There is first the cruel mandate of the third Lateran council for the exclusion of lepers from society, and then a shadow as dark as Bergman's *The Seventh Seal* is cast over this period. It comes from an account of the even crueller rite implementing this exclusion: its words are quoted, the leper stands in an open grave, and in some places spadefuls of earth are thrown over the leper's head.[45] The eloquence of these unforgettable pages comes from Moore, whose footnote indicates that he is using at this point Brody's *Disease of the Soul*.[46] In fact, the Lateran council – which was trying to provide support for *leprosaria* – is misrepresented. And according to the leading historian of medieval leprosy, Carol Rawcliffe, the existence and performance of the segregation ritual in the high medieval period is a nineteenth- and twentieth-century myth.[47]

Now, what is wrong here originated with Brody, not the author of *The Formation of a Persecuting Society*. But it constitutes a warning about what may happen as the focus of a work widens. *The War on Heresy* sometimes deals with its author's specialist areas. But it is less at home in scholastic theological treatises and inquisition trials. Its consequent reliance on a Sydney dissertation, when dealing with dualist theology in scholastic writings, and on

---

[45] Moore, *Persecuting Society*, pp. 58–9. See C. Rawcliffe, *Leprosy in Medieval England* (Woodbridge, 2006), pp. 257–8, on the Council; for extensive discussion of both the myth and the modern pervasiveness of belief in it (which is largely the result of its being retailed by very influential modern historians), see ibid., pp. 19–21, 23, 25, 27, 28, 29, 34, 38, 39–40, 42, 132, 136, 355. The presentation in the *Persecuting Society*'s second edition, pp. 54–5, remains the same.

[46] S. N. Brody, *The Disease of the Soul: Leprosy in Medieval Literature* (Ithaca NY, 1974), pp. 64–7.

[47] Moore, *Persecuting Society*, pp. 58–9; 2nd edn, pp. 54–5; C. Rawcliffe, *Leprosy in Medieval England*, pp. 19–21, 23, 25, 27–9, 34, 38–40, 42, 132, 136, 257–8, 355; F. Bériac, *Histoire des lépreux au Moyen Âge: une société des exclus* (Paris, 1988), pp. 215–21.

The Corruption of Angels for much of its interpretation of inquisition records, brings a danger: repetition of their weaknesses.

The War on Heresy is written for general readers, and quite properly it aims at lightness and readability, darting from one topic to another, recounting episodes in a lively and witty way, using a breezy style and incorporating many apt quotations from or allusions to Shakespeare *et al*. While the more elaborate annotation is presented on its author's website,[48] because of its target audience the book does not proceed like a disciplined academic monograph, starting with a direct account of previous scholarship and then proceeding to a systematic statement of the propositions it is going to argue. This is not a criticism, merely a warning that the extraction of the book's theses is sometimes a slippery business.

What *The War on Heresy* argues is that the dualist Cathars of Languedoc existed in the minds of the persecutors, not out there in reality (though some ground is ceded in the last chapter, which allows some dualism and ecclesial structure, but only in later Catharism). The constituent propositions are these (section numbers indicate the location of discussions below):

i. The eastern origins are a myth (§5).
ii. It was not heresy that was stronger in the Toulousain than elsewhere, but political preoccupation with this region (§6).
iii. The Church projected onto the heretics its own view of their doctrines. This was based on the coalescence of two things: an account of dualism distilled in the schools of twelfth-century Paris, and a picture of the heretics that had been developed by the Cistercians (§7).
iv. The Church's view was not derived from local observation and knowledge (§8).
v. In the early stages the heretics did not have a strong ecclesial and, in particular, episcopal structure, and the so-called adoration ritual used by inquisitors to identify followers was a misunderstanding of traditional courtesies (§9).

Let us look at these in turn.

§5 *The War on Heresy* and the East

'The putrescent cadaver of the wretched Bogomil horse continues to be mercilessly flogged.'[49] This is wittily put, but it does not remove the evidence.

---

[48] http://www.rimoore.net/War.html.
[49] 'Text and Context in Early Popular Heresy', paper presented at the Leeds International Conference in 2009; http://www.rimoore.net/TextandContext.html.

Goodbye to Catharism?

Leaving aside the various treatises attesting the eastern connections of the Cathars, which have been eruditely analysed by Bernard Hamilton, let us look at some of the less direct traces. There was common talk. Under the year 1201 Robert of Auxerre wrote in his chronicle about a man called Évrard – a man, he said 'versed in the ways of the world and quite an oppressor of lesser people. In front of a legate he was accused of what they call "the heresy of the Bulgars"'.[50] The word was *bougres* in the vernacular, and it was only much later on – in England first in 1555 – that it came to have a sexual connotation. In the early decades of the thirteenth century it denoted heretics, and it was in very widespread usage. It was what people said. Their talk rested on broad awareness that the heretics had once been indebted to missionaries who came from Bulgaria. As Anselm of Alessandria wrote in the 1260s, 'Because the French were originally led astray in Constantinople by Bulgars, throughout France these persons are called Bulgarian heretics.'[51] How does *The War on Heresy* deal with this? It states that the word 'was beginning to be used of heretics in northern France around this time [early thirteenth century] and ⟨it⟩ acquired its pejorative sexual connotation from the tales of orgies conducted by the heretics and their alleged condemnation of procreative sex'.[52] Space is occupied by the red herring of the much *later* sexual connotation, enabling the omission of the straightforward vernacular reflection of Bulgarian origins.

When writing about the heretics of Languedoc around 1223, Durand of Huesca referred to the eastern churches of heretics, including Bulgaria.[53] *The War on Heresy* is silent about this. In the same year the papal legate Conrad of Porto wrote of large numbers of Albigensians having recourse to a leader 'within the confines of the Bulgars'.[54] This is removed from discussion by assertion that the text is 'rightly discounted as a florid specimen of Cistercian invective'.[55]

Another trace is the texts that the Cathars shared with the Bogomils:

> What the heresiarchs secretly read to their believers about the seven lands, which they falsely pretend Isaiah said is not true nor verisimilar, nor did the holy Isaiah think such lies. Rather it was fabricated by the evil spirit in the

---

[50] Robert of Auxerre, *Chronicon*, ed. O. Holder-Egger, Monumenta Germaniae Historica, Scriptores 26 (Hanover, 1882), p. 260. The widespread use of the words *Bulgari* and *Burgari* (in French, *Bougres*) to denote heretics in France has been taken to be rooted in broad awareness of their sect's indebtedness to the Bogomil heretics of Bulgaria and the eastern Roman Empire; Borst, *Katharer*, pp. 249–50, lists the occurrences of the word.
[51] Translated in *Heresies of the High Middle Ages*, ed. Wakefield and Evans, pp. 168–9.
[52] *War*, p. 282. Comment is confined to a brief online note: http://rimoore.net/Chapter17.html.
[53] *Une somme anti-cathare*, ed. Thouzellier, pp. 138–9, 174–5, 210–11, 217.
[54] F. Sanjek, 'Albigeois et "chrétiens" bosniaques', *Revue d'histoire de l'église de France* 59 (1973), 251–67 (p. 254).
[55] *War*, p. 289; see the online note, http://rimoore.net/Chapter17.html.

mind of some heresiarch, and given a title with the name of Isaiah in order more easily to infatuate the ignorant.[56]

This is one of the passages where Durand of Huesca refers to the heretics of Languedoc using the so-called *Vision of Isaiah*, which was also used by the Bogomils and Italian Cathars.[57] *The War on Heresy* does not discuss this. A colophon to a Bogomil apocryphon, the *Interrogatio Iohannis*, states that it was brought from Bulgaria by the bishop of the heretics of Concorezzo, Nazarius.[58] Having come from Bulgaria to Italian Cathars, the text came over to the Cathars of Languedoc and, it appears, was seized by inquisitors, since a copy ended up in the archive of the Dominican inquisitors in Carcassonne.[59] *The War on Heresy* does not detail this. Just once, an inquisition deposition preserves the muddled impression this had made on the mind of a follower. A woman called Anglesia had referred to a book heretics had, 'and this in Bulgaria' ('et hoc in Bulgaria'), and a deponent interrogated in 1276 remembered her talking about it.[60] *The War on Heresy* does not mention this.

The War on Heresy further minimizes this topic by postponing it until the last chapter and dealing with it only fleetingly: 'Manuscripts containing legends and rituals associated with the Bulgarian Bogomil heretics circulated in northern Italy and Provence, but none can be confidently dated before the middle of the thirteenth century.'[61] Nazarius had been active from about 1190, and up to about 1240; Durand had written about something contemporary in the early 1220s. Omitting the details, ignoring Durand and Anglesia, and pivoting this sentence on the dates of the extant manuscripts enable *The War on Heresy* to make this phenomenon appear both vaguer and much later than it was in reality.

A good modern scholarly account of the dualist heretics provides an account of their rituals based on the juxtaposition of the thousands of accounts of their *mise-en-scène* in depositions, and the two liturgical books that survive, one providing the services in Latin in a manuscript once owned by Italian dualist heretics, the other in a manuscript providing in Occitan the services followed in Languedoc.[62] But all these manuscripts are accorded in

---

[56] *Une somme anti-cathare*, ed. Thouzellier, pp. 256–7, 287–8.

[57] B. Hamilton, 'Wisdom from the East: The Reception by the Cathars of Eastern Dualist Texts', in *Heresy and Literacy, 1000–1530*, ed. P. Biller and A. Hudson (Cambridge, 1994), pp. 38–60 (pp. 52–3); L. Paolini, 'Italian Catharism and Written Culture', in *Heresy and Literacy*, pp. 83–103 (p. 93).

[58] *Le livre secret des cathares:* Interrogatio Iohannis, *apocryphe d'origine bogomile*, ed. E. Bozóky (Paris, 1980), p. 86: 'Explicit secretum hereticorum de Concorresio portatum de Bulgario Nazario suo episcopo plenum erroribus.'

[59] Ibid., pp. 19–21.

[60] See n. 40 above.

[61] *War*, p. 323; note in http://rimoore.net/Chapter18.html.

[62] The ritual used in Italy is edited and studied in *Le Rituel cathare*, ed. C. Thouzellier,

Goodbye to Catharism?

The War on Heresy is the passing reference quoted in the previous paragraph. Otherwise there is silence. Rituals in these books are Janus heads, black and white: the large shadow of the modern myth of a leper's ritual in the pages of the *Formation of a Persecuting Society*, as opposed to the fleeting allusion allowed to the heretics' not-named manuscript, MS Bibliothèque municipale de Lyon PA 36.[63]

§6 *Heresy in the Toulousain*

'There is no real reason to think that the region [the Toulousain] was especially given to heresy', according to *The War on Heresy*.[64] Since there was so much action against heresy in the Toulousain, establishing that heresy was not *specially* rampant in the regions around Toulouse is an important part of *The War on Heresy*'s 'all in the eye of the persecutor' argument. It is important, then, to see how *The War on Heresy* manages the long series of texts produced during the twelfth century that connect heresy with Toulouse and the Toulousain. Here we shall list the major ones, noting in each case the methods by which *The War on Heresy* makes them not mean what they appear to mean.

In 1119 a council at Toulouse condemned heretics who rejected the Eucharist, baptism, ordination and marriage, expelling them from the Church and ordering them and their supporters to be constrained by the secular powers.[65] Here *The War on Heresy* uses assertion: 'There is no reason to think that it was directed against or inspired by any particular heretic or group of heretics.'[66]

A letter by Geoffrey of Auxerre described Bernard of Clairvaux's preaching in Languedoc in 1145, partly against the heretic Henry of Lausanne, partly against another heresy. Where the letter turned to the city of Toulouse, Geoffrey wrote that Henry had little support in Toulouse, but that another heresy had some support, especially among the powerful of the city. There are good grounds for investigating and following Herbert Grundmann's

---

Sources Chrétiennes 236 (Paris, 1977); the one used in Languedoc is best used in the online edition provided by M. R. Harris, http://www.rialto.unina.it/prorel/CatharRitual, and both are translated in *Heresies of the High Middle Ages*, ed. Wakefield and Evans, pp. 465–94. For model modern discussion, see Barber, *The Cathars*, pp. 90–4.

[63] Bibliothèque municipal de Lyon, MS PA 36; two manuscripts survive, one with the rituals of the dualist heretics of Languedoc, in Occitan, the other with those of the dualist heretics of Italy, in Latin; they are translated in *Heresies of the High Middle Ages*, ed. Wakefield and Evans, pp. 465–94. They are also ignored in *Corruption*.

[64] *War*, p. 248; see also, e.g., p. 203.

[65] *Corpus documentorum inquisitionis Neerlandicae*, ed. P. Frédéricq, 5 vols. (Ghent, 1889–1903), I, 29; repeated at the second Lateran Council, see *Decrees of the Ecumenical Councils*, ed. N. Tanner, 2 vols. (London, 1990), I, 202.

[66] *War*, pp. 145; see also p. 123.

understanding of this second group as Cathars. Be that as it may, within *The War on Heresy* it is not even an area for investigation, since its presentation is based on a mistranslation of this passage. In the mistaken version, there is one group only in Toulouse, the followers of Henry. *The War on Heresy* therefore just says, 'Henry had won many followers there.'[67] The mistranslation and correct translation are detailed in Appendix C below.

A decree of the Council of Tours in 1163 stated, 'Some time ago a damnable heresy arose in the regions of Toulouse [...] we order the bishops and all the Lord's priests living in those regions to be vigilant against them.'[68] For *The War on Heresy*, this was just politics. Wanting to get at the count of Toulouse, Henry II leant on the pope, Alexander III, who leant on the bishops at the council to be geographically specific in the decree.[69]

The 'Acts of the council of Lombers' state that in 1165 at Lombers, about eighty kilometres north-north-east of Toulouse and just to the south of Albi, there was a formal encounter and debate between bishops and men accused of heresy, who 'had themselves called the "Good Men"'.[70] This was also just politics, an attempt by count of Toulouse to use heresy accusations against a dangerous rival.[71]

In 1167 the (heretical) Church of Toulouse brought an eastern heretic into the *castrum* of Saint-Félix, and a great multitude of men and women of the Church of Toulouse and of other neighbouring Churches gathered themselves there in order to receive the *consolamentum*. At a conference in Nice in 1999, held in order to debate the forgery of the charter that described *Le supposé concile cathare de Saint-Félix*,[72] a team of experts in the words and forms of high medieval texts from the Institut de recherche et d'histoire des textes produced an unwelcome verdict. They pronounced the document genuine.[73] Although its author was present at this conference, *The War on Heresy* does not mention this, and simply declares, 'There is no doubt it is a forgery.'[74]

---

[67] *War*, p. 121.
[68] *Corpus documentorum inquisitionis Neerlandicae*, I, 39.
[69] *War*, pp. 185–8.
[70] *Heresies of the High Middle Ages*, ed. Wakefield and Evans, p. 190, where the translation is 'chose to be called'; see the Latin in n. 7, above.
[71] *War*, p. 188.
[72] The purpose of the conference was made clear by M. Zerner, 'Avant-propos', in *Histoire du catharisme en discussion*, ed. Zerner, p. 7.
[73] J. Dalarun *et al.*, 'La "Charte de Niquinta", analyse formelle', in *Histoire du catharisme en discussion*, ed. Zerner, pp. 135–201. Julien Roche's account ('La charte de Niquinta: un point sur la controverse', *Slavica Occitania* 16 (2003), 229–45) is clear and the most authoritative, combining as it does his own professional expertise as Archiviste-paléographe and his unparalleled knowledge both of the activities of heretics in the diocese of Carcassonne in the 1220s, and of the precise context within which the heretics felt the need to have a *vidimus* of this charter in 1223.
[74] *War*, p. 289.

Goodbye to Catharism?

In 1177 Count Raymond V of Toulouse wrote to the Cistercian General Chapter, complaining of the strength of heresy in his regions, in a letter that was preserved in a chronicle written by Gervase of Canterbury:

> Further, in our regions gold is obscured, so it is spread like dirt under the feet of the devil. For those who discharge the office of priesthood are corrupted by the filth of heresy, and the ancient and once to be venerated places of churches lie without worship and in ruins, baptism is denied, the Eucharist is abominated, penance is regarded as negligible, the creation of man and the resurrection of the flesh are denied and rejected, and all ecclesiastical sacraments are reduced to nothing, and also – even to say it is impious! – two principles are introduced.

The last phrase is significant as the earliest completely clear statement of dualism: 'et, quod dici nefas est, duo etiam principia introducuntur'.[75] As has long been realized, the sequence of events here began with the role of the Council of Saint-Félix in radicalizing the heretics of Languedoc, followed by a growing awareness of this which found expression in the count's letter. *The War on Heresy* produces a conditional clause about this – 'If the letter was authentic and unedited' – and expresses surprise that the letter was not mentioned by Roger of Howden.[76] It does not investigate Gervase's work as a historian and copyist of texts, to assess whether he was in the habit of forging or editing letters. But, having produced its conditional clause, it sexes it up into the declaration that the count's letter is 'of questionable authenticity'.[77]

In 1178 a mission headed by a papal legate, Peter of Chrysogonus, and Henry, abbot of Clairvaux, and backed by Louis VII, Henry II and the count of Toulouse went to Toulouse. Two heretics – Bernard Raymond (who had been consecrated bishop at the allegedly 'forged' Council of Saint-Félix) and Raymond of Baymac – appeared with safe-conduct, were questioned about their faith, and answered in an orthodox fashion. Some of the others who were present there, including the count of Toulouse, said they were lying and that they had heard heresies from them (or some of them). These included that 'There were only two Gods, the one good and the other bad, the good one having made only things invisible, the bad one the heavens, the earth,

---

[75] *The Historical Works of Gervase of Canterbury*, ed. W. Stubbs, 2 vols. (London, 1879–80), I, 270–1.

[76] *War*, p. 199. John Gillingham suggests that this is not odd. Although Roger was an assiduous collector of letters, he was disturbed in the latter part of 1177, and the manuscript of the *Gesta* that Gervase used comes to an abrupt end with the death by drowning, in September, of a master Robert, to whom Roger was perhaps closely attached. Gillingham suggests that the church of Canterbury received its copy of the count of Toulouse's letter in a dossier dispatched from Cîteaux to Canterbury [personal communication].

[77] *War*, p. 192.

man and other visible things' ('Quidam enim constanter proposuerunt se a quibusdam illorum audisse, quod duo dii existerent, alter bonus et alter malus: bonus [qui] invisibilia tantum, et ea quae mutari aut corrumpi non possunt fecisset; malus qui coelum, terram, hominem et alia visibilia condidisset'). The accusers also claimed they had 'heard them denying that a man and his wife could be saved if either renders to each other the [conjugal] debt' ('negantes audisse, virum cum uxore salvari, si alter alteri debitum reddat').[78] Once again, for *The War on Heresy*, this was just politics. Count Raymond had appealed to Henry II and Louis VII to intervene, using heresy as the excuse, 'to secure leverage against two rivals'.[79] 'It *may* be the case that the doctrine of two principles had been preached or professed in Toulouse' (my italics), *The War on Heresy* says, but 'none of those examined in 1178 was directly accused or convicted of doing either'; the spectre of dualism may simply have come from the visiting papal legate.[80]

Canon 27 of the third Lateran council (1179) stated that 'in Gascony and the regions of Albi and Toulouse and in other places the loathsome heresy of those whom some call Cathars, others the Patarenes, others the Publicani [...] has grown so strong that they no longer practice their wickedness in secret.'[81] *The War on Heresy* claims that 'The regions of Albi and Toulouse [...] owed their prominence in it to the reports' of the 1178 mission, with the implication that the canon does not add to the evidence.[82]

'We hear little more about heresy in the lands of the count of Toulouse for almost two decades' concludes *The War on Heresy*'s survey of heresy and the Toulousain in the twelfth century. Here the more elderly witnesses interrogated in the 1240s are being excluded, people whose long memories peopled the Toulousain with heretics well before 1200.[83]

Declamatory assertion, questioning the authenticity of evidence and silence constitute some of the techniques used here. 'Just politics' is the most frequent manœuvre. It rests on *The War on Heresy*'s use of the view that 'the traditional function of heresy accusations [was] as a vehicle for the rivalries of the powerful'.[84] One weakness of the application of this as an analytical tool is its simplicity, its binary either/or. If a political context can be sketched, the substantive and geographic specificity of a heresy charge is taken no longer to exist. Another weakness is the contemporary map of political rivalries in Latin Christendom, and the availability in every diocese of Cistercians equipped to do the dirty work of the heresy charges. Why was the accusation of heresy not

---

[78] *Chronica Magistri Rogeri de Houedene*, ed. W. Stubbs, 4 vols. (London, 1868–71), II, 158.
[79] *War*, p. 192.
[80] *War*, p. 201.
[81] *Ecumenical Councils*, ed. Tanner, I, 224.
[82] *War*, p. 207.
[83] *War*, p. 241; see n. 16 above.
[84] *War*, p. 295.

§7 Ivory-tower dualism

We turn now to *The War on Heresy*'s ivory-tower theology idea. The book looks to two sources for the theology which it claims the Church projected onto the Good Men. The first source was the schools of Paris. Carefully judged rhetoric is used. The schools are characterized and imported by allusiveness and suggestion. 'We *cannot exclude the possibility* that the spectre [of dualism], by now regularly deployed as target practice in the classrooms of Paris, had been raised by the legate's party' (Peter of Chrysogonus), in Toulouse in 1178.[85] 'It *would have* been in Peter's retinue [...] that *we would expect* to find clerks from the Paris schools, where rebuttal of the "Manichaean" heresy, based in descriptions of it by St Augustine and other early fathers of the Church, was now a routine academic exercise.'[86] (The italics are mine.)

The War on Heresy does not cite evidence or examples. From the annotation and praise we know that the author's trust is being placed in a Sydney MA dissertation, part of which has been published in an article entitled 'Alan of Lille's Academic Concept of the Manichee'. This argues against the possibility of academic theological treatises engaging with and responding to the views of contemporary heretics. Paris scholars manufactured contemporary dualism out of patristic writings. The essential point about this work is that it is programmatic: the claims are made,[87] but, as we shall see in a moment in the case of Alan of Lille, the basic research has not yet been done.

The second source considered by *The War on Heresy* was the creation and development by Cistercians – from Bernard of Clairvaux in the 1140s to Peter of les Vaux-de-Cernay seventy years later – of a picture of heresy which was then projected onto the heretics of Languedoc. The Cistercians' preoccupation with heresy is a very important strand in the history of heresy and its repression, one part of which was put on the map for anglophone readers by Kienzle's study of Cistercian preaching against heresy in Languedoc.[88] Surveying the sources for polemicists' knowledge of heretics in 1968, Marie-Humbert Vicaire identified and thought up the apt phrase, describing one source as 'le dossier Cistercien'; he provided a rapid overview of the texts

---

[85] *War*, p. 201.
[86] *War*, p. 219.
[87] H. Chiu, in *Journal of Religious History* 35 (2011), 492–506. His as yet unpublished MA dissertaton is 'The Intellectual Origins of Medieval Dualism' (University of Sidney, 2009).
[88] B. M. Kienzle, *Cistercians, Heresy and Crusade in Occitania, 1145–1229: Preaching in the Lord's Vineyard* (York, 2001). Inquisition records show continuing involvement by southern Cistercian abbots.

constituting this dossier, preserved at Clairvaux and amplified by what was in the southern 'archives Cisterciennes'.[89] How is this handled in *The War on Heresy*?

According to *The War on Heresy*, the 'development [of the Cistercian tradition] has been traced in these pages from the time of Bernard of Clairvaux'.[90] Peter of les Vaux-de-Cernay is the latest in this line, and his systematic account of the doctrines and practices of the heretics is presented and discussed. *The War on Heresy* veers between being tentative (one sentence begins, 'Stripped of everything that *might have been* only his uncle's interpretation based on the account developed by his Cistercian predecessors')[91] and asserting that its commentary is established fact ('His description of the Albigensian heresy is obviously derived').[92] This is throwing dust in our eyes. The essential questions are obvious. What does close comparison of the texts in this 'dossier Cistercien' show about their relationship? Do we find one author recycling whole passages from a previous one? Do the results point conclusively to a closed tradition? The textual analysis has not been done. It is not provided by *The War on Heresy*. The identification of sources in the apparatus of the Latin edition of les Vaux-de-Cernay does not support the contention of *The War on Heresy*.[93] There is one point where *The War on Heresy* does grapple very closely with a text in this tradition of the writings and thought of the Cistercians: Geoffrey of Vigeois's copy of a lost letter of Henri de Marcy. *The War on Heresy*'s handling of the text (outlined in Appendix C below) does not instil confidence in its capacity to investigate a textual tradition.

The War on Heresy's link for the two traditions was provided by Alan of Lille (d. 1202/3), a Paris scholastic who became a Cistercian,[94] and his four-part treatise *On Faith*, which he wrote late in his life. Two parts of the treatise were directed against heretics: one against 'heretics' (Cathars) and one against Waldensians. *The War on Heresy*'s source is the article 'Alan of Lille's Academic Concept of the Manichee'. According to this, Alan's book on heretics only retails the concerns of earlier academic theology, not of contemporary heretics. It is a hold-all, containing doctrines not relevant to contemporary 'Cathars'. Here further fundamental scholarship needs to be noted, absent from *The War on Heresy*'s discussion. There is a shorter version of Alan of Lille's book which is probably the earlier recension. Fifty years ago Marie-Thérèse d'Alverny

---

[89] M.-H. Vicaire, 'Les cathares vus par les polémistes', *Cathares en Languedoc = Cahiers de Fanjeaux* 3 (1968), 105–28 (pp. 110–11).
[90] *War*, p. 255.
[91] *War*, p. 257.
[92] *War*, p. 254.
[93] *Petri Vallium Sarnaii monachi hystoria Albigensis*, ed. P. Guébin and E. Lyon, 3 vols. (Paris, 1926–39), I, 9–19. There is a fine account of Peter's sources in the third volume, pp. i–xxxix.
[94] *War*, p. 219.

pointed out that this version has a narrower focus than the text printed in the *Patrologia Latina*; it omits the chapters on penance, confirmation, extreme unction and prayer.[95] One of the other books in Alan's *On Faith's* was directed against another group of contemporary heretics, Waldensians, who were also present in southern France. Investigation of Alan's handling of *them* seems an obvious thing to do: what he knew about the Waldensians and how he dealt with them would be indicative of him as a writer on contemporary heretics. There has not been a systematic account of Alan on the Waldensians, but we can offer a trial drilling. Alan wrote about Waldensians' objection to killing, and he ascribed to them the authorities and arguments they used to support their position. Looking at these, we can see that some of them derive from Gratian's *Decretum*.[96] Our first hypothesis can be that this is an example of ivory-tower projection. The scholastic theologian Alan was attributing academic texts to simple heretics. In fact, the earliest surviving letter written by Waldensians themselves comes soon afterwards, 1218. And in this letter the Waldensian authors were in fact accessing patristic material through Gratian's *Decretum*.[97] Alan's account simply deepens our knowledge of the culture of some early Waldensians. And it is indicative: it shows Alan possessing precise knowledge of another group of contemporary heretics.

It is very important to both 'Alan of Lille's Academic Concept of the Manichee' and *The War on Heresy* to remove Alan from southern France, for the former in order to remove the possibility that local observation underpinned what he wrote, for the latter on account of its anxiety to establish a 'yawning chasm of incomprehension between occitanians and outsiders'.[98] D'Alverny had paraded a trickle of evidence about Alan and southern France, judiciously not making too much of it but also making it clear that it did show Alan spent some time in the region. Alan dedicated *On Faith* to the count of Montpellier. He dedicated his *Distinctiones* to the abbot of a great Benedictine monastery in lower Languedoc, Saint-Gilles. Two posthumous *exempla* depict him lecturing in the schools at Montpellier. Most telling is the fact that in his *Distinctiones* he glosses a Latin word with its equivalent in vernacular Occitan.[99] 'Alan of Lille's Academic Concept of the Manichee' omits all this evidence apart from the first dedication, and this enables it to present doubt: 'whether he [Alan] ever went to the south is contentious.'[100] When following this article *The War on Heresy* converts this question into a declamatory

---

[95] M.-T. d'Alverny, *Alain de Lille: textes inédits* (Paris, 1965), p. 159.
[96] The borrowings from the *Decretum*, the *Glossa ordinaria* and Roman law are detailed in P. Biller, *The Waldenses, 1170–1530* (Aldershot, 2001), p. 83 n. 14.
[97] *Quellen zur Geschichte der Waldenser*, ed. A. Patschovsky and K.-V. Selge (Gütersloh, 1973), p. 40 n. 226.
[98] *War*, p. 261.
[99] D'Alverny, *Alain de Lille*, pp. 13–14, 16–17, 19 n. 48.
[100] Chiu, 'Alan of Lille's Academic Concept of the Manichee', p. 496 n. 12.

statement. 'There is nothing in Alan of Lille's disappointingly undocumented life to connect him with the Languedoc.'[101]

§8 The alternative: local knowledge

Vicaire listed three sources for writers' knowledge of the Cathars of Languedoc, the first two being the dossier of the Cistercians and that of prelates and legates. His phrase for the third was 'l'expérience vivante', and for him that was the most important: 'Issue d'une polémique tenace et constamment renouvelé pendant plus de quarante années, cette mine est de loin la plus riche, la mieux tenue à jour' ('The product of a persistent and constantly renewed polemic that lasted for more than forty years, this was by far the richest and best maintained repository [of texts]').[102]

The War on Heresy mentions a few of the debates, but avoids them as a source of the Church's knowledge about the Cathars. We need therefore to look briefly at what is being swept under the carpet. The earlier history of exchanges about doctrine in Languedoc goes back a long way, to Lombers in 1165, Toulouse in 1178 and Narbonne about 1190 (Catholics and Waldensians),[103] and the chronicles of Peter of les Vaux-de-Cernay and William of Puylaurens detail a sequence of debates in the first decade of the thirteenth century.[104] The bigger issue is what lay beyond the large formal occasions of theological two- and three-way debates between Cathars, Waldensians and Catholics. Debates happened among ordinary and humble people, in their homes and workshops. Here are a few examples among the ordinary people lay people who received penances from the inquisitor Peter Sellan in 1241–2 for earlier (undated) offences:

> Francis Clergue was present at a debate between heretics and Waldensians. [...] The Cahorsin Rigald saw debates of the heretics and Waldensians. [...] James Carbonel said that he had frequently gone to the schools of the Waldensians and read with them. Item, he was present at a disputation of Waldensians and heretics [...] Bernard Remon [...] debated with someone about the faith of the heretics and the Waldensians, and he supported the

---

[101] *War*, p. 220. Compare the declaration about Moneta of Cremona's treatise (*War*, p. 314), that 'it is doubtful whether it addressed any real heresy at all', a verdict for which no grounds are provided. Compare the chapter in this book by L. J. Sackville, 'The Textbook Heretic'.

[102] See n. 77 above.

[103] *Heresies of the High Middle Ages*, ed. Wakefield and Evans, pp. 210–13.

[104] Peter of les Vaux-de-Cernay, *The History of the Albigensian Crusade*, ed. and trans. W. A. Sibly and M. D. Sibly (Woodbridge, 1998), part II, pp. 17–20, 25–30; *The Chronicle of William of Puylaurens*, ed. and trans. W. A. Sibly and M. D. Sibly (Woodbridge, 2003), chs. 8–9, pp. 23–7.

faith of the heretics. [...] William of Brouil [...] saw heretics, and heard their preaching, and he debated with them about the creation. [...] The brothers Bernard Durand and Gaubert received three heretics [...] who remained in their house for a day and a night, and there was a debate between them and the priest of the place for virtually the whole day.[105]

Theology question-time was their substitute for TV and football. They talked theology to each other, and they had been talking thus for a long time. Doubtless some were better listeners, some worse. But neither a Cathar nor a Waldensian nor a Catholic in Languedoc needed a northern French Cistercian or academic theologian to introduce them to what their neighbours were saying.

On a more formal occasion, such as the solemn debate held between Catholics and Cathars at Montréal in 1207, written positions were exchanged. The texts are lost,[106] but the surviving *Summae auctoritatum* drawn up for the use of Catholic preachers allow us to conjecture their character:

I say that x is the case [x = a theological proposition]. These are the *auctoritates* [authorities = quotations from the Bible] which support it, and these the *rationes* [arguments]. You, O heretic, say that y is the case [y = theological proposition], and these are your authorities and arguments.[107]

This was Punch and Judy stuff, with each party hitting the other on the head with quotations. Its boring nature may explain why it is used so little in modern scholarship. But it was very significant at the time, significant in the diffusion of knowledge. Its simple and repetitive nature will have dinned into the heads of many ordinary people the basic tenets of the opposed parties.

A considerable role was played both at grass-roots level and on the big occasions by Waldensians. One of these, Durand of Huesca, was involved in these debates over many years. His first polemical treatise, the *Liber antiheresis*, written in the 1190s, already alludes to debates,[108] and he was described by William of Puylaurens as playing a leading role at the debate of Pamiers in 1207.[109] Although his next work, written around 1223, was about theology,

---

[105] *L'inquisition en Quercy: le registre des pénitences de Pierre Cellan, 1241–1242*, ed. J. Duvernoy (Castelnaud La Chapelle, 2001) – folio numbers provided for ease of location: fols. 219v, 234v, 243r, 263r, 296v.

[106] *Chronicle of William of Puylaurens*, ed. Sibly and Sibly, pp. 26–7.

[107] See the Albi *Summa auctoritatum* cited in n. 4 above, and *Heresies of the High Middle Ages*, ed. Wakefield and Evans, pp. 296–300.

[108] K.-V. Selge, 'Der *Liber antiheresis* des Durandus von Osca', in K.-V. Selge, *Die ersten Waldenser*, 2 vols., Arbeiten zur Kirchengeschichte 37 (Berlin, 1967), II, pp. xxi–xxii; see index-entry 'Dispute', I, 281.

[109] *Chronicle of William of Puylaurens*, ed. Sibly and Sibly, p. 24. The translation (he wrote 'a tract') makes a plural singular – 'Durandus de Osca [...] composuit contra hereticos quedam scripta'; Guillaume de Puylaurens, *Chronique*, ed. and trans. J. Duvernoy (Paris, 1976), p. 48.

the passing allusions he makes in it reveal his deep and detailed knowledge of the Good Men of Languedoc. He names some of the leading Good Men, lists the dioceses in which they were living, and talks about their economic activities. We have already cited his semantic precision. Durand had read their books, and he notes their use of the *Vision of Isaiah*. Quite extraordinary knowledge is displayed at one moment, where he bases a point on his observation of a word present in some of their manuscripts but erased in others.[110] What is most important is that Durand had in his hands a work of theology written by a Languedocian Cathar around 1220, the *Contradiction* (*Antifrasis*). Chapter after chapter of Durand's treatise uses this, not making short excerpts but quoting large sections. These can be extracted and put together to build a survival of a Languedocian Cathar treatise, incomplete but still consisting of about 5,000 words in Latin.[111] It is a text of extraordinary importance. It is entirely missing from *The War on Heresy*, and entirely ignored in its theory of the projection onto the heretics of Languedoc of ivory-tower dualism constructed by Cistercians and Paris theologians.

§9 *The War on Heresy and Church structure: the bishops*

The heretics talked of their church (*ecclesia*), they had a hierarchical structure, held councils, and had written theology and books containing their rituals. These are not prominent features in *The Corruption of Angels* and *The War on Heresy*, either absent or minimized as far as possible. Here we shall examine *The War on Heresy* and bishops.

The War on Heresy's view of Cathars and bishops has three stages:

i. Early on, there is no hierarchy among the Good Men.[112]
ii. By the 1220s there may have been moves towards a more hierarchical structure, as a way of coping with the terrible losses suffered during the early years of the Albigensian crusade.[113]
iii. There is an episcopal hierarchy by the second half of the thirteenth century.[114]

---

[110] *Une somme anti-cathare*, ed. Thouzellier, p. 91: 'in nonnullis hereticorum libris ipsum *hunc* scriptum vidimus. Sed quia multum est contra pravum intellectum eorum, postquam audierunt sibi obici, de suis codicibus abraserunt.'
[111] An excellent translation is provided in *Heresies of the High Middle Ages*, ed. Wakefield and Evans, pp. 494–510, but Durand's surrounding text is not translated. Since both texts emerged from hostile dialogues, they are more clearly understood when read together.
[112] *War*, p. 257.
[113] *War*, pp. 289–90: 'it is quite credible that [...] destruction of local bases [...] had driven the good men to adopt a supra-communal and more hierarchical organisation.'
[114] *War*, p. 322; http://rimoore.net/Chapter18.html.

Goodbye to Catharism?

How does *The War on Heresy* deal with the usually cited evidence?

The text bearing on the council at Saint-Félix in 1167 reveals an already elaborate episcopal structure. As we have seen, *The War on Heresy* removes this by declaring the document to be a forgery. Next, there are several references to the heretics' bishops in the decade 1200–10. Pedro II of Aragon met heretics and Waldensians in Carcassonne in 1204, referring in his letter to 'Bernard Simorre, bishop of the heretics' ('Bernardus Decimorra hereticorum episcopus'). *The War on Heresy* describes the meeting. It refers to good men and but does not mention the 'bishop of the heretics'.[115] Deponents interrogated by inquisitors recalled seeing the bishop of heretics Gaucelin, meeting him in the street in Toulouse around 1203, and seeing him maintaining his house openly in Saint-Paul-Cap-de-Joux around 1207.[116] Gaucelin is listed as a bishop by Borst[117] and in other standard histories. *The War on Heresy* does not mention him. Writing around 1223 and about heretics in the dioceses of Albi, Carcassonne and Toulouse, Durand of Huesca named several high-ranking heretics, including bishops – Sicard Cellarer, Gaucelin, Bernard of Simorre and Vigouroux of La Bouconne.[118] *The War on Heresy* does not mention Durand's comment.

Two examples of silence are worth further reflection. First of all, there is the deposition of a lay man, Raymond John of Albi, about events in 1225. Along with some heretics, he went to Pieusse, and there

> they entered the house of heretics. And they found there many heretics congregated, up to a hundred. Among them were Guilabert of Castres, and Pons Bernard, and Benedict of Termes, and Bertrand Martin of Tarabel, and Raymond Agulher, and Bonfils of Cassès, and others whom the same witness did not know. And there and then the heretics held a General Council. In this council the heretics of Razès petitioned and requested for a Bishop to be given to them. For ⟨they said⟩ it was not expedient for them that, when necessities arose among them, heretics had to come or be free to come from the Toulousain or Carcassès. For they did not know to whom they should be subject or obedient. And some of them would go to the heretics of the Toulousain, others to the heretics of the Carcassès. And so it was determined that a bishop should be granted to these heretics of Razès, and that a person should be taken from the Carcassès heretics and that they

---

[115] C. Compayré, *Études historiques et documents inédits sur l'albigeois, le castrais de l'ancien diocese de Lavaur* (Albi, 1841), doc. 54, pp. 227–8; *War*, p. 242.

[116] Paris, BnF, Collection Doat, MS 24, fol. 112v (a witness deposing in 1237): 'dicit se vidisse apud sanctum Paulum Gaucelinum episcopum haereticorum tenentem hospicium [...] publice in castro praedicato [...] triginta anni.' Also ibid., fol. 123r (a witness deposing in 1243): 'dum iret apud Tholosam invenit in via Gaucelinum episcopum haereticorum [...] quadraginta anni.' The references in this manuscript are used in all the modern deposition-based histories of the heretics.

[117] Borst, *Die Katharer*, p. 232.

[118] *Une somme anti-cathare*, ed. Thouzellier, pp. 76, 78.

should provide for this person the *consolamentum* and imposition of hands or ordination of the bishop of the Toulousan heretics. When this had been done they granted to the aforesaid heretics of Razès Benedict of Termes as bishop – Guilhabert of Castres, bishop of the Toulousan heretics, provided him the *consolamentum* and imposition of hands or ordination. When this had happened, they made Raymond Agulher Elder Son and Peter [*should be* Pons] Bernard Younger Son.

(Inde venerunt praefati haeretici, et ipse testis cum eis, apud Puissanum, et intraverunt domum haereticorum, et invenerunt ibi plures haeretici congregatos usque ad centum, inter quos erat Guilabertus de Castris, et Poncius Bernardi, et Benezet de Termino, et Bertrandus Martini de Taravello, et Raymundus Agulerii, et Bonus Filius de Casser, et alii quos ipse testis non cognovit. Et ibi tunc haeretici fecerunt concilium generale, in quo concilio haeretici de Redesio petierunt et postularunt episcopum sibi dari, dicentes quod non erat expediens eis quod pro necessitatibus suis adirent vel vacarent haeretici vel de Tholosano vel Carcassensi, quia nesciebant cui debebant esse submissi vel obedientes, et aliqui eorum ibant ad haereticos de Tholosano, et alii ad haereticos de Carcasses. Et ita fuit deffinitum quod episcopus concederetur eisdem haereticis de Redesio, et quod persona assumeretur de haereticis Carcassensibus et illi personae praestarent consolamentum et manus impositionem seu ordinationem episcopi haeretcorum Thoosanorum. Quo facto, concesserunt praefatis de Redesio Benedictum de Termino in episcopum, cui Guilabertus de Castris, haereticorum Tholosanorum episcopus, praestitit consolamentum et manus impositionem seu ordinationem. Hoc facto, fecerunt Ramundum Agulerium filium maiorem et Petrum Bernardum filium minorem.)[119]

This has been quoted at length because it is the most important evidence about the heretics' episcopal structure in these years. This General Council was tinkering with an existing episcopal structure, not inventing it. It is well known and prominent in deposition-based histories. *The War on Heresy* does not mention it.

Catholic and heretical bishops of Toulouse were at the centre of the story about one terrible event in 1234 that was recounted by William Pelhisson. A woman who was a believer in heretics was suffering from a serious illness in her son-in-law's house in Dry Elm Street in Toulouse, currently rue Romiguières. Advised that heretics were visiting the house to hereticate a sick woman, the Dominican bishop of Toulouse started off for the house. Someone warned the sick woman, 'Look, my lady, the lord bishop is coming to see you' ('Domina, videatis quod dominus episcopus venit ad vos'). But he did not have the opportunity to be more specific. She had peace of mind, because she had already been hereticated. And so she spoke freely about her beliefs,

---

[119] Paris, BnF, Collection Doat, MS 23, fols. 269v–270r.

Goodbye to Catharism?

as the chronicler wrote, 'perhaps because she had understood what had been said to mean that it was the bishop of heretics who was visiting her' ('quia illa intellexerat forsitan de episcopo hereticorum sibi dictum fuisse quod visitaret eam'). The Catholic bishop condemned her as a heretic, and she was carried out on the bed in which she lay, and burnt to death.[120]

The War on Heresy recounts the tale. The Catholic bishop

> hastened to the death-bed of an old woman rumoured to be a believer. In her fever she mistook him for the good man come to give her the last rites, and he secured her confession in time to have her 'carried on the bed in which she lay to the count's meadow and burned at once'.

Readers of *The War on Heresy* are going to be aghast at the horror of this terrible tale. But will they notice that *The War on Heresy* does not mention the heretic's *bishop*? He has been quietly disappeared from the story.[121]

Two sects have predominated in the historiography of heresy in the high Middle Ages – Catharism and Waldensianism – and, since the last few decades have seen some scholars trying to say 'Goodbye' to both sects, it is worth comparing them.[122] The leader in the new approach to Waldensianism, the Italian scholar of medieval religion Grado Merlo, has spent many years hauling its study into the modern world. Since the 1970s he has been taking a critical approach to the original evidence as texts emanating from clerical and inquisitorial culture, investigating historiographically the underlying assumptions of modern historians of the Waldensians, depicting the specifically local characteristics of Waldensian communities, and using his research in all these areas as the means whereby to scrutinize existing assumptions about Waldensian 'identity'.

Differences between the movement Merlo led and the Cathar demolition squad immediately emerge. Merlo was attempting an *aggiornamento* of the field, opening everything to question. Drawing on critical scholarship, especially German and Italian, he investigated *all* the evidence and historiography, doing this exhaustively and reporting both with scrupulous precision. His two books on Waldensian identity are ethically and academically unimpeachable.[123] Neither of them attempts to persuade at all costs, through rhetoric, artful omission and resort to 'it is a forgery' to remove adverse evidence. Further, Merlo was listening to other historians of the Waldensians, especially

---

[120] Translation: W. L. Wakefield, *Heresy, Crusade and Inquisition in Southern France, 1100–1250* (London, 1974), pp. 215–16. Latin: Guillaume Pelhisson, *Chronique (1229–1244)*, ed. and trans. J. Duvernoy (Paris, 1994), p. 62.

[121] *War*, p. 292.

[122] P. Biller, 'Goodbye to Waldensianism?', *Past and Present* 192 (2006), 3–33.

[123] *Valdesi e valdismi medievali: itinerari e proposte di ricerca* (Turin, 1984); *Valdesi e valdismi medievali II: Identità valdesi nella storia e storiografia: studi e discussioni* (Turin, 1991).

at decennial conferences.¹²⁴ As a result, over several decades encrustations were removed from 'medieval Waldensianism'. Scrubbed clean, it is now seen by Merlo as having possessed some unitary identity, alongside the local pluralism for which he coined the word 'Waldenianisms' ('Valdismi').¹²⁵ There has been a real advance in understanding.

The contrast with the debate about Cathars is not just ethical. Take the example of the last section of this paper, which went through pieces of evidence cited in *The War on Heresy* and showed that references to bishops were being omitted. Such work should not have to be done. If they were not busy with all this clear-up work, scholars would be free to devote their energy to investigating the interesting questions. In this case, for example, they could have been getting on with enquiry into what 'bishops' meant. In this way the study of Cathars could progress, as that of Waldensians undoubtedly has: but only if driven forward by very different scholarship.

---

[124] Aix-en-Provence 1988 and 1998, Milan 2008, the first and the third resulting in *Les vaudois des origines à leur fin (XIIe–XVIe siècles)*, ed. G. Audisio (Turin, 1990), and *Valdesi medievali: bilanci e prospettiva di ricerca*, ed. M. Benedetti (Turin, 2009). With a shorter interval, the series continued in 2015 at Torre Pellice with the conference 'Identità Valdese tra passato e presente'.

[125] G. G. Merlo, 'Itinerari storiografici dell'ultimo decennio', in *Valdesi medievali*, ed. Benedetti, pp. 11–21 (pp. 13–14).

Appendixes

Appendix A
Bernard Gui and names

Use of patristic terms when writing about contemporary heresy has been taken as a straightforward and incontrovertible sign that medieval Church writers mechanically projected patristic dualism onto contemporary heretics. Bernard Gui has come in for particular criticism here, as someone describing heretics of his time as Manichees.[1]

Names were one of Bernard's favourite topics. He wrote several treatises with *Nomina* in their titles.[2] In his treatise on inquisition he borrowed from an Italian inquisitor to discuss one point about naming heretics, the use of the past participle *perfectus* (perfected, finished) to denote the 'fully fledged' heretic in *any* sect.[3] Then, in his own practice as an inquisitor, he followed this, calling a fully fledged Waldensian a *Valdensis perfectus*.[4] His curiosity and fastidious semantic precision is reflected in the evidence of confessions made to him as an inquisitor. They call themselves 'Brothers', people call them 'The Poor of Lyons' and the Church persecutes them and calls them 'Waldensians': these are the distinctions of different groups naming a 'heretical' group in different ways which come up time and again in his inquisition records.[5] When dealing with members of another group, not Waldensian, his records are again littered with his nominal precision. 'He wanted to become a Good Christian [...] by which he understood he wanted to become a heretic' ('volebat fieri bonus Christianus [...] per quod ipse intellexit quod volebat fieri hereticus'), and 'They were of those "Good Men" who are called by others "heretics"' ('ipsi erant de illis bonis hominibus qui vocantur ab aliis heretici').[6]

Two very interesting points emerge from Bernard Gui's interest in names. The first is the contrast between his vocabulary when sentencing a fully fledged Waldensian and a fully fledged Good Man. When sentencing John Breyssan in 1315, he used specific names to define him. Breyssan had been

---

[1] Pegg, 'On Cathars, Albigenses and the Good Men of Languedoc', p. 184.
[2] T. Käppeli and A. Panella, *Scriptores Ordinis Praedicatorum Medii Aevi*, 4 vols. (Rome, 1970–93), I, 208, 224–5 (nos. 610, 635–6).
[3] Bernard Gui, *Practica inquisitionis* iv, ed. C. Douais (Paris, 1886), p. 218.
[4] For example, *Le livre des sentences*, ed. Pales-Gobilliard, II, 1046.
[5] Ibid., 1022, 1078, 1498, 1552.
[6] *Livre des sentences*, I, 816, 266.

in 'that heresy which is called the sect of the Waldensians or Poor of Lyons'.[7] When sentencing Amiel of Perles and Peter Autier in 1309 and 1310 he was able to refer to Church usage: 'the Roman Church calls them "heretics", and they were fully fledged and consoled ones.'[8] He then went on to use their dualist beliefs to define them. When dealing with these dualist heretics, then, he lacked a sect name that he was willing to use when acting as an inquisitor and sentencing two men to death.[9]

Peter Autier's sentence appears twice. The sentence itself is identical, with the words that have just been discussed. But the text is contained in two different texts, and the rubric changes. In Bernard's *Liber sententiarum*, the rubric is 'Sentence on Peter Autier, heretic' ('Sententia Petri Auterii heretici'), and in his *Practica inquisitionis*, the rubric is 'Form of a Sentence on some Manichee, a heretic' ('Forma sententie alicujus manichei heretici').[10] Never anywhere in his inquisition records does Bernard use the word Manichee. Why then does he use it in the *Practica inquisitionis*?

The solution appears when the question is recast. Given Bernard's fastidiousness about names, what light does his choice of name in this case cast on his view of his *Practica inquisitionis*? This work is usually taken to be a 'how to' manual to be used by inquisitors. But it is a square peg in the round hole. Manuals were short practical anthologies, of a size to fit in the pocket. Bernard's work was very long and elaborate. He was very unhappy with the provisions of the Council of Vienne restricting inquisitors, and his work was a long apologia for the inquisition of Languedoc, demonstrating how orderly and correct it was. It was a *Tractatus de practica* rather than a *Practica*, a *treatise* on what practice had been. As such, it was a discursive treatise, and it was in discursive treatises, especially works of theology like Aquinas's *Summa contra gentiles*, that the word Manichee was used to denote dualist heretics. This is the significance of Bernard's use of the word. He was providing the reader with a sign of the genre of text to which he wanted his treatise to belong: a discursive one.[11]

---

[7] Ibid., 952.
[8] Ibid., 326, 538.
[9] Bernard Gui would have understood the precise and sharp question posed by Julien Théry in the title of his article, 'L'hérésie des bons hommes: comment nommer l'hérésie non vaudoise ni béguine en Languedoc (XIIe–début XIVe siècle)', *Heresis* 36–7 (2002), 75–117.
[10] Bernard Gui, *Practica inquisitionis* iii, p. 129.
[11] This is developed further in my forthcoming article 'Bernard Gui, 15 Jan 1307'.

Appendix B
Heretics at Montségur: A Summary

Although fine modern accounts of Montségur can be found in the books of Wakefield, Barber and Roquebert, the fact that it is kept off centre-stage in *The Corruption of Angels* and *The War on Heresy* means that the reader of this chapter may find it useful to have a reminder of the key pieces of evidence.

The first stage in Montségur's use by the heretics was planned around 1204–6. When testifying in 1246 Peter William D'Arvigna, co-lord of Dun, said that forty years earlier 'he saw at Mirepoix a great gathering of heretics, up to six hundred heretics who had come there to decide some question which the heretics were dealing with among themselves'.[1] This huge heretics' council was almost certainly connected with what was stated by the co-lord of Montségur, Raymond of Péreille, deposing in 1244. Forty years earlier 'he rebuilt the castle of Montségur, which had previously been in ruins, at the behest and the requests of Raymond of Mirepoix and Raymond Blasquo and other heretics'.[2]

The second stage was its relaunching in 1232. The details were given by Berengar of Lavelanet, deposing in 1244:

> He saw that Guilhabert of Castres, bishop of heretics, and Bernard of Lamothe, Elder Son, and John Cambiaire, ⟨Younger⟩ Son, Vigoroux[3] of La Bouconne, Elder Son of the heretics of the Agennais, and Pons Guilabert, deacon of the heretics of Vilamur, and Tento, bishop of the heretics of the Agennais, and many other heretics, went into the *castrum* of Montségur and petitioned and supplicated Raymond of Péreille, former Lord of said *castrum*, to receive heretics within the *castrum* of Montségur to this end, that the Church of the heretics could have its residence and headquarters in the said *castrum*, and could send out from there and protect its preachers.[4]

---

[1] 'Vidit apud Mirapicem magnam congregationem haereticorum, usque ad sexcentos haereticos, qui venerant ibi pro quadam quaestione determinanda, quam faciebant haeretici inter se'; Paris, BnF, Collection Doat, MS 24, fols. 240v–241r.

[2] 'Ad instantiam et ad praeces Raimundi Blasquo et aliorum haereticorum rehedificavit castrum Montis Securi, quod antea destructum extiterat'; Paris, BnF, Collection Doat, MS 22, fol. 217v.

[3] The manuscript's 'Hugonis' (for Hugh) is emended here to 'Vigorosus' (Vigoroux).

[4] 'Dicit se vidisse quod Guilabertus de Castris, episcopus haereticorum, et Bernardus de Motta, filius maior, et Johannes Cambiaire, filius ⟨junior⟩, Hugonis de la Bacona, filius

Heretics at Montségur: A Summary

Montségur was the ecclesiastical headquarters of the heretics. What we are told about this safe haven provides our clearest glimpse of the through-flow of ordinations and the system of succession, as described by witnesses interrogated about life within the castle. Here, for example, is Raymond of Péreille, co-lord of Montségur:

> he received and maintained at Montségur Gaucelin, bishop of the Tolousan heretics, and Guilabert of Castres who succeeded him in the episcopate of the heretics of Toulouse, and John Cambiaire and Bertrand Martin, bishops of the heretics, who succeeded similarly.[5]

And Berengar of Lavelanet:

> the aforesaid heretics made their ordinations [*ordinationes*] there. They ordained John Cambiaire ⟨Younger⟩ Son, and Bernard Bonafos deacon of Toulouse, and Tento bishop of the heretics of Agennais, and they made Raymond of Montouty, whom they called Raymond Donat, deacon of heretics.[6]

The final stage in Montségur's history was its siege and eventual capture, which took place from May 1243 to March 1244. This was being followed by fellow dualist heretics in northern Italy, and at the highest level, as we learn from Imbert of Salles, deposing in 1244:

> John Reg of Saint-Paul-Cap-de-Joux entered Montségur with a letter from the bishop of the heretics of Cremona, and gave it to Bertrand Martin, bishop of the heretics of Toulouse. And the letter said that the Church of the

---

maior haereticorum Agennensium, et Poncius Guilaberti, diachonus haereticorum de Vilamur, et Tento, episcopus haereticorum Agennensium, et multi alii haeretici venerunt in castrum Montis Securi. Et postulaverunt, et postulaverunt [*sic*], et supplicaverunt Ramundo de Perella, domino olim dicti castri, quod receptaret dictos haereticos infra castrum Montis Securi, ad hoc ut in ipso castro posset ecclesia haereticorum habere domicilium et caput, et inde posset transmittere et deffendere praedicatores suos'; Paris, BnF, Collection Doat, MS 24, fols. 43v–44r.

5 'Dicit se receptasse et tenuisse apud Montem Securum Gaucelinum, episcopum haereticorum Tholosanorum, et Guilabertum de Castris, qui successit ei in episcopatu haereticorum de Tholosa, et Johannem Cambiaire et Bertrandum Martini, episcopos haereticorum, qui successerunt similiter'; Paris, BnF, Collection Doat, MS 22, fols. 217v–218r.

6 'Praedicti haeretici fecerunt ibi ordinationes suas. Ordinaverunt Johannem Cambiaire, et [*sic*] filium ⟨juniorem⟩, et Bernardum Bonafos, diachonum de Tholosa, et Tento, episcopum haereticorum Agennensium, et Ramundum de Montota, quem vocaverunt Ramundum Donatum, fecerunt diaconum haereticorum'; Paris, BnF, Collection Doat, MS 24, fol. 44v.

heretics of Cremona was in tranquillity and peace, and that Bertrand Martin should send two of his brother heretics, through whom he [Bertrand] could inform him [the bishop of the heretics of Cremona] about the state they were in.[7]

---

[7] 'Johannes Reg de Sancto Paulo de Cadaious intravit castrum Montis Securi cum litteris episcopi haereticorum de Cremona, et dedit eas Bertrando Martino, episcopo haereticorum de Tholosa. Et in litteris continebatur quod ecclesia haerticorum de Cremona erat in tranquillitate et in pace, et quod Bertrandus Martini mitteret episcopo de Cremona duos de fratribus suis haereticis, per quos redderet eum certum de statu suo'; Paris, BnF, Collection Doat, MS 24, fols. 171v–172r. Note the later instance of French and Italian Cathar bishops jointly administering a *consolamentum*, given in *Inquisitors and Heretics*, ed. Biller, Bruschi and Sneddon p. 865.

Appendix C
Translations of Geoffrey of Auxerre and Geoffrey of Vigeois

Two mistranslations of texts need attention.[1]

I. Geoffrey of Auxerre

Geoffrey of Auxerre wrote a letter about Bernard of Clairvaux's mission to Languedoc in 1145. It is clear Bernard was preaching against the heretic Henry of Lausanne. What is at issue is whether he was preaching against another group of heretics as well, and if he was, what sort of heretics they were. At a point where the letter has been referring to Henry, it moves onto the city of Toulouse. This sentence follows. Punctuation and capitalization are modern, and alterable. We provide the text as presented by Herbert Grundmann, first of all in 1935 in his *Religiöse Bewegungen*, and then repeated in later editions of this work and ultimately its English translation.

> Paucos quidem habebat civitas illa [Toulouse], qui heretico faverent; de Textoribus, quos Arrianos ipsi nominant, nonnullos; ex his vero, qui favebant heresi illi, plurimi erant et maximi civitatis illius.[2]

This is the translation in *The Birth of Popular Heresy*:[3]

> There were only a few in the city who favoured the heresy, some of the weavers [*de textoribus*], whom they called *Ariani*. A great many of these supported the heresy in the city, including some of its most prominent citizens.

This translation misses the distinction between 'heretic' and 'heresy', and the contrast between the 'few' who favoured the heretic and the 'not few' who favoured the *Textores*. Literally:

> Indeed, that city [Toulouse] had few who favoured the heretic [Henry]; ⟨it had⟩ not a few of the Weavers, whom they call 'Arians'; and, in fact, of

---

[1] I owe a debt to Shelagh Sneddon at every point to do with the Latin discussed in this appendix.
[2] Grundmann, *Religious Movements*, pp. 260–1 n. 35.
[3] R. I. Moore, *The Birth of Popular Heresy* (London, 1975), p. 43.

those who favoured that heresy many were also the greatest men in that city.

Grundmann's part translation part paraphrase makes it clear:

> The heretic Henry had few followers in Toulouse; but there were some heretics, who are called 'Textores' by us, but 'Arriani' in Provence, in Toulouse; and these heretics had very many adherents, even among the most important residents.

The letter clearly distinguishes two groups: a small group containing the few who were supporters of the heretic Henry; and another group containing some, many of them the elite of the city, who were supporters of the heresy of the Weavers, locally known as 'Arians'. This patristic label had come to mean 'extreme heretics'. What of 'Weavers'? Eckbert of Schönau wrote of this semantic usage, referring to heretics thus: '"Piphles", and in France "Tisserands", because of their connection with weaving'.[4] The correct translation and Grundmann's paraphrase allow investigation of the possibility that this passage in the letter attests large and important support for 'Cathars' in Toulouse in 1145, while the mistranslation disseminated by *The Birth of Popular Heresy* and relied upon by *The War on Heresy* forecloses this.

II. Geoffrey of Vigeois

The tradition and development of a Cistercian view of heretics is an important strand in *The War on Heresy*, and one link in this is Geoffrey of Vigeois's chronicle, containing a copy of a lost letter by Henri of Marcy, which recounts the views of heretics.[5] The numbers in square brackets refer to sections in Geoffrey's text and the translation provided below.

First, *The War on Heresy*'s presentation. The letter is introduced as having described the heresy 'as rejecting, predictably enough, the teaching of the Roman Church on the sacrifice of the Mass, the baptism of infants, marriage and the other sacraments' [see 2 below]. Then we read how the letter 'quotes them as saying that it taught that':

> Satan, the great Lucifer, who because of his pride and wickedness had fallen from the throne of the good angels, is the creator of heaven and earth, of all things visible and invisible, and of the evil spirits.[6] It was he who had given the law of Moses [3].

---

[4] *War* keeps these texts apart: Geoffrey on p. 121, Eckbert on p. 168.
[5] *Recueil des historiens des Gaules et de France*, ed. M. Bouquet et al., 24 vols., 2nd edn (Paris, 1840–1904), XII, 448; *War*, pp. 217–18.
[6] *War*'s compression of the Latin text at this point is understandable as a way of dealing with an apparently garbled statement about the heretics' views of Satan.

Christ had only the appearance of humanity; he did not experience hunger, thirst or other bodily needs; he did not undergo the passion, was not crucified, did not die and has not risen again. Everything claimed by the Gospels and the apostles is fantasy [1].

Finally, 'Raymond and Bernard also claimed that the heretics indulged in sexual orgies and justified abortion and infanticide on the grounds that giving life was the work of the devil' [4].

In the direct translation *The War on Heresy* changes the sequence of points to [3] then [1]. The translation begins as a fairly accurate but not literal rendering. It compresses [3] in order to avoid the problem of the garbled proposition about belief in Satan as creator. The last sentence of [1] ('Everything claimed …') is wrong. The final paraphrase [4] garbles what Geoffrey wrote.

The War on Heresy is right to draw attention to Geoffrey. Both text and a more literal translation are provided below.

Translation	Geoffrey of Viegois
They confessed that … [1] Christ was not born a true man, nor did he eat, or drink, or truly experience anything else in the way of human function or need. They did not believe that he suffered, was crucified, died, [and] rose again. But they say that everything the Gospels and the apostles assert about Christ is illusory.	Confessi sunt … [1] Christum natum haud verum fuisse hominem, nec comedisse aut bibisse, aut aliud humanae actionis aut necessitatis in veritate sustinuisse; passum, crucifixum, mortuum, surrexisse non credunt; sed omnia quae evangelia seu apostoli de Christo asserunt, fantastica dicunt.
[2] They totally reject and condemn what the sacrosanct Roman Church has instituted and all Catholics believe, receive and observe about the sacrifice of the altar, the baptism of babies, marriages and other sacraments and divine offices.	[2] Quod de sacrificio altaris, baptismate parvulorum, conjugiis aliisque sacramentis et divinis officiis sacrosancta Romana Ecclesia constituit et universitas Catholicorum credit, recipit et servat, omnino reprobant et condemnant.

[3] They professed that Satan, the great Lucifer, who fell from the throne of the good angels on account of his pride and wickedness, was the creator of heaven and earth and all things visible and invisible,[7] [and] was the creator and Prince and God of the evil spirits, and they assert that he gave the law to Moses.	[3] Sathanum magnum Luciferum, qui propter elevationem et nequitiam suam de throno bonorum cecidit angelorum, creatorem coeli et terrae omniumque visibilium et invisibilium, spirituum malorum creatorem et Principem et Deum esse profitebantur, ipsumque legem Moysi dedisse asseverant.
[4] They say that in the carnal intercourse of any male and any female the misdeed is the same, whether parents, or brothers, or common mothers,[8] or in whatever [relation] of consanguinity or affinity the women are [with the men]. The women among them who conceive kill the foetus. However it was said that this was avoided by the more skilled among them; although evidently many among them will have conceived, offspring does not appear.	[4] In carnali consuetudine cujuslibet maris et foeminae, sive parentes, sive fratres, sive communes matres, aut cujuslibet consanguinitatis vel affinitatis mulieres existant, par dicunt esse delictum. Mulieres quae inter eos concipiunt, foetus interimunt: tamen dicebatur a peritioribus eorum id evitari: cum manifeste inter illas multae conceperint, proles non comparet.

---

[7] The text is probably corrupt at this point.
[8] The explanation here (sex between a man and a women who have a mother but not father in common) casts light retrospectively on 'whether parents or brothers'. Although the phrase is too compressed for clarity, the author is clearly driving at heterosexual sex normally regarded as illicit because of close family relationship.

Index

Contributors have used English, French, and Occitan forms of name for medieval people; the index reflects these variant forms, but provides cross-references where appropriate

Abbé, J.-L., 84 n.13
Acerbi, A., 176 n.80
Ad abolendam, papal bull (1184), 231, 236
Ad extirpanda, papal bull (1252), 98
Adam, 120
Adcock, C. S., 22 n.4
Adhemar (Adémar) of Chabannes, 133, 134
adoration/*adoratio,* 10, 11, 13, 39–40, 91, 285, 288 *see also melioramentum, melhoramen*
aparelhamen/apparellamentum, 45
Agen, 142, 144, 145
Agenais, 46, 145, 272
Agout, 96 n.45
Agout, river, 80
Agreement of Belino Polje, 149
Aimergarda de Mazerolles, 11
Aitzetmüller, R., 162 n.28
Aix-en-Provence, 304
Alan of Lille, OCist, 59, 64 n.28, 193, 219 n.39, 232, 243 n.3, 295, 296, 297
'Albanenses', 145, 150, 190 n.29, 195 n.58, 199 and n.72, 202, 204 and n.92, 205 and n.94, 206, 256
Alberic of Ostia, Cardinal and legate, 211
Albi, Albigeois, 4, 31, 35, 34, 63, 65, 79, 80, 83, 84, 85, 86, 87, 88, 91, 94, 95, 96, 102, 103, 104, 105 and n.80, 106 and nn.80, 81, 107 n.82, 108, 109, 110 and n.88, 142, 144, 150, 211, 231, 256, 275 and n.4, 292, 294, 299 n.107, 301
'Albigenses'/Albigensians, 22, 29, 30, 31, 34, 50, 57, 99, 101, 112, 113, 118, 125, 129, 134, 144, 193, 211, 239, 244, 256, 260, 269, 275 and n.5, 282, 284, 289, 296, 305
Albigensian Crusade (1209–1229), 3, 4, 11, 27, 30 and n.42, 31 and n.43,
38, 45, 49, 64 n.25, 71, 81, 82, 103, 113 n.2, 125, 129, 135, 142 n.45, 144, 230, 231, 234, 236, 237, 240, 241, 247, 257, 258, 261 267, 269, 272, 282, 298, 300
crusaders, 27, 30, 34, 40, 235, 239, 256, 258, 270, 279
Alessandria, 190 n.29
Alexander II, Pope, 136
Alexander III, Pope, 97, 100, 231, 292
Alexander IV, Pope, 186, 201
Alexius I Emperor, 132
Alphandéry, P. D., 34 and n.61
Amalarius of Metz, 59
Amalfi, 132
Amargier, P.-A., 63 n.24
Ambrose, 206
Amiel of Perles, 306
Amselle, J.-L., 2 and n.6
Anatolia, 153, 155
Andersen, F., 170 n.63, 171 n.66
Andrew II, King of Hungary, 149
Angelov, B. S., 157 n.15, 162 n.29, 167 n.47
Angelov, D., 160 n.20
Angelovska-Panova, M., 273 n.38
angels, 64, 167, 169, 170, 171, 172, 181, 311, 313
Angold, M., 155 nn.11, 12
Anna Comnena, 140 n.36, 154 n.7
Alexiad, 140 n.36, 154 n.7
Anonymous of Laon, 220
Anonymous of Passau, 186, 220
Anselm of Alessandria, OP, inquisitor, 139, 140, 145, 146, 149, 186 and n.6, 186, 189, 190, 191, 192, 194, 195, 196 n.62, 199, 202, 203 and n.87, 212, 218 and n.35, 289
Antić, V., 161 n.22, 24 25, 162 n.26
anti-clericalism, 14, 82–3, 102
Antioch, 127

Index

apocryphal texts, 147, 156, 157, 159, 160, 161, 162, 163, 164, 165, 166, 167, 172, 173
apostolic life (apostolic poverty, evangelical poverty), 23, 89, 95, 115, 260, 263, 265, 266
Aragon, 46 n.106, 144
Ardorel, Cistercian abbey, 248
Arialdus, Patarene leader, 136
Arians, 29, 247, 310, 311
Ariège, 35
aristocrats, heretics among, 10, 108, 122, 311
Arles, 239
Armenia, 152, 153, 155, 156
Armitage, D., 30 n.40
Arnalda de la Mota, of Lamothe, 117
Arnaldus de Castillo, 120
Arnaldus Sarralhier, 121
Arnold Garner, 251
Arnold, J. H., 5, 36 and n.66, 42 n.90, 56 n.10, 59 n.15, 63 n.24, 67 n.36, 71 n.40, 77 n.53, 85 n.15, 92 n.32, 95 n.42, 101 n.66, 198 n.68, 271 n.33, 274, 283 n.35
Arnold Velh, 251
Arnulf, historian of Milan, 136
Arras, 58, 261
asceticism, 28, 89, 133, 154, 155
Asia Minor, 155, 242
Audisio, G., 100, 118, 304
Augustine of Hippo, St., 61, 62, 63, 77, 229, 235 and n.22, 263, 264, 295
 On Heresies 64 and n.26, 133, 135
Aurimonde of Moissac, 249, 250
Auxerre, 236, 237
Ava of Baziège, heretic, 5, 41, 44, 123–7
Avignonet, 47
Ax, 13
Aymare of Montlauzun, 250
Aymerici, G., 121 n.48

'Bagnolenses', Cathars of Mantua, 150, 206
Baietto, L., 14 n.21
Balkans, 1, 2, 6, 16, 56 n.9, 112, 131 n.2, 144, 153, 155
Ban Kulin, 149, 153
Banat, 153
baptism
 Bogomil beliefs about, 132
 Cathar beliefs about, 43, 67 n.34, 134, 135, 139, 195, 230, 247, 253, 283, 291, 293, 311, 312
Barber, M., 1 n.1, 203 n.89, 237 n.32, 240 n.48, 242 n.2, 264 n.18, 277, 281 n.27, 291 n.62, 307
Baronio, C., 152 n.2
Barth, F., 8 n.11
Bartholomaeus de Posaca, 122
Bartholomew of Carcassonne, 145
Basil, Bogomil leader, 132
Basil II, Emperor, 132
Baziège family, 5, 123–7
Baziège village 41 and n.88, 123–7, 129
Beauvais, 33
Becker, H., 81
Becquet, J., 100 n.60
beguines, 110, 115
Begunov, I., 160 n.20, 161 n.26, 168 n.50
Bélibaste, G., 176 n.80
Benad, M., 86 n.18
Benedetti, M., 185 n.1, 186 nn.2, 7, 188 nn.14, 15, 18, 189 n.21, 24, 190 n.26, 198 n.69, 200 n.75, 206 n.99, 304 n.124
Benedict d'Alignan, OSB, Bishop of Marseille, 63, 64, 65, 246
Benedict of Termes, Cathar Bishop, 301, 302
Beneit Ioculator, 121
Benoist, J., 152 and n.3, 156 n.13
Bentevenga de Bentivegni, OFM, Cardinal and apostolic penitentiary, 99
Berengar of Lavelanet, 307, 308
Bérenguier Azémar, 95
Bergamo, 206
Bériac, F., 287 n.47
Berman, C., 28 n.33, 71 and n.41
Bernard Bonafos, Cathar deacon, 308
Bernard de Combret, 102, 103
Bernard de Montmirat, 98
Bernard de Simorra, Cathar Bishop, 144, 301
Bernard Délicieux, OFM, 109, 110
Bernard Gui, OP, inquisitor, 42, n.93, 62, 63, 101 n.64, 116, 187 and n.8, 193, 194 n.51, 196 n.63, 213 and nn.14, 17, 223, n.56, 255, 284, 305–6
Bernard Manhe, 249
Bernard of Castanet, Bishop of Albi, 79, 83, 84, 85, 86, 102, 103, 104, 105, 106, 107, 108, 109, 110

Index

Bernard of Caux, OP, inquisitor, 37, 38 and n.79, 39, 41, 47, 116, 250, 251, 258, 283

Bernard of Clairvaux, OCist, St., 61, 134, 233, 235 and n.22, 260, 262–3, 291, 295, 296, 310

Bernard of Fontcaude, OPraem, 219

Bernard of Lamothe, Cathar Bishop, 66 n.32, 307

Bernard of Lasmartres, 250

Bernard Raymond, Cathar Bishop (later Canon of Toulouse), 142, 143, 293

Bernardus Tessender, 120

Bertran de Montagut, 90

Bertrand Aleman, 12

Bertrand Martin, Cathar Bishop, 301, 308 and n.5, 309 and n.7

Besse, G., 46, 71, 141, 142, 253

Beziérs, Council of (1232), 198

Bianchi, U., 166 n.43

Bible, 164, 299
  evangelical message, 5, 15, 89
  Genesis, Book of, 156, 172, 178, 179
  Gospel of St. John, 131–2
  heretical rejection of Old Testament, 1, 6, 64, 131, 137, 149, 182, 230
  in Occitan, 147
  New Testament, 1, 59, 64, 131, 157, 161, 173, 179, 182, 230, 312

Biget, J.-L., 2 n.2, 31 n.43, 57 and n.11, 78, 79 n.1, 81 and n.8, 83 and n.11, 84 and n.13, 85 n.14, 86 nn.16, 17, 89 n.23, 90 n.24, 91 n.28, 94 nn.36, 38, 39, 95 nn.41, 42, 96 nn.45, 46, 101 n.66, 103 and nn.69, 70, 71, 104 nn.74, 76, 105 n.78, 108 nn.83, 84, 110 nn.87, 91, 92, 117 n.22, 242 and n.1, 245 nn.11, 12, 262 nn.12, 13, 273, 280

Biller, P., 2 n.5, 5 and n.9, 7 n.10, 18 n.41, 19 n.44, 23 n.6, 24 n.12, 25 and n.18, 35, 36 nn.67, 69, 37 n.72, 42 and nn.90, 93, 43 n.97, 46 n.106, 47 n.110, 48 and n.114, 50 and nn.121, 122, 123, 51 n.125, 60 nn.17, 18, 66 n.31, 67 n.36, 72 n.43, 84 n.12, 85–6 n.15, 92 nn.29, 32, 101 n.66, 103 n.70, 118 nn.24, 29, 173 n.74, 174 n.76, 176 nn.81, 82, 186 n.4, 191 n.36, 193 n.43, 208 n.2, 210 n.6, 213 and n.16, 214 n.18, 215 n.24, 216 n.25, 219 n.39, 220 nn.41, 42, 221 n.45, 222 n.50, 231 n.4, 233 n.9, 236 n.30, 243 n.3, 244 n.8, 253 n.53, 257 n.1, 264 and n.18, 267, 268 n.25, 270, 271, 272 n.37, 273, 282 n.30, 283 n.35, 284 n.37, 285 n.40, 290 n.57, 297 n.96, 303 n.122, 309 n.7

birth control, Church condemnation and prevention of, 92, 106

Bisson, T. N., 10 and n.18, 73 and n.46

Blagoev, D., 153 n.5

Blagoev, N. P., 153 n.4

Bogomilism, 1, 2 and n.5, 32, 47 and n.110, 48 n.111, 56, 112, 128 n.75, 131–8, 140, 142, 145, 148–150, 152–76, 180, 211, 230, 258, 261, 288–91
  Apocryphon 156, 163, 164, 166, 171–2, 290
  Christology 163, 167, 172
  cosmology of multiple heavens, 169 and n.56, 170, 171, 172, 181
  diabology, 155, 163, 166, 167, 168, 169
  Ordo, 140–1, 144–5, 145–6
  rejection of sacraments, 131, 135, 137
  similarity to Catharism, 72

Bologna, 201, 203, 223, university of 213, 232, Dominican *studium* 221 and n.47

Bonacursus of Milan, 193, 209

Bonfils of Cassès, Cathar deacon, 301

Boniface VIII, Pope, 74, 82

Bonn, 135, 264

books and texts:
  Apocalypse of Abraham, 158 and n.17, 170, 171, 172
  Apocryphal Old Testament, 159
  Battle Between Archangel Michael and Satanael, 163, 166–72
  Book of the Secrets of Enoch, 157–8
  Cathar Ritual, 36, 147, 148 and n.72, 253, 254, 290–1 and n.62
  Contradiction, 300
  De heresi Catharorum in Lombardia, 139, 206
  Dogmatic Panoply/Panoplia Dogmatica, 132, 168 n.51, 170, 175 *see also* Euthymios Zigabenos
  Greek Apocalypse of Baruch, 158–9 and n.19, 168, 170, 171, 172
  Interrogatio Iohannis/Secret Book from Bulgaria, 48, 146, 147, 156 and

316

Index

n.13, 163, 166, 170, 171, 172, 176, 181, 284, 290
Liber de duobus principiis, 178, 184, 193–4, 216–17, 252–3 *see also* John of Lugio
Martyrdom and Ascension of Isaiah, 147, 158–9 and n.18
Martyrdom of St. Paul and St. Juliana, 168
Questions of Bartholomew, 168 and n.52, 169, 171, 172
Sea of Tiberias, 163, 166, 170, 171, 172
Secret Book of the Heretics of Concorezzo, 146, 181
Sermon against the Bogomils for the Sunday of All Saints, 169
Summa adversus catharos et valdenses, 6, 208–28 *passim*, *see also* Moneta of Cremona
Summa de Catharis et Pauperibus de Lugduno, 139, 185–207 *passim*, 209 *see also* Ranier Sacconi
summae auctoritatum, 225, 226, 299
Tractatus de Hereticis, 139 *see also* Anselm of Alessandria
Vision of Isaiah, 158–9 and n.18, 163, 169, 170, 171, 172, 176 and n.80, 216, 290, 300
Borst, A., 29 and nn.36, 37, 38, 30 and n.39, 47 n.110, 56 n.9, 113 and n.3, 148 and n.70, 210 n.6, 211 and nn.9, 11, 213 n.15, 214 n.20, 216 n.28, 222, 245, 275–6, 278, 280, 281, 289 n.50, 301 and n.117
Bose, M., 54 n.5
Bosnia, 145, 149, 150
Bossuet, J. B., Bishop of Meaux, 152 and nn.2, 3
Bourdieu, P., 17 n.40, 92 and n.30
Boureau, A., 99 n.54
Bourges, 31
Bourin, M., 10 n.16, 39 n.82, 57, 99 n.57, 100 n.58
Bozóky, E., 147 n.64, 156 n.13, 174 n.76, 176 n.80, 290 n.58
bread
  Cathar blessing of, 67, 90
  Cathar communal eating of, 120
Brescia, 14, 206
Brody, S. N., 287 and n.46
Broeckx, E., 34 n.63
Brooke, C. N. L., 183, 220 n.40

Brown, E. A. R., 26 n.25
Brown, P., 43 n.95
Brown, W. C., 8 n.11
Brungs, A., 222 n.49
Brunn, U., 7 n.10, 61 n.21, 81 n.6, 101 and n.65, 112 and n.1, 208 n.2, 210 n.6, 243 n.5, 262 n.15, 263, 264 nn.17, 20, 267 and n.22, 268, 269
Bruno de Renneville, 47
Bruschi, C., 18 n.41, 36 and n.66, 37 n.71, 45 nn.102, 103, 48 and n.114, 66 n.31, 67 n.36, 85–86 n.15, 101 n.66, 103 n.70, 176 n.79, 186 n.4, 190 nn.27, 29, 191 n.36, 193 nn.43, 44, 48, 198 n.69, 201 n.80, 203 n.89, 219 n.39, 282 n.30, 285 n.40, 309 n.7
Buddha, 34
Buddhism, 22
Bueno, I., 81 n.6, 101 n.66
Bulgaria, 32, 131, 140, 143, 144, 145, 146, 149 n.76, 150, 153, 155 n.10, 156, 157 n.14, 162, 168 n.49, 181, 190 and n.26, 230, 275 and n.5, 286, 289 and n.50, 290
  debate about *Vulgaria* as a possible reading for, 18–19 and n.43, 48 and n.114, 72 n.43, 284
Bulgarian Empire, 132
Bulgarian missionaries, 16, 48
Bulgarian *Ordo*, 140, 145, 146
Bulgarian sect 180
Bulgars, 274, 275, 289
Burnham, L. A., 73 n.45
Burrus, V., 57 n.12
Buslaev, F. I., 160 n.21
Byzantium, 48, 131, 132, 133, 138, 145, 150, 152, 153, 155, 156, 163, 165, 175, 181, 230, 259, 260
  Bogomilism, origins of, 47, 132, 134, 135, 136
  demonology, 155
  dualism, 140, 144
  heresiarch, heresiology, 46, 175
  mysticism, 155
  sources, 138, 157, 259
  theology 156
  see also Constantinople

Cabaret, 144
caena, specific ritual of the Waldensians 119, 120, 122
  see also Holy Supper

317

Index

Cahors, 249
Caldwell Ames, C., 28 n.33, 49 and n.116, 52 n.127, 187 n.10, 191 n.32, 215 n.24, 224 n.60, 226 nn.70, 71
Callahan, D. F., 134 n.12
Callixtus II, Pope, 20
Calvin, John, 95
Cameron, A., 154 n.7, 175 n.77
Campi, P. M., 189 n.23
Candeil, Cistercian abbey, 248
Cantarella, G. M., 20 n.45
Canterbury, 117, 293 n.76
Capetians, 111
Capitani, O., 1 n.1, 20 n.46
Carcassès, 35, 45, 46, 301, 302
Carcassonne, 59 n.16, 63, 65, 66 n.32, 86, 93 n.33, 97 n.48, 99, 107, 109, 110, 141, 142, 143, 144, 146, 150, 156 n.13, 171, 186 n.4, 260, 275 and n.3, 290, 292 n.73, 301
Carolingians 73
  empire, 69, 73
Caseneuve, M., 141
Cassidy-Welch, M., 45 n.102
Castres, 79, 80, 100 n.61
Catalonia, 10, 176
Cathars
  as a hierarchical organisation, 40–1, 260–1, 269–70, 300–1
  beliefs, *see* creation, extreme unction, baptism
  Cathar bishops, 45, 46, 47, 66 and n.32, 72, 127–9, 134, 138 n.26, 139–46, 180 and n.15, 188 and n.13, 189, 190 n.25, 194, 198, 217, 230, 263, 270, 274, 282, 286, 290, 293, 300–4, 307–9 *see also individually named people*
  Cathar confession, 199
  churches, 47, 57, 142, 190 n.29, 195 n.58, 280, 300, 308 n.4, 309 n.7
  conventicula, 97 n.49
  deacons, 45, 66 n.32, 139, 195 n.58, 230, 307, 308 *and individually named people*
  dioceses, 46, 63, 66, 72, 230, 275, 301
  Ordo, 139, 140
  perfects, 11, 42 and n.94, 57, 114 and n.6, 145 n.57, 150, 230, 237, 247, 248 n.23, 275 n.6, 284, 305
  problem of the existence and circulation of Cathar texts, 3, 5, 6, 21–2, 30, 36, 37, 42, 52, 72, 75–6, 85, 131–84, 289–90
  problems with the term, 1, 4, 7, 28–31, 54–5, 101, 135–6, 138, 152, 196, 215, 227, 229–32, 240, 242–56, 260, 268, 274, 277
  refusal to eat meat, eggs, or dairy products, 64, 87, 89, 120, 135, 179 n.9, 180 n.13, 230, 249
  rejection of sacraments, 83, 91 and n.28, 198, 230, 263, 293, 311, 312
  rejection of the Holy Cross, 137
  rite/sacrament of initiation, 139, 147–8, 148–9, 240
  rituals, *see* adoration, *apparellamentum, consolamentum, melioramentum, cortesia,* courtliness, genuflection
  sacraments, 198
  see also 'Albanenses', 'Albigenses', 'Bagnolenses'
Caturcinus de la Vernha, 120
Caucasus, 154
celibacy of the clergy, 136
Cessi, R., 18 n.43
Chabot, J.-D., 127 nn.72, 73
Chapman, A., 37 n.73
Charles, R. H., 147 n.65
Chassanion, J., 151 n.1
Chénon, É., 236 n.30
Cheyette, F. L., 41 nn.88, 89, 124 n.62, 126 n.68
Chiffoleau, J., 82 n.10, 84 n.13, 280
Chiu, H., 44 and n.98, 243 n.3, 295 n.87, 297 n.100
Christendom, 23, 25 n.20, 30, 44, 47, 48, 61, 81, 173, 174, 175, 176, 189, 225, 244, 261, 272, 282, 294
Christian discourse on heresy, 13, 58, 61, 62
Cistercians, 5, 38, 71, 225, 255, 256, 262, 274, 288, 294, 295, 296, 298, 300
  preaching 41, 44, 125, 295
  views on heresy, 35, 225, 311
Cîteaux, Cistercian abbey, 143, 261, 293 n.76
Clairvaux, Cistercian abbey, 247
Clédat, L., 36 n.71, 148 n.69, 253 nn.53, 54, 254
Clement V, Pope, 109, 110
clerical hierarchy, 22, 115
clericalism, protest against, 82, 83, 94, 102, 106, 109, 110, 111

318

Index

Clericis laicos, papal bull (1296), 82
Coffey, J., 37 n.73
Cohn, N., 55 and n.8
Cole, A., 54 n.5
Colin, A., 176 n.80
Cologne, 101, 104, 134, 135, 138, 262, 263, 264
Collingwood, R. G., 23 n.9
Collinson, P., 54 and n.4
Compayré, C., 301 n.115
Concorezzo, 146, 147, 150, 290 and n.58
confession, sacrament of, 105, 185 n.1, 230
Confucianism, 22
consolamentum (*consolamen, consolament*), 34, 40, 60, 86, 91, 94, 97, 139, 145, 148, 148, 180, 195, 195, 236, 237, 240, 253, 277, 283, 292, 309
Conrad of Marburg, 262
Conrad of Porto, OCist, Cardinal, legate, 145, 289
Constable, G., 23 n.6, 26 n.24, 27 n.28, 44 and n.99, 100 n.59, 235 n.22, 265 n.21
Constantine, Emperor, 1, 57
Constantine of Orvieto, OP, 248
Constantinople, 46, 117, 132, 132, 133, 136, 137, 138, 140, 142, 145, 148, 149, 150, 180, 267, 272, 289
Conybeare, F., 34 and nn.61, 62
Cordes, 110 and n.88
Corpus iuris canonici, 64 n.28, 97 n.49, 98 n.51, 220 n.41, 235 n.21
cortesia, cortezia, courtesy, courtliness, 10, 11, 12, 13, 39, 40, 41, 42, 45, 74, 125, 285
Cosmas the Priest, 131, 161 and n.26, 168, 169
Councils
  of the Church, *see* Beziérs, Lateran, Lombers, Toulouse, Tours, Vienne
  Concilium Generale of Pieusse, 45, 47, 66 n.32, 203
  Council of Saint Félix-de-Caraman, 19, 46, 142, 203, 240, 258
    acts of 71, 140, 240, 292
  held by Cathars, 19, 46, 66 and n.32, 71–2, 122, 141–5, 203, 204–5, 240, 252–3, 293, 300–2, 307
Cowdrey, H. E. J., 136 n.19
creation, heretic beliefs about, 6, 16, 55, 131, 149, 156, 167, 170, 171, 178, 179–80, 259, 293

Cremascoli, G., 222 nn.49, 52, 223 n.54
Cremona, 103, 223, 308, 309 and n.7
Crowley, A., 135

D'Acunto, N., 8 n.11
d'Alverny, M.-T., 243 n.3, 296, 297 and nn.95, 99
d'Avray, D., 6, 181 n.19, 183 nn.29, 30
Dalarun, J., 141 and n.41, 142 n.46, 201 n.81, 203 n.88, 292 n.72
Dalmatia, 143, 145, 149
Dando, M., 169 n.52
Daniele of Giussano, OP, inquisitor, 217 n.32
Davidson, N., 74 n.47
Davis, G. W., 87 n.19, 89 n.23, 90 n.24, 91 n.26, 93 n.33, 95 n.40
Davis, J. C. D., 54 and n.4
Del Col, A., 223 n.59
Delumeau, J., 279
Delle Donne, F., 18 n.43
Demetrius of Lampe, 136
demons, demonology, *see* Byzantium
Derrida, J., 53 n.1
Desiderius, heretic bishop of Concorezzo, 146, 189, 216, 217, 218
Despy, G., 82 n.10, 236 n.30
Devic, C., OSB, 141 n.43
Devil, Lucifer, Satan, Satanael, 9, 64 and n.27, 81, 127, 128, 131, 135, 156, 166, 167, 168 and n.49, 169 and nn.52, 54, 170, 171, 172, 177, 178, 181, 184, 215, 266, 293, 311 and n.6, 312, 313
Diehl, P. D., 189 and n.22, 201 n.80
Dillmann, A., 147 n.67
Dimitrov, P., 160 n.20, 161 n.23, 162 nn.26, 29, 163 n.32
Dimitrova, D., 160 n.20, 161 n.23, 163 n.32
discipline of clerics, 81, 92, 104, 106, 261
  see also celibacy of the clergy
Ditchfield, S., 102
Divine Chariot, *see* Merkabah
Dmitrewski, M. de, 110 n.89
Doat, J. de, 284
Doat manuscripts, 18, 45, 46, 48, 49, 59, 60, 66, 72, 88, 91, 116, 117, 195, 203, 249, 250, 251, 252, 278, 281, 284, 285, 301, 302, 307, 308, 309–10
Docetism/docetic Christology, 135, 151

319

von Döllinger, J. J. I., 22 and n.5, 24, 33 and n.54, 35, 210 and n.7, 211, 280 n.21
Dominic Guzman, Dominic of Caleruega, St., 40, 223, 238 n.33, 248, 255–6
Dominicans, 77, 103, 114, 139, 187, 191, 193, 199, 200 and n.79, 213, 221, 222, 223, 226, 227, 228, 302
  anti-heretical writings, 208
  as inquisitors 36, 37, 42, 44, 45, 48, 115, 125, 129, 263, 270, 290
  Christology, 226
  preachers, 226
  studium, 220
  see also individually named Dominicans
Donation of Constantine, 95
donatus, 126
Dondaine, A., OP, 47 n.110, 139 n.30, 140 nn.33, 38, 144 n.54, 145 n.59, 146 nn.61, 63, 149 n.74, 180 and nn.15, 16, 186 n.6, 192 and n.39, 193 n.47, 211, 217 and nn.31, 33, 218 nn.35, 36, 219 n.39, 253 n.52
Dossat, Y., 5 n.9, 32 n.48, 35 n.64, 46 n.107, 95 n.42, 116 n.14, 123 n.61, 141 n.40, 145 n.58, 186 n.6, 193 n.47, 208 n.2, 217 n.31, 235 n.21, 258 n.3, 282 and n.33
Douais, Célestin, Bishop of Beauvais, 33, 35, 42, 60, 101, 116, 125, 196, 210, 211, 225, 249, 255, 279, 281, 305
Douglas, M., 2–3 and n.6, 22 n.2, 27 n.28, 283
Dragojlović, D., 161 n.22
Dragometia, *see* Drugunthia
Dragovitsa, *see* Drugunthia
Drinov, M., 152–3 n.4
Drugunthia, church of, 140, 142, 145, 147, 149, 150
du Cange, C., 79 n.2, 152 n.2, 189 n.20
dualism, dualist beliefs, 3, 4, 5, 6, 15, 24, 25 n.20, 28, 29, 32, 35, 43 and n.97, 44, 62–7, 74–5 and n.48, 77, 91–2 and n.29, 96, 112, 114, 133, 138, 143, 144, 151–84, 199, 210, 211, 215, 230, 240–2, 244, 245, 257, 259–60, 264 and n.19, 267–9, 272, 273, 274, 286, 288, 293, 294, 295–8, 300, 305
  see also creation
Dujčev, I., 138 and n.25, 140 and n.35
Dun, 307

Durand de Beaucaire, Bishop of Albi, 102
Durand de Bordis, 11
Durand of Huesca, Waldensian, later Poor Catholic, 37 n.71, 63, 143, 147, 182, 215, 219 n.38, 275, 277, 289, 290, 299, 300 and n.111, 301
Durkheim, É., 92 and n.30
Duvernoy, J., 46, 53, 55, 86, 100 n.61, 116 and n.12, 143 n.51, 148 and n.73, 176 n.80, 203 n.88, 212 and n.12, 219 n.38, 242 n.1, 245 n.12, 251 nn.43, 44, 256 and nn.71, 72, 279 and n.16, 281, 283 n.34, 299 nn.105, 109, 303 n.120
Dvornik, F., 157 n.14
Dykema, P. A., 82 n.10

Eastern Christianity, 127, 151, 152–3, 153, 155, 155–6, 163, 165–6, 175–6
Eberwin, Abbot of Steinfeld, OPraem, 61, 63, 134, 135, 260, 262, 264, 265, 266, 267
Eckbert, Abbot of Schönau, OSB, 101, 135, 147, 209, 243, 244, 264, 311
Ehrle, F., SJ, Cardinal, 222 nn.49, 51
Elgin, C., 48 n.113
Ellenhard of Utrecht, 262
Emery, R. W., 145 n.57
England, 54, 100, 246, 264, 268, 277, 286, 289
Erlembald, Patarene leader, 136
Ermengart Boer, 41
Ermengaud of Béziers, Poor Catholic, 248
Ermengaud Vena, 87
Étienne de Muret, St., founder of Order of Grandmont, 100
Eubel, C., 99 n.56
eucharist, heretic beliefs about and rejection of, 91 n.28, 134, 283, 291, 293
Europe, 1, 2 and n.5, 3, 5, 6, 10 n.16, 13, 15, 16, 20, 24, 34, 53, 66, 76, 77, 113 n.2, 122, 133, 142, 150, 173, 177, 183, 186, 196, 202, 210, 239, 243, 257, 259, 263, 264, 265, 268, 272 n.37
Eustathius of Thessalonica, 133
Euthymius of Peribleptos, 162, 169
Euthymius Zigabenus, 32, 132, 148, 162, 168, 169, 170, 172, 175
Evans, A. P., 30 and n.39, 58 n.13, 60 n.19,

Index

61 n.22, 213 n.15, 246 n.15, 253 n.53, 254, 277 n.7, 289 n.50, 291 nn.62, 63, 292 n.70, 298 n.103, 299 n.107, 300 n.111
Eve, 172
excommunication/damnation of sinners, 14, 22, 92, 97, 104, 105, 137, 189, 205, 231
extreme unction, Cathar beliefs about, 230
Ezzelino of Romano, 201

Fantis, A. de, 147 n.67, 159 n.18
Farmer, S., 23 n.6
Feuchter, J., 5, 25 and n.22, 26 and n.23, 29 n.38, 73 and n.45, 112 n.1, 115 n.7, 245 n.12, 250 n.37, 272 and n.35, 278, 284 n.37
Ficker, G., 132 n.6, 162 n.27, 168 n.51
Fichtenau, H., 174 n.76, 261 n.10, 264 n.19
Filthaut, E., 222 n.52, 223 n.55, 224 n.61
Fine, J. V., 149 n.76
Flanders, 135
Fleury, C., 152 n.2
Florence, 138, 150, 191, 192, 255
Fontevraud, Fontevrault, 100 n.59
Fontfroide, Cistercian abbey, 248
fornication, 139, 145
Forrest, I., 70 n.39
Fossier, A., 99 n.56
Foucault, M., 81
Fox, R., 33 n.57
France, 31, 33, 104, 109, 122, 135, 159 n.15, 196, 204, 246, 247, 289 and n.50, 311
 Northern France, 142, 150, 211, 236 n.30, 289
 Southern France, 1 and n.1, 3, 4, 5, 6, 7, 13, 15, 16, 18, 31, 32, 37, 59, 60, 72 and n.44, 74 n.48, 77, 81, 122, 123 n.61, 127–9, 135, 177, 181, 182, 211, 223, 225, 230, 231, 232, 234, 235, 236, 237, 238, 239, 240, 241, 243, 244 nn.8, 10, 269, 297
Franciscans, 7, 77, 110, 177, 276
 Spiritual Franciscans, 56, 110
Franciscus Arisius, 208 n.1
Frassetto, M., 176 n.80
Frazer, J., 34
Frederick, Archbishop of Cologne, 265
Free Spirit, so-called heresy, 51, 53, 65, 278

Freedman, G., 28 n.32
Freedman, P., 28 and n.32
Friedlander, A. R, 65 n.30, 109 n.85, 110 nn.89, 90
'friends of God', 92, 99, *see also* Good Men
Friuli, 10
Frugoni, A., 30 and n.41
Fuchs, W. P., 24 n.11

Gaja-la-Selve, 67
Galdinus, Archbishop of Milan, 138
Galvano Fiamma, OP, 188, 190, 199
Gambara family, 14
Garattus, Cathar bishop, 145, 180
Garnier de Talapie, 88, 89, 91
Garonne, river, 15, 29, 30, 34, 39, 42, 43, 44, 46, 112, 113, 125, 130, 203, 248, 258, 260, 272
Garsoïan, N., 154 n.9, 155 n.11
Gascony, 97, 231, 294
Gaster, M., 160 n.20
Gattedo, near Milan, 189, 217
Gaucelin/Gaucelm, Cathar bishop, 144, 301, 308
Gaunt, S., 43 n.96
Gauthier, R.-A., OP, 222 n.51
Gaylord, H., 159 n.19, 169 n.52
Geertz, C., 27 n.28
Genoa, 132, 192
genuflection as part of *adoratio*, 39, 80–1, 90, 91, 118, 285–6
Geoffrey of Auxerre, OCist, 218, 291, 310
Geoffrey of Vigeois, OSB, 296, 310, 311
Geoffroy d'Ablis, OP, 11, 67
Georgiev, E., 162 n.29
Gerald Mercier of Carcassonne, 142
Geralda de Biele, 120
Geralda Manhe, 249–50
Gerard (II), Bishop of Arras-Cambrai, 58, 261
Gerard of Frachet, OP, 187, 213
Germany, 23, 135, 267
Gervase of Canterbury, OSB, 129, 143, 247, 293
Ghibellines, 103
Ghobrial, J.-P. A., 26 n.23
Ghosh, K., 54 n.5
Giambelluca Kossova, A. 159 n.18
Gibbon, E., 151 n.1
Gieseler, J. K. L., 32 and n.53
Gilchrist, J., 236 n.29

Gilles, H., 100 n.58
Gilli, P., 98, 103 n.72
Gillingham, J., 246 n.17, 262 and n.14, 293 n.76
Ginzburg, C., 26 n.23, 95 n.44, 283
Giraut de Borneil, 44–5
Given, J., 267 n.22
Gnosticism, 22 and n.4, 32, 57, 147, 157, 159, 164, 171 and n.64, 172, 210, 270, 272
God, 39, 45, 82, 90, 133, 136, 137, 170, 178, 196 n.58, 197, 199, 200, 213, 251, 252, 285
  Bogomil beliefs about, 131, 132, 155, 168 and n.49, 169, 171, 177
  Cathar beliefs about, 1, 6, 63, 64, 67 and n.34, 87, 128, 139, 179, 181, 230, 259, 283, 285, 293
Goffman, E., 81
Golubinskii, E., 160 n.120
Good Men (*boni homines, bos home, probi homines, prodome*), 3, 7, 9, 11, 38, 39, 40, 41, 42, 43 and n.97, 44, 45 and n.102, 46, 47, 49, 52, 55, 60 n.18, 66 n.32, 67 and n.34, 68, 75, 77, 80, 83, 84, 85, 86, 87–111, 125, 126, 196, 230, 245–56, 261, 268, 272, 276, 277 and n.7, 279, 282, 284, 285, 292, 295, 300 and n.113, 301, 303, 305
Good Women, 7, 38, 40 and n.86, 41, 42, 43, 44, 45, 49, 52, 67, 129, 249, 250, 251, 252
Goodman, N., 48 n.113
Gordoz Vidal, 251
Górecki, P., 8 n.11
Gorskii, A., 157 n.15, 162 n.29
Göttingen, religious historical school, *see* Gieseler, J. K. L, Monod, G., Scheider, H. H., Schramm, P. E., Waitz, G.
Gouillard, J., 154 n.10, 169 n.57
Gourdon, 118
Gouron, A., 123 n.61
Grabmann, M., 221 n.43
Grafton, A., 24 n.11
Grandmont, Order of, 100
Gratian, 64 n.28, 235 n.21, 297
Greco, A., 149 n.78, 174 n.76
Greece, 134, 263
Greek Orthodoxy, 63–4
Greenfield, R. P. H., 155 n.12

Gregorian Reform, 42, 81, 83, 89, 111
Gregory VII, Pope, 16, 267
Gregory IX, Pope, 98, 230, 271
Gregory, B., 37 n.73
Griffe, É., 141 n.43, 142 n.45, 144 n.53, 279 and n.16, 281
Grundmann, H., 23 and nn.6, 7, 24 and n.13, 25 and nn.16, 17, 28, 29 and n.37, 51 and n.125, 55 and n.9, 113 and n.3, 114 and nn.5, 6, 115, 211, 232 n.8, 245 and n.13, 246, 247 and n.23, 248 and n.23, 249 and n.30, 252, 255, 256, 265 n.21, 278 and nn.10, 12, 14, 291, 310 and n.2, 311
Guébin, P., 31 n.45, 248 n.23, 296 n.93
Guibert de Nogent, 61, 63
Guido, Archbishop of Milan, 136
Guido da Sesto, 191
Guilhabert of Castres, Cathar bishop, 145, 301, 307
Guilhabert Lantar, 79, 80 and n.4, 89
Guilhelm de La Grasse, 12
Guilhem de Maurian, 87, 88 n.20, 90 n.26, 93, 94
Guillaume Bernard d'Airoux, 60 and n.18
Guillelma Maurina, 121
Guillou, A., 100 n.58
Guiraud Delort, 87, 88–9, 90, 95
Guiraud, J., 248, 249, 279 and n.16, 281
Guitalens, 79, 80, 94–5

Hacking, I., 48 n.113
Hageneder, O., 16 nn.34, 35, 232 n.9
Hahn, C. U., 156 n.13, 208 and n.3, 210
Hamilton, B., 2 n.5, 6, 32 n.48, 36 and n.69, 37 n.72, 38, 46 n.106, 47 n.110, 48 n.114, 72 n.43, 133 n.11, 136 n.20, 140 n.37, 141 n.40, 142 n.44, 143 n.48, 145 n.58, 154 n.8, 155 n.12, 162 n.26, 168 nn.49, 50, 51, 174 n.76, 176 n.80, 242 n.2, 243 n.6, 253 n.53, 258 n.3, 272, 277, 284 and n.37, 289, 290 n.57
Hamilton, J., 46 n.106, 72, n.43, 136 n.20, 154 n.8, 155 n.12, 162 n.26, 168 nn.49, 50, 51
Hamilton, S., 46 n.106, 72, n.43, 136 n.20, 273 n.39
Harlow, D. C., 159 n.19
Harris, R., 33 n.58, 34 n.61, 148 and n.70, 291 n.62

Index

Harrison, R., 243 n.5, 264 n.16
Harvey, R., 43 n.96
Haskins, C. H., 27 and n.27, 236 n.30
Head, T., 61 n.21, 261 n.10
Helis of Mazerolles, 281
Henri of Marcy, 126, 129, 143, 247, 296, 311
Henry of Lausanne, 291, 310
Henry II, King of England, 100, 246, 262, 292, 293–4, 294
Heresy
  as a disease, 133, 234, 236, 238
  as political and social dissent, 4, 54
  persecution of, 15–17, 40–1, 27–8, 33–4, 38–9, 49–50, 55–8, 81
hereticatio, 42, 67, 91, 92, 93, 94, 97, 237 *see also consolamentum*
heretics
  confessions before the inquisitors, 48, 79, 80, 83, 87–8, 90 and nn.25, 26, 91, 94 and n.38, 95, 96 n.46, 192, 281, 303
  credentes/'believers' of heretics, 38, 45, 49, 55, 77, 96 and n.48, 97 and n.49, 98 and n.51, 102, 106, 114 and n.6, 125, 197 and n.66, 199 and n.73, 204, 205 and n.94, 206, 237, 263, 283, 289
  defensores of heretics, 97, 98
  heretical houses, 40 n.86, 97 n.49, 301
  heretici perfecti, 41–2
  'partisans' of heretics (*fautores*) 98
  receptatores (hosts of heretics) 97–8, 197
Hincmar, Archbishop of Reims, 183
Hinduism, 22
Hoécker, C. 219 n.38, 220 and n.42, 225 n.66, 226 and n.70
Hoffman Berman, C., 28 n.33
Holder-Egger, O., 19 n.43, 289 n.50
Holy Land, 239
Holy Spirit as part of Cathar (and Bogomil) baptism, 132, 134, 135, 139, 148, 195, 247
holy supper, Waldensian ritual, 119, 120, 121, 122 *see also caena*
Honorius II, Pope, 20
Honorius III, Pope, 14, 16, 230, 232, 237–8 n.33, 239, 240, 241, 271
Hornbeck III, J. P., 54 n.6
Housley, N. J., 16 n.37
Hübinger, G., 32 n.52
Hudson, A., 54 and n.5

Hugh Eteriano, Pisan theologian, 46, 47, 72, 136, 137, 138, 307
Hugh of Canelle, 251
Huguenots, 152
Hull, D., 48 n.113
Humbert of Romans, OP, 187 and n.11, 199 n.75
Humfress, C., 58 n.12
Humiliati, 231
Hussites, 56
Hutchinson, C. A., 100 n.60
Hyrlanda, 4
Hysarn de Gibel, 12

Iacobus Carbonel, 123
Iatsimirskii, I. I., 157 n.15, 162 n.30
Iggers, G. G., 24 n.11
Ilarino da Milano, OFM, 37 n.71
Ilić, D., 153 n.5
Imbert of Salles, 308
Innocent I, Pope, 101
Innocent II, Pope, 20
Innocent III, Pope, 16, 23, 30, 98, 113 n.2, 149, 230, 232, 233, 238, 239, 240, 241 271
Innocent IV, Pope, 98, 186, 189, 200, 217 and n.32, 224
Innocent V, Pope, 103
inquisition records, 3, 18 n.42, 29, 35, 36, 37, 38, 43 n.97, 60, 65, 66, 67, 74 n.48, 85, 86, 88, 89, 90 n.25, 91, 96, 99, 105 n.79, 110 n.88, 113, 115, 116, 118, 122, 129 n.81, 141, 144, 145, 191, 210, 230, 249, 259, 278, 279, 280, 281 and n.25, 282, 283, 288, 295 n.88, 305, 306
  Paenitenciae by Peter Sellan, 115–23
inquisitorial discourse 68, 85, 220, 234, 245, 261
inquisitorial manuals, 29, 35, 63, 194
interdict, 106, 138
Ioan Ekzarkh, 162, 167
Ioannes Austorcs, 120
Ioannes Toset, 120
Iogna-Prat, D., 61 n.21, 225 n.65, 261 n.9
Isidore, St., Bishop of Seville, 61, 63, 64 n.28, 206
Isaiah, Prophet 147, 167, 216, 233, 289, 290
Islam, 63
Italy, 1 and n.1, 13, 14, 16, 72 and n.44, 74 n.48, 77, 102, 132, 136, 138, 146, 147, 149, 159 n.18, 177, 181, 196,

323

221, 222, 223, 225, 227, 228, 230, 240, 255, 258, 270, 271, 286, 290 and n.62, 291 n.63, 308
Italian Communes, 14, 16, 201, 224, 271
podestà, 16, 190, 191, 201
Ivanov, I., 156 n.13, 160 nn.20, 21, 161 n.23, 162 nn.28, 29, 163, 168 n.49

Jacobites, *see* Syrian Orthodox
Jacques Fournier, OCist, bishop of Pamiers, inquisitor, Pope Benedict XII, 67, 86, 281 n.25
Jagić, V., 160 n.20, 162 n.29
James, M. R., 159 n.19, 220 n.41
Jean de Dieu, 221
Jean Galand, OP, inquisitor, 86
Jerusalem, 127 and n.73
Jesus Christ
  Bogomil beliefs about, 131, 132, 168, 169
  Cathar beliefs about, 1, 43, 64, 67 n.34, 137, 139, 146, 217–18 and n.35, 253, 264, 266, 283, 312
Jiménez-Sanchez, P., 46 n.106, 173 n.75, 174 n.76, 176 n.80, 242 and n.1
John Breyssan, 305
John Cambiaire, 307, 308
John Cassian, St., 206 n.97
John of Cucullio, 219 n.38
John of Lugio, Cathar theologian, 149, 188 n.13, 193 n.42, 194, 195, 199, 202 and n.84, 204, 219 n.38
John of Saint-Pierre, OP, inquisitor, 37, 38 and n.79, 39, 251, 258, 283
John of Turin, OP, 192 and n.39
John of Vicenza, OP, inquisitor, 224
John Reg of St-Paul-Cap-de-Joux, 308
John the Baptist, 9, 64 and n.26
John the Fair, heretic, 145
John Xiphilinus, Byzantine monk and preacher, 169
John XXII, Pope, 110, 150
Jonas of Cambrai, 264
Jordan of Vilar, 11
Jurkowski, M., 73 n.45

Käppeli, T. OP, 186 and nn.3 5, 187 n.8, 191 nn.30, 31, 32, 192 and nn.37, 38, 193 n.50, 196 n.62, 202 nn.85, 86, 213 nn.14, 15, 219 n.39, 223 n.57, 305 n.2
Kehr, P. F., 100 n.58

Kelly, H. A., 99 n.54
Kienzle, B. M., 126 n.68, 225 n.65, 262 n.12, 295 and n.88
King, K. L., 22 n.4, 54 and n.3
Kliment of Okhrid, 167
Klincharov, I., 153 n.5
Knight, J., 147 n.65
Knowles, D., OSB, 26 and n.24, 27
Kobiak, N. A., 157 n.15
Koleva, T., 161 n.25
Kuhn, T., 21 and n.1
Kulik, A., 158 n.17, 159 n.19
Kundera, M., 52 and n.128
Kusabu, H., 154 n.7, 155 n.11, 175 n.78

La Salvetat, 94–5
Lagrasse, Benedictine monastery, 64 n.25
Lake, P., 54 n.4
Lambert, M., 25 n.17, 174 n.76, 182 n.22, 233 n.10, 234 n.18, 242 n.2, 277
Landes, R., 69 n.37
Languedoc, 5, 33 and n.59, 81, 82, 83, 84, 89, 90 n.25, 93, 95, 96, 99, 100, 101, 103, 109, 110, 111, 112–31, 135, 140, 142, 143, 144, 145, 146, 210 n.8, 222, 223, 230, 242–56, 258, 259, 260, 270, 274, 275, 276, 277, 278, 279, 281 and n.25, 283, 284, 288, 289, 290, 291 and nn.62, 63, 293, 295, 297, 298, 299, 300, 306
Lansing, C., 25 and n.21, 38 and n.77
Lateran Councils
  Second Lateran Council, 97, 291–2
  Third Lateran Council, 59, 97 and n.59, 98, 127, 129, 138, 196, 220, 231, 232, 236, 240, 241, 287, 294
  Fourth Lateran Council, 98, 231, 240, 241, 272
Lauragais, 4, 35, 244 n.9, 251, 274, 284, 285, 286
Lavaur, 126, 142, 143
Le Puy, 83, 109, 110, 117
Le Roy Ladurie, E., 35 and n.65, 75, 86 n.18, 279 n.16, 283
Lea, H. C., 33 n.56
Leclerc, A., 100 n.60
Léger, J., 151 n.1
Léglu, C., 42 n.45, 230 n.2
Lerner, R. E., 23 nn.6, 8, 51 and n.125, 53 and n.2, 55, 65, 268 n.27, 278 and n.13

Lézat, abbey, 126
Liège, 264
Lincoln, diocese 286
Livre Rouge of Montauban, 118
Lobrichon, G., 261 and n.10
Loire, 262
Lollardy, *see* Wycliffism
Lombardy, 96, 140, 142, 145, 146, 150, 180, 185, 186, 188, 189, 190 n.29, 192, 220, 223, 224, 256, 259, 260, 286
Lombers, 143, 247, 292
   Council of (1165), 126, 246, 247, 255, acts of 277, 292
Loos, M., 161 n.22, 168 n.49, 169 n.54, 174 n.76
Lorenz, M., 48 n.112
Lošek, F., 18 n.43
Louis VII, King of France, 246, 293, 294
Louis VIII, King of France, 271
Louis IX, St., King of France, 103, 122
Low Countries, 263, 264
Lucifer, *see* Devil
Lucius III, Pope, 231, 236
Lutz, E. C., 82 n.10
Lyon, E., 31 n.45, 248 n.23, 296 n.93
Lyons, 118, 147

Mabillon, J., OSB, 141
Magdalino, P., 133 n.7
Magdeburg, Archbishopric of, 265
Mahul, M., 59 n.16, 60 n.18
Mai, A., 158 n.18
Maisonneuve, H., 59 n.15, 99 n.54
Maitland, S. R., 31 n.47
Mani, 214
Manichaeism, 16, 22, 24 n.12, 29, 31, 32, 42, 56, 61, 63, 64 n.26, 65, 101, 131, 133, 135, 137, 152, 154, 162 n.28, 168 and n.49, 210, 211, 222, 243, 263, 295, 296, 297, 305, 306
Manselli, R., 1 n.1, 91 n.29, 225 n.67, 264 n.16, 277
Mansi, J.-D., 97 n.49, 99 n.55, 145 n.56, 191 n.35, 246 n.14, 277 n.7
Mantua, 145, 206, 223
Manuel I, Emperor, 136
Manuel II, Emperor, 137
Marcabru, trubadour, 43
Marchand, S., 22 nn.3, 4, 24 nn.10, 15, 32 n.50
Marches, region of Italy, 140, 180, 190 n.29
Mark of Lombardy, 142

Marquesa, 250
marriage, views on, 1, 6, 16, 34 n.60, 40, 43, 64, 67 and n.34, 134, 135, 137, 177, 178, 179, 180, 181, 182, 183, 184, 283, 291, 311, 312
Marseille, 63
Marsh, C. W., 54 n.4
Martinez Sopena, P., 10 n.16
Marvin, L. W., 30 n.42
Mas-Saintes-Puelles, 283
Masuzawa, T., 22 n.4
Matfred Baudrac, 95
Matheude, 251
Mathieu de Marly, 60 n.18
Mauguio, 41
Maundy Thursday, 119
McAlhany, J., 61 n.22
McCormick, M., 69 n.37
McNulty, P. A., 133 n.11
Melenguia, Church of, 142–3
melioramentum, melhoramen, 11 and n.20, 13, 39, 40, 41, 45, 67, 253 *see also* adoration
Melville Jones, J. R., 133 n.7
Merkabah, 159, 172
Merlo, F., 223 n.57
Merlo, G. G., 4 n.8, 9 n.15, 15 n.32, 16 n.35, 30 n.41, 95 n.43, 200 n.75, 277, 303, 304 and n.125
Merville, castle, 249
Mesopotamia, 155
Messalianism, 154–5 and n.10
metempsychosis, 55
Michael the Great, Syrian Patriarch, 127
Migne, J.-P., 129 n.80, 132 n.6, 134 n.13, 162 n.27, 193 n.45, 232 n.9, 243 n.3, 260 n.5
Miladinova, N., 168 n.51
Milam, E. L., 21 n.1
Milan, 136, 138, 147, 189, 190 and n.26, 200 and n.77, 201, 206, 217, 223 n.55, 224
Milobar, F., 153 n.6
Miltenova, A., 161 n.23, 163 n.32, 165 nn.38, 39
Minissi, N., 161 n.24
Miramon, C. de, 126 n.70
Mirepoix, 307
Molinier, A., 33 nn.58, 59, 141 n.43, 211, 254–5
Molinier, C., 33 and n.57, 255 and nn.68, 69

Momigliano, A., 51 and n.126
Moneta of Cremona, OP, 6, 7, 37 n.71, 65, 147, 147 n.66, 193, 194 and n.51, 195, 208–8, 273, 298 n.101
Monod, G., 33 n.57
Montaillou, 10, 279 n.16
Montauban, 25, 115–23, 126 n.69, 245 n.12, 272
Montcuq, 118 n.25
Montdragon, 95
Montesquieu, 66 n.32
Montgaillard, 124, 252
Montpellier, 103, 141, 297
Montréal, 299
Montségur, 60 n.18, 189, 274, 280, 282, 307–9
Moore, R. I., 2 and nn.2, 4, 3, 19 and n.44, 27, 28 and n.29, 32 n.48, 44 n.100, 49 and n.118, 50 and nn.122, 123, 51, 53, 56, 60, 61 n.21, 71, 72 n.44, 73, 74, 75, 76, 78, 81 n.6, 82 n.10, 89 n.22, 92 n.31, 99 n.57, 100 n.59, 103 n.71, 112 and n.1, 113 and n.2, 129 nn.80, 81, 130 and n.82, 133 and nn.8, 10, 134 and n.12, 135 and n.14, 140 and n.39, 177 and n.1, 178, 180 and nn.14, 16, 181, 182 n.20, 183 and nn.27, 32, 184, 226 n.70, 229 n.1, 234 n.17, 244 and nn.8, 9, 257 n.1, 260 nn.4, 6, 262 n.14, 264 nn.16, 18, 267 n.24, 268 n.27, 269 n.29, 270 and n.30, 274 and n.2, 277, 280 n.22, 287 and nn.45, 47, 310 n.3
Morghen, R., 1 n.1, 211, 259, 260 n.4, 277
Moses, 177, 311, 313
Mulchahey, M. M., 221 n.48, 226 n.70
Müller, P., 24 n.11
Mundy, J. H., 25 and n.19, 30 and n.39, 39 n.81, 84 n.13
Muratori, L. A., 152 n.2
Murko, M., 160 n.20
Musca, G., 100 n.58
Muslims, 234, 238–9
Musson, A., 70 n.39
Muzerelle, D., 142 n.47
Mynors, R. A. B., 220 n.41

Narbonne, 145 n.57, 275, 298
Naufressa Hospitalaria, 121
Nazarius, heretic bishop of Concorezzo, 146, 189, 190 and n.25, 204, 217, 218, 289–90, 290
Nehlsen-von Stryk, K., 100 n.58
Neo-Manichaeans, 131–2
Neo-Platonism, 154–5
Nevostruev, K., 157 n.15, 162 n.29
Nicetas/Niquinta, heretic bishop, 46, 140, 142 and n.46, 143, 144, 145, 147, 149, 180
    charter of, 46 and nn.106, 107, 47, 72 n.42 *see also* Council of St Felix
Nickelsburg, G. W. E., 164 n.35
Nickson, M. A. E., 186 n.3
nicodemism, 95
Nicolas d'Abbeville, OP, inquisitor, 86
Niel, F., 268, 269 n.28
Nirenberg, D., 49 and n.118, 50 and n.119, 120
Norbert of Xanten, Archibishop of Magdeburg, founder of Premonstratensians, 265
Norelli, E., 158 n.18
Novaković, S., 158 n.16, 159 n.19
Novatians, 135
Novatus, 135
Novick, P., 27 n.28

oaths and oath-taking, 122, 136, 137, 282–3
Oberman, H. A., 82 n.10
Oberste, J., 126 n.70
Oberto Pallavicino, Ghibelline podestà of Milan, 189, 190, 201
Obolensky, D., 131 and n.3, 140 n.34, 155 n.11, 157 n.14, 160 n.20, 168 n.49
Odilo, St. Abbot of Cluny, 261
Oeder, J. L., 151 n.1
Oriani family, 14
Origen, 172 n.68
Orléans, 259
Orlov, A., 158 nn.16, 17, 159 nn.18, 19
Ormrod, W. M., 70 n.39
Orvieto, 25
Osma, 144
Ourliac, P., 100 n.58
Oxford, 264

P. de Pomareda, 121
P. Magistris, 121
Palès-Gobilliard, A., 11 n.20, 13 n.30, 110 n.88, 285 n.43, 305 n.4
Pamiers, 86, 299

Panella, E., OP, 186 n.3, 213 n.15
Paolini, L., 174 n.76, 176 nn.81, 82, 196
    nn.59, 63, 198 n.61, 201 nn.80, 81,
    203 n.90, 204 and n.91, 206 nn.95,
    96, 207 n.101, 216 n.25, 223 n.59,
    224 n.62, 225 and n.66, 277, 290 n.57
papacy, 5, 13, 14, 16, 23, 27, 59, 132, 186,
    190 and n.28, 201, 207, 231, 236,
    238, 240, 241
  papal chaplain, 83, 103
  papal curia, 109
  papal legate, 143, 145, 149, 236, 247,
    289, 293
  plenitudo potestatis, 74, 82, 103
  popes, 7, 14, 16, 20, 65, 82, 102, 103,
    109, 127, 128, 131, 145, 146, 150,
    188, 192, 220, 230, 231, 232, 233,
    234, 237, 239, 240, 241, 263 *see also
    individually named popes*
Papini, C., 118 n.24
parabiblical texts, 6, 151–76
Paradise, 147, 172
parascriptural texts, 6, 151–76
Paris, University of, 5, 136, 221, 222, 232,
    271, 274, 278, 288, 295, 296, 300
Parmeggiani, R., 221 n.48, 222 n.52, 223
    n.59
Patarenes (also *Patareni, Patarini*), 16, 29,
    97 n.50, 136, 137, 138, 196 n.62, 203
    n.90, 230, 231, 255, 275, 294
Paterson, L., 43 n.96
Patschovsky, A., 59 n.17, 135 and n.16,
    182 n.21, 219 nn.39, 40, 278 and
    n.12, 297 n.97
Paulicianism, 31, 32, 56, 140, 152, 153,
    154, 155, 156, 168 n.49, 175, 210,
    211
Pavia, 188
Peace of God, movement, 69
Peace of Lorris (1243), 122
Peace of Paris (1229), 261
Pedro II, King of Aragon, 301
Pegg, M. G., 3 and n.7, 4, 5 n.9, 6, 8, 9
    n.12, 10 n.17, 11 nn.21, 22, 17 n.39,
    18 n.42, 22 n.2, 29 n.34, 30 n.42,
    31 nn.43, 44, 34 n.60, 38 n.74, 39
    nn.80, 82, 83, 40 n.84, 41 n.88, 42
    n.91, 43 n.97, 47 n.109, 49 n.115,
    50 n.123, 66 n.31, 67 and n.35, 68,
    72 and n.43, 73, 74 and n.48, 75
    and n.51, 78, 81 and n.8, 85 n.15,
    90 n.25, 99 n.57, 101 nn.63, 66, 112
    and n.1, 13 and n.4, 114 and n.4,
    115, 116 n.14, 124 n.62, 125 and
    nn.66, 67, 129 n.81, 224 and nn.7,
    8, 9, 245 n.12, 251 n.44, 258, 260
    and n.7, 268 n.26, 272 and n.34,
    273, 274 and n.1, 275 n.4, 279 n.15,
    280 n.21, 281 n.27, 282 n.30, 284
    n.40, 285 nn.41, 42, 305 n.1
Peire Astruc, 88, 90
Peire Aymeric, 94
Peire Baudier, 95
Peire de Mézens, 93
Peire Enjalran, 105
Peire Ferreol, 106 n.81
Peire Izarn, Peter Isarn, Cathar Bishop,
    46, 47, 49, 141, 144
Peire Perrin, 18, 48
Pelagianism, 229
penance, sacrament of, 95, 110, 116 and
    n.13, 117 and n.16, 121, 122, 185
    n.1, 193
  Cathar penance, 197, 293, 296
Périgord, 261
Perrin, J., 151 n.1
Perrone, L., 158 n.18
Peter Autier, 176 n.80, 306
Peter Berardi, 12
Peter Damian, OSB, 183
Peter Gardog of Montgaillard, 252
Peter Isarn, *see* Peire Izarn
Peter Martyr, *see* Peter of Verona
Peter of Bruys, 211
Peter of Castelnau, Bl., OCist, legate, 236
Peter of Chrysogonus, OCist, Cardinal,
    legate, 293, 295
Peter of les Vaux-de-Cernay, OCist, 31
    and n.45, 42 and n.92, 219 n.39,
    237 and n.32, 247, 255, 295, 296,
    298 and n.104
Peter of Verona, OP, St., 185 n.1, 186 and
    n.5, 187 and n.8, 188 and n.16, 189,
    190 and n.28, 191, 192, 193, 194,
    195, 196 n.62, 199, 201, 202, 205
    n.93, 206, 217 and n.32, 218 n.35,
    219 n.39, 224
Peter Pollan, Cathar Younger Son and
    Bishop, 141
Peter the Chanter, 232
Peter the Venerable, OSB, 59, 235 and
    n.22
Peter William D'Arvigna, 307
Peters, E., 33 n.56

Petkov, K., 181 nn.17, 18
Petracius, heretic 145
Petranović, B., 153 n.6
Petrović, L., 153 n.6
Petrus Carbonelz, 120
Peter Sellan, OP, inquisitor, 115 and nn.7, 8, 117, 121, 123, 249, 250, 258, 272, 298
Philadelphia, Church of, 149 n.76
Philip IV of France, 65
Philippopolis, 140
Philippus Donadeu, 123
Philonenko, M., 158 n.17
Philonenko-Sayar, B., 158 n.17
Piacenza, 103, 185, 187, 188, 190 and nn.26, 29, 191 and n.31, 201, 204, 223 n.55, 224
Picard, J.-C., 159 n.19
Pierre de Mazerolles, 67 n.34 [= Peter of Mazerolles, 281, 283]
Pierre Garcias of Toulouse, 60 and n.20, 67
Pieusse, 47, 301
Piphles, 135, 311
Pisa, 132
Polakova, I., 161 n.25
Pons Bernard, 301
Pons de Parnac, OP, inquisitor, 48
Pons Grimoard, 250
Poor Lombards, 205
Poor (Men) of Lyon, 89, 121, 195, 202, 205 n.94, 231, 305, 306 see also Waldenses
pop, Orthodox priest 131 and n.2, 140
Popov, A. I., 159, 158 n.16, 159 n.18, 162 n.29
Popov, A. N., 167 n.48
Popović, M., 153 n.5
Popruzhenko, M. G., 160 n.20, 162 n.28
Porfir'ev, I. I., 157 n.15
Porro, P., 222 n.51
Portal, C., 105 n.77
Porto, 110
Pott, S., 31 n.46
Power, D., 31 n.43
preaching
  against heretics, 41, 43, 59, 125, 222, 223 n.55, 224, 230, 236, 263, 291, 295, 310
  by heretics, 3, 13, 41, 55, 67, 87, 90, 91, 114, 120, 121, 122, 131, 137, 138, 143, 157, 190, 204, 205, 217, 250, 266, 294, 299

see also sermons
Praemonstratensians, 264, 265
procreation, condemnation of, 6, 181, 259, 263
Prouille, Dominican monastery, 40 and n.86, 248
Prudlo, D., 185 n.1, 188 nn.14, 15, 16, 190 n.24, 191 n.30, 192 n.37, 199 n.75, 217 n.32
pseudepigraphic literature, 6, 151–76
Pseudo-David of Augsburg, 219 n.39
Pseudo-James Capelli, 193 and n.49
Publicani, 138, 230, 231, 294
Puech, H.-C., 160 n.20, 161 n.26, 169 n.53
Puritanism, 54, 57, 268
Puylaurens, 18, 45, 48
Pypin, A., 157 n.15, 160 n.20, 162 n.29
Pythagoras, 214

Quercy, 25, 35, 115 and n.8, 117, 118, 250, 272

Rački, F., 152 n.4, 160 n.20
Radchenko, K. F., 160 n.21
radical evangelism, 81
Radoslav the Christian, 148
Raimon Augier, 93
Raimon Baudier, 107 n.82
Raimon Calvière, 87, 95
Raimon de Baffignac, 79, 80, 83, 89, 90 n.25, 93
Raimon de Eclezia, 40
Raimon del Boc, 87, 89
Raimon Delort, 105
Raimon Didier, 89
Raimon Joan, 45
Raimundus Gastaudz, 121, 122
Ranier Sacconi, OP, 6, 7, 62, 139 and nn.30, 31, 32, 146 and nn.60, 62, 149 nn.76, 77, 150 and n.80, 177, 178, 185–207, 209, 210, 212, 217 and n.32, 218 n.34, 228
Rancière, J., 75 and n.50
Ranke, L. von, 23, 24 n.11
Ranters, 54
Ranulf de Plassac, OP, inquisitor, 49
Raoul Ardent, 211
Rawcliffe, C., 287 and nn.45, 47
Raymond Affre, 144
Raymond Agulher, 301
Raymond Blasquo, 307

Index

Raymond de Casalis, 142
Raymond de Saint-Martin, 60
Raymond John of Albi, 66 n.32, 301
Raymond of Barmiac/Baymac, 143, 293
Raymond of Mirepoix, 307
Raymond of Montouty, 308
Raymond of Péreille, co-lord of
  Montségur, 307, 308
Raymond V, Count of Toulouse, 129 n.78,
  143, 262, 293
Raymond VI, Count of Toulouse, 30, 234,
  235, 239
Raymond VII, Count of Toulouse, 102–3,
  122, 124, 238
Raymund Autier of Ax, 13Razès, 45, 66
  n.32, 301, 302
Réalmont, 87, 88
Reddy, W. M., 44 n.97
Reginald of Orléans, OP, 213
Reilly, D. J., 262 n.11
Reitzenstein, R., 156 n.13
Renneville, 124
Reusch, O., 157 n.15
Rexroth, F., 24 n.11
Rhine valley, 135, 147
Rhineland, 103, 129 n.81, 134, 135, 230,
  243 and n.5, 260, 262, 263, 264
Rhône, river, 15, 29, 31 n.43, 34, 38, 39,
  42, 43, 44, 112, 113 n.2, 125, 130,
  258, 260, 262, 272
Ricchini, T. A., OP, 37 n.71, 147 n.66, 194
  n.51, 208 and n.1, 228
Richard of Poitiers, OSB, 219 n.39
Riches, T. M., 261 n.11
Rieti, 286
Rigo, A., 154 n.10
Rimini, 14, 201, 203
Rist, R., 7, 42 n.94, 230 n.2
Roach, A., 33 nn.58, 59, 50 n.123, 75
  n.51, 173 n.75, 203 n.89, 272–3
  and n.38
Robert Aleman, 12
Robert de Spernone, Cathar Bishop, 142
Robert Le Bougre, OP, 27
Robert of Arbrissel, founder of Abbey of
  Fontevrault, 211
Robert of Auxerre, OPraem, 289
Robertson Smith, W., 34
Roche, J., 292 n.73
Rodenberg, C., 14 n.31
Roger Calcagni, 191
Roger of Howden, 99 n.55, 100 n.59, 143
  n.50, 246 and n.17, 247, 255, 262,
  293
Roland of Cremona, OP, 221, 224
Romagnoli, P., 193 n.49
Romania (Byzantine empire of Nicaea),
  149 n.76, 150
Rome, 14, 117, 127 and n.73, 128, 136,
  145, 208, 232, 240
Roquebert, M., 46 n.107, 53 n.1, 279 and
  n.16, 281, 307
Rosenwein, B. H., 23 n.6
Rottenwöhrer, G., 156 n.13, 159 n.18, 176
  n.80, 216 nn.25, 28, 217 nn.29, 31,
  218 n.37, 219 n.38, 223 n.58, 224
  nn.63, 64, 266–7 n.22
Rougemont, D. de, 75 n.48
Roumengoux, 11
Rovetta, A. OP, 191
Rubinkiewicz, R., 158 n.17, 163 n.33
Rubinstein, J., 61 n.22
Rüdiger, J., 126 n.69
Runciman, S., 47 n.110, 133 and n.8, 160
  n.20, 243 n.2

Sabapathy, J., 70 n.39
Sackville, L. J., 7, 42 and n.94, 59 n.14, 65
  n.29, 85 n.15, 101 n.66, 185 n.1, 186
  n.3, 188 nn.13, 16, 194 and n.34,
  196 n.59, 206 n.97, 208 n.1, 214
  n.19, 215 n.23, 219 n.38, 225 nn.65,
  67, 68, 248 n.25, 273 and n.40,
  297–8 n.101
sacraments, 139, 214, 226, 263, 267 *see also
  individually named sacraments*
Sadnik, L., 167 n.46
Saint-Gilles, Benedictine abbey, 297
Saint-Sernin, 11
salvation, 20, 43–4, 67–68, 82–3, 90, 92–3,
  95–6, 102, 114–15, 200
Salvo Burci, 37 n.71, 193 n.48, 205 n.94,
  207 n.100, 219 n.39
Šanjek, F., 139 n.30, 142 n.47, 185 n.1, 186
  n.3, 188 and nn.13, 17, 189 nn.19,
  22, 190 nn.25, 29, 191 n.34, 193
  n.42, 195 nn.55, 58, 196 nn.60, 63,
  197 n.64, 198 n.70, 201 n.83, 204
  n.92, 206 nn.96, 98, 218 n.34, 275
  n.4, 289 n.54
Santiago de Compostela, 117
Santos Otero, A. de, 169 n.52
Satan/ Satanael, *see* Devil
Sayce, A. H., 33–4

Index

Sclavonia, 145, 146, 149 and n.76, 150
Scott, J. C., 10 n.19, 13 n.29, 15 n.33
Schaeder, H. H., 29 and n.38
Scharff, T., 15 n.32
Schmidt, C., 31, 32 and nn.48, 49, 51, 53, 208 and nn.2, 3, 209 and nn.4, 5, 210 n.6, 211, 212, 228, 243 and n.6, 258 and n.3, 259, 268, 272, 277 and n.8
Schmitt, J.-C., 81 n.7
Schramm, P. E., 29
Segonne, M., 64 n.25
Selge, K.-V., 182 and n.23, 183 n.25, 219 nn.39, 40, 220 n.41, 297 n.97, 299 n.108
Sennis, A., 41 n.88
sermons
 against heretics, 58, 59, 135, 136, 161, 225 n.65, 233, 261
 by heretic 46, 66 n.32, 87, 91, 118, 119, 120, 121, 122
 see also preaching
Sharman, R. V., 45 n.101
Shaw, J. D., 24 n.11
Sicard Cellarier, Cathar Bishop, 142, 143, 144
Siegel, A., 2 n.2
Simeon Agulher, 122
Simon de Montfort, 31, 236, 239
simony, 89, 136
Simpson, J. R, 173 n.75
Sinibald of Lacu, OFM, inquisitor, 255
Skinner, Q., 37 n.73
Slavonic Orthodox, 157, 160, 167
Smith, D. J., 46 n.106, 48 n.111
Sneddon, S., 18, 48 and n.114, 86 n.15, 103 n.70, 191 n.36, 193 n.43, 285 n.40, 309 n.7
Sokolov, M., 156 n.13, 160 n.21, 162 n.29, 170 n.62, 171 n.65
Somerset, F., 54 n.6
Sorrel, C., 102 n.68
soul, 44, 64, 67 and n.34, 91, 104, 131, 132, 139, 215, 217, 220, 221, 230, 237
Soula, R., 75 n.51
Southern, R. W., 36 and n.70
Sparks, C., 18 n.42, 36 and n.66, 47 n.108, 284 and n.39
Sparks, H. F. D., 159 n.18
Spasovich, V. D., 160 n.20, 162 n.29
Spiegel, G., 28

Spivak, G. C., 76 n.52
Spoleto, 150
Sreznevskii, I., 158 n.17
St. John the Evangelist, 146, 148
St. Luke the Evangelist, 168, 169, 233
St. Mark the Evangelist, 233
St. Matthew the Evangelist, 170, 233, 238 n.38
St. Paul, 16, 234
St. Paul Cap-de-Joux, 301
St. Peter, 233, 238
Steinfeld, Praemonstratensian monastery, 134, 264, 265
Stenton, D. M., 246 n.17
Stephen Confalonieri, 189, 192
Stephen Katromanić, 150
Stephen of Anse, 59, 219 n.39
Stephen of Bourbon, OP, 219 n.39, 248, 255, 275, 276
Stephen of Salagnac, OP, 187 n.8, 193, 194 n.51, 208 n.1, 213 and nn.14, 17, 223 n.36
Stoyanov, Y., 6, 131 nn.1, 3, 150 n.79, 154 n.8, 158 nn.16, 17, 159 nn.18, 19, 166 nn.40, 43, 44, 172 nn.70, 71, 174 n.76, 176 n.80, 273
Strayer, J. R., 26 and n.25, 27 and nn.25, 26, 51
Strohm, P., 54 n.5
Stubbs, W., 99 n.55, 129 n.78, 143 nn.49, 50, 246 n.16, 247 nn.17, 20, 293 n.75, 294 n.78
Sun, A., 22 n.4
Swindler, J. K., 17 n.38
Sylvester I, Pope, 9
Syria, 155
Syrian Orthodox, 127

Tanchelm, 262
Tanner, N., SJ, 138 n.29, 196 n.61, 231 n.3, 232 n.6, 291 n.65, 294 n.81
Tarsus, 127
Tarragona, Council of, (1242), 198
Tatianus, 214
Taylor, C., 7, 25 and n.20, 29 n.35, 38 and n.76, 42 n.94, 43 n.97, 46 n.106, 47 n.110, 50 n.124, 51 n.125, 118 n.25, 173 n.75, 176 n.79, 230 n.2, 244 n.8, 261 n.10, 272 and n.36
Templars, Order of, 126
Tetricus, 37 n.71, 216–7 and n.29
Teulet, A., 124 n.62, 233 n.11

Index

Texerant, 135
Theophylact Lecapenus, 154 n.7
Théry, J., 38 n.78, 81 nn.6, 9, 96 n.45, 98
    n.53, 99 n.57, 101 nn.62, 63, 103
    n.72, 104 nn.73, 75, 105 nn.78, 79,
    109 n.86, 110 nn.88, 90, 112 and
    n.1, 242 n.1, 245 nn.11, 12, 258,
    273, 280, 306 n.9 *see also* Théry-
    Astruc, J.
Théry-Astruc, J., 3, 4
Thilo, J. C., 156 n.13
Thomas Aquinas, OP, 217–18, 306–7
Thomas Caudier, 122
Thouzellier, C., 16 n.34, 36–7 n.71, 63
    n.23, 144 nn.52, 53, 147 n.66, 148
    and nn.69, 72, 178 and n.2, 253
    n.53, 275 n.3, 277 n.7, 289 n.53, 290
    nn.56, 62, 300 n.110, 301 n.118
Tikhonravov, N. S., 157 n.15, 158 n.17
tithes, 26, 104, 265
Tocco, F., 33 and n.55, 191 n.33
Torrey, C., 164 n.34
Toulousain, 35, 41, 45, 467, 115, 117, 250,
    274, 282, 288, 291, 294, 301
Toulouse, 25, 37, 39, 46, 63, 84 n.13, 97
    n.49, 115, 123, 126, 128, 129, 141,
    222, 231, 239, 246, 260, 262, 272,
    275, 291, 293, 294, 295, 298, 301,
    302
  Cathar Church of, 142, 143, 144, 145
    and n.57, 150, 292, 301, 308, 310,
    311
  Council of, (1119) 291, (1229) 198,
    (1246) 191 n.35
  MS 609 of the Bibliothèque
    municipale de Toulouse, 5 n.9, 9
    nn.13, 14, 11 n.23, 40 n.85, 41 n.87,
    47 n.108, 66 n.32, 67 nn.33, 34, 72,
    73, 75, 116 n.14, 124 n.63, 125 n.64,
    210 n.8, 251 and nn.42, 43, 44, 45,
    252, 258, 260, 279 nn.15, 17, 285
    nn.43, 44
Toulouse-Lautrec, H. de, 34
Tours, 234
  Council of (1163), 97 n.49, 234 262, 292
transubstantiation, 15, 129
Transylvania, 153
Tremp, E., 82 n.10
Trencavel family, 103, 128, 129 n.78
Treviso, 16
Trier, 264
Trivellone, A., 262 n.12, 280 n.19

Troeltsch, E., 24 and n.12
Troyes, 236
Tsar Peter, 131
Tsukhlev, D., 160 n.20, 162 n.29
Tugwell, S., OP, 40 n.86
Turdeanu, É., 161 nn.22, 24, 163 n.33, 169
    n.52
Turner, H. J. M., 155 n.11
Turner, J., 22 n.3
Tuscany, 13, 140, 146, 150, 180, 191

Ubertino Landi, 201
Ugo of Baziège, 123
Ugoni family, 14
Ulturale, M., 185 n.1, 193 n.49
Unam sanctam, papal bull (1302), 74
Urban II, Pope, 136
Urban IV, Pope, 186, 187
Urbino, 187
usury, 92

Vaillant, A., 160 n.20, 161 n.26, 169 n.53
Vaissète, J., OSB, 141 and n.43
Val d'Aran, 142
Valdes, 59, 211, 219 and n.39, 220
Valentinus, 214
van Engen, J., 23 n.6, 77 and n.54
Vanderputten, S., 262 n.11
Vaneigem, R., 53 n.2
Vassiliev, A. V., 167 n.48, 168 n.52, 171
    n.67, 172 n.69
Venckeleer, T., 37 n.71
Venice, 132
Vermes, G., 164 n.35
Verona, 190 n.29, 203, 206
Vicaire, M.-H., OP, 295, 296 n.89, 298
Vicenza, 145, 150
Vidal, J.-M., 279
Vienne, 239
  Council of, 306
Vigouroux de Bacona/Vigouroux of La
    Bouconne 144, 145, 301, 307
Vilandrau, C., 2 n.2, 86 n.16, 96 n.47, 101
    n.66
Villelongue, 59
Villeneuve-Minervois, 59 n.16
Violante, C., 1 n.1, 16 n.36
Vital Vignal, 94 n.38
Viterbo, 192

Waitz, G., 33 n.57, 220 n.41
Wakefield, W. L., 58 n.13, 60 nn.19, 20, 61

n.22, 82 n.10, 213 n.15, 215 n.22, 216 nn.25, 28, 219 nn.38, 40, 222 nn.49, 53, 234 n.19, 246 n.15, 253 n.53, 254, 277 and n.7, 289 n.5, 291 nn.62, 63, 292 n.70, 298 n.103, 299 n.107, 300 n.111, 303 n.120, 307
Walahfrid Strabo, 59
Waldenses/Valdenses/Valdensians, 7, 15, 24 n.12, 25, 29, 31, 32, 38, 56, 62, 89, 100, 101 and n.64, 116, 118 and n.24, 119, 120, 121, 122, 123, 129, 151, 152, 182, 188, 191, 202, 214, 219, 220, 227, 232, 245 n.10, 250 and n.34, 259, 276, 278 n.9, 283, 296, 297, 298, 299, 301, 303, 304, 305, 306 *see also* Poor (Men) of Lyons
Waldensianism, 22, 25, 38, 219, 257, 276, 303, 304
Walker Bynum, C., 28 and n.30
Walter Map, 219 n.39, 220 and n.41
Wanegffelen, T., 95 n.44
Wazo, Bishop of Liège, 58
Webb, D. M., 14 n.31, 82 n.10
Weingart, M., 162 n.26
Weltecke, D., 127 n.72, 128 n.75, 129 n.79
White, H., 24 n.11
Wickham, C., 10 n.19, 13 n.29, 271 n.33
Wild, G., 161 n.25

William, Bishop of Albi, 143
Willelma Forneira, 12
William of Auvergne, Bishop of Paris, 221 and n.43, 222
William of Auxerre, 221, 222
William of Newburgh, OSA, 264
William of Puylaurens, 143 and n.51, 298, 299
William of Tudela, 144 and n.55
William Pelhisson, 222 n.53, 302
Wills, G., 33 n.60
Wolsky, J., 155 n.10
Wycliffism, 54

Young, S. E., 221 n.46

Zambon, F., 203 n.88
Zanella, G., 102 and n.67
Zbíral, D., 47 n.107, 173 n.75, 203 n.88
Zerner, M., 19 n.44, 46 nn.106, 107, 57 n.11, 72 n.42, 81 n.6, 103 n.71, 112 and n.1, 141 and nn.41, 42, 142 nn.44, 46, 47, 142, 203 n.88, 242 and n.1, 253 n.51, 261 and nn.8, 11, 262 n.12, 269, 273 n.37, 280 and nn.18, 20, 292 nn.72, 73
Zlatar, Z., 43 n.97
Zwicker, P., OCelest., 213 n.16

YORK MEDIEVAL PRESS: PUBLICATIONS

Heresy and Inquisition in the Middle Ages

1 *Heresy and Heretics in the Thirteenth Century: The Textual Representations*, L. J. Sackville (2011)

2 *Heresy, Crusade and Inquisition in Medieval Quercy*, Claire Taylor (2011)

3 *Heresy, Inquisition and Life Cycle in Medieval Languedoc*, Chris Sparks (2014)

4 *Cathars in Question*, ed. Antonio Sennis (2016)

Details of other York Medieval Press volumes are available from Boydell & Brewer Ltd.

www.ingramcontent.com/pod-product-compliance
Lightning Source LLC
Chambersburg PA
CBHW051558230426
43668CB00013B/1893